T0094194

Advances in Computer Vision and Pattern Recognition

For further volumes:
www.springer.com/series/4205

A. Ardeshir Goshtasby

Image Registration

Principles, Tools and Methods

 Springer

Prof. A. Ardeshir Goshtasby
Dept. Computer Science and Engineering
  303 Russ Engineering Center
Wright State University
Dayton, OH
USA

Series Editors
Professor Sameer Singh, PhD
Research School of Informatics
Loughborough University
Loughborough
UK

Dr. Sing Bing Kang
Microsoft Research
Microsoft Corporation
Redmond, WA
USA

ISSN 2191-6586   e-ISSN 2191-6594
Advances in Computer Vision and Pattern Recognition
ISBN 978-1-4471-2457-3   e-ISBN 978-1-4471-2458-0
DOI 10.1007/978-1-4471-2458-0
Springer London Dordrecht Heidelberg New York

British Library Cataloguing in Publication Data
A catalogue record for this book is available from the British Library

Library of Congress Control Number: 2011946223

Printed on acid-free paper

Springer is part of Springer Science+Business Media (www.springer.com)

To My Wife,
My Parents,
Charles E. Spearman,
and Larry L. Schumaker

Preface

Image registration is the process of finding correspondence between all points in two images of a scene. This correspondence is required in stereo depth perception, 3-D scene reconstruction, object detection and recognition, change detection, image fusion, object tracking and motion analysis. Analysis of two or more images of a scene often depends on the ability to find correspondence between points in the images.

This monograph overviews principles, tools and methods in image registration. In addition to reviewing past tools and methods and comparing their performances, new tools and methods are introduced and evaluated.

Chapter 1 describes the problem of image registration, identifies the steps involved in registering two images, defines the terminologies used in the book and categorizes image registration methods. This monograph focuses on point-based methods to image registration, although other methods are also reviewed in Chap. 11.

Chapter 2 reviews various similarity and dissimilarity measures used to register two images or find correspondence between local neighborhoods in two images. Chapter 3 reviews various point detectors and compares their performances.

Chapter 4 reviews methods for extracting various image features and Chap. 5 discusses various image descriptors that can be associated with the detected points. Chapter 6 shows that not all image features are equally informative. Some features carry more information than others or are invariant under intensity and geometric changes. Chapter 6 also describes various methods for selecting small subsets of image features to make the point correspondence process more efficient.

Chapter 7 discusses methods for finding correspondence between points in two images where each point has a feature vector associated with it. Robust matching and robust estimation of transformation parameters are discussed in Chap. 8 and various transformation models in image registration are discussed in Chap. 9.

Chapter 10 discusses the image resampling and intensity blending steps in image registration. Chapters 2–10 review various tools needed to design a particular image registration method. Specific methods that use the described tools to register images are reviewed in Chap. 11.

This monograph covers the fundamentals of digital image registration. It does not discuss applications of image registration nor does it discuss characteristics of various types of images. However, a researcher familiar with principles, tools, and methods covered in this book should be able to design an effective method for registering a particular type of imagery and for a given application.

The content of this monograph is intended for students, image analysis software developers, engineers, and researchers who would like to analyze two or more images of a scene. It provides the basic knowledge to find corresponding points in two images and spatially align them.

The satellite images used in the examples are courtesy of NASA, the medical images are courtesy of Kettering Medical Center, Kettering, Ohio, and the aerial images are courtesy of Image Registration and Fusion Systems, Dayton, Ohio. The remaining images are those of the author. The images may be found at http://www.imgfsr.com/book2.html and may be downloaded and used in research and scientific publications without a restriction.

Dayton, OH, USA   A. Ardeshir Goshtasby

Acknowledgements

I would like to thank NASA for the satellite images, Kettering Medical Center, Kettering, Ohio, for the medical images, and Image Registration and Fusion Systems for the aerial images used in this book. The support from the National Science Foundation, the National Institutes of Health, the Air Force Research Laboratory, and the State of Ohio at different stages of the author's career that enabled him to put together pieces of this monograph is greatly appreciated. I also would like to thank Libby Stephens for editing the grammar and style of this book.

A. Ardeshir Goshtasby

Contents

Acronyms

AAID	Average absolute intensity difference
ACC	Accuracy
ASIFT	Affine-invariant SIFT
BLUE	Best linear unbiased estimation
CCH	Contrast context histogram
DCT	Discrete cosine transform
DFT	Discrete Fourier transform
DoG	Difference of Gaussians
DOLP	Difference of low pass
DT	Distance transform
DTCWT	Dual tree complex wavelet transform
EM	Expectation maximization
FN	False negative
FP	False positive
FPR	False positive rate
GLD	Gray-level difference
GLOH	gradient location and orientation histogram
GLSD	Gray-level spatial-dependence
GSBS	Generalized sequential backward selection
GSFS	Generalized sequential forward selection
HSV	Hue, saturation, value
HT	Hadamard transform
JCPD	Joint conditional probability density
JPD	Joint probability distribution
k-NN	k-nearest neighbor
LoG	Laplacian of Gaussian
LMS	Least median of squares
LTS	Least trimmed square
M	Maximum likelihood
MAD	Median of absolute differences
MLESAC	Maximum likelihood estimation sample consensus

MQ	Multiquadric
MSD	Median of square differences
MSIFT	Multispectral SIFT
MSS	Multi-spectral scanner
MST	Minimum-spanning tree
NASA	National Aeronautics and Space Administration
OLS	Ordinary least-squares
OSID	Ordinal spatial intensity distribution
PCA	Principal component analysis
PROSAC	Progressive sample consensus
R	Rank
R-RANSAC	Randomized RANSAC
RaG	Rational Gaussian
RANSAC	Random sample and consensus
RGB	Red, green, blue
RIFT	rotation-invariant feature transform
RLM	Run-length matrix
RM	Repeated median
RMSE	Root-mean-squared error
RMSID	Root-mean-squared intensity difference
S	Scale
SBS	Sequential backward selection
SFS	Sequential forward selection
SIFT	Scale-invariant feature transform
SUSAN	Smallest univalue segment assimilating nucleus
TM	Thematic Mapper
TP	True positive
TPR	True positive rate
TPS	Thin-plate spline
USGS	United States Geological Survey
WLD	Weber local descriptor
WLIN	Weighted linear
WLS	Weighted least-squares

Chapter 1
Introduction

Image registration is the process of spatially aligning two images of a scene so that corresponding points assume the same coordinates. This process enables finding, for each point in the first image, the corresponding point in the second image. In this monograph, the first image will be referred to as the *reference image* and the second image will be referred to as the *sensed image*. The reference image is kept unchanged and the sensed image is transformed to take the geometry and spatial coordinates of the reference image.

If the images represent different views of a 3-D scene, or if the scene represents a dynamic environment, it may not be possible to find correspondence between all points in the images. Image registration aims to find correspondence between points that are present in both images.

An example of image registration is given in Fig. 1.1. The reference image is a Landsat multispectral (MSS) image of Kalkaska County, Michigan, and the sensed image is a Landsat thematic mapper (TM) image of the same area. Registration involves spatially aligning the TM image with the MSS image. By registering the images, it becomes possible to fuse information in the images or identify differences between the images.

Another example of image registration is given in Fig. 1.2. Reference and sensed images show downtown Honolulu, Hawaii. By registering the images using their overlap area, an image mosaic is created that contains areas covered by both images.

The word *registration* can be traced back to the year 1900 in a US patent by Becker [5]. In this patent, Becker discloses a focusing camera that uses a half-mirror and a full mirror to create two images of a scene on the viewer's retina. By changing the orientation of one mirror with respect to the other, images from the two mirrors are aligned on the viewer's retina. The mechanism that changes the orientation of one mirror with respect to the other also changes the distance of the image plane to the lens. The mechanism is designed in such a way that when images from the two mirrors perfectly align on the viewer's retina, the film also moves to the right distance to the lens, enabling creation of a sharp image of the scene on the film.

The next advancement in image registration is observed in the film industry in the production of a double-coated color film. In an apparatus disclosed by Kelley

A.A. Goshtasby, *Image Registration*,
Advances in Computer Vision and Pattern Recognition,
DOI 10.1007/978-1-4471-2458-0_1, © Springer-Verlag London Limited 2012

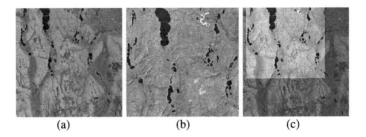

Fig. 1.1 (a) A Landsat MSS image and (b) a Landsat TM image of Kalkaska County, Michigan. (c) The TM image is geometrically transformed to spatially align the MSS image

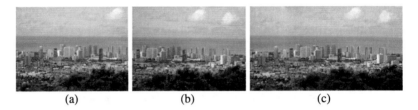

Fig. 1.2 (a), (b) Images of downtown Honolulu, Hawaii. (c) Registration of the images and creation of an image mosaic

and Mason in a US patent in 1917 [15], a color film is created by recording the blue band on one side of the film and a combination of red and green bands on the opposite side of the film. The challenge in creating a color film is to print two images of the same scene taken separately in perfect alignment on the film. The disclosed apparatus achieved alignment of different color bands with high precision using two registration pins that fit into the perforations in the edges of the films.

The next natural use of image registration happened in printing. Seaman, in a US patent in 1937 [29], disclosed an apparatus for printing overlapping images of a scene captured separately into a more complete image. The invention not only allowed the creation of an image mosaic from two or more overlapping images, a masking mechanism was introduced that made it possible to add figures captured from one scene to the photograph of another scene.

Image registration as we know it today emerged as an electronic image comparison device. Dressler, in a US patent in 1956 [7], disclosed an electronic device for comparing and combining two overlapping images. The images were provided on films. Through the use of a half mirror and a full mirror, the images were projected to an image subtraction circuitry that produced an output with an amplitude proportional to the degree of match between the images. By providing the means to translate and rotate one film with respect to the other and by observing the output of the subtraction circuitry, the capability to align and combine images from two films into a larger image was provided.

The electronic image comparison idea of Dressler was later extended to an image correlator. Link and Smith, in a US patent in 1962 [18], disclosed an electronic tube that could store a reference image and correlate it with a sensed image, producing an output signal with its strength a function of the correlation between the images. Steiner, in a US Patent in 1965 [31], further advanced the tube to make it possible to move the sensed image with respect to the reference image and align the images. Johnson, in a US Patent in 1969 [14], further improved the apparatus to normalize the correlation measure so that the output amplitude would be independent of the amplitude of the sensed image, thereby measuring the degree of match between the reference and sensed images more accurately.

The first example of digital image registration is traced back to the work of Roberts at MIT in 1963 [27]. By aligning the projections of edges of model polyhedral solids with image edges, Roberts developed a computational method for locating and recognizing predefined polyhedral objects in an image.

Methods for registering full digital images first appeared in the remote sensing literature. Anuta [1, 2] developed an automatic method for registering images with translational differences. Efforts to speed up the method and make it less sensitive to intensity differences between the images were made by Leese et al. [16], Barnea and Silverman [4], and Pratt [26] shortly after. The use of image registration in robot navigation was pioneered by Mori et al. [23], Levine et al. [17], and Nevatia [24]. Image registration found its way to medical imaging as data from medical scanners became digitally available [3, 30, 35].

While registration activities during 1970s focused on alignment of satellite images using rigid, similarity, and affine transformation functions, increased production of low-altitude aerial images during 1980s was the driving force behind invention of methods that could spatially align images with local geometric differences [9–13]. Due to the increased use of medical images during 1990s and the need for spatially aligning multimodality image, considerable advances were made in formulation of information theoretic similarity/dissimilarity measures that could compare and register multimodality images [8, 19, 20, 22, 25, 32, 34].

During the last decade, due to the increased use of videos in surveillance and other real-time applications, image registration became a necessary step in analysis of single and multi source videos. Advances in the imaging technology to increase resolution and quality of images, also increased the complexity of methods that can register such images. Intensity-based registration methods gradually lost ground to point-based registration methods that could accommodate local geometric differences between images.

During the past several years, considerable efforts have gone into locating unique points in images [28, 33] and finding the correspondence between them [6, 21]. Locally unique points in two images that are used to register the images will be referred to as *control points* in this monograph.

The general steps involved in image registration and the relation between them are shown in Fig. 1.3. An image registration system can be considered a black box that receives a reference image and a sensed image and resamples the sensed image to spatially align with the reference image. This operation assigns the same coordinates to corresponding points in the images, defining both images in the same coordinate system.

Fig. 1.3 Components of an
image registration system and
the relation between them

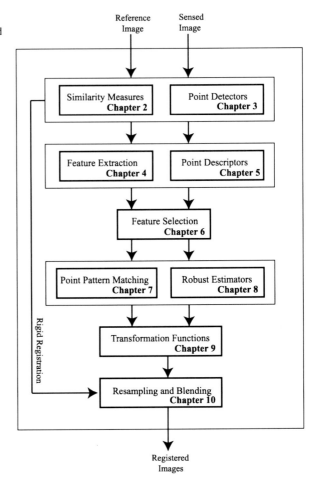

Depending on the severity of the intensity and geometric differences between the reference and sensed images, different steps may be needed to register the images. If the images can be treated as rigid bodies, they will have only translational and rotational differences. By translating and rotating the sensed image with respect to the reference image, the images can be registered. Early methods achieved image registration in this manner. The process is simple but it is not efficient. It is also limited to images that have only translational and rotational differences. Moreover, the presence of outliers in one or both images can break down the registration process.

A more robust approach will select a number of control points in the reference image and will try to locate them in the sensed image. This is achieved by selecting small windows centered at the points in the reference image and searching for the windows in the sensed image. If the images have only translation and rotational differences, each correct match will produce the same rotational parameter. By matching multiple windows in the images, the rotation parameter shared by two or more matches can be used to register the images even in the presence of outliers.

If the geometries of the images are not related by a rigid transformation, a sequence of steps as shown in Fig. 1.3 are needed to register the images. First, a number of control points is selected in each image. Then, features describing the neighborhoods of the points are calculated and the most informative features are selected. Initial correspondence is established between the points using the features of the points. Additional information about the images is then used in the form of constraints to distinguish the correct correspondences from the incorrect ones. Once a set of corresponding points in the images is found, the parameters of a nonlinear function to transform the space of the sensed image to that of the reference image are determined. The chapters containing the details of each step in image registration are also included in Fig. 1.3.

Chapters 2–10 describe the tools needed to design image registration methods for various applications and the underlying principles. Well-known registration methods that are designed by these tools are reviewed in Chap. 11.

References

1. Anuta, P.E.: Registration of multispectral video imagery. Soc. Photo-Opt. Instrum. Eng. J. **7**, 168–175 (1969)
2. Anuta, P.E.: Spatial registration of multispectral and multitemporal digital imagery using fast Fourier transform techniques. IEEE Trans. Geosci. Electron. **8**(4), 353–368 (1970)
3. Barber, D.C.: Automatic alignment of radionuclide images. Phys. Med. Biol. **27**, 387–396 (1982)
4. Barnea, D.I., Silverman, H.F.: A class of algorithms for fast digital image registration. IEEE Trans. Comput. **21**(2), 179–186 (1972)
5. Becker, J.: Focusing Camera. US Patent 1,178,474, Filed 11 Aug. 1900; Patented 4 Apr. 1916
6. Chum, O., Matas, J.: Optimal randomized RANSAC. IEEE Trans. Pattern Anal. Mach. Intell. **30**(8), 1472–1482 (2008)
7. Dressler, R.: Image Matching Apparatus. US Patent 2,989,890, Filed 13 Nov. 1956; Patented 27 June 1961
8. Gerlot, P., Bizais, Y.: Image registration: a review and a strategy for medical applications. In: de Graaf, C.N., Viergever, M.A. (eds.) Information Processing in Medical Imaging, pp. 81–89. Plenum Press, New York (1988)
9. Goshtasby, A.: Piecewise linear mapping functions for image registration. Pattern Recognit. **19**(6), 459–466 (1986)
10. Goshtasby, A.: Piecewise cubic mapping functions for image registration. Pattern Recognit. **20**(5), 525–533 (1987)
11. Goshtasby, A.: Geometric correction of satellite images using composite transformation functions. In: Proc. Twenty First Int'l Sym. Remote Sensing of Environment, October, pp. 825–834 (1987)
12. Goshtasby, A.: Registration of image with geometric distortion. IEEE Trans. Geosci. Remote Sens. **26**(1), 60–64 (1988)
13. Goshtasby, A.: Image registration by local approximation methods. Image Vis. Comput. **6**(4), 255–261 (1988)
14. Johnson, H.R.: Dual-Image Registration System. US Patent 3,636,254, Filed 12 Nov. 1969; Patented 18 Jan. 1972

15. Kelley, W.V.D., Mason, J.: Photographic Printing. US Patent 1,350,023, Filed 26 Jul. 1917, Patented 17 Aug. 1920
16. Leese, J.A., Novak, G.S., Clark, B.B.: An automatic technique for obtaining cloud motion from geosynchronous satellite data using cross correlation. Appl. Meteorol. **10**, 110–132 (1971)
17. Levine, M.D., O'Handley, D.O., Yagi, G.M.: Computer determination of depth maps. Comput. Graph. Image Process. **2**, 131–150 (1973)
18. Link, T.V., Smith, R.H.: Cathod Ray Tube Image Matching Apparatus. US Patent 3,290,546, Filed 25 Oct. 1962; Patented 6 Dec. 1966
19. Maes, F., Collignon, A., Vandermeulen, D., Marchal, G., Suetens, P.: Multimodality image registration by maximization of mutual information. IEEE Trans. Med. Imaging **16**(2), 187–198 (1997)
20. Maintz, J.B.A., Viergever, M.A.: A survey of medical image registration. Med. Image Anal. **2**(1), 1–36 (1988)
21. Matas, J., Chum, O.: Randomized RANSAC with Td:d test. Image Vis. Comput. **22**(10), 837–842 (2004)
22. Maurer, C.R. Jr., Fitzpatrick, J.M. A review of medical image registration. In: Interactive Image-Guided Neurosurgery, pp. 17–44 (1993)
23. Mori, K.I., Kidode, M., Asada, H.: An iterative prediction and correction method for automatic stereocomparison. Comput. Graph. Image Process. **2**, 393–401 (1973)
24. Nevatia, R.: Depth measurement by motion stereo. Comput. Graph. Image Process. **15**, 203–214 (1976)
25. Pluim, J.P.W., Maintz, J.B.A., Viergever, M.A.: Mutual-information-based image registration of medical images: A survey. IEEE Trans. Med. Imaging **22**(8), 986–1004 (2003)
26. Pratt, W.K.: Correlation techniques for image registration. IEEE Trans. Aerosp. Electron. Syst. **10**(3), 353–358 (1974)
27. Roberts, L.G.: Machine Perception of 3-D Solids. Ph.D. Thesis, MIT (1963)
28. Rohr, K.: Landmark-Based Image Analysis: Using Geometric and Intensity Models. Kluwer Academic, Boston (2001)
29. Seaman, O.J.L.: Method of Producing Composite Photographs. US Patent 2,314,663, Filed 23 Dec. 1937; Patented 17 Dec. 1940
30. Singh, M., Frei, W., Shibata, T., Huth, G.C.: A digital technique for accurate change detection in nuclear medical images with application to myocardial perfusion studies using Thallium-201. IEEE Trans. Nucl. Sci. **26**, 565–575 (1979)
31. Steiner, W.L.: Electron Image Correlator Tube. US Patent 3,424,937, Filed 8 Jan. 1965; Patented 28 Jan. 1969
32. Studholme, C., Hill, D.L.G., Hawkes, D.J.: Automated 3D registration of truncated MR and CT images of the head. In: Proc. British Machine Vision Conf., pp. 27–36 (1995)
33. Tuytelaars, T., Mikolajczyk, K.: Local invariant feature detectors: A survey. Found. Trends Comput. Graph. Vis. **3**(3), 177–280 (2007)
34. van den Elsen, P.A., Pol, E.-J.D., Viergever, M.A.: Medical image matching: A review with classification. In: IEEE Engineering in Medicine and Biology, pp. 26–39 (1993)
35. Venot, A., Devaux, J.Y., Herbin, M., Lebruchec, J.F., Dubertret, L., Raulo, Y., Roucayrol, J.C.: An automated system for the registration and comparison of photographic images in medicine. IEEE Trans. Med. Imaging **7**(4), 298–303 (1988)

Chapter 2
Similarity and Dissimilarity Measures

Given two sequences of measurements $X = \{x_i : i = 1, \ldots, n\}$ and $Y = \{y_i : i = 1, \ldots, n\}$, the similarity (dissimilarity) between them is a measure that quantifies the dependency (independency) between the sequences. X and Y can represent measurements from two objects or phenomena. In this chapter, we assume they represent images and x_i and y_i are intensities of corresponding pixels in the images. If X and Y represent 2-D images, the sequences can be considered intensities in the images in raster-scan order.

A similarity measure S is considered a metric if it produces a higher value as the dependency between corresponding values in the sequences increases. A metric similarity S satisfies the following [92]:

1. *Limited Range*: $S(X, Y) \leq S_0$, for some arbitrarily large number S_0.
2. *Reflexivity*: $S(X, Y) = S_0$ if and only if $X = Y$.
3. *Symmetry*: $S(X, Y) = S(Y, X)$.
4. *Triangle Inequality*: $S(X, Y)S(Y, Z) \leq [Z(X, Y) + S(Y, Z)]S(X, Z)$.

S_0 is the largest similarity measure between all possible X and Y sequences.

A dissimilarity measure D is considered a metric if it produces a higher value as corresponding values in X and Y become less dependent. A metric dissimilarity D satisfies the following for all sequences X and Y [23, 92]:

1. *Nonnegativity*: $D(X, Y) \geq 0$.
2. *Reflexivity*: $D(X, Y) = 0$ if and only if $X = Y$.
3. *Symmetry*: $D(X, Y) = D(Y, X)$.
4. *Triangle Inequality*: $D(X, Y) + D(Y, Z) \geq D(X, Z)$.

Although having the properties of a metric is desirable, a similarity/dissimilarity measure can be quite effective without being a metric. Similarity/dissimilarity measures that are insensitive to radiometric changes in the scene or invariant to sensor parameters are often not metrics. For instance, ordinal measures are not metrics but are quite effective in comparing images captured under different lighting conditions, and measures that are formulated in terms of the joint probability distribution of image intensities are not metrics but are very effective in comparing images captured by different sensors.

A.A. Goshtasby, *Image Registration*,
Advances in Computer Vision and Pattern Recognition,
DOI 10.1007/978-1-4471-2458-0_2, © Springer-Verlag London Limited 2012

Fig. 2.1 (a) Observed image
X and saved images
$\{Y_i : i = 1, \dots, N\}$ are given
and it is required to find the
saved image most similar to
the observed image.
(**b**) Template X and windows
$\{Y_i : i = 1, \dots, N\}$ in an
observed image are given and
it is required to find the
window that is most similar
to the template

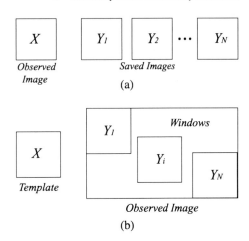

Various similarity/dissimilarity measures have been formulated throughout the years, each with its own strengths and weaknesses. Some measures use raw image intensities, some normalize the intensities before using them, some use the ranks of the intensities, and some use joint probabilities of corresponding intensities.

The similarity and dissimilarity measures are discussed in the context of two real problems. In one problem, an observed image and a number of saved images are given and it is required to determine the saved image that best matches the observed image (Fig. 2.1a). The saved images could be images in a database and the observed image could be the one that is being viewed by a camera.

The second problem involves locating an object of interest in an observed image where the model of the object is given in the form of a template and the observed image is an image being viewed by a camera (Fig. 2.1b). To locate the object within the observed image, there is a need to find the best-match position of the template within the observed image.

The two problems are similar in the sense that both require determination of the similarity between two images or between a template and a window in a larger image. We will denote the observed image in the first problem and the template in the second problem by X and denote a saved image in the first problem and a window within the observed image in the second problem by Y. We will also assume X and Y contain n pixels ordered in raster-scan order. Moreover, we assume the images do not have rotational and scaling differences. Therefore, if images X and Y truly match, corresponding pixels in the images will show the same scene point.

In the following sections, properties of various similarity and dissimilarity measures are reviewed and their strengths and weaknesses are identified. In addition to reviewing measures in the literature, four additional measures are newly introduced. The discrimination powers of the measures are determined using synthetic and real images and their sensitivities to noise and image blurring as well as to intensity and geometric differences between images are determined and compared.

2.1 Similarity Measures

2.1.1 Pearson Correlation Coefficient

The correlation coefficient between sequences $X = \{x_i : i = 1, \ldots, n\}$ and $Y = \{y_i : i = 1, \ldots, n\}$ is defined by

$$r = \frac{\sum_{i=1}^{n}(x_i - \bar{x})(y_i - \bar{y})}{\{\sum_{i=1}^{n}(x_i - \bar{x})^2\}^{\frac{1}{2}}\{\sum_{i=1}^{n}(y_i - \bar{y})^2\}^{\frac{1}{2}}}, \tag{2.1}$$

where $\bar{x} = \frac{1}{n}\sum_{i=1}^{n} x_i$, and $\bar{y} = \frac{1}{n}\sum_{i=1}^{n} y_i$. Correlation coefficient was first discovered by Bravais in 1846, "Memoires par divers savants," T, IX, Paris, 1846, pp. 255–332 [86] and later shown by Pearson [65] to be the best possible correlation between two sequences of numbers.

Dividing the numerator and denominator of (2.1) by n, we obtain

$$r = \frac{\frac{1}{n}\sum_{i=1}^{n}(x_i - \bar{x})(y_i - \bar{y})}{\{\frac{1}{n}\sum_{i=1}^{n}(x_i - \bar{x})^2\}^{\frac{1}{2}}\{\frac{1}{n}\sum_{i=1}^{n}(y_i - \bar{y})^2\}^{\frac{1}{2}}}, \tag{2.2}$$

which shows the sample covariance over the product of sample standard deviations. Equation (2.2) can also be written as

$$r = \frac{1}{n}\sum_{i=1}^{n}\left(\frac{(x_i - \bar{x})}{\sigma_x}\right)\left(\frac{(y_i - \bar{y})}{\sigma_y}\right), \tag{2.3}$$

or

$$r = \frac{1}{n}\bar{X}^t\bar{Y}, \tag{2.4}$$

where $\bar{X}$ and $\bar{Y}$ are X and Y after being normalized with respect to their means and standard deviations, and t denotes transpose.

Correlation coefficient r varies between -1 and $+1$. The case $r = +1$, called *perfect positive correlation*, occurs when $\bar{X}$ and $\bar{Y}$ perfectly coincide, and the case $r = -1$, called the *perfect negative correlation*, occurs when $\bar{X}$ and negative of $\bar{Y}$ perfectly coincide. Under perfect positive or negative correlation:

$$\frac{x_i - \bar{x}}{\sigma_x} = \pm\frac{y_i - \bar{y}}{\sigma_y}, \tag{2.5}$$

or

$$y = \pm\frac{\sigma_y}{\sigma_x}(x - \bar{x}) + \bar{y}, \tag{2.6}$$

showing that corresponding x and y values are related linearly.

When r is not equal to 1 or -1, the line best fitting corresponding values in X and Y is obtained from [38]:

$$y' = r\frac{\sigma_y}{\sigma_x}(x - \bar{x}) + \bar{y}. \tag{2.7}$$

Therefore, correlation coefficient can be considered the coefficient of the linear relationship between corresponding values in X and Y.

If X and Y represent intensities in two images obtained under different lighting conditions of a scene and corresponding intensities are linearly related, a high similarity will be obtained between the images. When images are in different modalities so that corresponding intensities are nonlinearly related, perfectly matching images may not produce high-enough correlation coefficients, causing mismatches. Therefore, Pearson correlation coefficient is suitable for determining the similarity between images with intensities that are known to be linearly related.

Pearson correlation coefficient is a relatively efficient similarity measure as it requires a small number of additions and multiplication at each pixel. Therefore, its computational complexity for images of size n pixels is on the order n. If correlation coefficient is to be used to locate a template in an image, and if N subimages or windows exist in the image that can be compared to the template, the time required to locate the template inside the image will be proportional to Nn. This computation time can be considerable, especially when N and n are large. A two-stage process to speed up this search has been proposed [35].

To speed up template-matching search by correlation coefficient, Anuta [3] took advantage of the high speed of the fast Fourier transform (FFT) algorithm. Assuming V represents the 2-D image inside which a 2-D template is to be found and U represents the template padded with zeros to be the same size as V, the result of correlating the template with the best-matching window in the image (Fig. 2.1b) can be computed by locating the peak of

$$C = \mathscr{F}^{-1}\big[\mathscr{F}(U) \cdot \mathscr{F}^*(V)\big], \tag{2.8}$$

where $\mathscr{F}$ implies 2-D Fourier transform, $\mathscr{F}^{-1}$ implies 2-D inverse Fourier transform, $*$ implies complex conjugate, and $\cdot$ implies point-by-point multiplication. Note that use of FFT requires that images U and V be the same size and have dimensions that are powers of 2. If dimensions of the images are not powers of 2, the images are padded with zeros so their dimensions become powers 2.

Use of FFT requires that the images be treated as 2-D arrays rather than 1-D arrays. Also note that when FFT is used, individual windows in an image cannot be normalized with respect to their means and standard deviations because all widows are collectively compared to the template. However, because Fourier transform measures the spatial frequency characteristics of the template and the image, the process is not sensitive to the absolute intensities but rather to the spatial variations of intensities in the images.

Kuglin and Hines [48] observed that information about the displacement of one image with respect to another is included in the phase component of the cross-power spectrum of the images. If $\phi = \phi_1 - \phi_2$ is the phase difference between two images, the inverse Fourier transform of e^{ϕ} will create a spike at the point showing the displacement of one image with respect to the other. Denoting $\mathscr{F}(U)$ by F and $\mathscr{F}(V)$ by G, then phase correlation

$$C_p = \mathscr{F}^{-1}\left[\frac{F \cdot G^*}{|F \cdot G^*|}\right], \tag{2.9}$$

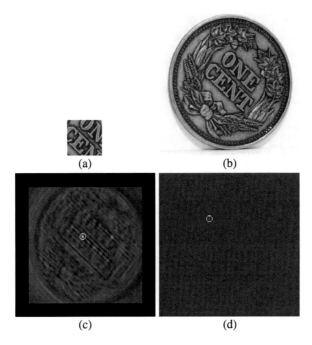

Fig. 2.2 (**a**) A template. (**b**) An image containing the template. (**c**) The correlation image with intensity at a pixel showing the correlation coefficient between the template and the window centered at the pixel in the image. The *dark boundary* in the correlation image represents pixels where matching is not possible because a part of the window centered there will fall outside the image. The pixel with the highest correlation coefficient, which shows the location of the center of the window best matching the template is encircled. (**d**) The real part of image C_p calculated by formula (2.9), showing the phase correlation result with the location of the spike encircled. The spike shows the location of the upper-left-hand corner of the template within the image

where division is carried out point-by-point, separates the phase from the magnitude in Fourier transform. The relative position of the template within the observed image will appear as a spike in image C_p exactly at the location where the correlation will peak when searching for the template within the image. This is demonstrated in an example in Fig. 2.2.

Although phase correlation is already very fast compared to iterative search with correlation coefficient, Alliney and Morandi [1] made the computations even faster by projecting the images into the x and y axes and matching the projections using 1-D Fourier transform. To reduce the boundary effects, Gaussian weights were used.

The phase correlation idea has been extended to images with rotational differences [21] and images with rotational and scaling differences [12, 72]. Stone [87] has provided an excellent review of phase correlation and its use in registration.

To make the matching process less dependent on absolute intensities in images, Fitch et al. [26] used intensity gradients rather than raw intensities in the calculations. The operation, which is known as *orientation correlation*, creates a complex image using gradients along x and y of each image and uses the complex gradient images in the calculations. If U and V represent the template and the image inside which the template is to be found, and the template is padded with zeros to have the same dimensions as the image, then complex images

$$U_d(x, y) = \text{sgn}\left(\frac{\partial U(x, y)}{\partial x} + j\frac{\partial U(x, y)}{\partial y}\right) \qquad (2.10)$$

and

$$V_d(x, y) = \text{sgn}\left(\frac{\partial V(x, y)}{\partial x} + j\frac{\partial V(x, y)}{\partial y}\right), \qquad (2.11)$$

are prepared, where $j = \sqrt{-1}$ and $\text{sgn}(a) = 0$ if $a = 0$ and $\text{sgn}(a) = a/|a|$, otherwise. If F and G are Fourier transforms of U_d and V_d, respectively, then

$$h = \mathcal{F}^{-1}(F \cdot G^*) \qquad (2.12)$$

will represent a complex image, the real part of which will have a spike at the point showing the location of the upper-left-hand corner of the template within the image [26].

2.1.2 Tanimoto Measure

The Tanimoto measure between images X and Y is defined by [92]:

$$S_T = \frac{X^t Y}{\|X\|^2 + \|Y\|^2 - X^t Y} \qquad (2.13)$$

$$= \frac{X^t Y}{(X - Y)^t (X - Y) + X^t Y} \qquad (2.14)$$

$$= \frac{X^t Y}{\|X - Y\|^2 + X^t Y}, \qquad (2.15)$$

where t implies transpose.

Comparing S_T with r, we see that although the numerators of both represent inner product, the one in correlation coefficient uses intensities that are normalized with respect to their means and the one in Tanimoto measure uses the raw intensities. While the denominator in correlation coefficient shows the product of the standard deviations of X and Y, the denominator in the Tanimoto measure represents the square Euclidean distance between X and Y plus the inner product of X and Y.

Tanimoto measure is proportional to the inner product of X and Y and inversely proportional to the sum of the squared Euclidean distance and the inner product of X and Y. The squared Euclidean distance between X and Y has the same effect as the product of the standard deviations of X and Y and normalizes the measure with respect to the scales of X and Y. Adding the inner product to the denominator in the Tanimoto measure has an effect similar to normalizing X and Y with respect to their means when divided by the inner product of X and Y. Therefore, Tanimoto measure and correlation coefficient produce similar results. The Tanimoto measures

Fig. 2.3 The similarity image obtained while searching for the template of Fig. 2.2a in the image of Fig. 2.2b using the Tanimoto measure. The best-match position of the template within the image is encircled

obtained by matching the template in Fig. 2.2a to windows in the image in Fig. 2.2b are shown in the similarity image in Fig. 2.3. The point of highest similarity, which shows the best-match position of the template within the image, is encircled.

The computational complexity of Tanimoto measure is on the order of n. Similar to correlation coefficient, it requires the calculation of the inner product, but rather than calculating the standard deviations of X and Y it calculates the squared Euclidean distance between X and Y, and rather than normalizing X and Y with respect to their means it calculates the inner product of X and Y.

2.1.3 Stochastic Sign Change

If images X and Y are exactly the same except for one being a noisy version of the other, the values in the difference image $D = \{x_i - y_i : i = 1, \ldots, n\}$ will frequently change between positive and negative values due to noise. If Y is a shifted version of X, there will be fewer sign changes in the difference image than when X and Y perfectly align. This suggests that the number of sign changes can be used as a similarity measure to quantify the degree of match between the two images. The larger the number of sign changes in the difference image, the higher the match-rating between the images will be [98, 99].

Contrary to other similarity measures that produce a higher matching accuracy as image detail increases, this measure performs best when the images contain smoothly varying intensities with added zero-mean noise of a small magnitude. Strangely, this measure works better on images containing a small amount of noise than on noise-free images. The template-matching result by this similarity measure using the template of Fig. 2.2a and the image of Fig. 2.2b is shown in Fig. 2.4a. The best-match position of the template within the image is encircled.

This measure can be implemented efficiently by simply finding the number of zero-crossings in the difference image. Since no sign changes are obtained when $X = Y$, in addition to the zero-crossings, points of zero difference are counted as a part of the similarity measure. Determination of the similarity between two images requires a few additions and comparisons at each pixel. Therefore, the computational complexity of the measure is on the order of n.

Fig. 2.4 Similarity images
obtained by matching the
template of Fig. 2.2a to
windows in the image of
Fig. 2.2b using (**a**) stochastic
sign change and
(**b**) deterministic sign change.
The best-match position of
the template within the image
in each case is encircled

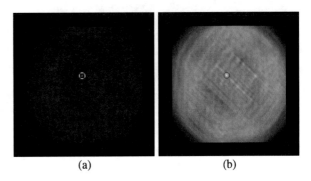

(a)   (b)

2.1.4 Deterministic Sign Change

This measure is similar to stochastic sign change except that noise is intentionally
added to one of the images to produce more sign changes in perfectly matching
images. Therefore, given images $X = \{x_i : i = 1, \ldots, n\}$ and $Y = \{y_i : i = 1, \ldots, n\}$,
a new image $Z = \{z_i : i = 1, \ldots, n\}$ is created from X by setting

$$z_i = x_i + q(-1)^i. \tag{2.16}$$

This operation will add q to every other pixel in X while subtracting q from pixels
adjacent to them, simulating the addition of noise to X. The number of sign changes
in the difference image $D = \{z_i - y_i : i = 1, \ldots, n\}$ is counted and used as the
similarity measure [100]. The choice of parameter q greatly affects the outcome. q
should be taken larger than noise magnitude in Y, while smaller than the intensity
variation between adjacent pixels in X.

Since q is a fixed number, it can be estimated through a training process using
images where coordinates of corresponding points are known. During the training
process, q is varied until results closest to those expected are obtained. If estimation
of q through a training process is not possible, it should be set to twice the standard
deviation of noise, and if standard deviation of noise is not known, q should be set
to twice the standard deviation of intensity differences between X and its smoothed
version [100].

The similarity image obtained by matching the template of Fig. 2.2a to windows
of the same size in the image of Fig. 2.2b by deterministic sign change is shown in
Fig. 2.4b. Because the template is a cutout of the same image, stochastic sign change
has produced a more distinct peak at the best-match position than the deterministic
sign change. In general, however, experiments have shown that deterministic sign
change succeeds more frequently than stochastic sign change in matching [100].

Although the computational complexity of deterministic sign change is on the
order of n for images of size n pixels, it has a much larger coefficient than that by
stochastic sign change because of the need to estimate parameter q and create a
noisy version of the template using (2.16).

Fig. 2.5 Template-matching
using the template of
Fig. 2.2a, the image of
Fig. 2.2b, and the minimum
ratio similarity measure. The
best-match position of the
template within the image is
encircled

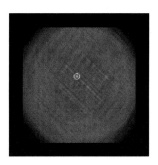

2.1.5 Minimum Ratio

If image $Y = \{y_i : i = 1, \ldots, n\}$ is a noisy version of image $X = \{x_i : i = 1, \ldots, n\}$ and if amplitude of noise is proportional to signal strength, then by letting $r_i = \min\{y_i/x_i, x_i/y_i\}$, and calculating

$$m_r = \frac{1}{n} \sum_{i=1}^{n} r_i, \tag{2.17}$$

we see that m_r measures the dependency between X and Y. When noise is not present, r_i will be equal to 1 and so will m_r. When X and Y do not depend on each other, y_i/x_i and x_i/y_i will be quite different, one becoming much smaller than the other. As a consequence, when the sum of the smaller ratios is calculated, it will become much smaller than 1. Therefore, the closer m_r is to 1, the more similar the images will be. Since ratios of intensities are considered in the calculation of the similarity measure, noise that varies with image intensities will have a relatively smaller effect on the calculated measure than measures that are calculated from the difference of image intensities.

Although resistant to noise, minimum ratio is sensitive to intensity difference between images and so is not suitable for matching images captured of a scene under different lighting conditions or with different sensors. It, however, should do well if the images are obtained under the same lighting condition and by the same sensor, such as stereo images or frames in a video. The template-matching result using the template of Fig. 2.2a and the image of Fig. 2.2b by minimum ratio similarity measure is shown in Fig. 2.5.

Computation of minimum ratio requires only a small number of simple operations at each pixel. Therefore, its computational complexity is on the order of n.

Proposition 2.1 *Minimum ratio is a metric.*

Proof To be a metric, minimum ratio has to (1) have a limited range, (2) be reflexive, (3) be symmetric, and (4) satisfy the triangle inequality.

First, minimum ratio has a limited range because the highest value it can have at a pixel is 1, and so the maximum value it can produce for images of size n according to formula (2.17) is 1, which happens when intensities of corresponding pixels in the images are exactly the same. Second, minimum ratio is reflexive because when $X = Y$, we obtain $m_r = 1$. When $m_r = 1$, we have to have $r_i = 1$ for all i, and that means $x_i = y_i$ for all i; therefore, $X = Y$. Third, minimum ratio is symmetric because switching X and Y will result in the same measure since $\max\{a_i, b_i\}$ is the same as $\max\{b_i, a_i\}$. Finally, to show that minimum ratio satisfies triangle inequality, we have to show that

$$\left(\frac{1}{n} \sum_i \min\left\{ \frac{x_i}{y_i}, \frac{y_i}{x_i} \right\} \right)\left(\frac{1}{n} \sum_i \min\left\{ \frac{y_i}{z_i}, \frac{z_i}{y_i} \right\} \right)$$

$$\leq \left(\frac{1}{n} \sum_i \min\left\{ \frac{x_i}{y_i}, \frac{y_i}{x_i} \right\} + \frac{1}{n} \sum_i \min\left\{ \frac{y_i}{z_i}, \frac{z_i}{y_i} \right\} \right)\left(\frac{1}{n} \sum_i \min\left\{ \frac{x_i}{z_i}, \frac{z_i}{x_i} \right\} \right). \quad (2.18)$$

For the extreme cases when $X = Y = Z$, we obtain $m_r = 1$ when comparing any pair of images and so (2.18) reduces to $1 \leq 2$. For the extreme case where images X, Y, and Z are least similar so that $m_r = 0$ for any pair of images, relation (2.18) reduces to $0 \leq 0$. As the images become more similar, the difference between left and right sides of (2.18) increases, and as the images become less similar, the left and right sides of (2.18) get closer, satisfying relation (2.18). While values on the left-hand side of (2.18) vary between 0 and 1 from one extreme to another, values on the right-hand side of (2.18) vary between 0 and 2 from one extreme to another, always satisfying relation (2.18). $\qquad\square$

2.1.6 Spearman's Rho

A similarity measure relating to the Pearson correlation coefficient is Spearman rank correlation or Spearman's Rho [86]. If image intensities do not contain ties when they are ordered from the smallest to the largest, then by replacing the intensities with their ranks and calculating the Pearson correlation coefficient between the ranks in two images, Spearman rank correlation will be obtained. This is equivalent to calculating [16]:

$$\rho = 1 - \frac{6 \sum_{i=1}^{n} [R(x_i) - R(y_i)]^2}{n(n^2 - 1)}, \quad (2.19)$$

where $R(x_i)$ and $R(y_i)$ represent ranks of x_i and y_i in images X and Y, respectively. To eliminate possible ties among discrete intensities in images, the images are smoothed with a Gaussian of a small standard deviation, such as 1 pixel, to produce unique floating-point intensities. Compared to r, ρ is less sensitive to outliers and, thus, less sensitive to impulse noise and occlusion. It is also less sensitive to nonlinear intensity difference between images than Pearson correlation coefficient.

Spearman rank correlation has been used to measure trends in data as a function of time or distance [29, 45, 110]. When comparing two images, ρ can be used to determine the dependency of corresponding intensities in the images.

Computationally, ρ is much slower than r primarily due to the need for ordering intensities in X and Y, which requires on the order of $n \log_2 n$ comparisons.

Therefore, if images X and Y do not contain impulse noise or occluding parts and intensities in the images are related linearly, no gain in accuracy is achieved by using ρ instead of r. However, under impulse noise, occlusion, and nonlinear intensity differences between images, the additional computational cost of ρ over r may well be worth it.

In a facial recognition study, Ayinde and Yang [4] compared Spearman rank correlation and Pearson correlation coefficient, finding that under considerable intensity differences between images, occlusion, and other random differences between images, Spearman's ρ consistently produced a higher discrimination power than Pearson correlation coefficient. Muselet and Trémeau [62] observed that the rank measures of color components of images captured under different scene illuminations remain relatively unchanged. Based on this observation, they develop a robust object recognition system using the rank correlation of color components.

2.1.7 Kendall's Tau

If x_i and y_i, for $i = 0, \ldots, n$, show intensities of corresponding pixels in X and Y, then for $i \neq j$, two possibilities exist: (1) $\text{sign}(x_j - x_i) = \text{sign}(y_j - y_i)$ or (2) $\text{sign}(x_j - x_i) = -\text{sign}(y_j - y_i)$. The first case is called concordance and the second case is called discordance. If a large number of corresponding intensity pairs are chosen from X and Y and there are more concordants than discordants, this is an indication that intensities in X and Y change together, although the magnitude of the change can differ from X to Y. Assuming that out of possible $\binom{n}{2}$ combinations, N_c pairs are concordants and N_d pairs are discordants, Kendall's τ is defined by [41]:

$$\tau = \frac{N_c - N_d}{n(n-1)/2}. \tag{2.20}$$

A variation of the Kendall's τ has been proposed [84] that places more emphasis on high (low) ranking values than on low (high) rankings ones. If, for example, noise is known to be influencing low-rank intensities more than high-rank intensities, the weighted τ makes it possible to put more emphasis on less noisy pixels than on noisy ones.

It has been shown [47] that if bivariate (X, Y) is normally distributed, Kendall's τ is related to Pearson correlation coefficient r by

$$r = \sin(\pi \tau / 2). \tag{2.21}$$

This relation shows that if (X, Y) is normally distributed, Pearson correlation coefficient can more finely distinguish images that represent different scenes than Kendall's τ because the sinusoidal relation between τ and r enables finer detection of changes in r in the neighborhoods of $\tau = 0$ compared to the neighborhood of $\tau = 1$. Conversely, Kendall's τ can more finely distinguish similar images from each other when compared to Pearson correlation coefficient. Chen [11], Fredricks

Fig. 2.6 Similarity images
obtained when matching the
template of Fig. 2.2a to
windows in the image of
Fig. 2.2b using
(**a**) Spearman's Rho, and
(**b**) Kendall's Tau. The
best-match position of the
template within the image in
each case is encircled

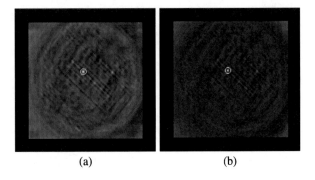

(a)   (b)

and Nelsen [27], and Kendall [42] have shown that when X and Y are independent, ρ/τ approaches $3/2$ as n approaches infinity. This result implies that Spearman's ρ and Kendall's τ have the same discrimination power when comparing images of different scenes.

Kendall's τ and Spearman's ρ both measure the association between two ordinal variables [31]. Both ρ and τ vary between -1 and $+1$, but for a considerable portion of this range, the absolute value of ρ is 1.5 times that of τ. Therefore, ρ and τ are not directly comparable. Gilpin [33] has provided formulas for converting Kendall's τ to Spearman's ρ and to Pearson's r.

An example comparing Spearman's ρ and Kendall's τ in template matching is given in Fig. 2.6. Figure 2.2a is used as the template and Fig. 2.2b is used as the image. The similarity images obtained by Spearman's ρ and Kendall's τ are shown in Figs. 2.6a and 2.6b, respectively. Compared to the similarity images obtained so far we see that the similarity images obtained by Spearman's ρ and Kendall's τ show most distinct peaks at the best-match position, and among the two, the Kendall's peak is more distinct.

Kendall's τ is one of the costliest similarity measures tested in this chapter. It requires computation of the concordants and discordants out of $n(n-1)/2$ combinations of corresponding intensity pairs in images of size n pixels. Therefore, the computational complexity of Kendall's τ is on the order of n^2 operations. In comparison, Pearson correlation coefficient requires on the order of n operations, and Spearman rank correlation requires on the order of $n \log_2 n$.

2.1.8 Greatest Deviation

Suppose intensities in an image are replaced by their ranks from 1 to n, where n is the number of pixels in the image. Suppose no ties exist among the intensities. Since ties are possible in a digital image, to remove them, the image is convolved with a Gaussian of a small standard deviation, such as 1 pixel. This will maintain image details while removing the ties by converting the intensities from integer to

Fig. 2.7 Template-matching results of (**a**) the greatest deviation and (**b**) the ordinal measure when using the template of Fig. 2.2a and the image of Fig. 2.2b

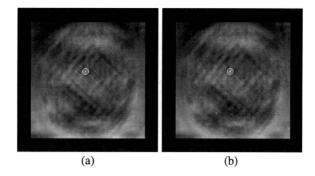

(a)   (b)

float. Assuming $R(x_i)$ is the rank of intensity x_i in image X and $R(y_i)$ is the rank of intensity y_i in image Y, let

$$d_i = \sum_{j=1}^{i} I\big[R(x_i) \leq i < R(y_j)\big], \tag{2.22}$$

where $I[E] = 1$ if E is true and $I[E] = 0$ if E is false. Also, let

$$D_i = \sum_{j=1}^{i} I\big[n + 1 - R(x_i) > R(y_i)\big], \tag{2.23}$$

then the greatest deviation between X and Y is calculated from [32]:

$$R_g = \frac{\max_i(D_i) - \max_i(d_i)}{n/2}. \tag{2.24}$$

As an example, consider the following:

$$
\begin{array}{lllllllllllllllll}
i\colon & 1 & 2 & 3 & 4 & 5 & 6 & 7 & 8 & 9 & 10 & 11 & 12 & 13 & 14 & 15 & 16 \\
x_i\colon & 1 & 2 & 3 & 4 & 5 & 6 & 7 & 8 & 9 & 10 & 11 & 12 & 13 & 14 & 15 & 16 \\
y_i\colon & 14 & 11 & 16 & 2 & 12 & 13 & 7 & 9 & 10 & 3 & 8 & 1 & 15 & 6 & 4 & 5 \\
d_i\colon & 1 & 2 & 3 & 3 & 4 & 5 & 5 & 6 & 6 & 5 & 4 & 3 & 3 & 2 & 1 & 0 \\
D_i\colon & 1 & 2 & 1 & 2 & 2 & 1 & 2 & 2 & 2 & 2 & 2 & 3 & 3 & 2 & 1 & 0 \\
\end{array} \tag{2.25}
$$

In this example, we find $R_g = (3 - 6)/8 = -3/8$. It has been shown that R_g varies between -1 and 1. $R_g = 1$ if y_i monotonically increases with x_i as i increases, and $R_g = 0$ if X and Y are independent. Similar to Spearman's ρ and Kendall's τ, this similarity measure is less sensitive to impulse noise (or occlusion in images) than correlation coefficient. However, for this same reason, it dulls the similarity measure and in the absence of impulse noise or outliers it may not be as effective as correlation coefficient. The similarity image obtained by searching the template of Fig. 2.2a in the image of Fig. 2.2b using this similarity measure is shown in Fig. 2.7a. The best-match position of the template within the image is encircled.

The greatest deviation similarity measure is computationally the costliest measure tested in this chapter. It first requires ordering the intensities in the images, which requires on the order of $n \log_2 n$ comparisons. Then, it requires on the order of n^2 comparisons to calculate d_i and D_i. Therefore, the computational complexity of the greatest deviation is on the order of n^2 with a coefficient larger than that in Kendall's τ.

2.1.9 Ordinal Measure

This similarity measure is the same as the greatest deviation except that it uses only D_i to define the similarity between two images [6]:

$$R_o = \frac{\max_i(D_i)}{n/2}. \tag{2.26}$$

The discrimination power of the ordinal measure is comparable to that of greatest deviation, with half the computations because it does not calculate d_i, which takes about the same time as calculating D_i. An example of template matching using this similarity measure is given in Fig. 2.7b. Figure 2.2a is used as the template and Fig. 2.2b is used as the image. The position of the highest ordinal value, which identifies the best match position of the template within the image is encircled. Greatest deviation and ordinal measure have produced very similar results.

2.1.10 Correlation Ratio

Correlation ratio is a similarity measure that quantifies the degree at which Y is a single-valued function of X and was first proposed by Pearson [66]. To find the correlation ratio between images X and Y, for entries in X with intensity i, intensities at the corresponding entries in Y are found. If mapping of intensities from X to Y is unique, this mapping will be a single-valued function; however, if an intensity in X corresponds to many intensities in Y, the mapping will not be unique. If intensities in Y are a single-valued function of intensities in X with a small amount of zero-mean noise, a narrow band will appear centered at the single-valued function. The standard deviation of intensities in Y that correspond to each intensity i in X can be used to measure the width of the band at intensity i:

$$\sigma_i = \left\{ \frac{1}{n_i} \sum_{x_i} (Y[x_i] - m_i)^2 \right\}^{\frac{1}{2}}, \tag{2.27}$$

where x_i shows an entry in X with intensity i, and $Y[x_i]$ shows the intensity at the corresponding entry in Y, and n_i is the number of entries in X with intensity i. m_i is the mean of intensities in Y corresponding to intensity i in X. σ_i measures the scatter of intensities in Y that map to intensity i in X. Therefore, average scatter over all intensities in X will be

$$\sigma_m = \frac{1}{256} \sum_{i=0}^{255} \sigma_i, \tag{2.28}$$

and variance of σ_i for $i = 0, \ldots, 255$ will be

$$D^2 = \left\{ \frac{1}{n} \sum_{i=0}^{255} \left(n_i \sigma_i^2 \right) \right\}, \tag{2.29}$$

where $n = \sum_{i=0}^{255} n_i$. Then, correlation ratio of Y on X is defined by

$$\eta_{yx} = \sqrt{1 - D^2}. \tag{2.30}$$

η_{yx} lies between 0 and 1 and $\eta_{yx} = 1$ only when $D = 0$, showing no variance in intensities of Y when mapping to intensities in X, and that implies a unique mapping from X to Y.

Given images X and Y of size n pixels, the steps to calculate the correlation ratio between the images can be summarized as follows:

1. Find entries in X that have intensity i; suppose there are n_i such entries, for $i = 0, \ldots, 255$.
2. If x_i is an entry in X that has intensity i, find the intensity at the corresponding entry in Y. Let this intensity be $Y[x_i]$. Note that there are n_i such intensities.
3. Find the average of such intensities $Y[x_i]$: $m_i = \frac{1}{n_i} \sum_{x_i} Y[x_i]$.
4. Find the variance of intensities in Y corresponding to intensity i in X: $\sigma_i^2 = \frac{1}{n_i} \sum_{x_i} (Y[x_i] - m_i)^2$.
5. Finally, calculate the correlation ratio from $\eta_{yx} = \sqrt{1 - \frac{1}{n} \sum_{i=0}^{255} n_i \sigma_i^2}$.

As the variance of intensities in Y that map to each intensity in X decreases, the correlation ratio between X and Y increases. This property makes correlation ratio suitable for comparing images that have considerable intensity differences when the intensities of one is related to the intensities of the other by some linear or nonlinear function. Combining Pearson correlation coefficient r and correlation ratio η, we can determine the linearity of intensities in X when mapped to intensities in Y. The measure to quantify this linearity is $(\eta^2 - r^2)$ [18] with the necessary condition for linearity being $\eta^2 - r^2 = 0$ [7].

Woods et al. [107] were the first to use correlation ratio in registration of multimodality images. Roche et al. [75, 76] normalized D^2 in (2.29) by the variance of intensities in Y. That is, they replaced D^2 with D^2/σ^2, where σ^2 represents the variance of intensities in Y.

A comparative study on registration of ultrasound and magnetic resonance (MR) images [61] found correlation ratio producing a higher percentage of correct matches than mutual information (described below). The superiority of correlation ratio over mutual information was independently confirmed by Lau et al. [50] in registration of inter- and intra-modality MR images. Matthäus et al. [57] used correlation ratio in brain mapping to identify cortical areas where there is a functional relationship between the electrical field strength applied to a point on the cortex and the resultant muscle response. Maps generated by correlation ratio were found to be in good agreement with maps calculated and verified by other methods.

Template-matching result using correlation ratio as the similarity measure, the template of Fig. 2.2a, and the image of Fig. 2.2b is shown in Fig. 2.8. Among the

Fig. 2.8 The similarity
image obtained when using
the correlation ratio as the
similarity measure and
searching for the template of
Fig. 2.2a in the image of
Fig. 2.2b

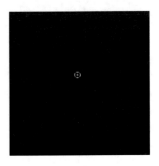

template-matching results presented so far, this similarity image shows the most
distinct peak, identifying the correct location of the template within the image with
least ambiguity.

Computationally, this measure requires calculation of 256 variances, each proportional to $256n_i$ additions and multiplications. n_i is on average $n/256$, therefore,
the computational cost of correlation ratio is proportional to $256n$.

2.1.11 Energy of Joint Probability Distribution

The relationship between intensities in two images is reflected in the joint probability distribution (JPD) of the images. After obtaining the joint histogram of the
images, each entry in the joint histogram is divided by n, the number of pixels in
each image to obtain the JPD of the images. If a single-valued mapping function exists that can uniquely map intensities in X to intensities in Y, the JPD of the image
will contain a thin density of points, showing the single-valued mapping function.
This is demonstrated in an example in Fig. 2.9.

If images X and Y are shifted with respect to each other, corresponding intensities will not produce a single-valued mapping but will fall irregularly in the joint
histogram and, consequently, in the JPD of the images. This is demonstrated in an
example in Fig. 2.9d. Therefore, when intensities in two images are related by a
single-valued function and the two images perfectly align, their JPD will contain
a thin density of points, showing the single-valued mapping function that relates
intensities of corresponding pixels in the images. When the images do not match,
the JPD of the images will show a scattering of points. This indicates that the JPDs
of correctly matching and incorrectly matching images can be distinguished from
each other by using a scatter measure of their JPD. Correlation ratio was one way
of measuring this scattering. Energy is another measure that can be used to achieve
this. The energy of the JPD of two images is defined by [83]:

$$E = \sum_{i=0}^{255} \sum_{j=0}^{255} p_{ij}^2, \tag{2.31}$$

Fig. 2.9 (**a**), (**b**) Two images
with intensities related by a
sinusoidal function. (**c**) The
JPD of intensities in (**a**)
and (**b**). The darker a point is,
the higher the count is at the
point. (**d**) The JPD of
intensities in image (**a**) and a
translated version of
image (**b**)

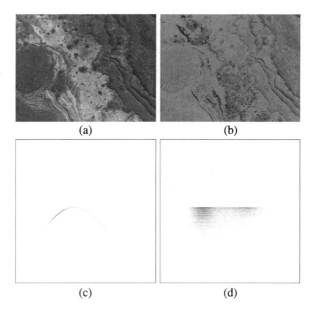

(a)   (b)

(c)   (d)

Fig. 2.10 The similarity
image obtained when using
the energy of JPD as the
similarity measure to search
for the template of Fig. 2.2a
in the image of Fig. 2.2b

where p_{ij} is the value at entry (i, j) in the JPD of the images. Therefore, given
an observed image and many saved images, the saved image best matching the observed image will be the one producing the highest JPD energy.

Energy of JPD can withstand considerable intensity differences between images,
but it quickly degrades with noise as noise causes intensities to shift from their true
values and produce a cloud of points in the JPD. This in turn, reduces the energy of
perfectly matching images, causing mismatches.

An example of template matching using the template of Fig. 2.2a and the image
of Fig. 2.2b with this similarity measure is given in Fig. 2.10. The presence of high
energy at the four corners of the similarity image, which corresponds to homogeneous areas in the image, indicates that any image can produce a high energy when
paired with a homogeneous image. If the homogeneous windows can be filtered out
through a preprocessing operation before calculating the energy, this similarity measure can be very effective in comparing multimodality images as evidenced by the

very distinct and robust peak at the best-match position, with very small similarities everywhere else.

Proposition 2.2 *Energy of JPD is not a metric.*

Proof Energy of the JPD of two images is not a metric because it is not reflexive. When $X = Y$ or $x_i = y_i$ for $i = 0, \ldots, n$, the JPD of the images will contain a 45-degree line, resulting in an entropy, which we denote by E_0. A 45-degree line in a JDP, however, can be obtained by adding a constant value to or multiplying a constant value by intensities in Y. This means, the same energy E_0 can be obtained from different images Y when compared to X. Therefore, energy of JPD is not a metric. For this same reason, any measure that is formulated in terms of the JPD of two images is not a metric.   □

Computationally, calculation of energy of JPD requires calculation of the JPD itself, which is on the order of n, and calculation of the energy from the obtained JPD, which is on the order of 256^2 multiplications. Therefore, the computational complexity of energy of JPD is on the order of n with an overhead, which is proportional to 256^2. This shows that the computational complexity of energy of JPD varies linearly with n.

2.1.12 Material Similarity

We know that when two noise-free multimodality images perfectly match, their JPD will contain a thin density of points, depicting the relation between intensities in the images. Under random noise, the thin density converts to a band of points with the width of the band depending on the magnitude of the noise. If noise is zero-mean, the band will be centered at the single-valued curve representing the mapping. To reduce the effect of noise, we smooth the JPD and look for the peak value at each column. Assuming the horizontal axis in a JPD shows intensities in X and the vertical axis shows intensities in Y, this smoothing and peak detection process will associate a unique intensity in Y to each intensity in X, thereby removing or reducing the effect of noise. The value at the peak can be used as the strength of the peak. This is demonstrated in an example in Fig. 2.11.

If two images match perfectly, very close mapping functions will be obtained when visiting every kth pixel once starting from 0 and another time starting from $k/2$. Figure 2.11d shows such peaks when $k = 4$. If two images do not match, the peaks detected in the two JPDs will be weaker and different. Taking this property into consideration, we define a similarity measure, appropriately named *material similarity*, which quantifies agreement between scene properties at corresponding pixels in images captured by the same or different sensors:

$$S_m = \sum_{i=0}^{255} \frac{\min\{p_{ij_1}, q_{ij_2}\}}{|j_1 - j_2| + d}, \tag{2.32}$$

Fig. 2.11 (**a**) The JPD of the image in Fig. 2.9a and the image in Fig. 2.9b after being corrupted with a Gaussian noise of standard deviation 10. *Darker points* show higher probabilities. The *horizontal axis* shows intensities in Fig. 2.9a and the *vertical axis* shows intensities in Fig. 2.9b. (**b**) Smoothing of the JPD with a Gaussian of standard deviation 3 pixels. (**c**) Detected peaks of the smoothed JPD. Stronger peaks are shown *darker*. (**d**) Overlaying of the peaks obtained in the JPDs of the images when visiting every fourth entry, once starting from entry 0 (*red*) and another time starting from entry 2 (*light blue*)

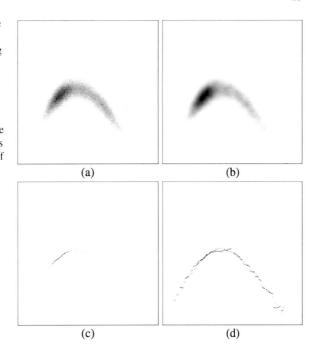

(a)   (b)

(c)   (d)

where i is the column number in a JPD and represents intensities in X. j_1 and j_2 are the row numbers of the peaks in column i in the two JPDs. The magnitudes of the peaks are shown by p_{ij_1} and q_{ij_2} in the two JPDs. d is a small number, such as 1, to avoid a possible division by 0. The numerator in (2.32) takes the smaller peak from the two JPDs at each column i. Therefore, if both peaks are strong, a higher similarity will be obtained than when only one of the peaks is strong. The denominator will ensure that as the peaks in the two JPDs at a column get closer and show the same mapping, a higher similarity measure is obtained.

Because only the peak value in each column is used to calculate S_m, when noise is zero-mean, the peak in the two JPDs is expected to coincide or be close to the peak when the same image without noise is used. Therefore, this similarity measure is less sensitive to zero-mean noise than the energy of JPD and other measures that are based on JDP of image intensities. Experimental results show that when n is sufficiently large, peaks in the JPDs with and without smoothing coincide, so there is no need to smooth the JPDs before detecting the peaks. Smoothing is recommended when n is small, typically smaller than 256. Template-matching results by material similarity using the template of Fig. 2.2a and the image of Fig. 2.2b without and with smoothing are shown in Figs. 2.12a and 2.12b. When noise is not present and the template is sufficiently large, smoothing the JPDs does not affect the outcome. Compared to the energy of JPD, we see that material similarity produces low similarities everywhere except at the best-match position, showing a robust measure that is not degraded when one of the images is homogeneous.

Computation of this similarity measure requires calculation of the two JPDs, which is on the order of n, and detection of the peaks with or without smoothing,

Fig. 2.12 (**a**) Template
matching with the material
similarity using the template
of Fig. 2.2a and the image of
Fig. 2.2b without smoothing
of the JPDs. (**b**) The same but
with smoothing of the JPDs.
The best-match position of
the template within the image
in each case is encircled

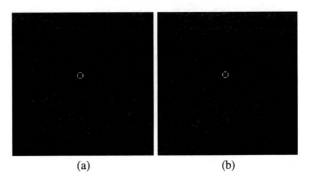

(a)   (b)

which is proportional to 256^2. Therefore, similar to energy of JPD, the computational complexity of material similarity is a linear function of n but with larger coefficients.

2.1.13 Shannon Mutual Information

Based on the observation that the JPD of registered images is less dispersed than the JPD of misregistered images, Collignon et al. [15] devised a method for registering multimodality images. Relative joint entropy or mutual information was used to quantify dispersion of JPD values and by maximizing it found best-matching images. Dispersion is minimum when dependency of intensities of corresponding pixels in images is maximum. Studholme et al. [88], Wells III et al. [104], Viola and Wells III [101], and Maes et al. [53] were among the first to use mutual information to register multimodality images.

Mutual information as a measure of dependence was introduced by Shannon [82] and later generalized by Gel'fand and Yaglom [30]. The generalized Shannon mutual information is defined by [24, 55]:

$$S_{\mathrm{MI}} = \sum_{i=0}^{255} \sum_{j=0}^{255} p_{ij} \log_2 \frac{p_{ij}}{p_i p_j}, \tag{2.33}$$

where p_{ij} is the probability that corresponding pixels in X and Y have intensities i and j, respectively, and shows the value at entry ijth in the JPD of the images; p_i is the probability of intensity i appearing in image X and is equal to the sum of entries in the ith column in the JDP of the images; and p_j is the probability of intensity j appearing in image Y and is equal to the sum of entries in the jth row of the JPD of the images.

Equation (2.33) can be written as follows also:

$$S_{\mathrm{MI}} = \sum_{i=0}^{255} \sum_{j=0}^{255} p_{ij} \log_2 p_{ij}$$
$$- \sum_{i=0}^{255} p_i \log_2 p_i - \sum_{j=0}^{255} p_j \log_2 p_j, \tag{2.34}$$

where

$$p_i = \sum_{j=0}^{255} p_{ij} \qquad (2.35)$$

and

$$p_j = \sum_{i=0}^{255} p_{ij}. \qquad (2.36)$$

Therefore, letting

$$E_i = -\sum_{j=0}^{255} p_j \log_2 p_j, \qquad (2.37)$$

$$E_j = -\sum_{i=0}^{255} p_i \log_2 p_i, \qquad (2.38)$$

and

$$E_{ij} = -\sum_{i=0}^{255} \sum_{j=0}^{255} p_{ij} \log_2 p_{ij}, \qquad (2.39)$$

we have

$$S_{\mathrm{MI}} = E_i + E_j - E_{ij}, \qquad (2.40)$$

which defines mutual information as the difference between the sum of Shannon marginal entropies and the joint entropy. Shannon's mutual information is a powerful measure for determining the similarity between multimodality images, but it is sensitive to noise. As noise in one or both images increases, dispersion in the JDP of the images increases, reducing the mutual information between perfectly matching images, causing mismatches.

When calculating the mutual information of images X and Y, the implied assumption is that the images represent random and independent samples from two distributions. This condition of independency is often violated because x_i and x_{i+1} depend on each other, and y_i and y_{i+1} depend on each other. As a result, calculated mutual information is not accurate and not reflective of the dependency between X and Y. To take into account the spatial information in images, rather than finding the JPD of corresponding intensities in images, the JPD of intensity pairs of adjacent pixels has been suggested [81]. The obtained mutual information, which is called *high-order mutual information* has been shown to produce more accurate registration results than traditionally used first-order mutual information [81].

Note that the JPD of intensity pairs becomes a 4-D probability distribution and to obtain a well populated 4-D JPD, the images being registered should be sufficiently large to create a meaningful probability distribution. Otherwise, a very

Fig. 2.13 Template matching
using Shannon mutual
information, the template of
Fig. 2.2a, and the image of
Fig. 2.2b. The best-match
position of the template
within the image is encircled

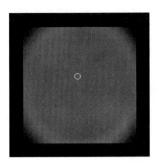

sparse array of very small numbers will be obtained, making the process ineffective and perhaps not any better than the regular entropy, if not worse. The requirement that images used in high-order mutual information be large makes high-order
mutual information unsuitable for registration of images with nonlinear geometric
differences because the subimages to be compared for correspondence cannot be
large.

To include spatial information in the registration process when using mutual information, Pluim et al. [68] used the product of mutual information and a gradient term instead of the mutual information alone. It should be noted that different-
modality images produce different gradients at corresponding pixels. Therefore, if
gradient information is used together with mutual information, the images to be registered should be of the same modality. This, however, beats the purpose of using
mutual information, which is designed for registration of different-modality images.
If images are in the same modality, other more powerful and computationally efficient similarity measures are available for their registration.

Since mutual information between two images varies with the content and size
of images, Studholme et al. [89] provided a means to normalize mutual information
with respect to the size and content of the images. This normalization enables effective localization of one image with respect to another by sliding one image over the
other and determining the similarity between their overlap area.

Shannon mutual information is one of the most widely used similarity measures
in image registration. Point coordinates [71], gradient orientation [52], and phase
[60] have been used in the place of intensity to calculate mutual information and register images. Shannon mutual information has been used to register multiresolution
[14, 54, 93, 108], monomodal [28, 112], multimodal [58, 103, 109], temporal [13],
deformed [17, 20, 43, 51, 85, 90, 96], and dynamic images [46, 105]. An example
of template matching using Shannon mutual information as the similarity measure
is given in Fig. 2.13.

The computational complexity of Shannon mutual information is proportional
to $256^2 + n$ because creation of the JPD of two images of size n pixels takes
on the order of n additions and calculation of E_3 takes on the order of 256^2
multiplications and logarithmic evaluations. Its computational complexity, therefore, is a linear function of n but with larger coefficients than those of the energy
of JPD.

Fig. 2.14 The similarity image obtained when using Rényi mutual information of the order $\alpha = 2$ to search for the template of Fig. 2.2a in the image of Fig. 2.2b. The best-match position of the template within the image is encircled

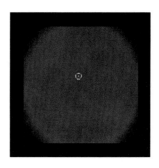

2.1.14 Rényi Mutual Information

Rényi mutual information is defined in terms of Rényi entropy, and Rényi entropy of order α of a finite discrete probability distribution $\{p_i : i = 0, \ldots, 255\}$ is defined by [73]:

$$E_\alpha = \frac{1}{1-\alpha} \log_2 \left(\sum_{i=0}^{255} p_i^\alpha \right), \qquad (2.41)$$

which is a generalization of Shannon entropy to a one-parameter family of entropies. As parameter α of the entropy approaches 1, Rényi entropy approaches Shannon entropy [73]. Moreover, as α is varied, Rényi entropy varies within range $\log_2(p_{\max}) \leq E_\alpha \leq \log_2(256)$, where $p_{\max} = \max_{i=0}^{255}\{p_i\}$ [39, 113]. Rényi mutual information is defined by [102]:

$$R_\alpha = \frac{E_\alpha^i + E_\alpha^j}{E_\alpha^{ij}}, \qquad (2.42)$$

where E_α^i is the Rényi entropy of order α of probability distribution $p_i = \sum_{j=0}^{255} p_{ij}$ for $i = 1, \ldots, 255$, E_α^j is the Rényi entropy of order α of $p_j = \sum_{i=0}^{255} p_{ij}$ for $j = 0, \ldots, 255$, and E_α^{ij} is the Rényi entropy of order α of probability distribution $\{p_{ij} : i, j = 0, \ldots, 255\}$. Equation (2.42) is based on the normalized mutual information of Studholme et al. [89]: $S_{\mathrm{NMI}} = (E_1 + E_2)/E_3$, where E_1 and E_2 are the marginal entropies and E_3 is the joint entropy. An example of Rényi mutual information with $\alpha = 2$ in template matching using the template of Fig. 2.2a and the image of Fig. 2.2b is given in Fig. 2.14.

As the order α of Rényi mutual information is increased, entries in the JPD with higher values are magnified, reducing the effect of outliers that randomly fall in the JPD. Therefore, under impulse noise and occlusion, Rényi mutual information is expected to perform better than Shannon mutual information. Under zero-mean noise also, Rényi mutual information is expected to perform better than Shannon mutual information for the same reason though not as much. Computationally, Rényi mutual information is about 20 to 30% more expensive than Shannon mutual information, because it requires power computations in addition to the calculations required by the Shannon mutual information.

Fig. 2.15 The similarity
image obtained when using
Tsallis mutual information to
search for the template of
Fig. 2.2a in the image of
Fig. 2.2b. The best-match
position of the template
within the image is encircled

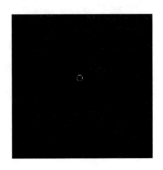

2.1.15 Tsallis Mutual Information

If instead of Shannon or Rényi entropy, Tsallis entropy is used to calculate the
mutual information, Tsallis mutual information will be obtained [102]. Tsallis entropy of order q for a discrete probability distribution $\{p_{ij} : i, j = 0, \dots, 255\}$ with
$0 \le p_{ij} \le 1$ and $\sum_{i=0}^{255} \sum_{i=0}^{255} p_{ij} = 1$ is defined by [94]:

$$S_q = \frac{1}{(q-1)} \left(1 - \sum_{i=0}^{255} \sum_{j=0}^{255} p_{ij}^q \right), \tag{2.43}$$

where q is a real number and as it approaches 1, Tsallis entropy approaches Shannon
entropy. S_q is positive for all values of q and is convergent for $q > 1$ [8, 70]. In the
case of equiprobability, S_q is a monotonic function of the number of intensities i
and j in the images [22]. Tsallis mutual information is defined by [19, 102]:

$$R_q = S_q^i + S_q^j + (1-q)S_q^i S_q^j - S_q, \tag{2.44}$$

where

$$S_q^i = \frac{1}{q-1} \sum_{j=0}^{255} p_{ij} \left(1 - p_{ij}^{q-1} \right) \tag{2.45}$$

and

$$S_q^j = \frac{1}{q-1} \sum_{i=0}^{255} p_{ij} \left(1 - p_{ij}^{q-1} \right). \tag{2.46}$$

Tsallis entropy makes outliers less important than Rényi entropy when q takes a
value larger than 1 because of the absence of the logarithmic function in the formula.
Therefore, Tsallis mutual information will make the similarity measure even less
sensitive to noise than Rényi mutual information and, therefore, more robust under
noise compared to Shannon mutual information and Rényi mutual information.

An example of template matching using Tsallis mutual information with $q = 2$ is
given in Fig. 2.15. Compared to the similarities discussed so far, this similarity measure has produced the most distinct peak when matching the template of Fig. 2.2a
to the windows of the same size in the image of Fig. 2.2b.

Fig. 2.16 The similarity
image obtained using I_α as
the similarity measure with
$\alpha = 2$ and when searching for
the template of Fig. 2.2a in
the image of Fig. 2.2b. The
best-match position of the
template within the image is
encircled

The performance of Tsallis mutual information in image registration varies with parameter q. Generally, the larger the q is the less sensitive measure R_q will be to outliers. The optimal value of q, however, is image dependent. In registration of functional MR images, Tedeschi et al. [91] found the optimal value for q to be 0.7.

Computationally, Tsallis mutual information is as costly as Rényi mutual information, because it replaces a logarithmic evaluation with a number of multiplications. When the problem is to locate the position of one image inside another through an iterative process, Martin et al. [56] have found that a faster convergence speed is achieved by Tsallis mutual information than by Shannon mutual information due to its steeper slope of the similarity image in the neighborhood of the peak.

2.1.16 F-Information Measures

The divergence or distance between the joint distribution and the product of the marginal distributions of two images can be used to measure the similarity between the images. A class of divergence measures that contains mutual information is the f-information or f-divergence. F-information measures include [69, 95]:

$$I_\alpha = \frac{1}{\alpha(\alpha - 1)} \left(\sum_{i=0}^{255} \sum_{j=0}^{255} \frac{p_{ij}^\alpha}{(p_i p_j)^{\alpha-1}} - 1 \right), \tag{2.47}$$

$$M_\alpha = \sum_{i=0}^{255} \sum_{j=0}^{255} \left| p_{ij}^\alpha - (p_i p_j)^\alpha \right|^{\frac{1}{\alpha}}, \tag{2.48}$$

$$\chi^\alpha = \sum_{i=0}^{255} \sum_{j=0}^{255} \frac{|p_{ij} - p_i p_j|^\alpha}{(p_i p_j)^{\alpha-1}}. \tag{2.49}$$

I_α is defined for $\alpha \neq 0$ and $\alpha \neq 1$ and it converges to Shannon information as α approaches 1 [95]. M_α is defined for $0 < \alpha \leq 1$, and χ^α is defined for $\alpha > 1$. Pluim et al. [69] have found that for the proper values of α these divergence measures can register multimodality images more accurately than Shannon mutual information. An example of template matching using I_α with $\alpha = 2$ is given in Fig. 2.16.

Computationally, f-information is costlier than Shannon mutual information, because in addition to calculating the JPD of the images, it requires multiple power computations for each JPD entry. The computational complexity of f-information is still proportional to $256^2 + n$ and, therefore, a linear function of n but with higher coefficients compared to Shannon mutual information.

2.2 Dissimilarity Measures

2.2.1 L_1 Norm

L_1 norm, Manhattan norm, or sum of absolute intensity differences is one of the oldest dissimilarity measures used to compare images. Given sequences $X = \{x_i : i = 1, \ldots, n\}$ and $Y = \{y_i : i = 1, \ldots, n\}$ representing intensities in two images in raster-scan order, the L_1 norm between the images is defined by [92]:

$$L_1 = \sum_{i=1}^{n} |x_i - y_i|. \tag{2.50}$$

If images X and Y are obtained by the same sensor and under the same environmental conditions, and if the sensor has a very high signal to noise ratio, this simple measure can produce matching results that are as accurate as those produced by more expensive measures. For instance, images in a video sequence or stereo images obtained under low noise level can be effectively matched using this measure. An example of template matching with L_1 norm using the template of Fig. 2.2a and the image of Fig. 2.2b is given in Fig. 2.17a.

Computationally, this measure requires determination of n absolute differences and n additions for an image of size n pixels. Barnea and Silverman [5] suggested ways to further speed up the computations by abandoning a case early in the computations when there is evidence that a correct match is not likely to obtain. Coarse-to-fine and two-stage approaches have also been proposed as a means to speed up this measure in template matching [77, 97].

2.2.2 Median of Absolute Differences

At the presence of salt-and-pepper or impulse noise, L_1 norm produces an exaggerated distance measure. For images of a fixed size with n pixels, L_1 norm which measures the sum of absolute intensity differences between corresponding pixels in two images is the same as the average absolute intensity difference between corresponding pixels in the images. To reduce the effect of impulse noise on the calculated dissimilarity measure, instead of the average of absolute differences, the median of

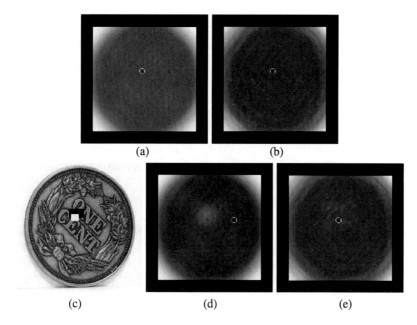

(a) (b)

(c) (d) (e)

Fig. 2.17 Dissimilarity images obtained when using (**a**) L_1 norm and (**b**) MAD in template matching using the template of Fig. 2.2a and the image of Fig. 2.2b. (**c**) Same as image of Fig. 2.2b but with introduction of occlusion near the best-match position. Determination of the best match position of the template within the occluded image by (**c**) the L_1 norm and (**d**) by MAD, respectively

absolute differences (MAD) may be used to measure the dissimilarity between two images. MAD measure is defined by

$$MAD = med_{i=1}^{n} |x_i - y_i|. \tag{2.51}$$

Although salt-and-pepper noise considerably affects L_1 norm, its effect on MAD is minimal. Calculation of MAD involves finding the absolute intensity differences of corresponding pixels in images, ordering the absolute differences, and taking the median value as the dissimilarity measure. In addition to impulse noise, this measure is effective in determining dissimilarity between images containing occluded regions. These are regions that are visible in only one of the images. For example, in stereo images, they appear in areas where there is a sharp change in scene depth. Effectiveness of MAD in matching of stereo images has been demonstrated by Chambon and Crouzil [9, 10]. This is a robust measure that does not change at the presence of up to 50% outliers [36, 80].

An example of template matching with MAD using the template of Fig. 2.2a and the image of Fig. 2.2b is given in Fig. 2.17b. Comparing this dissimilarity image with that obtained by L_1 norm, we see that the best-match position in the MAD image is not as distinct as that in the L_1 image. This implies that when salt-and-pepper noise or occlusion is not present, MAD does not perform as well as L_1 norm. While MAD uses information about half of the pixels that have the most similar intensities, L_1 norm uses information about all pixels with similar and dissimilar intensities to measure the dissimilarity between two images.

By introducing occlusion in Fig. 2.2b near the best-match position, we observe that while L_1 norm misses the best match position as depicted in Fig. 2.17d, MAD correctly locates the template within the image without any difficulty. Presence of occlusion barely affects the dissimilarity image obtained by MAD, indicating that MAD is a more robust measure under occlusion than L_1 norm.

Computationally, MAD is much slower than L_1 norm. In addition to requiring computation of n absolute differences, it requires ordering the absolute differences, which is on the order of $n \log_2 n$ comparisons. Therefore, the computational complexity of MAD is $O(n \log_2 n)$.

2.2.3 Square L_2 Norm

Square L_2 norm, square Euclidean distance, or sum of squared intensity differences of corresponding pixels in sequences $X = \{x_i : i = 1, \dots, n\}$ and $Y = \{y_i : i = 1, \dots, n\}$ is defined by [23]:

$$L_2^2 = \sum_{i=1}^{n} (x_i - y_i)^2. \tag{2.52}$$

Compared to L_1 norm, square L_2 norm emphasizes larger intensity differences between X and Y and is one of the popular measures in stereo matching. Compared to Pearson correlation coefficient, this measure is more sensitive to the magnitude of intensity difference between images. Therefore, it will produce poorer results than correlation coefficient when used in the matching of images of a scene taken under different lighting conditions.

To reduce the geometric difference between images captured from different views of a scene, adaptive windows that vary in size depending on local intensity variation have been used [64]. Another way to deemphasize image differences caused by viewing differences is to weigh intensities in each image proportional to their distances to the image center, used as the center of focus in matching [63].

An example of template matching using square L_2 norm, the template of Fig. 2.2a, and the image of Fig. 2.2b is given in Fig. 2.18a. The obtained dissimilarity image is very similar to that obtained by L_1 norm.

The computational complexity of square L_2 norm is close to that of L_1 norm. After finding the difference of corresponding intensities in X and Y, L_1 norm finds the absolute of the differences while L_2 norm squares the differences. Therefore, the absolute-value operation in L_1 norm is replaced with a multiplication in L_2 norm.

2.2.4 Median of Square Differences

The median of square differences (MSD) is the robust version of the square L_2 norm. When one or both images are corrupted with impulse noise, or when one

Fig. 2.18 Dissimilarity images obtained when using (**a**) L_2 norm and (**b**) MSD in template matching with the template of Fig. 2.2a and the image of Fig. 2.2b. Template-matching results by (**c**) L_2 norm and (**d**) MSD when using the same template but the image of Fig. 2.17c

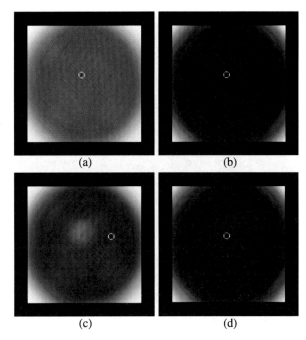

(a)   (b)

(c)   (d)

image contains occluded regions with respect to the other, by discarding half of the largest square differences, the influence of noise and occlusion is reduced. This distance measure is defined by

$$MSD = med_{i=1}^{n}(x_i - y_i)^2. \tag{2.53}$$

When the images are not corrupted by noise and do not contain occluded regions, MSD does not perform as well as square L_2 norm, because MSD uses information about the most similar half of pixel correspondences, while L_2 norm uses information about similar as well as dissimilar pixels, and dissimilar pixels play as important a role in template matching as similar pixels.

Using the template of Fig. 2.2a and the image of Fig. 2.2b, the dissimilarity image shown in Fig. 2.18b is obtained. We see the best match position determined by L_2 norm is more distinct than that obtained by MSD. In the absence of noise and occlusion, L_2 norm is generally expected to perform better than MSD in matching.

At the presence of occlusion or impulse noise, MSD is expected to perform better than L_2 norm. To verify this, template-matching is performed using the template of Fig. 2.2a and the image of Fig. 2.17c, which is same as the image of Fig. 2.2b except for introducing occlusion near the best-match position. The dissimilarity images obtained by L_2 norm and MSD are shown in Figs. 2.18c and 2.18d, respectively. Although the dissimilarity image of the L_2 norm has changed considerably under occlusion, the dissimilarity image of MSD is hardly changed. Use of MSD in matching of stereo images with occlusions has been reported by Lan and Mohr [49]. This dissimilarity measure is based on the well-established least median of squares distance measure used in robust regression under contaminated data [79].

The computational complexity of MSD is similar to that of MAD. After finding n square intensity differences of corresponding pixels in the given sequences, the intensity differences are squared and ordered, which requires on the order of $n \log_2 n$ comparisons. Therefore, the computational complexity of MSD is $O(n \log_2 n)$.

The performance of MSD is similar to that of MAD. This is because the smallest 50% absolute intensity differences used in MAD and the smallest 50% square intensity differences used in MSD both pick the same pixels in a template and a matching window to measure the dissimilarity between the template and the window. Also, both have the same computational complexity except for MAD using absolute intensity difference while MSD using square intensity difference, which are computationally very close if not the same.

2.2.5 Normalized Square L_2 Norm

Pearson correlation coefficient uses intensities in an image normalized with respect to the mean intensity. This makes correlation coefficient invariant to bias in image intensities. It also divides the inner product of the mean-normalized intensities by the standard deviation of intensities in each image. This process normalizes the measure with respect to image contrast. Another way to make the measure insensitive to image contrast, as suggested by Evangelidis and Psarakis [25], is to divide the mean-normalized intensities in each image by the standard deviation of the intensities. The sum of squared differences of bias and scale normalized intensities in each image is then used to measure the dissimilarity between the images.

Given images $X = \{x_i : i = 1, \ldots, n\}$ and $Y = \{y_i : i = 1, \ldots, n\}$, assuming average intensities in X and Y are $\bar{x}$ and $\bar{y}$, respectively, and letting

$$\sigma_x = \sqrt{\frac{1}{n} \sum_{i=1}^{n} (x_i - \bar{x})^2}, \qquad (2.54)$$

$$\sigma_y = \sqrt{\frac{1}{n} \sum_{i=1}^{n} (y_i - \bar{y})^2}, \qquad (2.55)$$

the normalized square L_2 norm is defined by [25]:

$$\text{Normalized } L_2^2 = \sum_{i=1}^{n} \left(\frac{x_i - \bar{x}}{\sigma_x} - \frac{y_i - \bar{y}}{\sigma_y} \right)^2. \qquad (2.56)$$

Normalizing the intensities in an image first with respect to its mean and then with respect to its standard deviation normalizes the intensities with respect to bias and gain/scale. Therefore, similar to correlation coefficient, this measure is suitable for comparing images that are captured under different lighting conditions. An example of template matching using normalized square L_2 norm is given in Fig. 2.19.

Compared to correlation coefficient, this measure is somewhat slower because it requires normalization of each intensity before calculating the sum of squared

Fig. 2.19 The dissimilarity image obtained using normalized square L_2 norm to search for the template of Fig. 2.2a in the image of Fig. 2.2b. The best-match position of the template within the image is encircled

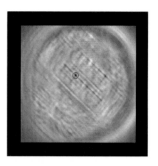

Fig. 2.20 The dissimilarity image obtained using incremental sign distance when searching for the template of Fig. 2.2a in the image of Fig. 2.2b. The best-match position of the template within the image is encircled

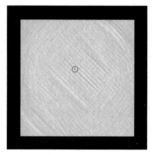

differences between them. In the calculation of correlation coefficient, scale normalization is performed once after calculating the inner product of the normalized intensities.

2.2.6 Incremental Sign Distance

Given image X with intensities $\{x_i : i = 1, \ldots, n\}$, create a binary sequence $B_X = \{b_i : i = 1, \ldots, n - 1\}$ with b_i showing the sign of the intensity difference between entries x_i and x_{i+1}. That is, let $b_i = 1$ if $x_{i+1} > x_i$ and $b_i = 0$ otherwise. Similarly, replace image Y with binary image B_Y. The Hamming distance between B_X and B_Y can then be used to measure the dissimilarity between the images [40].

Use of intensity change rather than raw intensity at each pixel makes the calculated measure insensitive to additive changes in scene lighting. Use of the sign changes rather than the raw changes makes the measure insensitive to sharp lighting changes in the scene caused by, for example, shadows. However, due to the use of intensity difference of adjacent pixels, the process is sensitive to noise in homogeneous areas.

Incremental sign distance is a relatively fast measure as it requires on the order of n comparisons, additions, and subtractions. The measure is suitable for comparing images that are not noisy but may have considerable intensity differences. The result of template matching using the template of Fig. 2.2a and the image of Fig. 2.2b with this dissimilarity measure is shown in Fig. 2.20.

Fig. 2.21 Template matching
using intensity-ratio variance,
the template of Fig. 2.2a, and
the image of Fig. 2.2b. The
best-match position of the
template within the image is
encircled

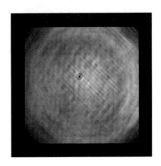

2.2.7 Intensity-Ratio Variance

If intensities in one image are a scaled version of intensities in another image, the
ratio of corresponding intensities across the image domain will be a constant. If two
images are obtained at different exposures of a camera, this measure can be used to
effectively determine the dissimilarity between them. Letting $r_i = (x_i + \varepsilon)/(y_i + \varepsilon)$,
where ε is a small number, such as 1 to avoid division by 0, intensity-ratio variance
is defined by [106]:

$$R_V = \frac{1}{n} \sum_{i=1}^{n} (r_i - \bar{r})^2, \qquad (2.57)$$

where

$$\bar{r} = \frac{1}{n} \sum_{i=1}^{n} r_i. \qquad (2.58)$$

Although invariant to scale difference between intensities in images, this measure is sensitive to additive intensity changes, such as noise. The computational
complexity of intensity-ratio variance is on the order of n as it requires computation
of a ratio at each pixel and determination of the variance of the ratios.

An example of template matching by intensity-ratio variance using the template
of Fig. 2.2a and the image of Fig. 2.2b is given in Fig. 2.21.

2.2.8 Intensity-Mapping-Ratio Variance

This measure combines correlation ratio, which measures intensity-mapping variance, with intensity-ratio variance [37]. Use of intensity ratios rather than raw intensities makes the measure less sensitive to multiplicative intensity differences between images, such as difference in gains of the sensors. Use of mapping-ratio variance rather than ratio variance makes the measure insensitive to differences in sensor
characteristics. By minimizing the variance in intensity-mapping ratios, the measure
is made insensitive to differences in sensor characteristics and the gain parameters
of the sensors or the exposure levels of the cameras capturing the images.

Fig. 2.22 The dissimilarity image obtained by the intensity-mapping-ratio variance when searching the template of Fig. 2.2a in the image of Fig. 2.2b. The best-match position of the template within the image is encircled

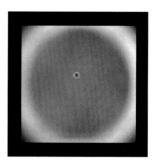

Computationally, this measure is slightly more expensive than the correlation ratio for the additional calculation of the intensity ratios. A template matching example by this dissimilarity measure using the template of Fig. 2.2a and the image of Fig. 2.2b is given in Fig. 2.22.

2.2.9 Rank Distance

This measure is defined as the L_1 norm of rank ordered intensities in two images. Given images $X = \{x_i : i = 1, \dots, n\}$ and $Y = \{y_i : i = 1, \dots, n\}$, intensity x_i is replaced with its rank $R(x_i)$ and intensity y_i is replaced with its rank $R(y_i)$. To reduce or eliminate ties among ranks in an image, the image is smoothed with a Gaussian of a small standard deviation, such as 1 pixel. The rank distance between images X and Y is defined by:

$$D_r = \frac{1}{n} \sum_{i=1}^{n} |R(x_i) - R(y_i)|. \tag{2.59}$$

Since $0 \le |R(x_i) - R(y_i)| \le n$, D_r will be between 0 and 1. The smaller is the rank distance between two images, the less dissimilar the images will be. Rank distance works quite well in images that are corrupted with impulse noise or contain occlusion. In addition, rank distance is insensitive to white noise if noise magnitude is small enough not to change the rank of intensities in an image. Furthermore, rank distance is insensitive to bias and gain differences between intensities in images just like other ordinal measures.

A template-matching example with rank distance using the template of Fig. 2.2a and the image of Fig. 2.2b is given in Fig. 2.23. Among the distance measures tested so far, rank distance finds the location of the template within the image most distinctly.

Rank distance is one of the fastest ordinal measures as it requires only a subtraction and a sign check at each pixel once ranks of the intensities are determined. The major portion of the computation time is spent on ranking the intensities in each image, which is on the order of $n \log_2 n$ comparisons for an image of size n pixels. Therefore, the computational complexity of rank distance is on the order of $n \log_2 n$.

Fig. 2.23 Template matching
with rank distance using the
template of Fig. 2.2a and the
image of Fig. 2.2b. The
best-match position of the
template within the image is
encircled

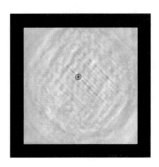

Proposition 2.3 *Rank distance is not a metric.*

Proof Rank distance is not a metric because it is not reflexive. When $X = Y$, we
have $x_i = y_i$ for $i = 1, \ldots, n$, and so $D_r = 0$. However, when $D_r = 0$, because
D_r is the sum of n non-negative numbers, it requires $|R(x_i) - R(y_i)| = 0$ for all i.
$|R(x_i) - R(y_i)|$ can be 0 when $y_i = a + x_i$ or $y_i = bx_i$, where a and b are constants;
therefore, $D_r = 0$ does not necessarily imply $X = Y$. For this same reason, none of
the ordinal measures is a metric.   □

2.2.10 Joint Entropy

Entropy represents uncertainty in an outcome. The larger the entropy, the more informative the outcome will be. Joint entropy represents uncertainty in joint outcomes. The dependency of joint outcomes determines the joint entropy. The higher
the dependency between joint outcomes, the lower the uncertainty will be and, thus,
the lower the entropy will be. When joint outcomes are independent, uncertainty
will be the highest, producing the highest entropy. Given an observed image and a
number of saved images, the saved image that produces the lowest joint entropy with
the observed image is the image best matching the observed image. Joint entropy
is calculated from the JPD of the images. Assuming p_{ij} represents the probability
that intensities i and j appear at corresponding pixels in the images, Shannon joint
entropy is defined by [74, 82]:

$$D_E = -\sum_{i=0}^{255}\sum_{j=0}^{255} p_{ij} \log_2 p_{ij}. \tag{2.60}$$

Similar to mutual information, the performance of joint entropy quickly degrades
with increasing noise. The measure, however, remains relatively insensitive to intensity differences between images and, thus, is suitable for comparing multimodality
images.

An example of template matching by minimizing the entropy of JPD of the template of Fig. 2.2a and windows of the same size in the image of Fig. 2.2b is given in

Fig. 2.24 Template matching
using entropy of JPD of the
template of Fig. 2.2a and
windows of the same size in
the image of Fig. 2.2b. The
center of the window best
matching the template is
encircled

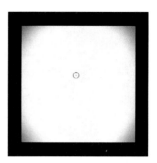

Fig. 2.24. The intensity at a pixel in the dissimilarity image is proportional to the entropy of the JDP of the template and the window centered at the pixel in the image. Relatively small values at the four corners of the dissimilarity image indicate that any image will produce a low entropy when compared with a homogeneous image. A preprocessing operation that marks the homogeneous windows so they are not used in matching is needed to reduce the number of mismatches by this measure.

The computational cost of joint entropy is proportional to both 256^2 and n. It requires on the order of n comparisons to prepare the JDP and on the order of 256^2 multiplications and logarithmic evaluations to calculate the joint entropy from the obtained JPD.

2.2.11 Exclusive F-Information

Information exclusively contained in images X and Y when observed jointly is known as exclusive f-information. Exclusive f-information $D_f(X, Y)$ is related to joint entropy $E(X, Y)$ and mutual information $S_{MI}(X, Y)$ by [78]:

$$D_f(X, Y) = E(X, Y) - S_{MI}(X, Y). \tag{2.61}$$

Since mutual information is defined by [95]:

$$S_{MI}(X, Y) = E(X) + E(X) - E(X, Y), \tag{2.62}$$

we obtain

$$D_f(X, Y) = 2E(X, Y) - E(X) - E(Y). \tag{2.63}$$

The larger the exclusive f-information between images X and Y, the more dissimilar the images will be. Therefore, in template matching, the window in an image that produces the lowest exclusive f-information with a template will be the window most similar to the template and locates the position of the template within the image. An example of template matching by exclusive f-information using the template of Fig. 2.2a and the image of Fig. 2.2b is given in Fig. 2.25.

Computational cost of exclusive f-information is proportional to both 256^2 and n as it requires computation of the same terms as in mutual information as shown in (2.62) and (2.63).

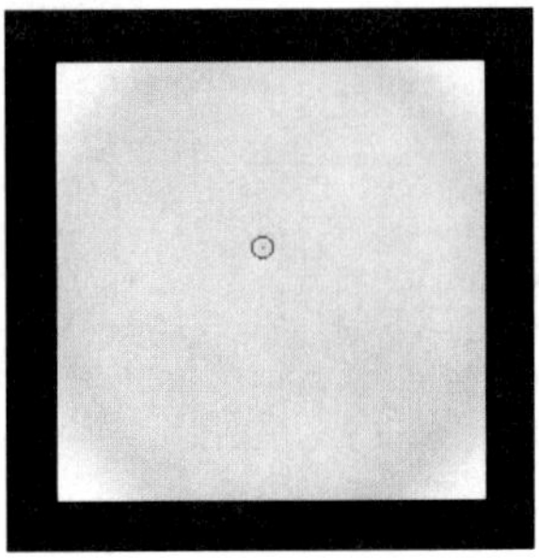

Fig. 2.25 Template matching
using exclusive
f-information, the template
of Fig. 2.2a, and the image of
Fig. 2.2b. The best-match
position of the template
within the image is encircled

2.3 Performance Evaluation

To evaluate the performances of the similarity and dissimilarity measures described
in the preceding sections, the accuracies and speeds of the measures are determined
on a number of synthetic and real images and the results are compared.

2.3.1 Experimental Setup

To create image sets where correspondence between images is known, the image
shown in Fig. 2.26a is used as the base. This image, which shows a Martian rock,
contains various intensities and intensity variations. To evaluate the sensitivity of
the measures to zero-mean noise, Gaussian noise of standard deviations 5, 10, and
20 were generated and added to this image to obtain the noisy images shown in
Figs. 2.26b–d.

Images in Figs. 2.26a and 2.26b are considered Set 1, images in Figs. 2.26a and
2.26c are considered Set 2, and images in Figs. 2.26a and 2.26d are considered
Set 3. These image sets will be used to measure the sensitivity of the similarity and
dissimilarity measures to low, moderate, and high levels of noise.

To find the sensitivity of the measures to intensity differences between images,
intensities of the base image were changed as follows:

1. Intensities at the four quadrants of the base image were changed by -30, -10,
   10, and 30 to obtain the image shown in Fig. 2.27b. Intensities below 0 were set
   to 0 and intensities above 255 were set to 255. These images simulate images
   taken at different exposures of a camera. Sharp intensity changes between the
   quadrants can be considered intensity changes caused by shadows.
2. Intensities in the base image were changed based on their locations using a
   sinusoidal function. Assuming the base image has n_r rows and n_c columns,
   and the intensity at (x, y) is I, intensity I was replaced with $O = I +
   50 \sin(4\pi y/n_r) \cos(4\pi x/n_c)$ to obtain Fig. 2.27c. This simulates smoothly vary-
   ing radiometric changes in a scene between times images 2.27a and 2.27c were
   captured.
3. Intensities in the base image were changed by a sinusoidal function based on
   their values. Assuming I is the intensity at a pixel in the base image, intensity

Fig. 2.26 (**a**) A relatively noise-free image of a Martian rock, courtesy of NASA. This image is used as the base. (**b**)–(**d**) The images obtained after adding Gaussian noise of standard deviations 5, 10, and 20, respectively, to the base image. These images are of size 400×300 pixels. Image (**a**) when paired with images (**b**)–(**d**) constitute Sets 1–3

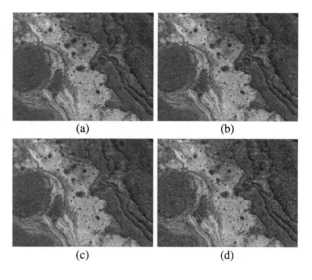

(a)   (b)

(c)   (d)

Fig. 2.27 (**a**) The Martian rock image is again used as the base image. (**b**) Intensities in the four quadrants of the base image are changed by -30, -10, 10, and 30. (**c**) Assuming the base image contains n_r rows and n_c columns, intensity I at pixel (x, y) in the base image is replaced with $O = I + 50 \sin(4\pi y/n_r) \cos(4\pi x/n_c)$. (**d**) Intensity I in the base image is replaced with $O = I(1 + \cos(\pi I/255))$. These images are of size 400×300 pixels. Image (**a**) when paired with images (**b**)–(**d**) constitute Sets 4–6

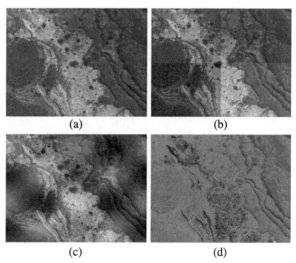

(a)   (b)

(c)   (d)

at the same pixel in the output was calculated from $O = I(1 + \cos(\pi I/255))$ to obtain the image shown in Fig. 2.27d. This image together with the base image can be considered images in different modalities.

Images in Figs. 2.27a and 2.27b are used as Set 4, images in Figs. 2.27a and 2.27c are used as Set 5, and images in Figs. 2.27a and 2.27d are used as Set 6. These images are used to determine the sensitivity of various measures to intensity differences between images.

To further evaluate the accuracy of the measures in matching multimodality images, bands 2 and 4 of the Landsat thematic mapper (TM) image shown in Figs. 2.28a and 2.28b were used. To test the measures against changes in camera

Fig. 2.28 (**a**) Band 2 and
(**b**) band 4 of a Landsat
thematic mapper image of a
desert city scene, courtesy of
USGS. These images are of
size 532 × 432 pixels and
constitute the images in Set 7

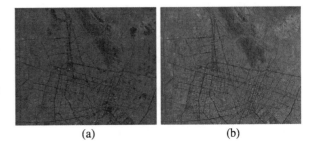

(a)   (b)

Fig. 2.29 (**a**), (**b**) Images
obtained of an outdoor scene
by different exposures of a
stationary camera. These
images are of size 307 × 131
pixels and constitute the
images in Set 8

(a)   (b)

Fig. 2.30 (**a**) The same base
image as in Fig. 2.26a.
(**b**) The base image after
smoothing with a Gaussian of
standard deviation 1 pixel.
These images represent Set 9

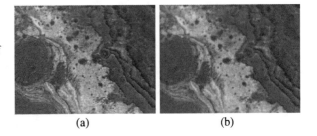

(a)   (b)

exposure, the images in Figs. 2.29a and 2.29b, which were obtained at different
exposures of a static scene by a stationary camera, are used.

The Landsat TM bands 2 and 4 in Fig. 2.28 are used as Set 7 and the multi-
exposure images in Fig. 2.29 are used as Set 8 to further evaluate the sensitivity of
the measures to intensity differences between images.

To determine the sensitivity of the measures to image blurring caused by camera defocus or change in image resolution, the Martian rock image shown again in
Fig. 2.30a was smoothed with a Gaussian of standard deviation 1 pixel to obtain the
image shown in Fig. 2.30b. The images in Figs. 2.30a and 2.30b are used as Set 9 to
determine the sensitivity of the measures to image blurring.

To determine the sensitivity of the measures to occlusion and local geometric
differences between images, stereo images of a Mars scene, courtesy of NASA,
and aerial stereo images of the Pentagon, courtesy of CMU Robotics Institute, were
used. These images are shown in Fig. 2.31. The Mars images represent Set 10 and
the Pentagon images represent Set 11.

Fig. 2.31 (**a**), (**b**) Stereo images of a Mars scene, courtesy of NASA. These images are of size 433 × 299 pixels. (**c**), (**d**) Stereo aerial images of the Pentagon, courtesy of CMU Robotics Institute. These images are of size 512 × 512 pixels. The Mars images represent Set 10 and the Pentagon images represent Set 11

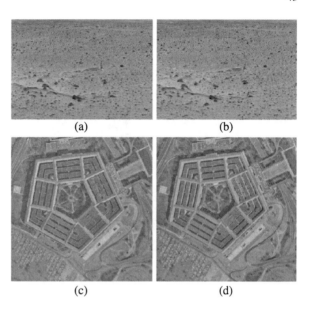

(a)   (b)

(c)   (d)

2.3.2 Evaluation Strategy

To measure and compare the performances of various similarity and dissimilarity measures, a number of template-matching scenarios were considered. Given two images, a template centered at each pixel (x, y) in the first image was taken and compared with windows of the same size in the neighborhood of (x, y) in the second image. Knowing true corresponding points in images in Sets 1–9, the percentage of correctly determined correspondences by each measure were determined.

As templates, square subimages of side 31 pixels were considered at each pixel in the first image in each set. Each such template was then searched for in the second image in the same set. Assuming a selected template was centered at pixel (x, y) in the first image, the search was performed in a square neighborhood of side 11 pixels centered at (x, y) in the second image. For stereo images, the search was performed only horizontally along corresponding scanlines in the images. In the Mars image set, the search area size was 81 pixels, and in the Pentagon data set, the search area size was 21 pixels centered at column x in scanline y in the second image. The search areas in the stereo images were selected in this manner in order to include the correct match within the search neighborhood.

Since the objective is to find the correspondence between centers of square regions in two images, when possible, intensities are weighted based on their distances to the centers of the matching template and window to allow intensities closer to the center of focus to influence the outcome more than intensities farther away. Gaussian weights of standard deviation equal to half the side of a template was used. For the Pearson correlation coefficient, Tanimoto measure, L_1 norm, square L_2 norm, and normalized square L_2 norm, intensities in a template and the pairing window were multiplied by Gaussian weights to reduce the effect of pixels away from the centers of the template and window on a calculated measure. Gaussian weights were not used in measures that used the ratios or ranks of the intensities.

In measures that are formulated in terms of the JPD or the joint histogram of two images, instead of incrementing entry (i, j) in the joint histogram of two images by 1, if corresponding pixels in a pairing template and window had intensities i and j, entry (i, j) in the joint histogram was incremented by the Gaussian weight at the pixel location in template with intensity i or in window with intensity j. Incrementing the joint histogram entries in this manner counts pixels away from template and window center by a smaller amount than pixels closer to the template and window centers when creating the joint histogram. In this way, the JPD produces measures that are less sensitive to local geometric differences between images and, thus, improves matching of images with geometric differences, such as stereo images.

Since correspondence between pixels in images in Sets 1–9 are known, it is possible to tell the correctness of a template-matching outcome. The number of correct matches over the total number of matches attempted multiplied by 100 is used as the percent correct matches.

For image sets with unknown correspondences, such as the stereo images in Sets 10 and 11, the root-mean-squared intensity differences (RMSID) between corresponding pixels are used as the matching error. The smaller the RMSID is, the smaller the matching error and so the more accurate the correspondences will be.

2.4 Characteristics of Similarity/Dissimilarity Measures

Percent correct matches (true positives) for images in Sets 1–9 by the 16 similarity measures and the 11 dissimilarity measures are summarized in Tables 2.1 and 2.2. The value at an entry, for example, Pearson correlation and Set 1, was obtained by selecting square templates of side 31 pixels centered at pixels in the first image and searching for them in square search areas of side 11 pixels in the second image, and finding the percent matches that were correct. Since images in Set 1 are of size 400×300 pixels, $(400 - 30 - 5) \times (300 - 30 - 5)$ or 96725 possible templates of side 31 pixels are selected in the first image and searched for in the second image. Templates selected in this manner in the first image appear in their entirety in the second images. The number of correct matches over 96725 was multiplied by 100 to obtain the percent correct matches. This number was then entered at the entry for Pearson correlation and Set 1.

Because the correct correspondences are not known for the images in Sets 10 and 11, the RMSID between corresponding pixels obtained by various measures were used to characterize matching accuracy. Average RMSID for all correspondences in a set was then used as the average RMSID for that set. For example, the entry for Pearson correlation and Set 11 was computed as follows. Since images in Set 11 are of size 512×512, using square templates of side 31 pixels and search areas of width 21 pixels, $(512 - 30) \times (512 - 30 - 10)$ or 227504 templates can be selected in the first image and searched in the second image. The RMSID for each match

Table 2.1 Percent correct matches (true positives) of different similarity (*top*) and dissimilarity (*bottom*) measures using noisy image Sets 1–3, and intensity transformed image Sets 4 and 5. Newly introduced measures are shown in *bold*. Template size in each experiment was 31×31 pixels and search area size was 11×11 pixels. The three measures producing the most number of correct matches in each set are shown in *bold*, unless more than three measures produce 100% correct matches

Method	Set 1	Set 2	Set 3	Set 4	Set 5
Pearson correlation	100.00	100.00	99.92	100.00	100.00
Tanimoto measure	100.00	100.00	99.95	100.00	100.00
Stochastic sign change	83.51	58.43	43.24	0.00	0.70
Deterministic sign change	98.50	99.05	85.81	48.20	49.45
Minimum ratio	100.00	100.00	99.61	42.29	50.41
Spearman's Rho	100.00	100.00	**99.96**	99.97	100.00
Kendall's Tau	100.00	100.00	**100.00**	100.00	100.00
Greatest deviation	99.92	99.36	91.18	97.17	94.01
Ordinal measure	99.98	99.25	90.35	94.66	87.75
Correlation ratio	100.00	100.00	99.90	100.00	99.49
Energy of JPD	100.00	82.13	16.91	100.00	87.59
Material similarity	100.00	97.82	56.06	100.00	73.11
Shannon MI	93.50	50.91	5.59	100.00	61.82
Rényi MI	98.11	54.12	5.93	100.00	73.66
Tsallis MI	100.00	83.61	17.46	100.00	90.16
I_α-information	99.85	98.06	77.72	100.00	98.92
L_1 norm	100.00	100.00	99.95	57.70	57.46
MAD and MSD	100.00	99.26	85.42	2.29	37.45
Square L_2 norm	100.00	100.00	**100.00**	95.18	75.34
Normalized square L_2 norm	100.00	100.00	99.75	99.91	100.00
Incremental sign dist.	100.00	99.49	93.34	100.00	100.00
Intensity-ratio var.	99.84	98.50	56.15	99.43	91.59
Intensity-mapping-ratio var.	100.00	100.00	99.84	99.45	97.73
Rank distance	100.00	100.00	99.86	99.61	99.78
Joint entropy	100.00	95.43	31.34	100.00	92.85
Exclusive F-information	100.00	83.37	14.07	100.00	88.88

was found and the average of the 227504 RMSIDs was calculated and entered into the entry for Pearson correlation and Set 11.

If three or fewer measures produce 100% correct matches under an image set, the accuracies of the best three measures are shown in bold. For the stereo images (Sets 10 and 11), the three measures with the lowest average RMSID are shown in bold.

Table 2.2 Same as Table 2.1 except for using intensity transformed image Set 6, different band image Set 7, different exposure image Set 8, different resolution image Set 9, and stereo image Sets 10, and 11. For the stereo images in Sets 10 and 11 the average RMSIDs of corresponding pixels are shown. The smaller the average RMSID, the more accurate the correspondences are expected to be. For stereo images, the search was carried out in 1-D horizontally. For Set 10, the search area was 81 pixels, while for Set 11, the search area was 21 pixels. The three measures producing the least RMSID under stereo data sets are shown in *bold*

Method	Set 6	Set 7	Set 8	Set 9	Set 10	Set 11
Pearson correlation	52.78	96.87	**98.96**	100.00	**8.44**	9.81
Tanimoto measure	52.55	96.88	95.16	100.00	**8.43**	**9.80**
Stochastic sign change	13.06	0.27	9.61	93.17	10.30	11.83
Deterministic sign change	2.25	0.00	12.33	88.24	9.00	10.01
Minimum ratio	100.0	0.10	2.81	100.00	8.60	**9.77**
Spearman's Rho	56.19	97.28	97.53	99.97	8.66	9.98
Kendall's Tau	59.44	98.64	98.23	100.00	9.04	10.08
Greatest deviation	45.39	96.16	89.15	93.62	11.66	10.92
Ordinal measure	44.05	95.24	88.71	96.07	11.31	10.91
Correlation ratio	100.00	98.27	**99.78**	100.00	10.81	10.70
Energy of JPD	100.00	98.21	79.25	85.51	12.08	11.23
Material similarity	100.00	**100.00**	**98.73**	93.84	16.52	15.46
Shannon MI	100.00	98.36	83.59	61.61	20.33	14.12
Rényi MI	100.00	98.30	79.57	67.84	17.75	12.99
Tsallis MI	100.00	98.30	84.31	89.06	10.87	10.86
I_α-information	100.00	97.59	91.18	86.71	11.14	11.59
L_1 norm	0.28	8.88	11.83	100.00	8.55	**9.78**
MAD and MSD	1.32	0.04	0.03	98.06	11.78	13.20
Square L_2 norm	28.30	74.47	36.34	100.00	8.85	9.95
Normalized square L_2 norm	52.91	96.65	98.45	100.00	**8.40**	9.92
Incremental sign dist.	60.96	**99.97**	93.90	98.78	10.23	10.56
Intensity-ratio var.	45.30	98.85	82.67	100.00	11.70	10.50
Intensity-mapping-ratio var.	100.00	96.96	97.60	99.53	13.18	11.17
Rank distance	56.52	97.72	98.54	100.00	9.85	10.36
Joint entropy	100.00	98.74	89.37	94.24	12.07	10.83
Exclusive F-information	100.00	**99.00**	95.79	89.14	16.19	11.12

2.4.1 Sensitivity to Noise

Results in Table 2.1 show that under zero-mean noise, Kendall's Tau and square L_2 norm tie for the most number of correct matches, followed by Spearman's Rho. Under zero-mean noise, measures that use intensity ranks generally perform well, while measures that are based on the JPD of image intensities perform poorly. Among the measures that are based on JPD, I_α-information appears least sensitive to noise, followed by material similarity and Tsallis mutual information.

2.4.2 Sensitivity to Scene Lighting/Camera Exposure

Sets 4 and 5 contain images simulating differences in scene lighting. Set 4 shows changes in scene lighting by fixed amounts at the four image quadrants and sharp changes across the boundary between the quadrants, while Set 5 shows changes that vary smoothly across the image domain. Measures that are formulated in terms of JPD perform well on Set 4 although ordinal measures perform equally well. For Set 5, the best measures are Pearson correlation, Tanimoto measure, Spearman's Rho, Kendall's Tau, normalized square L_2 norm, and incremental sign distance.

Set 8 contains images obtained at different exposures of a camera. Changing the exposure has the same effect as changing scene lighting. Although no measure was able to produce 100% correct matches for this image set, many measures performed quite well, with the best measure being correlation ratio, followed by Pearson correlation and material similarity.

2.4.3 Sensitivity to Image Modality

Images in Sets 6 and 7 represent simulated and real multimodality images with intensities of corresponding pixels related by nonlinear mapping functions. Measures that are based on JPD work best on these image sets, as expected. The surprising result is from the incremental sign distance, which also performs quite well on Set 7, although it does not perform that well on Set 6. The best measure for Set 7 is the material similarity, the only measure producing 100% correct matches.

2.4.4 Sensitivity to Image Blurring

Set 9 contains images with blurring differences. This represents images at different resolutions. Measures that are computed from JPD generally perform poorly, while ordinal measures generally perform well. Among the ordinal measures, Kendall's Tau and rank distance tie for the most number of correct matches. Other methods that produce 100% correct matches are Pearson correlation, Tanimoto measure, minimum ratio, L_1 norm, square L_2 norm, normalized square L_2 norm, and intensity-ratio variance.

Fig. 2.32 (**a**) Overlaying of
the stereo images in Set 10.
The *left* image is shown in *red*
and the *right* image is shown
in *green*. (**b**)–(**d**) Overlaying
of the *left* image and the *right*
image after being resampled
according to the
correspondences found by
normalized square L_2 norm,
Tanimoto measure, and
Pearson correlation,
respectively

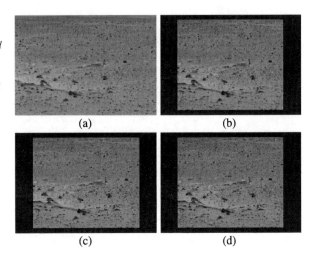

(a)   (b)

(c)   (d)

2.4.5 Sensitivity to Imaging View

Images from different views of a 3-D scene contain local geometric differences.
Stereo images have this characteristic. Tests on the stereo images in Sets 10 and
11 reveal that traditionally used measures such as Pearson correlation and L_1 norm
perform well, while measures that are based on JPD perform the worst. Surpris-
ingly, ordinal measures do not perform that well when applied to images with local geometric differences. The best measure for Set 10 was normalized square L_2
norm followed by Tanimoto measure and Pearson correlation. The best measure for
Set 11 was minimum ratio followed by L_1 Norm and Tanimoto measure. Examining results in Table 2.2 we see Pearson correlation, Tanimoto measure, minimum
ratio, L_1 norm, square L_2 norm, and normalized square L_2 norm all have very
close performance measures with the remaining measures producing much worse
results.

To visually evaluate the quality of stereo correspondences obtained by these measures, after finding the correspondences, the right image in a stereo pair was resampled to align with the left image. The overlaid images are shown in Figs. 2.32
and 2.33. Image (a) in each case shows overlaying of the original stereo images.
Figs. 2.32b–d show resampling of the right image to the space of the left image
using the correspondences obtained by normalized square L_2 norm, Tanimoto measure, and Pearson correlation, respectively. The left image in a stereo pair is shown
in red, while the right image is shown in green. Yellow pixels show overlaid pixels with very close intensities, most likely representing correct correspondences,
and red and green pixels show overlaid pixels with quite different intensities. These
pixels most likely represent incorrect correspondences. The red boundary region
in each overlaid image shows pixels where matching was not performed because
parts of templates centered at those pixels fall outside the image during matching.

Fig. 2.33 (**a**) Overlaying of
the original *left* and *right*
stereo images in Set 11.
(**b**)–(**d**) Stereo-matching
results using minimum ratio,
L_1 norm, and Tanimoto
measure, respectively

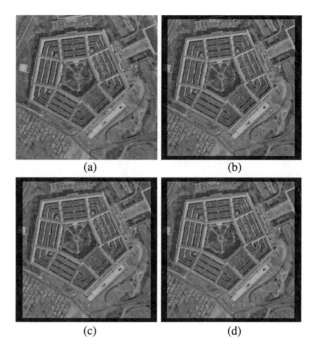

(a)   (b)

(c)   (d)

The matching results in Fig. 2.33 show correspondences obtained by minimum
ratio, L_1 norm, and Tanimoto measure. Most mismatches seem to be occurring at
points visible to only one of the cameras due to occlusion, or in homogeneous regions, where there is lack of sufficient detail for accurate matching.

It is interesting to note that the median of absolute differences and the median of
square differences have not performed as well as L_1 norm and square L_2 norm. Due
to very small occlusions in these stereo images, by discarding half of the pixels that
produce the highest 50% differences, not only the occluded pixels are discarded,
pixels that are critical in distinguishing adjacent neighborhoods from each other are
discarded, dulling the matching process.

2.4.6 Dependency on Template Size

As template size is increased, more image information is used in template matching, increasing the correspondence accuracy. This is only true when the images
do not have geometric differences. When the images have geometric differences
and the images are overlaid at a point of interest, points farther away from the
point of interest will displace more, confusing the matching process. When dealing with stereo images, matching accuracy increases as template size is increases
up to a point, beyond which increasing template size decreases matching accuracy.

Table 2.3 Similar to Table 2.1 except for using square templates of side 51 pixels

Method	Set 1	Set 2	Set 3	Set 4	Set 5
Pearson correlation	100.00	100.00	100.00	100.00	100.00
Tanimoto measure	100.00	100.00	100.00	100.00	100.00
Stochastic sign change	94.29	73.37	54.51	0.00	0.00
Deterministic sign change	99.94	100.00	96.31	47.69	54.43
Minimum ratio	100.00	100.00	100.00	49.23	65.94
Spearman's Rho	100.00	100.00	100.00	100.00	100.00
Kendall's Tau	100.00	100.00	100.00	100.00	100.00
Greatest deviation	100.00	99.94	99.26	98.31	91.46
Ordinal measure	100.00	99.97	99.11	94.22	83.37
Correlation ratio	100.00	100.00	100.00	100.00	99.66
Energy of JPD	100.00	99.97	69.46	100.00	92.77
Material similarity	100.00	100.00	72.14	100.00	81.51
Shannon MI	100.00	98.29	64.60	100.00	89.43
Rényi MI	100.00	99.09	54.83	100.00	90.83
Tsallis MI	100.00	100.00	69.26	100.00	95.34
I_α-information	100.00	99.97	94.14	100.00	99.69
L_1 norm	100.00	100.00	100.00	74.97	75.49
MAD or MSD	100.00	100.00	97.41	5.08	60.68
Square L_2 norm	100.00	100.00	100.00	99.43	89.97
Normalized square L_2 norm	100.00	100.00	100.00	100.00	100.00
Incremental sign dist.	100.00	100.00	99.69	100.00	100.00
Intensity-ratio var.	99.71	98.60	55.51	99.94	89.94
Intensity-mapping-ratio var.	100.00	100.00	100.00	100.00	97.97
Rank distance	100.00	100.00	100.00	99.89	100.00
Joint entropy	100.00	100.00	87.63	100.00	96.51
Exclusive F-information	100.00	100.00	83.94	100.00	98.09

Increasing template size from 31 to 51 pixels in Sets 1–9, and decreasing the template size from 31 to 21 pixels for Sets 10 and 11, the results shown in Tables 2.3 and 2.4 are obtained. Increasing template size clearly improves matching accuracy for Sets 1–9. Improvement is observed the most among measures that are formulated in terms of JPD. In particular, the accuracies of I_α-information and exclusive f-information improve considerably, even under high noise level. The accuracy of ordinal measures also increases considerably, especially that for Spearman's Rho, which produces perfect matches for all 9 image sets and surpasses the performances of Kendall's Tau and correlation ratio. Least affected by change in template size are minimum ratio, correlation ratio, incremental sign distance, and rank distance. Since these measures already perform quite well with small templates, if small templates are required, they are the measures to use.

Table 2.4 Similar to Table 2.2 except for using square templates of side 51 pixels in Sets 6–9 and square templates of side 21 pixels in Sets 10 and 11

Method	Set 6	Set 7	Set 8	Set 9	Set 10	Set 11
Pearson correlation	73.43	99.24	100.00	100.00	8.12	9.45
Tanimoto measure	73.46	99.22	99.66	100.00	**8.04**	**9.41**
Stochastic sign change	18.03	0.00	1.24	97.69	10.34	11.44
Deterministic sign change	2.80	0.00	9.05	97.86	8.55	9.53
Minimum ratio	0.00	0.00	3.05	100.00	**8.05**	**9.23**
Spearman's Rho	100.00	100.00	100.00	100.00	8.23	9.62
Kendall's Tau	78.69	99.87	100.00	100.00	8.42	9.64
Greatest deviation	37.69	98.33	98.29	97.26	11.49	10.81
Ordinal measure	35.63	97.62	98.42	98.69	11.01	10.62
Correlation ratio	100.00	99.34	100.00	100.00	9.50	10.64
Energy of JPD	100.00	99.85	90.61	99.11	13.13	12.92
Material similarity	100.00	100.00	100.00	100.00	16.32	16.49
Shannon MI	100.00	99.99	100.00	100.00	23.89	20.98
Rényi MI	100.00	99.93	99.21	99.63	22.65	19.84
Tsallis MI	100.00	99.94	95.48	99.57	11.90	11.94
I_α-information	100.00	99.17	99.89	93.69	12.99	12.18
L_1 norm	0.66	21.19	15.16	100.00	**8.04**	**9.23**
MAD or MSD	1.05	0.07	1.64	99.94	13.50	11.20
Square L_2 norm	40.17	87.48	46.27	100.00	8.26	9.47
Normalized square L_2 norm	47.66	97.72	100.00	100.00	**8.00**	**9.32**
Incremental sign dist.	59.63	100.00	100.00	100.00	9.64	10.50
Intensity-ratio var.	35.43	99.97	89.82	100.00	10.23	10.13
Intensity-mapping-ratio var.	100.00	98.84	100.00	100.00	12.11	11.08
Rank distance	53.97	99.54	100.00	100.00	8.78	9.96
Joint entropy	100.00	100.00	99.55	99.96	12.57	11.96
Exclusive F-information	100.00	100.00	100.00	100.00	21.48	15.75

2.4.7 Speed

In addition to accuracy, speed determines the performance of a similarity or dissimilarity measure. Computation time in milliseconds needed by a Windows PC with a 3.2 GHz processor to find a pair of corresponding points in the images for each case in Tables 2.1–2.4 is determined and shown in Tables 2.5–2.8, respectively.

From the contents of Tables 2.5–2.8, we can conclude that ordinal measures are the most expensive measures followed by measures that are based on the JPD of image intensities. The three fastest methods are square L_2 norm, L_1 norm, and intensity-ratio variance. The fact that square L_2 norm is widely used in stereo match-

Table 2.5 Computation time in milliseconds needed to find a pair of corresponding points in Table 2.1 on a Windows PC with a 3.2 GHz processor

Method	Set 1	Set 2	Set 3	Set 4	Set 5
Pearson correlation	5.09	5.09	5.05	5.13	5.13
Tanimoto measure	5.09	5.14	5.15	5.18	5.13
Stochastic sign change	4.29	4.30	4.36	3.86	3.87
Deterministic sign change	28.91	29.10	29.20	28.86	28.83
Minimum ratio	4.10	4.15	4.18	3.77	3.80
Spearman's Rho	107.94	107.93	108.18	107.85	108.80
Kendall's Tau	627.81	635.34	651.70	628.30	620.28
Greatest deviation	722.73	734.50	751.02	713.62	705.72
Ordinal measure	435.64	439.70	446.60	432.86	430.86
Correlation ratio	84.52	84.55	84.50	84.49	84.57
Energy of JPD	110.25	109.71	109.58	109.57	109.43
Material similarity	241.43	242.35	241.65	242.84	239.38
Shannon MI	172.97	172.58	172.96	172.41	172.59
Rényi MI	220.40	220.96	228.79	229.01	226.82
Tsallis MI	226.82	226.56	227.07	226.44	228.40
I_α-information	456.45	467.89	496.96	453.30	460.40
L_1 norm	**3.06**	**3.05**	**3.07**	**2.88**	**2.78**
Median of absolute diff.	18.06	19.13	19.21	19.18	18.12
Square L_2 norm	**2.71**	**2.71**	**2.71**	**2.72**	**2.71**
Median of square diff.	19.49	19.58	19.54	19.20	18.94
Normalized square L_2 norm	6.15	6.21	6.18	6.19	6.19
Incremental sign dist.	4.50	4.54	4.54	4.49	4.51
Intensity-ratio var.	**3.63**	**3.64**	**3.64**	**3.64**	**3.63**
Intensity-mapping-ratio var.	84.65	84.56	84.57	86.44	85.71
Rank distance	108.99	109.16	109.08	112.19	114.35
Joint entropy	105.88	106.02	106.11	106.62	107.07
Exclusive F-information	172.45	172.64	177.13	177.42	176.87

ing is no surprise as it has the fastest speed among the measures tested with accuracy that is very close to the best accuracy achievable.

Changing template size changes the computation time. Computation time varies from a linear function of template size n to a quadratic function of n. Computation time when using templates of side 51 pixels in Sets 1–9 and templates of side 21 pixels in Sets 10 and 11 are shown in Tables 2.7 and 2.8. When compared with Tables 2.5 and 2.6, we see that again square L_2 norm is the fastest and the gap between slower and faster measures widens for Sets 1–9. For Sets 10 and 11, the gap in computation time between slow and fast measures narrows as template size is decreased.

Table 2.6 Computation time in milliseconds needed to find a pair of corresponding points in Table 2.2 on a Windows PC with a 3.2 GHz processor

Method	Set 6	Set 7	Set 8	Set 9	Set 10	Set 11
Pearson correlation	5.12	6.69	4.49	4.92	3.49	2.18
Tanimoto measure	5.09	6.67	4.48	4.98	3.50	2.19
Stochastic sign change	3.61	4.30	3.30	4.13	2.97	2.06
Deterministic sign change	28.52	52.67	12.06	29.12	28.63	57.37
Minimum ratio	3.60	4.66	3.02	3.78	2.77	1.96
Spearman's Rho	108.67	110.39	103.21	110.14	74.83	21.05
Kendall's Tau	629.60	642.28	552.20	624.68	442.79	111.94
Greatest deviation	738.69	764.53	643.89	714.55	518.37	128.17
Ordinal measure	444.00	459.51	360.63	439.40	319.03	81.52
Correlation ratio	84.58	86.12	81.90	86.36	57.67	16.73
Energy of JPD	110.36	111.17	106.39	112.33	80.66	21.39
Material similarity	234.08	234.60	223.35	250.50	135.91	37.41
Shannon MI	171.90	173.52	166.53	176.41	116.72	32.83
Rényi MI	226.20	222.73	220.77	228.22	150.14	40.91
Tsallis MI	227.59	222.73	220.47	227.86	154.03	41.12
I_α-information	392.71	352.34	398.74	432.19	289.03	77.62
L_1 norm	**2.83**	**3.68**	**2.46**	**3.14**	**2.29**	**1.87**
Median of absolute diff.	19.29	19.56	22.54	19.23	20.11	5.26
Square L_2 norm	**2.71**	**3.58**	**2.44**	**2.86**	**2.07**	**1.77**
Median of square diff.	19.89	19.83	22.89	19.53	20.44	5.64
Normalized square L_2 norm	6.18	7.01	5.86	6.44	4.50	2.08
Incremental sign dist.	4.48	5.31	4.06	4.59	3.35	1.98
Intensity-ratio var.	**3.62**	**4.51**	**3.31**	**3.85**	**2.73**	**1.93**
Intensity-mapping-ratio var.	84.87	85.28	81.24	88.37	58.81	16.45
Rank distance	109.52	110.92	104.74	115.12	72.88	20.25
Joint entropy	105.91	104.48	99.71	106.05	70.69	19.91
Exclusive F-information	173.36	172.92	166.76	183.66	118.33	32.94

The smallest increase in computation time as template size is increased is observed in measures that use JPD. This is because a portion of the computation time is spent by these measures to create the JPD, which is a linear function of template size n, and a portion of the computation time that is independent of n is spent on calculating a similarity or dissimilarity measure from the obtained JPD. Increase in template size, therefore, only linearly increases the time for creating the JPD, which is a small portion of the overall computation time. Measures that have computational complexities a linear function of n, such as correlation coefficient, Tanimoto measure, minimum ratio, L_1 norm, square L_2 norm, and intensity ratio variance also have the smallest increase in computation time with an increase in n.

Table 2.7 Computation time in milliseconds needed to find a pair of corresponding points in Table 2.3 on a Windows PC with a 3.2 GHz processor

Method	Set 1	Set 2	Set 3	Set 4	Set 5
Pearson correlation	12.13	12.29	12.13	12.03	11.94
Tanimoto measure	12.15	12.03	12.05	12.03	12.05
Stochastic sign change	10.78	10.75	10.96	9.53	9.67
Deterministic sign change	36.63	36.75	36.92	36.38	36.33
Minimum ratio	9.96	10.03	10.19	9.02	9.15
Spearman's Rho	320.36	320.39	320.87	320.37	319.26
Kendall's Tau	4547.6	4608.7	4641.3	4471.3	4447.1
Greatest deviation	4873.3	4956.9	5110.9	4834.7	4708.7
Ordinal measure	2718.3	2778.2	2762.6	2627.6	2616.3
Correlation ratio	224.92	224.91	224.94	225.01	224.92
Energy of JPD	118.89	119.73	119.01	119.92	120.25
Material similarity	273.27	268.75	268.92	272.66	272.58
Shannon MI	192.60	193.41	194.57	192.71	190.21
Rényi MI	232.93	235.06	232.08	231.32	231.32
Tsallis MI	230.17	230.74	231.66	229.94	231.04
I_α-information	534.25	536.42	578.38	520.28	546.20
L_1 norm	**7.95**	**7.89**	**7.96**	**7.37**	**7.45**
Median of absolute diff.	124.65	124.12	122.97	122.28	120.08
Square L_2 norm	**7.25**	**6.90**	**6.90**	**6.94**	**6.93**
Median of square diff.	125.12	126.32	126.06	124.43	121.72
Normalized square L_2 norm	15.61	15.56	15.62	15.59	15.60
Incremental sign dist.	11.20	11.24	11.27	11.19	11.11
Intensity-ratio var.	**8.96**	**8.94**	**8.95**	**8.94**	**8.92**
Intensity-mapping-ratio var.	231.14	231.05	230.48	231.97	232.40
Rank distance	346.73	351.22	346.45	325.22	323.55
Joint entropy	119.45	120.38	120.66	118.67	119.58
Exclusive F-information	195.25	197.11	198.02	196.86	198.36

The largest increase in computation time as a function of n is observed by measures that use ranks of intensities, especially those that are quadratic functions of n, such as greatest deviation, Kendall's Tau, and the ordinal measure.

2.5 Choosing a Similarity/Dissimilarity Measure

Each similarity/dissimilarity measure has its strengths and weaknesses. A measure that performs well on one type of images may perform poorly on another type of

Table 2.8 Computation time in milliseconds needed to find a pair of corresponding points in Table 2.4 on a Windows PC with a 3.2 GHz processor

Method	Set 6	Set 7	Set 8	Set 9	Set 10	Set 11
Pearson correlation	11.94	12.74	11.17	13.00	1.86	1.75
Tanimoto measure	12.02	12.72	11.12	12.98	1.90	1.74
Stochastic sign change	9.02	10.03	8.36	10.32	1.72	1.67
Deterministic sign change	35.74	59.01	18.36	36.17	28.42	56.06
Minimum ratio	8.54	9.28	7.80	9.41	**1.46**	1.60
Spearman's Rho	320.86	321.68	297.40	344.80	74.35	9.53
Kendall's Tau	4550.9	4675.4	3809.5	4468.6	95.43	25.35
Greatest deviation	5035.3	5144.4	4008.0	4645.8	118.24	31.21
Ordinal measure	2742.3	2877.2	2058.5	2601.5	80.46	21.56
Correlation ratio	224.98	225.43	213.48	241.97	27.74	8.50
Energy of JPD	118.51	121.18	113.72	113.37	70.14	20.42
Material similarity	264.89	273.22	258.00	339.64	137.62	36.79
Shannon MI	185.32	183.75	174.74	181.89	116.16	31.21
Rényi MI	230.75	225.78	213.29	224.32	150.83	39.99
Tsallis MI	231.12	231.07	222.11	233.37	157.88	39.90
I_α-information	427.03	375.91	464.31	488.50	255.86	69.33
L_1 norm	**7.30**	**8.15**	**6.41**	**7.92**	**1.28**	**1.55**
Median of absolute diff.	121.18	125.88	122.01	125.73	5.08	1.75
Square L_2 norm	**7.01**	**7.67**	**6.31**	**6.73**	**1.20**	**1.52**
Median of square diff.	122.20	126.55	123.53	123.51	5.42	2.02
Normalized square L_2 norm	15.57	16.29	14.53	15.56	2.28	1.75
Incremental sign dist.	11.15	11.72	10.25	10.87	1.80	1.64
Intensity-ratio var.	**8.92**	**9.72**	**8.27**	**8.96**	1.48	**1.56**
Intensity-mapping-ratio var.	233.46	242.16	228.98	239.13	26.99	8.09
Rank distance	325.58	328.92	301.42	324.32	31.36	8.99
Joint entropy	116.46	115.26	109.89	119.41	69.48	18.99
Exclusive F-information	194.40	193.40	185.59	196.25	117.23	31.02

images. Therefore, an absolute conclusion cannot be reached about the superiority of one measure against another. However, the experimental results obtained on various image types and various image differences reveal that Pearson correlation coefficient, Tanimoto measure, minimum ratio, L_1 norm, square L_2 norm, and intensity ratio variance overall perform better than other measures. If the images are captured under different exposures of a camera or under different lighting of a scene, the results show that Pearson correlation coefficient, Tanimoto measure, normalized square L_2 norm, and incremental sign distance perform better than others.

Different-modality images are most efficiently and accurately matched by intensity-mapping-ratio variance, joint entropy, energy of JPD, correlation ratio, and Spearman's Rho. Although in the past, measures solely based on JPD have been used to match images in different modalities, experimental results obtained in this chapter show that ordinal measures such as correlation ratio and Spearman's Rho are equally effective and more efficient than many of the JPD measures in the matching of multimodality images.

Stereo images are most efficiently and accurately matched using Pearson correlation, Tanimoto measure, minimum ratio, L_1 norm, square L_2 norm, and normalized square L_2 norm. It is clear that when the images being matched are stereo, the measures to avoid are those that are based on JPD as not only are they computationally very expensive, they are the least accurate. Outliers and noise quickly degrade such measures. Some of the ordinal measures such as Spearman's Rho, Kendall's Tau, and rank distance produce accuracies that are close to those obtained by Pearson correlation, Tanimoto measure, minimum ratio, L_1 norm, square L_2 norm, and normalized square L_2 norm, but they are not as efficient and so are not recommended in stereo matching.

Considering the accuracies of the measures obtained using the images in Sets 1–9, we find that correlation ratio followed by intensity-mapping-ratio variance produce the best accuracy when template size is relatively small (side 31 pixels). At a larger template size (side 51 pixels), Spearman's Rho takes the lead followed by correlation ratio. Therefore, if a single measure is to be used to compare images containing noise and intensity differences but no geometric differences, correlation ratio, Spearman's rho, and Kendall's Tau are the ones to choose. Considering computational efficiency as well as accuracy, correlation ratio is clearly the choice followed by Spearman's Rho.

If a single measure is to be used to match all 11 image sets, we see that Pearson correlation and Tanimoto measure receive the highest score as they manage to match 7 out of 11 image sets either perfectly or better than all other measures. This is followed by Kendall's Tau and correlation ratio. At a larger template size, Spearman's Rho takes the lead, either perfectly matching 9 out of 11 images sets or matching them better than any other measure. This is followed by normalized square L_2, which manages to match 8 out of 11 sets either perfectly or better than other measures.

Among the four newly introduced measures, minimum ratio was found the best in matching the stereo images in Set 11 when using small templates and the best in matching the stereo images in Sets 10 and 11 when using moderate size templates. Also, because of its very low computational cost it is the similarity measure of choice when matching stereo images. Energy of JPD when compared to Shannon mutual information produces a better accuracy on 10 out of the 11 image sets for small templates and 8 out of the 11 image sets for moderate size templates. Considering that it requires nearly half the computation time of Shannon mutual information, it can replace Shannon mutual information to increase both speed and accuracy. Material similarity produced the highest accuracy in matching multimodality images in Sets 7 and 8 when using a relatively small template size and produced perfect matches for the same image sets at a larger template size, thus making it the most accurate measure in matching multimodality images. Material similarity is,

Fig. 2.34 (**a**), (**b**) A noise-free image and its noisy version. These images are the same as those in Figs. 2.26a and 2.26d. (**c**) Smoothing of image (**b**) by an adaptive Gaussian filter of standard deviation 1 pixel. (**d**) Smoothing of image (**b**) by the traditional Gaussian filter of standard deviation 1 pixel

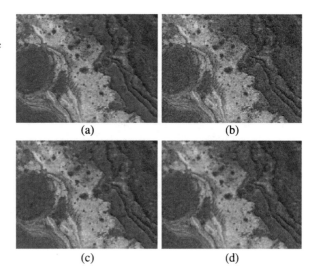

(a)   (b)

(c)   (d)

however, computationally more expensive than Shannon mutual information. Rank distance is an ordinal measure that has the fastest speed among the ordinal measures and has an accuracy that falls somewhere in the middle among the ordinal measures tested.

2.6 Preprocessing Considerations

Similarity and dissimilarity measures that are based on JDP or intensity ranks are not sensitive to sensor characteristics or scene lighting but are computationally very expensive. On the other hand, measures that use raw image intensities are fast but are sensitive to differences in sensor characteristics and scene lighting. In order to take advantage of the fast speed of the latter and the robustness of the former, the images may be preprocessed, normalizing the intensities before using them in the calculation of a measure.

If the images are known to contain noise, one may filter out the noise before attempting to compute the similarity/dissimilarity between them. If the images are known to contain impulse noise, median filtering may be used to reduce or remove noise, and if the images are known to contain zero-mean noise, Gaussian filtering may be used to reduce the effect of noise. Since image filtering changes intensities even at pixels that are not affected by noise, the filter kernel should be sufficiently small to avoid smoothing the image structures but large enough to reduce sufficient noise to produce an accurate similarity/dissimilarity measure.

To preserve image structures while reducing noise, filter kernels that change in shape and size are most desirable [2, 34, 59, 67]. Figure 2.34 compares adaptive smoothing versus traditional smoothing at the presence of zero-mean noise.

If the images are obtained under different lighting conditions, through a preprocessing operation image intensities can be normalized to remove global intensity

Fig. 2.35 (**a**), (**b**) Images
with smoothly varying
intensity differences. These
images are the same as those
shown in Figs. 2.27a and
2.27c. (**c**), (**d**) Rank transform
intensity mapping of (**a**)
and (**b**), respectively, using
17×17 windows and setting
ranks greater than 255 to 255

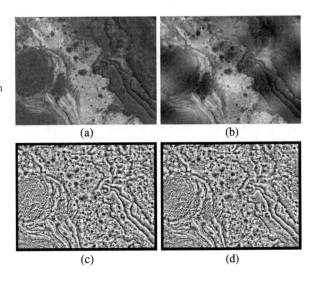

(a)   (b)

(c)   (d)

differences between them. In the *monotonicity operation* proposed by Kories and
Zimmerman [44], a 3×3 window is considered at a pixel, and the intensity at the
pixel is replaced by a number between 0 and 8 depending on the number of intensities within the 3×3 window that are smaller than the intensity at the pixel.
Intensities are newly assigned that depend on their relative values within a small
neighborhood rather than their absolute values globally. This process will reduce or
remove global intensity differences between images.

The *rank transform* proposed by Zabih and Woodfill [111], replaces the local
intensity distribution of an image with values in the range 0 to $d^2 - 1$ similar to
monotonicity operation, where $d = 2r + 1$ is an odd number showing the side of the
square window centered at the pixel under consideration. This mapping is particularly effective when high-dynamic range images are used. The method brightens
areas that are too dark and darkens areas that are too bright.

Suppose the center pixel in a $d \times d$ neighborhood is denoted by **p** and the inten-
sity at **p** is $I(\mathbf{p})$. Also, suppose the intensity at pixel $\mathbf{p}'$ ($\mathbf{p}' \neq \mathbf{p}$) in that neighborhood
is $I(\mathbf{p}')$. If the number of pixels within the neighborhood where $I(\mathbf{p}') < I(\mathbf{p})$ is m,
then m is considered the rank of **p** and assigned to **p**. This is the same as monotonicity operation except for using a neighborhood larger than 3×3.

If a 16×16 neighborhood is selected, the center pixel can be considered the
128th pixel within the neighborhood when counted in raster scan order. Then, the
rank of the intensity at the center pixel will have a value between 0 and 255 depending on whether from none to all intensities within the neighborhood are smaller than
the intensity at the center pixel. Mapping intensities in this manner enables removing global intensity differences between images. An example of intensity mapping
using 17×17 neighborhoods is given in Fig. 2.35. Ranks greater than 255, which
rarely occur, are set to 255. Figures 2.35a and 2.35b after rank transform are shown
in Figs. 2.35c and 2.35d, respectively. The images after rank transform are indistin-
guishable.

At the presence of outliers (occlusions), rank transform has been found to improve matching accuracy [111]. This can be attributed to the fact that at occluded boundaries there are sharp intensity changes and rank transform dulls the sharp changes, reducing the occlusion effect and producing more accurate matches. However, this dulling effect can worsen matching accuracy when applied to images that do not contain occlusions. Rank transform intensity mapping when applied to high-contrast and noise-free images may reduce image information sufficiently to worsen matching accuracy. Therefore, care should be taken when choosing a preprocessing operation in image matching.

References

1. Alliney, S., Morandi, C.: Digital image registration using projections. IEEE Trans. Pattern Anal. Mach. Intell. **8**(2), 222–233 (1986)
2. Alvarez, L., Lions, P.-L., Morel, J.-M.: Image selective smoothing and edge detection by nonlinear diffusion II. SIAM J. Numer. Anal. **29**(3), 845–866 (1992)
3. Anuta, P.E.: Spatial registration of multispectral and multitemporal digital imagery using fast Fourier transform techniques. IEEE Trans. Geosci. Electron. **8**(4), 353–368 (1970)
4. Ayinde, O., Yang, Y.-H.: Face recognition approach based on rank correlation of gabor-filtered images. Pattern Recognit. **35**, 1275–1289 (2002)
5. Barnea, D.I., Silverman, H.F.: A class of algorithms for fast digital image registration. IEEE Trans. Comput. **21**(2), 179–186 (1972)
6. Bhat, N., Nayar, S.K.: Ordinal measures for image correspondence. IEEE Trans. Pattern Anal. Mach. Intell. **20**(4), 415–423 (1998)
7. Blakeman, J.: On tests for linearity of regression in frequency distributions. Biometrika **4**(3), 332–350 (1905)
8. Borland, L., Plastino, A.R., Tsallis, C.: Information gain within nonextensive thermostatistics. J. Math. Phys. **39**(12), 6490–6501 (1998)
9. Chambon, S., Crouzil, A.: Dense matching using correlation: new measures that are robust near occlusions. In: Proc. British Machine Vision Conference, vol. 1, pp. 143–152 (2003)
10. Chambon, S., Crouzil, A.: Similarity measures for image matching despite occlusions in stereo vision. Pattern Recognit. **44**, 2063–2075 (2011)
11. Chen, Y.-P.: A note on the relationship between Spearman's ρ and Kendall's τ for extreme order statistics. J. Stat. Plan. Inference **137**, 2165–2171 (2007)
12. Chen, Q.-S.: Matched filtering techniques. In: Le Moigne, J., Netanyahu, N.S., Eastman, R.D. (eds.) Image Registration for Remote Sensing, pp. 112–130. Cambridge University Press, Cambridge (2011)
13. Chen, H.-M., Varshney, P.K., Arora, M.K.: Performance of mutual information similarity measure for registration of multitemporal remote sensing images. IEEE Trans. Geosci. Remote Sens. **41**(11), 2445–2454 (2003)
14. Cole-Rhodes, A.A., Johnson, K.L., LeMoigne, J., Zavorin, I.: Multiresolution registration of remote sensing imagery by optimization of mutual information using a stochastic gradient. IEEE Trans. Image Process. **12**(12), 1495–1511 (2003)
15. Collignon, A., Maes, F., Delaere, D., Vandermeulen, D., Suetens, P., Marchal, A.: Automated multi-modality image registration based on information theory. In: Proc. Information Processing in Medicine Conf., pp. 263–274 (1995)
16. Conners, R.W., Harlow, C.A.: A theoretical comparison of texture algorithms. IEEE Trans. Pattern Anal. Mach. Intell. **2**(3), 204–222 (1980)
17. Coselmon, M.M., Balter, J.M., McShan, D.L., Kessler, Marc L.: Mutual information based CT registration of the lung at exhale and inhale breathing states using thin-plate splines. Med. Phys. **31**(11), 2942–2948 (2004)

18. Crathorne, A.R.: Calculation of the correlation ratio. J. Am. Stat. Assoc. **18**(139), 394–396 (1922)
19. Cvejic, N., Canagarajah, C.N., Bull, D.R.: Information fusion metric based on mutual information and Tsallis entropy. Electron. Lett. **42**(11), 626–627 (2006)
20. D'Agostino, E., Maes, F., Vandermeulen, D., Suetens, P.: A viscous fluid model for multimodal non-rigid image registration using mutual information. Med. Image Anal. **7**, 565–575 (2003)
21. De Castro, E., Morandi, C.: Registration of translated and rotated images using finite Fourier transforms. IEEE Trans. Pattern Anal. Mach. Intell. **9**(5), 700–703 (1987)
22. dos Santos, R.J.V.: Generalization of Shannon's theorem of Tsallis entropy. J. Math. Phys. **38**(8), 4104–4107 (1997)
23. Duda, R.O., Hart, P.E., Stork, D.G.: Pattern Classification, 2nd edn., p. 187. Wiley-Interscience, New York (2001)
24. Duncan, T.E.: On the calculation of mutual information. SIAM Journal. Appl. Math. **19**(1), 215–220 (1970)
25. Evangelidis, G.D., Psarakis, E.Z.: Parametric image alignment using enhanced correlation coefficient maximization. IEEE Trans. Pattern Anal. Mach. Intell. **30**(10), 1858–1865 (2008)
26. Fitch, A.J., Kadyrov, A., Christmas, W.J., Kittler, J.: Orientation correlation. In: British Machine Vision Conf., vol. 1, pp. 133–142 (2002)
27. Fredricks, G.A., Nelsen, R.B.: On the relationship between Spearman's rho and Kendall's tau for pairs of continuous random variables. J. Stat. Plan. Inference **137**, 2143–2150 (2007)
28. Gao, Z., Gu, B., Lin, J.: Monomodal image registration using mutual information based methods. Image Vis. Comput. **26**, 164–173 (2008)
29. Gauthier, T.D.: Detecting trends using Spearman's rank correlation, coefficient. Environ. Forensics **2**, 359–362 (2001)
30. Gel'fand, I.M., Yaglom, A.M.: Calculation of the amount of information about a random function contained in another such function. Am. Math. Soc. Trans. **2**(12), 199–246 (1959)
31. Gibbons, J.D.: Nonparametric Methods for Quantitative Analysis, 2nd edn., p. 298. American Science Press, Columbus (1985)
32. Gideon, R.A., Hollister, R.A.: A rank correlation coefficient. J. Am. Stat. Assoc. **82**(398), 656–666 (1987)
33. Gilpin, A.R.: Table for conversion of Kendall's tau and Spearman's rho within the context of measures of magnitude of effect for meta-analysis. Educ. Psychol. Meas. **53**, 87–92 (1993)
34. Goshtasby, A., Satter, M.: An adaptive window mechanism for image smoothing. Comput. Vis. Image Underst. **111**, 155–169 (2008)
35. Goshtasby, A., Gage, S., Bartholic, J.: A two-stage cross-correlation approach to template matching. IEEE Trans. Pattern Anal. Mach. Intell. **6**(3), 374–378 (1984)
36. Harter, H.L.: Nonuniqueness of least absolute values regression. Commun. Stat. Theor. Math. **A6**(9), 829–838 (1977)
37. Hill, D.L.G., Hawkes, D.J., Harrison, N.A., Ruff, C.F.: A strategy for automated multimodality image registration incorporating anatomical knowledge and image characteristics. In: Proc. 13th Int'l Conf. Information Processing in Medical Imaging, pp. 182–196 (1993)
38. Huntington, E.V.: Mathematics and statistics, with an elementary account of the correlation coefficient and the correlation ratio. Am. Math. Mon. **26**(10), 421–435 (1919)
39. Jizba, P., Arimitsu, T.: Observability of Rényi entropy. Phys. Rev. E **69**, 026128 (2004), pp. 1–12
40. Kaneko, S., Murase, I., Igarashi, S.: Robust image registration by increment sign correlation. Pattern Recognit. **35**(10), 2223–2234 (2002)
41. Kendall, M.G.: A new measure of rank correlation. Biometrika **30**, 81–93 (1938)
42. Kendall, M.G.: Rank Correlation Methods, 3rd edn., p. 12. Charles Birchall and Sons, Liverpool (1962)
43. Klein, S., Staring, M., Pluim, J.P.W.: Evaluation of optimization methods for nonrigid medical image registration using mutual information and B-splines. IEEE Trans. Image Process. **16**(12), 2879–2890 (2007)

44. Kories, R., Zimmerman, G.: A versatile method for the estimation of displacement vector fields from image sequences. In: Workshop on Motion Representation and Analysis, pp. 101–107 (1986)

45. Kotlyar, M., Fuhrman, S., Ableson, A., Somogyi, R.: Spearman correlation identifies statistically significant gene expression clusters in spinal cord development and injury. Neurochem. Res. **27**(10), 1133–1140 (2002)

46. Krotosky, S.J., Trivedi, M.M.: Mutual information based registration of multimodal stereo video for person tracking. Comput. Vis. Image Underst. **106**, 270–287 (2007)

47. Kruskal, W.: Ordinal measures of association. J. Am. Stat. Assoc. **53**, 814–861 (1958)

48. Kuglin, C.D., Hines, D.C.: The phase correlation image alignment method. In: Proc. Int'l Conf. Cybernetics and Society, pp. 163–165 (1975)

49. Lan, Z.-D., Mohr, R.: Robust matching by partial correlation. In: Proc. 6th British Machine Vision Conf., pp. 651–660 (1995)

50. Lau, Y.H., Braun, M., Hutton, B.F.: Non-rigid image registration using a median-filtered coarse-to-fine displacement field and a symmetric correlation ratio. Phys. Med. Biol. **46**, 1297–1319 (2001)

51. Likar, B., Pernuš, F.: A hierarchical approach to elastic registration based on mutual information. Image Vis. Comput. **19**, 33–44 (2001)

52. Liu, L., Jiang, T., Yang, J., Zhu, C.: Fingerprint registration by maximization of mutual information. IEEE Trans. Image Process. **15**(5), 1100–1110 (2006)

53. Maes, F., Collignon, A., Vandermeulen, D., Marchal, G., Suetens, P.: Multimodality image registration by maximization of mutual information. IEEE Trans. Med. Imaging **16**(2), 187–198 (1997)

54. Maes, F., Vandermeulen, D., Suetens, P.: Comparative evaluation of multiresolution optimization strategies for multimodality image registration by maximization of mutual information. Med. Image Anal. **3**(4), 373–386 (1999)

55. Maes, F., Vandermeulen, D., Suetens, P.: Medical image registration using mutual information. Proc. IEEE **91**(10), 1699–1722 (2003)

56. Martin, S., Morison, G., Nailon, W., Durrani, T.: Fast and accurate image registration using Tsallis entropy and simultaneous perturbation stochastic approximation. Electron. Lett. **40**(10), 595–597 (2004)

57. Matthäus, L., Trillenberg, P., Fadini, T., Finke, M., Schweikard, A.: Brain mapping with transcranial magnetic stimulation using a refined correlation ratio and Kendall's τ. Stat. Med. **27**, 5252–5270 (2008)

58. McLaughlin, P.W., Narayana, V., Kessler, M., McShan, D., Troyer, S., Marsh, L., Hixson, G., Roberson, P.L.: The use of mutual information in registration of CT and MRI datasets post permanent implant. Brachytherapy **3**, 61–70 (2004)

59. Meer, P., Park, R.H., Cho, K.: Multiresolution adaptive image smoothing. CVGIP, Graph. Models Image Process. **56**(2), 140–148 (1994)

60. Mellor, M., Brady, M.: Phase mutual information as a similarity measure for registration. Med. Image Anal. **9**, 330–343 (2005)

61. Milko, S., Melvaer, E.L., Samset, E., Kadir, T.: Evaluation of the bivariate correlation ratio similarity measure metric for rigid registration of US/MR images of the liver. Int. J. Comput. Assisted Radiol. Surg. **4**, 147–155 (2009)

62. Muselet, D., Trémeau, A.: Rank correlation as illumination invariant descriptor for color object recognition. In: Proc. 15th Int'l Conf. Image Processing, pp. 157–160 (2008)

63. Nalpantidis, L., Sirakoulis, G.Ch., Gasteratos, A.: A dense stereo correspondence algorithm for hardware implementation with enhanced disparity selection. In: Lecture Notes in Computer Science, vol. 5138, pp. 365–370. Springer, Berlin (2008)

64. Okutomi, M., Kanade, T.: A locally adaptive window for signal matching. Int. J. Comput. Vis. **7**(2), 143–162 (1992)

65. Pearson, K.: Contributions to the mathematical theory of evolution, III, Regression, heredity, and panmixia. Philos. Trans. R. Soc. Lond. Ser. A **187**, 253–318 (1896)

66. Pearson, K.: Mathematical contributions to the theory of evolution, XIV, on the general theory of skew correlation and non-linear regression. In: Drapers' Company Research Memoirs, Biometric Series, II. Dulau and Co., London (1905), 54 p.

67. Perona, P., Malik, J.: Scale-space and edge detection using anisotropic diffusion. IEEE Trans. Pattern Anal. Mach. Intell. **12**(7), 629–639 (1990)

68. Pluim, J.P.W., Antoine, J.B., Viergever, M.: Image registration by maximization of combined mutual information and gradient information. IEEE Trans. Med. Imaging **19**(8), 809–814 (2000)

69. Pluim, J.P.W., Maintz, J.B.A., Viergever, M.A.: f-information measures in medical image registration. IEEE Trans. Med. Imaging **23**(12), 1506–1518 (2004)

70. Raggio, G.A.: Properties of q-entropies. J. Math. Phys. **36**(9), 4785–4791 (1995)

71. Rangarajan, A., Chui, H., Duncan, J.: Rigid point feature registration using mutual information. Med. Image Anal. **3**(4), 425–440 (1999)

72. Reddy, B.S., Chatterji, B.: An FFT-based technique for translation, rotation and scale invariant image registration. IEEE Trans. Image Process. **5**(8), 1266–1271 (1996)

73. Rényi, A.: On measures of entropy and information. In: Proc. Fourth Berkeley Symposium on Mathematical Statistics Probability, vol. 1, pp. 547–561. University of California Press, Berkeley (1961). Also available in Selected Papers of Alfréd Rényi **2**, 525–580 (1976)

74. Rényi, A.: Probability Theory. American Elsevier Publishing, North Holland, Amsterdam (1970)

75. Roche, A., Malandain, G., Pennec, X., Ayache, N.: The correlation ratio as a new similarity measure for multimodal image registration. Lect. Notes Comput. Sci. **1496**, 1115–1124 (1998). Also, see Multimodal Image Registration by Maximization of the Correlation Ratio, Report No. 3378, Institute de Research en Informatique et en Automatique, Aug. 1998

76. Roche, A., Pennec, X., Malandain, G., Ayache, N.: Rigid registration of 3-D ultrasound with MR images: A new approach combining intensity and gradient information. IEEE Trans. Med. Imaging **20**(10), 1038–1049 (2001)

77. Rosenfeld, A., Vanderburg, G.J.: Coarse-fine template matching. IEEE Trans. Syst. Man Cybern. **7**(2), 104–107 (1977)

78. Rougon, N.F., Petitjean, C., Preteux, F.: Variational non-rigid image registration using exclusive f-information. In: Proc. Int'l Conf. Image Processing, Los Alamitos, CA, pp. 703–706 (2003)

79. Rousseeuw, P.J.: Least median of squares regression. J. Am. Stat. Assoc. **79**(388), 871–880 (1984)

80. Rousseeuw, P.J., Leroy, A.M.: Robust Regression and Outlier Detection. Wiley, New York (1987)

81. Rueckert, D., Clarkson, M.J., Hill, D.L., Hawkes, D.J.: Non-rigid registration using high-order mutual information. In: Proc. SPIE Image Processing: Medical Imaging, vol. 3979, pp. 438–447 (2000)

82. Shannon, C.E.: The mathematical theory of communication. In: Shannon, C.E., Weaver, W. (eds.) The Mathematical Theory of Communication, pp. 29–125. University of Illinois Press, Urbana (1949), reprint 1998

83. Shapiro, L.G., Stockman, G.C.: Computer Vision, p. 219. Prentice Hall, Upper Saddle River (2001)

84. Shieh, G.S.: A weighted Kendall's tau statistic. Stat. Probab. Lett. **39**, 17–24 (1998)

85. Skouson, M.B., Guo, Q., Liang, Z.-P.: A bound on mutual information for image registration. IEEE Trans. Med. Imaging **20**(8), 843–846 (2001)

86. Spearman, C.: The proof and measurement of association between two things. Am. J. Psychol. **15**(1), 72–101 (1904)

87. Stone, H.S.: Fast correlation and phase correlation. In: Le Moigne, J., Netanyahu, N.S., Eastman, R.D. (eds.) Image Registration for Remote Sensing, pp. 79–111. Cambridge University Press, Cambridge (2011)

88. Studholme, C., Hill, D.L.G., Hawkes, D.J.: Automated 3D registration of truncated MR and CT images of the head. In: Proc. British Machine Vision Conf., pp. 27–36 (1995)

89. Studholme, C., Hill, D.L.G., Hawkes, D.J.: An overlap invariant entropy measure of 3D medical image alignment. Pattern Recognit. **32**, 71–86 (1999)

90. Tao, G., He, R., Datta, S., Narayana, P.A.: Symmetric inverse consistent nonlinear registration driven by mutual information. Comput. Methods Programs Biomed. **95**, 105–115 (2009)

91. Tedeschi, W., Müller, H.-P., de Araujo, D.B., Santos, A.C., Neves, U.P.C., Erné, S.N., Baffa, O.: Generalized mutual information fMRI analysis: A study of the Tsallis q parameter. Physica A **344**, 705–711 (2004)

92. Theodoridis, S., Koutroumbas, K.: Pattern Recognition, 4th edn. Academic Press, New York (2009), pp. 602, 605, 606

93. Thévenaz, P., Unser, M.: Optimization of mutual information for multiresolution image registration. IEEE Trans. Image Process. **9**(12), 2083–2099 (2000)

94. Tsallis, C.: Possible generalization of Boltzmann-Gibbs statistics. J. Stat. Phys. **52**, 479–487 (1988)

95. Vajda, I.: Theory of Statistical Evidence and Information, p. 309. Kluwer Academic, Dordrecht (1989)

96. van Hecke, W., Leemans, A., D'Angostino, E., De Backer, S., Vandervliet, E., Parizel, P.M., Sijbers, J.: Nonrigid coregistration of diffusion tensor images using a viscous fluid model and mutual information. IEEE Trans. Med. Imaging **26**(11), 1598–1612 (2007)

97. Vanderburg, G.J., Rosenfeld, A.: Two-stage template matching. IEEE Trans. Comput. **26**, 384–393 (1977)

98. Venot, A., Leclerc, V.: Automated correction of patient motion and gray values prior to subtraction in digitized angiography. IEEE Trans. Med. Imaging **3**, 179–186 (1984)

99. Venot, A., Lebruchec, J.F., Golmard, J.L., Roucayrol, J.C.: An automated method for the normalization of scintigraphic images. J. Nucl. Med. **24**, 529–531 (1983)

100. Venot, A., Devaux, J.Y., Herbin, M., Lebruchec, J.F., Dubertret, L., Raulo, Y., Roucayrol, J.C.: An automated system for the registration and comparison of photographic images in medicine. IEEE Trans. Med. Imaging **7**(4), 298–303 (1988)

101. Viola, P., Wells, W.M. III: Alignment by maximization of mutual information. Int. J. Comput. Vis. **24**(2), 137–154 (1997)

102. Wachowiak, M.P., Smolikova, R., Tourassi, G.D., Elmaghraby, A.S.: Similarity metrics based on nonadditive entropies for 2D-3D multimodal biomedical image registration. In: Medical Imaging Conf., Proc. SPIE, vol. 5032, San Diego, CA, pp. 1090–1100 (2003)

103. Walimbe, V., Zagrodsky, V., Raja, S., Jaber, W.A., DiFilippo, F.P., Garcia, M.J., Brunken, R.C., Thomas, J.D., Shekhar, R.: Mutual information-based multimodality registration of cardiac ultrasound and SPECT images: a preliminary investigation. Int. J. Card. Imaging **19**, 483–494 (2003)

104. Wells, W.M. III, Viola, P., Atsumi, H., Nakajima, S., Kikinis, R.: Multi-modal volume registration by maximization of mutual information. Med. Image Anal. **1**(1), 35–51 (1996)

105. Wong, K.K., Yang, E.S., Wu, E.X., Tse, H.-F., Wong, S.T.: First-pass myocardial perfusion image registration by minimization of normalized mutual information. J. Magn. Reson. Imaging **27**, 529–537 (2008)

106. Woods, R.P., Cherry, S.R., Mazziotta, J.C.: Rapid automated algorithm for aligning and reslicing PET images. J. Comput. Assist. Tomogr. **16**, 620–633 (1992)

107. Woods, R.P., Mazziotta, J.C., Cherry, S.R.: MRI-PET registration with automated algorithm. J. Comput. Assist. Tomogr. **17**(4), 536–546 (1993)

108. Xu, P., Yao, D.: A study on medical image registration by mutual information with pyramid data structure. Comput. Biol. Med. **37**, 320–327 (2007)

109. Yokoi, T., Soma, T., Shinohara, H., Matsuda, H.: Accuracy and reproducibility of co-registration techniques based on mutual information and normalized mutual information for MRI and SPECT brain images. Ann. Nucl. Med. **18**(8), 659–667 (2004)

110. Yue, S., Pilon, P., Cavadias, G.: Power of the Mann-Kendall and Spearman's rho tests for detecting monotonic trends in hydrological series. J. Hydrol. **259**, 254–271 (2002)

111. Zabih, R., Woodfill, J.: Non-parametric local transforms for computing visual correspondence. In: European Conf. Computer Vision, Stockholm, Sweden, pp. 151–158 (1994)
112. Zhu, H., Shu, H., Xia, T., Luo, L., Coatrieux, J.L.: Translation and scale invariants of Tchebichef moments. Pattern Recognit. **40**, 2530–2542 (2007)
113. Zyczkowski, K.: Rényi extrapolation of Shannon entropy. Open Syst. Inf. Dyn. **10**, 297–310 (2003)

Chapter 3
Point Detectors

Feature points in an image carry critical information about scene structure [7] and are widely used in image analysis. In image registration, knowledge about corresponding points in two images is required to spatially align the images. It is important that detected points be independent of noise, blurring, contrast, and geometric changes so that the same points can obtained in images of the same scene taken under different environmental conditions and sensor parameters.

A large number of point detectors have been developed throughout the years. These detectors will be reviewed and their sensitivities to noise, blurring, and intensity and geometric changes will be compared. A number of surveys have appeared in the literature comparing point detectors in different contexts. These include the papers by Rajan and Davidson [122], Heyden and Rohr [71], Schmid and Mohr [135], Schmid et al. [137], Fraundorfer and Bischof [58], Moreels and Perona [108], Tuytelaars and Mikolajczyk [157], and Gauglitz et al. [60].

Feature points have also been referred to as *critical points, interest points, key points, extremal points, anchor points, landmarks, control points, tie points, corners, vertices*, and *junctions* in the literature. We will refer to feature points as *control points* in this chapter and elsewhere in this book.

In the following, point detectors appeared in the literature are reviewed chronologically while classifying them. A number of new point detectors are also introduced. Next, the performances of widely used detectors under noise and intensity and geometric changes are determined and compared. Finally, the detectors are characterized and a guide to their selection is provided.

3.1 Categorization of Point Detectors

3.1.1 Correlation-Based Detectors

One of the earliest point detectors was designed using the correlation of concentric circles [165]. Examples of two concentric circles are given in Fig. 3.1. If pixel (x, y)

A.A. Goshtasby, *Image Registration*,
Advances in Computer Vision and Pattern Recognition,
DOI 10.1007/978-1-4471-2458-0_3, © Springer-Verlag London Limited 2012

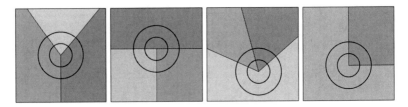

Fig. 3.1 Examples of concentric circles used in the correlation-based detector of Winston and Lerman [165]

represents a vertex or a junction, intensities of two or more concentric circles at the pixel will correlate highly. Suppose there are n pixels along the smallest circle, the angle between the line connecting pixel (x, y) to the ith pixel on the smallest circle and the x-axis is θ_i, and the intensity at the ith pixel is $I_1(\theta_i)$. To determine whether (x, y) represents a corner, first, intensities along each circle are normalized to have a mean of 0. If $\bar{I}_j(\theta_i)$ represents the normalized intensity at θ_i in the jth circle, then

$$C(x, y) = \sum_{i=1}^{n} \prod_{j=1}^{m} \bar{I}_j(\theta_i) \tag{3.1}$$

is used to measure the strength of a vertex or a junction at (x, y). Pixel (x, y) is then considered a corner if $C(x, y)$ is locally maximum.

To reduce the effect of noise, intensities along a circle are smoothed with a Gaussian of standard deviation proportional to the radius of the circle. This detector is invariant to image rotation. As larger circles are used, junctions at larger scales are detected, and as more concentric circles are used, fewer but more robust junctions are obtained. An even number of circles should be used so that when $\bar{I}_j(\theta_i)$ is negative for all j, a positive value is obtained.

It should be mentioned that although a low correlation correctly rejects a junction, a high correlation does not necessarily mean the presence of a junction. This is because correlation of concentric circles in a homogeneous area or along a line is also high. Therefore, a detected junction should be rejected when (1) the interior circle does not contain a sufficient number of high-gradient pixels, and (2) gradient directions at and around the detected point form a single mode in the histogram of the gradient directions.

Examples of the kind of points detected by the correlation-based detector of Winston and Lerman [165] with four concentric circles of radii 2, 4, 8, and 16 pixels are given in Fig. 3.2. The images were smoothed with a Gaussian of standard deviation 2 pixels to reduce the effect of image noise. *Smoothing is performed similarly on all images tested in this chapter.* Centers of the small circles depicted in Fig. 3.2 show the detected points. Black circles are shown in high intensity areas and white circles are shown in low intensity areas to enhance viewing of the detected points. Only the strongest 100 points that are also well dispersed over the image domain are shown. *In all the examples given in this chapter, the 100 strongest and well-dispersed points will be displayed.* Some of the detected points represent visually obvious vertices

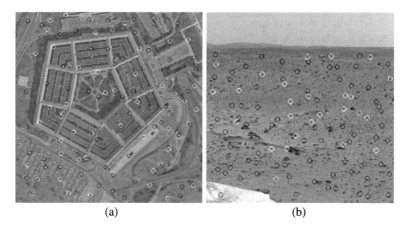

(a)   (b)

Fig. 3.2 Points detected by the detector of Winston and Lerman [165] using correlation of four concentric circles in (**a**) an image of the Pentagon (courtesy of CMU Robotics Institute) and (**b**) an image of the surface of Mars (courtesy of NASA). The centers of the small *circles* in the images represent the detected points

and junctions, while some of the other points represent vertices and junctions that are not visually obvious.

In image registration it is important to select points that are widely spread over the image domain. If too many points are detected in an image, some of the points detected in high density areas may be eliminated. Different approaches have been proposed to achieve this. Fonseca and Kenney [54] suggested clustering the points into a required number of clusters and selecting the strongest point within each cluster. Brown et al. [24] selected a desired number of well-dispersed points in an image by examining the strength of each point and keeping a point only if it has the highest strength within a neighborhood of radius r. Starting from the entire set of detected points and radius $r = 1$, the neighborhood radius is gradually increased to eliminate weak points in dense areas until the desired number of points is reached. Eliminating points in this manner selects well-dispersed points that are locally the strongest. *In all the experiments reported in this chapter, the method of Brown et al. [24] is used to select the 100 strongest and well-dispersed points in an image from among the detected points.*

3.1.2 Edge-Based Detectors

Edge information can be used to detect points in an image. In an edge-based point detector developed by Horn [73], first, edges are detected by correlating various edge masks with an image. Then, lines are fitted to the edges. When two line end-points appear near each other, the intersection of the lines is used as a vertex. If three or more line end-points appear near each other, their average intersection is used as an initial estimate to a vertex. A search is then made for all lines that have an end-point near the vertex and whose extensions fall sufficiently close to the vertex. Finally, the accurate position of the vertex is calculated by least-squares fitting. T-junctions are formed by locating a line end-point near another line and extending the line at the end-point to intersect the line. Further, heuristics are used to form K- and X-junctions. The heuristics are determined empirically with tolerances that are functions of image resolution and image noise.

An edge-based point detector developed by Beymer [19] analyzes image gradients to fill gaps between Canny edges [26] or LoG zero-crossings [102] after removing the false edges [32]. Since at a junction, edges become disconnected due to the absence of a unique gradient direction, a disconnected edge's gradient ridge is traced until it reaches another junction edge. For junctions with vanishing gradients, the minimum direction of the nearby saddle point is traced to bridge the gap between disconnected edges and form junctions.

An edge-based point detector developed by Xie et al. [167] finds edge contours in an image and calculates a cost function at each edge point using the gradient magnitude, curvature, and similarity of regions on the two sides of the contour. Then, maximum and minimum costs are determined over the image domain and through a thresholding process, edges that are not likely to represent a vertex are suppressed. Finally, the optimal position, orientation, and angular opening of a vertex are determined through a simulated annealing optimization process.

3.1.3 Model-Based Detectors

One of the earliest model-based point detectors is due to Perkins and Binford [119]. A model corner is defined by two or three lines, angles between the lines, directions of the lines (showing which side of a line is darker than the other), and unit vectors along the lines pointing toward the corner. To find a corner in a neighborhood, Hueckel [76] edges are determined in the neighborhood. Lines are formed from the edges by the Hough transform [45, 74], and from among the detected lines those that are quite different from the lines in the model are discarded. The remaining lines are then used to form corners. From among the created corners, the one best matching the model is taken as the final result. The method has been found to perform quite well in images of textureless polyhedral scenes. The weakness of the method is in requiring the approximate location of the model corner and the strength of the method is in being invariant to the orientation of the image and, up to a point, to its scale.

A model-based point detector that uses the plot of an ordered list of image intensities against the positions of the intensities within the list is described by Paler et al. [116]. For each model corner centered at a 5×5 or 7×7 window, intensities of the window are ordered from the smallest to the largest. Then a plot is created with the horizontal axis showing the intensities and the vertical axis showing the positions of the intensities within the list. This plot is then used as a rotation invariant model of the corner. Use of a circular window rather than a square one will make the model more independent of the orientation of the image. To locate corners in an image similar to the model corner, windows containing intensity plots similar to that of the model corner are located. Since windows with different intensity arrangements can produce the same plot, the process can pick false corners. This method, therefore, may be used as a preprocessor to select likely corner positions in an image. A more elaborate method can then be used to reject the false corners from among the likely ones.

To locate L-shaped corners in an image, first, templates representing models of L-shaped corners at various orientations are created. Then the models are searched for in an image via template matching [88]. In the implementation of Singh and Shneier [144], first a template representing the desired corner type is created. The template is then rotated about its center by $\pi/4$ increments to obtain eight model templates. A corner is declared at a pixel if the largest correlation coefficient between the eight templates and the window of the same size centered at the pixel is sufficiently high and locally maximum. A circular template with a smaller rotational increment may be used to create more model templates and find the locations of the desired corner type in an image independent of the image's orientation more accurately.

The idea of adaptable models with parameters that adjust to local image details is proposed by Rohr [128, 129]. Parametric models of L-, T-, Y-, and W-shaped junctions are developed. Points in an image where variation in intensity is locally maximum and sufficiently high are taken as the initial positions of junctions. The initial values for the angles in a model junction are estimated by fitting straight lines to linked edges within the window centered at an estimated junction. Then, the accurate position and orientation of the junction are determined iteratively by varying the model parameters and minimizing the sum of squared intensity differences between the model and the image via Levenberg-Marquardt optimization [101]. Based on the same ideal, a parametric model of a ring-shaped structure is developed [44].

Olague and Hernández [115] developed a parametric model of L-shaped corners similar to the parametric model of Rohr but relying more on the geometric relation between edges in a window than the differential property of their intensities. Vincent and Laganière [160] segmented a neighborhood that was believed to contain a corner into foreground and background regions using the mean intensity as the threshold value. Then, a model wedge-corner best fitting the boundary between foreground and background regions was determined through functional minimization.

Baker et al. [11] represented L-shaped corners by a parametric manifold in a lower dimensional subspace of a Hilbert space. Image information within a small window centered at a pixel is projected to the subspace and if the projection is sufficiently close to the manifold, a corner is declared. The manifold point closest to the projected point is used to estimate the corner parameters.

Cooper and Kitchen [35] modeled a corner by two templates on opposing sides of a pixel. If the gradient magnitude at the pixel is not sufficiently high, a corner is rejected at the pixel. Otherwise, if templates at opposing sides of the pixel and in the gradient direction are not sufficiently similar, a corner is declared at the pixel. Similarity is measured using the sum of absolute intensity differences between the templates.

Brand and Mohr [23] modeled L-shaped corners by a blurred region that is separated by two regions of higher and lower intensities. They first estimate the initial
location of a corner by an existing method. They then refine the initial corner parameters by iteratively determining the location, orientation, and opening of a wedge
corner that best fits image intensities in the window centered at the initial corner.

Parida et al. [117] modeled a corner by a circular template of piecewise constant
wedge-shaped regions emanating from the template center with unknown template
radius, center location, number of wedges, angular direction of lines creating the
wedges, and intensity of each wedge. The best-fit corner parameters are determined
by optimally partitioning the template into wedges using gradient information and
dynamic programming. The radius of the best-fit model determines the scale of the
corner and the wedge angles determine the orientation of the corner. Therefore, in
addition to determining the location of a corner, this detector determines the scale
and orientation of a corner.

3.1.4 Uniqueness-Based Detectors

To select unique points in an image, the correlation values of the window centered
at a pixel with windows centered at surrounding pixels may be used. If the smallest
correlation value is locally minimum and sufficiently small, the pixel is considered
locally unique and used as a control point [68].

Directional variance can be used to identify unique points in an image also [106,
107]. If the minimum variance at a pixel when measured in horizontal, vertical, and
the two diagonal directions is sufficiently high and locally maximum, the pixel is
considered locally unique and used as a control point. Variance in a direction is
measured using the sum of squared intensity differences of overlapping windows at
opposing sides of a pixel in that direction. Variance at a pixel is set to the minimum
variance calculated in the four directions. Experiments carried out by Barnard and
Thompson [14] have confirmed the distinctiveness and effectiveness of the unique
points determined by directional variance in stereo matching.

Because the directional variance of Moravec [106, 107] finds intensity variance
in only four directions, the method is not fully rotation invariant. Trajković and
Hedley [153] used variances in 8, 12, and 16 orientations in a multigrid approach
to make the detector more rotation invariant. A pixel where the minimum gradient
when considering all directions is sufficiently high and locally maximum is taken
as a control point. First, a 3×3 neighborhood with 8 directions is used. A detected
point is considered robust if it is also detected when using a 5×5 neighborhood
with 12 directions and a 7×7 neighborhood with 16 directions.

3.1.5 Curvature-Based Detectors

Information about second derivative image intensities or curvature along isointen-
sity contours can be used to detect control points in an image. A point detector in-

troduced by Beaudet [18] calculates the cornerness measure at pixel (x, y) in image I by the determinant of the Hessian matrix defined by

$$\mathbf{H}(x, y) = \begin{bmatrix} I_{xx}(x, y) & I_{xy}(x, y) \\ I_{xy}(x, y) & I_{yy}(x, y) \end{bmatrix}. \tag{3.2}$$

That is

$$DET(x, y) = I_{xx}(x, y)I_{yy}(x, y) - I_{xy}^2(x, y). \tag{3.3}$$

This detector, which is also known as the *Hessian detector*, finds image locations where the absolute value of DET becomes maximum and larger than a prespecified threshold value. Deriche and Blaszka [39] used points obtained by this detector as initial estimates to corners. Edges passing through each estimated corner are then used to find the optimal corner model with two or three edges by an iterative gradient descent algorithm. The model parameters producing the least error are then used as the corner parameters.

Nagel [112] showed that the determinant of the Hessian matrix at (x, y) is proportional to the Gaussian curvature of the patch centered at (x, y). That is,

$$DET(x, y) \propto \kappa_{\max}(x, y)\kappa_{\min}(x, y), \tag{3.4}$$

where $\kappa_{\max}(x, y)$ and $\kappa_{\min}(x, y)$ represent principal curvatures at (x, y). Guiducci [67] showed that the principal curvatures at pixel (x, y) in an image are related to the components of the Hessian matrix by,

$$\kappa_{\max}(x, y) = I_{xx}(x, y)\cos^2(\theta) + 2I_{xy}(x, y)\sin(\theta)\cos(\theta)$$
$$+ I_{yy}(x, y)\sin^2(\theta), \tag{3.5}$$
$$\kappa_{\min}(x, y) = I_{xx}(x, y)\sin^2(\theta) - 2I_{xy}(x, y)\sin(\theta)\cos(\theta)$$
$$+ I_{yy}(x, y)\cos^2(\theta), \tag{3.6}$$

where

$$\theta = \frac{1}{2}\tan^{-1}\left\{\frac{2I_{xy}(x, y)}{I_{xx}(x, y) - I_{yy}(x, y)}\right\}. \tag{3.7}$$

Deriche and Giraudon [40] find $1/(1 + I_x^2 + I_y^2)$ to be the proportionality term between the Gaussian curvature and the determinant of the Hessian matrix; therefore,

$$\kappa_{\max}(x, y)\kappa_{\min}(x, y) = \frac{DET(x, y)}{1 + I_x^2(x, y) + I_y^2(x, y)}. \tag{3.8}$$

Both Gaussian curvature extrema and DET extrema detect saddle points in an image when intensities are treated as height values. Through experimentation, Dreschler and Nagel [43] found that when the product of the two principal curvatures is used to detect corners and one of the principal curvatures is much larger than the other, the detected corner can fall along a line of very high gradient, which does not represent a true corner. They also note that curvature maxima and minima come in pairs. Therefore, rather than taking both as corners, they suggest taking the point

Fig. 3.3 The point on the line connecting pairing Gaussian curvature extrema where the curvature changes sign is taken as the location of a wedge corner. Alternatively, the zero curvature point along the line connecting points of curvature maxima at two resolutions is used as the corner. **P** and **P′** are points of maximum curvature obtained at two different resolutions, **N** is the point of minimum curvature obtained at the same resolution as **P**, and **C** is the point of zero curvature. The three figures from *top* to *bottom* show wedge corners with aperture equal to, less than, and greater than $\pi/2$

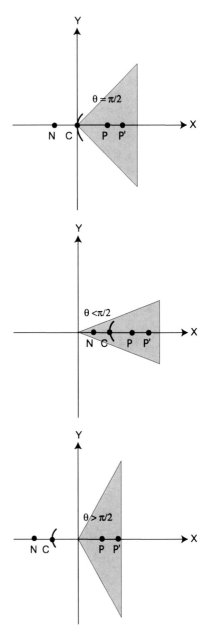

on the line connecting pairing curvature extrema and taking the point where curvature changes sign as the location of a wedge corner (Fig. 3.3). Although the location of a curvature extremum may change considerably as resolution is changed, the point where curvature extremum changes sign remains relatively stationary. Therefore, points of zero curvature represent more stable control points than points of curvature extremum.

Deriche and Giraudon [40] found through further analysis of the Gaussian curvature that although a locally maximum curvature point is unique, a locally minimum curvature point is not. Therefore, they suggest using two curvature maxima determined at two different resolutions and finding the curvature zero-crossing on the line connecting the two curvature maxima. This is demonstrated in Fig. 3.3. Instead of using locally maximum curvature point **P** and locally minimum curvature point **N** to find curvature zero-crossing **C**, locally maximum curvature points **P** and **P′** obtained at two resolutions are used to find the point of zero curvature. Giraudon and Deriche [64] and Deriche and Giraudon [41] later extended this method to detect Y-junctions by finding neighborhoods that contained two curvature maxima for each curvature minimum.

Dreschler and Nagel [43] compared the local curvature extrema of LoG zero-crossings and zero-crossings of lines connecting pairing Gaussian curvature extrema. Since LoG zero-crossings correspond to locally maximum intensity gradients and corner points represent saddle points of image intensities, which may not necessarily have locally maximum gradients, they used the zero-crossings of the Gaussian curvature rather than the curvature extrema of zero-crossing contours as feature points. Because curvature extrama of LoG zero-crossings displace more than other points along a zero-crossing contour when changing image resolution, curvature extrema of the LoG zero-crossings are sensitive to image resolution. Gaussian curvature zero-crossings and LoG zero-crossings follow rather similar paths as image resolution is changed, although they are not exactly the same. Points detected under both methods shift as image resolution is changed; therefore, although these detectors are invariant to image rotation, they are sensitive to changes in image resolution.

Kitchen and Rosenfeld [80] and later Fang and Huang [48] used the product of the rate of change of the gradient direction (curvature) and the gradient magnitude at a pixel as the cornerness measure:

$$k = \frac{I_{xx}I_y^2 + I_{yy}I_x^2 - 2I_{xy}I_xI_y}{I_x^2 + I_y^2}. \tag{3.9}$$

Mathematical derivation of this cornerness measure from image intensities was later provided by Torre and Poggio [152] and Clark [32]. Zuniga and Haralick [172] take curvature extrema along an edge contour independent of their gradient magnitudes as corners. Nagel [112] showed that the extremum of the product of curvature and gradient magnitude used by Kitchen and Rosenfeld [80] is the same as the zero-crossing of the Gaussian curvature along the line connecting pairing Gaussian curvature extrema as described by Dreschler and Nagel [43].

Examples of points detected by the method of Kitchen and Rosenfeld [80] are given in Fig. 3.4. Although many of the detected points represent visually unique and high-curvature points, the detector selects also some points that do not appear visually unique or highly curved.

Wang and Brady [162, 163] showed that the total curvature of a surface representing intensities in a neighborhood is proportional to the second derivative of intensities in the gradient tangent (k in (3.9)) and inversely proportional to the gra-

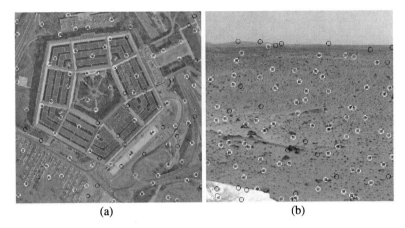

(a)   (b)

Fig. 3.4 Points detected by the detector of Kitchen and Rosenfeld [80] in (**a**) the Pentagon image and (**b**) the Mars image

dient magnitude. That is

$$\kappa = \frac{k}{[I_x^2 + I_y^2]^{1/2}}$$
$$= \frac{I_{xx} I_y^2 + I_{yy} I_x^2 - 2I_{xy} I_x I_y}{[I_x^2 + I_y^2]^{3/2}}. \tag{3.10}$$

They then take pixels where total curvature is locally extremum as corners.

Brunnström et al. [25] used the numerator of (3.9) as curvature that is scaled by square gradient. Possible locations of junctions are found in an image by tracing isovalued scaled curvature contours. The junctions are located by further analyzing the isovalued curvatures.

Fidrich and Thirion [52] took the zero-crossing of the curvature gradient in the direction normal to the gradient tangent as a corner. Assuming $(\kappa_x(x, y), \kappa_y(x, y))$ represent the curvature gradients in x- and y-directions at (x, y), and $I_x(x, y)$ and $I_y(x, y)$ represent the intensity gradients in x- and y-directions at the same point, image pixels satisfying

$$\big(\kappa_x(x, y), \kappa_y(x, y)\big) \cdot \big(-I_y(x, y), I_x(x, y)\big) = 0, \tag{3.11}$$

where the dot indicates inner product, are taken as loci of curvature extrema of isovalued intensity contours in the direction tangent to the contour. The point where such contours meet (Fig. 3.5) is taken as a control point. This point is invariant to image rotation and scale. Intensities and gradients along contours associated with each control point can be used as rotation-invariant descriptors in matching.

It is often required to smooth an image before finding its derivatives to reduce the effect of noise. Therefore, I_x is calculated by convolving image I with Gaussian G and then determining the derivative of the convolved image with respect to x. This is equivalent to convolving image I with the first derivative of a Gaussian with respect to x, that is, $G_x(x, y)$ or $G_x(x)G(y)$. Similarly, I_y, I_{xx}, I_{yy}, and I_{xy} are obtained by convolving image I with $G(x)G_y(y)$, $G_{xx}(x)G(y)$, $G(x)G_{yy}(y)$, and

Fig. 3.5 Paths of curvature maxima and minima satisfying (3.11) are shown in *solid* and *dashed contours*, respectively. The point where the curvature extrema contours meet represents a point that is invariant of the orientation and scale of an image

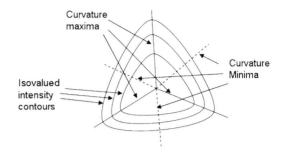

$G_x(x)G_y(y)$. Stammberger et al. [147] showed that the Gaussian derivatives can be combined into orthogonal operators and used to detect curvature-based corners in an image. The first derivatives of a 2-D Gaussian are already orthogonal. The orthogonal operators obtained from the Gaussian second derivatives are

$$A_0(x, y) = \frac{1}{\sqrt{2}}\big[G_{xx}(x)G(y) + G(x)G_{yy}(y)\big], \tag{3.12}$$

$$A_1(x, y) = \frac{1}{\sqrt{2}}\big[G_{xx}(x)G(y) - G(x)G_{yy}(y)\big], \tag{3.13}$$

$$A_2(x, y) = G_x(x)G_y(y). \tag{3.14}$$

Using these orthogonal operators, the cornerness measure k of Kitchen and Rosenfeld [80] can be calculated from

$$k(x, y) = \bigg\{\frac{1}{\sqrt{2}}\big[G_x^2(x)G^2(y) + G^2(x)G_y^2(y)\big]A_0$$
$$+ \frac{1}{\sqrt{2}}\bigg[G_x^2(x)G^2(y) - G^2(x)G_y^2(y)\bigg]A_1$$
$$- 2G_x(x)G_y(y)A_2\bigg\} \Big/ \big\{G_x^2(x)G^2(y) + G^2(x)G_y^2(y)\big\} \tag{3.15}$$

and the cornerness measure of Beaudet [18] can be computed from

$$DET(x, y) = \frac{1}{2}\big[A_0^2(x, y) - A_1^2(x, y)\big] - A_2^2(x, y). \tag{3.16}$$

In relations (3.15) and (3.16), for notational convenience, $I \oplus G$ and $I \oplus A$ are denoted by G and A, respectively, where $\oplus$ implies convolution.

Florack and Kuijper [53] note that image pixels where the Hessian determinant is positive represent peak intensities, while pixels where the Hessian determinant is negative represent saddle points. As image resolution is decreased (the standard deviation of the Gaussian smoother is increased), adjacent peak and saddle points approach each other and merge. The point at which a peak point and a saddle point merge represents a unique point in an image called a *top point*. Top points are points in an image where the image gradient vanishes and the Hessian matrix becomes 0.

Therefore, if (x, y) is a top point, then

$$I_x(x, y) = 0, \tag{3.17}$$

$$I_y(x, y) = 0, \tag{3.18}$$

$$I_{xx}(x, y)I_{yy}(x, y) - I_{xy}^2(x, y) = 0. \tag{3.19}$$

The point in an image where gradients vanish in scale-space forms a path. Platel et al. [120] called such a path a critical path and showed that local maxima and minima of a critical path correspond to the top points. Platel et al. showed that top points are invariant under affine transformation as well as gray value scaling and offset. They also showed that top points have a high repeatability rate under image rotation and random noise. Since top points correspond to local maxima and minima of curves representing critical paths in scale-space, and at the neighborhood of such points a path is relatively flat, the location of a minimum or maximum cannot be accurately determined. The matching process that uses top points as feature points should allow some positional difference between them. Platel et al. [121] created directed acyclic graphs (DAGs) from the points and use DAGs in matching. For two DAGs to match, it is important that similar top points are obtained, although corresponding points may be slightly displaced with respect to each other. DAGs of top points can be used to match images representing different views of a 3-D scene for recognition purposes.

3.1.6 Laplacian-Based Detectors

A number of detectors use either the Laplacian of Gaussian (LoG) or the difference of Gaussians (DoG) to detect points in an image. The DoG operator is an approximation to the LoG operator, first suggested by Marr and Hildreth [102]. The best approximation to the LoG operator of standard deviation σ is the difference of Gaussians of standard deviations σ and 1.6σ. That is

$$\nabla^2 G(\sigma) = \frac{1.6[G(1.6\sigma) - G(\sigma)]}{\sigma^2}. \tag{3.20}$$

Local extrema of LoG or its approximation DoG detect centers of bright or dark blobs in an image. Examples of points detected by the LoG operator with a Gaussian of standard deviation 2 pixels are given in Fig. 3.6. Points that represent centers of round blobs in an image are not as much influenced by noise as points representing corners and junctions. Therefore, points detected by the LoG operator are generally more resistant to noise than points detected by vertex and junction detectors. However, points detected by the LoG operator do not always represent round blobs. They sometime represent elongated and branching structures. Such points are influenced by noise just like points detected by vertex and junction detectors.

The response of the LoG to a circular blob reaches a peak when the size of the LoG matches the size of the blob. The relation between the scale σ of LoG and diameter D of the blob is $D = 2\sqrt{2}\sigma$ [21]. The LoG operator, therefore, can be tuned to detect center points of blobs of a desired size in an image.

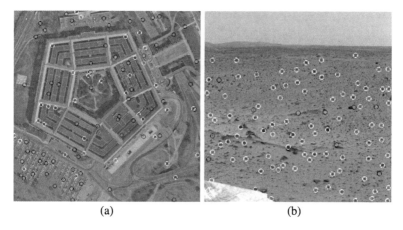

(a)   (b)

Fig. 3.6 Points representing the local extrema of the LoG of (**a**) the Pentagon image and (**b**) the Mars image

Therefore, the LoG operator of a particular scale responds the highest to blobs of the matching size [91]. To detect blobs of various sizes in an image simultaneously, the response of the LoG operator of scale σ is scaled by σ^2.

Crowley and Parker [37] described a detector that uses a bandpass filter created by the difference of low-pass (DOLP) filters, such as Gaussians, to detect points in an image. They convolved an image with bandpass filters of standard deviations increasing by a factor of $\sqrt{2}$. They then tracked local extrema of the filtered images in scale-space from high to low resolution. The paths tracking different extrema from high to low resolution form a tree structure. They then used the tree to characterize the contents of an image. Points where paths from different extrema meet in scale-space represent unique points that are independent of the scale and orientation of an image. Such points only depend on the image content and can be used as scale- and rotation-invariant points.

Lowe [97, 98] used the difference of Gaussians (DoG) to find points in an image. Since DoG is an approximation to LoG, the obtained detector behaves like the blob detector of Lindeberg [91]. Lowe calls the detector obtained from the DoG operator SIFT for scale-invariant feature transform. In SIFT, a local extremum at a resolution is considered a feature point if its value is smaller (larger) than all its 26 neighbors in scale-space. The SIFT detector has been extended to color [1] and hyperspectral images [109].

The difference between DOLP and SIFT points is depicted in Fig. 3.7. In SIFT, a feature point is only required to be locally maximum or minimum within a $3 \times 3 \times 3$ neighborhood in scale-space, while in DOLP a feature point is obtained when two or more extrema at a higher resolution meet and produce a single extremum at a lower resolution.

To find the size of a round blob, rather than tracking the extrema of the DoG or LoG, Bay et al. [17] suggested taking the locally maximum determinant of the Hessian matrix (4.121) in scale-space and using the scale at which the determinant

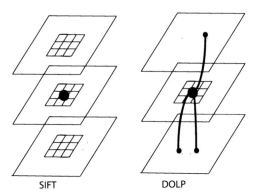

SIFT   DOLP

Fig. 3.7 The difference between SIFT [97, 98] and DOLP [37] points. In SIFT, a point is selected if it is locally extremum within a $3 \times 3 \times 3$ neighborhood in scale-space. In DOLP, a point is selected if it connects to two or more feature points in one level higher resolution and also connects to a feature point in one level lower resolution. In the above figures, image resolution increases downward

becomes maximum. They show that this detector has a repeatability comparable to or better than that of SIFT while being computationally faster. Increased speed is achieved by approximating the Gaussian second derivatives used in the calculation of the Hessian matrix by box filters that contain only -1, 0, and 1 values, thereby performing all computations with additions and subtractions.

When the LoG or DoG points represent centers of round blobs in an image, they are relatively immune to noise. Therefore, their positional accuracy is high under noise and changes in resolution. However, if a LoG or a DoG point belongs to an elongated or a branching structure, noise and changes in image scale/resolution can significantly affect the location of the detected point. To distinguish stable SIFT points from unstable ones, Li et al. [90] ranked the points using their differential features in a training process.

To make the detected LoG or DoG points less dependent on image contrast, Voorhees and Poggio [161] suggested using the logarithm intensities rather than the raw intensities in the calculations. Difference of logarithm intensities is the same as the logarithm of intensity ratios, and intensity ratios remove the luminance component of recorded intensities and use only the albedo component to find the points, making the detected points less dependent on scene luminance that influences image contrast.

3.1.7 Gradient-Based Detectors

A number of detectors use the first derivative image intensities to find control points in an image. Förstner [55] and Förstner and Gülch [57] used distinctiveness, invariance, stability, and seldomness to select points in an image. Distinctiveness is considered local uniqueness and is measured using correlation [68] or directional

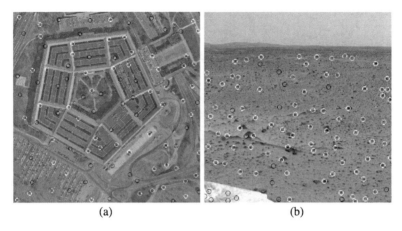

(a) (b)

Fig. 3.8 Points found in (**a**) the Pentagon image and (**b**) the Mars image by the detector of Förstner and Gülch [57]

variance [106]. Invariance is considered insensitivity to geometric and radiometric changes. This property makes it possible to find the same points in images that may have been obtained from different views, by cameras with different radiometric characteristics, or under different lighting conditions. Stability ensures robustness under noise, and seldomness ensures that selected points are widely spread over an image rather than being clustered in a few areas. Based on these properties, a detector was designed that first finds optimal windows in an image and then determines the optimal location of a point within each window using intensity gradients. To find the optimal windows, first the square gradient matrix defined by

$$\mathbf{N}(x, y) = \begin{bmatrix} \sum I_x^2(x, y) & \sum I_x(x, y)I_y(x, y) \\ \sum I_y(x, y)I_x(x, y) & \sum I_y^2(x, y) \end{bmatrix}, \tag{3.21}$$

is calculated, where the sum is over a small neighborhood, such as 5×5. Assuming $\lambda_1(x, y)$ and $\lambda_2(x, y)$ are the eigenvalues of $\mathbf{N}(x, y)$ with $\lambda_1(x, y) > \lambda_2(x, y)$, and the determinant and trace of $\mathbf{N}$ are denoted by $\text{Det}(\mathbf{N})$ and $\text{Tr}(\mathbf{N})$, respectively, letting,

$$r(x, y) = \text{Det}\big(\mathbf{N}(x, y)\big) / \text{Tr}\big(\mathbf{N}(x, y)\big), \tag{3.22}$$

$$s(x, y) = 1 - \left[\frac{\lambda_1(x, y) - \lambda_2(x, y)}{\lambda_1(x, y) + \lambda_2(x, y)}\right]^2, \tag{3.23}$$

and if both r and s are sufficiently high and r is locally maximum, (x, y) is considered a corner. A large r avoids selection of homogeneous windows, and a large s ensures that the selected window contains a well-defined corner with strong intensity gradients in orthogonal directions.

Examples of points detected by the method of Förstner and Gülch [57] are given in Fig. 3.8. Local maxima of $r(x, y)$ where $s(x, y) > 0.5$ are shown. Detected points correlate well with visual corners. Interestingly, the process detects small spots in the images also.

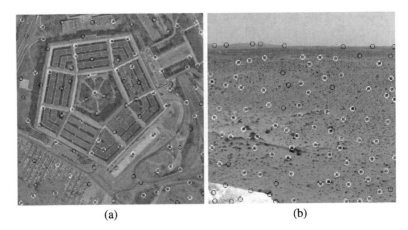

(a)   (b)

Fig. 3.9 Points found by the detector of Rohr [131] in (**a**) the Pentagon image and (**b**) the Mars image

Rohr [130] finds the localization accuracy of the detector of Förstner to be superior to those of the detectors appearing before it. Rohr [131] also shows that $\mathrm{Det}(\mathbf{N})/\mathrm{Tr}(\mathbf{N})$ is one of the principal invariants of matrix $\mathbf{N}$. He finds another principal invariant of $\mathbf{N}$ to be $\mathrm{Det}(\mathbf{N})$ and suggests maximizing it to detect points of least uncertainty in an image. The points detected in the Pentagon image and the Mars image by this method are shown in Fig. 3.9. The process has detected points representing visual corners as well as small spots in the images.

Nobel [113] calls the detector that uses the cornerness measure r (see (3.22)) the Plessey detector and demonstrates its ability to locate L-shaped, T-shaped, and Y-shaped junctions in an image.

Harris and Stephens [70] defined the cornerness measure at pixel (x, y) by

$$R(x, y) = \mathrm{Det}\big[\mathbf{N}(x, y)\big] - h\,\mathrm{Tr}^2\big[\mathbf{N}(x, y)\big] \qquad (3.24)$$

and selected points where $R(x, y)$ is locally maximum as corners. Numbers such as 0.04 and 0.06 have been used for h. Zheng et al. [171] let $h = t/(1+t)^2$ and set t to a value satisfying $t > \lambda_1/\lambda_2 > 1/t$, where λ_1 and λ_2 represent the eigenvalues of $\mathbf{N}$.

The Harris detector was originally designed to detect both edges and corners. Analysis of $R(x, y)$ reveals that parameter h can assume values between 0 and 0.25 and when $h = 0$ only points are detected and when $h = 0.25$ only edges are detected. As h is increased from 0 to 0.25 more points along edges are obtained [93].

Brown et al. [24] defined corner strength by

$$B(x, y) = \frac{\mathrm{Det}[\mathbf{N}(x, y)]}{\mathrm{Tr}[\mathbf{N}(x, y)]} \qquad (3.25)$$

and selected points with locally maximum $B(x, y)$ as corners. Loog and Lauze [95] find that the points detected by the method of Harris and Stephens are the most salient when compared to points detected by many other point detectors. Examples of corners detected by the method of Harris and Stephens [70] with $h = 0.08$ are given in Fig. 3.10.

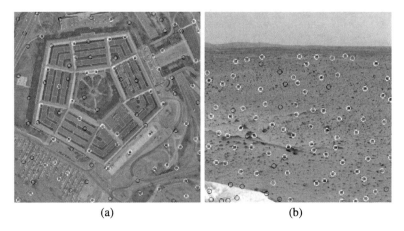

Fig. 3.10 Points found in (**a**) the Pentagon image and (**b**) the Mars image by the detector of Harris and Stephens [70]

While the Plessey detector considers all image locations where measure r is locally maximum as corners, the Förstner detector rejects those locations where measure s is not sufficiently high; thus, filtering out points that fall along edges with one eigenvalue substantially larger than the other. The detector of Harris and Stephens [70], which maximizes measure R, has the same weakness in that it may pick points along strong edges. To ensure that detected points do not lie along edges, Tomasi and Kanade [151] as well as Shi and Tomasi [143] selected only points where the smaller of the two eigenvalues was sufficiently high and also locally maximum. Since the eigenvalues are very much image dependent, selection of the threshold value for the smaller eigenvalue will be image dependent. To make the process less dependent on image contrast, Carneiro and Jepson [27] normalized the smaller eigenvalues in an image so their values vary between 0 and 1:

$$C(x, y) = \frac{2\lambda_2(x, y)}{\lambda_1(x, y) + \lambda_2(x, y)}. \qquad (3.26)$$

Point (x, y) is selected if $C(x, y) \geq 0.5$ and $C(x, y)$ is locally maximum.

Examples of corners detected by the method of Tomasi and Kanade [151] are given in Fig. 3.11. Rather than using a threshold value to avoid detection of weak corners, the 100 corners with the highest λ_2 that were also well dispersed over the image domain were selected. The corners found by the detectors of Harris and Stephens [70] and Tomasi and Kanade [151] have considerable overlap.

Rather than selecting corners using only a cornerness measure that is a function of the eigenvalues of the square gradient matrix and is dependent on image contrast, Bastanlar and Yardimci [15] suggested selecting corners if, in addition to producing high cornerness measures, they have a sufficiently high match-rating with an ideal corner, created beforehand. This process selects only well-defined corners in an image.

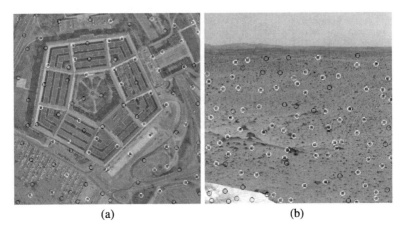

Fig. 3.11 Points found in (**a**) the Pentagon image and (**b**) the Mars image by the detector of Tomasi and Kanade [151]

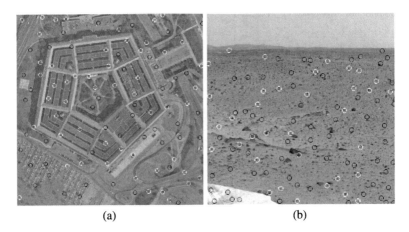

Fig. 3.12 Various types of points found by the detector of Ando [5] in (**a**) the Pentagon image and (**b**) the Mars image

Ando [5] showed that the dimensionless measure

$$Q(x, y) = \frac{4\lambda_1(x, y)\lambda_2(x, y)}{[\lambda_1(x, y) + \lambda_2(x, y)]^2} \tag{3.27}$$

varies between 0 and 1 and produces a high response at the center of a blob or a saddle-shaped region. Q also produces a high response at the center of regions containing L-, T-, and X-shaped junctions. This measure is, therefore, suitable for detecting various types of points in an image. Examples of points found by the detector of Ando [5] are given in Fig. 3.12.

Experimental results obtained by Schmid et al. [135–137] on various images show that Harris detector is the most repeatable when compared to a number of other detectors. They also find that rather than calculating I_x and I_y from the raw image intensities, if the intensities are convolved with the first derivative of a Gaussian filter of a small standard deviation in x- and y-directions, more repeatable and distinct points will be obtained.

I_x in (3.21) can be calculated by convolving I with $g_x = G'(\sigma, x) \oplus G(\sigma, y)$ [46, 56], where $\oplus$ denotes convolution, G' is the first derivative of Gaussian G, and σ is the standard deviation of G. I_y is calculated similarly. Therefore,

$$\mathbf{N}_1(x, y) = \begin{bmatrix} \sum [I \oplus g_x]^2 & \sum [I \oplus g_x][I \oplus g_y] \\ \sum [I \oplus g_x][I \oplus g_y] & \sum [I \oplus g_y]^2 \end{bmatrix} \qquad (3.28)$$

can be used in place of $\mathbf{N}(x, y)$. The sum in (3.28) can be replaced by Gaussian smoothing also. For instance $\sum [I \oplus g_x]^2$ can be considered finding $[I \oplus g_x]^2$ at each pixel and smoothing the obtained image with a Gaussian of standard deviation σ'. Therefore, images corresponding to $[I \oplus g_x]^2$, $[I \oplus g_x][I \oplus g_y]$, and $[I \oplus g_y]^2$ are obtained and smoothed with a Gaussian of standard deviation σ'. Then, corresponding entries in the images are used to find the equivalent square gradient matrix:

$$\mathbf{N}_1(x, y) = \begin{bmatrix} G_{\sigma'} \oplus [I \oplus g_x]^2 & G_{\sigma'} \oplus [I \oplus g_x][I \oplus g_y] \\ G_{\sigma'} \oplus [I \oplus g_x][I \oplus g_y] & G_{\sigma'} \oplus [I \oplus g_y]^2 \end{bmatrix} \qquad (3.29)$$

where $G_{\sigma'}$ denotes the 2-D Gaussian smoother of standard deviation σ'. The larger the σ', the fewer the number of detected points and, thus, the larger the spacing between the points.

Mikolajczyk and Schmid [103, 105] further adapted the square gradient matrix to local scale, making the detector less dependent on changes in image resolution. The scale-adapted square gradient matrix is defined by

$$\mathbf{N}_2(x, y) = \sigma^2 \begin{bmatrix} G_{\sigma'} \oplus [I \oplus g_x]^2 & G_{\sigma'} \oplus [I \oplus g_x][I \oplus g_y] \\ G_{\sigma'} \oplus [I \oplus g_x][I \oplus g_y,] & G_{\sigma'} \oplus [I \oplus g_y]^2 \end{bmatrix}. \qquad (3.30)$$

Use of scaling factor σ^2 in (3.30) enables comparing the eigenvalues of the gradient matrix at different resolutions. Mikolajczyk and Schmid use matrix $\mathbf{N}_2$ to find the Harris points at various resolutions. They then determine the Laplacian at various resolutions at each Harris point and find the resolution at which the Laplacian becomes extremum when compared to Laplacians at lower and higher resolutions. The location of the Harris point is used as the location of the point obtained at the optimal Laplacian scale. If a local extremum is not found among the resolutions tested, the Harris point is not selected. This has shown to filter out weak and noisy Harris points and retain points that are strong and well defined. The process chooses Harris points that appear more like round spots and so remain relatively stable under changes in resolution when compared to acute corners that displace as image resolution is changed. Experimental results by Mikolajczyk and Schmid [103] show that this new detector, which is called the Harris–Laplacian detector, has a higher repeatability than those of the Laplacian detector and the Harris detector.

To increase the robustness of a detector, Goshtasby [66] found corners at two different resolutions, σ_1 and σ_2 ($\sigma_2 > \sigma_1$). A corner is considered stable and retained if it does not move by more than $2(\sigma_2 - \sigma_1)$ pixels from one resolution to another; otherwise, the point is discarded. Stable corners remain stationary over changes in image resolution, while weak and noisy corners displace or disappear as image resolution is changed.

When images from different views of a scene are available and the objective is to find the same scene points in the images, the corresponding neighborhood must produce the same cornerness measure. To make this possible, Lindeberg and Gårding [92] suggested adapting the neighborhood shape to the local gradient information and proposed an iterative algorithm for achieving that. Baumberg [16] normalized local intensity patches using the affine-adapted square gradient matrix. After this normalization, two patches that are related by an affine transformation have only rotational differences, enabling detection of the same scene points in two images by a rotationally invariant detector. Based on this local image normalization idea, Mikolajczyk and Schmid [104, 105] developed an affine invariant Harris detector. They take the neighborhood centered at a Harris point and allow the iterative process to gradually warp the neighborhood and reposition the point within the neighborhood until the gradient matrix produces identical eigenvalues. The detector is found suitable for determining correspondence between images representing different views of a scene where corresponding local neighborhoods in the images can be related by an affine transformation.

Experimental results by Mikolajczyk and Schmid [104, 105] reveal that as view-angle difference between two images is increased, the affine-adapted Harris points more accurately correspond to each other when compared to points detected by the regular Harris detector. This is confirmed by the experimental results of Moreels and Perona [108]. The experimental results by Fraundorfer and Bischof [58], however, show that the regular Harris detector produces more repeatable results than its affine-adapted version. This can be attributed to the use of information in a larger neighborhood by the affine-adapted Harris detector when compared to the regular Harris detector. As neighborhood size is increased, various geometric and intensity differences between images cause corresponding points in images to displace with respect to each other. Smaller detectors reduce global image differences and, as a result, produce points in two images that more closely represent the same scene points than detectors that use larger neighborhoods to find the points.

To make the Harris detector less sensitive to radiometric changes, Faille [47] suggested using the logarithm of the intensities rather than the raw intensities when calculating the square gradient matrix. Alternatively, Faille suggested replacing I_x by $I_x/\bar{I}$ and I_y by $I_y/\bar{I}$ in $\mathbf{N}$, where $\bar{I}$ denotes the average intensity of pixels in a small circular window centered at the pixel under consideration to make the detector invariant to radiometric changes, Gevrekci and Gunturk [61] suggested stretching image intensities in the range [0, 1] by sigmoid function

$$I_c(x, y) = \frac{1}{1 + e^{-\gamma(I(x,y)-c)}} \tag{3.31}$$

where c is the contrast center and γ is the slope of the sigmoid function. The Harris cornerness measure is then calculated at each pixel at a range of contrast centers, and a point (x, y) where the sum of the cornerness measures at the contrast centers is maximum is selected as a corner. Although this process slows down the Harris detector by a factor of n where n is the number of contrast centers used, results on high-dynamic range images obtained by Gevrekci and Gunturk [61] show that this intensity mapping can increase the repeatability of the Harris detector by up to 25% in some images.

Since Harris points are found in high-gradient areas in an image, to speed up the process Rémi and Bernard [127] preprocessed an image to identify low-gradient areas and by avoiding computation in such areas reduced computation time. The gradient across resolutions is built into a hierarchical structure using the Haar wavelets. The structure is then used to access high-gradient image regions at different resolutions and detect the Harris points.

A method that does not use the square gradient matrix but uses image gradients to find corners is described by Achard et al. [4]. In this method the sum of square of the cross-product of the gradient vector at a pixel is replaced with gradient vectors of the surrounding pixels to calculate a cornerness measure. Local maxima of this cornerness measure are detected and used as corners. This method can be easily extended to color, multispectral, and hyperspectral images by calculating the gradient magnitude and gradient direction using color, multispectral, or hyperspectral data.

3.1.8 Hough Transform-Based Detectors

Hough transform-based detectors rely on global information in images to detect points. A detector introduced by Davies [38] uses the Hough transform [12, 45, 74] to detect L-shaped corners in an image. The detector first uses a boundary-following algorithm to find the boundary contour of an object or region. Lines are formed from the contour points using the Hough transform and corners are detected from the intersections of the lines. Davies makes the Hough space and the image space the same and for each contour point in the image space draws a line through the point and normal to the gradient direction in the Hough space. If a corner with aperture θ is present in a contour, pixels contributing to the corner will produce lines that go through the corner. Therefore, after drawing a line for each point in the contour, points in the Hough space where a sufficiently large number of lines meet are identified and among them those with locally maximum counts are used as corners.

Because global information is used in the method of Davies, the process can detect dull and defective corners where local detectors fail. Also, the method is invariant to homography because under homography straight lines remain straight and the locations where the lines meet remain unchanged. In addition, since image gradients and edges are used to draw the lines, the process is resistant to radiometric changes. Therefore, this detector can detect similar corners in two images obtained from different views and under different lighting conditions of a scene. However, because of the global nature of the method, the likelihood for detecting false corners exists, especially when many contours are present in an image. To reduce the likelihood of producing false corners, each contour should be processed independent of other contours.

Shen and Wang [141] used subimages to find lines via Hough transform and then formed corners from the lines. They consider a corner to be the point where two or more lines meet. For each image pixel, edges within a small window centered at the pixel are found and possible lines passing through the pixel are determined. The window center is used as the local coordinate system, enabling representation of a line by only one parameter, its orientation with respect to the x-axis. The orientations of the detected lines are determined and if two or more sufficiently strong lines intersect at the window center, the window center is taken as a corner. This method is also invariant to homography and linear changes in image intensity.

3.1.9 Symmetry-Based Detectors

Detectors inspired by psychophysical evidence on symmetry and fixation point by primates have been proposed also. A detector proposed by Reisfeld et al. [125, 126] finds points of high radial symmetry and uses them as control points. Operators based on intuitive notion of radial symmetry are proposed that assign a symmetry score to a pixel based on its local symmetry. Points that have a sufficiently high and locally maximum symmetry score are detected.

The detector proposed by Reisfeld et al. [125] uses image gradients to calculate symmetry. Since image gradients change with image contrast, a lower symmetry score is obtained for a darker circular region than for a brighter one. To make the symmetry scores independent of image contrast, Kovesi [83] observed that symmetry points give rise to patterns of local phase, which can be used to construct a contrast-invariant measure that depends on the level of symmetry of a spot rather than its contrast.

In a later study, Reisfeld [123] described a method for relating symmetry to phase using the local phase response of filters in quadrature. Image locations producing a consistent symmetry phase across resolutions were then used as control points.

Oh and Chien [114] improved the localization accuracy of Reisfeld points by using a parametric corner model defined in terms of two intersecting lines. The parameters of the lines forming a symmetry point were then determined via Hough transform using edges in the neighborhood of the point.

The intersection of symmetry lines in a neighborhood of interest has been used as a control point also [138]. Inspired by this method, Loy and Zelinsky [99] introduced a point detector that calculates radial symmetry at a pixel using the symmetry contributions of pixels around it.

Given a radial distance r, an orientation image and a magnitude image are calculated as follows. For each pixel $\mathbf{p} = (x, y)$ in the image and in the gradient direction, the pixel at distance r from it is located. Let's denote this pixel by $\mathbf{p}_+$. Also, the pixel opposing $\mathbf{p}_+$ with respect to $\mathbf{p}$ and at distance r is found (Fig. 3.13). Let's denote this pixel by $\mathbf{p}_-$. Then, assuming initial values of the orientation image O_r and the magnitude image M_r are 0, for each pixel $\mathbf{p}$ in the image, entries $\mathbf{p}_+$ and $\mathbf{p}_-$ of O_r are incremented and decremented by 1, respectively. Also, entry $\mathbf{p}_+$ of M_r is

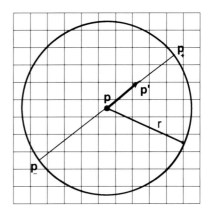

incremented by gradient magnitude $\|\mathbf{p}'\|$ and entry $\mathbf{p}_-$ of M_r is decremented by
$\|\mathbf{p}'\|$, where $\mathbf{p}'$ denotes the gradient vector at $\mathbf{p}$. Next, the orientation and magnitude
images are normalized to have maximum value 1:

$$\tilde{O}_r(\mathbf{p}) = \frac{O_r(\mathbf{p})}{\max_{\mathbf{p}}\{\|O_r(\mathbf{p})\|\}}, \tag{3.32}$$

$$\tilde{M}_r(\mathbf{p}) = \frac{M_r(\mathbf{p})}{\max_{\mathbf{p}}\{\|M_r(\mathbf{p})\|\}}. \tag{3.33}$$

Then,

$$F_r(\mathbf{p}) = \left\|\tilde{O}_r(\mathbf{p})\right\|^{\alpha} \tilde{M}_r(\mathbf{p}) \tag{3.34}$$

and

$$S_r = F_r \oplus G_\sigma \tag{3.35}$$

are calculated, where $\oplus$ implies convolution and α is the radial strictness parameter
and determines the degree of circularity of a region from which a symmetry point
is found. The larger the value for α is, the fewer will be the number of detected
symmetry points. Typically, $\alpha = 2$ and G_σ is a 2-D Gaussian of standard deviation
$\sigma = r/4$ pixels.

After calculating S_r for a number of radial distances, the full symmetry measure
is calculated from

$$S = \sum_{r=r_1}^{r_n} S_r. \tag{3.36}$$

Typically, $r_1 = 1$ pixel and $r_n \leq 16$ pixels. Local extrema of image S identify points
of locally maximum radial symmetry. These points are invariant to image rotation
and small changes in scale. The symmetry detector of Loy and Zelinsky [99] is
found to be an order of magnitude faster than the symmetry detector of Reisfeld
et al. [124, 126] while producing a larger number of points [99]. Examples of points
detected by the detector of Loy and Zelinsky [99] are given in Fig. 3.14 when letting

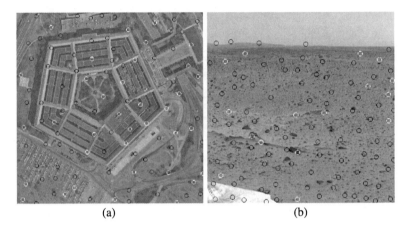

(a)   (b)

Fig. 3.14 The strongest and well-dispersed 100 local extrema of the radial symmetry measure S of Loy and Zelinsky [99] in (**a**) the Pentagon image and (**b**) the Mars image

$r = 2, 4, 8$, and 16 pixels. Local extrema of S, which represent the symmetry points, are encircled.

Johansson and Granlund [77] detect points of radial symmetry in an image by finding the local orientation at each pixel, correlating the orientation image with rotational symmetry filters, and allowing filter responses to inhibit each other and enhance points of radial symmetry and facilitating their detection.

3.1.10 Intensity-Based Detectors

If intensities in an image represent height values in a scene, the intensity extrema of the image will represent unique points that are independent of the scale and orientation of the image. Kweon and Kanade [84] used the extrema of the height map of a terrain to find the peaks and pits in the terrain.

Smith and Brady [145] described a heuristic point detector using raw image intensities called SUSAN for Smallest Univalue Segment Assimilating Nucleus. They consider a pixel a control point if the sum of absolute intensity differences between that pixel and pixels within a circular region centered at the pixel is not only sufficiently high but is also locally maximum. If the pixel at the center of a window is not influenced by noise, the summation process reduces the effect of noise at non-center pixels. If the center pixel is corrupted by noise, the calculated sum will overestimate/underestimate the determined measure. This detector is invariant to rotation and small scale changes. The detector is fast but is sensitive to noise.

Tuytelaars and Van Gool [158] take local intensity extrema in an image as control points. They describe a method for selecting regions related by the affine transformation in two images. Points of local intensity extremum are used as anchors. A measure of intensity is calculated at each pixel along a ray emanating from the

Fig. 3.15 Selection of an
affine-invariant region
centered at an anchor point.
Points of extremum intensity
calculated by $f(r)$ along rays
emanating from the anchor
point are selected and an
ellipse is fitted to the points to
create the affine-invariant
region

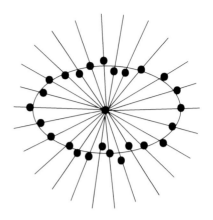

anchor point and the pixel with locally extremum value is located. An ellipse is then
fitted to such points and the image region within the ellipse is taken as an affine invariant region (Fig. 3.15). The intensity measure used to select the extremum point
along a ray is computed from

$$f(r) = \frac{|I(r) - I(0)|}{1 + \frac{1}{r} \sum |I(r) - I(0)|}, \quad d > r > 1. \tag{3.37}$$

$I(0)$ in (3.37) represents the intensity at the anchor point and $I(r)$ represents the
intensity at distance r from the anchor point along the ray. The addition of 1 in the
denominator is to avoid a possible division by 0. Parameter d specifies the radius of
the local neighborhood inside which the affine region should be found.

If the images have unknown scale differences, since corresponding elliptic regions will be different in size, parts of an ellipse in one image may fall outside the
circular regions of radius d. Therefore, intensity extrema along rays emanating from
corresponding anchor points in two images may produce different points within regions of radius d. This makes the method unsuitable for images that have scale
differences. Instead of using an anchor point as a feature point, the center of the
ellipse fitting the extremum points is suggested as the control point. Since this detector relies on intensity extremum at an anchor point and also on intensity extrema
along rays emanating from the anchor point, the process is sensitive to noise.

Bae et al. [9] determined the responses of a 3×3 neighborhood to a '+' operator and a '×' operator and identified corners in an image through a non-maxima
suppression process. Due to the small size of the neighborhoods tested for corners,
false corners are possible to obtain at the presence of noise. Larger neighborhoods
can be used to detect more robust corners.

A detector is described by Rosten et al. [133] that selects a pixel as a corner if
intensities of n contiguous pixels along a circle of radius 3 pixels centered at the
pixel are all greater than the intensity of the center pixel plus a threshold value
(or less than the intensity of the center pixel minus a threshold value). A circle of
radius 3 pixels has 16 pixels, and n is typically set to a value between 9 and 12. The
threshold value is image dependent and is determined experimentally. This detector

is sensitive to noise as the process does not include an averaging process, although use of a proper threshold value can make the process less sensitive to noise.

Under homography and small amounts of noise, the detector of Rosten et al. is shown to be more repeatable than the detector of Harris and Stephens [70] and the detector of Smith and Brady [145]. Under noise, however, the repeatability of this detector falls below those of Harris and Stephens, and Smith and Brady. The detector is made faster and more repeatable later [134] by rejecting image pixels that are not likely to be corners.

Li et al. [89] suggested ordering pixels in a neighborhood in a list according to their intensities, finding the intensity difference of adjacent pixels in the list, and locating adjacent pixels in the list that have the highest intensity difference. If this difference is lower than a prespecified threshold value, it is concluded that the neighborhood does not contain a corner. Otherwise, the list is partitioned into two at the point where the largest intensity difference is obtained and the ratio of the number of pixels in the two sublists is determined (ratio of the smaller over the larger). If this ratio is larger than a second threshold value, again the presence of a corner is rejected. Otherwise, a corner is declared at the center of the neighborhood. The two threshold values are determined experimentally.

3.1.11 Filtering-Based Detectors

A number of detectors use oriented filters to find points in an image. Rosenthaler et al. [132] convolved oriented filters with an image and analyzed the filtered outputs to detect line end-points, corners, and junctions. Noting that edges in a particular orientation respond the highest to matching oriented filter, line end-points, corners, and junctions were located in an image by analyzing the response of the image to various oriented filters.

Assuming n oriented filters are used and the response of the image at pixel $\mathbf{p}$ to orientation θ_i is $E_i(\mathbf{p})$, first and second derivatives of $E_i(\mathbf{p})$ in filter direction are determined:

$$E_i'(\mathbf{p}) = \left| \frac{\partial E_i(\mathbf{p})}{\partial \theta_i} \right|, \qquad E_i''(\mathbf{p}) = \left[-\frac{\partial^2 E_i(\mathbf{p})}{\partial \theta_i^2} \right]^+, \tag{3.38}$$

where $[A]^+$ implies $\max(0, A)$. The responses of the image at $\mathbf{p}$ to the n filters are determined and the cornerness measure at $\mathbf{p}$ is calculated from

$$\hat{K}(\mathbf{p}) = \max_{i=0}^{n-1} \sqrt{E_i'(\mathbf{p})^2 + E_i''(\mathbf{p})^2}. \tag{3.39}$$

Image points where $\hat{K}(\mathbf{p})$ is locally maximum and sufficiently high are taken as control points. To avoid detection of false points when filter orientations do not perfectly match the edges of a corner, a correction is made to $\hat{K}(\mathbf{p})$ using the derivatives of $E_i(\mathbf{p})$ in the gradient direction:

$$K(\mathbf{p}) = \left[\hat{K}(\mathbf{p}) - \hat{C}(\mathbf{p}) \right]^+, \tag{3.40}$$

where

$$\hat{C}(\mathbf{p}) = \sum_{i=0}^{n-1} \left[O_i'(\mathbf{p}) + O_i''(\mathbf{p}) \right], \tag{3.41}$$

$$O_i'(\mathbf{p}) = \left| \frac{\partial E_i(\mathbf{p})}{\partial \theta_{i_\perp}} \right|, \qquad O_i''(\mathbf{p}) = \left[-\frac{\partial^2 E_i(\mathbf{p})}{\partial \theta_{i_\perp}^2} \right]^+, \tag{3.42}$$

and $\theta_{i_\perp}$ represents the direction normal to θ_i. If measure $K(\mathbf{p})$ is sufficiently high and is locally maximum, $\mathbf{p}$ is considered a control point, which may represent a line endpoint, a corner, or a junction.

A filtering-based detector developed by Felsberg and Sommer [50] estimates the local orientation at each pixel. The orientation is then used to steer quadrature filter responses. Linear combinations of the filter responses are then used to detect various types of image features including corners and points of isotropy.

3.1.12 Transform Domain Detectors

The detectors described so far analyze information in the spatial domain to find control points in an image. A number of detectors analyze information in the frequency domain to find control points in an image. Based on a simple observation that an edge in the spatial domain contributes to a line through the origin in the frequency domain, Yang et al. [169] and Chabat et al. [29] considered a corner to be the center of a neighborhood if gradient magnitude there is high and gradient directions of pixels within the neighborhood are not dominant in only one direction. They calculate the orientations of the arms of a corner or junction in a neighborhood by measuring the likelihood that pixels in that neighborhood will belong to a corner or junction.

A detector based on Hilbert transform is described by Kohlmann [82]. The Hilbert transform of 1-D image I with N pixels is defined by:

$$h[k] = \mathcal{F}^{-1}\{H[n]\mathcal{F}[I]\}, \quad k = 0, \dots, N-1, \tag{3.43}$$

where $\mathcal{F}$ and $\mathcal{F}^{-1}$ denote Fourier and inverse Fourier transforms,

$$H[n] = \begin{cases} -j & \text{for } n = 1, \dots, N/2 - 1, \\ 0 & \text{for } n = 0, N/2, \\ j & \text{for } n = N/2 + 1, \dots, N-1, \end{cases} \tag{3.44}$$

and $j = \sqrt{-1}$. Similarly, the Hilbert transform of 2-D image I with M rows and N columns is defined by

$$h[k_1, k_2] = \mathcal{F}^{-1}\{H[m,n]\mathcal{F}[I]\} \tag{3.45}$$

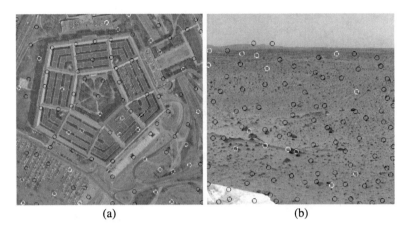

Fig. 3.16 Points detected by the Hilbert transform [82] in (**a**) the Pentagon image and (**b**) the Mars image

where

$$
H[m,n] = \begin{cases}
-1 & \text{for } m = 1, \ldots, M/2 - 1,\ n = 1, \ldots, N/2 - 1, \\
& \text{or } m = M/2 + 1, \ldots, M - 1,\ n = N/2 + 1, \ldots, N - 1, \\
0 & \text{for } m = 0, M/2,\ n = 0, N/2, \\
1 & \text{for } m = 1, \ldots, M/2 - 1,\ n = N/2 + 1, \ldots, N - 1, \\
& \text{or } m = M/2 + 1, \ldots, M - 1,\ n = 1, \ldots, N/2 - 1.
\end{cases}
\tag{3.46}
$$

Since 2-D Fourier and inverse Fourier transforms can be calculated from 1-D Fourier and inverse Fourier transforms, the 2-D Hilbert transform of an image can be calculated very efficiently. The Hilbert transform of an image produces sharp extremas at corner points.

Examples of points detected by the Hilbert transform are given in Fig. 3.16. Local maxima of the absolute transform coefficients are detected and used as control points. Being primarily a corner detector, the method of Kohlmann [82] detects some of the well-defined corners in the Pentagon image. It also detects some points in the Mars image that do not visually appear like corners but have locally extremum Hilbert-transform coefficients.

Chen et al. [31] detected corners in an image by analyzing the wavelet transform coefficients of the image at two different scales. Loupias et al. [96] noted that points representing global variations contribute to coarser wavelet coefficients and points representing local variations contribute to finer wavelet coefficients. Based on this observation, they developed a detector capable of finding a desired number of points at different resolutions in an image.

Fauqueur et al. [49] detected points in an image by analyzing the dual tree complex wavelet transform (DTCWT) coefficients of the image. Energies of the points are computed from the decimated DTCWT coefficients at different scales and accumulated into a smooth energy map. The peaks of the map are then considered control points. Scales of the control points are determined from the gradient of the accumulated energy map. This detector finds blobs, corners, and junctions. Experimental results show that this detector produces more robust points under image rotation than the SIFT detector of Lowe [97]. Generally, fewer points are reported by DTCWT compared to SIFT. The number of points detected by SIFT increases with noise, while the number of points detected by DTCWT remains relatively unchanged. DTCWT tends to remove noisy points and keep points that persist over changes in image resolution, thus detecting more stable points. Bharath and Kingsbury [20] extended the method of Fauqueur et al. [49] to include a circular measure.

3.1.13 Pattern Recognition-Based Detectors

Point detection in an image can be considered a pattern recognition problem [86]. Consider a 2-D feature vector that represents the gradient magnitude and gradient direction at a pixel. Since corners have rather high gradient magnitudes, first, all feature vectors with small gradient magnitudes are removed. Then, the remaining feature vector are classified into corners and non-corners as follows. A feature vector X is classified to corner (c_0) or non-corner (c_1) based on whether

$$\lambda_{01} P(X|c_0) P(c_0) - \lambda_{10} P(X|c_1) P(c_1) > 0 \qquad (3.47)$$

is true or false. λ_{01} represents the cost of incorrectly classifying a pixel to a corner, and λ_{10} is the cost of incorrectly classifying a pixel to a non-corner. $P(c_0)$ and $P(c_1)$ are the a-priori probabilities that a feature vector represents a corner and a non-corner, respectively, and $P(X|c_0)$ and $P(X|c_1)$ are class conditional probability density functions of corners and non-corners, respectively.

Instead of 0 on the right-hand side in (3.47), a threshold value T may be used to avoid detection of weak corners. The cost functions are empirically determined and the class-conditional probability densities are estimated by fuzzy logic. The a-priori probabilities $P(c_0)$ and $P(c_1)$ are estimated by finding the number of true corners and non-corners among the feature vectors selected in representative images. The class conditional probability density functions $P(X|c_0)$ and $P(X|c_1)$ are estimated using gradient information in small patches that represent both corners and non-corners in training data.

A neural network approximation to the Bayesian classifier for L-shaped corners has been proposed by Chen and Rockett [30] with a performance close to that of the detector of Harris and Stephens [70].

Dias et al. [42] defined a corner as the point of intersection of straight edges at angles in multiples of 45° and trained a neural network with 8×8 subimages containing known corners as well as non-corners. Detection rate is found to be 97% when using noise-free images containing corners with edge slopes in multiples of 45° and 71% for images containing some noise and edges that do not have slopes in multiples of 45°.

Trujillo and Olague [154–156] developed a genetic programming learning algorithm for automatically detecting corners in an image by optimizing repeatability and global separability of the corners. Repeatability rate of this detector is reported to be comparable to that of the detector of Harris and Stephens [70].

Based on the observation that intensity gradient in the neighborhood of an edge has a single dominant direction, while those in the neighborhood of a corner have multiple dominant directions, Banerjee et al. [13] designed a support vector learning machine to distinguish corners from non-corners using four-dimensional feature vectors. The four components of a feature vector show the number of pixels within a small neighborhood of an edge point that have gradient directions closest to 0, 45, 90, and 135 degrees. Only points along edge contours are tested for corners to avoid detection of weak and noisy corners.

3.1.14 Moment-Based Detectors

Moment-based detectors use geometric information in an image to detect patterns of interest. A detector proposed by Ghosal and Mehrotra [62, 63] projects intensities within a circular neighborhood to orthogonal and rotationally symmetric Zernike moments and by analyzing the moments detects various types of points. Because Zernike moments are orthogonal, a small number of them can describe various local intensity patterns, detecting various types of points. Overall brightness in a neighborhood is reflected in the zeroth-order moment, a discontinuity in intensities is reflected in the first-order moments, and a discontinuity in gradients is reflected in the second-order moments for the neighborhood.

Denoting the Zernike moment of order n and repetition m by A_{nm}, Ghosal and Mehrotra [62, 63] show that Zernike moments A_{11}, A_{20}, A_{22}, and A_{31} are sufficient to detect rotationally invariant edges and points in an image. In particular, they show that neighborhoods centered at unique points in an image produce a high $|A_{22}|$ and have locally maximum $|A'_{22}/A_{20}|$, where $A'_{22} = A_{22}e^{j\phi}$, $j = \sqrt{-1}$, and $\phi = \tan^{-1}(\text{Im}[A_{22}])/\text{Re}[A_{22}])$. $\text{Re}[A]$ and $\text{Im}[A]$ are the real and imaginary parts of A.

Due to the integral nature of Zernike moments, this detector is resistant to uncorrelated noise. This is in contrast to derivative-based detectors, which are sensitive to noise. This detector has proven effective in detecting corners in range images, which are often missed by derivative-based operators due to very small gradients at range corners.

3.1.15 Entropy-Based Detectors

Entropy measures information content and can be used to limit search for the points. Kadir and Brady [78] developed a salient point detector that relies on the entropy of

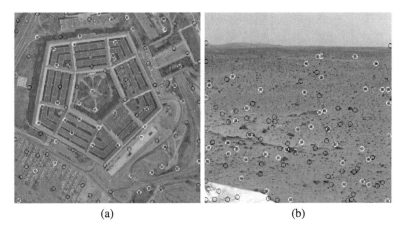

(a)   (b)

Fig. 3.17 Points found by the detector of Goshtasby [66], identifying highly informative and locally unique neighborhoods in (**a**) the Pentagon image and (**b**) the Mars image

circular neighborhoods. Entropy over a range of resolutions is determined for each neighborhood and neighborhoods where the entropy exhibits a peak under change in resolution are selected. Then, magnitude change in the histogram of the neighborhood at a peak is determined, the product of entropy and magnitude change in histogram is used as the saliency measure, and the peaks are ordered according to their saliency measures. Since histogram and entropy of circular neighborhoods are invariant to the orientation of an image, and since the peaks are calculated at various resolutions, the process is expected to be invariant to image orientation and resolution.

Kadir et al. [79] later extended the method to affine invariant points. This extension involved replacing circular areas with elliptic ones. Starting from each circular region, the region is iteratively revised to an ellipse while maximizing saliency using local image information.

Although entropy can locate informative (detailed) areas in an image, detected neighborhoods may lack uniqueness. Kadir et al. [78, 79] used change in the probability density function (histogram) of intensities within a neighborhood as resolution was varied to identify unique neighborhoods from non-unique ones. Goshtasby [66] measured uniqueness by determining the normalized correlation of a window centered at pixel (x, y) with windows centered at the eight neighboring pixels. If maximum correlation obtained at (x, y) is r, $1 - r$ is used as the uniqueness of the neighborhood centered at (x, y). Points detected in this manner in the Pentagon and Mars images are shown in Fig. 3.17. Detected points represent centers of highly informative and unique neighborhoods.

3.2 New Point Detectors

Efforts to detect points in an image in the past have focused mostly on visually identifiable points, such as corners, junctions, centers of blobs, etc. In many applications, however, it is not the visual identity of the points but the invariance property of the points that is important. It does not matter whether a point is visually identifiable or not, but it is important that the point be stable under various image changes. As long as the same points are detected in two images of a scene independent of their intensity and geometric differences, the points will be valuable.

If an image property assumes a maximum or a minimum value in a neighborhood, the extremum point will be locally unique and can be used as a control point. Some of these properties, have been explored in the past, such as curvature, symmetry, filter response, and entropy. By measuring an image property and through non-maxima suppression, many other point detectors can be designed. In the following sections, a number of point detectors designed in this manner are introduced.

3.2.1 Moment Invariant-Based Detectors

Moment invariants naturally provide invariance under various geometric transformations and should make good point detectors. The moment of order (p, q) of image $I(x, y)$ of dimensions $M \times N$ is defined by [75]:

$$M_{pq} = \sum_{x=0}^{M-1} \sum_{y=0}^{N-1} x^p y^q I(x, y). \tag{3.48}$$

M_{00} is equal to the total image intensity, and the coordinates of the center of gravity of the image (x_0, y_0) are obtained from $x_0 = M_{10}/M_{00}$ and $y_0 = M_{01}/M_{00}$. To make the moments shift invariant, they are calculated with respect to the center of gravity of the image. Such moments are called *central moments* [75]:

$$\mu_{pq} = \sum_{x=0}^{M-1} \sum_{y=0}^{N-1} (x - x_0)^p (y - y_0)^q I(x, y). \tag{3.49}$$

These moments vary with the orientation of an image. A set of rotationally invariant second and third order moments has been derived by Hu [75]:

$$\phi_1 = (\mu_{20} + \mu_{02}), \tag{3.50}$$

$$\phi_2 = (\mu_{20} - \mu_{02})^2 + 4\mu_{11}^2, \tag{3.51}$$

$$\phi_3 = (\mu_{30} - 3\mu_{12})^2 + (3\mu_{21} - \mu_{03})^2, \tag{3.52}$$

$$\phi_4 = (\mu_{30} + \mu_{12})^2 + (\mu_{21} + \mu_{03})^2, \tag{3.53}$$

$$\begin{aligned} \phi_5 = {} & (\mu_{30} - 3\mu_{12})(\mu_{30} + \mu_{12}) \\ & \times \left[(\mu_{30} + \mu_{12})^2 - 3(\mu_{21} + \mu_{03})^2 \right] \\ & + (3\mu_{21} - \mu_{03})(\mu_{21} + \mu_{03}) \\ & \times \left[3(\mu_{30} + \mu_{12})^2 - (\mu_{21} + \mu_{03})^2 \right], \end{aligned} \tag{3.54}$$

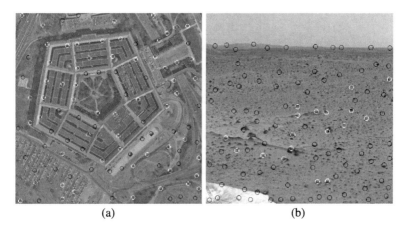

Fig. 3.18 Points found in (**a**) the Pentagon image and (**b**) the Mars image by the Hu invariant moment ϕ_4 [75]

$$\phi_6 = (\mu_{20} - \mu_{02})\big[(\mu_{30} + \mu_{12})^2 - (\mu_{21} + \mu_{03})^2\big]$$
$$+ 4\mu_{11}(\mu_{30} + \mu_{12})(\mu_{21} + \mu_{03}), \tag{3.55}$$

$$\phi_7 = (3\mu_{21} - \mu_{03})(\mu_{30} + \mu_{12})$$
$$\times \big[(\mu_{30} + \mu_{12})^2 - 3(\mu_{21} + \mu_{03})^2\big]$$
$$- (\mu_{30} - 3\mu_{12})(\mu_{21} + \mu_{03})$$
$$\times \big[3(\mu_{30} + \mu_{12})^2 - (\mu_{21} + \mu_{03})^2\big]. \tag{3.56}$$

Any of the above invariant moments can be calculated locally within circular windows, and through non-maxima suppression control points can be detected. For instance, the 100 strongest and widely dispersed points in the Pentagon and Mars images detected using ϕ_4 are shown in Fig. 3.18. Circular neighborhoods of radius 8 pixels are used to calculate ϕ_4. These points show locations where ϕ_4 is locally maximum. Since ϕ_4 is always positive, only local maxima of ϕ_4 are detected. Although the detected points do not represent any particular visual patterns, due to the rotationally invariant nature of these moments, we expect to detect the same points under different orientations of the same images.

When calculating invariant moments, it is important that circular images/windows are used so that if two images/windows have rotational differences they will contain the same scene parts.

Maitra [100] extended the rotationally invariant moments of Hu (ϕ_1–ϕ_7) to moments that are invariant to image scale as well as image contrast. The relation between these new moments and ϕ_1–ϕ_7 are:

$$\beta_1 = \frac{\sqrt{\phi_2}}{\phi_1}, \tag{3.57}$$

$$\beta_2 = \frac{\phi_3\mu_{00}}{\phi_2\phi_1}, \tag{3.58}$$

$$\beta_3 = \frac{\phi_4}{\phi_3}, \tag{3.59}$$

$$\beta_4 = \frac{\sqrt{\phi_5}}{\phi_4}, \tag{3.60}$$

$$\beta_5 = \frac{\phi_6}{\phi_4 \phi_1}, \tag{3.61}$$

$$\beta_6 = \frac{\phi_7}{\phi_5}. \tag{3.62}$$

The maxima of any one of these invariant moments when considered locally can be used as control points. In addition to Zernike moments with complex values (Sect. 3.1.14), complex moments formulated in terms of Hu invariant moments produce complex numbers that can be used to detect control points in an image. Complex moments are defined by [2, 3]

$$C_{pq} = \sum_x \sum_y (x + jy)^p (x - jy)^q I(x, y), \tag{3.63}$$

or equivalently by

$$C_{pq} = \sum_{x}^{\cdot} \sum_y r^{p+q} e^{j(p-q)\theta} I(x, y), \tag{3.64}$$

where $j = \sqrt{-1}$, and $r = \sqrt{x^2 + y^2}$ and $\theta = \tan^{-1}(y/x)$ are the polar coordinates of pixel (x, y). Note that under this definition, C_{qp} becomes the complex conjugate of C_{pq}. Rotating the image by ϕ counter-clockwise will change the pqth order moment from C_{pq} to $C_{pq} e^{-j(p-q)\phi}$. Therefore, rotating an image about its center will only change the phase of the complex moments, without changing their magnitudes. Since C_{pq} is the complex conjugate of C_{qp}, we get about half as many rotationally invariant complex moments of a particular order. In addition to

$$C_{pq} C_{qp} \tag{3.65}$$

being rotationally invariant,

$$C_{rs} C_{tu}^k + C_{sr} C_{ut}^k, \tag{3.66}$$

conditioned that $(r - s) + k(t - u) = 0$, is invariant to rotation. Image properties defined by (3.65) and (3.66) have exponents that reduce to 0 under any rotational angle, thus, making them real-valued properties [3]. Complex moments are made invariant to image contrast and image scale, by normalizing them as follows [2]:

$$C_{pq}^n = C_{pq} \left[\frac{1}{C_{00}} \left(\frac{C_{00}}{C_{11}} \right)^{(p+q)/2} \right], \tag{3.67}$$

where C_{pq}^n is the normalized complex moment of order (p, q), C_{pq} is the complex moment of order (p, q) computed when origin of the local coordinate system is at the center of the neighborhood under consideration. The term inside the bracket shows normalization with respect to image contrast and scale. Therefore, if $C_{pq} C_{qp}$

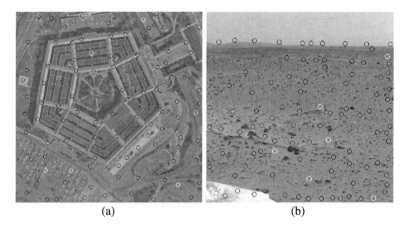

(a)   (b)

Fig. 3.19 Points found in (**a**) the Pentagon image and (**b**) the Mars image by the normalized complex moment [2]

is translation and rotation invariant,

$$C_{pq}^n C_{qp}^n \tag{3.68}$$

will be invariant to translation, rotation, scale, and contrast.

The 100 widely dispersed local maxima of property (3.68) detected in the Pentagon and Mars images are shown in Fig. 3.19. Again, the points do not identify visually distinct patterns, but they are locally maximum values of property (3.68), calculated within circular neighborhoods of radius 8 pixels. Knowing that property (3.68) is invariant to translation, rotation, scale, and contrast of an image, the same points are expected in images with translational, rotational, and scaling differences as well as differences in contrast.

In addition to the above invariant moments, Legendre moments [149], Gaussian-Hermite moments [142, 166], Tchebichef moments [110], Krawtchouk moments [170], and wavelet moments [51, 140] can be used to measure local image properties and by non-maxima suppression of the properties unique points in an image can be detected.

3.2.2 Filtering-Based Detectors

In Sect. 3.1.11, the use of oriented filters [50, 132] in design of point detectors was discussed. In addition to oriented filters, image responses to steerable filters [28, 33, 59], Gabor filters [22, 139, 164], and masks [34, 85] may be used in a non-maxima suppression algorithm to detect points in an image. Responses to masks are of particular interest because of their simplicity.

Masks can be designed to capture desired spatial frequencies in an image. Cohen et al. [34] used the following 2×2 orthogonal masks to capture low frequencies as well as high frequencies horizontally, vertically, and diagonally.

$$\mathbf{H}_1 = \begin{bmatrix} 1 & 1 \\ 1 & 1 \end{bmatrix}, \qquad \mathbf{H}_2 = \begin{bmatrix} 1 & 1 \\ -1 & -1 \end{bmatrix},$$

$$\mathbf{H}_3 = \begin{bmatrix} 1 & -1 \\ 1 & -1 \end{bmatrix}, \qquad \mathbf{H}_4 = \begin{bmatrix} 1 & -1 \\ -1 & 1 \end{bmatrix}. \tag{3.69}$$

Assuming $I(x, y)$ is an image normalized to have mean of 0 and letting $I^{(d)}(x, y)$ represent the image at resolution d, the following measures for $i = 1, \ldots, 4$ can be used to capture low and high spatial frequencies at (x, y) in an image.

$$F_i(x, y, d) = \mathbf{H}_i \oplus I^{(d)}(x, y), \quad i = 1, \ldots, 4, \tag{3.70}$$

where $\oplus$ denotes convolution. By finding the responses of these masks to different resolutions of an image, local frequency characteristics of the image can be determined.

Laws [85] created 3×3, 5×5, and 7×7 masks and used responses of a 15×15 neighborhood to the masks to characterize multi-scale frequency characteristics of a neighborhood. For instance, to create 5×5 masks, the following 1-D masks were used:

$$\begin{aligned}
B_0 &= [\ 1 \quad 4 \ 6 \quad 4 \quad 1\ ], \\
B_1 &= [\ -1 \ -2 \ 0 \quad 2 \quad 1\ ], \\
B_2 &= [\ -1 \quad 0 \ 2 \quad 0 \ -1\ ], \\
B_3 &= [\ -1 \quad 2 \ 0 \ -2 \quad 1\ ], \\
B_4 &= [\ \ 1 \ -4 \ 6 \ -4 \quad 1\ ].
\end{aligned} \tag{3.71}$$

By convolving any one of the above masks horizontally with any of the masks vertically, a 5×5 mask is obtained. Overall, 25 such 2-D masks are obtained from the combinations. All created masks have mean of 0 except for mask $B_{00} = B_0^t \oplus B_0$, which has a nonzero mean. t denotes matrix transpose. The B_{00} convolution result is used to normalize the convolution results of other 5×5 masks and to reduce the effect of image contrast on the calculated measures. Therefore, denoting $B_i^t \oplus B_j$ by B_{ij} for $i, j = 0, \ldots, 4$, and letting

$$F_0(x, y) = I(x, y) \oplus B_{00}, \tag{3.72}$$

the following 24 measures

$$G_{ij}(x, y) = \left[I(x, y) \oplus B_{ij} \right] / F_0(x, y), \tag{3.73}$$

where $i, j = 0, \ldots, 4$, and $i + j > 0$ can be used to characterize frequencies in a 5×5 neighborhood centered at (x, y). Similar features can be calculated from 3×3 and 7×7 masks [85].

The feature points representing the local extrema of G_{22} in the Pentagon and Mars images are shown in Fig. 3.20. Responses of an image to mask B_{22} are determined and the local extrema of the responses are detected. Since B_{22} is actually a Laplacian operator, G_{22} tends to detect centers of small bright and dark spots in an image.

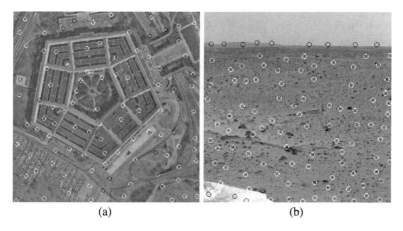

(a)   (b)

Fig. 3.20 Local extrema of the responses of Laws mask B_{22} [85] in (**a**) the Pentagon image and (**b**) the Mars image

3.2.3 Intensity-Based Detectors

Various image properties can be calculated from raw image intensities and used to detect points in an image.

1. *Smoothed intensity*: By smoothing an image $I(x, y)$ with a Gaussian of standard deviation σ ($G_\sigma(x, y)$) an image will be obtained that will be resistant to noise and invariant to image rotation.

$$\bar{I}(x, y) = G_\sigma(x, y) \oplus I(x, y) \qquad (3.74)$$

2. *Gradient magnitude of smoothed intensity*: The gradient magnitude of a smoothed image is also resistant to noise and invariant to rotation.

$$\bar{g}(x, y) = \sqrt{\bar{I}_x^2(x, y) + \bar{I}_y^2(x, y)} \qquad (3.75)$$

3. *Center contrast*: The average difference between the center pixel and other pixels in a neighborhood [65].

$$c(x, y) = \frac{1}{N-1} \sum_x \sum_y \left(I(x, y) - I_c\right), \qquad (3.76)$$

where I_c is the intensity at the center of the neighborhood and N is the number of pixels within the neighborhood under consideration.

Examples of points detected in the Pentagon and the Mars images by non-extrema suppression of smoothed intensities and non-maxima suppression of gradient magnitude are shown in Figs. 3.21 and 3.22, respectively. A Gaussian of standard deviation 2 pixels was used to smooth the images. Local extrema of the center contrast measure calculated in the Pentagon and the Mars images using circular neighborhoods of radius 8 pixels are shown in Fig. 3.23.

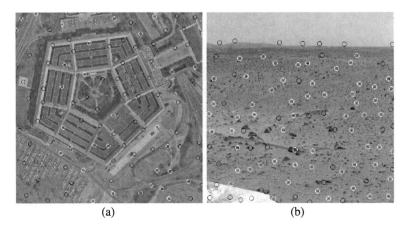

(a)   (b)

Fig. 3.21 Points detected in (**a**) the Pentagon image and (**b**) the Mars image using the local extrema of smoothed intensities

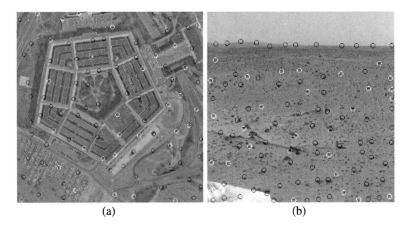

(a)   (b)

Fig. 3.22 Points detected in (**a**) the Pentagon image and (**b**) the Mars image using the local maxima of the gradient magnitude of the smoothed intensities

3.2.4 Other Point Detectors

A large number of other point detectors can be designed through non-maxima or non-extrema suppression of other image properties. These properties can be statistical [69, 148, 159], geometric [75, 87, 168], algebraic [6, 111], differential [81, 150], fractal dimension [118, 146], and spatial frequency content [10, 72, 94].

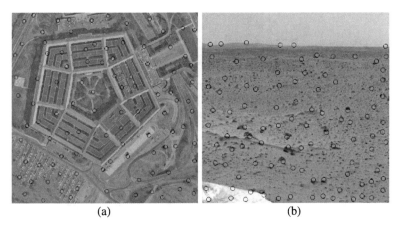

Fig. 3.23 Points detected in (**a**) the Pentagon image and (**b**) the Mars image using the local extrema of the center contrast measure when computed in circular neighborhoods of radius 8 pixels

3.3 Performance Evaluation

The most important information about a control point is its location. Detectors that identify the same points in two images of a scene independent of the intensity and geometric differences between the images are most desired. Detected points do not have to be visually identifiable to be valuable, they only have to identify the same physical points in two images so that accurate correspondence can be established between the images.

The number of same points found by a detector in two images of a scene determines the repeatability of the detector. The detectors described in the preceding sections are all highly repeatable in the absence of noise and geometric and intensity differences between the images. However, some detectors perform better than others in the presence of image differences. Detectors that include image smoothing as a part of the detection process are usually more resistant to noise than detectors that do not include smoothing in the detection process.

Detectors that are based on intensity gradients are generally more invariant to image contrast than detectors that are based on raw image intensities. Also, detectors that use properties invariant to image geometric transformations are generally more repeatable under changes in imaging view-angle than other detectors.

A number of studies have compared the performances of various point detectors. Fraundorfer and Bischof [58] find that when images have view-angle differences, the detectors of Harris and Stephens [70] and Beaudet [18] produce more repeatable points than the SIFT detector [97, 98] and the affine-adapted Harris detector [104, 105]. This can be attributed to the fact that the simpler detectors use more local information that is immune to image geometric differences than more complex detectors that use information in larger neighborhoods. Due to occlusion and sharp changes in scene depth, larger neighborhoods that are centered at the same scene point in two images cannot contain the same scene parts, producing points that are displaced with respect to each other.

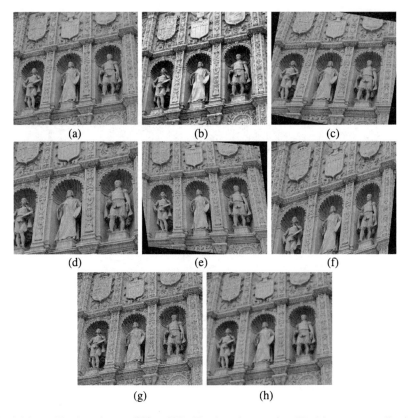

Fig. 3.24 (**a**) The base image (932 × 820). The base image after (**b**) histogram equalization, (**c**) rotation by 10 degrees clockwise, (**d**) scaling by 1.25, (**e**) transformations by affine, (**f**) transformation by homography, (**g**) addition of 20% zero-mean uniform noise, and (**h**) smoothing by a Gaussian of standard deviation 2 pixels

In the following sections, a number of experiments are performed using various synthetic and real data sets. The experiments are performed using a number of well-known and promising detectors. The repeatability, localization accuracy, and speed of the detectors are determined and compared.

3.3.1 Experimental Setup

To create a controlled data set where the coordinates of corresponding points in the images are known, an image containing various details as shown in Fig. 3.24a is selected. The intensity and the geometry of the image are then transformed to obtain the images shown in Figs. 3.24b–f. In addition, noise is added to the image to obtain Fig. 3.24g, and the image is blurred to obtain Fig. 3.24h. The repeatability and accuracy of the detectors under these image variations are determined and compared.

Histogram equalization is used to change intensities in the base image. This mapping nonlinearly changes the intensities but in a monotonic manner. The noisy image is obtained by adding 20% zero-mean uniform noise to the base image. 20% zero-mean uniform noise implies generating random numbers between -255 and 255, multiplying the numbers by 0.20, and adding them to the image intensities. If by this addition a pixel intensity becomes larger than 255, it is set to 255, and if the intensity becomes smaller than 0, it is set to 0 to keep the intensities between 0 and 255.

Six widely used detectors in the literature and five newly proposed detectors are subjected to a series of tests and their repeatabilities, localization accuracies, and computational speeds are measured and compared. The detectors used in the experiments are:

1. The curvature-based detector of Kitchen and Rosenfeld [80], which detects corners in an image (4.124).
2. The LoG detector of standard deviation 2 pixels, which locates small dark and bright blobs in an image.
3. The SIFT detector of Lowe [97, 98], which also locates dark and bright blobs in an image.
4. The gradient-based detector of Harris and Stephens [70], which finds corners using measure $R = \text{Det}(\mathbf{N}) - h \, \text{Tr}^2(\mathbf{N})$. $h = 0.08$ is assumed in the experimental results reported here.
5. The gradient-based detector of Tomasi and Kanade [151], which uses the smaller of the two eigenvalues of the square gradient matrix $\mathbf{N}$ to locate corners in an image.
6. The Hilbert-transform-based detector of Kohlmann [82], which detects corners in an image.
7. Local maxima of the invariant moment ϕ_4 of Hu [75] (3.53) computed within circular neighborhoods of radius 8 pixels.
8. Local maxima of the normalized complex moment invariant of order $(1, 1)$ (3.68). Again the invariant moments are calculated within circular neighborhoods of radius 8 pixels.
9. Local extrema of the response of an image to the Laws mask B_{22} (3.73).
10. Local extrema of image intensities after being smoothed with a Gaussian of standard deviation 2 pixels (3.74).
11. Local extrema of the center-contrast measure calculated within circular neighborhoods of radius 8 pixels (3.76).

Since a control point cannot appear in a homogeneous area in an image, if the gradient magnitude at a pixel is less than 1, the pixel is not tested for the presence of a point and further computation at the pixel is abandoned. In implementation of the gradient-based methods, (3.29) is used to calculate the square gradient matrix by letting $\sigma = \sigma' = 2$ pixels.

3.3.2 Performance Measures

A detector is required to find the same points in two images of a scene. If a detector finds N_1 points in one image and N_2 points in another image in their overlap area, and if N of the points are the same, then the ratio of the number of points common in the two sets and the number of points in the smaller set defines the repeatability of the detector. That is

$$R = \frac{N}{\min(N_1, N_2)}. \tag{3.77}$$

A pair of points in two images is considered to represent the same scene point if they fall within a small distance ε of each other after proper transformation. ε depends on the resolution of the provided images and the application under consideration. In an application where symbolic matching is sufficient without the need for accurate correspondence between the points, such as object recognition by graph matching, a larger ε may be used than in an application where accurate coordinates of corresponding points in the images are needed, such as image registration.

In the following discussion, a point in the reference image is denoted by $\mathbf{p} = (x, y)$, the corresponding point in the sensed image is denoted by $\mathbf{P} = (X, Y)$, and the geometric relation between the images is denoted by $\mathbf{f}$. If the geometric relation between two images is known, from the coordinates of points in the reference image, the coordinates of the corresponding points in the sensed image can be determined from,

$$\mathbf{P} = \mathbf{f}(\mathbf{p}). \tag{3.78}$$

$\mathbf{f}$ has two components f_x and f_y satisfying

$$X = f_x(x, y), \tag{3.79}$$

$$Y = f_y(x, y). \tag{3.80}$$

If the geometric relation $\mathbf{f}$ between two images of a scene is known and a detector finds point $\mathbf{p}_i$ in the reference image and point $\mathbf{P}_i$ in the sensed image, and if $\mathbf{p}_i$ and $\mathbf{P}_i$ approximately represent the same scene point, then the localization error of $\mathbf{P}_i$ with respect to $\mathbf{p}_i$ will be $\|\mathbf{P}_i - \mathbf{f}(\mathbf{p}_i)\|$. If N corresponding points are found in two images, the average localization error of points in the reference image with respect to those in the sensed image will be

$$E = \frac{1}{N} \sum_{i=1}^{N} \|\mathbf{P}_i - \mathbf{f}(\mathbf{p}_i)\|. \tag{3.81}$$

The smaller measure E is, the smaller the correspondence error will be, implying a higher accuracy in localization of the detected points.

Representing the geometric relation between two images in Fig. 3.24 by $\mathbf{f}$, points $\mathbf{p}$ and $\mathbf{P}$ in two images will be considered corresponding points if

$$\|\mathbf{P} - \mathbf{f}(\mathbf{p})\| \leq \varepsilon, \tag{3.82}$$

where ε is the desired error tolerance. In the event that two or more points in the reference image after transformation by **f** fall within the distance tolerance of a point in the sensed image, the sensed point closest to the transformed reference points is taken as the correspondence point. In the experiments conducted in this chapter, ε is set to $2\sqrt{2}$ pixels. In many applications, such as stereo depth perception and image registration, correspondences that are apart by more than a few pixels are not useful.

3.4   Characterization of Point Detectors

Repeatability R (3.77), localization error E (3.81), and number of corresponding points found in the overlap area between two images of a scene N are included in Table 3.1. Knowing the exact locations of corresponding points in various image pairs, these performance measures can be calculated from the detected points in the images.

The computation time C for each detector is also measured and entered into Table 3.1. The computation time in a table entry shows the time in seconds needed to detect points in an image by a detector on a 3.2 GHz PC. Results reported in the table for the SIFT detector are the ones obtained from the program provided by David Lowe, University of British Colombia (US Patent 6,711,293, March 23, 2004). The program finds the point locations with subpixel accuracy. The remaining point detectors were implemented by the author and provide only pixel accuracy. The SIFT program does not report the computation time; therefore, the table does not include the computation time for the SIFT detector. Since computation of LoG and DoG require the same time and the SIFT detector computes DoG at least three times, computation time of SIFT is expected to be at least 3 times that of the LoG detector.

From the performance measures in Table 3.1, the following conclusions can be reached.

3.4.1   Sensitivity to Intensity Changes

The images depicted in Figs. 3.24a and 3.24b have intensity differences. Intensities in the images are related nonlinearly but the relation is monotonic. By comparing the points detected by various detectors in these images, we see that under the applied intensity transformation, the lowest localization error and the highest repeatability are achieved by the Laws B_{22} mask. Among all detectors tested the Laws mask has also produced the most correspondences in the shortest time. It is interesting to note that the Laws B_{22} mask is actually a Laplacian that is defined within a 5×5 neighborhood. LoG and SIFT provide properties similar to those of Laws B_{22} mask but in larger neighborhoods. Consequently, the localization accuracy and repeatability of LoG and SIFT are also high, although not as high as those of Laws

Table 3.1 P: performance, E: localization error, R: repeatability, N: number of corresponding points in two images, and C: computation time in seconds. Histogram equalized (Fig. 3.24b), rotated (Fig. 3.24c), scaled (Fig. 3.24d), affine transformed (Fig. 3.24e), projective transformed (Fig. 3.24f), noisy (Fig. 3.24g), and smoothed (Fig. 3.24h) images were compared individually to the base image (Fig. 3.24a) to obtain these performance measures. The *bold* numbers in a column show the best performance measures obtained for an image

Method	P	3.24b	3.24c	3.24d	3.24e	3.24f	3.24g	3.24h
Kitchen and	E	0.358	0.986	0.862	0.975	0.955	1.060	1.314
Rosenfeld	R	0.718	0.450	0.751	0.486	0.462	0.427	0.435
[80]	N	2478	1534	2590	1675	1593	1017	1501
	C	0.816	0.805	1.270	0.801	0.789	0.811	0.790
LoG	E	0.327	0.567	0.870	0.787	0.922	0.877	1.117
	R	0.913	0.858	0.916	0.837	0.713	0.756	0.907
	N	9389	7943	9412	7882	6951	7766	5088
	C	0.833	0.826	1.291	0.822	0.823	0.837	0.830
SIFT [97]	E	0.378	**0.366**	0.578	**0.693**	**0.645**	0.930	1.063
	R	0.798	0.774	**0.952**	0.723	0.647	0.557	0.916
	N	8251	8001	9848	7474	6689	4756	2242
Harris and	E	0.563	0.802	0.735	0.901	0.888	0.902	1.266
Stephens	R	0.833	0.687	0.846	0.721	0.657	0.704	0.544
[70]	N	3079	2347	3126	2468	2202	2603	1629
	C	1.031	1.024	1.605	1.030	1.063	1.108	1.080
Tomasi and	E	0.667	0.836	0.711	0.884	0.931	0.927	1.291
Kanade	R	0.826	0.675	0.926	0.732	0.664	0.683	0.538
[151]	N	3173	2431	3557	2692	2445	2622	2047
	C	1.043	1.039	1.636	1.042	1.043	1.051	1.041
Kohlmann	E	0.476	1.451	0.696	1.279	1.127	0.684	**0.912**
[82]	R	0.850	0.329	0.793	0.419	0.505	0.812	0.908
	N	3502	1234	3269	1650	1949	3345	1955
	C	1.878	1.873	6.931	1.878	1.895	1.866	1.863
Hu	E	0.775	0.691	1.349	1.017	1.224	0.878	0.980
invariant	R	0.820	0.873	0.826	0.831	0.650	0.799	**0.925**
moment	N	6380	6096	6430	5709	4718	6218	4521
[75]	C	183.9	203.3	289.4	199.4	191.0	184.4	184.0
Complex	E	0.713	0.834	1.423	1.075	1.240	1.092	1.320
moment	R	0.847	0.805	0.818	0.774	0.584	0.737	0.627
[2]	N	4035	5064	5611	4816	3963	5056	3609
	C	186.1	185.7	291.1	184.9	184.6	185.1	184.8

Table 3.1   (Continued)

Method	P	3.24b	3.24c	3.24d	3.24e	3.24f	3.24g	3.24h
Laws	E	**0.230**	0.563	**0.529**	0.727	0.694	0.611	1.653
mask	R	**0.994**	**0.979**	0.834	**0.975**	0.883	**0.999**	0.405
response	N	98482	82757	118741	92637	78641	98975	47847
[85]	C	**0.416**	**0.407**	**0.638**	**0.406**	**0.407**	**0.415**	**0.397**
Smoothed	E	0.556	0.733	0.832	0.839	0.902	0.651	1.133
intensity	R	0.504	0.462	0.577	0.529	0.434	0.500	0.487
	N	1851	1391	2119	1526	1594	1838	415
	C	0.566	0.556	0.877	0.557	0.560	0.569	0.551
Center	E	0.283	0.632	0.551	0.947	1.000	**0.606**	1.642
contrast	R	0.939	0.885	0.914	0.973	**0.941**	0.997	0.698
[65]	N	37202	23888	27883	30400	25714	39505	4570
	C	3.087	3.085	4.852	3.089	3.161	3.215	3.141

mask. Image changes outside a 5×5 window do not affect the Laws mask response but do affect the LoG and SIFT responses.

The Laws mask, by operating in very small neighborhoods detects a large number of points. We have considered two points corresponding if they are within a threshold distance of $\varepsilon = 2\sqrt{2}$ pixels. By reducing the threshold distance to 1 pixel, the number of correspondences obtained by the Laws mask is 91627, which is not much lower than 98482 correspondences found under the threshold distance of $\varepsilon = 2\sqrt{2}$ pixels. This implies that the majority of the correspondences found by Laws mask accurately correspond to each other. To reduce the number of detected points, one may keep points with stronger responses and discard points with weaker responses.

Another impressive detector under the applied intensity transformation is center contrast, which produces a very low localization error and has a very high repeatability.

3.4.2 Sensitivity to Geometric Changes

The images in Figs. 3.24a and 3.24c have rotational differences. Under rotation, SIFT produces the most accurately localized points, while the Laws mask finds the most repeatable points and the most correspondences in the shortest time among all detectors tested. Note that SIFT point locations are determined with subpixel accuracy while point locations of other detectors are determined with pixel accuracy. Some of the gains achieved by the SIFT detector can be the result of localizing the points with subpixel accuracy.

Figures 3.24a and 3.24d have scaling differences. By comparing the points found in these images by the various detectors, we see that Laws mask localizes the points most accurately, produces the largest number of correspondences, and is the fastest. The SIFT detector has the highest repeatability closely followed by the detector of Tomasi and Kanade and center contrast.

Images in Figs. 3.24a and 3.24e are related by the affine transformation. Comparing the points in these images, we see that SIFT points are most accurately localized, but the points detected by Laws mask are most repeatable. Laws mask also produces the largest number of correspondences and has the fastest speed among all detectors. Center contrast also has a very high repeatability.

Under the applied homography (Figs. 3.24a and 3.24f), the SIFT detector finds the most accurately localized points, but center contrast finds the most repeatable points, and the Laws mask produces the largest number of correspondences in the shortest time.

3.4.3 Sensitivity to Noise

The image in Fig. 3.24g is obtained after adding 20% zero-mean uniform noise to the image in Fig. 3.24a. Under the applied noise, center contrast finds the most accurate points, while the Laws mask produces the most repeatable points, finds the largest number of correspondences, and is the fastest.

3.4.4 Sensitivity to Blurring

The image in Fig. 3.24h is obtained after smoothing the image in Fig. 3.24a with a Gaussian of standard deviation 2 pixels. Image smoothing blurs and reduces image details. Under the applied blurring, the Kohlmann detector finds the most accurately localized points, while the Hu moment invariant finds the most repeatable points. Laws mask finds the most correspondences and has the shortest computation time.

3.5 Performance Analysis

Examining the results in Table 3.1, we see that the LoG detector has a relatively high performance in each category, but it is not the highest in any of the categories. The LoG detector finds the extrema of intensity second derivatives after being smoothed. As the standard deviation of the Gaussian smoother is changed, the positional accuracy of some points improve. This can be attributed to the improved positional accuracy of the SIFT detector when compared to the LoG detector under image intensity and geometric transformation and also under blurring. The improved positional accuracy of SIFT points over LoG points can also be because the SIFT points are determined with subpixel accuracy while the LoG points are determined with pixel accuracy. The positional accuracy of SIFT points can be further improved by improving the accuracy of the interpolation that determines the subpixel position of a point from the feature values of pixels around it [36].

Responses of an image to Laws B_{22} mask remain most invariant under various image changes, except under image blurring. Since Laws mask is a local operator, it is greatly influenced by blurring. LoG and SIFT on the other hand are larger operators, making them less sensitive to blurring. Image blurring causes extrema points to displace [8], reducing the localization accuracy of the Laws mask and, to a lesser degree, the localization accuracies of LoG and SIFT.

The SIFT detector first estimates the scale and orientation of a blob and then calculates its center. To determine the accuracy of an estimated scale or orientation for a blob by the SIFT detector, images in Figs. 3.24a, 3.24b, 3.24g, and 3.24h, which have exactly the same geometry were used. Corresponding points in these images have exactly the same coordinates. To determine the accuracy with which the scale and orientation of points in these images are estimated, the maximum and mean differences between the scales and orientations of corresponding points in image 3.24a and in images 3.24b, 3.24g, and 3.24h were determined. The maximum difference between estimated scales in images 3.24a and 3.24b was 38.1 while the maximum difference in estimated orientations was 3.14 radians. On average, estimated error in scale was 0.23, while estimated error in orientation was 0.52 radians.

Comparing the scales and orientations of points detected in Figs. 3.24a and 3.24g by the SIFT detector, we find that maximum error in estimated scale is 22.8, while maximum error in estimated orientation is 3.14 radians. Average error in estimated scale is 0.34, while average estimated error in orientation is 0.65 radians. Images 3.24a and 3.24h have blurring differences. Comparing the scales and orientations of SIFT points detected in these images, we find that maximum error in scale estimation is 24.0, while maximum error in orientation estimation is 3.14 radians. Average error in estimated scale is 0.84, while average estimation error in orientation is 0.77 radians.

Although estimated errors at some points may be acceptable, estimated error at some other points are considerably higher than many applications can handle. Such large errors in scale could displace a detected point. This can be the reason for obtaining a lower repeatability for SIFT when compared to LoG in some of the images.

Examining the performances of the two moment-based detectors in Table 3.1, we see that these detectors are highly repeatable under all image variations, although they are very time consuming. When comparing the localization errors and repeatabilities of the various corner detectors with those of various blob detectors, we see that blob detectors, in general, perform better than corner detectors.

3.6 Further Observations

From the experimental results obtained in this chapter, we can conclude that overall, the SIFT detector is the most accurate, closely followed by the LoG detector and the Laws mask. Some of the superior accuracy of SIFT can be attributed to its subpixel localization implementation. One should note that other detectors can also be implemented to provide subpixel localization accuracy. SIFT detector, however, can displace a detected point from its true position by estimating the scale of the blob incorrectly and over- or under-smoothing a neighborhood. When blobs are nonsymmetric, elongated, or contain branches, detected points shift with respect to each other in images if corresponding neighborhoods are not smoothed by the same amount. If a blob is not round, branches or segments of it can fall off under blurring [8], displacing the detected point.

The LoG detector smoothes all areas in an image similarly while the SIFT detector, in effect, applies different smoothing to different areas in an image. When images are known to have about the same scale, the LoG detector is expected to produce a higher repeatability than the SIFT detector, as evidenced by the results in Table 3.1. However, if the images have unknown scaling differences, the SIFT detector is expected to produce more repeatable points than the LoG detector.

Repeatability under changes in scale/resolution is low for many of the detectors because image information in local neighborhoods is changed by changing the scale or resolution of an image. The same image structure is not simply scaled up or down, image details are reduced or added to an area as image resolution is changed. This change instead causes a feature point in one image to displace or disappear in another image. The problem of scale is that it is often unknown, and an attempt to estimate it, as done in SIFT [98] and some other detectors, could involve inaccuracies. Scale estimation will be accurate only for round blobs. To distinguish points representing round blobs from points representing non-round blobs, one may associate a roundness score with a blob, measuring the radial symmetry of the blob. The user can then choose only those points that are associated with round/symmetric blobs.

The solution to the unknown scale is to choose a property that does not change with scale or changes very gradually with scale. Invariant moments are intrinsically invariant to scale. However, even with invariant moments, when the scale difference between two images is not known, the neighborhoods inside which calculations should be performed cannot be chosen, and if the same neighborhood size is chosen in two images at different scales, the neighborhoods cannot contain the same pattern, producing different moments for corresponding neighborhoods. Examining the contents of Table 3.1 we observe that if the scaling difference between two images is not very large, invariant moments still produce better results than other detectors. We also observe that the Kohlmann [82] detector has a high performance under unknown scale. The Kohlmann detector measures the spatial frequency characteristics of a neighborhood, and it appears that if the scaling difference between two images is not very high, the frequency characteristics of corresponding neighborhoods will not be very different, detecting the same points in the images.

References

1. Abdel-Hakim, A.E., Farag, A.A.: CSIFT: A SIFT descriptor with color invariant characteristics. In: Proc. IEEE Conf. Computer Vision and Pattern Recognition, vol. 2, pp. 1978–1983 (2006)

2. Abo-Zaid, A., Hinton, O., Horne, E.: About moment normalisation and complex moment descriptors. In: Proc. 4th Int'l Conf. Pattern Recognition, pp. 399–407 (1988)

3. Abu-Mostafa, Y.S., Psaltis, D.: Recognitive aspects of moment invariants. IEEE Trans. Pattern Anal. Mach. Intell. **6**(6), 698–706 (1984)

4. Achard, C., Bigorgne, E., Devars, J.: A sub-pixel and multispectral corner detector. In: 15th Int'l Conf. Pattern Recognition, vol. 3, pp. 959–962 (2000)

5. Ando, S.: Image field categorization and edge/corner detection from gradient covariance. IEEE Trans. Pattern Anal. Mach. Intell. **22**(2), 179–190 (2000)

6. Andrews, H.C., Patterson, C.L.: Singular value decomposition and digital image processing. In: IEEE Trans. Acoustics, Speech, and Signal Processing, pp. 26–53 (1976)

7. Attneave, F.: Some informational aspects of visual perception. Psychol. Rev. **61**(3), 183–193 (1954)

8. Babaud, J., Witkin, A.P., Baudin, M., Duda, R.O.: Uniqueness of the Gaussian kernel for scale-space filtering. IEEE Trans. Pattern Anal. Mach. Intell. **8**(1), 26–33 (1986)

9. Bae, S.C., Kweon, S., Yoo, C.D.: COP: A new corner detector. Pattern Recognit. Lett. **23**, 1349–1360 (2002)

10. Bajcsy, R.: Computer description of textured surfaces. In: Proc. 3rd Int'l J. Conf. Artificial Intelligence, pp. 572–579 (1973)

11. Baker, S., Nayar, S.K., Murase, H.: Parametric feature detection. Int. J. Comput. Vis. **27**(1), 27–50 (1998)

12. Ballard, D.H.: Generalizing the Hough transform to detect arbitrary shapes. Pattern Recognit. **13**, 111–122 (1981)

13. Banerjee, M., Kundu, M.K., Mitra, P.: Corner detection using support vector machines. In: Proc. Int'l Conf. Pattern Recognition (ICPR), vol. 2, pp. 819–822 (2004)

14. Barnard, S.T., Thompson, W.B.: Disparity analysis of images. IEEE Trans. Pattern Anal. Mach. Intell. **2**(4), 333–340 (1980)

15. Bastanlar, Y., Yardimci, Y.: Corner validation based on extracted corner properties. Comput. Vis. Image Process. **112**, 243–261 (2008)

16. Baumberg, A.: Reliable feature matching across widely separated views. In: IEEE Conf. Computer Vision and Pattern Recognition, vol. 1, pp. 774–781 (2000)

17. Bay, H., Tuetelaars, T., van Gool, L.: SURF: Speeded up robust features. In: Proc. European Conf. Computer Vision (2006). Also in Comput. Vis. Image Underst. **110**, 346–359 (2006)

18. Beaudet, P.R.: Rotationally invariant image operators. In: Proc. Int'l Conf. Pattern Recognition, pp. 579–583 (1978)

19. Beymer, D.J.: Finding junctions using the image gradient. In: Proc. IEEE Conf. Computer Vision and Pattern Recognition, Maui, Hawaii (1991). Also see MIT AI Lab Memo No. 1266, December 1991

20. Bharath, A.A., Kingsbury, N.: Phase invariant keypoint detection. In: Proc. 15th Int'l Conf. Digital Signal Processing, pp. 447–450 (2007)

21. Blostein, D., Ahuja, N.: A multiscale region detector. Comput. Vis. Graph. Image Process. **45**, 22–41 (1989)

22. Bovik, A.C., Clark, M., Geisler, W.S.: Multichannel texture analysis using localized spatial filters. IEEE Trans. Pattern Anal. Mach. Intell. **12**(1), 55–73 (1990)

23. Brand, P., Mohr, R.: Accuracy in image measure. In: Proc. SPIE Videometrics III, Boston, MA, pp. 218–228 (1994)

24. Brown, M., Szeliski, R., Winder, S.: Multi-image matching using multi-scale oriented patches. In: Proc. IEEE Conf. Computer Vision and Pattern Recognition, vol. 1, pp. 510–517 (2005) Also see Microsoft Research Technical Report MSR-TR-2004-133

25. Brunnström, K., Lindeberg, T., Eklundh, J.O.: Active detection and classification of junctions by foveation with head-eye system guided by the scale-space primal sketch. In: Proc. 2nd European Conf. Computer Vision. Lecture Notes in Computer Science, vol. 588, pp. 701–709 (1992)

26. Canny, J.F.: A computational approach to edge detection. IEEE Trans. Pattern Anal. Mach. Intell. **8**(6), 679–698 (1986)

27. Carneiro, G., Jepson, A.D.: Phase-based local features. In: European Conf. Computer Vision, Copenhagen, Denmark, pp. 282–296 (2002)
28. Carneiro, G., Jepson, A.D.: Multi-scale phase-based local features. In: Proc. Computer Vision and Pattern Recognition, vol. 1, pp. 736–743 (2003)
29. Chabat, F., Yang, G.Z., Hansell, D.M.: A corner orientation detector. Image Vis. Comput. **17**, 761–769 (1999)
30. Chen, W.-C., Rockett, P.: Bayesian labeling of corners using a grey-level corner image model. In: IEEE Int'l Conf. Image Processing, vol. 1, pp. 687–690 (1997)
31. Chen, C.-H., Lee, J.-H., Sun, Y.-N.: Wavelet transformation for gray-level corner detection. Pattern Recognit. **28**(6), 853–861 (1995)
32. Clark, J.J.: Authenticating edges produced by zero-crossing algorithms. IEEE Trans. Pattern Anal. Mach. Intell. **11**(1), 43–57 (1989)
33. Coggins, J.M., Jain, A.K.: A spatial filtering approach to texture analysis. Pattern Recognit. Lett. **3**(3), 195–203 (1985)
34. Cohen, P., LeDinh, C.T., Lacasse, V.: Classification of textures by means of two-dimensional orthogonal masks. IEEE Trans. Acoust. Speech Signal Process. **37**(1), 125–128 (1989)
35. Cooper, S.J., Kitchen, L.: Early jump-out corner detectors. IEEE Trans. Pattern Anal. Mach. Intell. **15**(8), 823–828 (1993)
36. Cordes, K., Müller, O., Rosenhahn, B., Ostermann, J.: HALF-SIFT: High accurate localized features for SIFT. In: Proc. IEEE Conf. Computer Vision and Pattern Recognition, pp. 31–38 (2009)
37. Crowley, J.L., Parker, A.C.: A representation for shape based on peaks and ridges in the difference of low pass transform. IEEE Trans. Pattern Anal. Mach. Intell. **6**(2), 156–170 (1984)
38. Davies, E.R.: Application of the generalized Hough transform to corner detection. IEE Proc. **135**(1), 49–54 (1988)
39. Deriche, R., Blaszka, T.: Recovering and characterizing image features using an efficient model based approach. In: Proc. IEEE Conf. Computer Vision and Pattern Recognition, New York, NY, pp. 530–535 (1993). Also see T. Blaszka and R. Deriche, Recovering and characterizing image features using an efficient model based approach, INRIA Technical Report No. 2422 (1994)
40. Deriche, R., Giraudon, G.: Accurate corner detection: An analytical study. In: Proc. 3rd Int'l Conf. Computer Vision, Osaka, Japan, pp. 66–70 (1990)
41. Deriche, R., Giraudon, G.: A computational approach for corner and vertex detection. Int. J. Comput. Vis. **10**(2), 101–124 (1993)
42. Dias, P., Kassim, A., Srinivasan, V.: A neural network based corner detection method. In: IEEE Int'l Conf. Neural Networks, Perth, Australia, vol. 4, pp. 2116–2120 (1995)
43. Dreschler, L., Nagel, H.H.: Volumetric model and 3D-trajectory of a moving car derived from monocular TV-frame sequences of a street scene. In: Proc. Int'l J. Conf. Artificial Intelligence, Vancouver, Canada, pp. 692–697 (1981)
44. Drewniok, C., Rohr, K.: High-precision localization of circular landmarks in aerial images. In: Wachsmuth, I., Rollinger, C.-R., Brauer, W. (eds.) Proc. 19th Conf. on Artificial Intelligence, KI-95: Advances in Artificial Intelligence, Bielefeld, Germany. Lecture Notes in Artificial Intelligence, vol. 981, pp. 259–268. Springer, Berlin (1995)
45. Duda, R.O., Hart, P.E.: Use of the Hough transformation to detect lines and curves in pictures. Commun. ACM **15**(1), 11–15 (1972)
46. Dufournaud, Y., Schmid, C., Horaud, R.: Matching images with different resolutions. In: Proc. Conf. Computer Vision and Pattern Recognition, Hilton Head Island, South Carolina, pp. 612–618 (2000)
47. Faille, F.: A fast method to improve the stability of interest point detection under illumination changes. In: Int'l Conf. Image Processing, pp. 2673–2676 (2004)
48. Fang, T.J., Huang, Z.H., Kanal, L.N., Lavine, B.D., Stockman, G., Xiong, F.L.: Three-dimensional object recognition using a transform clustering technique. In: Proc. 6th Int'l Conf. Pattern Recognition, pp. 678–681 (1982)

49. Fauqueur, J., Kingsbury, N., Anderson, R.: Multiscale keypoint detection using the dual-tree complex wavelet transform. In: Proc. IEEE Int'l Conf. Image Processing, pp. 1625–1628 (2006)
50. Felsberg, M., Sommer, G.: Image features based on a new approach to 2-D rotation invariant quadrature filters. In: Lecture Notes in Computer Science, vol. 2350, pp. 369–383. Springer, Berlin (2002)
51. Feng, Z., Shang-qian, L., Da-bao, W., Wei, G.: Aircraft recognition in infrared image using wavelet moment invariants. Image Vis. Comput. **27**, 313–318 (2009)
52. Fidrich, M., Thirion, J.-P.: Multiscale extraction and representation of features from medical images. INRIA Technical Report No. 2365 (1994)
53. Florack, L., Kuijper, A.: The topological structure of scale-space images. J. Math. Imaging Vis. **12**(1), 65–79 (2000)
54. Fonseca, L., Kenney, C.: Control point assessment for image registration. In: Proc. XII Brazilian Symp. Computer Graphics and Image Processing, pp. 125–132 (1999)
55. Förstner, W.: A feature based correspondence algorithm for image matching. Int. Arch. Photogramm. Remote Sens. **26**, 150–166 (1986)
56. Förstner, W.: A framework for low level feature extraction. In: European Conf. Computer Vision. Lecture Notes in Computer Science, vol. 801, pp. 383–394 (1994)
57. Förstner, W., Gülch, E.: A fast operator for detection and precise location of distinct points, corners and centers of circular features. In: Intercommission Conf. Fast Processing of Photogrammetric Data, Interlaken, Switzerland, pp. 281–305 (1987)
58. Fraundorfer, F., Bischof, H.: Evaluation of local detectors on nonplanar scenes. In: Proc. 28th Workshop of the Austrian Association for Pattern Recognition, pp. 125–132 (2004)
59. Freeman, W.T., Adelson, W.H.: The design and use of steerable filters. IEEE Trans. Pattern Anal. Mach. Intell. **13**(9), 891–906 (1991)
60. Gauglitz, S., Höllerer, T., Turk, M.: Evaluation of interest point detectors and feature descriptors for visual tracking. Int. J. Comput. Vis. **94**, 335–360 (2011)
61. Gevrekci, M., Gunturk, K.: Illumination robust interest point detection. Comput. Vis. Image Underst. **113**, 565–571 (2009)
62. Ghosal, S., Mehrotra, R.: Zernicke moment-based feature detectors. In: Int'l Conf. Image Processing, pp. 934–938 (1994)
63. Ghosal, S., Mehrotra, R.: A moment based unified approach to image feature detection. IEEE Trans. Image Process. **6**(6), 781–793 (1997)
64. Giraudon, G., Deriche, R.: On corner and vertex detection. In: Proc. IEEE Conf. Computer Vision and Pattern Recognition, pp. 650–655 (1991)
65. Gong, P., Howarth, P.J.: An assessment of some small window-based spatial features for land-cover classification. In: Int'l Conf. Geoscience and Remote Sensing Symposium, vol. 4, pp. 1668–1670 (1993)
66. Goshtasby, A.: 2-D and 3-D Image Registration for Medical, Remote Sensing, and Industrial Applications. Wiley, New York (2005)
67. Guiducci, A.: Corner characterization by differential geometry techniques. Pattern Recognit. Lett. **8**(5), 311–318 (1988)
68. Hannah, M.J.: Computer matching of areas in stereo images. Ph.D. Dissertation, Stanford University, Department of Computer Science (1974)
69. Haralick, R.M., Shanmugam, K., Dinstein, I.: Texture features for image classification. IEEE Trans. Syst. Man Cybern. **3**(6), 610–621 (1973)
70. Harris, C., Stephens, M.: A combined corner and edge detector. In: Proc. 4th Alvey Vision Conf. (AVC88), Univ. Manchester, pp. 147–151 (1988)
71. Heyden, A., Rohr, K.: Evaluation of corner extraction schemes using invariance methods. In: Proc. 13th Int'l Conf. Pattern Recognition (ICPR'96), Vienna, Austria, vol. 1, pp. 895–899 (1996)
72. Horikawa, Y.: A feature of 2D and 3D image invariant to similarity transformations based on the bispectrum. Syst. Comput. Jpn. **33**(3), 1–10 (2002)
73. Horn, B.K.P.: The Binford-Horn Line-finder, MIT Artificial Intelligence Laboratory AI Memo No. 285, July 1971, revised December 1973

74. Hough, P.V.C.: Method and means for recognizing complex patterns. US Patent 3,069,654, 1 December 1962
75. Hu, M.K.: Visual pattern recognition by moment invariants. IEEE Trans. Inf. Theory **8**, 179–187 (1962)
76. Hueckel, M.H.: An operator which locates edges in digitized pictures. J. ACM **18**(1), 113–125 (1971)
77. Johansson, B., Granlund, G.: Fast selective detection of rotational symmetries using normalized inhibition. In: Proc. 6th European Conf. Computer Vision, vol. 1, pp. 871–887 (2000)
78. Kadir, T., Brady, J.M.: Scale saliency and image description. Int. J. Comput. Vis. **45**(2), 83–105 (2001)
79. Kadir, T., Zisserman, A., Brady, M.: An affine invariant salient detector. In: Proc. 8th European Conf. Computer Vision, pp. 228–241 (2004)
80. Kitchen, L., Rosenfeld, A.: Gray level corner detection. Technical Report #887, Computer Science Center, University of Maryland (1980). Also in Pattern Recogn. Lett. **1**, 95–102 (1982)
81. Koenderink, J.J., van Doorn, A.J.: Representation of local geometry in the visual system. Biol. Cybern. **55**, 367–375 (1987)
82. Kohlmann, K.: Corner detection in natural images based on the 2-D Hilbert transform. Signal Process. **48**, 225–234 (1996)
83. Kovesi, P.: Detection of interest points using symmetry. In: Proc. 3rd Int'l Conf. Computer Vision, pp. 62–65 (1990)
84. Kweon, I., Kanade, T.: Extracting topologic terrain features from elevation maps. CVGIP, Image Underst. **59**(2), 171–182 (1994)
85. Laws, K.I.: Rapid texture identification. In: Image Processing for Missile Guidance, Proc. SPIE, vol. 238, pp. 376–380 (1980)
86. Lee, K.-J., Bien, Z.: A gray-level corner detector using fuzzy logic. In: Pattern Recognition Letters, vol. 17, pp. 939–950 (1996)
87. Li, Y.: Reforming the theory of invariant moments for pattern recognition. Pattern Recognit. **25**(7), 723–730 (1992)
88. Li, X., Wu, T., Madhavan, R.: Correlation measure for corner detection. In: Proc. IEEE Conf. Computer Vision and Pattern Recognition, pp. 643–646 (1986)
89. Li, Q., Ye, Y., Kambhamettu, C.: Interest point detection using imbalance selection. Pattern Recognit. **41**, 672–688 (2008)
90. Li, R., Xiao, R., Li, Z., Cai, R., Lu, B.-L., Zhang, L.: Rank-SIFT: Learning to rank repeatable local interest points. In: Proc. IEEE Conf. Computer Vision and Pattern Recognition, pp. 1737–1744 (2011)
91. Lindeberg, T.: Feature detection with automatic scale selection. Int. J. Comput. Vis. **30**(2), 79–116 (1998)
92. Lindeberg, T., Gårding, J.: Shape-adapted smoothing in estimation of 3-D shape cues from affine deformations of local 2-D brightness structure. Image Vis. Comput. **15**(6), 415–434 (1997)
93. Linden, T.: A triangulation-based approach to nonrigid image registration. M.S. Thesis, Department of Computer Science and Engineering, Wright State University, Dayton, OH (2011)
94. Lohmann, A.W., Wirnitzer, B.: Tripple correlations. Proc. IEEE **72**(7), 889–901 (1984)
95. Loog, M., Lauze, F.: The improbability of Harris interest points. IEEE Trans. Pattern Anal. Mach. Intell. **32**(6), 1141–1147 (2010)
96. Loupias, E., Sebe, N., Bres, S., Jolion, J.-M.: Wavelet-based salient points for image retrieval. In: IEEE Int'l Conf. Image Processing, pp. 518–521 (2000)
97. Lowe, D.G.: Object recognition from local scale-invariant features. In: Proc. Int'l Conf. Computer Vision, vol. 2, pp. 1150–1157 (1999)
98. Lowe, D.: Distinctive image features from scale-invariant keypoints. Int. J. Comput. Vis. **60**(2), 91–110 (2004)
99. Loy, G., Zelinsky, A.: A fast radial symmetry transform for detecting points of interest. In: 7th European Conf. Computer Vision, pp. 358–368 (2002)

100. Maitra, S.: Moment invariants. Proc. IEEE **67**(4), 697–699 (1979)
101. Marquardt, D.: An algorithm for least-squares estimation of nonlinear parameters. SIAM J. Appl. Math. **11**, 431–444 (1963)
102. Marr, D., Hildreth, E.: Theory of edge detection. Proc. R. Soc. Lond. B **207**, 187–217 (1980)
103. Mikolajczyk, K., Schmid, C.: Indexing based on scale invariant interest points. In: Proc. Int'l Conf. Computer Vision, pp. 525–531 (2001)
104. Mikolajczyk, K., Schmid, C.: An affine invariant interest point detector. In: European Conf. Computer Vision, vol. 1, pp. 128–142 (2002)
105. Mikolajczyk, K., Schmid, C.: Scale and affine invariant interest point detectors. Int. J. Comput. Vis. **60**(1), 63–86 (2004)
106. Moravec, H.P.: Towards automatic visual obstacle avoidance. In: Proc. Int'l Joint Conf. Artificial Intelligence, p. 584 (1977)
107. Moravec, H.P.: Rover visual obstacle avoidance. In: Proc. Int'l Joint Conf. Artificial Intelligence, pp. 785–790 (1981)
108. Moreels, P., Perona, P.: Evaluation of features detectors and descriptors based on 3D objects. In: Proc. Int'l Conf. Computer Vision, vol. 1, pp. 800–807 (2005)
109. Mukherjee, A., Velez-Reyes, M., Roysam, B.: Interest points for hyperspectral image data. IEEE Trans. Geosci. Remote Sens. **47**(3), 748–760 (2009)
110. Mukundan, R., Ong, S.H., Lee, P.A.: Image analysis by Tchebichef moments. IEEE Trans. Image Process. **10**(9), 1357–1364 (2001)
111. Murase, H., Nayar, S.: Visual learning and recognition of 3-D objects from appearance. Int. J. Comput. Vis. **14**, 5–24 (1995)
112. Nagel, H.H.: Displacement vectors derived from second order intensity variations in image sequences. Comput. Vis. Graph. Image Process. **21**, 85–117 (1983)
113. Nobel, J.A.: Finding corners. In: Proc. 3rd Alvey Vision Conference, Cambridge, England, pp. 267–274 (1988)
114. Oh, H.-H., Chien, S.-I.: Exact corner location using attentional generalized symmetry transform. Pattern Recognit. Lett. **23**(11), 1361–1372 (2002)
115. Olague, G., Hernández, B.: A new accurate and flexible model based multi-corner detector for measurement and recognition. Pattern Recognit. Lett. **26**(1), 27–41 (2005)
116. Paler, K., Föglein, J., Illingworth, J., Kittler, J.V.: Local ordered grey levels as an aid to corner detection. Pattern Recognit. **17**(5), 535–543 (1984)
117. Parida, L., Geiger, D., Hummel, R.: Junctions: Detection, classification, and reconstruction. IEEE Trans. Pattern Anal. Mach. Intell. **20**(7), 687–698 (1998)
118. Pentland, A.: Fractal-based description of natural scenes. IEEE Trans. Pattern Anal. Mach. Intell. **6**(6), 661–674 (1984)
119. Perkins, W.A., Binford, T.O.: A corner finder for visual feedback, Stanford Artificial Intelligence Laboratory, Memo AIM-214, Computer Science Department, Report No. CS-386 (1973)
120. Platel, B., Balmachnova, E., Florack, L., Kanters, F., ter Haar Romeny, B.M.: Using top-points as interest points for image matching. In: Deep Structure, Singularities, and Computer Vision, pp. 211–222 (2005)
121. Platel, B., Fatih Demirci, M., Shokoufandeh, A., Florack, L.M.J., Kanters, F.M.W., Dickinson, S.J.: Discrete representation of top points via scale space tessellation. In: Proc. 5th Int'l Conf. Scale Space Methods in Computer Vision, Germany, pp. 73–84 (2005)
122. Rajan, P.K., Davidson, J.M.: Evaluation of corner detection algorithms. In: IEEE Proc. 21st Southeastern Symposium on System Theory, pp. 29–33 (1989)
123. Reisfeld, D.: The constrained phase congruency feature detector: Simultaneous location, classification, and scale determination. Pattern Recognit. Lett. **17**(11), 1161–1169 (1996)
124. Reisfeld, D., Yeshurun, Y.: Preprocessing of face images: Detection of features and pose normalization. Comput. Vis. Image Underst. **71**(3), 413–430 (1998)
125. Reisfeld, D., Wolfson, H., Yeshurun, Y.: Detection of interest points using symmetry. In: Proc. 3rd Int'l Conf. Computer Vision, Osaka, Japan, pp. 62–65 (1990)
126. Reisfeld, D., Wolfson, H., Yeshurun, Y.: Context-free attention operators: The generalized symmetry transform. Int. J. Comput. Vis. **14**(2), 119–130 (1995)

127. Rémi, T., Bernard, M.: Accelerated keypoint extraction. In: 9th Int'l Workshop on Image Analysis for Multimedia Interactive Services (WIAMIS'08), pp. 183–186 (2008)

128. Rohr, K.: Recognizing corners by fitting parametric models. Int. J. Comput. Vis. **9**(3), 213–230 (1992)

129. Rohr, K.: Modelling and identification of characteristic intensity variations. Image Vis. Comput. **10**, 66–76 (1992)

130. Rohr, K.: Localization properties of direct corner detectors. J. Math. Imaging Vis. **4**, 139–150 (1994)

131. Rohr, K.: Extraction of 3D anatomical point landmarks based on invariance principles. Pattern Recognit. **32**, 3–15 (1999)

132. Rosenthaler, L., Heitger, F., Kubler, O., van Heydt, R.: Detection of general edges and keypoints. In: Proc. European Conf. Computer Vision, pp. 78–86 (1992)

133. Rosten, E., Drummond, T.: Machine learning for high-speed corner detection. In: European Conf. Computer Vision, pp. 430–443 (2006)

134. Rosten, E., Porter, R., Drummond, T.: Faster and better: A machine learning approach to corner detection. IEEE Trans. Pattern Anal. Mach. Intell. **32**(1), 105–119 (2010)

135. Schmid, C., Mohr, R.: Local gray-value invariants for image retrieval. IEEE Trans. Pattern Anal. Mach. Intell. **19**(5), 530–535 (1997)

136. Schmid, C., Mohr, R., Bauckhage, C.: Comparing and evaluating interest points. In: Int'l Conf. Computer Vision, pp. 230–235 (1998)

137. Schmid, C., Mohr, R., Bauckhage, C.: Evaluation of interest point detectors. Int. J. Comput. Vis. **37**(2), 151–172 (2000)

138. Sela, G., Levine, M.D.: Real-time attention for robotic vision. Real-Time Imaging **3**, 173–194 (1997)

139. Serre, T., Wolf, L., Poggio, T.: Object recognition with features inspired by visual cortex. In: Proc. Conf. Computer Vision and Pattern Recognition, vol. 2, pp. 994–1000 (2005)

140. Shen, D., Ip, H.H.S.: Discriminative wavelet shape descriptors for recognition of 2-D patterns. Pattern Recognit. **32**, 151–165 (1999)

141. Shen, F., Wang, H.: Corner detection based on modified Hough transform. Pattern Recognit. Lett. **23**, 1039–1049 (2002)

142. Shen, J., Shen, W., Shen, D.: On geometric and orthogonal moments. Int. J. Pattern Recognit. Artif. Intell. **14**(7), 875–894 (2000)

143. Shi, J., Tomasi, C.: Good features to track. In: Proc. IEEE Conf. Computer Vision and Pattern Recognition, Seattle, WA, pp. 593–600 (1994)

144. Singh, A., Shneier, M.: Grey level corner detection: A generalization and a robust real time implementation. Comput. Vis. Graph. Image Process. **51**(1), 54–59 (1990)

145. Smith, S.M., Brady, J.M.: SUSAN—A new approach to low level image processing. Int. J. Comput. Vis. **23**(1), 45–78 (1997)

146. Soille, P., Rivest, J.-F.: On the validity of fractal dimension measurements in image analysis. J. Vis. Commun. Image Represent. **7**(3), 217–229 (1996)

147. Stammberger, T., Michaelis, M., Reiser, M., Englmeier, K.-H.: A hierarchical filter scheme for efficient corner detection. Pattern Recognit. Lett. **9**, 687–700 (1998)

148. Tang, F., Lim, S.H., Chang, N.L., Tao, H.: A novel feature descriptor invariant to complex brightness changes. In: Proc. Computer Vision and Pattern Recognition, pp. 2631–2638 (2009)

149. Teague, M.R.: Image analysis via the general theory of moments. J. Opt. Soc. Am. **70**(8), 920–930 (1980)

150. ter Haar Romeny, B.M., Florack, L.M.J., Salden, A.H., Viergever, M.A.: High order differential structure of images. In: 13th Int'l Conf. Information Processing in Medical Imaging, pp. 77–93 (1993)

151. Tomasi, C., Kanade, T.: Shape and motion from image streams: a factorization method—part 3. Technical Report CMU-CS-91-132, April 1991

152. Torre, V., Poggio, T.: On edge detection. IEEE Trans. Pattern Anal. Mach. Intell. **8**(2), 147–163 (1986)

153. Trajković, M., Hedley, M.: Fast corner detection. Image Vis. Comput. **16**, 75–87 (1998)
154. Trujillo, L., Olague, G.: Using evolution to learn how to perform interest point detection. In: Int'l Conf. Pattern Recognition, Hong Kong, China, pp. 211–214 (2006)
155. Trujillo, L., Olague, G.: Synthesis of interest point detectors through genetic programming. In: Genetic and Evolutionary Computation Conference, Seattle, WA, pp. 887–894 (2006)
156. Trujillo, L., Olague, G., Hammoud, R., Hernandez, B.: Automatic feature localization in thermal images for facial expression recognition. In: 2nd Joint IEEE Int'l Workshop on Object Tracking and Classification in and Beyond the Visible Spectrum (OTCBVS), in conjunction with CVPR2005, vol. 3, pp. 14–20 (2005)
157. Tuytelaars, T., Mikolajczyk, K.: Local invariant feature detectors: A survey. Found. Trends Comput. Graph. Vis. **3**(3), 177–280 (2007)
158. Tuyterlaars, T., van Gool, L.: Wide baseline stereo matching based on local, affinely invariant regions. In: British Machine Vision Conference (2000)
159. Unser, M.: Sum and difference histograms for texture classification. IEEE Trans. Pattern Anal. Mach. Intell. **8**(1), 118–125 (1986)
160. Vincent, E., Laganière, R.: Detecting and matching feature points. J. Vis. Commun. Image Represent. **16**, 38–54 (2005)
161. Voorhees, H., Poggio, T.: Detecting textons and texture boundaries in natural images. In: 1st Int'l Conf. Computer Vision, pp. 250–258 (1987)
162. Wang, H., Brady, M.: A practical solution to corner detection. In: Proc. 5th Int'l Conf. Image Processing, vol. 1, pp. 919–923 (1994)
163. Wang, H., Brady, M.: Real-time corner detection algorithm for motion estimation. Image Vis. Comput. **13**(9), 695–703 (1995)
164. Wang, W., Li, J., Huang, F., Feng, H.: Design and implementation of Log-Gabor filter in fingerprint image enhancement. Pattern Recognit. Lett. **29**, 301–308 (2008)
165. Winston, P.H., Lerman, J.B.: Circular scan, Vision Flash 23, Artificial Intelligence Laboratory, Robotics Section, Massachusetts Institute of Technology (1972)
166. Wu, Y., Shen, J.: Properties of orthogonal Gaussian-Hermite and their applications. EURASIP J. Appl. Signal Process. **4**, 588–599 (2005)
167. Xie, X., Sudhakar, R., Zhuang, H.: Corner detection by a cost minimization approach. Pattern Recognit. **26**, 1235–1243 (1993)
168. Xu, D., Li, H.: Geometric moment invariants. Pattern Recognit. **41**, 240–249 (2008)
169. Yang, G.Z., Burger, P., Firmin, D.N., Underwood, S.R.: Structure adaptive anisotropic image filtering. Image Vis. Comput. **14**, 135–145 (1996)
170. Yap, P.-T., Paramesran, R., Ong, S.-H.: Image analysis by Krawtchouk moments. IEEE Trans. Image Process. **12**(11), 1367–1377 (2003)
171. Zheng, Z., Wang, H., Teoh, E.K.: Analysis of gray level corner detection. Pattern Recognit. Lett. **20**, 149–162 (1999)
172. Zuniga, O.A., Haralick, R.M.: Corner detection using the facet model. In: Proc. IEEE Conf. Computer Vision and Pattern Recognition, Washington, DC, pp. 30–37 (1983)

Chapter 4
Feature Extraction

Image features provide a critical source of information for various recognition tasks. A feature may measure a global or a local image property, revealing statistical, algebraic, geometric, spatial, differential, and spectral information about an image or subimage.

Features that are stable under noise and invariant to changes in geometry and contrast of an image are most useful. Invariant features enable comparison of images taken from different views, under different lighting conditions, and with different sensors.

Among the many types of features that can be extracted from an image, one is faced with the problem of selecting those features that carry the most information about the image. This chapter covers topics relating to only feature extraction. Topics relating to feature selection will be covered in the subsequent chapter.

For a feature to be useful, it should produce the same value for images of the same scene while producing different values for images of different scenes. By comparing a set of features in two images, it is possible to measure the degree of similarity/match between the images without knowing the correspondence between pixels in the images.

To study the behaviors of various image features under changes in imaging conditions, the images shown in Fig. 4.1 will be used in various experiments. Figure 4.1a is a 128×128 image of a coin. This will be used as the base image. Figure 4.1b is a blurred version of the base image obtained by smoothing the coin image with a Gaussian of standard deviation 1.5 pixels. Figure 4.1c is the image obtained by adding Gaussian noise of standard deviation 20 to the base image. To keep intensities of the noisy image within $[0, 255]$, intensities above 255 are set to 255 and intensities below 0 are set to 0. Figure 4.1d shows the base image after histogram equalization. This process nonlinearly but monotonically transforms intensities in the base image. Figure 4.1e shows the base image after rotation clockwise by $30°$, and Fig. 4.1f shows the base image after scaling by factor of 1.5. Resampling of geometrically transformed images are achieved via bilinear interpolation. These images contain the same pattern but have different intensities and geometries.

In order to evaluate the invariance properties of a feature under intensity and geometric changes of an image, a window of radius 8 pixels is taken centered at each

A.A. Goshtasby, *Image Registration*,
Advances in Computer Vision and Pattern Recognition,
DOI 10.1007/978-1-4471-2458-0_4, © Springer-Verlag London Limited 2012

Fig. 4.1 (**a**) The base image. The base image after (**b**) blurring, (**c**) addition of noise, (**d**) histogram equalization, (**e**) rotation, and (**f**) scaling

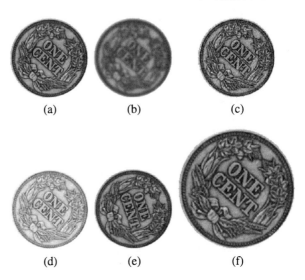

(a)   (b)   (c)

(d)   (e)   (f)

pixel and the feature value calculated within the window is saved at the pixel to create a *feature image*. A feature image, therefore, shows the feature values calculated everywhere in the image domain using windows of radius 8 pixels. Values in a feature image are mapped to [0, 255] so they can be visually compared. Since windows in these images contain a wide range of patterns, the obtained feature images show the responses of a feature to a wide range of intensity patterns.

The blurring invariance (BI) property of a feature is measured by finding the average absolute difference between feature images obtained for the base image and its blurred version. Change in blurring can be considered change in resolution also.

The noise invariance (NI) property of a feature is measured by finding the feature images for the base image and its noisy version and calculating the average absolute difference between the two. The intensity invariance (II) property of a feature is measured by comparing the feature images of the base image and its histogram equalized version.

The rotation invariance (RI) and scale invariance (SI) properties of a feature are determined by computing the average absolute difference between corresponding feature values in the base image and its rotated and scaled versions. Note that since the rotational difference between Fig. 4.1e and the base image, and the scaling difference between Fig. 4.1f and the base image are known, correspondence between pixels in these images is known.

To convert the invariance properties to numbers between 0 and 1, first, the feature values in a feature image are mapped to [0, 255]. Then, the average absolute difference between two feature images is determined and divided by 255. This will produce a value between 0 and 1, with a larger value showing a larger difference between the feature images. Finally, the obtained value is subtracted from 1 to associate a higher value with a higher invariance.

In addition to being resistant to noise and invariant to changes in the geometry and contrast of an image, a feature is required to be highly repeatable. To measure repeatability, local extrema of a feature image are determined. Extremum locations form a unique geometric network that can be used to characterize and recognize an image. If similar extrema networks are obtained in feature images before and after an intensity or geometric transformation, the feature is considered highly repeatable. If the number of extrema detected in the base image and in its transformed version are N_1 and N_2, and N of the extrema remain unchanged from one image to another, the repeatability of the feature is measured by

$$R = \frac{N}{\min(N_1, N_2)}. \tag{4.1}$$

Repeatabilities of a feature under image blurring, intensity transformation, noise, rotation, and scaling will be denoted by BR, IR, NR, RR, and SR, respectively. Generally, the higher the invariance property of a feature, the higher will be its repeatability; however, exceptions are possible. While invariance is calculated using all corresponding values in two feature images, repeatability is calculated using only the locations of extrema in two feature images.

In the following sections, various image features are reviewed, categorized, and evaluated. Earlier review, categorization, and evaluation of image features may be found at [72, 107, 159, 198, 230]. The features will be denoted by L_x, with x uniquely identifying a feature. 122 different features are studied in this chapter. Therefore, index x varies between 1 to 122.

4.1 Statistical Features

The first- and second-order statistics of image intensities characterize the statistical properties of an image. The probability that a pixel will have a particular intensity in an image is considered a first-order statistic, and the probability that two pixels in predefined positions with respect to each other in an image will have particular intensities is considered a second-order statistic. The first-order statistic represents a 1-D probability distribution, while the second-order statistic represents a 2-D probability distribution. Features calculated from a 1-D or a 2-D probability distribution can be used to characterize and recognize an image.

4.1.1 First-Order Statistical Features

4.1.1.1 Histogram Features

If an $M \times N$ image $f(x, y)$ contains intensities in the range $[0, 255]$, then

$$H(i) = \sum_{x=0}^{M-1} \sum_{y=0}^{N-1} \delta\big(f(x, y) = i\big), \quad i = 0, \ldots, 255 \tag{4.2}$$

shows the number of pixels in the image with intensity i, where $\delta(a)$ is a binary function returning a 1 if a is true and a 0 otherwise. The histogram of an image is defined by array $H(i)$ for $i = 0, \ldots, 255$.

To make a histogram independent of an image's size, its entries are divided by the image size. Therefore, if the number of pixels in an image is $S = MN$, then

$$p(i) = H(i)/S, \tag{4.3}$$

shows the probability that if a pixel is randomly selected in the image it will have intensity i, and $\{p(i) : i = 0, \ldots, 255\}$ shows the probability distribution of intensities in the image.

Peak entries in a histogram or a probability distribution are often the consequence of regions of homogeneous intensities in an image. The most dominant intensity

$$L_1 = i \quad \text{such that} \quad p(i) = \max_{k=0}^{255}\{p(k)\} \tag{4.4}$$

in an image is a useful feature. More than one peak may be selected from a histogram or a probability distribution. Intensities corresponding to local peaks often correspond to homogeneous regions of different intensities in an image and may be used as features. To avoid selection of noisy peaks, a peak may be required to have a value at least twice those appearing about the same distance to it on its left and right sides. To avoid detection of noisy peaks, Goshtasby and O'Neill [69] decomposed a signal (a probability distribution in this case) into Gaussians and used the positions of the Gaussians as the locations of the peaks.

Given the probability distribution of intensities in an image, the mean intensity

$$L_2 = \mu = \sum_{i=0}^{255} ip(i), \tag{4.5}$$

the variance intensity

$$\sigma^2 = \sum_{i=0}^{255} (i - \mu)^2 p(i), \tag{4.6}$$

or the standard deviation

$$L_3 = \sigma \tag{4.7}$$

are unique features that can be used to characterize the image. Other unique features that can be calculated from a probability distribution are skewness [86]

$$L_4 = \gamma = \frac{1}{\sigma^3} \sum_{i=0}^{255} (i - \mu)^3 p(i), \tag{4.8}$$

which measures asymmetry, and kurtosis [86]

$$L_5 = \kappa = \frac{1}{\sigma^4} \sum_{i=0}^{255} (i - \mu)^4 p(i) - 3, \tag{4.9}$$

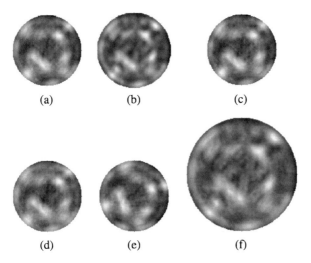

(a)   (b)   (c)

(d)   (e)   (f)

Fig. 4.2 (**a**)–(**f**) Mean (L_2) feature images computed for the images in Figs. 4.1a–f. The more similar features images (**b**)–(**f**) are when compared to feature image (**a**), the more invariant the mean feature is to blurring, noise, change in intensity, rotation, and scaling. The invariance measures obtained from feature images (**b**)–(**f**) when compared with feature image (**a**) are BI = 0.97, NI = 0.98, II = 0.98, RI = 0.99, SI = 0.93. The repeatability measures computed for the same images are BR = 1.00, NR = 0.75, IR = 0.86, RR = 0.88, SR = 0.12, respectively

which shows the degree of similarity of a distribution to a normal distribution. A distribution with a distinct peak at or near the mean that sharply declines and has long tails on both sides has a high kurtosis, while a distribution that is flat near the mean without a distinct mean, such as a uniform distribution, has a low kurtosis.

Mean intensity varies with image brightness, and standard deviation intensity varies with image contrast. An image with a high mean intensity implies a bright image, and an image with a high standard deviation implies a high-contrast image. An image with a high skewness implies an image with a dominant dark or bright intensity, and an image with a high kurtosis implies an image with an intensity distribution similar to a normal distribution.

The feature images obtained from the mean, standard deviation, skewness, and kurtosis of the images in Fig. 4.1 are shown in Figs. 4.2, 4.3, 4.4, 4.5. Although the invariance properties of these features are consistently high under noise as well as under intensity and geometric changes, the repeatabilities of the features vary greatly under these changes. The mean feature is highly repeatable under blurring, but the standard deviation, skewness, and kurtosis features are not.

The repeatabilities of these features are especially low under image scaling because fixed circular windows of radius 8 pixels are used to calculate the features independent of the image scale. When centers of two windows in two images with scaling differences coincide, the windows will have some overlap but they do not contain exactly the same scene parts, resulting in different intensity distributions. This change in intensity distribution does not affect the invariance properties of the features as much as it does the repeatabilities of the features. A change in the lo-

Fig. 4.3 (**a**)–(**f**) Standard
deviation (L_3) feature
images, producing invariance
measures BI $= 0.81$,
NI $= 0.92$, II $= 0.94$,
RI $= 0.93$, SI $= 0.88$, and
repeatability measures
BR $= 0.39$, NR $= 0.61$,
IR $= 0.69$, RR $= 0.63$,
SR $= 0.17$

Fig. 4.4 (**a**)–(**f**) Skewness
(L_4) feature images,
producing invariance
measures BI $= 0.84$,
NI $= 0.95$, II $= 0.93$,
RI $= 0.97$, SI $= 0.93$, and
repeatability measures
BR $= 0.19$, NR $= 0.57$,
IR $= 0.71$, RR $= 0.55$,
SR $= 0.11$

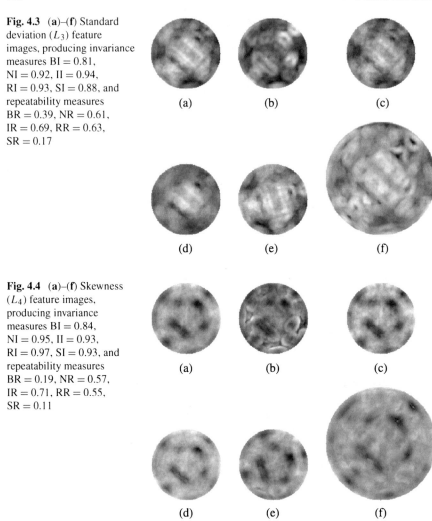

cal intensity distribution displaces extrema locations and such displacements bring
down the repeatability measure. Since the scales of images being registered are often not known, degradation in repeatability measure due to change in image scale is
inevitable.

Other related features have been proposed. Unser [206] considered image intensities as random variables. Since the sum and difference of two random variables
define the principal axes of their joint probability density, Unser suggests scanning
an image at a desired orientation, finding the sum and difference of adjacent intensities, creating two 1-D histograms, and using the histograms to characterize the
intensity distribution of the image in the scanned direction.

Since a histogram does not contain information about local intensity distribution
but rather provides a global intensity distribution of an image, to capture some local

Fig. 4.5 (a)–(f) Kurtosis
(L_5) feature images,
producing invariance
measures BI $= 0.89$,
NI $= 0.93$, II $= 0.91$,
RI $= 0.96$, SI $= 0.88$, and
repeatability measures
BR $= 0.25$, NR $= 0.57$,
IR $= 0.43$, RR $= 0.56$,
SR $= 0.17$

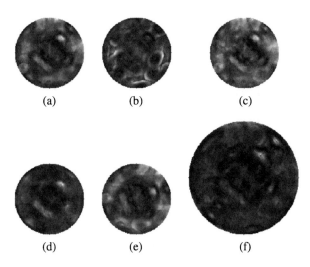

intensity characteristics of an image Lazebnik et al. [100] used the spin-image idea
of Johnson and Hebert [88] to map image intensities to a 2-D histogram with the
horizontal axis showing distances of pixels to the image center and the vertical axis
showing the intensities. Thus, entry (d, i) in the histogram shows the number of
pixels in the image that have intensity i and are of distance d to the image center.
That is,

$$H(d, i) = \sum_x \sum_y \delta\big(D(x, y) = d \ \& \ f(x, y) = i\big), \tag{4.10}$$

where $D(x, y)$ denotes the distance of pixel (x, y) to the image center and $\delta(a \ \& \ b)$
is a binary function that returns a 1 when both a and b are true, and it returns a 0
otherwise. Since $H(d, i)$ is invariant to the orientation of an image, it can be used
as a rotation-invariant feature in recognition tasks. Tang et al. [190] suggested using
the histogram of angularly scanned ordinal intensities to characterize the intensity
distribution of an image. Ordinal intensities as opposed to raw intensities make the
calculated features invariant to nonlinear but monotone intensity changes.

Local peaks of $H(d, i)$ are unique and can be used as features to characterize
an image. To avoid detection of noisy peaks, $H(d, i)$ may be decomposed into 2-D
Gaussians [68] and the locations of the Gaussians can be used as the peaks. Alternatively, $H(d, i)$ may be smoothed to suppress noise before detecting its peaks.

In a color image, the histogram will be a 3-D array. If the image is small, most
entries in the 3-D array will be 0. To avoid creation of a very sparse histogram,
values in each color component are mapped to a smaller range such as $[0, 7]$. This
will produce a 3-D array with 512 entries, creating a denser histogram.

In spite of the fact that different images can produce the same histogram, the
likelihood that images of two different scenes have exactly the same or very similar
histograms is very low. Images captured from different views of a scene, or images
representing small changes in the shape or position of objects in the scene, will
produce very similar histograms. Swain and Ballard [187] demonstrated the power
of image histograms in recognition of objects of the same class.

4.1.1.2 Gray-Level Difference Features

Gray-level difference (GLD) of adjacent pixels in different directions can be used
to characterize an image also. Weszka et al. [218] used the absolute intensity difference of adjacent pixels in horizontal, vertical, and diagonal directions to char-
acterize intensity variations in an image. Letting $H(g|\theta)$ denote the number of ad-
jacent pixels in direction θ that have absolute intensity difference g, and letting
$h(g|\theta) = H(g|\theta)/\sum_g H(g|\theta)$ be the probability that adjacent pixels when scanned
in θ direction have absolute intensity difference g, the following image features have
been proposed [38, 218]:

1. *Gradient contrast*:

$$L_6(\theta) = \sum_g g^2 h(g \mid \theta). \tag{4.11}$$

2. *Gradient second moment*:

$$L_7(\theta) = \sum_g [h(g \mid \theta)]^2. \tag{4.12}$$

3. *Gradient entropy*:

$$L_8(\theta) = -\sum_g h(g \mid \theta) \log h(g \mid \theta). \tag{4.13}$$

4. *Gradient mean*:

$$L_9(\theta) = \sum_g h(g \mid \theta) g. \tag{4.14}$$

5. *Inverse-difference moment*:

$$L_{10}(\theta) = \sum_g \frac{h(g \mid \theta)}{(g^2 + 1)}. \tag{4.15}$$

To make these features less dependent on scene lighting, Funt and Finlayson
[60] suggested using the ratio of intensities rather than the difference of intensities.
The ratio of the intensities represent changes in local scene albedo and capture the
property of the scene rather than that of the lighting. To make the process rotation
invariant, instead of finding the difference of intensities in an image in a particular
direction, the image is convolved with a Laplacian or a Laplacian of a Gaussian of
standard deviation 0.5 pixels. For a color image, the same is performed on each color
component and the histogram of the ratios in each component is used to calculate
features invariant to scene lighting.

Instead of using intensity differences or ratios, Schiele and Crowley [171, 172]
convolved an image with various filters and used the histograms of the filtered images to characterize the image. Worthy and Singzinger [220] used histograms of
polar image gradients and saturation-weighted hues scanned angularly to characterize an image.

4.1.2 Second-Order Statistical Features

4.1.2.1 Gray-Level Spatial-Dependence Features

To determine the second-order statistical features of image $f(x, y)$ with intensities in the range $[0, 255]$, first a gray-level spatial-dependence (GLSD) or co-occurrence matrix is created with entry (i_1, i_2) in the matrix showing the number of adjacent pixels in the image, when scanned in the desired direction, having intensity i_1 at the first pixel and intensity i_2 at the second pixel [72, 73]. For instance, given image

$$
\begin{array}{c|cccc}
y \diagdown x & 0 & 1 & 2 & 3 \\
\hline
0 & 0 & 0 & 10 & 10 \\
1 & 0 & 0 & 10 & 10 \\
2 & 0 & 20 & 20 & 20 \\
3 & 20 & 20 & 30 & 30
\end{array}
\tag{4.16}
$$

the co-occurrence matrix obtained at direction $\theta = 0°$ (horizontally), $h(i_1, i_2 | \theta = 0)$ will be:

$$
\begin{array}{c|cccc}
i_1 \diagdown i_2 & 0 & 10 & 20 & 30 \\
\hline
0 & 2 & 2 & 1 & 0 \\
10 & 0 & 2 & 0 & 0 \\
20 & 0 & 0 & 3 & 1 \\
30 & 0 & 0 & 0 & 1
\end{array}
\tag{4.17}
$$

The sum of the entries of a co-occurrence matrix of an image with M columns and N rows calculated in this manner in direction $0°$ will be $(M-1)N$. Similarly, co-occurrence matrices for directions $\theta = 45°, 90°$, and $135°$ can be calculated. Since $h(i_1, i_2 | \theta + \pi) = h(i_2, i_1 | \theta)$, the co-occurrence matrices for θ and $\theta + \pi$ contain the same information. Haralick et al. [73] used the sum of the two, that is, the sum of $h(i_1, i_2 | \theta)$ and its transpose $h(i_2, i_1 | \theta)$ as the co-occurrence matrix for direction θ. Therefore,

$$
\begin{array}{c|cccc}
i_1 \diagdown i_2 & 0 & 10 & 20 & 30 \\
\hline
0 & 4 & 2 & 1 & 0 \\
10 & 2 & 4 & 0 & 0 \\
20 & 1 & 0 & 6 & 1 \\
30 & 0 & 0 & 1 & 2
\end{array}
\tag{4.18}
$$

will be the co-occurrence matrix for image (4.16) when calculated in direction $\theta = 0°$.

When entries of a co-occurrence matrix are divided by the sum of its entries, the joint conditional probability density (JCPD) $p(i_1, i_2 | \theta)$ will be obtained. Therefore, using (4.18) as the co-occurrence matrix for direction $\theta = 0°$, the corresponding JCPD $p(i_1, i_2|0°)$ will be:

i_1	i_2			
	0	10	20	30
0	$\frac{4}{24}$	$\frac{2}{24}$	$\frac{1}{24}$	0
10	$\frac{2}{24}$	$\frac{4}{24}$	0	0
20	$\frac{1}{24}$	0	$\frac{6}{24}$	$\frac{1}{24}$
30	0	0	$\frac{1}{24}$	$\frac{2}{24}$

$$(4.19)$$

An image with intensities varying smoothly in the horizontal direction will produce a JCPD matrix calculated at $\theta = 0°$ that contains high values diagonally, and an image containing highly varying intensities in the horizontal direction will produce a JCPD matrix calculated at $\theta = 0°$ that has high values away from the diagonal elements.

The following features can be calculated from a co-occurrence matrix to characterize texture in an image [73]:

1. *Energy*:

$$L_{11}(\theta) = \sum_{i_1} \sum_{i_2} \left[p(i_1, i_2|\theta) \right]^2. \tag{4.20}$$

As the number of intensities in an image decreases, a higher energy is obtained.

2. *Contrast*:

$$L_{12}(\theta) = \sum_{i_1} \sum_{i_2} (i_1 - i_2)^2 p(i_1, i_2|\theta). \tag{4.21}$$

As the difference between intensities of adjacent pixels increases, a higher contrast is obtained.

3. *Correlation*:

$$L_{13}(\theta) = \sum_{i_1} \sum_{i_2} \frac{(i_1 - \mu_{i_1})(i_2 - \mu_{i_2})}{\sigma_{i_1} \sigma_{i_2}} p(i_1, i_2|\theta), \tag{4.22}$$

where μ_{i_1} and σ_{i_1} denote the mean and the standard deviation of $\sum_{i_2} h(i_1, i_2|\theta)$, and μ_{i_2} and σ_{i_2} denote the mean and the standard deviation of $\sum_{i_1} h(i_1, i_2|\theta)$. A higher correlation is obtained when intensities of adjacent pixels vary together, showing a slowly varying pattern.

4. *Entropy*:

$$L_{14}(\theta) = -\sum_{i_1} \sum_{i_2} p(i_1, i_2|\theta) \log p(i_1, i_2|\theta). \tag{4.23}$$

Maximum entropy is obtained when the probability of two intensities appearing next to each other becomes the same for any two intensities. As zero-mean noise in an image increases, entropy of the image increases.

Fig. 4.6 (a)–(f) The energy (L_{11}) feature images of the co-occurrence matrix computed for the images in Figs. 4.1a–f, respectively. The invariance measures obtained when comparing images (b)–(f) to image (a) are BI = 0.79, NI = 0.89, II = 0.86, RI = 0.86, SI = 0.87, and the corresponding repeatability measures are BR = 0.15, NR = 0.29, IR = 0.38, RR = 0.29, SR = 0.11

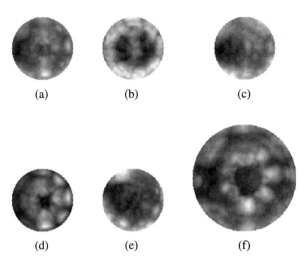

(a)   (b)   (c)

(d)   (e)   (f)

5. *Homogeneity*:

$$L_{15}(\theta) = \sum_{i_1} \sum_{i_2} \frac{p(i_1, i_2 | \theta)}{1 + (i_1 - i_2)^2}. \tag{4.24}$$

This feature is the inverse of contrast. It produces a higher value for a smoother image.

An image that contains a small number of repeated intensities has a higher energy than an image that contains about the same number of pixels in each intensity. This is the reverse of entropy which produces the highest value when an image contains the same number of pixels in each intensity. An image where many adjacent pixels have high intensity differences produces a high contrast and an image where intensities vary slowly produces a high homogeneity measure. Therefore, the values of the measures can be used to describe the intensity characteristics of an image. Note that these image features are for scanning an image in a particular direction. Therefore, an image and its rotated version may produce very different features.

Compared to GLSD features, GLD features are less dependent on absolute image intensities. Therefore, images of the same scene captured under different lighting conditions will produce more similar GLD features than GLSD features. On the other hand if the images are obtained under the same lighting conditions, GLSD features produce more distinct values than GLD features, providing a higher discrimination power. Conners and Harlow [38] find that GLSD features, in general, have a higher discrimination power than GLD features.

The feature images computed from the co-occurrence matrices of the images in Fig. 4.1 are depicted in Figs. 4.6, 4.7, 4.8, 4.9. Energy, contrast, correlation, and entropy feature images are shown. The feature value at a pixel is calculated using a circular window of radius 8 pixels centered at the pixel. To make the features less dependent on an image's orientation, a window is scanned horizontally, vertically, and in the two diagonal directions. Then, the highest feature value obtained by scan-

Fig. 4.7 (**a**)–(**f**) The contrast
(L_{12}) feature images of the
co-occurrence matrix
computed for the images in
Figs. 4.1a–f, producing
invariance measures
BI = 0.79, NI = 0.94,
II = 0.96, RI = 0.80,
SI = 0.90, and repeatability
measures BR = 0.19,
NR = 0.51, IR = 0.44,
RR = 0.19, SR = 0.11,
respectively

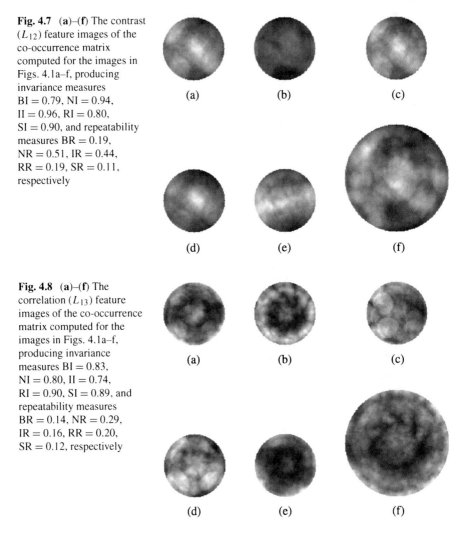

Fig. 4.8 (**a**)–(**f**) The
correlation (L_{13}) feature
images of the co-occurrence
matrix computed for the
images in Figs. 4.1a–f,
producing invariance
measures BI = 0.83,
NI = 0.80, II = 0.74,
RI = 0.90, SI = 0.89, and
repeatability measures
BR = 0.14, NR = 0.29,
IR = 0.16, RR = 0.20,
SR = 0.12, respectively

ning the window in the four directions is selected as the feature value at the center
of window.

Second-order statistical features generally produce invariance and repeatability
measures that are similar to those obtained by the first-order statistical features.
Noise as well as intensity and geometric changes influence second-order statistical
features slightly more than first-order statistical features. The repeatability measures
of first-order and second-order statistical features are both low. Therefore, these features should not be used when the images are noisy or have intensity and geometric
differences.

Co-occurrence matrices obtained by scanning an image in a particular direction
depend on the image orientation. To obtain features that are less dependent on the
orientation of an image, the image is scanned at $\theta = 0°$, 45°, 90°, and 135° direc-

Fig. 4.9 (**a**)–(**f**) The entropy
(L_{14}) feature images of the
co-occurrence matrix
computed for the images in
Figs. 4.1a–f, producing
invariance measures
BI = 0.83, NI = 0.91,
II = 0.87, RI = 0.88,
SI = 0.89, and repeatability
measures BR = 0.16,
NR = 0.30, IR = 0.35,
RR = 0.31, SR = 0.17,
respectively

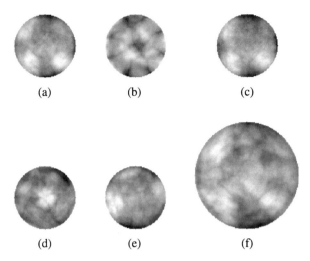

(a)   (b)   (c)

(d)   (e)   (f)

tions. Features are calculated for each direction and the maximum (or the minimum) feature in all directions is used as the feature value. To make the process less dependent on an image's orientation, circular images or windows should be used in the calculations so that the same pattern can be included in two images or two windows with rotational differences.

4.1.2.2 Run-Length Features

Consider creating a matrix with the value at an entry showing the number of runs of a particular length and intensity when scanning an image in a particular direction. Such a matrix can be used to characterize intensity variations in the image [62]. The value at entry (i, l) in the run-length matrix (RLM) when an image is scanned in direction $0°$ shows the number of runs of length l of intensity i appearing in the image horizontally. For example, the run-length matrix h of the 4×4 image shown in (4.16) when scanned at $\theta = 0°$ (horizontally) will be:

i	l			
	1	*2*	*3*	*4*
0	1	2	0	0
10	0	2	0	0
20	0	1	1	0
30	0	1	0	0

$$(4.25)$$

$h(i, l|\theta)$ shows the number of runs of intensity i of length l in direction θ. Note that sum of the entries of a run-length matrix when each entry is weighted by its run-length l will be equal to image size, MN. A joint conditional probability density function $p(i, l|\theta)$ can be obtained from a run-length matrix by dividing each entry of the matrix by the sum of the entries. Therefore, in the above example, we will have $p(i, l|0°)$ as below:

i	l			
	1	2	3	4
0	$\frac{1}{8}$	$\frac{2}{8}$	0	0
10	0	$\frac{2}{8}$	0	0
20	0	$\frac{1}{8}$	$\frac{1}{8}$	0
30	0	$\frac{1}{8}$	0	0

$$(4.26)$$

The following features have been proposed for $p(i, l|\theta)$ [62]:

1. *Short-runs emphasis*:

$$L_{16}(\theta) = \sum_i \sum_l \frac{p(i, l|\theta)}{l^2}.$$

$$(4.27)$$

This feature will be high when the image contains mostly short runs, implying a noisy or highly-varying image.

2. *Long-runs emphasis*:

$$L_{17}(\theta) = \sum_i \sum_l l^2 p(i, l|\theta).$$

$$(4.28)$$

This feature will increase as the number of longs runs in an image increase, implying a smoother image.

3. *Gray-level nonuniformity*:

$$L_{18}(\theta) = \frac{\sum_i (\sum_l h(i, l|\theta))^2}{\sum_i \sum_l h(i, l|\theta)}.$$

$$(4.29)$$

This feature increases as the number of runs of the same intensity increases, implying an image with highly varying intensities.

4. *Run-length nonuniformity*:

$$L_{19}(\theta) = \frac{\sum_l (\sum_i h(i, l|\theta))^2}{\sum_i \sum_l h(i, l|\theta)}.$$

$$(4.30)$$

This feature increases as the number of intensities of the same run-length increases, implying a noisy image or an image with highly varying and most likely repeated patterns.

5. *Run percentage*:

$$L_{20}(\theta) = \frac{100}{MN} \sum_i \sum_l h(i, l|\theta).$$

$$(4.31)$$

This feature shows the percentage of runs in direction θ in an image when normalized with respect to the image size. The smaller the percentage, the smaller the number of runs, implying a smoothly varying image or an image with large homogeneous regions.

Run-length features are effective in distinguishing images from each other if the images contain a small number of intensities. However, noise and blurring can greatly affect run-length features. When images contain a large number of intensities, a small amount of noise or blurring can considerably change the feature values.

Features that are computed from the histogram or the probability distribution of an image are invariant to the orientation of the image if circular images are used. If square or rectangular images are used and the images have rotational differences that are not a multiple of 90°, since the images cannot contain the same scene parts, they cannot produce the same features.

4.2 Geometric Features

Features that characterize the geometric layout of intensities in an image are known as geometric features. These include structural features, geometric moments, Legendre moments, Tchebichef moments, Krawtchouk moments, Zernike moments, and wavelet moments.

4.2.1 Structural Features

The fact that we can effortlessly identify objects in an image from their boundary shapes is evidence that structural features contain useful information about objects. Images of man-made scenes contain abundant lines, circles, and other simple shapes. The number of line segments of similar slope, the number of line segments of similar length, and the total number of line segments in an image are powerful features that can be used to describe an image independent of its orientation. The number of circles of similar radii, the number of circular arcs of similar radii, and the total number of circles or circular arcs are also useful in characterizing the contents of an image. These structural features are rotation invariant and can be used to effectively analyze images of man-made scenes.

The spatial relationship between structural features provides additional information that can be used in conjunction with the structural features to recognize objects. Relationships can be topological (e.g., adjacent, overlap), directional (e.g., north-of, east-of), and show proximity (e.g., close, far) [33]. The calculus-based topological relations, consisting of five relationships (in, overlap, cross, touch, and disjoint) are known to be complete and capable of describing all topological situations [34].

Zhang and Ghosh [228] used structural features and their spatial relations to recognize scene parts and build the floor map for a mobile robot; Peterson et al. [150] used structural features to detect road curbs, berms, and shoulders in an autonomous vehicle project; Chhabra et al. [31] used structural features to recognize handprinted characters; and Zhang and Chen [227] used multiple structure types in an image and the relationship between them to identify previously seen complex objects in an image.

To characterize an image based on its edges, Zhou et al. [233] found the distance of an edge point to the closest endpoint along a contour and assigned the obtained distance to the edge point. Distances assigned to edge points along a closed contour are all set to the length of the contour. Values assigned to edges in an image in this manner are relatively invariant to the orientation of the image. Zhou et al. [233] used the histogram of such edge images to characterize geometric structures in them.

Damon et al. [41] used local relations between various structural features (T-junction, V-junction, curve end point, etc.) in an image containing smooth or piecewise smooth surfaces to characterize the image. Using an alphabet of structural features and the spatial relationship between them, they provided a means to describe the contents of an image.

Structural features are invariant to the orientation of an image. Being extracted from image edges, they are also relatively insensitive to image contrast.

4.2.2 Geometric Moments

The geometric moment of order (p, q) of image $f(x, y)$ of dimensions $M \times N$ is defined by [80]:

$$L_{21}(p, q) = M_{pq} = \sum_{x=0}^{M-1} \sum_{y=0}^{N-1} x^p y^q f(x, y). \tag{4.32}$$

M_{00} is equal to the total image intensity, and the coordinates of the center of gravity of the image, (x_0, y_0), are obtained from $x_0 = M_{10}/M_{00}$ and $y_0 = M_{01}/M_{00}$. To make the moments invariant of the coordinate system origin, the moments are calculated with respect to the center of gravity of the image. Such moments are called *central moments* [80]:

$$L_{22}(p, q) = \mu_{pq} = \sum_{x=0}^{M-1} \sum_{y=0}^{N-1} (x - x_0)^p (y - y_0)^q f(x, y). \tag{4.33}$$

If an image is isotropically scaled by factor of s, that is, if

$$x' = sx, \tag{4.34}$$

$$y' = sy, \tag{4.35}$$

the central moment of the image in the new coordinate system will be

$$\mu'_{pq} = \sum_{x=0}^{Ms-1} \sum_{y=0}^{Ns-1} (x' - x'_0)^p (y' - y'_0)^q f(x', y') \tag{4.36}$$

$$= \sum_{x=0}^{M-1} \sum_{y=0}^{N-1} (sx - sx_0)^p (sy - sy_0)^q s^2 f(x, y) \tag{4.37}$$

$$= \sum_{x=0}^{M-1} \sum_{y=0}^{N-1} s^{p+q+2}(x - x_0)^p (y - y_0)^q f(x, y) \qquad (4.38)$$

$$= s^{p+q+2} \mu_{pq}. \qquad (4.39)$$

When $p = q = 0$, we have $\mu'_{00} = s^2 \mu_{00}$, or $s = \{\mu'_{00}/\mu_{00}\}^{1/2}$. Therefore, we can rewrite (4.39) by

$$\mu'_{pq} = \left\{ \frac{\mu'_{00}}{\mu_{00}} \right\}^{\frac{p+q}{2}+1} \mu_{pq}, \qquad (4.40)$$

or

$$\frac{\mu'_{pq}}{(\mu'_{00})^{\frac{p+q}{2}+1}} = \frac{\mu_{pq}}{(\mu_{00})^{\frac{p+q}{2}+1}}, \qquad (4.41)$$

or

$$\eta_{pq} = \frac{\mu_{pq}}{(\mu_{00})^{\frac{p+q}{2}+1}}, \qquad (4.42)$$

which is invariant of scale. The measure, however, still depends on the orientation of the image. A set of second-order and third-order moments that are invariant of the orientation of an image as well as its scale and coordinate system origin has been derived by Hu [80]:

$$L_{23} = (\eta_{20} + \eta_{02}), \qquad (4.43)$$
$$L_{24} = (\eta_{20} - \eta_{02})^2 + 4\eta_{11}^2, \qquad (4.44)$$
$$L_{25} = (\eta_{30} - 3\eta_{12})^2 + (3\eta_{21} - \eta_{03})^2, \qquad (4.45)$$
$$L_{26} = (\eta_{30} + \eta_{12})^2 + (\eta_{21} + \eta_{03})^2, \qquad (4.46)$$
$$L_{27} = (\eta_{30} - 3\eta_{12})(\eta_{30} + \eta_{12})$$
$$\times \left[(\eta_{30} + \eta_{12})^2 - 3(\eta_{21} + \eta_{03})^2 \right]$$
$$+ (3\eta_{21} - \eta_{03})(\eta_{21} + \eta_{03})$$
$$\times \left[3(\eta_{30} + \eta_{12})^2 - (\eta_{21} + \eta_{03})^2 \right], \qquad (4.47)$$
$$L_{28} = (\eta_{20} - \eta_{02})\left[(\eta_{30} + \eta_{12})^2 - (\eta_{21} + \eta_{03})^2 \right]$$
$$+ 4\eta_{11}(\eta_{30} + \eta_{12})(\eta_{21} + \eta_{03}), \qquad (4.48)$$
$$L_{29} = (3\eta_{21} - \eta_{03})(\eta_{30} + \eta_{12})$$
$$\times \left[(\eta_{30} + \eta_{12})^2 - 3(\eta_{21} + \eta_{03})^2 \right]$$
$$- (\eta_{30} - 3\eta_{12})(\eta_{21} + \eta_{03})$$
$$\times \left[3(\eta_{30} + \eta_{12})^2 - (\eta_{21} + \eta_{03})^2 \right]. \qquad (4.49)$$

To learn the invariance and repeatability of geometric moments, L_{23}–L_{26} feature images were computed for the images in Fig. 4.1 to obtain the images shown in Figs. 4.10, 4.11, 4.12, 4.13, respectively. Compared to the statistical features, we see that geometric features remain more invariant under image blurring and noise. They

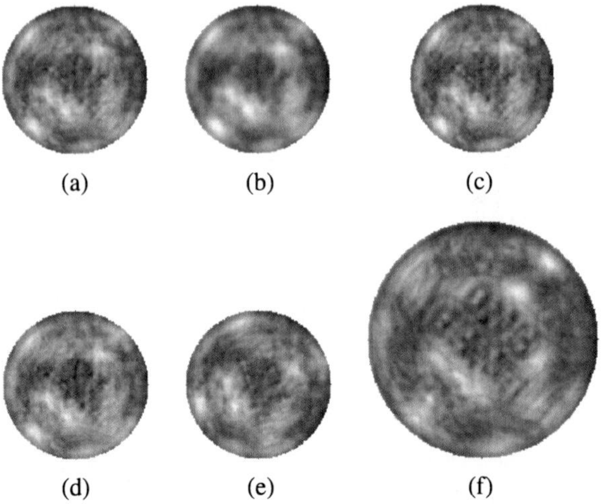

Fig. 4.10 (a)–(f) Hu
invariant moment (L_{23})
feature images obtained for
the images in Figs. 4.1a–f.
The invariance measures of
feature images (**b**)–(**f**) with
respect to feature image (**a**)
are BI $= 0.97$, NI $= 0.98$,
II $= 0.97$, RI $= 0.98$,
SI $= 0.91$, and the
corresponding repeatability
measures are BR $= 0.92$,
NR $= 0.79$, IR $= 0.90$,
RR $= 0.84$, SR $= 0.11$

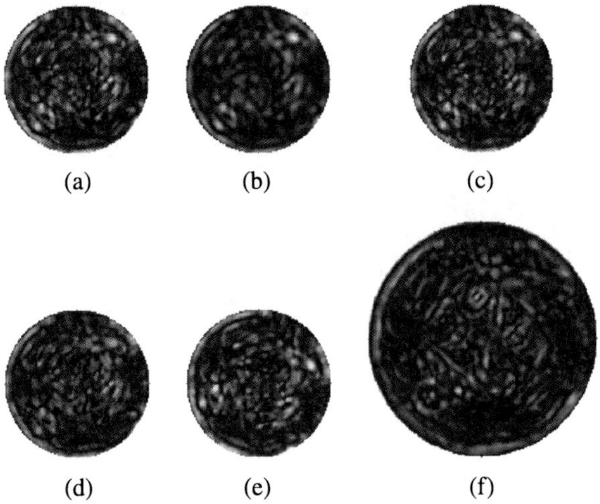

(a)   (b)   (c)

(d)   (e)   (f)

Fig. 4.11 (a)–(f) Hu
invariant moment (L_{24})
feature images. The
invariance measures are
BI $= 0.95$, NI $= 0.96$,
II $= 0.98$, RI $= 0.98$,
SI $= 0.89$, and the
repeatability measures are
BR $= 0.92$, NR $= 0.72$,
IR $= 0.83$, RR $= 0.75$,
SR $= 0.33$

(a)   (b)   (c)

(d)   (e)   (f)

are also more invariant under image rotation and scaling. Repeatability of geometric
features are also higher than those of statistical features. The very detailed nature of
geometric feature images is evidence of their distinctive nature. Adjacent windows
with considerable overlap have produced quite different geometric features compared to statistical features. Therefore, geometric features can discriminate images
with subtle differences better than statistical features.

Li [108] derived invariant moments of up to order 9, Jin and Tianxu [85] and
Papakostas et al. [146] proposed efficient algorithms for the calculation of geometric
moments, and Xu and Li [223] showed how to extend 2-D geometric moments to
3-D and use them to recognize 3-D objects.

Reddi [157] derived geometric moments in polar coordinates. Assuming a Cartesian coordinate system with origin at the center of the image, pixel (x, y) in the

Fig. 4.12 (**a**)–(**f**) Hu
invariant moment (L_{25})
feature images, producing
invariance measures
BI = 0.96, NI = 0.97,
II = 0.98, RI = 0.97,
SI = 0.90 and repeatability
measures BR = 0.84,
NR = 0.72, IR = 0.84,
RR = 0.74, SR = 0.47

Fig. 4.13 (**a**)–(**f**) Hu
invariant moment (L_{26})
feature images, producing
invariance measures
BI = 0.98, NI = 0.98,
II = 0.98, RI = 0.99,
SI = 0.93 and repeatability
measures BR = 0.88,
NR = 0.67, IR = 0.81,
RR = 0.81, SR = 0.40

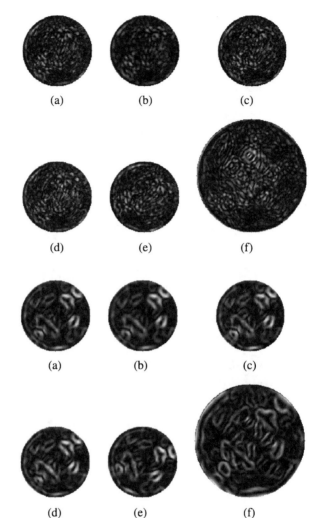

Cartesian coordinate system is represented by (r, θ) in the polar coordinate system,
where $r = \sqrt{x^2 + y^2}$ and $\theta = \tan^{-1}[(y - y_0)/(x - x_0)]$. Knowing $f(x, y) = f(r, \theta)$,
the radial moment of order k and orientation θ is obtained from [157]:

$$L_{30}(k, \theta) = \sum_{r=0}^{r_{max}} r^k f(r, \theta),\qquad(4.50)$$

where r_{max} is the radius of the circular image under consideration, and the angular
moment of order (p, q) at radial distance r is [157]:

$$L_{31}(p, q, r) = \sum_{\theta=0}^{2\pi} \cos^p(\theta) \sin^q(\theta) f(r, \theta).\qquad(4.51)$$

Fig. 4.14 (a)–(f) Normalize invariant moment (L_{32}) feature images obtained for the images in Figs. 4.1a–f, respectively. The invariance measures of feature images (b)–(f) with respect to feature image (a) are $BI = 0.94$, $NI = 0.95$, $II = 0.97$, $RI = 0.97$, $SI = 0.85$, and the corresponding repeatability measures are $BR = 0.93$, $NR = 0.76$, $IR = 0.86$, $RR = 0.85$, $SR = 0.41$

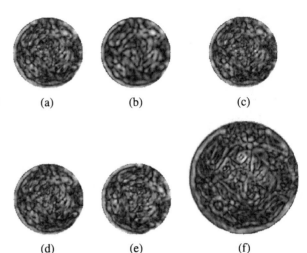

(a)   (b)   (c)

(d)   (e)   (f)

Reddi in this manner derived invariant moments in polar coordinates equivalent to Hu invariant moments in Cartesian coordinates.

When calculating invariant moments, it is important to use circular images and windows so that if the centers of two images or two windows correspond, they can contain the same pattern.

Maitra [120] extended the rotationally invariant moments of Hu, L_{23}–L_{29}, to moments that are invariant to image scale as well as image contrast. The relation between these new invariant moments and L_{23}–L_{29} are:

$$L_{32} = \frac{\sqrt{L_{24}}}{L_{23}}, \tag{4.52}$$

$$L_{33} = \frac{L_{25}\mu_{00}}{L_{24}L_{23}}, \tag{4.53}$$

$$L_{34} = \frac{L_{26}}{L_{25}}, \tag{4.54}$$

$$L_{35} = \frac{\sqrt{L_{27}}}{L_{26}}, \tag{4.55}$$

$$L_{36} = \frac{L_{28}}{L_{26}L_{23}}, \tag{4.56}$$

$$L_{37} = \frac{L_{29}}{L_{27}}. \tag{4.57}$$

To verify the effectiveness of the normalization of Maitra [120] on the invariance and repeatability properties of invariant moments, feature images were produced for L_{32}–L_{34} using the images in Figs. 4.1a–f, and the results are shown in Figs. 4.14, 4.15, 4.16. We observe that, in general, invariance measures slightly worsen while repeatability measures slightly improve after this normalization.

A consistent improvement in the repeatability of geometric moments after normalization can be attributed to the fact that the extrema points become more well-

Fig. 4.15 (a)–(f) Normalized invariant moment (L_{33}) feature images, shown in logarithmic scale. The invariance measures are BI = 0.94, NI = 0.95, II = 0.98, RI = 0.95, SI = 0.89, while the repeatability measures are BR = 0.90, NR = 0.81, IR = 0.87, RR = 0.83, SR = 0.53

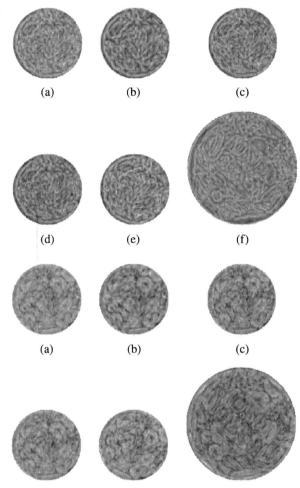

(a)   (b)   (c)

(d)   (e)   (f)

Fig. 4.16 (a)–(f) Normalized invariant moment (L_{34}) feature images, shown in logarithmic scale. Invariance measures are BI = 0.92, NI = 0.95, II = 0.97, RI = 0.90, SI = 0.90, while repeatability measures are BR = 0.90, NR = 0.78, IR = 0.86, RR = 0.81, SR = 0.52

(a)   (b)   (c)

(d)   (e)   (f)

defined and digital noise caused by geometric transformation of an image does not move the locations of the extrema. For a better viewing of L_{33} and L_{34} feature images, the values were logarithmically scaled and displayed. The very detailed nature of these feature images indicate their distinctiveness nature and their ability to discriminate images with subtle differences while remaining stable under noise, blurring, and intensity and geometric transformations.

Flusser and Suk [57] derived moments that were invariant to affine transformation:

$$L_{38} = \frac{\mu_{20}\mu_{02} - \mu_{11}^2}{\mu_{00}^4}, \qquad (4.58)$$

$$L_{39} = \left(\mu_{30}^2\mu_{03}^2 - 6\mu_{30}\mu_{21}\mu_{12}\mu_{03} + 4\mu_{30}\mu_{12}^3 \right.$$
$$\left. + 4\mu_{21}^3\mu_{03} - 3\mu_{21}^2\mu_{12}^2\right)/\mu_{00}^{10}, \qquad (4.59)$$

$$L_{40} = \left[\mu_{20}\left(\mu_{21}\mu_{03} - \mu_{12}^2\right) - \mu_{11}(\mu_{30}\mu_{03}\right.$$
$$\left. - \mu_{21}\mu_{12}) + \mu_{02}\left(\mu_{30}\mu_{12} - \mu_{21}^2\right)\right]/\mu_{00}^7. \tag{4.60}$$

In addition to affine invariance, Yuanbin et al. [226] derived moments that were invariant to projective transformation, and Wang et al. [216] found moments that were invariant to restricted projective transformations. Van Gool et al. [207] derived moments that were invariant to photometric scaling.

Higher order invariant moments are increasingly influenced by noise [2]. Abu-Mostafa and Psaltis [3] proposed means to normalizing invariant moments so they become less sensitive to noise and changes in imaging conditions.

Geometric moments suffer from information redundancy due to their dependency on each other. In the following section, moments are described in terms of orthogonal polynomials to minimize information redundancy.

4.2.3 Legendre Moments

While reconstructing an image from its moments, Teague [192] noticed that geometric moments contain redundant information, and in search for less redundant moments came up with Legendre moments. Considering an image a 2-D function, the function can be decomposed into orthogonal polynomials. After mapping coordinates (x, y) of an image to the range $[-1, 1]$, the image is decomposed into Legendre orthogonal polynomials:

$$f(x, y) = \sum_p \sum_q \lambda_{pq} K_p(x) K_q(y), \tag{4.61}$$

where $K_p(x) = \sum_{i=0}^p C_{pi} x^i$ is the Legendre polynomial of order p, x varies between -1 and 1, and C_{pi} for $i \le p$ are the Legendre coefficients of order p [4] and are computed from

$$C_{pi} = \frac{(p + i + 1)^{(i+1)}}{(2i + 1)p^{(i)}}. \tag{4.62}$$

$a^{(i)}$ is the backward factorial function of order i defined by

$$a^{(i)} = a(a - 1) \cdots (a - i + 1). \tag{4.63}$$

λ_{pq} in (4.61) is the Legendre moment of order (p, q) and is computed from the Legendre polynomials of order (p, q):

$$L_{41}(p, q) = \lambda_{pq} = \frac{(2p + 1)(2q + 1)}{4} \int_{-1}^{+1} \int_{-1}^{+1} K_p(x) K_q(y) f(x, y) \, dx \, dy. \tag{4.64}$$

Teague [192] showed that Legendre moments are related to geometric moments by:

$$\lambda_{pq} = \frac{(2p + 1)(2q + 1)}{4} \sum_{k=0}^p \sum_{l=0}^q C_{pk} C_{ql} M_{kl}, \tag{4.65}$$

where M_{kl} is the geometric moment of order (k, l). Since coordinate origin is assumed at $(0, 0)$, Legendre moments are invariant to translation. Since image coordinates are mapped to $[1, -1]$, one would expect that Legendre moments be invariant to image scale; however, larger images contain more pixels, so more terms are added together than a smaller image even though pixel coordinates in both vary between -1 and 1. Legendre moments change with blurring but by determining the relation between Legendre moments of an image an its blurred version it is possible to derive blur-invariant moments [232].

Legendre moments are not invariant to image rotation and they do not perform well under noise. Liao and Pawlak [110] show that given a noisy image, use of higher-order Legendre moments improves reconstruction accuracy but only up to a point, beyond which use of higher-order moments decreases reconstruction accuracy. They developed a procedure to determine the optimal number of Legendre moments that could reconstruct an image with the highest accuracy.

Direct computation of the Legendre moments can be quite costly. Papakostas et al. [147] proposed an efficient algorithm for computing the Legendre moments using the block representation of an image.

4.2.4 Gaussian–Hermite Moments

Hermite polynomials are defined by [188]:

$$H_p(x) = (-1)^p \exp(x^2) \frac{d^p}{dx^p} \exp(-x^2). \tag{4.66}$$

H_p is a polynomial of degree p for $p \geq 0$ and the polynomials are orthogonal with respect to weight function

$$w(x) = \exp(-x^2). \tag{4.67}$$

Therefore,

$$\int_{-\infty}^{\infty} H_p(x) H_q(x) w(x)\, dx = 0, \quad \text{when } p \neq q, \tag{4.68}$$

and

$$\int_{-\infty}^{\infty} H_p(x) H_p(x) w(x)\, dx = p! 2^p \sqrt{\pi} \quad \text{when } p = q. \tag{4.69}$$

The Hermite moment of order (p, q) of discrete image $f(x, y)$ with the coordinate system origin at the center of the image is defined by [178, 221]:

$$H_{pq} = \sum_x \sum_y H_p(x) H_q(y) f(x, y). \tag{4.70}$$

Note that Hermite moments are not orthogonal. To obtain orthogonal moments, term $w(x)w(y) = \exp(-x^2 - y^2)$ should be included in the computations. Therefore,

$$L_{42}(p, q) = G_{pq} = \sum_x \sum_y H_p(x) w(x) H_q(y) w(y) f(x, y). \tag{4.71}$$

Also note that since

$$w(x)w(y) = \exp(-x^2)\exp(-y^2)$$

$$= \exp\left\{-\frac{(x^2 + y^2)}{2(1/2)}\right\} \tag{4.72}$$

represents a 2-D Gaussian of standard deviation $\sqrt{2}/2$ and height 1, G_{pq} is called the Gaussian–Hermite moment of order (p, q) and represents orthogonal moments for various values of $p, q \geq 0$ [178]. Gaussian–Hermite moment G_{pq} of image $f(x, y)$ can be considered a linear combination of the convolution of the pth derivative in the x-direction and the qth derivative in the y-direction of a Gaussian with the image [221]. Different order moments, therefore, respond to objects of different sizes (different spatial frequencies) in an image. Shen et al. [178] find that the Gaussian smoothing in Gaussian–Hermite moments makes the moments less sensitive to noise and find Gaussian–Hermite moments to have a higher recognition power than the Legendre and geometric moments under noise. Gaussian–Hermite moments vary with rotation and scale of an image as well as with image contrast.

4.2.5 Tchebichef Moments

Tchebichef moments are the coefficients of an image represented by discrete Tchebichef polynomials [134]:

$$f(x, y) = \sum_{p=0}^{M}\sum_{q=0}^{N} T_{pq}t_p(x)t_q(y), \tag{4.73}$$

$t_p(x)$ is the Tchebichef polynomial of order p in x, $t_q(y)$ is the Tchebichef polynomial of order q in y, and T_{pq} for $0 \leq p \leq M$ and $0 \leq q \leq N$ are computed from:

$$T_{pq} = \frac{1}{\rho(p)\rho(q)}\sum_{x=0}^{M-1}\sum_{y=0}^{N-1} t_p(x)t_q(y)f(x, y), \tag{4.74}$$

where

$$\rho(p) = \sum_{x=0}^{M-1}\left[t_p(x)\right]^2 \tag{4.75}$$

and

$$\rho(q) = \sum_{y=0}^{N-1}\left[t_q(y)\right]^2. \tag{4.76}$$

The Tchebichef polynomial of order $p + 1$ is recursively defined in terms of Tchebichef polynomials of orders p and $p - 1$:

$$t_{p+1}(x) = \frac{(2p+1)(2x-M+1)}{(p+1)} t_p(x)$$

$$- \frac{p(M^2-p^2)}{(p+1)} t_{p-1}(x), \quad q = 1, \ldots, N-1. \quad (4.77)$$

Tchebichef polynomials calculated in this manner, however, quickly increase in magnitude because of term M^p in the recurrence formula. In order to obtain Tchebichef moments in the range $[-1, 1]$, Tchebichef polynomials are scaled by suitable terms $\beta(p)$ and $\beta(q)$ that adjust to p and q. That is

$$\tilde{t}_p(x) = \frac{t_p(x)}{\tilde{\rho}(p)}; \qquad \tilde{t}_q(y) = \frac{t_q(y)}{\tilde{\rho}(q)} \quad (4.78)$$

where

$$\tilde{\rho}(p) = \frac{\rho(p)}{\beta(p)^2}; \qquad \tilde{\rho}(q) = \frac{\rho(q)}{\beta(q)^2}. \quad (4.79)$$

Simple choices for $\beta(p)$ and $\beta(q)$ are M^p and N^q, although other choices are possible [134]. Using the scaled Tchebichef polynomials so they vary between -1 and 1, Tchebichef moments are calculated from [134]:

$$L_{43}(p,q) = T_{pq} = \frac{1}{\tilde{\rho}(p)\tilde{\rho}(q)} \sum_{x=0}^{M-1} \sum_{y=0}^{N-1} \tilde{t}_p(x)\tilde{t}_q(y)f(x,y), \quad (4.80)$$

for $p = 0, \ldots, M-1$ and $q = 0, \ldots, N-1$. Mukundan et al. [134] experimentally showed that Tchebichef moments encode more image information in a fixed number of coefficients than Legendre moments. Tchebichef moments, like Legendre moments, are not invariant to rotation and scaling of an image. Unlike Legendre moments, Tchebichef moments are not invariant to the location of the coordinate system origin. An extension of Tchebichef moments to make them invariant to scale is proposed by Zhu et al. [234]. Numerical stability of Tchebichef moments has been studied by Mukundan [133], proposing means to produce accurate high-order moments. Efficient algorithms for computing Tchebichef moments are described by Wang and Wang [214] and Shu et al. [181].

4.2.6 Krawtchouk Moments

Features obtained from the decomposition of an image into discrete orthogonal Krawtchouk polynomials is referred to as Krawtchouk moments [224]. The orthogonality of the polynomials ensures minimal redundancy. Since Krawtchouk polynomials are discrete, no numerical approximation is needed in their calculation. By scaling the Krawtchouk polynomials with local weight functions, Krawtchouk moments can be made to capture local image information. This scaling also eliminates the possibility of obtaining overflows when calculating high-order moments.

In the discrete domain, the Krawtchouk polynomial of order p, $K_p(x; u, M)$, for $x, p = 0, 1, \ldots, M - 1$ and $u \in [0, 1]$ is defined by [224]:

$$K_p(x; u, M) = HG(-p, -x; -M; 1/u), \tag{4.81}$$

where HG is a hypergeometric function defined by

$$HG(a, b; c; x) = \sum_{k=0}^{\infty} \frac{(a)_k (b)_k x^k}{(c)_k k!}, \tag{4.82}$$

and $(a)_k = a(a + 1) \cdots (a + k - 1)$.

Scaled Krawtchouk polynomials are defined by

$$\bar{K}_p(x; u, M) = K_p(x; u, M) \sqrt{\frac{w(x; u, M)}{\rho(p; u, M)}}, \tag{4.83}$$

where

$$w(x; u, M) = \binom{M}{x} u^x (1 - u)^{M - x} \tag{4.84}$$

and

$$\rho(p; u, M) = (-1)^p \left(\frac{1 - u}{u} \right)^p \frac{p!}{(-M)_p}. \tag{4.85}$$

Given a discrete image $f(x, y)$ of dimensions $M \times N$, the Krawtchouk moments of order (p, q) are defined in terms of the weighted Krawtchouk polynomials of orders p and q [224]:

$$L_{44}(p, q, u, v) = Q_{pq}(u, v) = \sum_{x=0}^{M-1} \sum_{y=0}^{N-1} \bar{K}_p(x; u, M)$$
$$\times \bar{K}_q(y; v, N) f(x, y), \tag{4.86}$$

where $p, x = 0, \ldots, M - 1$, $q, y = 0, \ldots, N - 1$, and $u, v \in [0, 1]$.

Experiments by Yap et al. [224] have revealed a higher recognition ability by the Krawtchouk moments than by the geometric moments in both noise-free and noisy images. Despite superior performance under noise when compared to invariant moments, Krawtchouk moments are not invariant to translation, rotation, and scale of an image.

4.2.7 Zernike Moments

If image coordinates are mapped to range $[-1, 1]$ and only the circular region of radius 1 centered at the image is used, then x can be considered the real part and y the imaginary part of complex number $z = x + jy$. In polar form, this can be written as $z = r(\cos\theta + j\sin\theta)$ or $z = re^{j\theta}$. With this notation, an image within the unit disk centered at the origin can be decomposed into [192, 193]

$$f(x, y) = \sum_{p=0}^{\infty} \sum_{q=-\infty}^{\infty} A_{pq} V_{pq}(r, \theta), \tag{4.87}$$

where A_{pq} is the Zernike moment of order (p, q), $V_{pq}(r, \theta) = R_{pq}(r)e^{jq\theta}$ is the Zernike polynomial of order (p, q) [191], and

$$R_{pq}(r) = \sum_{s=0}^{(p-|q|)/2} (-1)^s$$
$$\times \frac{(p-s)!}{s!(\frac{p+|q|}{2}-s)!(\frac{p-|q|}{2}-s)!} \times r^{p-2s}, \tag{4.88}$$

conditioned that $p - |q|$ be an even number and $|q| \le p$. Letting $k = p - 2s$, the above relation can be written as

$$R_{pq}(r) = \sum_{k=|q|}^{p} B_{p|q|k} r^k \tag{4.89}$$

conditioned that $p - k$ be an even number. Zernike polynomials are orthogonal within a unit disk. Therefore,

$$\int_0^{2\pi} d\theta \int_0^1 r\, dr\, V_{pq}(r, \theta) V_{p'q'}^*(r, \theta) = \frac{\pi}{q+1} \delta(q = q')$$
$$\times \delta(p = p'), \tag{4.90}$$

where $*$ implies complex conjugate, and $\delta(a = a')$ is equal to 1 when $a = a'$ and equal to 0, otherwise.

Given discrete image $f(x_i, y_i)$ or $f(r_i \cos\theta_i, r_i \sin\theta_i)$ for $i = 1, \ldots, N$, the Zernike moments of the image are computed from

$$A_{pq} = \frac{p+1}{\pi} \sum_{i=1}^{N} f(x_i, y_i) V_{pq}^*(r_i, \theta_i), \tag{4.91}$$

where $p = 0, 1, \ldots, \infty$ and q takes positive and negative values from $-\infty$ to $+\infty$ conditioned that $p - |q|$ is an even number and $|q| \le p$.

Zernike moments are related to geometric moments by [192, 193]:

$$L_{45}(p, q) = A_{pq} = \frac{p+1}{\pi} \sum_{k=|q|}^{p} \sum_{i=0}^{n} \sum_{m=0}^{|q|} w^m$$
$$\times \binom{n}{i}\binom{|q|}{m} B_{p|q|k} M_{k-2i-m, 2i+m}, \tag{4.92}$$

where $p - k$ is even, $w = -j$ when $q > 0$ and $w = +j$ when $q \le 0$, and $n = (k - |q|)/2$.

Zernike moments are complex numbers and by rotating an image within the unit disk centered at the origin by θ the Zernike moments will convert from A_{pq} to $A_{pq} \exp(-iq\theta)$, shifting the phase of the moments by $q\theta$ while keeping the magnitude of the moments unchanged [192]. Therefore, magnitude Zernike moments can be used as rotation-invariant features. When an image is reflected with respect to a line that makes angle ϕ with the x axis, its Zernike moments change from A_{pq} to $A_{pq}^* \exp(-i2q\phi)$ [192]. Therefore, the magnitude Zernike moments are invariant under reflection of the image also. This means having images that show the opposite sides of a symmetric object, such as a fish, will produce the same magnitude Zernike moments, facilitating recognition of such objects.

Teh and Chin [193] find that Zernike moments carry less redundancy than Legendre moments and, thus, fewer of them are sufficient to reconstruct an image with a required accuracy. Khotanzad and Hong [93] show through experimentation that if an equal number of geometric moments and magnitude Zernike moments are used, Zernike moments have a higher recognition ability and are less sensitive to noise than geometric moments.

Liao and Pawlak [111] and Wee and Paramesran [217] have pointed out the inherent precision limitation of Zernike moments and proposed means to improve it. Papakostas et al. [144] also studied the numerical accuracy of Zernike moments and found that as the order of the moments increase, the moments become less reliable due to propagation of overflow and finite precision in the calculations. They later [145] suggest replacing the factorials that result in overflows with their approximations, making the process computationally more stable while maintaining the invariance property of Zernike moments. Other efficient algorithms for the calculation of Zernike moments have been described by Belkasim et al. [16] and Mohammed and Jie [129]. Zernike moments were originally described in the polar coordinate system. Extension of the formulas to the Cartesian coordinate system makes it possible to formulate Zernike moments in terms of geometric moments [17]. Zernike moments have been extended to 3-D by Canterakis [22] as well as by Novotni and Klein [137].

If the real-valued radial polynomial R_{pq} of Zernike polynomials is replaced with

$$R_{pq}(r) = \sum_{s=0}^{p-|q|} (-1)^s$$

$$\times \frac{(2p+1-s)!}{s!(p-|q|-s)!(p+|q|+1-s)!} \times r^{p-s}$$

$$= \sum_{k=|q|}^{p} S_{p|q|k} r^k, \tag{4.93}$$

pseudo-Zernike polynomials will be obtained [193], where $p = 0, 1, \ldots, \infty$ and q takes on positive and negative values conditioned that $|q| \leq p$. There are $(p+1)^2$ linearly independent pseudo-Zernike polynomials of degree p or lower while there are only $(p+1)(p+2)/2$ linearly independent Zernike polynomials of degree p or lower due to the additional requirement that $p - |q|$ be an even number. Pseudo-Zernike moments are found to be less sensitive to noise than Zernike moments [193].

4.2.8 Complex Moments

Like Zernike moments complex moments have magnitude and phase, but unlike Zernike moments they are not defined in terms of orthogonal polynomials. Therefore, they suffer from information redundancy if a combination of them are used for recognition. However, they provide a computationally fast means of generating invariant moments [2].

Complex moments are defined by [1, 2]:

$$C_{pq} = \sum_x \sum_y (x + jy)^p (x - jy)^q f(x, y). \tag{4.94}$$

This can also be defined by:

$$L_{46}(p, q) = C_{pq} = \sum_x \sum_y r^{p+q} e^{j(p-q)\theta} f(x, y), \tag{4.95}$$

where $r = \sqrt{x^2 + y^2}$ and $\theta = \tan^{-1}(y/x)$ are the polar coordinates of pixel (x, y). Note that under this definition, C_{qp} becomes the complex conjugate of C_{pq}. Rotating an image by ϕ counter-clockwise will change the pqth order moment from C_{pq} to $C_{pq} e^{-j(p-q)\phi}$. Therefore, rotating an image about its center will only change the phase of the complex moments, without changing the magnitude. Since C_{pq} is the complex conjugate of C_{qp}, we get about half as many rotationally invariant complex moments of a particular order. In addition to

$$L_{47}(p, q) = C_{pq} C_{qp} \tag{4.96}$$

being rotationally invariant,

$$L_{48}(r, s, t, u, k) = C_{rs} C_{tu}^k + C_{sr} C_{ut}^k \tag{4.97}$$

are rotation invariant when $(r - s) + k(t - u) = 0$. Features L_{47} and L_{48} are designed to have exponents that reduce to 0 under any rotational angle, thus, they are real-valued features [2]. To obtain features invariant to image contrast and image scale, Abo-Zaid et al. [1] normalized complex moments as follows:

$$L_{49}(p, q) = C_{pq}^n = C_{pq} \left[\frac{1}{C_{00}} \left(\frac{C_{00}}{C_{11}} \right)^{(p+q)/2} \right], \tag{4.98}$$

where C_{pq}^n is the normalized complex moment of order (p, q), C_{pq} is the complex moment of order (p, q) computed when an image is centered at the origin. The term inside the brackets shows normalization with respect to image contrast and scale of the image. Therefore, since $C_{pq} C_{qp}$ is translation and rotation invariant,

$$L_{50}(p, q) = C_{pq}^n C_{qp}^n \tag{4.99}$$

will be invariant to translation, rotation, scale, and contrast.

Examples of complex invariant moments are given in Figs. 4.17, 4.18, 4.19. These are feature images obtained for L_{47} when using the images in Fig. 4.1 and letting (p, q) be $(2, 0)$, $(0, 2)$, and $(1, 1)$, respectively. Invariance and repeatability

Fig. 4.17 (a)–(f) Complex moment (L_{47}) feature images obtained for the images in Fig. 4.1 when $p = 2$ and $q = 0$. The invariance measures of feature images (b)–(f) when compared to feature image (a) are BI = 0.93, NI = 0.95, II = 0.97, RI = 0.97, SI = 0.84, and the corresponding repeatability measures are BR = 0.95, NR = 0.81, IR = 0.88, RR = 0.86, SR = 0.40

Fig. 4.18 (a)–(f) Complex moment (L_{47}) feature images obtained when $p = 0$ and $q = 2$, producing invariance measures BI = 0.93, NI = 0.95, II = 0.97, RI = 0.97, SI = 0.84, and repeatability measures BR = 0.95, NR = 0.79, IR = 0.88, RR = 0.86, SR = 0.40

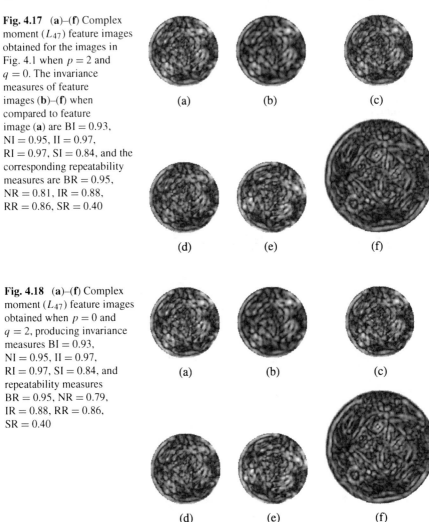

measures of these complex invariant moments are similar to those obtained by geometric invariant moments. The moment features tested so far have higher invariance and repeatability measures than the corresponding measures obtained from statistical features.

To show the amount of improvement achieved in the invariance and repeatability measures of complex moments after normalization, L_{50} was calculated for (p, q) equal to $(2, 0)$, $(0, 2)$, and $(1, 1)$ and displayed in Figs. 4.20, 4.21, and 4.22, respectively. Normalization has slightly improved the invariance property of complex invariant moments. Generally, the invariance and repeatability of complex moments and their normalized versions are not any better than those of the originally proposed Hu invariant moments [80].

Fig. 4.19 (**a**)–(**f**) Complex moment (L_{47}) feature images obtained when $p = 1$ and $q = 1$, resulting in invariance measures BI = 0.97, NI = 0.96, II = 0.97, RI = 0.98, SI = 0.91, and repeatability measures BR = 0.99, NR = 0.78, IR = 0.88, RR = 0.88, SR = 0.11

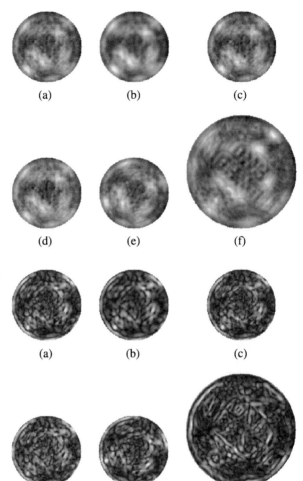

(a)   (b)   (c)

(d)   (e)   (f)

Fig. 4.20 (**a**)–(**f**) Normalized complex moment (L_{50}) feature images obtained for the images in Fig. 4.1 when $p = 2$ and $q = 0$. The invariance measures of feature images (**b**)–(**f**) when computed against feature image (**a**) are BI = 0.95, NI = 0.95, II = 0.98, RI = 0.97, SI = 0.86, and the corresponding repeatability measures are BR = 0.97, NR = 0.78, IR = 0.86, RR = 0.88, SR = 0.38

(a)   (b)   (c)

(d)   (e)   (f)

4.2.9 Wavelet Moments

Rotation invariant moments can be generally defined by [176]:

$$F_{pq} = \int_{\theta} \int_{r} f(r, \theta) A_p(r) e^{jq\theta} r \, dr \, d\theta, \tag{4.100}$$

where $A_p(r)$ is a function of radial variable r and integers p and q are the radial and angular orders of the moments. In the discrete domain, F_{pq} is defined by

$$L_{51}(p, q) = F_{pq} = \sum_{x} \sum_{y} f(x, y) A_p(r) e^{jq\theta} r, \tag{4.101}$$

where $r = \sqrt{x^2 + y^2}$ and $\theta = \tan^{-1}(y/x)$. $\|F_{pq}\|$, which is independent of θ, is a rotation invariant feature [176].

Fig. 4.21 (**a**)–(**f**) Normalized complex moment (L_{50}) feature images obtained for $p = 0$ and $q = 2$, producing invariance measures BI $= 0.95$, NI $= 0.96$, II $= 0.98$, RI $= 0.97$, SI $= 0.86$, and repeatability measures BR $= 0.97$, NR $= 0.79$, IR $= 0.86$, RR $= 0.88$, SR $= 0.38$

Fig. 4.22 (**a**)–(**f**) Normalized complex moment (L_{50}) feature images when $p = 1$ and $q = 1$, resulting in invariance measures BI $= 0.98$, NI $= 0.98$, II $= 0.98$, RI $= 0.99$, SI $= 0.93$, and repeatability measures BR $= 0.93$, NR $= 0.72$, IR $= 0.81$, RR $= 0.91$, SR $= 0.12$

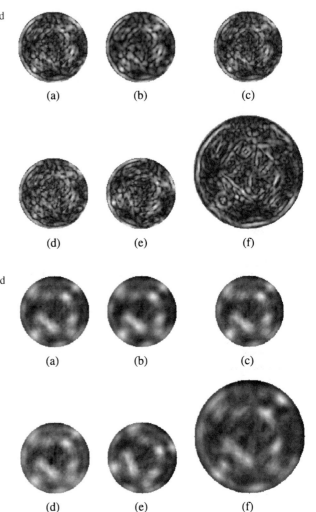

When $A_p(r) = r^p$ with some constraints on p and q [80], geometric moments are obtained, and when $A_p(r)$ is replaced with $R_{pq}(r)$ as defined in (4.93), Zernike moments are obtained [176]. $A_p(r)$ may be represented by other radial functions to produce additional moments. In particular, if $A_p(r)$ is replaced with wavelet functions, the obtained moments will contain image information at multiresolution.

Shen and Ip [176] suggest replacing $A_p(r)$ with

$$\psi_{m,n}(r) = 2^{m/2}\psi\left(2^m r - n/2\right) \qquad (4.102)$$

where $m = 0, \ldots, 3$, $n = 0, \ldots, 2^{m+1}$, and

$$\psi(r) = \frac{4a^{n+1}}{\sqrt{2\pi(n+1)}}\sigma_w \cos\left[2\pi f_0(2r-1)\right]\exp\left[-\frac{(2r-1)^2}{2\sigma_w^2(n+1)}\right]. \qquad (4.103)$$

If $n = 3$, $a = 0.697066$, $f_0 = 0.409177$, and $\sigma_w^2 = 0.561145$, a Gaussian approximation to the cubic B-spline function will be obtained. Using cubic B-spline wavelets, the wavelet moment invariants will be [176]:

$$L_{52}(m, n, q) = F_{m,n,q} = \int S_q(r)\psi_{m,n}(r)r\,dr, \tag{4.104}$$

where $m = 0, \ldots, 3$ is the scale index; $n = 0, \ldots, 2^{m+1}$ is the shift index; $q = 0, \ldots, 3$ shows resolution; and for a fixed r;

$$S_q(r) = \int_0^{2\pi} f(r, \theta)e^{jq\theta}\,d\theta \tag{4.105}$$

shows the qth frequency feature of image $f(r, \theta)$ angularly and $S_q(r)r$ represents the intensity distribution of image $f(r, \theta)$ radially for $0 \le r \le 1$. Note that

$$L_{53}(m, n, q) = \|F_{m,n,q}\| \tag{4.106}$$

is invariant to rotation.

Experimental results obtained by Shen and Ip [176] and Feng et al. [52] on various images reveal the superior discrimination power of wavelet moments over Zernike and geometric moments. Because different wavelet moments contain information about different scales in an image, by proper selection of wavelet moments, it is possible to ignore small differences between images and find image similarity based on large variations in them, or emphasize small differences between images and distinguish images with subtle differences from each other.

4.3 Algebraic Features

Algebraic features represent the intrinsic attributes of images. They are global features such as the singular values or the eigenvalues of an image, or they represent local features calculated from the inertia or Hessian matrices of local neighborhoods.

4.3.1 Singular Values

Treating image $f(x, y)$ as a matrix $\mathbf{f}$ and assuming $\mathbf{U}$ represents the row eigenvector system of $\mathbf{f}$ and $\mathbf{V}$ represents the column eigenvector system of $\mathbf{f}$, we can write [9, 185]:

$$\mathbf{UfV} = \begin{pmatrix} \Sigma & \mathbf{0} \\ \mathbf{0} & \mathbf{0} \end{pmatrix}, \tag{4.107}$$

where $\Sigma = \mathrm{diag}(\sigma_1, \sigma_2, \ldots, \sigma_r)$ and $\sigma_1 \ge \sigma_2 \ge \cdots \ge \sigma_r > 0$ are the singular values of the image. $\sigma_i = \lambda_i^{1/2}$, where λ_i is the ith largest eigenvalue of $\mathbf{f}$.

Note that since $\mathbf{U}$ and $\mathbf{V}$ are orthonormal matrices, we have

$$\mathbf{U}\mathbf{U}^t = \mathbf{I}, \quad \text{and} \tag{4.108}$$

$$\mathbf{V}^t\mathbf{V} = \mathbf{I}, \tag{4.109}$$

where t implies transpose and $\mathbf{I}$ implies unit matrix.

If $\mathbf{u}_i$ is the ith row eigenvector of $\mathbf{U}$ and $\mathbf{v}_i$ is the ith column eigenvector of $\mathbf{V}$, we can reconstruct the image from its eigenvectors and singular values:

$$\mathbf{f} = \sum_{i=1}^{r} \sigma_i \mathbf{u}_i \mathbf{v}_i. \tag{4.110}$$

Singular values of an image,

$$L_{54}(i) = \sigma_i, \quad i = 1, \ldots, r, \tag{4.111}$$

therefore, contain valuable information about an image, which can be used to characterize the image [10]. r, which shows the number of nonzero singular values of the image, is known as the rank of the image.

σ_i depends on image contrast. Features independent of image contrast can be obtained by finding the ratio of the singular values and the largest singular value. That is

$$L_{55}(i) = \sigma_i / \sigma_1, \quad i = 2, \ldots, r. \tag{4.112}$$

Although for a given image the singular values are unique [78], different images can produce the same singular values. Singular values of an image are more useful if they are used together with their eigenvectors [196].

If C images $\{\mathbf{f}_i : i = 1, \ldots, C\}$ are available, for example, showing different views of an object, each image can be opened into a long 1-D array in scan-order form, and if each image contains $S = M \times N$ pixels, then, letting $\mathbf{m}$ represent the pixel-by-pixel mean of the C images,

$$\mathbf{Q} = \frac{1}{C} \sum_{i=1}^{C} (\mathbf{f}_i - \mathbf{m})(\mathbf{f}_i - \mathbf{m})^t \tag{4.113}$$

will be an $S \times S$ matrix with $r \leq S$ nonzero singular values.

Considering the d-dimensional space defined by the eigenvectors representing the d largest singular values of $\mathbf{Q}$, where $d \leq r$, each image can be considered a point in the d-dimensional space obtained by opening it into a 1-D array and finding its dot product with each of the d eigenvectors of $\mathbf{Q}$.

The process of mapping the C images into the d-dimensional space can be considered a learning process. To determine whether an image contains an object of interest, it is opened to a 1-D array and its dot product is determined with eigenvectors corresponding to the d largest singular values of the image, producing a point in the d-dimensional space. If this point is sufficiently close to a model point obtained during the learning process, it is concluded that the object is the same as the model.

This method has been used [135] to recognize images containing arbitrary views of previously seen objects. A combination of eigenvectors and eigen/singular values is used to provide an effective means of recognizing various objects. This idea was first developed by Sirovich and Kirby [182] and was made popular by Turk and Pentland [199] in the recognition of human faces. Extension of the idea to a multi-class problem where training images are available in each class is provided by Liu et al. [113]. Representation of a sequence of images by $\mathbf{Q}$ in (4.113) and use of the eigenvectors and eigenvalues of $\mathbf{Q}$ to describe and characterize the images is known as Hotelling transform or Karhunen–Loève transform [66].

4.3.2 Inertia-Matrix Features

Denoting $\partial f(x, y)/\partial x$ by f_x and $\partial f(x, y)/\partial y$ by f_y, the *second moment matrix* or the *inertia matrix* of image f computed in the neighborhood of (x, y) is defined by

$$\mathbf{I}(x, y) = \begin{bmatrix} \sum f_x^2(x, y) & \sum f_x(x, y) f_y(x, y) \\ \sum f_y(x, y) f_x(x, y) & \sum f_y^2(x, y) \end{bmatrix}. \tag{4.114}$$

The sum is over a small circular neighborhood centered at pixel of interest, (x, y). The eigenvectors of $\mathbf{I}(x, y)$ show the dominant gradient directions in the neighborhood of (x, y). When a well-defined corner structure is present in a neighborhood, both eigenvalues will be high, while if a neighborhood contains an edge structure, only one of the eigenvalues will be high. Assuming $\lambda_1(x, y)$ and $\lambda_2(x, y)$ are the eigenvalues of $\mathbf{I}(x, y)$, and $\lambda_1(x, y) > \lambda_2(x, y)$, then

$$L_{56}(x, y) = \lambda_1(x, y) \quad \text{and}$$

$$L_{57}(x, y) = \lambda_2(x, y) \tag{4.115}$$

represent rotation-invariant features that can be used to describe the neighborhood. Shi and Tomasi [179] used the locations where $\lambda_2(x, y)$ was locally maximum as feature points for tracking.

Since $\lambda_1(x, y)$ and $\lambda_2(x, y)$ vary with image contrast, to make the detected feature points independent of an image's contrast, Carneiro and Jepson [23] normalized $\lambda_2(x, y)$:

$$L_{58}(x, y) = \frac{\lambda_2(x, y)}{[\lambda_1(x, y) + \lambda_2(x, y)]/2} \tag{4.116}$$

before using it. Ando [6] selected pixels where the following measure was locally maximum as feature points:

$$L_{59}(x, y) = \frac{4\lambda_1(x, y)\lambda_2(x, y)}{[\lambda_1(x, y) + \lambda_2(x, y)]^2}. \tag{4.117}$$

Ballester and González [12] used the direction of the eigenvector corresponding to the larger eigenvalue as the dominant direction in a neighborhood to segment a textured image. An elliptic neighborhood based on the directions and magnitudes of the eigenvectors was used to calculate an affine-invariant energy for texture discrimination. Various methods to select affine-invariant regions and compute affine-invariant features have been reported [14, 127, 169, 170, 201–204].

Fig. 4.23 (a)–(f) Second
eigenvalue of inertia matrix
(L_{57}) feature images obtained
using the images in Fig. 4.1.
The invariance measures of
feature images (b)–(f) with
respect to feature image (a)
are BI = 0.85, NI = 0.93,
II = 0.96, RI = 0.92,
SI = 0.92, and the
corresponding repeatability
measures are BR = 0.30,
NR = 0.65, IR = 0.75,
RR = 0.47, SR = 0.47

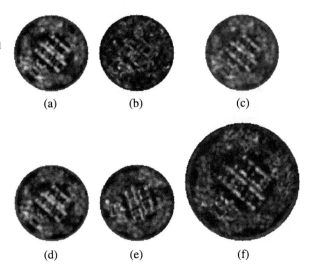

In addition to the eigenvalues of the inertia matrix, the determinant and the trace
of the inertia matrix show unique properties of a local neighborhood and may be
used as features.

$$L_{60}(x, y) = \text{Det}[\mathbf{I}(x, y)],$$
$$L_{61}(x, y) = \text{Tr}[\mathbf{I}(x, y)]. \quad (4.118)$$

Rohr [163] used locations in an image where the determinant of the inertia matrix
became locally maximum as control points. Harris and Stephens [74] used locations
where

$$L_{62}(x, y) = \text{Det}[\mathbf{I}(x, y)] - h \, \text{Tr}^2[\mathbf{I}(x, y)] \quad (4.119)$$

became locally maximum as control points. h is a small number, such as 0.05. Förstner [58] used locations in an image where

$$L_{63}(x, y) = \text{Det}[\mathbf{I}(x, y)] / \text{Tr}[\mathbf{I}(x, y)] \quad (4.120)$$

became locally maximum as control points.

Examples of inertia matrix features are given in Figs. 4.23, 4.24, 4.25, 4.26, 4.27,
4.28. Circular neighborhoods of radius 4 pixels were used to calculate the inertia
matrix at each pixel. Repeatability measures are calculated using the maxima (rather
than the extrema) in a feature image as is customary by point detectors. From the
obtained feature images and their invariance and repeatability measures, we observe
that these features behave similarly, and generally are less invariant and repeatable
than geometric features. Experimental results show that in general low repeatability
measures are obtained for these features, especially under blurring.

Fig. 4.24 (a)–(f) Normalized
second eigenvalue of inertia
matrix (L_{58}) feature images,
producing invariance
measures BI = 0.73,
NI = 0.88, II = 0.97,
RI = 0.83, SI = 0.84, and
repeatability measures
BR = 0.58, NR = 0.65,
IR = 0.85, RR = 0.67,
SR = 0.57

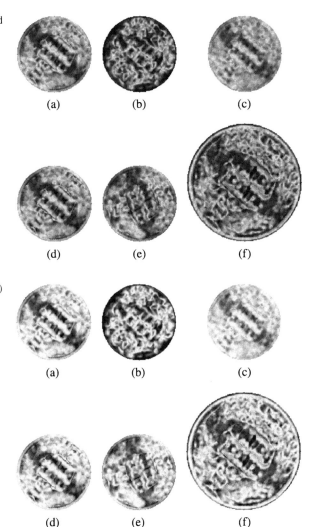

(a)   (b)   (c)

(d)   (e)   (f)

Fig. 4.25 (a)–(f) Ando (L_{59})
feature images, producing
invariance measures
BI = 0.70, NI = 0.89,
II = 0.97, RI = 0.84,
SI = 0.85, and repeatability
measures BR = 0.58,
NR = 0.66, IR = 0.85,
RR = 0.65, SR = 0.57

(a)   (b)   (c)

(d)   (e)   (f)

4.3.3 Hessian-Matrix Features

The Hessian matrix of image $f(x, y)$ at pixel (x, y) is defined by

$$\mathbf{H}(x, y) = \begin{bmatrix} f_{xx}(x, y) & f_{xy}(x, y) \\ f_{xy}(x, y) & f_{yy}(x, y) \end{bmatrix},$$ (4.121)

where f_{xx} denotes intensity second derivative with respect to x, f_{yy} denotes intensity second derivative with respect to y, and f_{xy} denotes intensity derivative with respect to both x and y. Beaudet [15] used image locations where determinant of the Hessian matrix

$$L_{64}(x, y) = \mathrm{Det}\big[\mathbf{H}(x, y)\big] = f_{xx}(x, y) f_{yy}(x, y) - f_{xy}^2(x, y)$$ (4.122)

Fig. 4.26 (a)–(f)
Determinant of inertia matrix
(L_{60}) feature images,
producing invariance
measures BI = 0.90,
NI = 0.94, II = 0.97,
RI = 0.96, SI = 0.94, and
repeatability measures
BR = 0.26, NR = 0.56,
IR = 0.72, RR = 0.63,
SR = 0.49

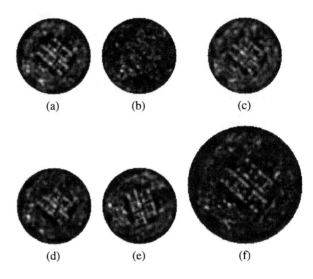

Fig. 4.27 (a)–(f) Harris and
Stephens (L_{62}) feature
images, producing invariance
measures BI = 0.74,
NI = 0.81, II = 0.98,
RI = 0.65, SI = 0.76, and
repeatability measures
BR = 0.30, NR = 0.64,
IR = 0.75, RR = 0.54,
SR = 0.51

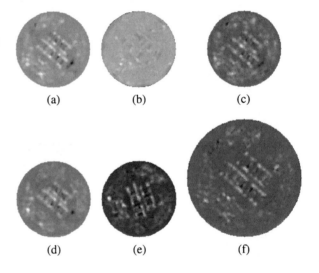

became locally maximum as feature points. It has been shown [136] that if image
intensities are considered height values, treating an image as a surface, the determinant of the Hessian matrix at a pixel is proportional to the Gaussian curvature of the
surface at the pixel. That is,

$$\text{Det}\big[\mathbf{H}(x, y)\big] \propto \kappa_{\max}(x, y)\kappa_{\min}(x, y), \qquad (4.123)$$

where $\kappa_{\max}$ and $\kappa_{\min}$ represent the principal curvatures of the surface at (x, y). Deriche and Giraudon [46] found this proportionality term to be $\frac{1}{1+f_x^2(x,y)+f_y^2(x,y)}$.

Fig. 4.28 (a)–(f) Förstner and Gülch (L_{63}) feature images, producing invariance measures BI = 0.84, NI = 0.93, II = 0.96, RI = 0.93, SI = 0.91, and repeatability measures BR = 0.31, NR = 0.62, IR = 0.71, RR = 0.55, SR = 0.50

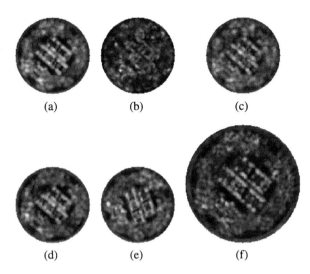

(a)   (b)   (c)

(d)   (e)   (f)

Kitchen and Rosenfeld [95] defined a cornerness measure that is a combination of image first and second derivatives:

$$L_{65}(x, y) = k(x, y)$$
$$= \frac{f_{xx}(x, y)f_y^2(x, y) + f_{yy}(x, y)f_x^2(x, y)}{f_x^2(x, y) + f_y^2(x, y)}$$
$$- \frac{2f_{xy}(x, y)f_x(x, y)f_y(x, y)}{f_x^2(x, y) + f_y^2(x, y)} \tag{4.124}$$

and selected image pixels where this measure was locally maximum as control points. Wang and Brady [212, 213] showed that total curvature κ is proportional to k, while inversely proportional to gradient magnitude. Therefore,

$$L_{66}(x, y) = \kappa(x, y) = \frac{k(x, y)}{[f_x^2(x, y) + f_y^2(x, y)]^{1/2}} \tag{4.125}$$

and used pixels with locally maximum total curvature as control points.

Examples of feature images obtained using feature L_{64} of Beaudet [15] and feature L_{65} of Kitchen and Rosenfeld [95] are given in Figs. 4.29 and 4.30, respectively. Invariance and repeatability measures of Hessian matrix features are generally higher than those of inertia matrix features. To quantify repeatability, in both cases, only peak feature locations are used.

4.4 Frequency-Domain Features

The features discussed so far are calculated in the spatial domain. Features may be calculated in the frequency domain also. The features discussed in the following sections are extracted from various image transforms.

Fig. 4.29 (a)–(f)
Determinant of
Hessian-matrix feature (L_{64})
images obtained using the
images in Fig. 4.1. The
invariance measures of
feature images (**b**)–(**f**) when
computed with respect to the
feature image (**a**) are
BI $= 0.87$, NI $= 0.90$,
II $= 0.95$, RI $= 0.93$,
SI $= 0.97$, and the
corresponding repeatability
measures are BR $= 0.89$,
NR $= 0.82$, IR $= 0.93$,
RR $= 0.74$, SR $= 0.87$

Fig. 4.30 (a)–(f)
Curvature-based feature (L_{65})
images, resulting in
invariance measures
BI $= 0.90$, NI $= 0.94$,
II $= 0.98$, RI $= 0.92$,
SI $= 0.96$, and repeatability
measures BR $= 0.81$,
NR $= 0.81$, IR $= 0.95$,
RR $= 0.78$, SR $= 0.86$

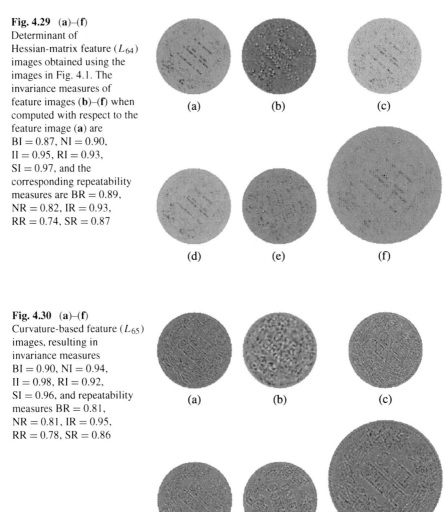

4.4.1 Transform Coefficients

Transform coefficients encode spatial frequencies in an image and can be used as features to describe the image. Image transform coefficients can be obtained by pre- and post-multiplying an image by a transform matrix. Transform matrices are often orthogonal, capturing non-redundant spatial information about an image. A typical transform matrix is the same size as the image itself. For instance, the transform

matrix for calculating the discrete Fourier transform (DFT) of an $N \times N$ image is
[112]:

$$\mathbf{W} = \frac{1}{\sqrt{N}} \begin{bmatrix} 1 & 1 & 1 & \cdots & 1 \\ 1 & w_N & w_N^2 & \cdots & w_N^{N-1} \\ \cdot & \cdot & \cdot & \cdot & \cdot \\ \cdot & \cdot & \cdot & \cdot & \cdot \\ \cdot & \cdot & \cdot & \cdot & \cdot \\ 1 & w_N^{N-1} & w_N^{2(N-1)} & \cdots & w_N^{((N-1)(N-1))} \end{bmatrix}, \tag{4.126}$$

where N is a power of 2 and $w_N = \exp(-\frac{2\pi j}{N})$. The DFT coefficients of image $\mathbf{f}$ are
obtained from $\mathbf{D}_f = \mathbf{WfW}$. Except for $\mathbf{D}_f[0,0]$, which contains information about
image contrast, transform coefficients

$$L_{67}(i, j) = \mathbf{D}_f[i, j] \tag{4.127}$$

for $i, j = 0, \ldots, N$ where $i + j > 0$ represent information about various spatial
frequencies in the image. Higher order coefficients measure higher frequencies in
the image. DFT coefficients are complex numbers, having magnitude and phase.
Changing the location of the coordinate system origin will change the phase component of a coefficient but not its magnitude. Through a log-polar mapping of DFT
coefficients, Reddy and Chatterji [158] derived features that were invariant to the
translation, rotation, and scale of an image.

The transform matrix for Hadamard transform (HT) is recursively defined by
[152]:

$$\mathbf{H}_n = \mathbf{H}_1 \otimes \mathbf{H}_{n-1}, \tag{4.128}$$

where $\otimes$ denotes the Kronecker product of two matrices. For example,

$$\mathbf{A} \otimes \mathbf{B} = \begin{bmatrix} a[1,1]\mathbf{B} & a[1,2]\mathbf{B} & \cdots & a[1,n]\mathbf{B} \\ \cdot & \cdot & \cdot & \cdot \\ \cdot & \cdot & \cdot & \cdot \\ a[N,1]\mathbf{B} & a[N,2]\mathbf{B} & \cdots & a[N,N]\mathbf{B} \end{bmatrix}, \tag{4.129}$$

where matrix $\mathbf{A}$ is assumed $N \times N$ with entries $a[1,1] \ldots a[N,N]$. Knowing that a
2×2 Hadamard matrix is defined by

$$\mathbf{H}_1 = \frac{1}{\sqrt{2}} \begin{bmatrix} 1 & 1 \\ 1 & -1 \end{bmatrix}, \tag{4.130}$$

we obtain

$$\mathbf{H}_2 = \mathbf{H}_1 \otimes \mathbf{H}_1 = \begin{bmatrix} \mathbf{H}_1 & \mathbf{H}_1 \\ \mathbf{H}_1 & -\mathbf{H}_1 \end{bmatrix}$$

$$= \frac{1}{2} \begin{bmatrix} 1 & 1 & 1 & 1 \\ 1 & -1 & 1 & -1 \\ 1 & 1 & -1 & -1 \\ 1 & -1 & -1 & 1 \end{bmatrix}, \tag{4.131}$$

and so on. HT coefficients, similar to DFT coefficients, capture spatial frequencies in an image. Given an image $\mathbf{f}$ of dimensions $N \times N$, where $N = 2^n$, the Hadamard transform of the image is obtained from $\mathbf{D}_h = \mathbf{H}_n \mathbf{f} \mathbf{H}_n$. Transform coefficients

$$L_{68}(i, j) = \mathbf{D}_h[i, j] \tag{4.132}$$

for $i, j = 0, \ldots, N$ and $i + j > 0$ contain information about various spatial frequencies in the image and can be used as image features. Note that DFT features represent complex numbers, while HT features represent real numbers. Also note that computation of HT features is much faster than computation of DFT features because HT matrices contain 1 and -1, requiring only addition and subtraction of image intensities. Computation of the DFT of an image involves complex multiplications.

Other transform coefficients can be used as features to characterize spatial frequencies in an image. These include discrete cosine transform (DCT) coefficients [5], Haar transform coefficients [8], Walsh transform coefficients [211], and slant transform coefficients [153]. Shen and Sethi [177] used DCT coefficients to determine the presence of edges of particular scales and orientations in an image, while Feng and Jiang [51] used the moments of DCT coefficients to retrieve compressed JPEG images from a database.

The number of transform coefficients equals the number of pixels in an image. Some transform coefficients contain more information about an image than other coefficients. For example, locations in the transform image where the magnitude transform become locally maximum show dominant horizontal and vertical spacial frequencies in the image. The magnitude of a peak coefficient indicates the abundance of the spatial frequencies represented by the peak. The number of such peaks and their spatial arrangement can be represented in a graph (such as a minimum spanning tree) and via graph matching, images can be compared independent of their contrast, translational, rotational, and scaling differences. To avoid detection of peaks caused by noise or changes in the scale/resolution of an image, rather than using all peaks, the n largest peaks may be used. Alternatively, peaks corresponding to very high frequencies may be excluded in the count as such peaks are often the result of image noise.

Assuming image $f(x, y)$ has Fourier transform $F(u, v)$, the magnitude coefficient at (u, v) will be $\sqrt{F(u, v)F^*(u, v)}$, where $*$ implies complex conjugate. A transform such as Hadamard transform, which produces real coefficients, the magnitude coefficient at (u, v) will be $|F(u, v)|$. The n largest locally peak coefficients ordered according to their angles with u axis when connected to $(0, 0)$ in the uv-domain will produce a feature vector that can be used in recognition and matching. Alternatively, the location (u, v) of a peak can be used as a complex number $(u + jv)$, and a feature vector of such complex numbers can be created by ordering them according to their magnitudes or phases for recognition or matching.

An example using

$$L_{69} = \text{Number of peaks in the magnitude DFT} \tag{4.133}$$

as the feature, computed in a 16×16 neighborhood, is shown in Fig. 4.31. The detail of the feature images is indicative of the distinctive nature of the feature;

Fig. 4.31 (a)–(f) Number of peaks of the DFT (L_{69}) feature images obtained from the images in Fig. 4.1. The invariance measures of feature images (**b**)–(**f**) when computed against feature image (**a**) are BI = 0.82, NI = 0.95, II = 0.93, RI = 0.93, SI = 0.93, and the corresponding repeatability measures are BR = 0.48, NR = 0.62, IR = 0.79, RR = 0.65, SR = 0.21

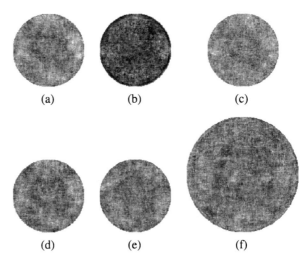

(a) (b) (c)

(d) (e) (f)

therefore, the process can distinguish images with small differences from each other. However, the abundance of similar features in a feature image indicates that different images can produce the same number of peaks. Therefore, although false negative probability is low when using this feature, false positive probability is high.

Examining the invariance and repeatability measures of the feature images, we observe that this simple spatial feature is highly invariant under monotone intensity transformation because such a transformation does not change spatial frequencies in the image noticeably. Although the repeatability measures of this feature under various image changes are relatively low, they are still higher than those obtained by statistical features. Since square windows rather than circular windows were used in the calculation of transform coefficients, some of the degradations in invariance and repeatability measures under rotation can be attributed to that. Influence of noise on invariance and repeatability properties can be reduced by not using the high-frequency regions in the transform domain as noise predominantly contributes to the high frequency coefficients.

4.4.2 Bispectrum Features

In the preceding section, we saw that the magnitude Fourier transform of an image is invariant to image translation and by log-polar mapping it can be made invariant to rotation and scale. It is important to note that most information in the Fourier transform of an image is kept in the phase rather than in the magnitude of the transform [140]. By discarding phase, we discard important information, weakening the discrimination power of the transform coefficients.

Bispectrum is an attempt to preserve phase information in frequency-domain features. The bispectrum of an image is a triple correlation measure, introduced by Lohmann and Wirnitzer [114]. Given image $f(\mathbf{x})$, where $\mathbf{x} = (x, y)$, and assuming

$\mathbf{u} = (u, v)$ and $F(\mathbf{u})$ is the Fourier transform of $f(\mathbf{x})$, the bispectrum of the image is defined by

$$B(\mathbf{u}_1, \mathbf{u}_2) = F(\mathbf{u}_1)F(\mathbf{u}_2)F(-\mathbf{u}_1 - \mathbf{u}_2). \tag{4.134}$$

The bispectrum of an image is invariant to image translation because Fourier transform is invariant to image translation. If image $f(\mathbf{x})$ is of dimensions $N \times N$, the bispectrum will be of dimensions $N \times N \times N \times N$, requiring considerable space and time for its computation. A solution provided by Marabini and Carazo [125] is to project the bispectrum in the direction $\mathbf{u}_1$, reducing the 4-D bispectrum space into a 2-D space. Therefore,

$$
\begin{aligned}
I(\mathbf{u}_2) &= \sum_{\mathbf{u}_1} B(\mathbf{u}_1, \mathbf{u}_2) \\
&= \sum_{\mathbf{u}_1} F(\mathbf{u}_1)F(\mathbf{u}_2)F(-\mathbf{u}_1 - \mathbf{u}_2) \\
&= F(\mathbf{u}_2) \sum_{\mathbf{u}_1} F(\mathbf{u}_1)F^*(\mathbf{u}_1 + \mathbf{u}_2).
\end{aligned} \tag{4.135}
$$

Now, letting $h(\mathbf{x}) = f(-\mathbf{x})$ and denoting F^* by H, we obtain

$$
\begin{aligned}
I(\mathbf{u}_2) &= F(\mathbf{u}_2) \sum_{\mathbf{u}_1} F(\mathbf{u}_1)F^*(\mathbf{u}_1 + \mathbf{u}_2) \\
&= F(\mathbf{u}_2) \sum_{\mathbf{u}_1} H^*(\mathbf{u}_1)H(\mathbf{u}_1 + \mathbf{u}_2) \\
&= F(\mathbf{u}_2)H \diamond H \\
&= F(\mathbf{u}_2)F\left(h^2(\mathbf{x})\right) \\
&= F(\mathbf{u}_2)F\left(f^2(-\mathbf{x})\right) \\
&= F\left(f(\mathbf{x})\right)F\left(f^2(-\mathbf{x})\right)
\end{aligned} \tag{4.136}
$$

where $*$ implies complex conjugate and $\diamond$ denotes correlation. Therefore,

$$L_{70}(\mathbf{u}) = I(\mathbf{u}), \tag{4.137}$$

which is obtained from point-by-point multiplication of the DFT of image $f(\mathbf{x})$ and the DFT of an inverted version of the same image with squared intensities can be used as translation invariant features. It has been shown [125] that these invariant features are capable of reconstructing an image up to its position.

Bispectrum features can be made invariant to the orientation and scale of an image. Since by scaling an image its Fourier transform is inversely scaled, the scaling will not change ratio $r = |\mathbf{u}_1|/|\mathbf{u}_2|$. If an image is rotated, its Fourier transform will rotate by the same amount, but the rotation will not change angle θ, where $\cos\theta = (\mathbf{u}_1 \cdot \mathbf{u}_2)/(|\mathbf{u}_1||\mathbf{u}_2|)$. By integrating the bispectrum in $(\mathbf{u}_1, \mathbf{u}_2)$ space where $|\mathbf{u}_1|/|\mathbf{u}_2| = r$ and $(\mathbf{u}_1 \cdot \mathbf{u}_2)/(|\mathbf{u}_1||\mathbf{u}_2|) = \cos\theta$, we will obtain features

$$J(r, \theta) = \sum_r \sum_\theta g\left(B(\mathbf{u}_1, \mathbf{u}_2)\right), \tag{4.138}$$

that are invariant to the orientation and scale of an image. Since B is invariant to translation, $J(r, \theta)$ is actually invariant to translation, rotation, and scale of an image. In the above equation $g(\cdot)$ can be any function. Since $B(\mathbf{u}_1, \mathbf{u}_2)$ is a complex number, to create real features, one may let g be the real part, the imaginary part, or the magnitude of B. $J(r, \theta)$ can be considered a 2-D histogram in the (r, θ) space and the entries of the histogram can be filled by going through $B(\mathbf{u}_1, \mathbf{u}_2)$, and for each $(\mathbf{u}_1, \mathbf{u}_2)$ finding the corresponding (r, θ) and incrementing $J(r, \theta)$ by $g(B(\mathbf{u}_1, \mathbf{u}_2))$.

Horikawa [79] suggested the following normalization to make the bispectrum features invariant to image contrast also:

$$L_{71}(r, \theta) = \frac{J(r, \theta)}{[\sum_r \sum_\theta J^2(r, \theta)]^{1/2}}. \qquad (4.139)$$

Again, some entries in the $J(r, \theta)$ histogram carry more information about the underlying image than other entries. Therefore, if there is a choice to be made on the entries of $J(r, \theta)$, one should choose local maxima entries. A feature vector representing maxima of $J(r, \theta)$ when ordered in increasing r or θ may be used for recognition or matching. Alternatively, the network of the peak entries in $J(r, \theta)$ can be used as a graph or a tree in recognition or matching.

4.4.3 Power-Spectrum Features

If $F(u, v)$ is the DFT of image $f(x, y)$ and $F^*(u, v)$ is the complex conjugate of $F(u, v)$, the power spectrum $\phi(u, v)$ of image $f(x, y)$ is defined by

$$\phi(u, v) = F(u, v)F^*(u, v) = \|F(u, v)\|^2. \qquad (4.140)$$

Since the angular variation of $\|F\|^2$ depends on the direction of the pattern in image $f(x, y)$, and values of $\|F\|^2$ at different distances to the 0 frequency show the presence of objects of different sizes, $\|F\|^2$ calculated angularly and within various rings can be used to characterize the spatial characteristics of objects in image $f(x, y)$.

Use of power spectrum features in texture discrimination was first suggested by Bajcsy [11]. Letting $r = \sqrt{u^2 + v^2}$ and $\theta = \tan^{-1}(v/u)$, typical features calculated from the power spectrum are [38, 50]:

1. *Annular-ring sampling geometry*:

$$L_{72}(r_0, \delta r) = \sum_r \sum_\theta \|F(r, \theta)\|^2, \qquad (4.141)$$

where $r_0 - \delta r \leq r < r_0 + \delta r$ and $0 \leq \theta < 2\pi$. This feature is invariant to image rotation as it is independent of parameter θ.

2. *Wedge sampling geometry*:

$$L_{73}(\theta_0, \delta\theta) = \sum_\theta \sum_r \|F(r, \theta)\|^2, \qquad (4.142)$$

Fig. 4.32 (a)–(f) Local power spectrum (L_{74}) feature images obtained for the images in Fig. 4.1. The invariance measures of feature images (b)–(f) when compared to feature image (a) are BI = 0.81, NI = 0.93, II = 0.94, RI = 0.95, SI = 0.93, and the corresponding repeatability measures are BR = 0.94, NR = 0.82, IR = 0.92, RR = 0.79, SR = 0.80

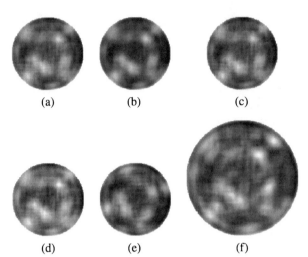

where $\theta_0 - \delta\theta \le \theta < \theta_0 + \delta\theta$, $0 \le r \le R$, and R is the maximum radius of the circular region enclosed in the image.

3. *Parallel-slit sampling geometry*:

$$L_{74}(u_0, \delta u; v_0, \delta v) = \sum_u \sum_v \|F(u, v)\|^2, \qquad (4.143)$$

where $u_0 - \delta u \le u < u_0 + \delta u$ and $v_0 - \delta v \le v < v_0 + \delta v$. This feature is only invariant to image translation and captures information within a range of frequencies horizontally and vertically.

4. *Frequency-domain entropy*: Letting $s_{uv} = \|F(u, v)\|^2$ and $p_{uv} = s_{uv}/\sum_u \sum_v s_{uv}$, entropy within a region in the frequency domain is calculated from [84]:

$$L_{75}(u_1, u_2; v_1, v_2) = -\sum_u \sum_v p_{uv} \log p_{uv}, \qquad (4.144)$$

where $u_1 \le u < u_2$ and $v_1 \le v < v_2$. This feature is also invariant to image translation.

Conners and Harlow [38] find that power spectrum features classify a larger number of textures than GLSD features (Sect. 4.1.2.1) and GLD features (Sect. 4.1.1.2). They also find textures that can be recognized by GLSD and GLD features but not by power spectrum features and vice versa. They find 50% of textures recognizable by power spectrum features are also recognizable by GLSD or GLD features.

Examples of power spectrum feature images are given in Figs. 4.32 and 4.33. Feature L_{74} is calculated for all u and v, producing the total power spectrum in each local neighborhood. Feature L_{75} is also calculated at all frequencies, producing the total entropy of the power spectrum in each local neighborhood. More specifically, to calculate the feature value at pixel (x, y) in an image, a 16×16 window is taken centered at the pixel, the Fourier transform of the window is calculated and L_{74} is calculated for all values of u and v. The obtained result is then saved at (x, y).

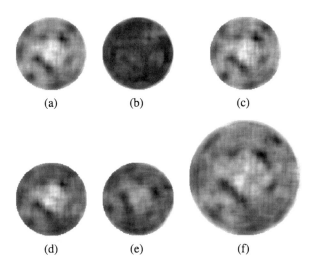

Fig. 4.33 (a)–(f) Local frequency-domain entropy (L_{75}) feature images, producing invariance measures BI = 0.87, NI = 0.92, II = 0.84, RI = 0.95, SI = 0.96, and repeatability measures BR = 0.96, NR = 0.85, IR = 0.98, RR = 0.82, SR = 0.76

(a)   (b)   (c)

(d)   (e)   (f)

Entry $(8, 8)$ within a 16×16 window is considered the center of the window. This produced the feature images depicted in Fig. 4.32 when using the images in Fig. 4.1. Feature values have been mapped to $[0, 255]$ for viewing purposes. The same was repeated for feature L_{75} over all frequencies within each neighborhood and for the images in Fig. 4.1 to produce the feature images shown in Fig. 4.33.

Examining L_{74} feature images and the calculated invariance measures, we see that this feature is highly invariant under image rotation, scale, noise, and monotone intensity transformation, but it is sensitive to blurring. Examining the repeatability measures of this feature under various image changes, we see that they are relatively low under noise, rotation, and scaling of the image but are relatively high under blurring and intensity transformation. This implies that although blurring and intensity transformation change power spectrum values, many of the same peak locations are obtained before and after image blurring and monotone intensity transformation.

Repeatability measures are rather low under rotation and scale because fixed square windows in images rotated by 30° or scaled by 1.5 with respect to each other cannot contain the same pattern, resulting in different peaks in the power spectra of the images. Decreased repeatability under noise can be attributed to change in the locations of many high-frequency peaks. Similar results are obtained for the frequency domain entropy feature L_{75} except that monotone intensity mapping affects the local frequency-domain feature more than the local power-spectrum feature.

4.4.4 Wavelet Transform Coefficients

Consider a set of 1-D real orthonormal bases, created by translating and scaling mother wavelet $\psi(x)$:

$$\psi_{i,n}(x) = 2^{-\frac{i}{2}} \psi\left(2^{-i}x - n\right). \tag{4.145}$$

Then, a 1-D signal $g(x)$ can be defined in terms of the bases by

$$g(x) = \sum_{i,k} d_{i,k} \psi_{i,k}(x), \tag{4.146}$$

where $d_{i,k}$ are the wavelet transform coefficient. Conversely, if the signal and the orthonormal bases are known, the wavelet coefficients can be computed from

$$d_{i,k} = f(x) \diamond \psi_{i,k}(x), \tag{4.147}$$

where $\diamond$ implies correlation.

The mother signal $\psi(x)$ is obtained by first determining a scaling function $\phi(x)$ that satisfies [43]

$$\phi(x) = \sqrt{2} \sum_{k} h(k)\phi(2x - k), \tag{4.148}$$

where coefficients $h(k)$ are specified in such a way that the wavelet bases are unique and orthonormal [186]. Then, the wavelet kernel is defined by

$$\psi(x) = \sqrt{2} \sum_{k} g(k)\phi(2x - k), \tag{4.149}$$

where

$$g(k) = (-1)^k h(1 - k). \tag{4.150}$$

Various sets of coefficients $h(k)$ satisfying these conditions have been found and reported [44, 122].

B-spline bases provide one example of scaling functions. A B-spline function of order d can be constructed from scaled and translated versions of itself [32]:

$$\phi(x) = \sum_{k=0}^{d} 2^{1-d} \binom{d}{k} B^d(2x - k). \tag{4.151}$$

Note that since a B-spline function of order $d > 1$ can be obtained from B-spline functions of order $d - 1$,

$$B_k^d(x) = \frac{x - x_k}{x_{k+d} - x_k} B_k^{d-1}(x) + \frac{x_{k+d+1} - x}{x_{k+d+1} - x_{k+1}} B_{k+1}^{d-1}(x), \tag{4.152}$$

the B-spline scaling functions can be recursively defined in terms of a scaling function of order 1,

$$\phi_k^1(x) = \begin{cases} 1 & \text{if } x_k \leq x < x_{k+1}, \\ 0 & \text{otherwise}, \end{cases} \tag{4.153}$$

where x_k are the knots of the B-spline and for uniform B-spline they are integers, and the first and last knots are repeated d times: $(x_0, x_1, \ldots, x_{2k+2d-2}) = 2^{-k}(0, \ldots, 0, 1, 2, \ldots, 2^k - 1, 2^k, \ldots, 2^k)$. The B-spline scaling functions of order 2 are shown in Fig. 4.34. Note that the sum of the scaling functions at any x is equal to 1.

Considering a separable multiresolution approximation where 2-D scaling function $\phi(x, y)$ is defined in terms of two 1-D scaling functions: $\phi(x, y) = \phi(x)\phi(y)$,

Fig. 4.34 Five B-spline scaling functions of order 2. Each scaling function is drawn with a different line width

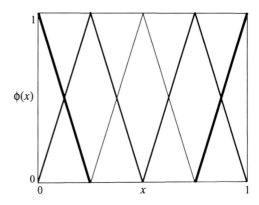

and assuming $\psi(x)$ and $\psi(y)$ are wavelets associated with $\phi(x)$ and $\phi(y)$, respectively, and letting

$$\phi_{i,k}(x) = 2^{-\frac{i}{2}}\phi(2^{-i}x - k), \tag{4.154}$$

and

$$\psi_{i,k}(x) = 2^{\frac{i}{2}}\psi(2^{-i}x - k), \tag{4.155}$$

three 2-D wavelets can be defined as follows [26, 121]:

$$\psi_{i,k,l}^1(x, y) = \phi_{i,k}(x)\psi_{i,l}(y), \tag{4.156}$$

$$\psi_{i,k,l}^2(x, y) = \psi_{i,k}(x)\phi_{i,l}(y), \tag{4.157}$$

$$\psi_{i,k,l}^3(x, y) = \psi_{i,k}(x)\psi_{i,l}(y). \tag{4.158}$$

An orthonormal basis set in 2-D, $\{\phi_{i,k,l}(x, y)\}$, can be constructed from various translation parameters k and l and scale parameter i:

$$\phi_{i,k,l}(x, y) = 2^{-i}\phi(2^{-i}x - k)\phi(2^{-i}y - l). \tag{4.159}$$

Knowing the wavelet basis set at scale i, the wavelet coefficients of 2-D image $f(x, y)$ at scale i can be obtained from [122]:

$$L_{76}(i, m, k, l) = d_i^m[k, l] = f \diamond \psi_{i,k,l}^m, \tag{4.160}$$

where $\diamond$ denotes correlation, $m = 1, 2, 3$, and $\psi_{i,k,l}^1(x, y)$, $\psi_{i,k,l}^2(x, y)$, and $\psi_{i,k,l}^3(x, y)$ are given in (4.156)–(4.158).

The wavelet coefficients at level or band i show image information at scale 2^i. Use of wavelets makes it possible to separate information at different scales from each other and use them to describe an image. Oren et al. [141] use Haar wavelet coefficients calculated at scales $2^i = 16$ and $2^i = 32$ in subimages of size 128×64

to detect pedestrians. The three 2-D Haar wavelets are:

$$
\begin{array}{|c|c|}\hline -1 & 1 \\\hline -1 & 1 \\\hline\end{array}, \quad
\begin{array}{|c|c|}\hline -1 & -1 \\\hline 1 & 1 \\\hline\end{array}, \quad
\begin{array}{|c|c|}\hline 1 & -1 \\\hline -1 & 1 \\\hline\end{array}.
\tag{4.161}
$$

Papageorgiou et al. [143] follow a similar approach to detect faces in an image.

Discrete wavelet transform coefficients are generally dependent on scene lighting, although Garcia et al. [63] show that they are relatively unaffected by small illumination changes. Shift-invariant features have been extracted from images using complex wavelets [94, 173]. To represent an object independent of its orientation and scale, Shokoufandeh et al. [180] made the wavelet coefficients the nodes of a tree so that an object present in two images creates similar branches in the trees, enabling comparison via graph-matching. To produce rotation-invariant wavelets, polar mapping [154, 167] has been proposed, and to produce rotation- and scale-invariant wavelets, log-polar mapping [104] has been used. Le Moigne et al. [103] explored use of wavelet features in image registration.

To verify the presence of objects of a given size, wavelet coefficients at the appropriate scale or subband should be examined. If wavelet coefficients at a subband are sufficiently high, it is an indication that objects (intensity variations) at that scale are present in the image. A threshold value may be used to count the coefficients that are sufficiently high. Assuming n_l is the number of coefficients that are higher than a prespecified threshold value at subband l, then

$$
L_{77}(l) = \frac{n_l}{n_{\max}}
\tag{4.162}
$$

may be used as a feature, where $n_{\max}$ is the number of pixels in the subband. This feature, which is relatively invariant to image rotation, can be used to characterize an image for the presence of objects of a given size [109].

For an image representation to be efficient, it should be local, directional, and multiresolution [47]. Wavelets are local and multiresolution but capture only limited directional information. To overcome this weakness, contourlet transform has been proposed [47]. After applying a multiscale transform, a local directional transform is performed to gather nearby basis functions at the same scale into linear structures, producing elongated supports. By repeating the process at multiresolution, supports at various scales, directions, and aspect ratios are formed to create contourlet filter banks. It is shown that contourlet representation can optimally reproduce piecewise boundaries that are continuous up to second derivatives. The contourlet transform proposed by Do and Vetterli [47] is not shift-invariant due to its filter bank structure. A shift-invariant version of the contourlet transform has been proposed by Cunha et al. [40].

The image transforms discussed above capture global image information, except for the wavelet transform, which captures both local and global information depending on the wavelet coefficients used. With wavelet coefficients it is possible to tell the presence of an object of a given size at a particular location in an image. Transform coefficients are generally not translation, rotation, and scale invariant, although means to produce translation, rotation, and scale invariant features have been proposed [79, 94, 154, 158, 167].

4.5 Filter Responses

The transform coefficients described above (except for the wavelet transform coefficients) capture global information about spatial frequencies in an image. To capture local spatial frequencies in an image, filter responses may be used.

4.5.1 Steerable Filter Responses

It is convenient to synthesize a filter of a desired orientation from a linear combination of a number of basis filters. The process can then steer a filter to any orientation, making it possible to determine the response of an image to a filter of an arbitrary orientation [59]. The process also makes it possible to determine the filter direction that produces the maximum response at any image pixel.

Consider a 2-D Gaussian of standard deviation σ:

$$G(x, y, \sigma) = \frac{1}{2\pi\sigma^2} \exp\left\{-\frac{(x^2 + y^2)}{2\sigma^2}\right\} \tag{4.163}$$

and oriented filters representing the derivatives of the Gaussian in x ($0°$) and y ($90°$) directions:

$$G_1^{0°}(x, y, \sigma) = \frac{\partial}{\partial x} G(x, y, \sigma)$$

$$= -\frac{x}{2\pi\sigma^4} \exp\left\{-\frac{(x^2 + y^2)}{2\sigma^2}\right\}, \tag{4.164}$$

$$G_1^{90°}(x, y, \sigma) = \frac{\partial}{\partial y} G(x, y, \sigma)$$

$$= -\frac{y}{2\pi\sigma^4} \exp\left\{-\frac{(x^2 + y^2)}{2\sigma^2}\right\}, \tag{4.165}$$

then, the filter representing the first derivative of a 2-D Gaussian at orientation θ can be obtained from

$$G_1^\theta(x, y, \sigma) = G_1^{0°}(x, y, \sigma)\cos\theta + G_1^{90°}(x, y, \sigma)\sin\theta. \tag{4.166}$$

This implies that the response of an image $f(x, y)$ to filter $G_1^\theta(\sigma)$ at (x, y) can be obtained by a weighted sum of the responses of the image to filters $G_1^{0°}(\sigma)$ and $G_1^{90°}(\sigma)$ at (x, y), with the weights being $\cos\theta$ and $\sin\theta$. That is,

$$L_{78}(x, y, \sigma, \theta) = f(x, y) \oplus G_1^\theta(x, y, \sigma)$$

$$= f(x, y) \oplus G_1^{0°}(x, y, \sigma)\cos\theta$$

$$+ f(x, y) \oplus G_1^{90°}(x, y, \sigma)\sin\theta$$

$$= A(x, y)\cos\theta + B(x, y)\sin\theta, \tag{4.167}$$

where $\oplus$ implies convolution. $A(x, y)$ and $B(x, y)$ represent the responses of image $f(x, y)$ to $G_1^{0°}$ and $G_1^{90°}$ at (x, y). The orientation producing the highest response can be determined by finding the derivative of $A(x, y)\cos\theta + B(x, y)\sin\theta$ with respect to θ, setting it to zero, and solving for θ. This results in $\theta = \tan^{-1}[B(x, y)/A(x, y)]$, which is the gradient direction at (x, y). Substituting this θ into (4.167), we obtain the gradient magnitude at (x, y) in direction θ.

Freeman and Adelson [59] created a filter of an arbitrary orientation θ by a weighted sum of a number of basis filters of appropriately oriented filters:

$$g^{\theta}(x, y) = \sum_{j=1}^{n} k_j(\theta)g^{\theta_j}(x, y), \tag{4.168}$$

where $g^{\theta_j}(x, y)$ is the jth basis filter with orientation θ_j, and $k_j(\theta)$ is the associating weight. For instance, the filter representing the second derivative of Gaussian calculated in orientation θ, $G_2^{\theta}(\sigma)$, is obtained from

$$G_2^{\theta}(x, y, \sigma) = \sum_{j=1}^{3} k_j(\theta)G_2^{\theta_j}(x, y, \sigma), \tag{4.169}$$

where $\theta_1 = 0, \theta_2 = 60°, \theta_3 = 120°$, $k_j(\theta) = [1 + 2\cos(2\theta - 2\theta_j)]/3$, and $G_2^{0°}(x, y, \sigma) = \sigma^{-2}(x^2\sigma^{-2} - 1)G(x, y, \sigma)$. $G_2^{60°}(x, y, \sigma)$ and $G_2^{120°}(x, y, \sigma)$ are obtained by rotating $G_2^{0°}$ by 60° and 120°, respectively. Therefore, the response of image $f(x, y)$ to a second derivative of a 2-D Gaussian at an arbitrary orientation θ can be computed from

$$L_{79}(x, y, \sigma, \theta) = f \oplus G_2^{\theta}(x, y, \sigma). \tag{4.170}$$

Note that L_{79} is a function of θ and, therefore, the orientation maximizing/minimizing this feature at each pixel can be determined by finding the derivative of L_{79} with respect to θ, setting it to 0, and solving the obtained equation for θ. The calculated θ will represent the maximum when G_1^{θ} is positive and it will represent the minimum when G_1^{θ} is negative. For image edges, since the second derivative image intensity at the edge points will be zero, to determine whether an edge is present at a pixel or not, one can solve $L_{79}(x, y, \sigma, \theta) = 0$ for θ. If a solution can be obtained, edge (x, y) will have direction θ.

Carneiro and Jepson [23, 24] proposed complex-valued steerable filters and used the phase of the complex responses as features. Assuming $G_2^{\theta}(x, y, \sigma)$ represents the second derivative of a 2-D Gaussian in θ direction and $H_2^{\theta}(x, y, \sigma)$ is the Hilbert transform of $G_2^{\theta}(x, y, \sigma)$, and also letting

$$g(x, y, \sigma, \theta) = G_2^{\theta}(x, y, \sigma) \oplus f(x, y), \tag{4.171}$$

$$h(x, y, \sigma, \theta) = H_2^{\theta}(x, y, \sigma) \oplus f(x, y), \tag{4.172}$$

then $g(x, y, \sigma, \theta) + jh(x, y, \sigma, \theta)$ represents a complex response at (x, y). This response can be written in polar form as

$$g(x, y, \sigma, \theta) + ih(x, y, \sigma, \theta) = \rho(x, y, \sigma, \theta)e^{i\phi(x, y, \sigma, \theta)}. \tag{4.173}$$

$\rho(x, y, \sigma, \theta)$ represents the amplitude and

$$L_{80}(x, y, \sigma, \theta) = \phi(x, y, \sigma, \theta) \tag{4.174}$$

Fig. 4.35 (**a**)–(**f**) Gradient magnitude (L_{78}) feature images obtained for the images in Fig. 4.1 when letting $\sigma = 2$ pixels. Invariance measures of feature images (**b**)–(**f**) with respect to feature image (**a**) are BI $= 0.97$, NI $= 0.98$, II $= 0.96$, RI $= 0.97$, SI $= 0.94$, and the corresponding repeatability measures are BR $= 0.91$, NR $= 0.77$, IR $= 0.92$, RR $= 0.80$, SR $= 0.85$

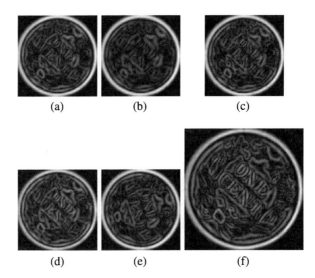

(a)   (b)   (c)

(d)   (e)   (f)

represents the phase at (x, y). It has been shown that the phase feature is less sensitive to noise than the amplitude feature and, thus, provides a more robust feature than the amplitude in recognition [23, 24].

To capture scale as well as orientation information in an image Coggins and Jain [35] used responses of the image to a combination of ring-shaped and wedge-shaped filters. The ring-shaped filters capture scale while the wedge-shaped filters capture orientation information about intensity variations in an image.

As an example of a steerable filter, the feature image obtained from L_{78} (the gradient magnitude in the gradient direction when $\sigma = 2$) is calculated and shown in Fig. 4.35. This is basically the gradient magnitude at each pixel after smoothing with a Gaussian of standard deviation 2 pixels. This feature is highly invariant under noise, monotone intensity transformation, and image rotation and scaling. The repeatability of this feature is also relatively high. Although highly invariant under noise, the repeatability of the feature degrades under noise as noise displaces some of the gradient peaks. The elongated region boundaries contribute to this degradation as a gradient ridge is formed along a boundary and the peaks along a ridge can displace due to noise. Interestingly, image scaling has preserved the locations of many of the peaks, producing relatively high repeatability measures.

4.5.2 Gabor Filter Responses

A Gabor filter is a complex sinusoidal function modulated by a Gaussian [21]:

$$h(x, y) = G(x', y') \exp\left[2\pi j (Ux + Vy)\right], \tag{4.175}$$

where

$$G(x, y) = \left(\frac{1}{2\pi\lambda\sigma^2}\right)\exp\left[-\frac{(x/\lambda)^2 + y^2}{2\sigma^2}\right] \tag{4.176}$$

is a 2-D Gaussian of standard deviation σ and aspect ratio λ and

$$x' = x\cos\phi + y\sin\phi, \tag{4.177}$$

$$y' = -x\sin\phi + y\cos\phi \tag{4.178}$$

represent rotation of the Gaussian coordinate system about the origin by ϕ. When $\lambda = 1$, the Gaussian is circularly symmetric, so $x' = x$ and $y' = y$.

The Fourier transform of $h(x, y)$ is

$$H(u, v) = \exp\{-2\pi^2\sigma^2[(u' - U')^2\lambda^2 + (v' - V')^2]\}, \tag{4.179}$$

where

$$u' = u\cos\phi + v\sin\phi, \tag{4.180}$$

$$v' = -u\sin\phi + v\cos\phi, \tag{4.181}$$

and (U', V') is rotation of (U, V) by ϕ. $H(u, v)$ is a bandpass Gaussian with the minor axis having angle ϕ with the u-axis, aspect ratio $1/\lambda$, radial frequency $F = \sqrt{U^2 + V^2}$ octave, and orientation $\theta = \tan^{-1}(V/U)$ radians.

If the modulating Gaussian has the same orientation as the complex sinusoidal grating, then $\theta = \phi$ and

$$h(x, y) = G(x', y')\exp(2\pi j F x') \tag{4.182}$$

has spatial frequency response

$$H(u, v) = \exp\{-2\pi^2\sigma^2[(u' - F)^2\lambda^2 + (v')^2]\}. \tag{4.183}$$

Gabor filter $h(x, y)$ has real and imaginary parts:

$$h_c(x, y) = G(x', y')\cos(2\pi F x'), \tag{4.184}$$

$$h_s(x, y) = G(x', y')\sin(2\pi F x'). \tag{4.185}$$

Filtering image $f(x, y)$ with $h(x, y)$ produces complex image $k(x, y) = k_c(x, y) + jk_s(x, y)$ with real and imaginary parts obtained from:

$$\begin{aligned} k_c(x, y) = \mathrm{Re}[k(x, y)] &= h_c(x, y) \oplus f(x, y) \\ &= [G(x', y') \oplus f(x, y)]\cos(2\pi F x'), \end{aligned} \tag{4.186}$$

$$\begin{aligned} k_s(x, y) = \mathrm{Im}[k(x, y)] &= h_s(x, y) \oplus f(x, y) \\ &= [G(x', y') \oplus f(x, y)]\sin(2\pi F x'). \end{aligned} \tag{4.187}$$

The amplitude $A(x, y)$ and phase $\psi(x, y)$ of the complex response $k(x, y)$ of an image with a Gabor filter of scale σ and orientation θ can be calculated at each pixel (x, y) and used as features to characterize the spatial frequency characteristic of the neighborhood of (x, y):

$$L_{81}(x, y, \sigma, \theta) = A(x, y) = \sqrt{k_c^2(x, y) + k_s^2(x, y)}, \quad (4.188)$$

$$L_{82}(x, y, \sigma, \theta) = \psi(x, y) = \tan^{-1}\left(\frac{k_s(x, y)}{k_c(x, y)}\right). \quad (4.189)$$

Serre et al. [174] used real sinusoids modulated by Gaussian:

$$G(x, y, \sigma, \theta, \gamma) = \exp\left(-\frac{X^2 + Y^2}{2\sigma^2}\right)\cos\left(\frac{2\pi X}{\gamma}\right) \quad (4.190)$$

to extract image features, where θ shows filter orientation, σ shows filter scale, $X = x\cos\theta + y\sin\theta$, $Y = -x\sin\theta + y\cos\theta$, and γ shows wavelength. The response of an image to such a filter is

$$L_{83}(x, y, \sigma, \theta, \gamma) = G(x, y, \sigma, \theta, \gamma) \oplus f(x, y), \quad (4.191)$$

which can be used to characterize the scale, orientation, and wavelength of the image in the neighborhood of (x, y). Serre et al. [174] found responses of the neighborhood of interest to such filters at 4 orientations, 16 scales, and 16 wavelengths, and used the maximum response at a pixel as the feature value at the pixel.

Gabor filters have Gaussian transfer functions in the linear frequency scale. Filters that have Gaussian transfer functions in the logarithmic frequency scale are known as Log-Gabor filters [54, 215]. A Log-Gabor filter in the polar coordinate system $G(r, \theta)$ is the product of a radial component $G(r)$ and an angular component $G(\theta)$, where the radial component is defined by

$$G(r) = \exp\left\{-\frac{[\log(r/f_0)]^2}{2\sigma_r^2}\right\} \quad (4.192)$$

and the angular component is defined by

$$G(\theta) = \exp\left\{-\frac{(\theta - \theta_0)^2}{2\sigma_\theta^2}\right\}. \quad (4.193)$$

f_0 is the center frequency, θ_0 is the orientation angle, σ_r is the scale bandwidth and σ_θ is the angular bandwidth. Therefore,

$$L_{84}(r, \theta) = f(r, \theta) \oplus G(r) \oplus G(\theta) \quad (4.194)$$

shows response of the Log-Gabor filter with center frequency f_0, orientation angle θ_0, scale bandwidth σ_r, and angular bandwidth σ_θ of image f with polar coordinates (r, θ).

A class of self-similar Gabor filters, known as Gabor wavelets, was designed by scaling and rotating a single Gabor filter $h(x, y)$ known as the mother filter [123]:

$$h_{mn}(x, y) = a^{-m}h(x', y'), \quad (4.195)$$

where $a > 1$,

$$x' = a^{-m}(x\cos\theta + y\sin\theta), \quad (4.196)$$

$$y' = a^{-m}(-x\sin\theta + y\cos\theta), \quad (4.197)$$

$\theta = n\pi/k$, k is the desired number of orientations, and m and n are indices of the filters. Parameters a and k are chosen in such way that the half-peak magnitude support of filter responses in the transform domain touch each other [82, 83, 123].

A bank of filters used in this manner produces an $m \times n$ matrix of features. Kyrki et al. [98] showed that feature matrices calculated at corresponding points in two images with rotational and scaling differences will have translational differences, providing an easy means of comparing local image neighborhoods irrespective of their orientations and scales. Dunn and Higgins [49] described the design of optimal Gabor filters for a known texture in a recognition task. The process finds the center frequency and bandwidth of each filter through a training process to produce minimum classification error.

Image features captured by Gabor filters of various scales and orientations characterize intensity variations in an image locally and have been used in texture discrimination [21, 76, 81, 142, 200], as well as in image matching [124] and object recognition [165, 231]. The 1-D version of the Gabor filter $h(x) = G(x)\exp(2\pi jUx)$ was introduced by Gabor [61] and shown to minimize combined uncertainty in the spatial and frequency domain. Gabor filter was extended to 2-D by Daugman [45], showing that in 2-D also the filter provides optimal localization in space and frequency. This property makes it possible to design filters that are spatially well localized and can provide narrow frequency and orientation responses. A comparative study carried out by Randen and Husøy [156] finds that optimal joint resolution in the spatial and frequency domain does not necessarily imply optimal recognition performance. The study finds that quadrature mirror filters [155] with sharper frequency responses compared to Gabor filters, but wider impulse responses have a superior discrimination power than Gabor filters.

Gabor filters have a number of nice properties. First, they are smooth and infinitely differentiable. Second, their modulus transforms are monomodal and have no side lobes in the frequency domain. Third, they are optimally joint-localized in the space and frequency domains. In spite of these nice properties, Gabor filters have a number of drawbacks. For example, it is not possible to build complete orthogonal bases and often non-orthogonal overlapping bases are used, involving redundancies. Gabor filters are bandpass filters, and as such they are inadequate in covering the lowest and the highest frequencies in an image. Moreover, it is difficult to cover the mid-frequencies uniformly. To overcome some of these drawbacks, Fischer et al. [55] proposed an overcomplete multiresolution scheme resembling the receptive field of simple cortical cells, using log-polar coordinates in the Fourier domain, uniformly covering the frequency domain.

4.5.3 Mask Correlation Responses

Masks can be designed to capture desired spatial frequencies in an image. Cohen et al. [36] used the following 2×2 orthogonal masks to capture low as well as high frequencies horizontally, vertically, and diagonally.

$$\mathbf{H}_1 = \begin{bmatrix} 1 & 1 \\ 1 & 1 \end{bmatrix}, \qquad \mathbf{H}_2 = \begin{bmatrix} 1 & 1 \\ -1 & -1 \end{bmatrix},$$

$$\mathbf{H}_3 = \begin{bmatrix} 1 & -1 \\ 1 & -1 \end{bmatrix}, \qquad \mathbf{H}_4 = \begin{bmatrix} 1 & -1 \\ -1 & 1 \end{bmatrix}. \tag{4.198}$$

Assuming $f(x, y)$ is an image normalized to have mean of 0 and letting $f^{(d)}(x, y)$ represent the image at resolution d, the following features for $i = 1, \ldots, 4$ capture low and high frequency characteristics at location (x, y) in an image.

$$L_{85}(x, y, d, i) = \mathbf{H}_i \oplus f^{(d)}(x, y), \quad i = 1, \ldots, 4. \tag{4.199}$$

By finding the responses of these masks to different resolutions of an image, local frequency characteristics of the image can be determined.

Laws [99] created 3×3, 5×5, and 7×7 masks and used responses of the masks within a 15×15 neighborhood to characterize multi-scale frequency characteristics of the neighborhood. For instance, to create 5×5 masks, the following 1-D masks

$$\begin{aligned}
B_0 &= (\ 1 \quad 4\ 6 \quad 4 \quad 1), \\
B_1 &= (-1\ -2\ 0 \quad 2 \quad 1), \\
B_2 &= (-1 \quad 0\ 2 \quad 0 -1), \\
B_3 &= (-1 \quad 2\ 0 -2 \quad 1), \\
B_4 &= (\ 1\ -4\ 6\ -4 \quad 1)
\end{aligned} \tag{4.200}$$

were used. By convolving any one of the above masks taken horizontally with any one of the masks taken vertically, a 5×5 mask will be obtained. Overall, 25 such 2-D masks will be obtained from all combinations. Created masks have mean of 0 except for mask $B_{00} = B_0^t \oplus B_0$, which has a nonzero mean. The B_{00} convolution result is used to normalize convolution results by other 5×5 masks and reduce the effect of image contrast on the calculated features. Therefore, denoting $B_i^t \oplus B_j$ by B_{ij} for $i, j = 0, \ldots, 4$, and letting

$$F_0 = f(x, y) \oplus B_{00}, \tag{4.201}$$

the following 24 features:

$$L_{86}(x, y, i, j) = \left[f(x, y) \oplus B_{ij} \right] / F_0, \tag{4.202}$$

where $i, j = 0, \ldots, 4$, and $i + j > 0$, can be used to characterize spatial frequencies in the 5×5 neighborhood centered at (x, y). Similar features can be calculated from 3×3 and 7×7 masks.

Examples of mask correlation feature images are given in Figs. 4.36, 4.37, 4.38 using Laws masks B_{11}, B_{22}, and B_{33} in L_{86}. As can be observed from the feature images, these masks capture details at different scales in an image. Invariance and repeatability measures of these features for lower-order masks are generally higher than those for higher-order masks.

Fig. 4.36 (**a**)–(**f**) Laws L_{86} feature images calculated by letting $B_{ij} = B_{11}$ and using the images in Fig. 4.1. The invariance measures of feature images (**b**)–(**f**) when computed with respect to feature image (**a**) are BI $= 0.86$, NI $= 0.96$, II $= 0.99$, RI $= 0.90$, SI $= 0.96$, and the corresponding repeatability measures are BR $= 0.93$, NR $= 0.83$, IR $= 0.95$, RR $= 0.62$, SR $= 0.95$

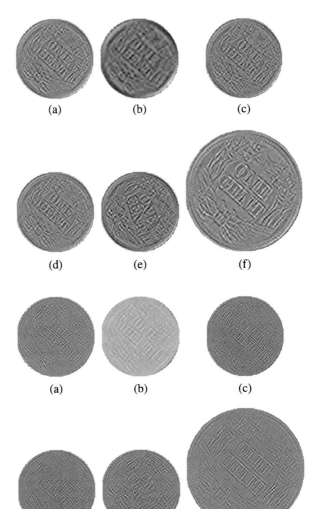

Fig. 4.37 (**a**)–(**f**) Laws L_{86} feature images when $B_{ij} = B_{22}$, producing invariance measures BI $= 0.75$, NI $= 0.95$, II $= 0.98$, RI $= 0.92$, SI $= 0.96$, and repeatability measures BR $= 0.93$, NR $= 0.89$, IR $= 0.95$, RR $= 0.81$, SR $= 0.93$

To emphasize center-symmetric patterns, Harwood et al. [75] used the following 3×3 mask.

g_3	g_2	g_4
g_1		g'_1
g'_4	g'_2	g'_3

g_i and g'_i denote opposing intensities with respect to the center pixel (x, y). Then, the covariance measure

$$L_{87}(x, y) = \frac{\frac{1}{4}\sum_{i=1}^{4}(g_i - \mu)(g'_i - \mu)}{VAR}, \tag{4.203}$$

Fig. 4.38 (a)–(f) Laws L_{86} feature images calculated by letting $B_{ij} = B_{33}$, resulting in invariance measures BI $= 0.93$, NI $= 0.94$, II $= 0.98$, RI $= 0.92$, SI $= 0.91$, and repeatability measures BR $= 0.83$, NR $= 0.85$, IR $= 0.91$, RR $= 0.87$, SR $= 0.93$

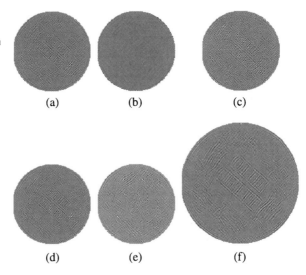

where

$$\mu = \frac{1}{8} \sum_{i=1}^{4} (g_i + g_i') \tag{4.204}$$

and

$$VAR = \frac{1}{8} \sum_{i=1}^{4} (g_i^2 + g_i'^2) - \mu^2 \tag{4.205}$$

are rotation invariant and produce a higher response in a more symmetric neighborhood.

The symmetry feature described in (4.203) is invariant to intensity scaling due to normalization by VAR. By using the rank-order of the intensities rather than the raw intensities, a symmetry feature is obtained that is invariant to monotone changes in intensities also [75].

Johansson et al. [87] used twenty 5×5 masks that represented different types of corners and by finding the correlation responses of the masks with an image identified various corners in an image.

Rather than using fixed masks, Benke et al. [18] and You and Cohen [225] used masks that adapted to local patterns. Ojala et al. [138, 139] created an adaptable 3×3 mask at a pixel by thresholding intensities within the mask with the center intensity, obtaining a binary mask. Values within the mask were then multiplied by prespecified values based on their positions within the mask to encode local intensity patterns to numbers that could identify different patterns. For example, the pattern in the following 3×3 neighborhood is given value 98.

10	15	3
12	13	8
15	25	9
$\longrightarrow$
0	1	0
0		0
1	1	0
$\times$
1	2	4
8		16
32	64	128

$=$
0	2	0
0		0
32	64	0
$\longrightarrow$ 98.

The leftmost mask shows intensities in a 3×3 neighborhood. Intensity at the center of the mask, in this case 13, is used as the threshold value. Entries with values higher than or equal to 13 are set to 1 and those below 13 are set to 0 as shown in the binary mask. The rightmost mask contains prespecified values that when multiplied by the binary mask produces the values shown in the bottom mask. Sum of values in the bottom mask will be the response of the adaptive filter to the neighborhood. The sum, which varies between 0 and 255, identifies various intensity patterns in a 3×3 neighborhood. Note that the measure is invariant to image contrast due to the thresholding step.

4.6 Differential Features

Koenderink and van Doorn [96] have shown that certain filter operations are equivalent to partial derivatives of image intensities after smoothing. They also show that concatenation of such filter operations are equivalent to higher order derivatives of image intensities with more smoothing. Based on this finding, ter Haar Romeny et al. [194] derived a number of derivative-based invariants by concatenating Gaussian derivatives of different degrees. Letting $\bar{f}(x, y)$ represent a Gaussian filtered image and denoting the derivatives of the smoothed image in x and y directions by $\bar{f}_x(x, y)$ and $\bar{f}_y(x, y)$, respectively, and second derivatives by $\bar{f}_{xx}(x, y)$, $\bar{f}_{xy}(x, y)$, and $\bar{f}_{yy}(x, y)$, the following are rotationally invariant features [194]:

$$L_{88}(x, y) = \bar{f}(x, y), \tag{4.206}$$

$$L_{89}(x, y) = \left\{ \bar{f}_x^2(x, y) + \bar{f}_y^2(x, y) \right\}^{\frac{1}{2}}, \tag{4.207}$$

$$L_{90}(x, y) = \bar{f}_{xx}(x, y) + \bar{f}_{yy}(x, y), \tag{4.208}$$

$$L_{91}(x, y) = \left\{ 2\bar{f}_x(x, y) \bar{f}_y(x, y) \bar{f}_{xy}(x, y) \right. $$
$$\left. - \bar{f}_x^2(x, y) \bar{f}_{yy}(x, y) - \bar{f}_y^2(x, y) \bar{f}_{xx}(x, y) \right\}$$
$$\left/ \left\{ \bar{f}_x^2(x, y) + \bar{f}_y^2(x, y) \right\}^{3/2}, \right. \tag{4.209}$$

$$L_{92}(x, y) = \left\{ \bar{f}_x(x, y) \bar{f}_y(x, y) \left(\bar{f}_{yy}(x, y) \right. \right. $$
$$\left. - \bar{f}_{xx}(x, y) \right) + \bar{f}_{xy} \left\{ \bar{f}_x^2(x, y) - \bar{f}_y^2(x, y) \right\} \right\}$$
$$\left/ \left\{ \bar{f}_x^2(x, y) + \bar{f}_y^2(x, y) \right\}^{3/2}. \right. \tag{4.210}$$

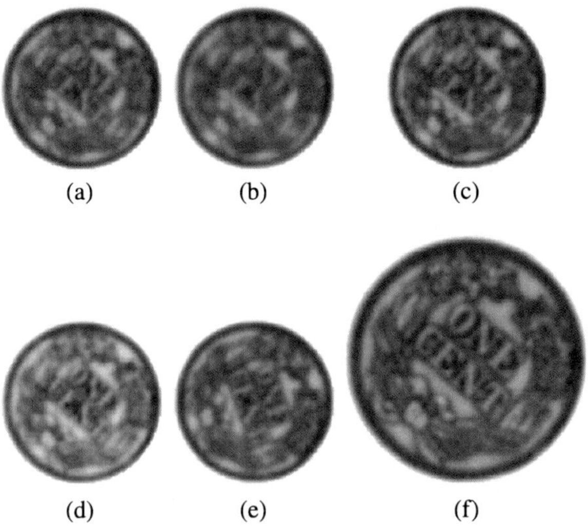

Fig. 4.39 (a)–(f) Smoothed intensity (L_{88}) feature images obtained from the images in Fig. 4.1 using a Gaussian smoother of standard deviation 2 pixels. The invariance measures of feature images (b)–(f) with respect to feature image (a) are BI = 0.98, NI = 0.98, II = 0.90, RI = 0.97, SI = 0.97, and the corresponding repeatability measures are BR = 0.84, NR = 0.65, IR = 0.81, RR = 0.73, SR = 0.82

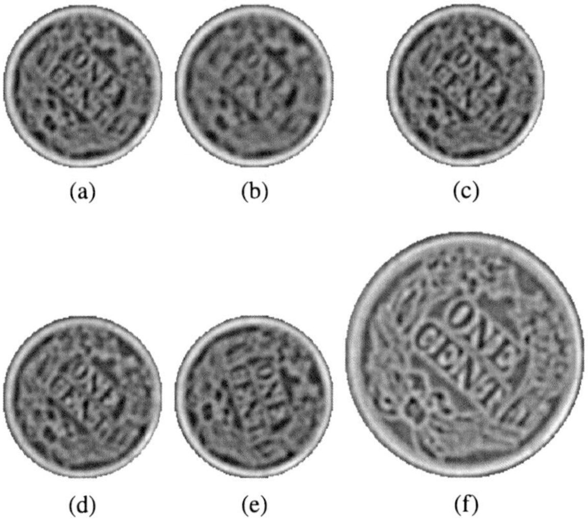

(a) (b) (c)

(d) (e) (f)

Fig. 4.40 (a)–(f) The LoG (L_{90}) feature images calculated using a Gaussian of standard deviation 2 pixels and the images in Fig. 4.1. Obtained invariance measures are BI = 0.97, NI = 0.97, II = 0.97, RI = 0.99, SI = 0.87, and the corresponding repeatability measures are BR = 0.87, NR = 0.72, IR = 0.87, RR = 0.89, SR = 0.85

(a) (b) (c)

(d) (e) (f)

Features L_{88}–L_{92} are called smoothed intensity, gradient magnitude, Laplacian, isophote curvature, and flowline curvature of smoothed intensity, respectively [194]. The intensity derivatives of various degrees after image smoothing are obtained by convolving Gaussian derivatives of various degrees with an image, combining both image smoothing and intensity derivative into one operation. By changing the standard deviation of the Gaussian, derivatives of an image at various resolutions are obtained, creating derivative-based features at different resolutions.

Examples of feature images obtained from the smoothed intensity (L_{88}) and the Laplacian (L_{90}) are shown in Figs. 4.39 and 4.40, respectively. The images in Fig. 4.39 were obtained by smoothing the images in Fig. 4.1 with a Gaussian of standard deviation 2 pixels. Note that the smoothed intensity feature (L_{88}) is not the same as the mean intensity feature (L_2). The mean intensity represents the global average of intensities in a window, while the smoothed intensity is a Gaussian weighted averaging of the intensities and so is a locally sensitive feature.

The images in Fig. 4.40 show the LoG of standard deviation 2 pixels of the images in Fig. 4.1. Although the repeatability measures of these features are relatively low, the invariance measures are quite high.

Differential features have been used to identify distinct or salient neighborhoods and to determine corresponding neighborhoods in two images of a scene [184, 209, 210].

Among the differential features, Laplacian of Gaussian (LoG) has received the most attention due to its ability to detect dark and bright blobs of different sizes in an image. When an image that contains varying sized blobs is convolved with a Laplacian of Gaussian (LoG), local maxima or minima will be obtained depending on whether the blob is darker or brighter than its surroundings. Local exterma of a LoG of an image identify the center points of the blobs.

Letting $\nabla^2 G_\sigma$ denote the LoG of standard deviation σ, the result of convolving $\nabla^2 G_\sigma$ with image $f(x, y)$ will be $g_\sigma(x, y) = \nabla^2 G_\sigma \oplus f(x, y)$. Quantity

$$L_{93}(x, y, \sigma) = g_\sigma(x, y) \tag{4.211}$$

can then be used as the feature value at (x, y) and local extrema of this feature, which identifies the centers of the blobs, can be used as control points in an image.

Blostein and Ahuja [19] have shown that the absolute response of a LoG at an extremum point increases as the diameter of the circular blob, D, approaches $2\sqrt{2}\sigma$. If the blob is not circular, D will be its effective diameter. This property makes it possible to determine the size of a blob by changing σ and finding the value of σ that produces the highest response. The location where $L_{93}(x, y, \sigma)$ becomes extremum as σ is varied, therefore, can be used as a control point with associating scale σ [115, 116].

The difference of Gaussians (DoG) has been used as an approximation to LoG for speed purposes. Since a circle under affine transformation converts to an ellipse, and the center of a circle under an affine transformation converts to the center of the ellipse, control points obtained for circular and elliptic blobs are invariant under affine transformation [64, 101, 102].

It should be mentioned that the LoG of an image produces extrema at non-circular and non-elliptic blobs also. However, extrema of non-circular and non-elliptic blobs are not guaranteed to remain invariant under affine transformation.

4.7 Spatial-Domain Features

Features can also be calculated from the raw image intensities. These include [65]:

1. *Deviation from mean*: The average absolute difference between the mean intensity and other intensities in an image

$$L_{94}(x, y) = \frac{1}{MN} \sum_{x=0}^{M-1} \sum_{y=0}^{N-1} |f(x, y) - \bar{f}|, \tag{4.212}$$

where $\bar{f}$ is the mean intensity.

2. *Absolute center contrast*: The average absolute difference between the center intensity and other intensities in an image

$$L_{95}(x, y) = \frac{1}{MN - 1} \sum_{x=0}^{M-1} \sum_{y=0}^{N-1} |f(x, y) - f_c|, \tag{4.213}$$

where f_c is the intensity at the center pixel in the image.

3. *Center contrast*: The average difference between the center pixel and other pixels

$$L_{96}(x, y) = \frac{1}{MN - 1} \sum_{x=0}^{M-1} \sum_{y=0}^{N-1} (f(x, y) - f_c). \tag{4.214}$$

4. *Average local contrast*: The average of absolute difference between intensities of adjacent pixels

$$L_{97}(x, y) = \frac{1}{MN} \sum_{x=0}^{M-1} \sum_{y=0}^{N-1} \frac{1}{n} \sum_{x',y'} |f(x, y) - f(x', y')|, \tag{4.215}$$

where (x', y') represents a pixel adjacent to (x, y) and n is the number of such pixels [65].

5. *Dominant intensity*: The dominant intensity in the image

$$L_{98} = i \quad \text{such that} \quad H(i) = \max_{k} \{H(k)\}, \tag{4.216}$$

where $H(k)$ is the number of pixels in the image with intensity k.

These features are typically calculated within small windows in an image and, thus, describe local spatial characteristics of the image. The features are rotation-invariant if circular neighborhoods are used in the calculations.

Examples of feature images obtained from features L_{94}–L_{98} using the images in Fig. 4.1 are given in Figs. 4.41, 4.42, 4.43, 4.44, 4.45. The invariance measures of these features are generally high, although their repeatability measures are low. There are exceptions though. For instance, the center contrast has a relatively high repeatability under noise and geometric transformation. Worst repeatability measures are obtained from the dominant intensity feature, since it remains unchanged with great variation in window position. The feature value at a window depends on a single intensity, ignoring other intensities in the window and producing the same (nonunique) feature in a wide area in an image, consequently producing poor repeatability measures.

Edges in an image also represent spatial features; however, edges appear at only a small number of pixels in an image. To assign a spatial feature value to all pixels in an edge image, the Euclidean distance of a pixel to the edge pixel closest to it can

Fig. 4.41 (**a**)–(**f**) Deviation
from mean (L_{94}) feature
images obtained using the
images in Fig. 4.1. The
invariance measures of
feature images (**b**)–(**f**) when
calculated against feature
image (**a**) are BI = 0.82,
NI = 0.94, II = 0.93,
RI = 0.93, SI = 0.93, and the
corresponding repeatability
measures are BR = 0.50,
NR = 0.59, IR = 0.71,
RR = 0.60, SR = 0.17

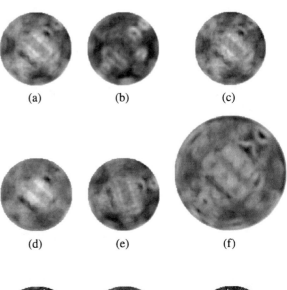

Fig. 4.42 (**a**)–(**f**) Absolute
center contrast (L_{95}) feature
images, producing invariance
measures BI = 0.81,
NI = 0.93, II = 0.94,
RI = 0.95, SI = 0.93, and
repeatability measures
BR = 0.87, NR = 0.75,
IR = 0.88, RR = 0.74,
SR = 0.70

be used. Distances of non-edge pixels to edge pixels in an image can be determined efficiently from the *distance transform* of the image [20, 42, 130]:

$$L_{99}(x, y) = DT(x, y), \tag{4.217}$$

where $DT(x, y)$ represents the Euclidean distance between pixel (x, y) and the edge pixel closest to it. Distances at edge pixels will be 0. Ridges in a distance transform image, which are also known as medial axis ridges, represent unique points that depend only on the edges in an image. A medial-axis point is a point that has two or more edge points at the same distance to it. A medial axis contour traces the center of a rolling circle that changes its radius to remain tangent to two or more edge

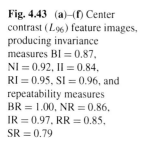

Fig. 4.43 (a)–(f) Center contrast (L_{96}) feature images, producing invariance measures BI = 0.87, NI = 0.92, II = 0.84, RI = 0.95, SI = 0.96, and repeatability measures BR = 1.00, NR = 0.86, IR = 0.97, RR = 0.85, SR = 0.79

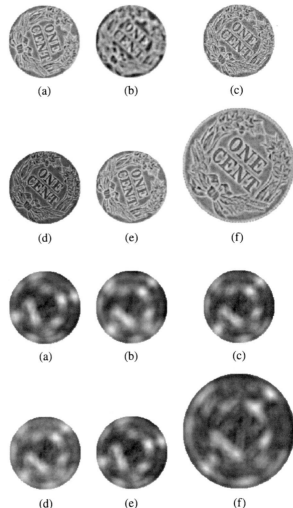

Fig. 4.44 (a)–(f) Average local contrast (L_{97}) feature images, resulting in invariance measures BI = 0.93, NI = 0.97, II = 0.95, RI = 0.98, SI = 0.94, and repeatability measures BR = 0.82, NR = 0.74, IR = 0.85, RR = 0.67, SR = 0.09

contours without ever intersecting an edge contour. Medial axis contours merge to create unique points in an image. A medial axis pixel

$$L_{100} = (x, y) \qquad (4.218)$$

that has more than two medial axis pixels adjacent to it can be used as a unique location and a unique feature.

Distance transform features are rotation-invariant and are useful when dealing with binary (edge) images. Such features are, however, very sensitive to noise. A single noisy edge pixel can drastically change the distance transform and so the medial axis structure of an edge image. A distance transform scheme that is defined in terms of a nonlinear function of distances has been proposed by Goshtasby [67], which is less sensitive to noise.

Fig. 4.45 (a)–(f) Dominant
intensity (L_{98}) feature
images, producing invariance
measures BI $= 0.86$,
NI $= 0.86$, II $= 0.81$,
RI $= 0.90$, SI $= 0.88$, and
repeatability measures
BR $= 0.09$, NR $= 0.08$,
IR $= 0.74$, RR $= 0.20$,
SR $= 0.20$

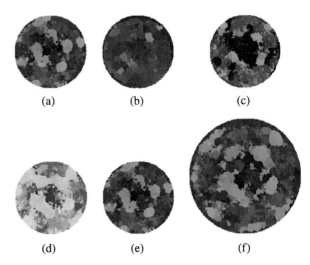

4.8 Color Features

Color images contain more information than gray scale images. Average color as
well as number of color edges have been used as features to recognize images [25].
Assuming red, green, and blue components of the color at pixel (x, y) are denoted by
$R(x, y)$, $G(x, y)$, and $B(x, y)$, average color at the pixel using a 3×3 neighborhood
will be

$$L_{101}(x, y) = \left(\bar{R}, \bar{G}, \bar{B} \right), \tag{4.219}$$

where

$$\bar{R} = \frac{1}{9} \sum_{k=-1}^{1} \sum_{l=-1}^{1} R(x + k, y + l), \tag{4.220}$$

$$\bar{G} = \frac{1}{9} \sum_{k=-1}^{1} \sum_{l=-1}^{1} G(x + k, y + l), \tag{4.221}$$

$$\bar{B} = \frac{1}{9} \sum_{k=-1}^{1} \sum_{l=-1}^{1} B(x + k, y + l). \tag{4.222}$$

Note that this feature is vector-valued and has three components.

To determine the number of color edges, first an image is separated into regions
of uniform color. To reduce the number of colors in an image, R, G, and B, values
are mapped from 0–255 to a smaller range, such as 0–15. Then the number of pixels
on the boundaries of regions of the same color are counted. Assuming k different
colors are available, and there are n_i pixels on the boundaries of regions of color i,
feature

$$L_{102} = \{n_i : i = 1, 2, \ldots, k\}, \tag{4.223}$$

which has k components, can be used to describe the color characteristics of the image. Note that since a boundary pixel is shared between two regions, it is counted twice.

Assuming $\mathbf{C}_1 = (R_1, G_1, B_1)$ and $\mathbf{C}_2 = (R_2, G_2, B_2)$ are average or representative colors of two regions,

$$L_{103}(\mathbf{C}_1, \mathbf{C}_2) = \{|R_2 - R_1|, |G_2 - G_1|, |B_2 - B_1|\} \tag{4.224}$$

measures the relative color of the regions. Cheng et al. [30] used relative color as the feature to distinguish malignant lesions from benign lesions in color skin images. Using the difference between the color of a lesion and the color of the normal skin surrounding the lesion, the lesion is classified into one of many categories and through a learning process malignant lesions are distinguished from the benign ones. Lu and Chang [118] used color distance $\|\mathbf{C}_1 - \mathbf{C}_2\|$ as the feature to discriminate images.

To segment microscopic bone marrow images, Zhang et al. [229] used the dominant color and the density of the dominant color. Dominant color represents the color with the most pixels in an image. Denoting the number of pixels of color $\mathbf{C}$ in an image or subimage by $N_{\mathbf{C}}$, dominant color is defined by

$$L_{104} = \mathbf{C}_i \quad \text{such that} \quad \max_k\{N_{\mathbf{C}_k}\} = N_{\mathbf{C}_i}. \tag{4.225}$$

Density of dominant color is the ratio of number of pixels with dominant color to the total number of pixels in the image. That is, if $\mathbf{C}_i$ denotes the dominant color and $N_{\mathbf{C}_i}$ is the number of pixels with the dominant color, then density of dominant color will be

$$L_{105} = \frac{N_{\mathbf{C}_i}}{\sum_k N_{\mathbf{C}_k}}. \tag{4.226}$$

To provide illumination invariant color features, Andreadis and Tsalides [7] converted colors in the RGB coordinate system to HSI (hue, saturation, intensity) colors, discarded the I component, which represents scene illumination, and used the H and S components that represent surface characteristics to segment an image. Given the RGB values at a pixel, and letting

$$\theta = \frac{0.5[(R - G) + (R - B)]}{[(R - G)^2 + (R - B)(G - B)]^{1/2}}, \tag{4.227}$$

the hue at the pixel is computed from

$$L_{106} = H = \cos^{-1}(\theta) \tag{4.228}$$

when $G > B$. Otherwise, hue is calculated from

$$L_{106} = H = 360° - \cos^{-1}(\theta). \tag{4.229}$$

Saturation at the same pixel is calculated from

$$L_{107} = S = 1 - \frac{3\min(R, G, B)}{(R + G + B)}. \tag{4.230}$$

Salvador et al. [164] proposed the following illumination invariant color features for image recognition.

$$L_{108} = \tan^{-1}\left\{\frac{R}{\max(G, B)}\right\},$$ (4.231)

$$L_{109} = \tan^{-1}\left\{\frac{G}{\max(R, B)}\right\},$$ (4.232)

$$L_{110} = \tan^{-1}\left\{\frac{B}{\max(R, G)}\right\}.$$ (4.233)

One may also convert RGB color coordinates to Lab color coordinates [92], discard the L component, which represents luminance, and use a and b, which represent chroma, as illumination-invariant features to recognize/match images.

Heo et al. [77] considered each component of the color at a pixel a product of (1) brightness ρ, which is a function of the angle between the direction of light and the surface normal, (2) a global scale factor s, which depends on quantization step in image acquisition, and (3) power γ of actual color at the pixel, which depends on the camera. For example, the red component of color at a pixels is defined by $\rho s R^{\gamma}$. If instead of colors, the logarithm of colors is used, the red component will be

$$R' = \log \rho + \log s + \gamma \log R.$$ (4.234)

$\log \rho$, which is a function of surface normal of the scene point being imaged can be removed from R' by subtracting the average of the three transformed color components from it. Therefore, if

$$I' = \frac{R' + G' + B'}{3}$$ (4.235)

is the average of the three color components, then

$$R'' = R' - I' = \alpha + \beta \log R,$$ (4.236)

will be a linear function of the logarithm of the actual color of the point. Representing colors in this manners makes matching of patches in different images by cross-correlation independent of the surface normal and differences in camera parameters capturing the images [77].

4.9 Fractal Dimension

Fractal dimension highly correlates with human perception of roughness [149] and can be used to characterize image details. Different methods for estimating the fractal dimension of an image have been proposed [183].

Consider an object that is of unit size and suppose reducing the size of the object by $1/\varepsilon$ in each spatial dimension. Then, if $N(\varepsilon)$ of the scaled-down objects perfectly fit inside the original object, the dimension D of the fractal structure will be

$$L_{111} = D = \lim_{\varepsilon \to 0} \frac{\log N_{\varepsilon}}{\log \frac{1}{\varepsilon}},$$ (4.237)

which is also known as the Hausdorff-Besicovitch dimension [183]. While the definition of fractal dimension via the notion of self-similarity is clear, its computation using image data is less straightforward.

A popular method for estimating the fractal dimension is via box counting [27, 166]. Consider an $M \times M$ image that is scaled down to an $L \times L$ image with $1 \leq L \leq M/2$. The scale ratio ε is, therefore, L/M. Treating intensities as the third dimension (z) and partitioning the (x, y) image space into an $L \times L$ grid, fractal dimension can be estimated as follows. Assuming there are G intensities in the image and there is a block of size $L' = \lfloor L \times G/M \rfloor$ at each grid element, and assuming intensities in the ijth grid element fall between k and l, define

$$n_\varepsilon(i, j) = l - k + 1 \tag{4.238}$$

and calculate

$$N_\varepsilon = \sum_i \sum_j n_\varepsilon(i, j). \tag{4.239}$$

N_ε is obtained for different values of ε (different values of L) and fractal dimension D is estimated from the linear least-squares fit of $\log(N_\varepsilon)$ versus $\log(1/\varepsilon)$.

In a method developed by Peleg et al. [148], the area of the intensity surface is determined at various resolutions and the rate of decrease in surface area as resolution is decreased is used to calculate fractal dimension.

Fractal dimension has been calculated using the image power spectrum by treating intensities as a fractional Brownian function f and noting that the power spectral density P of function f is proportional to its radial frequency [149, 208]. That is,

$$P_f(u, v) \propto \frac{1}{\rho^\beta}, \tag{4.240}$$

where $\beta \geq 0$, $\rho = \sqrt{u^2 + v^2}$ is the radial frequency, and (u, v) are the 2-D frequency coordinates. The exponent β in the above equation relates to the fractal dimension by [168]:

$$f_{112} = D = 3.5 - \beta/2. \tag{4.241}$$

Estimation of the fractal dimension by the power spectrum involves: (1) computing the power spectrum of the image, (2) taking the power spectrum along various radial directions $\theta = \tan^{-1}(v/u)$, (3) determining exponent β of the power-law curve that best fits each radial power spectrum, (4) finding average of β over various θ, and (5) estimating fractal dimension D from (4.241). Note that the fractal dimension of an image estimated in this manner is a rotation-invariant feature if β is estimated radially at a sufficiently large number of directions. Lundahl et al. [119] showed that a fractal dimension determined in this manner involves errors due to the discrete use of power spectrum rather than the continuous power spectrum and proposed a maximum likelihood estimation of the fractal dimension.

Fractal dimension has been estimated through wavelet analysis also [126, 195, 219]. Variances of wavelet coefficients are found to follow a power law, from which the fractal dimension is computed. An estimated fractal dimension is found to depend on the choice of the wavelet orthonormal bases [56]. It is also found that a

Fig. 4.46 (**a**)–(**f**) Fractal (L_{111}) feature images obtained using the images in Fig. 4.1. The invariance measures of feature images (**b**)–(**f**) when computed in reference to feature image (**a**) are BI = 0.85, NI = 0.98, II = 0.95, RI = 0.98, SI = 0.91, and the corresponding repeatability measures are BR = 0.05, NR = 0.47, IR = 0.59, RR = 0.48, SR = 0.06

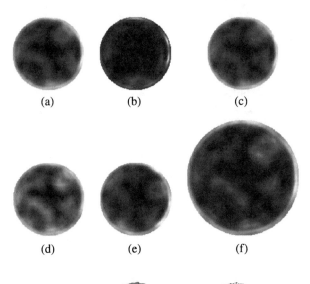

Fig. 4.47 (**a**) A 32 × 32 image displayed in intensity form. (**b**) The same image displayed as a 3-D surface by letting the intensities show the height values. (**c**) Triangulation of the height values. (**d**)–(**f**) The surfaces obtained at resolutions $\sigma = (1.5)^0$, $(1.5)^2$, and $(1.5)^4$. The surface points at the pixel locations are triangulated and the sum of the triangle areas is used as the area of the surface

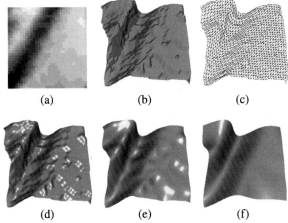

fractal dimension calculated from wavelet coefficients could overestimate the actual fractal dimension due to the local nature of the wavelet coefficients [56].

Examples of fractal feature images are given in Fig. 4.46 using the images in Fig. 4.1. Fractal dimension at a pixel is calculated using a circular window of radius 8 pixels centered at the pixel. To calculate the fractal dimension, intensities are considered height values, creating a surface from an array of intensities. The area of this surface changes as the resolution of the image is changed. The area of a surface is calculated by triangulating the height values, finding the area of each triangle, and finding the sum of the triangle areas over the image domain. This process is depicted in Fig. 4.47.

When the image is smoothed with a Gaussian of standard deviation σ_i, if the obtained surface area is S_{σ_i}, $x_i = \log(S_{\sigma_i})$ is calculated for $\sigma_i = (1.5)^{(i-1)}$ and $i = 0, \ldots, 7$. Therefore, $\sigma_0 = 1/1.5, \sigma_1 = 1, \sigma_2 = 1.5, \sigma_3 = (1.5)^2$, and so on. Letting

$y_i = \log(1/\sigma_i^2)$ for $i = 0, \ldots, 7$, and fitting a line to (x_i, y_i) for $i = 0, \ldots, 7$ by the least-squares method, the slope of the line will represent the fractal dimension of the image.

An estimated fractal dimension should be in the range 2–3. However, digital inaccuracies can cause the fractal dimension to become smaller than 2.0 or larger than 3.0 for some images. To minimize digital error, smoothing is performed with floating-point precision, and floating-point intensities are used in triangulating and computing the surface area. Moreover, rather than smoothing individual local neighborhoods (windows), the entire image is smoothed to eliminate boundary effects in smoothing. The fractal dimensions calculated in this manner for windows of radius 8 pixels using Fig. 4.1 are shown in Fig. 4.46. These figures show mapping of the fractal dimensions from [2, 3] to [0, 255] for viewing purposes.

The invariance property of fractal dimension is generally high, especially with respect to noise, intensity transformation, and rotation. Invariance property of fractal dimension is degraded by blurring and change in scale. The repeatability of fractal dimension is relatively low, especially under blurring and change in scale. Although fractal dimension cannot be used to compare images that have gone through resolution or scale changes, they can be used to segment an image with respect to local roughness by treating intensities in the image as height values.

Fractal dimension as a feature has been used in texture analysis. Chen et al. [29] used fractal dimension to segment ultrasound breast images, separating malignant from benign tissues; Chen et al. [28] used fractal dimension to segment CT liver images; and Lee et al. [105, 106] used fractal dimension to segment ultrasonic liver images. Wu et al. [222] experimentally demonstrate that fractal dimensions calculated at multiresolutions are able to segment liver images more accurately than features calculated from gray-level spatial dependence matrices (Sect. 4.1.2.1), gray-level run-length matrices (Sect. 4.1.2.2), and Fourier power spectrum (Sect. 4.4.3).

4.10   Information-Theoretic Features

Different neighborhoods in an image carry different information. The higher the information content in a neighborhood the less ambiguous it is. Information content in an image can be measured by entropy [175]:

$$L_{113} = -\sum_{i=0}^{255} P(i) \log_2 P(i), \qquad (4.242)$$

where $P(i)$ is the probability that if a pixel is randomly selected in the image it will have intensity i. The higher the entropy of an image, the more informative the image will be.

If the entropy calculated for a circular region of radius r is $E(r)$, the radius maximizing $E(r)$ is selected as the scale of the region. The calculated entropy can then be weighted by some measure of self-dissimilarity in scale-space and local

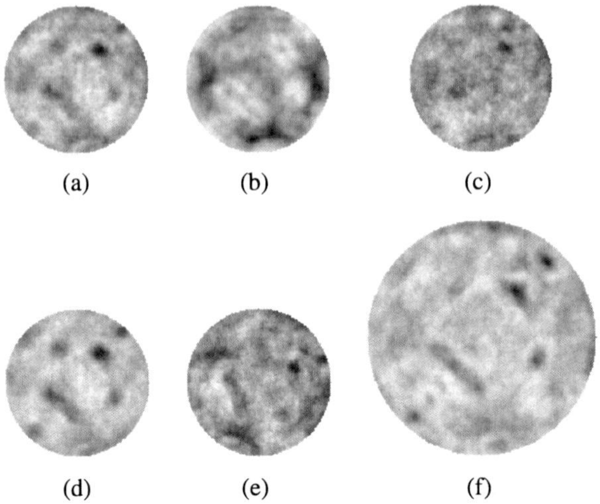

Fig. 4.48 (a)–(f) Local
entropy (L_{113}) feature images
obtained from the images in
Fig. 4.1. The invariance
measures of feature
images (b)–(f) when
computed with respect to
feature image (a) are
BI $= 0.82$, NI $= 0.89$,
II $= 0.97$, RI $= 0.88$,
SI $= 0.90$, and the
corresponding repeatability
measures are BR $= 0.25$,
NR $= 0.51$, IR $= 0.84$,
RR $= 0.46$, SR $= 0.32$

maxima of the weighted entropies can be chosen as salient points [89]. Fergus et al.
[53] selected a region of scale r centered at a salient point and by mapping it to a
region of a fix size, normalize the scales of all regions to the same, thereby providing
a means to compare regions of different scales to each other.

Saliency can also be measured by uniqueness, computed from the mutual information [37, 175] between two neighborhoods. Assuming $P_A(i)$ and $P_B(i)$ are
probabilities that intensity i appear in A and B, and $P_{AB}(i, j)$ is the probability that
corresponding pixels in A and B have intensities i and j, respectively, then mutual
information between A and B is computed from

$$L_{114} = \sum_i \sum_j P_{AB}(i, j) \log_2 \frac{P_{AB}(i, j)}{P_A(i) P_B(j)}. \tag{4.243}$$

The higher the mutual information between the neighborhoods, the more dependent intensities in the neighborhoods will be. A unique neighborhood A will,
therefore, have a small mutual information when compared with each neighborhood B adjacent to it. A neighborhood with 8 surrounding neighbors will be unique
if the maximum mutual information calculated with the 8 neighbors is sufficiently
small and locally minimum. Ullman et al. [205] found that when the size of a neighborhood is adjusted to the size of the pattern to be recognized the most accurate
recognition will be achieved when using mutual information to measure similarity
between patterns.

Uniqueness has also been measured using Pearson correlation [39, 70] and intensity variance [131, 132, 197]. Pixels belonging to unique neighborhoods produce
more robust matches than pixels belonging to not so unique neighborhoods [13].

Examples of entropy feature images are given in Fig. 4.48. The entropy of the
circular region of radius 8 pixels centered at each pixel in the images in Fig. 4.1 is
calculated and assigned to the pixel to obtain the feature images shown in Fig. 4.48.
Low entropies are obtained in homogeneous areas while high entropies are obtained

in detailed areas. Entropy remains highly invariant under monotone intensity transformation, while it is most influenced by blurring. The repeatability of entropy is also the lowest under blurring and generally low under other image changes.

4.11   Other Features

Other image features have been used in the past to analyze images. This includes scale-trace features, trace-transform features, extrema-based features, and psychologically inspired features.

4.11.1   Scale-Trace Features

A scale-trace is a sequence of numbers representing the property value at a pixel under changes in image resolution [71]. As image resolution is decreased, the intensity at a pixel is influenced by the intensities of pixels farther from it. A scale-trace of intensities at a pixel depends on the intensities of pixels surrounding the pixel.

If $f_\sigma(x, y)$ is the intensity at (x, y) after smoothing image $f(x, y)$ with a Gaussian of standard deviation σ, the scale trace at pixel (x, y) is defined by:

$$L_{115}(x, y, \sigma_1, \sigma_2, \Delta\sigma) = \{ f_\sigma(x, y) : \sigma = \sigma_1, \sigma_1 + \Delta\sigma,$$
$$\sigma_1 + 2\Delta\sigma, \dots, \sigma_2 \}. \tag{4.244}$$

Note that scale trace is a vector-valued feature, which can be determined for any image property. For instance, rather than the intensity, the gradient magnitude, the Laplacian, the entropy, or other image properties can be used. A scale trace is represented by an array of scalars and is invariant under image orientation if smoothing is performed using a circularly symmetric operator. Changing the scale of an image will shift values in a scale-trace array. Hansen and Morse [71] used scale-trace features to determine the scaling difference between two images.

4.11.2   Trace-Transform Features

Trace transform captures image information in a manner invariant to the image's orientation. To create a trace transform of an image, the image is scanned in all directions and intensities along each scan direction are evaluated according to a prespecified function [90, 91]. Given image $f(x, y)$, the trace transform of it is an image $g(\phi, \rho)$ where ϕ shows the scan direction with respect to the x-axis and ρ shows distance of the scanline to the origin. Therefore, for a circular image, assuming origin is at the image center and the prespecified function is averaging, the average intensity obtained in direction ϕ at distance ρ is saved at $g(\phi, \rho)$. Note

Fig. 4.49 (**a**)–(**f**) Extrema count ratio (L_{116}) feature images obtained using the images in Fig. 4.1. The invariance measures of feature images (**b**)–(**f**) when computed against feature image (**a**) are BI = 0.83, NI = 0.91, II = 0.96, RI = 0.91, SI = 0.89, and the corresponding repeatability measures are BR = 0.37, NR = 0.41, IR = 0.60, RR = 0.47, SR = 0.33

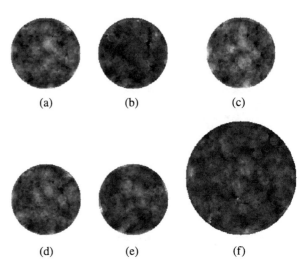

(a)   (b)   (c)

(d)   (e)   (f)

that trace transforms of two images with rotational differences will have only translational differences. Petrou and Kadyrov [151] described a method for calculating affine-invariant features from the trace transform of an image.

4.11.3 Extrema-Based Features

Mitchell et al. [128] used the number of intensity extrema in an image as a feature. They found that the ratio of the number of extrema in two resolutions of an image distinguish different textures from each other quite well. If the number of extrema obtained by convolving an image with Gaussians of standard deviations σ_1 and σ_2 are n_1 and n_2, respectively, and $\sigma_2 > \sigma_1$, then they define an extrema-based feature by:

$$L_{116}(\sigma_1, \sigma_2) = \frac{n_2}{n_1}. \tag{4.245}$$

This feature is invariant to image rotation if computed within circular neighborhoods. As the difference between the number of extrema intensities in two images increases, the images will have more spatial frequency differences. Using the extrema-based ratios obtained from six different resolutions of an image, Mitchell et al. [128] experimentally showed that extrema ratios have a higher discrimination power than the same number of other spatially dependent features.

Examples of extrema-based features are given in Fig. 4.49 using the images in Fig. 4.1. σ_1 and σ_2 were 1 pixel and 2 pixels, respectively. The ratio of extremum counts is highly invariant to intensity mapping and to a lesser degree to noise and image rotation. Its invariance property under blurring is relatively low. This feature is not very repeatable, especially under blurring and change in image scale. This is attributed to the displacement of extremum points under blurring or change in scale.

A measure similar to the extrema count is the busyness feature introduced by Dondes and Rosenfeld [48]. Busyness of a neighborhood is defined as the median of absolute intensity difference of adjacent pixel intensities measured horizontally, vertically, and diagonally within the neighborhood. Alternatively, the median of the gradient magnitude of pixels within the neighborhood may be used.

$$L_{117}(x, y) = median_{x, y}\{\|f'(x, y)\|\},\qquad(4.246)$$

where $\|f'(x, y)\|$ implies gradient magnitude at (x, y). If variations are abundant within a neighborhood, the median gradient magnitude will be high, and if intensity variations are rare, the median gradient magnitude will be low. This feature is also rotation invariant if calculations are performed in circular neighborhoods.

4.11.4 Psychologically Inspired Features

Computational features that simulate the measures used by the human visual system to distinguish different textures from each other have been proposed by Tamura et al. [189]. These features include coarseness, directionality, and symmetry.

4.11.4.1 Coarseness

To determine the coarseness or fineness of image $f(x, y)$ at a pixel, the difference of average intensities of regions on opposing sides of the pixel is calculated horizontally, vertically, and diagonally and under different region sizes. Then the region size producing the highest difference is chosen as the coarseness measure at the pixel. The average of coarseness values at all pixels in the image is then used as the coarseness of the image.

The average intensity of a neighborhood of size $2^k \times 2^k$ centered at (x, y) is

$$A_k(x, y) = \frac{1}{2^{2k}} \sum_i \sum_j f(i, j),\qquad(4.247)$$

where $x - 2^{k-1} \le i \le x + 2^{k-1} - 1$ and $y - 2^{k-1} \le j \le y + 2^{k-1} - 1$. Then, the absolute difference between average intensities of adjacent neighborhoods of size 2^k horizontally at (x, y) is computed

$$E_k^0(x, y) = |A_k(x + 2^{k-1}, y) - A_k(x - 2^{k-1}, y)|.\qquad(4.248)$$

Similarly, differences vertically, E_k^{90}, and diagonally, E_k^{45} and E_k^{135}, are calculated. Among directions 0, 45, 90, and 135 degrees, the k maximizing E is found and denoted by k_m. Finally, coarseness is calculated from

$$L_{118} = \frac{1}{MN} \sum_{x=0}^{M-1} \sum_{y=0}^{N-1} 2^{k_m(x,y)}.\qquad(4.249)$$

Fig. 4.50 (**a**)–(**f**) Scale (L_{119}) feature images obtained using the images in Fig. 4.1. The invariance measures of feature images (**b**)–(**f**) when computed with respect to feature image (**a**) are BI = 0.94, NI = 0.97, II = 0.98, RI = 0.96, SI = 0.90, and the corresponding repeatability measures are BR = 0.49, NR = 0.47, IR = 0.63, RR = 0.63, SR = 0.74

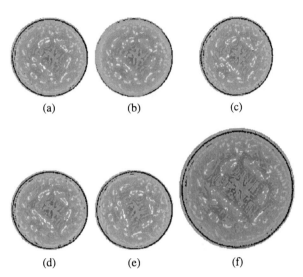

(a)   (b)   (c)

(d)   (e)   (f)

This coarseness measure shows the average diameter of different-sized texture elements in an image, and is approximately rotation invariant. The approximation is because of the use of square neighborhoods rather than circular ones in the calculations.

Note that parameter k_m is associated with the pixel between two regions of size 2^{k_m}. To associate such a parameter with the pixel at the center of a region, the absolute differences of a region with its 8 neighbors is determined and the minimum absolute difference is used as the value at the pixel. This minimum can then be calculated at a range of scales, and the scale producing the highest minimum is taken as the scale of the region centered at the pixel.

Rather than finding the absolute difference between the region at (x, y) and the regions surrounding it, the response of the image at (x, y) to a Laplacian of Gaussian (LoG) of an appropriate standard deviation can be used. Blostein and Ahuja [19] show that when the radius of the circle best approximating the region is r, highest response is obtained when standard deviation of the LoG is $\sigma = r/\sqrt{2}$. Assuming the response of image $f(x, y)$ to the LoG of standard deviation σ reaches an extremum when $\sigma = \sigma_m$, the radius of the region centered at (x, y) will be

$$L_{119} = r = \sigma_m \sqrt{2}, \qquad (4.250)$$

which can be taken as the scale feature at pixel (x, y). Lowe [116] approximated a LoG by the difference of two Gaussians and used the scale feature r at a pixel to create a scale-invariant descriptor at the pixel.

Examples of scale feature L_{119} calculated for the images in Fig. 4.1 are given in Fig. 4.50 starting from $\sigma = 1$ pixel and with increments of 0.5 pixels until $\sigma = D/2\sqrt{2}$, where D is the diameter of the local circular neighborhood used in the calculations. Gray pixels in these feature images correspond to detailed areas while dark and bright pixels correspond to dark and bright homogeneous regions in the image. Pixels where a minimum or a maximum is not found for the range of scales tested are set to black. The black ring around the boundary of the coin in the an image shows pixels where extrema were not detected due to the absence of circular regions at those pixels for the range of scales tested.

The invariance property of this scale feature is high under blurring, noise, and intensity and geometric transformations. Under changes in scale, the feature values change, degrading the invariance measure. The repeatability of the scale feature is relatively low under blurring, noise, and intensity and geometric transformations. This is because circular regions are scarce in these images and effective scales of non-circular regions change with noise and other image changes.

4.11.4.2 Directionality

This feature identifies one or more dominant directions in an image and is obtained from the histogram of gradient directions in the image. The most dominant direction in an image is found from the highest peak in the gradient direction histogram. A peak is required to have valleys on both sides with counts smaller than half that at the peak. Under this condition, an image may have no dominant direction or have more than one dominant direction. Therefore, the number of dominant directions in an image, n, can be used as a rotation-invariant feature to characterize the image

$$L_{120} = n, \quad \text{number of dominant directions.} \tag{4.251}$$

If $n > 1$, and denoting the peak directions by $\theta_0, \ldots, \theta_{n-1}$, with θ_0 denoting the most dominant direction, then all directions can be normalized with respect to the dominant direction to produce $n - 1$ rotationally invariant features

$$L_{121}(i) = \theta_i - \theta_0, \quad i = 1, \ldots, n - 1. \tag{4.252}$$

4.11.4.3 Symmetry

Inspired by psychophysical evidence on symmetry and fixation point by primates, Reisfeld et al. [160–162] suggested radial symmetry as a feature to characterize local neighborhoods in an image. Kovesi [97] observed that symmetry points give rise to patterns of local phase that can then be used to construct a contrast-invariant feature with a value that depends on the level of symmetry of a spot than its contrast.

Loy and Zelinsky [117] calculated radial symmetry at a pixel using the symmetry contributions of pixels around it. This was discussed in Sect. 3.1.9 in detail. Therefore, the symmetry feature S calculated in (3.36):

$$L_{122} = S = \sum_{r=r_1}^{r_n} S_r \tag{4.253}$$

can be used to characterize the degree of radial symmetric of a neighborhood. This symmetry feature is invariant to rotation and small changes in scale [117].

4.12 Performance Evaluation

Invariance and repeatability properties of a number of representative features were tested under image blurring, noise, and changes in image intensity and geometry. Although a single image is used in the experiments, because a large number of windows are taken from the image to calculate the features and the windows contain a vast variety of intensity patterns, the results obtained on other images are not expected to be very different from the results reported here.

4.12.1 Invariance

To compare the invariance properties of the features, the invariance measures of the tested features are calculated and tabulated in Table 4.1. The highest measure obtained under each category of image change is shown in bold. If the highest measure is shared by more than one feature, the measures for all those features are shown in bold. Some features are highly invariant under one image change, while some are highly invariant under a number of image changes.

4.12.1.1 Invariance Under Blurring

When an image is blurred, it loses some of its details. Although many features are highly invariant under blurring, a third-order Hu invariant moment (L_{26}), the normalized complex invariant moment of order $(p, q) = (1, 1)$ (L_{50c}), and the smoothed intensity (L_{88}) are the most invariant under image blurring. The least invariant feature under image blurring is the cornerness measure of Ando (L_{59}). Among the cornerness measures, those defined by Rohr (L_{60}) and Kitchen and Rosenfeld (L_{65}) are the most invariant under blurring.

4.12.1.2 Invariance Under Noise

Examining the results in Table 4.1, we see that mean intensity (L_2), the Hu invariant moments (L_{23}, L_{24}, L_{26}), the normalized complex invariant moment of order $(1, 1)$ (L_{50c}), the steerable filter response (L_{78}), smoothed intensity (L_{88}), and fractal dimension (L_{111}) are the least sensitive to noise. It is interesting to note that noise does not affect fractal dimension greatly as it does not change the repeated structural organization of an intensity pattern. The feature most sensitive to noise is the correlation of the co-occurrence matrix (L_{13}). Noise affects the co-occurrence matrix, and among the co-occurrence matrix features, it influences the correlation the most.

Table 4.1 Invariance properties of a number of representative features. Bold numbers show the highest invariance measure obtained in a particular category of image change. The following notations are used. $L_\#$: feature index; BI: blurring invariance; NI: noise invariance; II: intensity invariance; RI: rotation invariance; SI: scale invariance; $L_2–L_5$: mean, standard deviation, skewness, and kurtosis of image intensities; $L_{11}–L_{14}$: energy, contrast, correlation, and entropy of the co-occurrence matrix; $L_{23}–L_{26}$: two second-order and two third-order Hu invariant moments; $L_{32}–L_{34}$: contrast normalized invariant moments; $L_{47a}–L_{47c}$: complex invariant moments of orders $(p, q) = (2, 0)$, $(0, 2)$, and $(1, 1)$; $L_{50a}–L_{50c}$: normalized complex invariant moments of orders $(2, 0)$, $(0, 2)$, and $(1,1)$; $L_{57}–L_{60}$, $L_{62}–L_{65}$: cornerness measures of Shi and Tomasi, Carneiro and Jepson, Ando, Rohr, Harris and Stephens, Förstner and Gülch, Beaudet, and Kitchen and Rosenfeld; L_{69}: number of peaks in magnitude transform; L_{74}: local power spectrum; L_{75}: local frequency domain entropy; L_{78}: steerable filter response; $L_{86a}–L_{86c}$: correlation responses to Laws masks B_{11}, B_{22}, B_{33}; L_{88}: smoothed intensity; L_{90}: Laplacian; $L_{94}–L_{98}$: deviation from mean, absolute center contrast, center contrast, average local contrast, and dominant intensity; L_{111}: fractal dimension; L_{113}: image entropy; L_{116}: extrema count ratio; and L_{119}: local scale feature

$L_\#$	BI	NI	II	RI	SI	$L_\#$	BI	NI	II	RI	SI
L_2	0.97	**0.98**	0.98	**0.99**	0.93	L_{60}	0.90	0.94	0.97	0.96	0.94
L_3	0.81	0.92	0.94	0.93	0.88	L_{62}	0.74	0.81	0.98	0.65	0.76
L_4	0.84	0.95	0.93	0.97	0.93	L_{63}	0.84	0.93	0.96	0.93	0.91
L_5	0.89	0.93	0.91	0.96	0.88	L_{64}	0.87	0.90	0.95	0.93	**0.97**
L_{11}	0.79	0.89	0.86	0.86	0.87	L_{65}	0.90	0.94	0.98	0.92	0.96
L_{12}	0.79	0.94	0.96	0.80	0.90	L_{69}	0.82	0.93	0.93	0.93	0.93
L_{13}	0.83	0.80	0.74	0.90	0.89	L_{74}	0.81	0.93	0.94	0.95	0.93
L_{14}	0.83	0.91	0.87	0.88	0.89	L_{75}	0.87	0.92	0.84	0.95	0.96
L_{23}	0.97	**0.98**	0.97	0.98	0.91	L_{78}	0.97	**0.98**	0.96	0.97	0.94
L_{24}	0.97	**0.98**	0.97	0.98	0.91	L_{86a}	0.86	0.96	**0.99**	0.90	0.96
L_{25}	0.96	0.97	0.98	0.97	0.90	L_{86b}	0.75	0.95	0.98	0.92	0.96
L_{26}	**0.98**	**0.98**	0.98	**0.99**	0.93	L_{86c}	0.93	0.92	0.98	0.92	0.91
L_{32}	0.94	0.95	0.97	0.97	0.85	L_{88}	**0.98**	**0.98**	0.90	0.97	**0.97**
L_{33}	0.94	0.95	0.98	0.95	0.89	L_{90}	0.97	0.97	0.97	**0.99**	0.87
L_{34}	0.92	0.89	0.97	0.90	0.90	L_{94}	0.82	0.94	0.93	0.93	0.93
L_{47a}	0.93	0.95	0.97	0.97	0.84	L_{95}	0.81	0.93	0.94	0.95	0.93
L_{47b}	0.93	0.95	0.97	0.97	0.84	L_{96}	0.87	0.92	0.84	0.95	0.96
L_{47c}	0.97	0.97	0.97	0.98	0.91	L_{97}	0.93	0.97	0.95	0.98	0.94
L_{50a}	0.95	0.95	0.98	0.97	0.86	L_{98}	0.86	0.86	0.81	0.90	0.88
L_{50b}	0.95	0.96	0.98	0.97	0.86	L_{111}	0.85	**0.98**	0.95	0.98	0.91
L_{50c}	**0.98**	**0.98**	0.98	**0.99**	0.93	L_{113}	0.82	0.89	0.97	0.88	0.90
L_{57}	0.85	0.93	0.96	0.92	0.92	L_{116}	0.83	0.91	0.96	0.91	0.89
L_{58}	0.73	0.88	0.97	0.83	0.84	L_{119}	0.94	0.97	0.98	0.96	0.90
L_{59}	0.70	0.89	0.97	0.84	0.85						

4.12.1.3 Invariance under Intensity Transformation

The features have been tested under intensity transformation through histogram equalization. This is a nonlinear but monotone intensity transformation. Best performance has been achieved by a Laws mask (L_{86a}), which measures image gradient. For the kind of images used, the gradient of an image and the gradient of its histogram-equalized version seem to be very similar, producing the highest invariance measure. The feature least invariant under monotone intensity transformation is the correlation of the co-occurrence matrix (L_{13}). Since intensity mapping changes intensities of adjacent pixels, it greatly affects the co-occurrence matrix, and that appears to affect the correlation feature the most.

4.12.1.4 Invariance under Geometric Transformation

Since the features are calculated within small neighborhoods of radius 8 pixels, only rotation and scale changes are considered. Although in many real situations, images may have affine, projective, or even nonlinear geometric differences, often within such small neighborhoods, affine, projective, and nonlinear differences between images can be considered negligible and ignored. Therefore, results reported here apply to images where affine, projective, and nonlinear distortions within regions of radius 8 pixels are negligible.

Among the features tested, mean intensity (L_2), an invariant moment of Hu (L_{26}), the normalized complex invariant moment of order $(1, 1)$ (L_{50c}), and the Laplacian (L_{90}) are the most invariant under rotation. The features most invariant under scale are the Beaudet cornerness measure (L_{64}) and the smoothed intensity feature (L_{88}). The feature least invariant under rotation and scaling is the Harris and Stephens cornerness measure (L_{62}). This is an unexpected result since Harris corner detector is widely used in image registration. Results in Table 4.1, however, indicate that some of the Harris corners detected in images with rotational and scaling differences may point to different scene points.

4.12.1.5 Most Invariant Features

Although some features remain highly invariant under a particular type of image change, some features remain highly invariant under a wide range of image changes. Not knowing differences between two images, the feature that is most invariant under all image changes should be chosen to compare the images. Assuming an invariance measure of 0.9 or higher is required of a feature to be useful in a particular vision task, from Table 4.1 we see that features highly invariant under all image changes are L_2, L_{23}–L_{26}, L_{50c}, L_{60}, L_{65}, L_{78}, L_{86c}, L_{88}, L_{97}, and L_{119}. Among all the features tested, a third-order invariant moment of Hu (L_{26}) and the normalized complex invariant moment of order $(1, 1)$ (L_{50c}) are the most invariant under all image changes considered in the experiments.

4.12.1.6 Sensitivity of Invariance to Feature Parameters

The results reported in Table 4.1 are for circular windows of radius 8 pixels. Some features, such as inertia matrix features, use small fixed windows, but many features have free parameters that can affect their performances. Changing the window size in some features can change their invariance properties and change their ranking. In addition to window size, parameters such as the standard deviation of the Gaussian in derivative-based features, can influence the ranking of features. To determine the influence of the free parameters of the features on their invariance measures, experiments were carried out on the features identified as most invariant in the preceding section.

Specifically, window size (radius) was changed from 2 pixels to 32 pixels with an increment of 2 pixels, and the invariance measures for L_{26} and L_{50c} were calculated for each window size and plotted in Fig. 4.51. Results indicate that window size has very little effect on the invariance measures of these features under noise, image blurring, monotone intensity transformation, and image rotation. The invariance measures of these features decrease under unknown scaling. However, even with decreased invariance measures, we see that these features remain moderately invariant under unknown image scales.

4.12.2 Repeatability

Repeatability measures the stability of a feature extremum under various image changes. Locations of feature extrema represent unique points in an image that can be used as control points to register images. Since a feature can be measured at any pixel in an image, locations where a feature becomes locally minimum or maximum are of interest.

To measure repeatability, extrema feature locations are marked in the base image in Fig. 4.1a. The extrema locations are also marked in the images in Figs. 4.1b–f. If the number of extrema detected in the base image and in its transformed version are n_1 and n_2, and $n = \min(n_1, n_2)$, and also if m of the extrema detected in both images are verified to be the same, then repeatability is defined by

$$R = \frac{m}{n}. \tag{4.254}$$

Since the geometric relations between the base image in Fig. 4.1 and its transformed versions in Figs. 4.1b–f are known, corresponding extrema in the images can be identified. For images with rotational and scaling differences, to compensate for digital errors caused by image transformation, extrama falling within a pixel of each other are considered corresponding extrema. Repeatabilities of various features measured under various image changes are included in Table 4.2.

Fig. 4.51 Sensitivity of the invariance measures of (**a**) the Hu invariant moment L_{26} and (**b**) the normalized complex invariant moment L_{56c} on window size (radius)

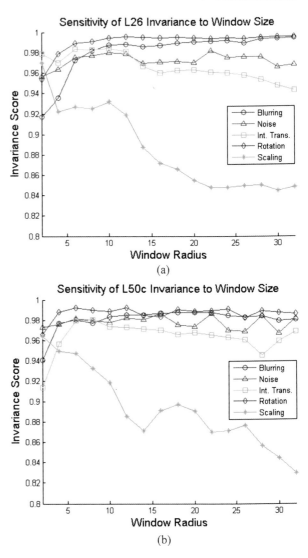

4.12.2.1 Repeatability Under Blurring

Repeatability under blurring varies vastly from feature to feature. The most repeatable features are local mean intensity (L_2) and center contrast (L_{96}). The least repeatable feature is fractal dimension (L_{111}). Fractal dimension varies relatively slowly from region to region, making the feature locally less unique. Although fractal dimension was found to be highly invariant under blurring, local extrema of fractal dimension move under image blurring, making the feature unsuitable for use as a point detector.

The repeatability measures of the features used in traditional point detectors L_{57}–L_{65} are not very high under image blurring. Extrema of the local mean (L_2),

Table 4.2 Repeatability measures of image features. The bold number under each category of image change shows the feature that is the most repeatable under that category of image change. The following notations are used. $L_\#$: feature index; BR: blurring repeatability; NR: noise repeatability; IR: intensity repeatability; RR: rotation repeatability; SR: scale repeatability; L_2–L_5: mean, standard deviation, skewness, and kurtosis of image intensities; L_{11}–L_{14}: energy, contrast, correlation, and entropy of the co-occurrence matrix; L_{23}–L_{26}: two second-order and two third-order Hu invariant moments; L_{32}–L_{34}: contrast normalized invariant moments; L_{47a}–L_{47c}: complex invariant moments of orders $(p, q) = (2, 0)$, $(0, 2)$, and $(1, 1)$; L_{50a}–L_{50c}: normalized complex invariant moments of orders $(2, 0)$, $(0, 2)$, and $(1, 1)$; L_{57}–L_{60}, L_{62}–L_{65}: cornerness measures of Shi and Tomasi, Carneiro and Jepson, Ando, Rohr, Harris and Stephens, Förstner and Gülch, Beaudet, and Kitchen and Rosenfeld; L_{69}: number of peaks in magnitude transform; L_{74}: local power spectrum; L_{75}: local frequency domain entropy; L_{78}: steerable filter response; L_{86a}–L_{86c}: correlation responses to Laws masks B_{11}, B_{22}, B_{33}; L_{88}: smoothed intensity; L_{90}: Laplacian; L_{94}–L_{98}: deviation from mean, absolute center contrast, center contrast, average local contrast, and dominant intensity; L_{111}: fractal dimension; L_{113}: image entropy; L_{116}: extrema count ratio; and L_{119}: local scale feature

$L_\#$	BR	NR	IR	RR	SR	$L_\#$	BR	NR	IR	RR	SR
L_2	**1.00**	0.75	0.86	0.88	0.12	L_{60}	0.26	0.56	0.72	0.63	0.49
L_3	0.39	0.61	0.69	0.63	0.17	L_{62}	0.30	0.64	0.75	0.54	0.51
L_4	0.19	0.57	0.71	0.55	0.11	L_{63}	0.31	0.62	0.71	0.55	0.50
L_5	0.25	0.57	0.43	0.56	0.17	L_{64}	0.89	0.82	0.93	0.74	0.87
L_{11}	0.15	0.29	0.38	0.29	0.11	L_{65}	0.81	0.81	0.95	0.78	0.86
L_{12}	0.19	0.51	0.44	0.19	0.11	L_{69}	0.48	0.62	0.79	0.65	0.21
L_{13}	0.14	0.29	0.16	0.20	0.12	L_{74}	0.94	0.82	0.92	0.79	0.80
L_{14}	0.16	0.30	0.35	0.31	0.17	L_{75}	0.96	0.85	**0.98**	0.82	0.76
L_{23}	0.92	0.79	0.90	0.84	0.11	L_{78}	0.91	0.77	0.92	0.80	0.85
L_{24}	0.92	0.72	0.83	0.75	0.33	L_{86a}	0.93	0.83	0.95	0.62	**0.95**
L_{25}	0.84	0.72	0.84	0.74	0.47	L_{86b}	0.93	**0.89**	0.95	0.81	0.93
L_{26}	0.88	0.67	0.81	0.81	0.40	L_{86c}	0.83	0.85	0.91	0.87	0.93
L_{32}	0.93	0.76	0.86	0.85	0.41	L_{88}	0.84	0.65	0.81	0.73	0.82
L_{33}	0.90	0.81	0.87	0.83	0.53	L_{90}	0.87	0.72	0.87	0.89	0.85
L_{34}	0.90	0.78	0.86	0.81	0.52	L_{94}	0.50	0.59	0.71	0.60	0.17
L_{47a}	0.95	0.81	0.88	0.86	0.40	L_{95}	0.87	0.75	0.88	0.74	0.70
L_{47b}	0.95	0.79	0.88	0.86	0.40	L_{96}	**1.00**	0.86	0.97	0.85	0.79
L_{47c}	0.99	0.78	0.88	0.88	0.11	L_{97}	0.82	0.74	0.85	0.67	0.09
L_{50a}	0.97	0.78	0.86	0.88	0.38	L_{98}	0.09	0.08	0.74	0.20	0.20
L_{50b}	0.97	0.79	0.86	0.88	0.38	L_{111}	0.05	0.47	0.59	0.48	0.06
L_{50c}	0.93	0.72	0.81	**0.91**	0.12	L_{113}	0.25	0.51	0.84	0.46	0.32
L_{57}	0.30	0.65	0.75	0.47	0.47	L_{116}	0.37	0.41	0.60	0.47	0.33
L_{58}	0.58	0.65	0.85	0.67	0.57	L_{119}	0.49	0.47	0.63	0.63	0.74
L_{59}	0.58	0.66	0.85	0.65	0.57						

center contrast (L_{96}), various moment invariants (L_{23}, L_{24}, L_{32}–L_{34}, L_{47a}–L_{47c}, L_{50a}–L_{50c}), local power spectrum (L_{74}), local frequency domain entropy (L_{75}), the steerable filter (L_{78}), and Laws masks B_{11} and B_{22} (L_{86a}, L_{86b}) are all more repeatable under blurring than the cornerness measures used by the point detectors.

4.12.2.2 Repeatability Under Noise

In general, repeatability of all features decrease under noise. Noise displaces the locations of the extrema in a feature image. The most repeatable feature under noise is correlation response to Laws first derivative mask (L_{86b}). The worst repeatable feature under noise is the correlation of the co-occurrence matrix (L_{13}). The co-occurrence matrix of an image is sensitive to noise, and the extrema of the correlation of the matrix are most influenced by noise.

4.12.2.3 Repeatability Under Intensity Transformation

Under the applied monotone intensity transformation, the most repeatable feature is the local frequency domain entropy (L_{75}). The applied intensity transformation does not change the spatial frequency characteristics of an image noticeably, and any such change appears to have the least effect on the extrema of the local entropy in the frequency domain. The least repeatable feature under this intensity transformation is correlation of the co-occurrence matrix (L_{13}).

4.12.2.4 Repeatability Under Geometric Transformation

Under rotation, the most repeatable feature is the normalized complex invariant moment of order $(1, 1)$ (L_{50c}). Overall, complex invariant moments and normalized complex invariant moments are the most stable under rotation, resulting in the most repeatable extrema due to their rotationally invariant property. The feature the least repeatable under image rotation is the contrast of the co-occurrence matrix (L_{12}). Although L_{12} is computed by taking the highest contrast of co-occurrence matrices obtained by scanning the image horizontally, vertically, and diagonally, but under $30°$ rotation the co-occurrence matrices obtained are different from those before the rotation, producing features that are sensitive to image rotation. The extrema of the contrast of the co-occurrence matrix is the least stable and, thus, the least repeatable under rotation.

The repeatability measures of the features tested in this chapter are relatively low under scaling. This can be attributed to the use of the same window of radius 8 pixels independent of an image's scale. Often in practice the scales of images to be compared are not known. Among the features tested in this study, correlation response to Laws B_{11} filter (L_{86a}) is the most repeatable. In general, we see that under image scaling, Laws masks (L_{86a}–L_{86c}) produce the most stable extrema when

Fig. 4.52 Sensitivity of the repeatability of the center contrast feature (L_{96}) on window size and various image changes

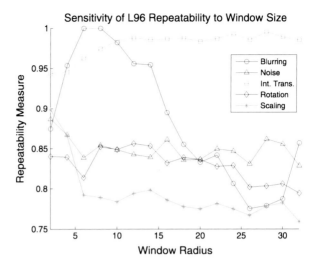

compared to other features. The least repeatable features under image scaling are skewness (L_4), the energy (L_{11}) and the contrast (L_{12}) of the co-occurrence matrix, a second-order invariant moment of Hu (L_{23}), and the complex invariant moment of order $(1, 1)$ (L_{47c}). Although invariant moments are formulated to be invariant to scale, under unknown scale since the proper window size cannot be chosen, windows containing the same pattern in the images cannot be chosen, causing a poor performance under unknown scaling.

4.12.2.5 Most Repeatable Features

Examining the contents of Table 4.2 and assuming repeatability measures of 0.9 and higher are needed in an application, we see that among all the features tested in this study, correlation responses to Laws masks ($L_{86a}-L_{86c}$) and the center contrast feature (L_{96}) produce the most repeatable results under all image changes. Invariant moments are generally the most repeatable except for unknown scaling. Least repeatable features under various image changes are the co-occurrence matrix features.

4.12.2.6 Sensitivity of Repeatability to Feature Parameters

The most repeatable features are found to be correlation responses to Laws masks ($L_{86a}-L_{86c}$) and the center contrast feature (L_{96}). The Laws masks in $L_{86a}-L_{86c}$ are 5×5 and any window of radius 2 and higher is going to produce the same repeatability measure. The repeatability of the center contrast feature, however, depends on the window size as depicted in Fig. 4.52. The repeatability of the center contrast feature remains relatively unchanged under noise, monotone intensity transformation, and image rotation. Under image blurring, the repeatability measure initially increases, then decreases, and then increases again. The feature is the most repeatable under Gaussian blurring of standard deviation 2 pixels when window radius is between 5 and 10 pixels. Under unknown scaling, the repeatability of the feature initially decreases, but then it remains relatively unchanged when window radius is larger than 7 pixels. The repeatability of the center contrast feature remains relatively high under all image changes and a wide range of window sizes.

4.13 Final Remarks

Image features provide a means of measuring the similarity between two images without establishing correspondence between pixels in the images. A feature measures a particular property of an image. A feature is ideal if it does not depend on an image's orientation or scale, is not affected by noise or image contrast, and is insensitive to image blurring that may have been caused by camera defocus.

Among the features tested, invariant moments are found to be highly invariant and repeatable under various image changes. Laws masks, although small and contain limited information, are highly invariant and repeatable under a variety of image changes. Simple features such as local and global intensity averaging are highly invariant and repeatable under various image changes.

This chapter examined the invariance and repeatability properties of various image features. The recognition ability of the features was not discussed. In addition to being invariant and repeatable, a feature should carry the most information about an image. We are interested in features that produce different values for different images and produce the same value for images containing the same pattern but are noisy and may have scale, rotational, contrast, and resolution (blurring) differences. The problem of finding features that can most unambiguously recognize an image is addressed by feature selection. In Chap. 6, those features that carry the most information about an image are searched and algorithms for selecting the best n features from among $N > n$ features for image recognition/matching are reviewed.

References

1. Abo-Zaid, A., Hinton, O., Horne, E.: About moment normalisation and complex moment descriptors. In: Proc. 4th Int'l Conf. Pattern Recognition, pp. 399–407 (1988)
2. Abu-Mostafa, Y.S., Psaltis, D.: Recognitive aspects of moment invariants. IEEE Trans. Pattern Anal. Mach. Intell. **6**(6), 698–706 (1984)
3. Abu-Mostafa, Y.S., Psaltis, D.: Image normalization by complex moments. IEEE Trans. Pattern Anal. Mach. Intell. **7**(1), 46–55 (1985)
4. Aburdene, M.F.: On the computation of discrete Legendre polynomial coefficients. Multidimens. Syst. Signal Process. **4**, 181–186 (1993)
5. Ahmed, N., Natarajan, T., Rao, K.R.: On image processing and a discrete cosine transform. IEEE Trans. Commun. **23**(1), 90–93 (1974)
6. Ando, S.: Image field categorization and edge/corner detection from gradient covariance. IEEE Trans. Pattern Anal. Mach. Intell. **22**(2), 179–190 (2000)

7. Andreadis, I., Tsalides, Ph.: Coloured object recognition using invariant spectral features. J. Intell. Robot. Syst. **13**, 93–106 (1995)

8. Andrews, H.C.: Computer Techniques in Image Processing. Academic Press, New York (1970)

9. Andrews, H.C., Patterson, C.L.: Singular value decomposition and digital image processing. In: IEEE Trans. Acoustics, Speech, and Signal Processing, pp. 26–53 (1976)

10. Andrews, H.C., Patterson, C.L.: Singular value decomposition (SVD) image coding. In: IEEE Trans. Communications, pp. 425–432 (1976)

11. Bajcsy, R.: Computer description of textured surfaces. In: Proc. 3rd Int'l J. Conf. Artificial Intelligence, pp. 572–579 (1973)

12. Ballester, C., González, M.: Affine invariant texture segmentation and shape from texture by variational methods. J. Math. Imaging Vis. **9**, 141–171 (1998)

13. Barnard, S.T., Thompson, W.B.: Disparity analysis of images. IEEE Trans. Pattern Anal. Mach. Intell. **2**(4), 333–340 (1980)

14. Baumberg, A.: Reliable feature matching across widely separated views. In: IEEE Conf. Computer Vision and Pattern Recognition, vol. 1, pp. 774–781 (2000)

15. Beaudet, P.R.: Rotationally invariant image operators. In: Proc. Int'l Conf. Pattern Recognition, pp. 579–583 (1978)

16. Belkasim, S.O., Ahmadi, M., Shridhar, M.: Efficient algorithm for fast computation of Zernike moments. J. Franklin Inst. **333B**(4), 577–581 (1996)

17. Belkasim, S., Hassan, E., Obeidi, T.: Explicit invariance of Vartesian Zernike moments. Pattern Recognit. Lett. **28**, 1969–1980 (2007)

18. Benke, K.K., Skinner, D.R., Woodruff, C.J.: Convolution operators as a basis for objective correlates of texture perception. IEEE Trans. Syst. Man Cybern. **18**(1), 158–163 (1988)

19. Blostein, D., Ahuja, N.: A multiscale region detector. Comput. Vis. Graph. Image Process. **45**, 22–41 (1989)

20. Borgefors, G.: Distance transforms in digital images. Comput. Vis. Graph. Image Process. **34**, 344–371 (1986)

21. Bovik, A.C., Clark, M., Geisler, W.S.: Multichannel texture analysis using localized spatial filters. IEEE Trans. Pattern Anal. Mach. Intell. **12**(1), 55–73 (1990)

22. Canterakis, N.: 3-D Zernike moments and Zernike affine invariants for 3D image analysis and recognition. In: Proc. 11th Scandinavian Conference on Image Analysis (1999)

23. Carneiro, G., Jepson, A.D.: Phase-based local features. In: European Conf. Computer Vision, Copenhagen, Denmark, pp. 282–296 (2002)

24. Carneiro, G., Jepson, A.D.: Multi-scale phase-based local features. In: Proc. Computer Vision and Pattern Recognition, vol. 1, pp. 736–743 (2003)

25. Chan, Y.-K., Chen, C.-Y.: Image retrieval system based on color-complexity and color-spatial features. J. Syst. Softw. **71**, 65–70 (2004)

26. Chang, T., Kuo, C.-C.: Texture analysis and classification with tree-structured wavelet transform. IEEE Trans. Image Process. **2**(4), 429–441 (1993)

27. Chen, C.-C., Daponte, J.S., Fox, M.D.: Fractal feature analysis and classification in medical imaging. IEEE Trans. Med. Imaging **8**(2), 133–142 (1989)

28. Chen, E.-L., Chung, P.-C., Chen, C.-L., Tsai, H.-M., Chang, C.-I.: An automatic diagnostic system for CT liver image classification. IEEE Trans. Biomed. Eng. **45**(6), 783–794 (1998)

29. Chen, D.-R., Chang, R.-F., Chen, C.-J., Ho, M.-F., Huo, S.-J., Chen, S.-T., Hung, S.-J., Moons, W.K.: Classification of breast ultrasound images using fractal feature. J. Clin. Imaging **29**, 235–245 (2005)

30. Cheng, Y., Swamisai, R., Umbaugh, S.E., Moss, R.H., Stoecker, W.V., Teegala, S., Srinivasan, S.K.: Skin lesion classification using relative color features. Skin Res. Technol. **14**, 53–64 (2008)

31. Chhabra, A.K., Zhigang, A., Balick, D., Genevieve, C., Loris, K., Sheppard, P., Smith, R., Wittner, B.: High-order statistically derived combinations of geometric features for hand-printed character recognition. In: Proc. Second Int'l Conf. Document Analysis and Recognition, pp. 397–401 (1993)

32. Chui, C.K., Wang, J.-Z.: On compactly supported spline wavelets and a duality principle. Trans. Am. Math. Soc. **330**(2), 903–915 (1992)
33. Clementini, E., Di Felice, P.: A model for representing topological relationships between complex geometric features in spatial databases. Inf. Sci. **90**, 121–136 (1996)
34. Clementini, E., Di Felice, P., van Oosterom, P.: A small set of formal topological relationships suitable for end-user interaction. Lect. Notes Comput. Sci. **692**, 277–295 (1993)
35. Coggins, J.M., Jain, A.K.: A spatial filtering approach to texture analysis. Pattern Recognit. Lett. **3**(3), 195–203 (1985)
36. Cohen, P., LeDinh, C.T., Lacasse, V.: Classification of textures by means of two-dimensional orthogonal masks. IEEE Trans. Acoust. Speech Signal Process. **37**(1), 125–128 (1989)
37. Collignon, A., Maes, F., Delaere, D., Vandermeulen, D., Suetens, P., Marchal, A.: Automated multi-modality image registration based on information theory. In: Proc. Information Processing in Medicine Conf, pp. 263–274 (1995)
38. Conners, R.W., Harlow, C.A.: A theoretical comparison of texture algorithms. IEEE Trans. Pattern Anal. Mach. Intell. **2**(3), 204–222 (1980)
39. Conover, W.J.: Practical Nonparametric Statistics, 2nd edn., p. 252. Wiley, New York (1980)
40. Cunha, A.L., Zhou, J., Do, M.N.: The nonsubsampled contourlet transform: Theory, design, and applications. IEEE Trans. Image Process. **15**, 3089–3101 (2006)
41. Damon, J., Giblin, P., Haslinger, G.: Local image features resulting from 3-dimensional geometric features, illumination, and movement: I. Int. J. Comput. Vis. **82**, 25–47 (2009)
42. Danielsson, P.E.: Euclidean distance mapping. Comput. Graph. Image Process. **14**, 227–248 (1980)
43. Daubechies, I.: Orthonormal bases of compactly supported wavelets. Commun. Pure Appl. Math. **41**, 909–996 (1988)
44. Daubechies, I.: The wavelet transform, time-frequency localization and signal analysis. IEEE Trans. Inf. Theory **36**, 961–1005 (1990)
45. Daugman, J.G.: Uncertainty relation for resolution in space, spatial frequency, and orientation optimized by two-dimensional visual cortical filters. J. Opt. Soc. Am. **2**, 1160–1169 (1985)
46. Deriche, R., Giraudon, G.: Accurate corner detection: An analytical study. In: Proc. 3rd Int'l Conf. Computer Vision, Osaka, Japan, pp. 66–70 (1990)
47. Do, M.H., Vetterli, M.: The contourlet transform: An efficient multiresolution image representation. IEEE Trans. Image Process. **14**, 2091–2106 (2005)
48. Dondes, P.A., Rosenfeld, A.: Pixel classification based on gray level and local 'busyness'. IEEE Trans. Pattern Anal. Mach. Intell. **4**(1), 79–84 (1982)
49. Dunn, D.F., Higgins, W.E.: Optimal Gabor filters for texture segmentation. IEEE Trans. Image Process. **4**(7), 947–964 (1995)
50. Dyer, C.R., Rosenfeld, A.: Fourier texture features: Suppression of aperature effects. IEEE Trans. Syst. Man Cybern. **6**, 703–705 (1976)
51. Feng, G., Jiang, J.: JPEG compressed image retrieval via statistical features. Pattern Recognit. **36**, 977–985 (2003)
52. Feng, Z., Shang-qian, L., Da-bao, W., Wei, G.: Aircraft recognition in infrared image using wavelet moment invariants. Image Vis. Comput. **27**, 313–318 (2009)
53. Fergus, R., Perona, P., Zisserman, A.: Object class recognition by unsupervised scale-invariant learning. In: Proc. IEEE Computer Society Conf. Computer Vision and Pattern Recognition, pp. II-264–II-271 (2003)
54. Field, D.J.: Relations between the statistics of natural images and the response properties of cortical cells. J. Opt. Soc. Am. A **4**, 2379–2394 (1987)
55. Fischer, S., Šroubek, F., Perrinet, L., Redondo, R., Cristóbal, G.: Self-invertible 2D log-polar wavelets. Int. J. Comput. Vis. **75**(2), 231–246 (2007)
56. Flandrin, P.: Wavelet analysis and synthesis of fractional Brownian motion. IEEE Trans. Inf. Theory **38**, 910–917 (1992)
57. Flusser, J., Suk, T.: Pattern recognition by affine moment invariant. Pattern Recognit. **26**(1), 167–174 (1993)

58. Förstner, W.: A feature based correspondence algorithm for image matching. Int. Arch. Photogramm. Remote Sens. **26**, 150–166 (1986)
59. Freeman, W.T., Adelson, W.H.: The design and use of steerable filters. IEEE Trans. Pattern Anal. Mach. Intell. **13**(9), 891–906 (1991)
60. Funt, B.V., Finlayson, G.D.: Color constant color indexing. IEEE Trans. Pattern Anal. Mach. Intell. **17**(5), 522–529 (1995)
61. Gabor, D.: Theory of communication. J. Inst. Electr. Eng. **93**(26), 429–457 (1946)
62. Galloway, M.M.: Texture analysis using gray level run lengths. Comput. Graph. Image Process. **4**, 172–179 (1975)
63. Garcia, C., Zikos, G., Tziritas, G.: A wavelet-based framework for face recognition. Image Vis. Comput. **18**, 289–297 (2000)
64. Gårding, J., Lindeberg, T.: Direct computation of shape cues using scale-accepted spatial derivative operators. Int. J. Comput. Vis. **17**(2), 163–191 (1996)
65. Gong, P., Howarth, P.J.: An assessment of some small window-based spatial features for land-cover classification. In: Int'l Conf. Geoscience and Remote Sensing Symposium, vol. 4, pp. 1668–1670 (1993)
66. Gonzalez, R.C., Wintz, P.: Digital Image Processing, 2nd edn., pp. 122–125. Addison-Wesley, Reading (1987)
67. Goshtasby, A.: 2-D and 3-D Image Registration for Medical, Remote Sensing, and Industrial Applications. Wiley, New York (2005)
68. Goshtasby, A., O'Neill, W.: Surface fitting to scattered data by a sum of Gaussians. Comput. Aided Geom. Des. **10**, 143–156 (1993)
69. Goshtasby, A., O'Neill, W.: Curve fitting by a sum of Gaussians. Graph. Models Image Process. **56**(4), 281–288 (1994)
70. Hannah, M.J.: Computer matching of areas in stereo images. Ph.D. Dissertation, Stanford University, Department of Computer Science (1974)
71. Hansen, B.B., Morse, B.S.: Multiscale image registration using scale trace correlation. In: Proc. Computer Vision and Pattern Recognition, pp. 202–208 (1999)
72. Haralick, R.M.: Statistical and structural approaches to texture. Proc. IEEE **67**(5), 786–807 (1979)
73. Haralick, R.M., Shanmugam, K., Dinstein, I.: Texture features for image classification. IEEE Trans. Syst. Man Cybern. **3**(6), 610–621 (1973)
74. Harris, C., Stephens, M.: A combined corner and edge detector. In: Proc. 4th Alvey Vision Conf. (AVC88), Univ. Manchester, pp. 147–151 (1988)
75. Harwood, D., Ojala, T., Pietikäinen, M., Kelman, S., Davis, L.S.: Texture classification by center-symmetric autocorrelation, using Kullback discrimination of distributions. Pattern Recognit. Lett. **16**, 1–10 (1995)
76. Hayley, G.M., Manjunath, B.M.: Rotation invariant texture classification using modified Gabor filters. In: Proc. of IEEE Int'l Conf. Image Processing, pp. 262–265 (1995)
77. Heo, Y.S., Lee, M., Lee, S.U.: Robust stereo matching using adaptive normalized cross-correlation. IEEE Trans. Pattern Anal. Mach. Intell. **33**(4), 807–822 (2011)
78. Hong, Z.: Algebraic feature extraction of image for recognition. Pattern Recognit. **24**, 211–219 (1991)
79. Horikawa, Y.: A feature of 2D and 3D image invariant to similarity transformations based on the bispectrum. Syst. Comput. Jpn. **33**(3), 1–10 (2002)
80. Hu, M.K.: Visual pattern recognition by moment invariants. IEEE Trans. Inf. Theory **8**, 179–187 (1962)
81. Jain, A.K., Farrokhnia, F.: Unsupervised texture segmentation using Gabor filters. In: Proc. Int'l Conf. Systems, Man, and Cybernetics, pp. 14–19 (1990)
82. Jain, A.K., Farrokhnia, F.: Unsupervised texture segmentation using Gabor filters. Pattern Recognit. **24**, 1167–1186 (1991)
83. Jain, A., Healey, G.: A multiscale representation including opponent color features for texture recognition. IEEE Trans. Image Process. **7**(1), 124–128 (1998)
84. Jernigan, M.E., D'Astous, F.: Entropy-based texture analysis in the spatial frequency domain. IEEE Trans. Pattern Anal. Mach. Intell. **6**(2), 237–243 (1984)

85. Jin, L., Tianxu, Z.: Fast algorithm for generation of moment invariants. Pattern Recognit. **37**, 1745–1756 (2004)
86. Joanes, D.N., Gill, C.A.: Comparing measures of sample skewness and kurtosis. J. R. Stat. Soc., Ser. D Stat. **47**(1), 183–189 (1998)
87. Johansson, B., Borga, M., Knutsson, H.: Learning corner orientation using canonical correlation. In: Proc. SSAB Symposium on Image Analysis, pp. 89–92 (2001)
88. Johnson, A.E., Hebert, M.: Recognizing objects by matching oriented points. In: Proc. Computer Vision and Pattern Recognition, pp. 684–689 (1997)
89. Kadir, T., Brady, J.M.: Scale, saliency and image description. Int. J. Comput. Vis. **45**(2), 83–105 (2001)
90. Kadyrov, A., Petrou, M.: The trace transform as a tool to invariant feature construction. In: Proc. 14th Int'l Conf. Pattern Recognition, vol. 2, pp. 1037–1039 (1998)
91. Kadyrov, A., Petrou, M.: The trace transform and its application. IEEE Trans. Pattern Anal. Mach. Intell. **23**(8), 811–828 (2001)
92. Kasson, J.K., Plouffe, W.: An analysis of selected computer interchange color spaces. ACM Trans. Graph. **11**(4), 373–405 (1992)
93. Khotanzad, A., Hong, Y.H.: Invariant image recognition by Zernike moments. IEEE Trans. Pattern Anal. Mach. Intell. **12**(5), 489–497 (1990)
94. Kingsbury, N.G.: Complex wavelets for shift invariant analysis and filtering of signals. J. Appl. Comput. Harmon. Anal. **10**(3), 234–253 (2001)
95. Kitchen, L., Rosenfeld, A.: Gray level corner detection. Technical Report #887, Computer Science Center, University of Maryland (1980). Also in Pattern Recogn. Lett. **1**, 95–102 (1982)
96. Koenderink, J.J., van Doorn, A.J.: Representation of local geometry in the visual system. Biol. Cybern. **55**, 367–375 (1987)
97. Kovesi, P.: Detection of interest points using symmetry. In: Proc. 3rd Int'l Conf. Computer Vision, pp. 62–65 (1990)
98. Kyrki, V., Kamarainen, J.-K., Kälviäinen, H.: Simple Gabor feature space for invariant object recognition. Pattern Recognit. Lett. **25**, 311–318 (2004)
99. Laws, K.I.: Rapid texture identification. In: Image Processing for Missile Guidance, Proc. SPIE, vol. 238, pp. 376–380 (1980)
100. Lazebnik, S., Schmid, C., Ponce, J.: Sparse texture representation using affine-invariant neighborhoods. In: Proc. Computer Vision and Pattern Recognition, pp. 319–324 (2003)
101. Lazebnik, S., Schmid, C., Ponce, J.: Semi-local affine parts for object recognition. In: British Machine Vision Conf., vol. 2, pp. 959–968 (2004)
102. Lazebnik, S., Schmid, C., Ponce, J.: Sparse texture representation using local affine regions. IEEE Trans. Pattern Anal. Mach. Intell. **27**(8), 1265–1278 (2005)
103. Le Moigne, J., Zavorin, I., Stone, H.: On the use of wavelets for image registration. In: Le Moigne, J., Netanyahu, N.S., Eastman, R.D. (eds.) Image Registration for Remote Sensing, pp. 240–264. Cambridge University Press, Cambridge (2011)
104. Lee, M.-C., Pun, C.-M.: Rotation and scale invariant wavelet feature for content-based texture retrieval. J. Am. Soc. Inf. Sci. Technol. **54**(1), 66–80 (2003)
105. Lee, W.-L., Chen, Y.-C., Hsieh, K.-S.: Ultrasonic liver tissues classification by fractal feature vector on M-band wavelet transform. IEEE Trans. Med. Imaging **22**(3), 382–392 (2003)
106. Lee, W.-L., Chen, Y.-C., Chen, Y.-C., Hsieh, K.-S.: Unsupervised segmentation of ultrasonic liver images by multiresolution fractal feature vector. Inf. Sci. **175**, 177–199 (2005)
107. Levine, M.D.: Feature extraction: A survey. Proc. IEEE **57**(8), 1391–1407 (1969)
108. Li, Y.: Reforming the theory of invariant moments for pattern recognition. Pattern Recognit. **25**(7), 723–730 (1992)
109. Liang, K.-C., Jay Kuo, C.-C.: WaveGuide: A joint wavelet-based image representation and description system. IEEE Trans. Image Process. **8**(11), 1619–1929 (1999)
110. Liao, S.X., Pawlak, M.: On image analysis by moments. IEEE Trans. Pattern Anal. Mach. Intell. **18**(3), 254–266 (1998)
111. Liao, S.X., Pawlak, M.: On the accuracy of Zernike moments for image analysis. IEEE Trans. Pattern Anal. Mach. Intell. **20**(12), 1358–1364 (1998)

112. Lim, J.S.: The discrete Fourier transform. In: Two-Dimensional Signal and Image Processing, pp. 136–183. Prentice Hall, New York (1990)
113. Liu, K., Cheng, Y.-Q., Yang, J.-Y.: Algebraic feature extraction for image recognition based on an optimal discriminant criterion. Pattern Recognit. **26**(6), 903–911 (1993)
114. Lohmann, A.W., Wirnitzer, B.: Tripple correlations. Proc. IEEE **72**(7), 889–901 (1984)
115. Lowe, D.G.: Object recognition from local scale-invariant features. In: Proc. Int'l Conf. Computer Vision, vol. 2, pp. 1150–1157 (1999)
116. Lowe, D.: Distinctive image features from scale-invariant keypoints. Int. J. Comput. Vis. **60**(2), 91–110 (2004)
117. Loy, G., Zelinsky, A.: A fast radial symmetry transform for detecting points of interest. In: 7th European Conf. Computer Vision, pp. 358–368 (2002)
118. Lu, T.-C., Chang, C.-C.: Color image retrieval technique based on color features and image bitmap. Inf. Process. Manag. **43**, 461–472 (2007)
119. Lundahl, T., Ohley, W.J., Kay, S.M., Siffert, R.: Brownian motion: A maximum likelihood estimator and its application to image texture. IEEE Trans. Med. Imaging **5**(3), 152–161 (1986)
120. Maitra, S.: Moment invariants. Proc. IEEE **67**(4), 697–699 (1979)
121. Mallat, S.G.: A theory for multiresolution signal decomposition: The wavelet representation. IEEE Trans. Pattern Anal. Mach. Intell. **11**(7), 674–693 (1989)
122. Mallat, S.: A Wavelet Tour of Signal Processing. Academic Press, New York (1998)
123. Manjunath, B.S., Ma, W.Y.: Texture features for browsing and retrieval of image data. IEEE Trans. Pattern Anal. Mach. Intell. **18**(8), 837–842 (1996)
124. Manjunath, B.S., Shekhar, C., Chellappa, R.: A new approach to image feature detection with applications. Pattern Recognit. **29**(4), 627–640 (1996)
125. Marabini, R., Carazo, J.M.: On a new computationally fast image invariant based on bispectrum projections. Pattern Recognit. Lett. **17**, 956–967 (1996)
126. Masry, E.: Wavelet transform of stochastic processes with stationary increments and its application to fractional Brownian motion. IEEE Trans. Inf. Theory **39**, 260–264 (1993)
127. Mikolajczyk, K., Tyetelaars, T., Schmid, C., Zisserman, A., Matas, J., Schaffalitzky, F., Kadir, T., Van Gool, L.: A comparison of affine region detectors. Int. J. Comput. Vis. **65**(1/2), 43–72 (2005)
128. Mitchell, R., Myer, C.R., Boyne, W.: A max-min measure for image texture analysis. IEEE Trans. Comput. **26**, 408–414 (1977)
129. Mohammed, A.-R., Jie, Y.: Practical fast computation of Zernike moments. J. Comput. Sci. Technol. **17**(2), 181–188 (2002)
130. Montanari, U.: A method for obtaining skeletons using a quasi-Euclidean distance. J. ACM **15**(4), 600–624 (1968)
131. Moravec, H.P.: Towards automatic visual obstacle avoidance. In: Proc. Int'l Joint Conf. Artificial Intelligence, p. 584 (1977)
132. Moravec, H.P.: Rover visual obstacle avoidance. In: Proc. Int'l Joint Conf. Artificial Intelligence, pp. 785–790 (1981)
133. Mukundan, R.: Some computational aspects of discrete orthogonal moments. IEEE Trans. Image Process. **13**(8), 1055–1059 (2004)
134. Mukundan, R., Ong, S.H., Lee, P.A.: Image analysis by Tchebichef moments. IEEE Trans. Image Process. **10**(9), 1357–1364 (2001)
135. Murase, H., Nayar, S.: Visual learning and recognition of 3-D objects from appearance. Int. J. Comput. Vis. **14**, 5–24 (1995)
136. Nagel, H.H.: Displacement vectors derived from second order intensity variations in image sequences. Comput. Vis. Graph. Image Process. **21**, 85–117 (1983)
137. Novotni, M., Klein, R.: Shape retrieval using 3D Zernike descriptors. Comput. Aided Des. **36**, 1047–1062 (2004)
138. Ojala, T., Pietikäinen, M.: Unsupervised texture segmentation using feature distribution. Pattern Recognit. **32**, 477–486 (1999)
139. Ojala, T., Pietikäinen, M., Harwood, D.: A comparative study of texture measures with classification based on feature distributions. Pattern Recognit. **29**(1), 51–59 (1996)

140. Oppenheim, A.V., Lim, J.S.: The importance of phase in signals. Proc. IEEE **69**(5), 529–541 (1981)
141. Oren, M., Papageorgiou, C., Sinha, P., Osuna, E., Poggio, T.: Pedestrian detection using wavelet templates. In: Proc. Computer Vision and Pattern Recognition, pp. 193–199 (1997)
142. Palm, C., Keysers, D., Lehmann, T., Spitzer, K.: Gabor filtering of complex hue/saturation images for color texture classification. In: Int. Conf. Computer Vision, Atlantic City, NJ, vol. 2, pp. 45–49 (2000)
143. Papageorgiou, C.P., Oren, M., Poggio, T.: A general framework for object detection. In: 6th Int'l Conf. Computer Vision, pp. 555–562 (1998)
144. Papakostas, G.A., Boutalis, Y.S., Papaodysseus, C.N., Fragoulis, D.K.: Numerical error analysis in Zernike moments computation. Image Vis. Comput. **24**, 960–969 (2006)
145. Papakostas, G.A., Boutalis, Y.S., Karras, D.A., Mertzois, B.G.: A new class of Zernike moments for computer vision applications. Inf. Sci. **177**, 1802–2819 (2007)
146. Papakostas, G.A., Karakasis, E.G., Koulouriotis, D.E.: Efficient and accurate computation of geometric moments on gray-scale images. Pattern Recognit. **41**, 1895–1904 (2008)
147. Papakostas, G.A., Karakasis, E.G., Koulouriotis, D.E.: Accurate and speedy computation of image Legendre moments for computer vision applications. Image Vis. Comput. **28**, 414–423 (2010)
148. Peleg, S., Naor, J., Hartley, R., Avnir, D.: Multiple resolution texture analysis and classification. IEEE Trans. Pattern Anal. Mach. Intell. **6**(4), 519–523 (1984)
149. Pentland, A.: Fractal-based description of natural scenes. IEEE Trans. Pattern Anal. Mach. Intell. **6**(6), 661–674 (1984)
150. Peterson, K., Ziglar, J., Rybski, P.E.: Fast feature detection and stochastic parameter estimation of road shape using multiple LIDAR. In: Proc. Int'l Conf. Intelligent Robot Systems, pp. 612–619 (2008)
151. Petrou, M., Kadyrov, A.: Affine invariant features from the trace transform. IEEE Trans. Pattern Anal. Mach. Intell. **26**(1), 30–44 (2004)
152. Pratt, W.K., Kane, J., Andrews, H.C.: Hadamard transform image coding. In: Proc. IEEE, pp. 58–70 (1969)
153. Pratt, W.K., Welch, L.R., Chen, W.H.: Slant transform for image coding. In: Proc. Symp. Application of Walsh Functions, pp. 229–234 (1972)
154. Pun, C.-M.: Rotation-invariant texture feature for image retrieval. Comput. Vis. Image Underst. **89**, 24–43 (2003)
155. Randen, T., Husøy, J.H.: Multichannel filtering for image texture segmentation. Opt. Eng. **33**(2), 2617–2625 (1994)
156. Randen, T., Husøy, J.H.: Filtering for texture classification: A comparative study. IEEE Trans. Pattern Anal. Mach. Intell. **21**(4), 291–310 (1999)
157. Reddi, S.S.: Radial and angular moment invariants for image identification. IEEE Trans. Pattern Anal. Mach. Intell. **3**(2), 240–242 (1981)
158. Reddy, B.S., Chatterji, B.: An FFT-based technique for translation, rotation and scale invariant image registration. IEEE Trans. Image Process. **5**(8), 1266–1271 (1996)
159. Reed, T.R., Du Buf, J.M.H.: A review of recent texture segmentation and feature extraction techniques. CVGIP, Image Underst. **57**(3), 359–372 (1993)
160. Reisfeld, D.: The constrained phase congruency feature detector: Simultaneous location, classification, and scale determination. Pattern Recognit. Lett. **17**(11), 1161–1169 (1996)
161. Reisfeld, D., Wolfson, H., Yeshurun, Y.: Detection of interest points using symmetry. In: Proc. 3rd Int'l Conf. Computer Vision, Osaka, Japan, pp. 62–65 (1990)
162. Reisfeld, D., Wolfson, H., Yeshurun, Y.: Context-free attention operators: The generalized symmetry transform. Int. J. Comput. Vis. **14**(2), 119–130 (1995)
163. Rohr, K.: Extraction of 3D anatomical point landmarks based on invariance principles. Pattern Recognit. **32**, 3–15 (1999)
164. Salvador, E., Cavallaro, A., Ebrahimi, T.: Cast shadow segmentation using invariant color features. Comput. Vis. Image Underst. **95**, 238–259 (2004)
165. Sarfaraz, M.S., Hellwich, O.: Estimation in face recognition across pose scenarios. In: Proc. Int'l Conf. Computer Vision Theory and Applications, vol. 1, pp. 235–242 (2008)

166. Sarkar, N., Chaudhuri, B.B.: An efficient differential box-counting approach to compute fractal dimension of image. IEEE Trans. Syst. Man Cybern. **24**, 115–120 (1994)
167. Sastry, Ch.S., Pujari, A.K., Deekshatulu, B.L., Bhagvati, C.: A wavelet based multiresolution algorithm for rotation invariant feature extraction. Pattern Recognit. Lett. **25**, 1845–1855 (2004)
168. Saupe, D.: Algorithms for random fractals. In: Peitgen, H., Saupe, D. (eds.) The Science of Fractal Images, pp. 71–136. Springer, New York (1988)
169. Schaffalizky, F., Zisserman, A.: Viewpoint invariant texture matching and wide baseline stereo. In: Proc. Int'l Conf. Computer Vision, vol. 2, pp. 636–643 (2001)
170. Schaffalitzky, F., Zisserman, A.: Multi-view matching for unordered image sets. In: European Conf. Computer Vision, pp. 414–431 (2002)
171. Schiele, B., Crowley, J.L.: Probabilistic object recognition using multidimensional receptive field histograms. In: Proc. 13th Int'l Conf. Pattern Recognition, vol. 2, pp. 50–54 (1996)
172. Schiele, B., Crowley, J.L.: Object recognition using multidimensional receptive field histograms. In: Proc. European Conf. Computer Vision (ECCV), vol. 1, pp. 610–619 (1996)
173. Selesnick, I.W., Baraniuk, R.G., Kingsburg, N.G.: The dual-tree complex wavelet transform—a coherent framework for multiscale signal and image processing. IEEE Signal Process. Mag. **22**(6), 123–151 (2005)
174. Serre, T., Wolf, L., Poggio, T.: Object recognition with features inspired by visual cortex. In: Proc. Conf. Computer Vision and Pattern Recognition, vol. 2, pp. 994–1000 (2005)
175. Shannon, C.E.: The mathematical theory of communication. In: Shannon, C.E., Weaver, W. (eds.) The Mathematical Theory of Communication, pp. 29–125. University of Illinois Press, Urbana (1949), reprint (1998)
176. Shen, D., Ip, H.H.S.: Discriminative wavelet shape descriptors for recognition of 2-D patterns. Pattern Recognit. **32**, 151–165 (1999)
177. Shen, B., Sethi, I.K.: Direct feature extraction from compressed images. In: SPIE Conf. Storage and Retrieval from Image and Video Databases IV, vol. 2670 (1996)
178. Shen, J., Shen, W., Shen, D.: On geometric and orthogonal moments. Int. J. Pattern Recognit. Artif. Intell. **14**(7), 875–894 (2000)
179. Shi, J., Tomasi, C.: Good features to track. In: Proc. IEEE Conf. Computer Vision and Pattern Recognition, Seattle, WA, pp. 593–600 (1994)
180. Shokoufandeh, A., Marsic, I., Dickinson, S.J.: View-based object recognition using saliency maps. Image Vis. Comput. **17**(5/6), 445–460 (1999)
181. Shu, H., Zhang, H., Haigron, P., Luo, L.: Fast computation of Tchebichef moments for binary and grayscale images. IEEE Trans. Image Process. **19**(12), 3171–3180 (2010)
182. Sirovich, L., Kirby, M.: Low-dimensional procedure for the characterization of human faces. J. Opt. Soc. Am. A **4**(3), 519–524 (1987)
183. Soille, P., Rivest, J.-F.: On the validity of fractal dimension measurements in image analysis. J. Vis. Commun. Image Represent. **7**(3), 217–229 (1996)
184. Staring, M., van der Heide, U.A., Klein, S., Viergever, M.A., Pluim, J.P.W.: Registration of cervical MRI using multifeature mutual information. IEEE Trans. Med. Imaging **28**(9), 1412–1421 (2009)
185. Stewart, G.W.: Introduction to Matrix Computations, p. 318. Academic Press, New York (1973)
186. Strang, G.: Wavelets and dilation equations: a brief introduction. SIAM Rev. **31**, 614–627 (1989)
187. Swain, M.J., Ballard, D.H.: Color indexing. Int. J. Comput. Vis. **7**(1), 11–32 (1991)
188. Szegö, G.: Orthogonal Polynomials, 4th edn. Am. Math. Soc., Providence (1981)
189. Tamura, H., Mori, S., Yamawaki, T.: Texture features corresponding to visual perception. IEEE Trans. Syst. Man Cybern. **8**(6), 460–473 (1978)
190. Tang, F., Lim, S.H., Chang, N.L., Tao, H.: A novel feature descriptor invariant to complex brightness changes. In: Proc. Computer Vision and Pattern Recognition, pp. 2631–2638 (2009)
191. Tango, W.J.: The circle polynomials of Zernike and their application in optics. Appl. Opt. **13**, 327–332 (1977)

192. Teague, M.R.: Image analysis via the general theory of moments. J. Opt. Soc. Am. **70**(8), 920–930 (1980)
193. Teh, C.-H., Chin, R.T.: On image analysis by the methods of moments. IEEE Trans. Pattern Anal. Mach. Intell. **10**(4), 496–513 (1988)
194. ter Haar Romeny, B.M., Florack, L.M.J., Salden, A.H., Viergever, M.A.: High order differential structure of images. In: 13th Int'l Conf. Information Processing in Medical Imaging, pp. 77–93 (1993)
195. Tewfik, A.H., Kim, M.: Correlation structure of the discrete wavelet coefficients of fractional Brownian motion. IEEE Trans. Inf. Theory **38**, 904–909 (1992)
196. Tian, Y., Tan, T., Wang, Y., Fang, Y.: Do singular values contain adequate information for face recognition. Pattern Recognit. **36**(3), 649–655 (2003)
197. Trajković, M., Hedley, M.: Fast corner detection. Image Vis. Comput. **16**, 75–87 (1998)
198. Tuceryan, M., Jain, A.K.: Texture analysis. In: Chen, C.H., Pau, L.F., Wang, P.S.P. (eds.) The Handbook of Pattern Recognition and Computer Vision, 2nd edn., pp. 207–248. World Scientific, Singapore (1998)
199. Turk, M., Pentland, A.P.: Eigenfaces for recognition. J. Cogn. Neurosci. **3**(1), 71–96 (1991)
200. Turner, M.R.: Texture discrimination by Gabor functions. Biol. Cybern. **55**, 71–82 (1986)
201. Tuytelaars, T., van Gool, L.: Content-based image retrieval based on local affinely invariant regions. In: Proc. Int. Conf. on Visual Information Systems, pp. 493–500 (1999)
202. Tuytelaars, T., van Gool, L.: Matching widely separated views based on affine invariant regions. Int. J. Comput. Vis. **59**(1), 61–85 (2004)
203. Tuyterlaars, T., van Gool, L.: Wide baseline stereo matching based on local, affinely invariant regions. In: British Machine Vision Conference (2000)
204. Tuytelaars, T., van Gool, L., D'haene, L., Koch, R.: Matching of affinely invariant regions for visual sevoing. In: Int'l Conf. Robotics and Automation, pp. 1601–1606 (1999)
205. Ullman, S., Vidal-Naquet, M., Sali, E.: Visual features of intermediate complexity and their use in classification. Nat. Neurosci. **5**(7), 682–687 (2002)
206. Unser, M.: Sum and difference histograms for texture classification. IEEE Trans. Pattern Anal. Mach. Intell. **8**(1), 118–125 (1986)
207. van Gool, L., Moons, T., Ungureanu, D.: Affine/photometric invariants for planar intensity patterns. In: Proc. European Conference on Computer Vision, pp. 642–651 (1996)
208. Voss, R.: Fractals in nature: From characterization to simulation. In: Peitgen, H., Saupe, D. (eds.) The Science of Fractal Images, pp. 21–70. Springer, New York (1988)
209. Walker, K.N., Cootes, T.F., Taylor, C.J.: Correspondence using distinct points based on image invariants. In: British Machine Vision Conference, pp. 540–549 (1997)
210. Walker, K.N., Cootes, T.F., Taylor, C.J.: Locating salient facial features using image invariants. In: Int. Conf. Automatic Face and Gesture Recognition, Nara, Japan (1998)
211. Walsh, J.L.: A closed set of orthogonal functions. Am. J. Math. **45**, 5–24 (1923)
212. Wang, H., Brady, M.: A practical solution to corner detection. In: Proc. 5th Int'l Conf. Image Processing, vol. 1, pp. 919–923 (1994)
213. Wang, H., Brady, M.: Real-time corner detection algorithm for motion estimation. Image Vis. Comput. **13**(9), 695–703 (1995)
214. Wang, G., Wang, S.: Recursive computation of Tchebichef moment and its inverse transform. Pattern Recognit. **39**, 47–56 (2006)
215. Wang, W., Li, J., Huang, F., Feng, H.: Design and implementation of Log-Gabor filter in fingerprint image enhancement. Pattern Recognit. Lett. **29**, 301–308 (2008)
216. Wang, Y.B., Zhang, B., Yao, T.S.: Moment invariants of restricted projective transformations. In: Int'l Sym. Information Science and Engineering, vol. 1, pp. 249–253 (2008)
217. Wee, C.-Y., Paramesran, R.: On the computational aspects of Zernike moments. Image Vis. Comput. **25**, 967–980 (2007)
218. Weszka, J.S., Dyer, C.R., Rosenfeld, A.: A comparative study of texture measures for terrain classification. IEEE Trans. Syst. Man Cybern. **6**(4), 269–285 (1976)
219. Wornell, G.W.: Wavelet-based representations for the $1/f$ family of fractal processes. Proc. IEEE **81**, 1428–1450 (1993)

220. Worthy, L., Sinzinger, E.: Scene identification using invariant radial feature descriptors. In: Proc. 8th Int'l Workshop Image Analysis for Multimedia Interactive Service, pp. 39–43 (2007)

221. Wu, Y., Shen, J.: Properties of orthogonal Gaussian–Hermite and their applications. EURASIP J. Appl. Signal Process. **4**, 588–599 (2005)

222. Wu, C.-M., Chen, Y.-C., Hsieh, K.-S.: Texture features for classification of ultrasonic liver images. IEEE Trans. Med. Imaging **11**(2), 141–152 (1992)

223. Xu, D., Li, H.: Geometric moment invariants. Pattern Recognit. **41**, 240–249 (2008)

224. Yap, P.-T., Paramesran, R., Ong, S.-H.: Image analysis by Krawtchouk moments. IEEE Trans. Image Process. **12**(11), 1367–1377 (2003)

225. You, J., Cohen, H.A.: Classification and segmentation of rotated and scaled textured images using texture 'tuned' masks. Pattern Recognit. **26**(2), 245–258 (1993)

226. Yuanbin, W., Bin, Z., Tianshun, Y.: Projective invariants of co-moments of 2D images. Pattern Recognit. **43**, 3233–3242 (2010)

227. Zhang, Y., Chen, T.: Efficient kernels for identifying unbounded-order spatial features. In: Proc. Conf. Computer Vision and Pattern Recognition, pp. 1762–1769 (2009)

228. Zhang, L., Ghosh, B.K.: Geometric feature based 2.5D map building and planning with laser, sonar, and tactile sensors. In: Proc. Int'l Conf. Intelligent Robots and Systems, vol. 1, pp. 115–120 (2000)

229. Zhang, X.-W., Song, J.-Q., Lyu, M.R., Cai, S.-J.: Extraction of karyocytes and their components from microscopic bone marrow images based on regional color features. Pattern Recognit. **37**, 351–361 (2004)

230. Zhang, J., Marszalek, M., Lazebnik, S., Schmid, C.: Local features and kernels for classification of texture and object categories: A comprehensive study. Int. J. Comput. Vis. **73**(2), 213–238 (2007)

231. Zhang, B., Shan, S., Chen, X., Gao, W.: Histogram of Gabor phase patterns (HGPP): A novel object representation approach for face recognition. IEEE Trans. Image Process. **16**(1), 57–68 (2007)

232. Zhang, H., Shu, H., Han, G.N., Gouenou, G., Luo, L., Coatrieux, J.L.: Blurred image recognition by Legendre moment invariants. IEEE Trans. Image Process. **19**(3), 596–611 (2010)

233. Zhou, X.S., Rui, Y., Huang, T.S.: Water-filling: A novel way for image structural feature extraction. In: Proc. Int'l Conf. Image Processing, vol. 2, pp. 570–574 (1999)

234. Zhu, H., Shu, H., Xia, T., Luo, L., Coatrieux, J.L.: Translation and scale invariants of Tchebichef moments. Pattern Recognit. **40**, 2530–2542 (2007)

Chapter 5
Image Descriptors

An image descriptor is a feature vector containing various information about an image. It is a compact representation that can be used to distinguish one image from another. Summary and characterization of image descriptors have been previously provided by Guyon and Elisseeff [20], Kittler [27], Mikolajczyk and Schmid [31], Saeys et al. [39], and Winder and Brown [56].

Descriptors are traditionally created from components of the same type, measuring statistical, geometric, algebraic, differential, or spatial properties of an image. This self-imposed restriction, however, is not necessary and the components of a descriptor can represent different types of information. Hörster and Lienhart [21] and Schiele and Crowley [42] have shown that two or more descriptors of different types provide a higher recognition power than any one of the descriptors when used alone. Descriptors that are composed of heterogenous components are discussed in the next chapter.

In image registration, descriptors are needed to determine the correspondence between control points in two images. Once control points are detected, windows centered at them are selected (Fig. 5.1). Information within the windows are then used to establish correspondence between points in the images. If the images do not have rotation and scaling differences, by finding the similarity between the windows, best-matching windows in the images can be identified by template-matching, as discussed in Chap. 2. However, when the images have unknown rotation and scaling differences, rotation and scale invariant descriptors are needed to find the correspondences.

Although our focus will be on windows centered at control points in images, the following discussions apply to whole images as well. Therefore, in the rest of this chapter, *image* and *window* will be used interchangeably. We consider circular rather than rectangular windows to ensure that windows centered at corresponding points in two images contain the same scene parts independent of their rotational differences.

To create scale and rotation invariant descriptors, various approaches have been proposed. One class of descriptors converts an image to a representation that is invariant to rotation and scale and characterizes the transformed image. An example

A.A. Goshtasby, *Image Registration*,
Advances in Computer Vision and Pattern Recognition,
DOI 10.1007/978-1-4471-2458-0_5, © Springer-Verlag London Limited 2012

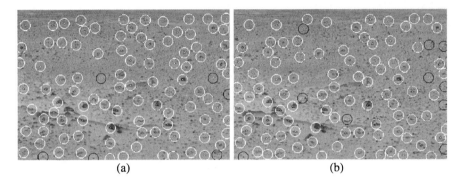

(a)   (b)

Fig. 5.1 (**a**), (**b**) Stereo images of a Mars scene, courtesy of NASA. Shown are detected control points and the circular windows centered at them

of such a representation is an image histogram. Another class of methods estimates the scale and orientation of an image first, normalizes the image with respect to scale and rotation, and then describes the normalized image. An example of such a representation is SIFT [30] (Sect. 5.2). Other descriptors use invariant features, such as invariant moments, to characterize a neighborhood.

5.1 Histogram-Based Descriptors

The color or intensity histogram of a circular window is a rotationally invariant vector that describes the window. Swain and Ballard [48] used the color histogram of an image to characterize the color distribution of the image. Image histograms are insensitive to small changes in imaging view angle, occlusion, and scale. The invariant property of the histogram, which is its strength, is also its weakness. Two images of the same scene could produce very different histograms due to different lighting conditions, while images of two different scenes could produce very similar histograms.

A color image with red (R), green (G), and blue (B) components has a 3-D histogram. When the image under consideration is very small, the obtained histogram will be very sparse, making histogram matching unreliable. In such a situation, each color component, which normally is in the range [0, 255], is mapped to a smaller range, such as [0, 7]. Since this quantization can cause two very similar colors to be mapped to different bins in a histogram, rather than letting the color at a pixel contribute to a single histogram bin, a Gaussian is centered at the histogram bin corresponding to the color at the pixel, contributing to different histogram bins by amounts inversely proportional to their distances to the bin representing the center of the Gaussian. Assuming $G_\sigma(R, G, B)$ is a 3-D Gaussian of standard deviation σ centered at bin (R, G, B) within the 3-D histogram, the image histogram is then calculated from

$$H(R, G, B) = \sum_x \sum_y G_\sigma\big(R(x, y), G(x, y), B(x, y)\big), \qquad (5.1)$$

where $(R(x, y), G(x, y), B(x, y))$ denote (R, G, B) color components at pixel (x, y). The sum is over all pixels in a circular window of a given radius centered at a control point. Note that G_σ does not have to be quantized to discrete values. Rather, their floating-point values can be used in the calculation of the histogram. The standard deviation of the Gaussian is typically a small number, such as 0.5 or 1. Also, note that instead of RGB, other color coordinates can be used in the same manner to create a color histogram.

The similarity between two color histograms is determined from their intersection. Given histograms H_1 and H_2, their intersection at entry (R, G, B) is computed from [48]

$$D(R, G, B) = \min\{H_1(R, G, B), H_2(R, G, B)\} \tag{5.2}$$

and the intersection at all entries is computed from:

$$I(H_1, H_2) = \sum_R \sum_G \sum_B D(R, G, B). \tag{5.3}$$

To obtain a measure between 0 and 1 independent of the size of a window, the above measure is normalized with respect to the window size. Therefore, if the windows used in matching are of size N pixels,

$$S_1(H_1, H_2) = \frac{I(R, G, B)}{N} \tag{5.4}$$

will be the normalized similarity measure. The closer S_1 is to 1, the more similar the color distributions in the windows being matched will be.

Schiele and Crowley [41] proposed methods for finding the dissimilarity or distance between two histograms. In one method, they suggested using the sum of squared differences between corresponding histogram bins as the dissimilarity measure:

$$S_2(H_1, H_2) = \sum_R \sum_G \sum_B [H_1(R, G, B) - H_2(R, G, B)]^2. \tag{5.5}$$

In another method, they suggested using the χ^2 test as the dissimilarity measure:

$$\chi^2(H_1, H_2) = \sum_R \sum_G \sum_B \frac{[H_1(R, G, B) - H_2(R, G, B)]^2}{H_1(R, G, B) + H_2(R, G, B)}. \tag{5.6}$$

The smaller the dissimilarity between two histograms, the more likely it is that their associating windows represent the same scene. Sebe and Lew [44] formulated the problem of finding the similarity between two histograms as a maximum likelihood estimation problem. In addition, they showed that hue-saturation-value (HSV) histograms more reliably match/recognize images than RGB histograms.

Note that two windows that contain the same pattern but have different contrasts can produce histograms that have a small overlap, while two windows that contain quite different patterns can produce histograms that have a large overlap. Therefore, histogram-based descriptors have the potential to produce high false positive and high false negative probabilities. However, Swain and Ballard [48] show that in real-life applications, if the images/windows under consideration are sufficiently large and histogram bins are finely spaced, such likelihoods are small, and histograms are, in general, effective rotation-invariant descriptors that can be used to match/recognize images.

The effect of image contrast on a computed similarity measure can be minimized by converting *RGB* to *HSV* (hue, saturation, value), discarding the *V* component, which varies with image contrast, and using only the *HS* components. It should be noted that by discarding the *V* component, considerable image information is lost. Therefore, if the images do not have contrast differences, *HSV* histograms rather than *HS* histograms should be used to find correspondence between image windows.

Although the preceding discussions centered at color images and color histograms, the same discussions apply to gray-scale images. A gray-scale image has a 1-D histogram, simplifying calculation of the intersection of two histograms.

Rather than using the raw intensities or colors at image pixels, one may use local image properties that are calculated from the intensities or colors. An example is the Weber local descriptor (WLD) of Chen et al. [10], where from image intensities in a window two properties are calculated. One property shows the ratio of the difference of the intensity at a pixel and average intensity of pixels around it, and the second property shows the gradient direction at the pixel. A 2-D histogram is then formed from pixels within the window with the two dimensions representing the two properties. WLD is inspired by the Weber's law, which states that the ratio of the just noticeable change in intensity observed by a human over the original intensity at a point is a constant. The descriptor, therefore, has some invariance properties that are shared by the human visual system.

5.2 Scale-Invariant Feature Transform (SIFT)

To detect points representing the centers of blobs in an image, the image is convolved with Gaussians of standard deviations $2^{n/2}$ for $n \geq 0$, creating a stack of images. From the stack of Gaussian smoothed images, another stack of images is produced with each image representing the difference of adjacent Gaussian smoothed images. The nth image in the new stack, which is a difference of Gaussian (DoG) smoothed images, approximates the Laplacian of Gaussian (LoG) image of standard deviation $2^{n/2}$. Pixel (x, y) in the original image is considered the center of a blob if an extremum is detected at (x, y, n) in the volumetric image obtained from the stack of DoG images [30].

As the size/scale of an image is changed, the parameter n obtained at an extremum will change. Therefore, n is an indicator of the scale of the image. However, n also depends on the scale of the local pattern centered at the point. If the same pattern of a larger size appears in another location in the same image, parameter n calculated there will be higher. Therefore, parameter n depends on the local scale of the pattern as well as the global scale of the image.

Considering that the same point (x, y) can be extremum at multiple scales, it may not be possible to find a unique scale at an image point. This is natural because concentric overlapping regions can produce multiple extrema at exactly the same point or at points very close to each other. Therefore, there may not be a one-to-one correspondence between an extremum at scale n and the actual scale of the blob there. Assuming that a single extremum is detected at an image point at scale n, by mapping an area of radius $2^{n/2}$ at the extremum to an area of a fixed size, the neighborhood can be normalized for its local and global scale.

To create a descriptor for the window centered at an extremum detected at scale n, first, the gradient magnitude and gradient direction of each pixel within the window at scale n are computed. This involves convolving the image with a Gaussian of standard deviation $\sigma_n = 2^{n/2}$ and calculating gradient magnitude and direction at each pixel in the smoothed image. The gradient magnitudes within a window of width $2\sigma_n$ centered at the extremum are then weighted by a Gaussian of standard deviation $1.5\sigma_n$ centered at the extremum. This weighting will make gradient contributions farther from the extremum smaller, making the descriptor less sensitive to geometric differences between two windows. This Gaussian weighting also reduces the difference between the contents of square windows in two images with coinciding centers but rotational differences.

The direction of the highest gradient magnitude sum within a window is then used as the direction of the window. This involves finding a 36-bin histogram of the gradient directions and locating the peak of the histogram. The histogram bin with the peak value identifies the direction where the gradient magnitude sum is maximum. This direction is normal to the direction of local structure. If the histogram does not possess a unique peak, the dominant gradient direction will not be unique. This happens when a symmetric pattern is centered at a point. If a unique peak is found, by rotating the image so that the peak gradient direction aligns with the y-axis, the local structure will align with the x-axis, and it becomes possible to measure gradient information in the window centered at the extremum independent of the image orientation. The process, in effect, makes it possible to generate a descriptor independent of the orientation of the image.

Knowing the orientation of a local structure with respect to the image coordinate axes, a square window of side $2^{1+n/2}$ pixels is considered at the calculated orientation (Fig. 5.2). Gradient magnitudes within the window are then accumulated into 8 directions after normalization with respect to the peak direction in each of the 4×4 blocks within the window (Fig. 5.2b). The bin corresponding to a direction within a block, therefore, contains the sum of the gradient magnitudes in that direction within the block. The process produces $4 \times 4 \times 8 = 128$ numbers overall, which are used as the descriptor for the window. Finally, the descriptor is normalized to have magnitude 1.

Since a proportionately larger window is selected for a larger scale n, a larger scale will produce a larger gradient sum. The normalization is meant to ensure that if the same pattern is scaled and the scale is known, by selecting the window size proportionately large, the same descriptor is obtained for the same pattern independent of its scale. However, local scale is not known and the only information available is the combined local and global scale.

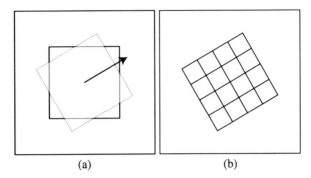

Fig. 5.2 A square window is selected centered at an extremum detected at scale n with its side equal to $2^{1+n/2}$. Gradient magnitudes and directions of pixels within the window are calculated. The gradient magnitudes are weighted by a Gaussian centered at the extremum and standard deviation equal to $1.5 \times 2^{n/2}$ and the histogram of the gradient-magnitude weighted gradient directions is computed with 36 bins. The direction represented by the histogram peak is taken as the direction for the window. A window of side equal to $2^{1+n/2}$ is then taken in the peak direction, as shown in (**a**), and gradient magnitudes within each of the 4 × 4 square blocks, shown in (**b**), are grouped into 8 bins according to their gradient directions with respect to the peak direction. This produces a histogram with 8 bins within each block, producing $4 \times 4 \times 8 = 128$ numbers overall, which are used as the descriptor of the window centered at the extremum

Assuming the images being registered are of the same scale and have the same orientation but have different local contrasts, the peak gradient sum obtained at corresponding points in the images can point to different gradient directions. Weighing gradient directions with their gradient magnitudes, therefore, works well when the images do not have spatially varying intensity differences. To reduce the influence of local image contrast on the generated descriptors, the histograms of the gradient directions at the 4 × 4 blocks within a window should be calculated without gradient-magnitude weighting. To make the generated descriptors invariant to smoothly varying image contrast, Toews and Wells III [52] used the ranks of the gradient magnitudes rather than their raw values. Improved matching accuracy was reported as a result of this new weighting, especially when images had nonlinear but monotone intensity differences.

Along with each SIFT descriptor, the scale and orientation of the window used in the calculations are saved. By normalizing the gradient directions with respect to the peak gradient direction and by normalizing the descriptors to have magnitude 1, a created descriptor is intended to be invariant to the scale and orientation of the image.

Since a SIFT descriptor is based on estimated scale and orientation of a local neighborhood, an error in the estimation of the scale or orientation parameter will result in inaccuracies in the created descriptor. The SIFT detector finds local extrema of the response of an image to LoG or its approximation, DoG, in scale-space. When the underlying structure is circular, the estimated scale is proportional to the size of the structure [4]. The same applies to elliptic structures. However, for more complex structures with branches, the process is very sensitive to changes in image view, image scale, and noise. Therefore, estimated scale and orientation parameters for a neighborhood can be quite different from their true values. Not knowing the shape of a local structure, it is not know how reliable the estimated scale and rotation parameters are.

Normally, when an extremum is detected from a round structure, by increasing or decreasing the scale of the image, the location of the extremum does not change. However, if an extremum is detected from a complex structure with branches, a small change in image scale can break the structure and displace the detected extremum. Therefore, if point (x, y, n) in scale-space is a locally extremum point, then we can consider the point at (x, y) stable if the same point will be locally extremum in the DoG images at scales $n - \Delta n$ and $n + \Delta n$ also, where Δn is a small increment in n, such as $\sqrt{2}$. This simple test makes it possible to distinguish a stable extremum and its descriptor from an unstable extremum and its descriptor.

To find a match to a sensed window from among many reference windows, Lowe [30] determined the Euclidean distance between the sensed descriptor and the two reference descriptors closest to it. Let's suppose the obtained distances are D_1 and D_2, where $D_1 \leq D_2$. Then the ratio of the smaller distance over the larger, $r = D_1/D_2$, is determined and $p = 1 - r$ is considered the likelihood that the closest reference descriptor corresponds to the sensed descriptor in a nearest-neighbor classifier. Correspondences where $p < 0.8$ are discarded to avoid mismatches. Note that matching in this manner will discard all similar reference windows and will keep only those that are globally unique. In effect, the process cannot find correspondence between local structures that are not globally unique.

To make the process use local rather than global uniqueness, ratio of distances of a control point to control points within a scale-adjusted threshold distance is taken and the similarity between the distance-ratios is used to determine correspondence between control points in images. If k reference windows produce $p > 0.8$ when matching with a sensed window, the reference window that produces the most similar distance-ratios when compared to that of the sensed window is chosen as the best-match window. Chin and Suter [12] used distances alone to find correspondence between control points in two images. Shin and Tjahjadi [45] used local distances of a control point to its surrounding control points to supplement the information provided by SIFT, improving the recognition/matching accuracy of the SIFT descriptor.

Pele and Werman [37] noticed that Euclidean distance between SIFT descriptors is based on the assumption that the SIFT descriptors are correctly aligned (i.e., the scale and orientation parameters are determined accurately). Otherwise, descriptors for corresponding points will be displaced with respect to each other. Pele and Werman suggested using the Earth Mover's distance rather than the Euclidean distance to compute the distance between SIFT descriptors, reporting improved matching accuracy.

Rather than using image gradients, Mutch and Lowe [35] and Moreno et al. [34] used responses to multi-scale Gabor filters to define a SIFT descriptor, reporting improved recognition/matching accuracy over the original SIFT descriptor.

The SIFT descriptor has been extended to color and multispectral images. Bosch et al. [5] computed SIFT descriptors over the three HSV color components, creat-

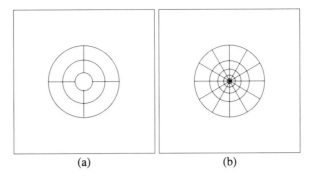

(a)   (b)

Fig. 5.3 (**a**) The log-polar grid with the 17 blocks used in the GLOH descriptor [31]. Gradient magnitudes in each block are grouped into 16 according to their gradient directions, producing $17 \times 16 = 272$ numbers. The dimensions of a descriptor are reduced to 128 by PCA. (**b**) The shape context of Belongie et al. [3] with 5 uniformly spaced rings in the log-polar space. Gradient magnitudes in each circular block are then grouped into 12 according to their gradient directions, producing a descriptor with $5 \times 12 = 60$ values

ing a descriptor with 3×128 components. Van de Weijer [54] concatenated the hue histogram with the luminance SIFT descriptor to create a new descriptor that contained both color and luminance information. Abdel-Hakim and Farag [1] used the gradients of the color invariance described by Geusebroek et al. [19] instead of the intensity gradients used in the SIFT descriptor to create a color descriptor invariant to change in contrast.

Van de Sande et al. [53] found that a SIFT descriptor based on opponent colors is most invariant to changes in color. The opponent and RGB color coordinates are related by

$$\begin{pmatrix} O_1 \\ O_2 \\ O_3 \end{pmatrix} = \begin{pmatrix} (R - G)/\sqrt{2} \\ (R + G - 2B)/\sqrt{6} \\ (R + G + B)/\sqrt{3} \end{pmatrix}. \tag{5.7}$$

Brown and Süsstrunk [6] followed the method of Van de Sande et al. but replaced the three-dimensional RGB vectors with four-dimensional RGB and near-infrared vectors, in a descriptor called multispectral SIFT or MSIFT.

An extension of the SIFT descriptor proposed by Mikolajczyk and Schmid [31] uses the gradient location and orientation histogram (GLOH) computed in a log-polar grid. At each extremum, a log-polar grid with rings of radii 6, 11, and 15 pixels is positioned. The grid has 2 blocks radially and 8 blocks angularly, plus the center block, creating 17 blocks overall (Fig. 5.3a). Then, gradient magnitudes at pixels in each block are grouped into 16 according to their gradient directions, producing a descriptor with $16 \times 17 = 272$ components. A component shows the sum of gradient magnitude of a particular direction at a particular block within the neighborhood under consideration. Finally, the number of components is reduced to 128 by principal component analysis (PCA). The covariance matrix for PCA is computed from the windows centered at the points in the reference image. Note that the window used by GLOH is circular while that used by SIFT is square but Gaussian weighted.

Belongie et al. [3] used a grid with 5 uniformly spaced radial blocks in the log-polar space and 12 uniformly spaced blocks angularly, creating a descriptor called *shape context* with 60 components (Fig. 5.3b). Radial spacing is made uniform in the log-polar space to increase the influence of information at and near the point of interest. Each component in the descriptor shows the number of edges in one of the 12 directions in one of the 5 circular blocks. Note that this descriptor also uses a circular neighborhood. Mikolajczyk and Schmid [31] find that if the images do not have intensity differences, the sum of the gradient magnitudes produces a better matching accuracy than the number of pixels of a particular gradient direction.

In some literature, SIFT, GLOH, and shape context are called histogram-based descriptors, although these descriptors do not possess the global properties of a histogram. In SIFT and GLOH, a histogram is formed within each block and the histogram bins from the blocks are concatenated in a prespecified order to create the descriptor. In shape context, 12-bin histograms are produced at each of the 5 radial blocks and the histograms are concatenated to create a sequence of 60 numbers. Therefore, although parts of these descriptors represent histograms, a created descriptor does not posses the properties of a histogram. Rather than being a weakness, this can be considered a strength. By ordering local histograms in a prespecified order in a descriptor, structural information in the underlying window is preserved.

Another extension of the SIFT descriptor is provided by Ke and Sukthanker [25] called PCA-SIFT. First, local scale and orientation are determined for the window centered at an extremum by SIFT. Then the neighborhood of the right size and orientation centered at the point is resampled to a 41×41 patch. This resampling normalizes the neighborhood with respect to scale and orientation. Next, gradients of pixels in the patch are horizontally and vertically calculated and ordered in a gradient vector of size $2 \times 39 \times 39 = 3042$. The dimension of the gradient vector is reduced to 36 by PCA. The covariance matrix for PCA is calculated using the gradient vectors for the windows centered at extrema in the reference image. Matching/recognition is achieved using a nearest-neighbor classifier.

A sensed window is represented by a point in the 36-dimensional eigenspace by projecting the gradient vector of the sensed window to the 36 principal components. The same is done for the reference windows, each producing a point in the eigenspace. Then, distances of the sensed point to the reference points are determined in the eigenspace and the reference point closest to a sensed point is taken to identify the sensed point and the window corresponding to the reference point is taken to correspond to the sensed window.

The rotation and scale invariant properties of the SIFT descriptor makes the descriptor suitable for determining the correspondence between local neighborhoods that are related by the similarity transformation. To enable matching of local neighborhoods in images captured from different views, an affine-invariant descriptor called ASIFT is proposed by Morel and Yu [33]. ASIFT normalizes image features with respect to shearing and leaves normalization of features with respect to translation, rotation, and scaling to SIFT, thus producing an affine-invariant descriptor. When the images to be matched represent different views of a scene, considerable improvement in matching has been reported by ASIFT when compared with SIFT.

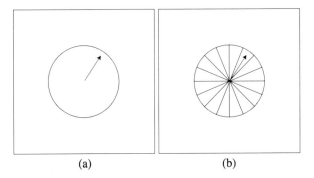

(a)   (b)

Fig. 5.4 (a) A circular window centered at a point of interest and the direction of the peak gradient magnitude sum are shown. (b) The window is quantized into 16 sectors, with the first sector aligned with the direction of peak gradient magnitude sum. Ordinal intensity histograms of the sectors are then concatenated in a prespecified order to create a descriptor for the window

Improvements to ASIFT have been proposed by Le Brese et al. [29] and Noury et al. [36].

Although many image descriptors are based on image gradients, other properties of an image may be used to create descriptors. Huang et al. [22] used central contrast in a log-polar grid similar to that of Belongie et al. [3] to define a descriptor called contrast context histogram (CCH). Contrast at a pixel is calculated from the intensity difference between that pixel and the center pixel within a window. The descriptor obtained from the contrast measure calculated in this manner will be insensitive to changes in scene lighting. This is because such changes affect all pixels in a window, including its center. The intensity difference between each pixel in a window and the intensity at the center of the window normalizes the intensities, creating a descriptor that is resistant to slowly varying image contrast.

Other descriptors that are formed from the concatenation of local histograms have been proposed. Tang et al. [49] first converted image intensities to 8 ordinal values to reduce the dependency of a descriptor on image contrast. Then, a circular window centered at a point was taken and subdivided into 16 sectors (Fig. 5.4). The histogram of the ordinal intensities within each sector was then determined and the histograms were concatenated in a prespecified order to create a descriptor with $8 \times 16 = 128$ components. The first sector is taken to be the peak gradient direction determined by SIFT. The obtained descriptor is called ordinal spatial intensity distribution (OSID). Use of ordinal intensities rather than the raw intensities is intended to make the descriptor independent of nonlinear but monotone intensity differences between two images in matching. Since the peak direction is taken to be the direction determined by SIFT, which is sensitive to local image contrast, the created descriptor will be sensitive to local image contrast even though ordinal intensities are used to create the histogram within each of the 16 sectors.

A similar structure was employed by Worthy and Sinzinger [57] using both gradient and color information in a sector. Gradient is calculated radially and tangentially. The circular window centered at a point is divided into 4 sectors, and a histogram with 8 bins is created from the gradients for each sector, each bin covering an angular range of $\pi/8$, producing overall $8 \times 4 = 32$ numbers. A similar vector is obtained using saturation-weighted hues within each sector, again, grouping the values into 8 bins and producing another 32 numbers. The two vectors are then concatenated to produce a descriptor with 64 components, containing both spatial and color information about a neighborhood in its descriptors. Use of only hue and saturation without luminance makes the descriptor invariant to changes in scene illumination, and concatenation of the histograms for different sectors in a prespecified order with respect to the peak gradient direction makes the descriptor invariant to rotation. Contrast invariance is achieved at the cost of discarding the rich luminance information that can potentially distinguish complex structures from each other. Other descriptors that have been inspired by the SIFT descriptor have used edge orientation [38] and gradient orientation [13, 14, 58].

When a window is subdivided into blocks, if the rotational difference between two windows is a multiple of the angle covered by a block, the descriptors will be rotation invariant. However, if the rotational difference between two windows is not an integer multiple of a block's angular width, the information contained in a block in one window will be split into adjacent blocks in the other window, dulling the matching process. To improve matching accuracy, the window can be subdivided into finer blocks, each covering a smaller angular range. This, however, will make the histograms sparser and will increase the dimensionality of the descriptor.

The key ideas *intended* in the SIFT descriptor are: (1) to use the histogram of an image property to make a created descriptor resistant to the local geometric deformation caused by imaging view or presence of occlusion, (2) to concatenate the local histograms in a window in a prespecified order to encode structural information in the window within the created descriptor, (3) to describe the contents of the window with respect to a local coordinate system that has its x-axis pointing in the direction of the local structure, and (4) to take window size proportional to the scale of the local structure. A descriptor obtained in this manner will be independent of the scale and orientation of the local structure and insensitive to local image deformation.

5.3 Spin-Image-Based Descriptors

Lazebnik et al. [28] used the spin-image idea of Johnson and Hebert [24] to map properties at pixels in a circular window to a rectangular grid where the horizontal axis shows the distance of a pixel in the circular grid to its center and the vertical axis shows the quantized property value at the pixel. An example of this mapping is given in Fig. 5.5. Property values of pixels in a circular block (pixels between two consecutive rings) are grouped into 8 bins in a histogram. This process, in effect, maps property values in a circular grid to a vector of $4 \times 8 = 32$ numbers.

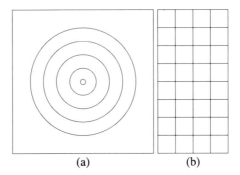

Fig. 5.5 (a) A grid containing 4 circular blocks and (b) its spin image. A rotation-invariant property, such as intensity or radial gradient, is chosen. A histogram of the property values at pixels within each circular block is obtained. In this example, the histogram has 8 bins. The histogram bins are then mapped to spin-image entries in a column. Therefore, different columns in the spin image represent different circular blocks in the grid, and a particular row in a column shows the value at the corresponding histogram bin obtained for the circular block representing that column. When the spin image entries are scanned in raster (or any other prespecified) order, a descriptor with 32 components called rotation-invariant feature transform (RIFT) is obtained

Note that if the property under consideration is invariant to image rotation, the information produced in the rectangular grid will be rotation invariant. Image intensity is an example of such a property. Lazebnik et al. [28] used gradient direction calculated radially in the outward direction and used that as the rotation invariant property. The gradient direction at a pixel is determined with respect to the direction obtained by connecting the pixel to the window center. The descriptor obtained as a result is called rotation-invariant feature transform (RIFT).

There is a similarity between the shape context of Belongie et al. [3] and RIFT in that both concatenate histograms of the property values between consecutive rings in a circular grid; however, their main difference is in the spacing between the rings. In the spin image the radii of the rings are uniformly spaced, but in the shape context the logarithm radii of the rings are uniformly spaced. Logarithm spacing emphasizes property values at and near the center of the window and deemphasizes property values far away from the center. When the centers of two windows with geometric differences correspond, since geometric differences between windows increase as one moves away from the window center, shape context will be less sensitive to image deformations than RIFT.

The desire to describe an object with respect to a local coordinate system rather than the global coordinate system of the image has led to the development of the spin image idea. A spin image is meant to produce the same representation for a window independent of its position within an image and the orientation of the image. All the descriptors discussed above provide this property as they are measured with respect to a coordinate system that is positioned at the center of the window under consideration and normalized in one way or another with respect to the orientation of the window.

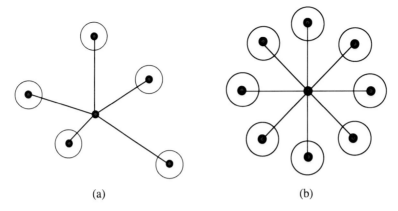

(a)   (b)

Fig. 5.6 (**a**) Arrangement of regions around a point of interest as considered by Schmid and Mohr [43]. The region centers can themselves be detected points closest to the point under consideration. (**b**) Arrangement of regions around a point of interest as considered by Carneiro and Jepson [8]. The regions are at fixed positions and orientations with respect to the point under consideration

5.4 Filtering-Based Descriptors

Florack et al. [17] used responses of an image window to rotationally invariant Gaussian derivative filters as the descriptor for the window. For instance, responses of a window to zeroth order and second order Gaussian filters are invariant to rotation. The sum of squares of the responses of a window to the first derivatives of a Gaussian in x- and y-directions is also rotationally invariant. Other filters created from combinations of Gaussian derivatives that are rotationally invariant have been found [17], some of which were outlined in Sect. 4.6. Consider convolving various rotationally invariant filters within a window. A feature vector constructed from the obtained responses can then be used as a descriptor to characterize the window.

Schmid and Mohr [43] used feature vectors representing responses of regions within a window to various Gaussian derivative filters to describe the window. Feature vectors were then used to establish correspondence between parts of two windows. As more correspondence is established between parts of the windows, correspondence between the windows is reinforced.

Carneiro and Jepson [8] used responses of regions around a point of interest to complex steerable filters as a descriptor for the window centered at the point. The difference between the regions used by Schmid and Mohr [43] and Carneiro and Jepson [8] is depicted in Fig. 5.6. While the regions used by Schmid and Mohr are centered at an unorganized set of points around a point of interest, the regions used by Carneiro and Jepson are centered at fixed locations and orientations with respect to the point under consideration. The feature vectors produced for the individual regions are then concatenated to create a descriptor for the neighborhood centered at the point. To produce a rotationally invariant descriptor, the reference direction is determined by one of the existing methods [18, 30].

Complex filter responses [2] and wavelet transform coefficients [31] are other filtering-based descriptors that have been used. The descriptor obtained from filter responses characterizes the spatial frequency characteristics of a neighborhood. Such descriptors are generally not invariant to image scale since a change in image scale results in changes in spatial frequencies in the neighborhood. In Sect. 5.8.2, a method for normalizing an image with respect to scale and orientation is described.

5.5 Moment-Based Descriptors

Various moments can be used to characterize the geometry of the pattern in a window. Chen and Sun [9] used Zernike moments to construct a descriptor for a circular window. Zernike moments provide orthogonal features that lack redundancy and, therefore, are very compact. Magnitude Zernike moments are invariant to image rotation [32]; therefore, they can be used to create rotation-invariant descriptors. However, by discarding phase, valuable information is lost. Therefore, in the descriptor of Chen and Sun [9], phase as well as magnitude Zernike moments are used. The rotational difference between two windows is determined from the phase difference between corresponding Zernike moments.

Assuming $f(\rho, \theta)$ shows intensity at polar coordinates (ρ, θ) measured with respect to the center of a circular window where ρ is normalized to vary between 0 and 1, and assuming A_{mn} is the Zernike moment of order (m, n) given by (4.91), the Zernike moment of the same order after rotating the window about its center by α will be $A_{mn} \exp(jn\alpha)$, where $j = \sqrt{-1}$. If two sets of Zernike moments describe two windows that are rotated with respect to each other by α, corresponding moments will be different in phase by α. Corresponding moments in descriptors that represent different patterns will not have the same phase difference. This provides a means to use Zernike moments to not only establish correspondence between circular windows in two images, but also to determine the rotational difference between them.

Noise and other image differences, however, can produce somewhat different phases even when the windows contain the same scene parts. Kim and Kim [26] suggested weighing the phase difference estimated for a corresponding Zernike moment of order (m, n) by the magnitude Zernike moment $\|A_{mn}\|$ and finding the weighted average of the phase differences of corresponding moments as the phase difference between matching windows. An advantage that this method has over the principal axis method or the gradient peak of SIFT is in its ability to determine the rotational difference between nearly symmetric windows.

Van Gool et al. [55] used affine invariant moments that were also invariant to image contrast as image descriptors. Other invariant moments discussed in Sect. 4.2.2 can be used to create descriptors in the same manner. It should be noted that, since the ranges of values the higher order moments can assume is much higher than that of lower order moments, when a descriptor is created from a combination of moments of different orders, the moments with highest orders will dominate the calculation of a similarity or dissimilarity measure. Either the moments used as features in a descriptor should be normalized so they all have the same dynamic range, or a similarity/dissimilarity measure that takes into consideration the dynamic ranges of the features should be used.

5.6 Composite Descriptors

To use various types of information in matching/recognition, a combination of descriptors may be used. Schiele and Crowley [40, 42] provide a means for determining the similarity between two images when using two or more descriptors from each image. Suppose $p(o_i|r_j)$ represents the probability density function of windows in the reference image corresponding to window o_i in the sensed image. Since window r_j is unique in reference image, $p(r_j) = 1/M$ for M windows in the reference image, and the probability that window o_i in the sensed image corresponds to window r_j in the reference image is estimated by the Bayes decision rule from [51]:

$$p(r_j|o_i) = \frac{p(o_i|r_j)p(r_j)}{p(o_i)}$$
$$= \frac{p(o_i|r_j)p(r_j)}{\sum_{j=1}^{M} p(o_i|r_j)p(r_j)}. \tag{5.8}$$

If two descriptors that provide different types of information about a window are available, both descriptors can be used to improve the correspondence accuracy. Schiele and Crowley [42] suggested using the joint probabilities of the normalized descriptors. Therefore, if descriptors o_{i1} and o_{i2} represent independent properties of a window i in the sensed image, and assuming that the corresponding descriptors for window j in the reference image are r_{j1} and r_{j2}, then the probability that windows i and j in the images correspond will be

$$p(r_{j1}, r_{j2}|o_{i1}, o_{i2}) = \frac{p(o_{i1}, o_{i2}|r_{j1}, r_{j2})p(r_j)}{\sum_{j=1}^{M} p(o_{i1}, o_{i2}|r_{j1}, r_{j2})p(r_j)}$$
$$= \frac{p(o_{i1}|r_{j1})p(o_{i2}|r_{j2})p(r_j)}{\sum_{j=1}^{M} p(o_{i1}|r_{j1})p(o_{i2}|r_{j2})p(r_j)}. \tag{5.9}$$

In general, if k descriptors are available, each of which provide independent information about a window, a sensed window can be identified from among M reference windows by finding the reference window r_j that maximizes [42]

$$p(r_{j1}, \ldots, r_{jk}|o_{i1}, \ldots, o_{ik}) = \frac{\prod_{l=1}^{k} p(o_{il}|r_{jl})p(r_j)}{\sum_{j=1}^{M} \prod_{l=1}^{k} p(o_{il}|r_{jl})p(r_j)}. \tag{5.10}$$

If the *a priori* probability $p(r_j) = 1/M$ for all j, the above relation reduces to

$$p(r_{j1}, \ldots, r_{jk}|o_{i1}, \ldots, o_{ik}) = \frac{\prod_{l=1}^{k} p(o_{il}|r_{jl})}{\sum_{j=1}^{M} \prod_{i=1}^{k} p(o_{il}|r_{jl})}. \tag{5.11}$$

To describe the contents of a window with moving parts, Fergus et al. [16] defined a descriptor for each part of the window and used a combination of the descriptors to represent the window. A Bayesian maximum-likelihood classifier was then used to find the class of a window using descriptors representing its parts. The same can be done to match windows with fixed parts and find the correspondence between windows centered at control points in two images.

Creating a descriptor from the responses of a window to Gaussian derivatives of various degrees and creating another descriptor from the responses of the window to a bank of Gabor filters, Schiele and Crowley [42] showed that if both descriptors are used, an unknown window can be more accurately identified. The same conclusion was reached by Hörster and Lienhart [21] using descriptors representing color histogram and SIFT features. Brown et al. [7] also showed that a combination of various descriptors provides a higher discrimination power than SIFT. In addition, they developed a learning mechanism to select the best combination of descriptors to minimize error in nearest-neighbor matching using a training data set.

Rather than using a single scale and orientation for the window centered at a point of interest, Cheng et al. [11] used multiple support regions around the point of interest, each with its own scale and orientation. Then a descriptor was computed for each support region and by concatenating the local descriptors, a global descriptor was formed. Similarity between two global descriptors was computed using a filtering step and a refinement step. The filtering step rejected those reference windows that were not likely to match a sensed window, and the refinement step narrowed down on the reference window that best matched the sensed window. This method was found to be particularly effective when matching windows with deformable parts.

Dickscheild et al. [15] compared local descriptors from the point of view of information completeness and found that a combination of descriptors that decode complimentary information reproduce the most complete information about an image.

5.7 Similarity/Dissimilarity Between Descriptors

When features in a descriptor have different dynamic ranges, the dynamic range of each feature should be taken into consideration when calculating the similarity or dissimilarity between the descriptors. If descriptors $\mathbf{x} = \{x_i : i = 1, \ldots, n\}$ and $\mathbf{y} = \{y_i : i = 1, \ldots, n\}$ have positive components, a dissimilarity or distance measure that normalizes each feature with respect to its scale is [46]:

$$d_1(\mathbf{x}, \mathbf{y}) = \left\{ \frac{1}{n} \sum_{i=1}^{n} \left(\frac{x_i - y_i}{x_i + y_i} \right)^2 \right\}^{\frac{1}{2}}. \tag{5.12}$$

The difference between corresponding features in the two descriptors is divided by the sum of the two features. This normalization ensures that the squared difference of corresponding features will vary between 0 and 1 independent of the scale of that feature.

Another dissimilarity/distance measure that provides this property is [46]:

$$d_2(\mathbf{x}, \mathbf{y}) = -\log\left(1 - \frac{1}{n}\sum_{i=1}^{n}\frac{|x_i - y_i|}{b_i - a_i}\right) \qquad (5.13)$$

where a_i and b_i are the minimum and maximum values of the ith feature and are obtained from all available descriptors, and log is in base 10. Distance measure d_2 becomes 0 when the two descriptors are exactly the same, and as the descriptors become less similar, the distance d_2 increases. Note that the scale normalization performed by d_1 is local to the two descriptor, while the scale normalization performed by d_2 is global to all descriptors. Therefore, d_1 will scale the same feature differently depending on the two descriptors being compared, while d_2 scales a feature independent of the particular descriptors being compared.

Schmid and Mohr [43] and Mikolajczyk and Schmid [31] used the Mahalanobis distance between two descriptors as the distance between the descriptors. Given two descriptors $\mathbf{x}$ and $\mathbf{y}$ with covariance matrix Σ, the Mahalanobis distance between $\mathbf{x}$ and $\mathbf{y}$ is computed from

$$d_3(\mathbf{x}, \mathbf{y}) = \sqrt{(\mathbf{y} - \mathbf{x})^t \Sigma^{-1}(\mathbf{y} - \mathbf{x})}. \qquad (5.14)$$

The covariance matrix Σ in the Mahalanobis distance takes into consideration not only the correlation between features, it normalizes the scale of each feature by its spread. When the range of values a feature takes in a descriptor varies from feature to feature, Mahalanobis distance is preferred over the Euclidean distance.

If features with different scales are used in a descriptor, since the feature with the largest scale has the most influence on a calculated Euclidean distance, small inaccuracies in features with large scales can degrade a calculated measure and have a significant effect on the outcome. If the true descriptor is $\mathbf{v}$ and the measured descriptor is $\widetilde{\mathbf{v}}$, we can write

$$\widetilde{\mathbf{v}} = \mathbf{v} + \mathbf{e}, \qquad (5.15)$$

where $\mathbf{e}$ is the error vector. Therefore, if error in the measurement of the ith feature is $e[i]$, we will have

$$\widetilde{v[i]} = v[i] + e[i]. \qquad (5.16)$$

Mahalanobis distance assumes that $\mathbf{e}$ has a multidimensional normal distribution. However, this assumption is violated when the features are calculated from windows centered at non-corresponding points. Terasawa et al. [50] suggested calculating the distance between feature vectors $\mathbf{v}_i$ and $\mathbf{v}_j$ from

$$d_4(\mathbf{v}_i, \mathbf{v}_j) = \sqrt{\sum_k \left(\frac{v_i[k] - v_j[k]}{s[k]}\right)^2}, \qquad (5.17)$$

where $s[k]$ is the scale of the kth feature.

When calculating the distance between two descriptors with features that have different scales, first the scale of each feature should be estimated. Assuming σ_i is the scale of the ith feature, then distance d_i between the ith feature in two descriptors should be normalized with respect to σ_i. Then the sum of the normalized feature distances

$$d_5 = \sum_{i=1}^{n} \frac{d_i}{\sigma_i} \tag{5.18}$$

can be used as the distance between the descriptors.

If the features represent different types of information, the similarity/dissimilarity measure between each type may be determined and an appropriate weighted sum of the measures can be used as the similarity/dissimilarity measure. For example, to determine the similarity between descriptors containing both shape and color information about two windows, Jain and Vailaya [23] calculated similarities of the windows using the shape features and the color features separately. Then they combined the individual similarity measures into a combined similarity measure using appropriate weights. Assuming S_c and S_s represent color and shape similarities of two windows, the combined similarity between the windows is determined from

$$S = \frac{W_c S_c + W_s S_s}{W_c + W_s}, \tag{5.19}$$

where weights W_c and W_s are determined empirically and show the importance of color and shape features in determining the similarity between two images or windows.

5.8 Estimating Global Scale and Rotation Parameters

If two windows have different scales and orientations, there is a need to either use scale and rotation invariant features or normalize the windows so they have the same scale and orientation before finding their features. The SIFT descriptor estimates the scale and orientation of a window, reorients the window, and normalizes the calculated features with respect to the estimated scale, generating a scale- and rotation-invariant descriptor for the window.

If the pattern within the window under consideration is round and symmetric, SIFT can localize the window quite accurately, but it cannot reliably estimate its orientation. If the pattern is elongated or has branches, it can find the local orientation reliably, but it cannot estimate the local scale reliably as a small change in image resolution can change local structure drastically.

Since the scale estimated by SIFT depends on the global scale of the image as well as the local scale of the pattern, it is not possible to tell the scale of the image from an estimated scale. The questions we would like to answer are: (1) Given estimates to dominant orientations of windows centered at control points in two images without knowledge about the correspondence between the points, is it possible to determine the rotational difference between the images? (2) Given estimates to the scales of windows centered at control points in two images without knowledge about correspondence between the points, is it possible to determine the scale ratio between the images?

Once the rotational difference and the scale ratio between two images are known, then one image can be resampled to the scale and orientation of the other, facilitating the correspondence process. Two approaches to global scale and rotation parameter estimation are provided below.

5.8.1 Scale and Rotation Estimation by Clustering

Suppose M control points are present in a reference image and N control points are present in a sensed image. Suppose the orientations estimated by SIFT or other methods at windows centered at the points in the reference and sensed images are $\{\alpha_i : i = 1, \ldots, M\}$ and $\{\beta_j : j = 1, \ldots, N\}$, respectively.

If we calculate $D_{ij} = \beta_j - \alpha_i$ for different values of i and j, we will see that when points i and j in the images truly correspond to each other, and the estimated orientations are relatively accurate, D_{ij} will produce about the same difference, forming a cluster around the true rotational difference between the images. However, when points i and j do not correspond to each other, D_{ij} for different values of i and j will fall randomly in the 1-D space. Therefore, clustering can be performed in 1-D to find the rotational difference between the images. This method was first proposed by Stockman et al. [47]. The process involves clustering D_{ij} for a large combination of i and j and finding the location of the highest peak.

When the orientations estimated at the points are not accurate, clustering may miss the correct rotational difference between the images due to lack of a clear peak. To enhance the peak, there is a need to avoid irrelevant angles that appear as noise in clustering. Rather than finding the rotational difference between random combinations of points in the images, points in the sensed image are only paired with points in the reference image that have similar local arrangements. Information about local arrangement of points in an image is reflected in the minimum spanning tree (MST) or the triangulation of the points. Such information is invariant of the orientation and scale of an image. Degree of a point **P** in an MST or a triangulation of a point set shows the number of edges with one end at **P**. Having a graph to represent the MST or the triangulation of the points in an image, each point becomes a vertex in the graph. We will determine and save the degree of each vertex with the vertex in the graph.

After finding the degrees of the points in both images, we will calculate D_{ij} only when the degree at point i in the reference image is within a small threshold of the degree of point j in the sensed image. The threshold value will be a small number such as 1. A small threshold value will reduce calculation of a large number of irrelevant angles that act as noise in clustering, while preserving the relevant angles in clustering and facilitating localization of the dominant peak.

To determine the scaling ratio between two images, we will determine the ratio of scales estimated at points i and j and use the logarithm of the ratio when clustering.

That is, we let $D_{ij} = \log(S_j/s_i) = \log(S_j) - \log(s_i)$, where s_i and S_j are the scales of windows centered at point i in the reference image and point j in the sensed image, respectively. The scale ratio between two images is then determined in the same manner the rotational difference between the images is determined.

Since D_{ij} for both rotation and scale represents a floating-point number, to map the numbers to discrete bins in the cluster space, if a cluster space with n bins is used and assuming $a = \min(D_{ij})$ and $b = \max(D_{ij})$, then values in $[a, b]$ are mapped to $[0, n-1]$ by letting $x_{ij} = (D_{ij} - a)(n-1)/(b-a)$ and incrementing entry $round(x_{ij})$ by $A_{ij} = \exp\{-(k-l)^2\}$. k and l represent the degrees of point i in the reference image and point j in the sensed image, respectively. The process will produce a weighted histogram, emphasizing point pairs that have closer degrees.

Clustering will find the rotational difference or the scale ratio between two images such that most points in the images are matched. The rotational difference $D_{\max}$ identified by the cluster peak shows the rotational difference of the sensed image with respect to the reference image. In the case of scale, $D_{\max}$ shows the logarithm of scale ratio of the sensed image with respect to the reference image. Therefore, $\exp(D_{\max})$ represents the scale of the sensed image with respect to the reference image.

Since bins in the cluster space represent discrete measures, to more accurately estimate the rotational difference or scale ratio of two images, rather than incrementing a single histogram bin by A_{ij} for D_{ij}, bin D is incremented by

$$A_{ij} \exp\left\{ -\frac{(D - D_{ij})^2}{2\sigma^2} \right\}, \tag{5.20}$$

for $D = 0, \ldots, n-1$, where σ is a small number such as 0.5 or 1. This will produce a "soft cluster" where a measured rotational difference or scale ratio contributes to more than one cluster bin and is proportional to the difference between the D_{ij} and the center of bin D.

The finer the clustering bins are, the more accurate the estimated rotational difference or scaling ratio between the images will be. Soft clustering with the increments shown by (5.20) avoids creation of sparse entries. Soft clustering ensures that values are obtained in all bins in the cluster space, reducing ambiguity in localization of the cluster peak.

Examples demonstrating use of clustering in determination of the unknown rotation of one image with respect to another are given in Fig. 5.7. Suppose Fig. 5.7a is a reference image, and Figs. 5.7b–e are various sensed images obtained by adding uniform noise of amplitude 10 to reference image, rotating reference image clockwise by 30 degrees, smoothing reference image with a Gaussian of standard deviation 1.5 pixels, and scaling reference image by 1.5. 10% uniform noise implies generating random numbers between -0.1 and 0.1, multiplying the numbers by 255, and adding the obtained numbers to the intensities. In the event that an intensity becomes larger than 255, it is set to 255, and in the event that it becomes smaller than 0, it is set to 0. The SIFT points detected in these images along with their local orientations and scales are shown in Figs. 5.7f–j, respectively. The orientation of the window centered at a point is shown by the arrow at the point and the scale of the pattern within the window is shown by the length of the arrow.

Fig. 5.7 (a) A circular image
showing a coin.
(b)–(e) Noisy, rotated,
smoothed, and scaled images
of the coin. (f)–(j) The SIFT
points of images (a)–(e),
respectively, along with their
orientations and scales

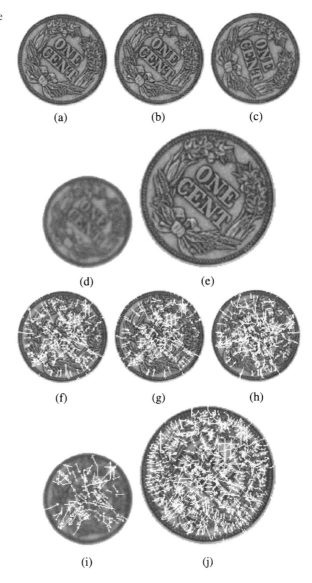

Assuming degree of point i in the reference image is k and degree of point j in the sensed image is l when $|k - l| \le 1$, the orientational differences between points i and j in the images are determined and clustered for all possible i and j. When using Fig. 5.7a as the reference and Fig. 5.7c as the sensed image, we obtain the clustering shown in Fig. 5.8a. Entry $round(D_{ij})$ in cluster space is incremented by $\exp(-|k - l|^2)$. Processing only point pairs in the images that have exactly the same degree, that is $k = l$, we obtained the clustering depicted in Fig. 5.8b. Although the location of the peak has not changed, the noise has decreased and the peak is more

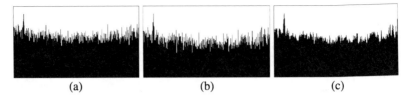

Fig. 5.8 (**a**) Rotational clustering of descriptors in images of Figs. 5.7a and 5.7c using points pairs that either have the same degree or have degrees that differ by 1. (**b**) The same as (**a**) but computed from point pairs that have exactly the same degree. (**c**) The same as (**b**) but using the soft clustering idea with $\sigma = 1$

Fig. 5.9 (**a**)–(**c**) Rotational clustering when using the image in Fig. 5.7c against the images in Figs. 5.7b, 5.7d, and 5.7e, respectively

pronounced. The soft clustering idea with $\sigma = 1$ produced a less noisy clustering as shown in Fig. 5.8c.

When using the image in Fig. 5.7c against the images in Figs. 5.7b, 5.7d, and 5.7e, the clustering results shown in Figs. 5.9a–c, respectively, are obtained. The cluster peak in each case corresponds to the 30° rotational difference between the images. Although the peaks find the correct answer in each case, the peaks are not pronounced and it is conceivable that the process could fail in other images. This is an indication that a great proportion of the dominant directions reported by the SIFT descriptor at the control points is not accurate.

Clustering was not able to find the scale ratio between the images in Fig. 5.7 using the scale parameters produced by the SIFT descriptor. Since a SIFT descriptor is generated based on the estimated scale and rotation, any inaccuracy in the estimated scale and/or rotation will carry over to the accuracy of the generated descriptor. Therefore, windows that have inaccurate rotation and/or scale parameters will have descriptors that are inaccurate.

To distinguish useful descriptors from noisy ones in SIFT, post-processing of the parameters is required. We know that if a point represents a round region, its scale can be more accurately estimated than a point that represents a complex structure with branches. Therefore, we will need to distinguish round regions from non-round ones to identify useful descriptors from other descriptors.

A characteristic of a round region is that its center will not move as the image resolution/scale is changed. Using this property, we can find SIFT points at two resolutions of an image, keep only those points that do not move, and discard the rest.

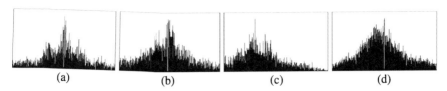

Fig. 5.10 (**a**)–(**d**) Scale clustering when using the image in Fig. 5.7c against the images in Figs. 5.7a, 5.7b, 5.7d, and 5.7e, respectively

The above process was repeated after filtering out the unstable points using a distance tolerance of 1 pixel and Gaussian smoothing of standard deviation 1 pixel. When using the image in Fig. 5.7c against images in Figs. 5.7a, 5.7b, 5.7d, and 5.7e, the clustering results shown in Figs. 5.10a–d are, respectively, obtained. Relatively well-defined histograms are created. The scale parameter for the original and noisy images are estimated correctly to be 1. However, the scale parameter estimated when the images have scale or resolution differences is not reliable. When using the images in Figs. 5.7c and 5.7d, a scale ratio of 1 should be obtained; however, the process finds a scale ratio of 0.66. The process thinks that the image in Fig. 5.7c is a scaled down version of the smoothed image in Fig. 5.7d. On the other hand, when using the images in Figs. 5.7c and 5.7e, the process finds a scale ratio of 1.0, even though the correct scale ratio is 1/1.5.

The conclusion to be reached by these experiments is that when the images do not have scale or resolution differences, the scale and rotation parameters generated by SIFT are useful and can be used to determine the rotational difference and the scale ratio of local neighborhoods. However, if the images have unknown scale and resolution differences, the scale parameters estimated by SIFT are not useful. Since the generated descriptors are based on the estimated rotation and scale parameters, this implies that SIFT descriptors are useful when comparing images with the same scale/resolution, and they are not useful when comparing images with scale/resolution differences.

5.8.2   Scale and Rotation Estimation by Log-Polar Mapping

A descriptor provides information about a window with respect to a coordinate system that is centered at the window. If two images have only translational differences, windows centered at corresponding points will contain the same scene parts, producing descriptors that are the same or very similar.

If the images have unknown rotational and scaling differences, windows containing the same scene parts cannot be selected at corresponding points and that makes generation of similar descriptors for windows centered at corresponding points impossible. One way to overcome this difficulty is to transform the window centered at each point into a form that is invariant to the orientation and scale of the image. A transformation that provides this property is log-polar mapping.

In log-polar mapping, an $M \times N$ window $f(x, y)$ in the Cartesian coordinate system is mapped to a $P \times Q$ array $g(u, v)$ in the log-polar coordinate system. First, the Cartesian coordinate system origin is moved to the image center. This involves a translation:

$$X = x - \bar{x}, \tag{5.21}$$

$$Y = y - \bar{y}, \tag{5.22}$$

where $\bar{x} = M/2$ and $\bar{y} = N/2$. Then, polar coordinates

$$r = \sqrt{X^2 + Y^2}, \tag{5.23}$$

$$\theta = \tan^{-1}(Y/X) \tag{5.24}$$

are calculated from the new Cartesian coordinates, and finally the log-polar coordinates are found:

$$u = a \log(r), \tag{5.25}$$

$$v = b\theta, \tag{5.26}$$

where $r \geq 1$ and a and b are parameters that determine the dimensions P and Q of the log-polar image. a and b can be considered units defining pixel dimensions in the log-polar map. Given a and b, the dimensions of the log-polar image are calculated from

$$P = \left[0.5 \log(M^2 + N^2) - \log 2\right] a, \tag{5.27}$$

$$Q = 2\pi b. \tag{5.28}$$

The center pixel, which represents the origin of the Cartesian coordinate system, is not processed in order to avoid calculation of $\log(0)$.

Note that isotropic scaling with respect to the center of a window implies replacing r with sr. Scaling in the Cartesian coordinate system will displace point $(a \log(r), b\theta)$ to $(a \log(r) + a \log(s), b\theta)$ in the log-polar map. Therefore, isotropically scaling a window by s causes its log-polar map to translate along the u-axis by $a \log(s)$. Rotating a window by α will move point $(a \log(r), b\theta)$ to $(a \log(r), b\theta + b\alpha)$ in the log-polar map, cyclically translating the log-polar map along the v-axis by $b\alpha$.

Examples of log-polar mapping are given in Fig. 5.11. Images (a)–(e) in this figure show the log polar maps of images (a)–(e) in Fig. 5.7, respectively. As can be observed, isotropic scaling causes the log-polar map to shift horizontally, and rotation causes the log-polar map to cyclically shift vertically. Therefore, images that have scaling and rotational differences but coincide at their centers will produce log-polar maps that are only translated with respect to each other.

Log-polar mapping can be considered a preprocessing operation that is applied to a window to normalize it with respect to scale and orientation of the underlying image. Note that this normalization is done with respect to a center point that is the control point location. Therefore, if circular windows are taken centered at corresponding control points, the produced log-polar maps will have only translational differences. The translational difference between two log-polar maps can

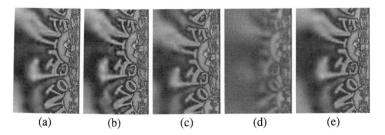

| (a) | (b) | (c) | (d) | (e) |

Fig. 5.11 (a)–(e) Log-polar maps of the images in Figs. 5.7a–e, respectively

Fig. 5.12 (**a**) The central
portion of Fig. 5.7e taken to
be the same size as that in
Figs. 5.7a–d. (**b**) The
log-polar map of image (**a**)

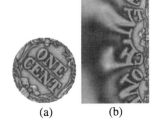

(a)   (b)

be determined by locating the peak in their cross-power spectrum, as discussed in
Sect. 2.1.1.

Since there is a one-to-one correspondence between points in a window and
points in its log-polar map, knowing the translational difference between two log-
polar maps, the rotational and scaling difference between the windows can be determined. For instance, if in the transformed domain the sensed image is translated
with respect to the reference image by (u, v), the scale ratio and rotational difference
between the original images will be:

$$s = e^{\frac{u}{a}}, \tag{5.29}$$

$$\theta = v/b. \tag{5.30}$$

Parameters a and b relate to the resolution of the log-polar map and determine
the accuracy in estimation of the rotational difference and scaling ratio between
the two images from the translational difference between their log-polar maps. The
larger parameters a and b are, the more accurate the estimated scale and rotation
parameters will be. Increased accuracy, however, will be at a higher computational
cost.

Cross-power spectra of log-polar map pairs in Fig. 5.11 correctly determined
the scaling and rotational differences between the images from which the log-polar
maps were found. Note that not knowing the scale ratio between two images, the
windows used to obtain the log-polar maps will be all the same size. This means that
instead of the image in Fig. 5.7e, we actually have to use the image in Fig. 5.12a. The
log-polar map of this image is shown in Fig. 5.12b. The cross-power spectrum of
this image and any of the images in Fig. 5.11 again correctly determine the rotational
difference and scaling ratio between the images.

While it was possible to determine the rotation and scale parameters between only some of the images in Fig. 5.7 by clustering of SIFT parameters, it was possible to determine the rotation and scale parameters between all images in Fig. 5.7 by clustering of parameters determined by log-polar mapping. For points that correspond, log-polar mapping determines the rotation and scale parameters accurately. The rotation and scale parameters determined by SIFT are often not accurate enough to produce unique and robust peaks in clustering to unambiguously determine the rotation and scale parameters.

References

1. Abdel-Hakim, A.E., Farag, A.A.: CSIFT: A SIFT descriptor with color invariant characteristics. In: Proc. IEEE Conf. Computer Vision and Pattern Recognition, vol. 2, pp. 1978–1983 (2006)
2. Baumberg, A.: Reliable feature matching across widely separated views. In: IEEE Conf. Computer Vision and Pattern Recognition, vol. 1, pp. 774–781 (2000)
3. Belongie, S., Malik, J., Puzicha, J.: Shape matching and object recognition using shape contexts. IEEE Trans. Pattern Anal. Mach. Intell. 24(4), 509–522 (2002)
4. Blostein, D., Ahuja, N.: A multiscale region detector. Comput. Vis. Graph. Image Process. 45, 22–41 (1989)
5. Bosch, A., Zisserman, A., Muñoz, X.: Scene classification using a hybrid generative/discriminative approach. IEEE Trans. Pattern Anal. Mach. Intell. 30(4), 712–727 (2008)
6. Brown, M., Süsstrunk, S.: Multi-spectral SIFT for scene category recognition. In: Proc. IEEE Conf. Computer Vision and Pattern Recognition, pp. 177–184 (2011)
7. Brown, M., Hua, G., Winder, S.: Discriminative learning of local image descriptors. IEEE Trans. Pattern Anal. Mach. Intell. 33(1), 43–57 (2010)
8. Carneiro, G., Jepson, A.D.: Phase-based local features. In: European Conf. Computer Vision, Copenhagen, Denmark, pp. 282–296 (2002)
9. Chen, Z., Sun, S.-K.: A Zernike moment phase-based descriptor for local image representation and matching. IEEE Trans. Image Process. 19(1), 205–219 (2010)
10. Chen, J., Shan, S., He, C., Zhao, G., Pietikäinen, M., Chen, X., Gao, W.: WLD: A robust local image descriptor. IEEE Trans. Pattern Anal. Mach. Intell. 32(9), 1705–1710 (2010)
11. Cheng, Y., Swamisai, R., Umbaugh, S.E., Moss, R.H., Stoecker, W.V., Teegala, S., Srinivasan, S.K.: Skin lesion classification using relative color features. Skin Res. Technol. 14, 53–64 (2008)
12. Chin, T.-J., Suter, D.: Keypoint induced distance profiles for visual recognition. In: Proc. Computer Vision and Pattern Recognition, pp. 1239–1246 (2009)
13. Dalal, N., Triggs, B.: Histograms of oriented gradients for human detection. In: Proc. Computer Vision and Pattern Recognition, pp. 886–893 (2005)
14. Dalal, N., Triggs, B., Schmid, C.: Human detection using oriented histograms of flow and appearance. In: Proc. European Conference Computer Vision, pp. 428–441 (2006)
15. Dicksheild, T., Schindler, F., Förstner, W.: Coding images with local features. Int. J. Comput. Vis. 94, 154–174 (2011)
16. Fergus, R., Perona, P., Zisserman, A.: Object class recognition by unsupervised scale-invariant learning. In: Proc. IEEE Computer Society Conf. Computer Vision and Pattern Recognition, pp. 1063–6919 (2003)
17. Florack, L., ter Haar Romeny, B., Koenderink, J., Viergever, M.: General intensity transformations and second order invariants. In: Proc. Seventh Scandinavian Conf. Image Analysis, pp. 338–345 (1991)
18. Freeman, W.T., Adelson, W.H.: The design and use of steerable filters. IEEE Trans. Pattern Anal. Mach. Intell. 13(9), 891–906 (1991)

19. Geusebroek, J.M., van den Boomgaard, R., Smeulders, A.W.M., Geerts, H.: Color invariance. IEEE Trans. Pattern Anal. Mach. Intell. **23**(12), 1338–1350 (2001)
20. Guyon, I., Elisseeff, A.: An introduction to variable and feature selection. J. Mach. Learn. Res. **3**, 1157–1182 (2003)
21. Hörster, E., Lienhart, R.: Fusing local image descriptors for large-scale image retrieval. In: Computer Vision and Pattern Recognition, pp. 1–8 (2007)
22. Huang, C.-R., Chen, C.-S., Chung, P.-C.: Contrast context histogram—an efficient discriminating local descriptor for object recognition and image matching. Pattern Recognit. **41**, 3071–3077 (2008)
23. Jain, A.K., Vailaya, A.: Image retrieval using color and shape. Pattern Recognit. **29**(8), 1233–1244 (1996)
24. Johnson, A.E., Hebert, M.: Recognizing objects by matching oriented points. In: Proc. Computer Vision and Pattern Recognition, pp. 684–689 (1997)
25. Ke, Y., Sukthankar, R.: PCA-SIFT: A more distinctive representation for local image descriptors. In: Proc. Conf. Computer Vision and Pattern Recognition, pp. 511–517 (2004)
26. Kim, W.-Y., Kim, Y.-S.: Robust rotation angle estimator. IEEE Trans. Pattern Anal. Mach. Intell. **21**(8), 768–773 (1999)
27. Kittler, J.: Feature set search algorithms. In: Chen, C.H. (ed.) Pattern Recognition and Signal Processing, pp. 41–60 (1978)
28. Lazebnik, S., Schmid, C., Ponce, J.: Sparse texture representation using local affine regions. IEEE Trans. Pattern Anal. Mach. Intell. **27**(8), 1265–1278 (2005)
29. Le Brese, C., Zou, J.J., Uy, B.: An improved ASIFT algorithm for matching repeated patterns. In: Proc. IEEE Int'l Conf. Image Processing, pp. 2949–2952 (2010)
30. Lowe, D.: Distinctive image features from scale-invariant keypoints. Int. J. Comput. Vis. **60**(2), 91–110 (2004)
31. Mikolajczyk, K., Schmid, C.: A performance evaluation of local descriptors. IEEE Trans. Pattern Anal. Mach. Intell. **27**(10), 1615–1630 (2005)
32. Mohan, V., Shanmugapriya, P., Venkataramani, Y.: Object recognition using image descriptors. In: Proc. Int'l Conf. Computing, Communication and Networking, pp. 1–4 (2008)
33. Morel, J.M., Yu, G.: ASIFT: A new framework for fully affine invariant image comparison. SIAM J. Imaging Sci. **2**, 438–469 (2009)
34. Moreno, P., Bernardino, A., Santos-Victor, J.: Improving the SIFT descriptor with smooth derivative filters. Pattern Recognit. Lett. **30**, 18–26 (2009)
35. Mutch, J., Lowe, D.G.: Multiclass object recognition with sparse, localized features. In: IEEE Computer Society Conf. Computer Vision and Pattern Recognition, vol. 1, pp. 11–18 (2006)
36. Noury, N., Sur, F., Berger, M.-O.: How to overcome perceptual aliasing in ASIFT. In: Proc. 6th Int'l Sym. Visual Computing, vol. 1 (2010)
37. Pele, O., Werman, M.: A linear time histogram metric for improved SIFT matching. In: European Conf. Computer Vision (2008)
38. Pinheiro, A.M.G.: Image descriptors based on the edge orientation. In: Int'l Workshop on Digital Object Identifier: Semantic Media Adaptation and Personalization, pp. 73–78 (2009)
39. Saeys, Y., Inza, I., Larrañaga, P.: A review of feature selection techniques in bioinformatics. Bioinformatics **23**(19), 2507–2517 (2007)
40. Schiele, B., Crowley, J.L.: Probabilistic object recognition using multidimensional receptive field histograms. In: Proc. 13th Int'l Conf. Pattern Recognition, vol. 2, pp. 50–54 (1996)
41. Schiele, B., Crowley, J.L.: Object recognition using multidimensional receptive field histograms. In: Proc. European Conf. Computer Vision (ECCV), vol. 1, pp. 610–619 (1996)
42. Schiele, B., Crowley, J.L.: Recognition without correspondence using multidimensional receptive field histograms. Int. J. Comput. Vis. **36**(1), 31–50 (2000)
43. Schmid, C., Mohr, R.: Local gray-value invariants for image retrieval. IEEE Trans. Pattern Anal. Mach. Intell. **19**(5), 530–535 (1997)
44. Sebe, N., Lew, M.S.: Robust color indexing. In: Int'l Multimedia Conf., pp. 239–242 (1999)
45. Shin, D., Tjahjadi, T.: Clique descriptor of affine invariant regions for robust wide baseline image matching. Pattern Recognit. **43**, 3261–3272 (2010)

46. Spath, H.: Cluster Analysis Algorithms. Ellis Horwood, Chichester (1980)
47. Stockman, G., Kopstein, S., Benett, S.: Matching images to models for registration and object detection via clustering. IEEE Trans. Pattern Anal. Mach. Intell. **4**(3), 229–241 (1982)
48. Swain, M.J., Ballard, D.H.: Color indexing. Int. J. Comput. Vis. **7**(1), 11–32 (1991)
49. Tang, F., Lim, S.H., Chang, N.L., Tao, H.: A novel feature descriptor invariant to complex brightness changes. In: Proc. Computer Vision and Pattern Recognition, pp. 2631–2638 (2009)
50. Terasawa, K., Nagasaki, T., Kawashima, T.: Error evaluation of scale-invariant local descriptor and its application to image indexing. Electron. Commun. Jpn., Part 3 **90**(2), 31–39 (2007)
51. Theodoridis, S., Koutroumbas, K.: Pattern Recognition, 4th edn. Academic Press, San Diego (2009), pp. 602, 605, 606
52. Toews, M., Wells, W. III: SIFT-Rank: Ordinal description for invariant feature correspondence. In: Computer Vision and Pattern Recognition Workshops, pp. 172–177 (2009)
53. van de Sande, K., Gevers, T., Snoek, C.G.M.: Evaluating color descriptors for object and scene recognition. IEEE Trans. Pattern Anal. Mach. Intell. **32**(9), 1582–1596 (2010)
54. van de Weijer, J., Gevers, T., Bagdanov, A.: Boosting color saliency in image feature detection. IEEE Trans. Pattern Anal. Mach. Intell. **28**(1), 150–156 (2006)
55. van Gool, L., Moons, T., Ungureanu, D.: Affine/photometric invariants for planar intensity patterns. In: Proc. European Conference on Computer Vision, pp. 642–651 (1996)
56. Winder, S.A.J., Brown, M.: Learning local image descriptors. In: Computer Vision and Pattern Recognition, pp. 1–8 (2007)
57. Worthy, L., Sinzinger, E.: Scene identification using invariant radial feature descriptors. In: Proc. 8th Int'l Workshop Image Analysis for Multimedia Interactive Service, pp. 39–43 (2007)
58. Zhu, Q., Avidan, S., Yeh, M.-C., Cheng, K.-T.: Fast human detection using cascade of histograms of oriented gradients. In: Computer Vision and Pattern Recognition (2006)

Chapter 6
Feature Selection and Heterogeneous Descriptors

Various image features were described and their invariances and repeatabilities were explored in Chap. 4. The question we would like to answer in this chapter is, if d features are to be selected from among $D > d$ features for inclusion in an image descriptor, which features should be chosen? Creation of image descriptors from homogeneous features was discussed in the previous chapter. Our focus in this chapter will be to create descriptors from heterogeneous features.

Feature selection is the problem of reducing the number of features in a recognition or matching task. Feature selection problems arise in regression analysis, independence analysis, discriminant analysis, cluster analysis and classification [3], inductive learning [15, 21], and image matching, which is of particular interest in image registration.

In regression analysis, features that add little to the regression accuracy are discarded. Independent analysis is the problem of determining whether a D-dimensional structure can be represented exactly or approximately by $d < D$ dimensions, and if so, which of the original dimensions should be used. In discriminant analysis, the objective is to find whether some features can be dropped without significantly changing the discrimination power of a recognition system. In clustering and classification also, there is a need to remove features that do not influence the final clustering or classification result.

In inductive learning, since a learner uses all available features, the presence of irrelevant information can decrease the learning performance [39]. Therefore, again, there is a need to remove the irrelevant features to improve the learning performance. For example, if feature x_2 is a linear function of feature x_1 or if $x_2 = x_1 + \varepsilon$, where ε represents random noise, then either x_1 or x_2 can be dropped with little change in the classification result.

Given a set of D features from an image or a window, the feature selection problem is that of selecting a subset $d < D$ of features that contains more discriminatory information than any other subset of d features. An exhaustive search for the optimal solution requires $\binom{D}{d}$ comparisons, which is prohibitively large even for moderate values of D and d.

A.A. Goshtasby, *Image Registration*,
Advances in Computer Vision and Pattern Recognition,
DOI 10.1007/978-1-4471-2458-0_6, © Springer-Verlag London Limited 2012

If the features are statistically independent, the problem may be solved by selecting individually the d best features out of D [26]. This involves first selecting the feature that maximizes a matching/recognition criterion. Among the remaining features, the next feature is then selected that maximizes the same criterion, and the process is repeated until the best d features are selected. However, Elashoff et al. [12] and Cover [6] show that the set of best two features do not necessarily contain the two best features. Toussaint [41] shows that the set of best two features may not even include the best feature. Therefore, the set of most informative d features out of D is not necessarily the set of the d individually most informative features. We would like to select the features in such a way as to achieve the smallest classification/matching error.

It is generally expected that the selected features (1) be independent of each other, and (2) when combined, provide the most complete information about the objects to be recognized. Condition 1 ensures that the selected features do not contain redundant information and condition 2 ensures that the selected features will least ambiguously distinguish different objects (or in our case, image windows) from each other.

Fourier transform and Zernike moments satisfy these conditions if a sufficient number of them are selected, but we know these features are not very efficient when used in recognition/matching. One can often find a combination of features that are not independent (orthogonal) but can provide more complete information about the objects or image windows. It has also been shown that informative class-specific features provide a higher discriminative power than generic features such as Zernike moments or wavelets [43]. We, therefore, will relax the orthogonality requirement and select rich features that may have some overlap with other features but when combined can provide the most complete information about the objects to be recognized or the windows to be located in an image.

Given M windows $\{O_i : i = 1, \ldots, M\}$ and D features $\{f_i : i = 1, \ldots, D\}$ from each window, we would like to determine the smallest subset d among D features that can distinguish the windows from each other with least ambiguity. We start by extracting features that are the least sensitive to changes in scale, orientation, contrast, noise, and blurring from the windows. Among the extracted features, we then select a subset that can best distinguish the windows from each other.

If the feature vector with d components is used to describe the contents of a window, the feature vector can be represented by a point in a d-dimensional space. By increasing the number of features, distance between the points in the feature space will increase, improving the recognition/matching accuracy. However, as the number of dimensions increases, the computational resources needed to solve a recognition/matching problem increase also. The key is to find the smallest d that can solve the problem with a required error tolerance.

Since it is possible for a pattern to appear repeatedly in an image, and knowing that a descriptor provides only information about a pattern local to a window, some kind of an information exterior to the window is needed to distinguish the pattern in different locations from each other. Assuming windows are taken centered at the control points in an image, examples of such exterior information are:

(1) distance of a control point to the control point closest to it, (2) the degree of a control point in the minimum-spanning tree (MST) or triangulation of the points, and (3) the largest/smallest angle between edges of the MST or triangulation at the control point. One or more of these exterior features, which are invariant to image scale and orientation, can be used together with the interior features of a window to distinguish windows containing the same pattern in different locations in an image from each other.

In the rest of this chapter, various feature selection methods are reviewed and their uses in creation of efficient heterogeneous image descriptors are explored.

6.1 Feature Selection Algorithms

Feature selection algorithms generally follow either a filter algorithm or a wrapper algorithm [8, 9, 21], although hybrid algorithms that take advantage of the strengths of both have been proposed also [27]. A filter algorithm selects features without regard to the final matching rate. For example, it may remove features that are highly dependent and retain only features that are independent. In a wrapper algorithm, features are selected taking into consideration the final matching outcome and will rely on the particular correspondence algorithm used. Wrapper algorithms are generally more accurate than filter algorithms, but they are computationally costlier.

Hybrid algorithms combine the strengths of the filter and wrapper algorithms and work well when a large feature set is provided. In a hybrid algorithm, first the best feature subset of a given cardinality is selected by removing redundant, irrelevant, or dependent features. Then by a wrapper algorithm and cross-validation, the final best features are selected [8, 18, 32, 47, 52].

6.1.1 Filter Algorithms

Given feature set $X = \{x_i : i = 1, \ldots, D\}$, we would like to select the feature subset $Y = \{y_j : j = 1, \ldots, d\}$ from X that is least redundant. Das [7] (also see [42]) measured redundancy by calculating linear dependency, while Heydorn [14] measured redundancy by calculating statistical dependency. A feature z in X is considered redundant with respect to feature subset Y if the probability distributions of (Y, z) and (Y) completely overlap. That is,

$$P\big[F(Y, z) = F(Y)\big] = 1, \tag{6.1}$$

where $F(Y)$ denotes the probability distribution of features in Y and $F(Y, z)$ denotes the cumulative distribution of Y and z. By adding feature z to feature subset Y, the distribution of Y does not change, and so Y still carries the same information. Koller and Sahami [22] remove redundant features in such a way that the class-conditional probability after removal of the redundant features is as close as possible to the class-conditional probability of the original features.

In an attempt to remove redundant features in a feature set, King [19] and Jolliffe [16] used a cluster merging idea. Initially, each feature is included in a cluster of its own. Then, the two closest clusters are merged to a new cluster. The cluster feature is then considered the average of the two features. The merging process is repeated by letting the feature representing the merged cluster be the average of the features in it. The process is stopped any time the desired number of clusters or features is reached. This method, in effect, merges similar features, producing features that are less similar. Note that this method transforms given features to new features while reducing redundancy.

Based on the clustering idea of King [19] and Jolliffe [16], Mitra et al. [30] used feature similarity to subdivide a feature set into clusters in such a way that the features in a cluster are highly similar, while those in different clusters are highly dissimilar. Similarity is measured using Pearson correlation. If N windows are available in the reference image, each with an associating feature vector, the correlation between features x any y is calculated from

$$r(x, y) = \frac{\sum_{i=1}^{N}(x_i - \bar{x})(y_i - \bar{y})}{\sigma_x \sigma_y} \tag{6.2}$$

where

$$\bar{x} = \frac{1}{N}\sum_{i=1}^{N} x_i, \qquad \bar{y} = \frac{1}{N}\sum_{i=1}^{N} y_i, \tag{6.3}$$

and

$$\sigma_x = \left(\frac{1}{N}\sum_{i=1}^{N}(x_i - \bar{x})^2\right)^{1/2}, \qquad \sigma_y = \left(\frac{1}{N}\sum_{i=1}^{N}(y_i - \bar{y})^2\right)^{1/2}. \tag{6.4}$$

Clustering of the features is achieved by the k-nearest neighbor (k-NN) method. First, the k-nearest features of each feature are identified and among them the feature with the most compact subset, determined by its distance to the farthest neighbor, is selected. Then, those k-neighboring features are discarded. Initially, k is set to $D - d$ and is gradually reduced until distance of a feature to the kth feature closest to it becomes larger than a required tolerance ε or k reaches 1.

Note that when Pearson correlation is used to measure the similarity between two features, the measure only detects linear dependency between features. If the features have nonlinear dependencies, a measure such as information gain or mutual information should be used.

Information gain is the amount of reduction in entropy of a feature x after observing feature y. That is,

$$IG(x|y) = H(x) - H(x|y), \tag{6.5}$$

where $H(x)$ is the entropy of feature x and is computed from

$$H(x) = -\sum_{i=1}^{N} P(x(i)) \log_2(P(x(i))). \tag{6.6}$$

$P(x(i))$ denotes the probability that feature x will have value $x(i)$ and $H(x|y)$ is the entropy of observing feature x after having observed feature y and is computed from

$$H(x|y) = -\sum_{j=1}^{N} P(y(j)) \sum_{i=1}^{N} \left[P(x(i)|y(j)) \log_2 \left(P(x(i)|y(j)) \right) \right]. \tag{6.7}$$

Given N windows in the reference image with associating feature vectors, the information gain for any pair of features can be calculated in this manner.

If two features are highly dependent, the obtained information gain will be smaller than when two less dependent features are used. Therefore, information gain can be used as a means to remove dependent (redundant) features from a set. Yu and Liu [48–50] normalized information gain $IG(x|y)$ with respect to the sum of the entropies of x and y to obtain a *symmetrical uncertainty* measure:

$$SU(x, y) = 2 \left[\frac{IG(x|y)}{H(x) + H(y)} \right] = 2 \left[\frac{IG(y|x)}{H(x) + H(y)} \right]. \tag{6.8}$$

This measure varies between 0 and 1, with 0 indicating that x and y are completely independent and 1 indicating that x and y are completely dependent. The closer the symmetrical uncertainly between two features is to 1, the more dependent the features will be, so one of them should be removed from the feature set. This process can be repeated until all features are sufficiently independent of each other. Note that accurate calculation of entropies for $H(x)$ and $H(y)$ as well as the conditional entropy $H(x|y)$ requires well populated probability distributions for $P(x), P(y)$, and $P(x|y)$, and that requires a large number of reference windows.

Dependency can be measured using generalized Shannon mutual information [11] also:

$$I(x, y) = H(x) + H(y) - H(x, y), \tag{6.9}$$

where $H(x)$ and $H(y)$ are entropies of features x and y and $H(x, y)$ is the joint entropy of features x and y, defined by

$$H(x, y) = -\sum_{i=1}^{N} \sum_{j=1}^{N} P(x(i), y(j)) \log_2 P(x(i), y(j)). \tag{6.10}$$

$P(x(i), y(j))$ is the probability that feature x has value $x(i)$ and feature y has value $y(j)$. Bonnlander and Weigend [5], Wang et al. [44], and Bell and Wang [4] used mutual information to measure feature dependency and relevance. Ding, Peng, and Long [10, 33, 34] considered relevance the inverse of redundancy and selected features in such a way that redundancy was minimized.

To select a representative subset from a set, Wei and Billings [45] first selected the feature that correlated with most features in the set. They then added features one at a time such that each newly selected feature correlated the most with the remaining features and correlated the least with features already selected. Least correlation was ensured through an orthogonalization process. They argue that if many features correlate with feature x, feature x represents those features and so should be included in the selected subset.

6.1.2 Wrapper Algorithms

Wrapper algorithms select features in a training step where correspondence between windows in the images are known. Given a set of corresponding windows in two images, a wrapper algorithm selects the features such that the number of incorrect matches is minimized. The matching process can be considered a nearest-neighbor classifier. To determine the window in the reference image that corresponds to a window in the sensed image, distances between all windows in the reference image to the window in the sensed image are determined and the reference window closest to the sensed window is selected as the corresponding window. Examples of distance measures are given in (5.12) and (5.13).

Perhaps the simplest wrapper algorithm is the *Max-Min* algorithm [2], which selects the features one at a time until the required number of features is reached.

Max-Min Algorithm Given features $X = \{x_i : i = 1, \ldots, D\}$ from each window and knowing the correspondence between windows in reference and sensed images, we would like to find feature subset $Y \subset X$, which is initially empty, and upon exit contains d features maximizing the number of correspondences. Let $J(x_i)$ show the number of correspondences obtained when using feature x_i, and let $J(x_i, x_j)$ show the number of correspondences obtained when using features x_i and x_j, where $i \neq j$. Then:

1. Select feature x_j in X and include in Y where $J(x_j) = \max_i(J(x_i))$.
2. Among the remaining features in X, select feature x_k and include in Y if for all features x_j in Y we obtain $J(x_k, x_j) = \max_k\{\min_j(\Delta J(x_k, x_j))\}$, where $\Delta J(x_k, x_j) = J(x_k, x_j) - J(x_j)$.
3. Repeat Step 2 until Y contains d features.

$\Delta J(x_k, x_j)$ is the increase in the number of correspondences by moving feature x_k from X to Y. The feature in X that maximizes the minimum increase in the number of correspondences when considered pairwise against all features in Y is selected and added to Y. The computational complexity of this algorithm is on the order of Dd operations, where each operation involves a few additions, multiplications, and comparisons.

A feature selection algorithm that is based on the search algorithm of Marill and Green [28] removes the least relevant features from X one at a time until the desired number of features remains. This algorithm is known as sequential backward selection (SBS) [20]. Similarly, an algorithm developed by Whitney [46] selects the most relevant features one at a time from a feature set to create the desired subset. This algorithm is known as sequential forward selection (SFS) [20].

SBS starts from the given feature set and removes the worst feature from the set at each iteration until the desired number of features remains. On the other hand, SFS starts from an empty subset, selects a feature from among the given set and moves it to the subset in such a way that the number of correspondences is maximized. Steps in the SFS and SBS algorithms are given below [40].

Sequential Forward Selection (SFS) Algorithm Given N corresponding windows in two images and feature set $X = \{x_i : i = 1, \ldots, D\}$ calculated for each window, we would like to select feature subset $Y = \{y_j : j = 1, \ldots, d\}$, such that $d < D$, $Y \subset X$, and the obtained feature subset maximizes the number of correct correspondences.

1. Choose a dissimilarity measure to determine the distance between two feature vectors.
2. Compute the number of correspondences using each feature individually. Move the feature from X to Y that produces the most correct correspondences, and let $k = 1$.
3. Select a feature from among the remaining $D - k$ features. There are $D - k$ such cases. Use the selected feature and the k features already in Y to determine the number of correct correspondences. Move the feature that produces the most correspondences from X to Y and incremented k by 1.
4. If $k = d$, return Y. Otherwise, go to Step 3.

Sequential Backward Selection (SBS) Algorithm Starting from feature subset Y containing all D features in X, remove features from Y one at a time until d features remain and the d features produce the smallest number of incorrect correspondences.

1. Choose a dissimilarity measure to determine the distance between two feature vectors.
2. Let Y contain all D features in X and $k = D$.
3. Eliminate one feature from Y. There are k possibilities. Find the number of correspondences obtained when using the remaining $k - 1$ features. Eliminate the feature that produces the minimum number of incorrect correspondences when using the remaining features in Y, and decrement k by 1.
4. If $k = d$, return the d features in Y. Otherwise, go to Step 3.

SFS starts from an empty subset and adds one feature at a time to it until the required number of features is reached, and SBS starts from the entire set and removes features one at a time from it until the required number of features remain.

The choice of forward or backward comes from the relative value of d with respect to D. If d is close to D, backward elimination is more efficient than forward selection. However, if d is very small compared to D, forward selection is more efficient than backward elimination.

Note that in backward elimination, once a feature is removed from the set of features, it never gets a chance to return to the set. Also, in forward selection, once a feature is included in the subset, it remains there and there is no chance for it to get out. This problem, which is known as *nesting*, may introduce considerable redundancy in the created subset.

To reduce redundancy in backward elimination, Pudil et al. [35] described a *floating algorithm* that revises SBS algorithm to exchange a feature already excluded from the subset with a feature in the subset if that increases the number of correspondences. This involves only a slight modification of the SBS algorithm. Insert a

step between Steps 3 and 4 in the SBS algorithm as follows: Replace each of the
k features remaining in the set, with one of the features already removed from the
set. There are $D - k$ such replacements for each of the k features. If a replacement
increases the number of correspondences, keep the replacement. The SFS can be
revised in the same manner to avoid nesting. Insert a step between Steps 3 and 4
in SFS algorithm as follows: Replace each of the k features in Y with one of the
$D - k$ features still remaining in X. If this replacement increases the number of
correspondences, keep it.

Generalized versions of SFS and SBS have also been proposed [20]. In the generalized SFS (GSFS), if k features are already selected, all subsets with $k + r$ features
are generated by adding r features from the remaining $D - k$ features to the existing
subset. Then the subset that maximizes the number of correspondences is selected.
In the generalized SBS (GSBS), if k features remain in the set after removing features from the set, all combinations of $k + r$ subsets are created by adding to the
subset all combinations of r features out of $D - k$. Again, the subset maximizing
the number of correspondences is chosen. As r, the number of features added or
removed in each iteration, is increased, a more optimal subset is obtained but at a
higher computational cost. Aha and Bankert [1] explored other variations of the SFS
and SBS algorithms.

Somol et al. [37] further improved the feature selection optimality by combining
the forward and backward steps, calling the new algorithm *adaptive floating feature
selection*. By carrying out a more thorough search in each selection step, a solution
closer to the optimal one is reached, at a higher computational cost.

An SFS algorithm that prevents nesting is proposed by Michael and Lin [29].
The idea is generalized by Stearns [38] into an algorithm appropriately called *plus l
take away r*, which adds l features to the subset at each iteration while removing r
features.

Plus l Take Away r Algorithm Assuming $l > r$, X represents a set of D features,
and $Y \subset X$ represents the feature subset containing $d < D$ features:

1. Choose a distance measure and initially let Y be an empty set. Also let $k = 0$.
2. Choose feature x in X and add to Y if new Y maximizes the number of correspondences, then increment k by 1. If $k = d$, return Y. Otherwise, repeat this step
   l times.
3. Remove that feature y from Y such that the new Y minimizes the number of
   incorrect correspondences, then decrement k by 1. Repeat this step r times.
4. Repeat Steps 2 and 3 in sequence as many times as needed until d features are
   obtained in Y.

Stearns [38] compared the computational complexities of plus-l-take-away-r and
SFS and SBS algorithms, finding that the computational complexity of plus-l-take-
away-r algorithm is only several times higher than those of the SFS and SBS algorithms. Kittler [20] found that the plus-l-take-away-r algorithm produces significantly better results than the SFS and SBS algorithms but only when $l \approx r$. When l
and r are too different, the process is incapable of avoiding nesting.

The above algorithms are suboptimal. To obtain the optimal solution, exhaustive search is needed, but that is not feasible when the feature set contains 100 or more features. A branch-and-bound algorithm developed by Narender and Fukunaga [31] selects the optimal feature subset without explicitly evaluating all possible feature subsets. The algorithm, however, requires the feature selection criterion be monotonic. That is, the provided features should be such that the correspondence algorithm would produce more correspondences when using $d + 1$ features than when using d features.

A branch-and-bound algorithm repeatedly partitions the solution space into smaller subspaces. Within each subspace, a lower bound is found for the solutions there. Those subspaces with bounds that exceed the cost of a feasible solution are excluded from future partitioning. Among all remaining subspaces, the subspace with the lowest cost is partitioned and the process is repeated until a solution is reached. The solution reached first will be the lowest-cost as any solution obtained subsequently will have a higher cost [25].

Narender and Fukunaga [31] used the branch-and-bound principle to develop an optimal feature selection algorithm that selects the feature subset maximizing the number of correspondences. The performance of the branch-and-bound algorithm is further improved by Yu and Yuan [51] by expanding the tree branches that are more likely to be a part of the solution subset. The algorithm adds one feature at a time to a subset, always keeping track of the subset producing the highest number of correspondences. The process will find the highest number of correspondences for a required number of features. The steps of this algorithm are as follows.

Branch-and-Bound Algorithm

1. Create the root of a tree T and an empty list L. Also, let $m = 0$ and $k = 0$. m shows the height of a node from the root and k shows the index of a selected feature. 0 implying that no feature has been selected.
2. Create $i = 1, \ldots, D - d + 1$ nodes, then save in the ith node x_i and the number of correspondences found using feature x_i. Also, increment m by 1 and save that at the nodes. Next, make a link from each newly created node to the root and save in L pointers to the created nodes in the descending order of the number of obtained correspondences. These nodes represent the leaves of the tree at height $m = 1$.
3. Take the first node in L and suppose the index of the node is k. If $m = d$, backtrack from that node to the root and return the indices of the features saved at the visited nodes. Otherwise continue.
4. Create $l = D - d - k + m + 1$ nodes pointing to node k in the tree and save at the created nodes feature indices $k + 1, \ldots, k + l$. Also, find the number of correspondences found for each node using the features from that node to the root and save that number at the node. Then, increment m by 1 and save m at the created nodes. Next, update L by inserting the newly created nodes in the list in such a way that the list remains ordered in descending order of the number of correspondences. L now points to nodes in the tree that represent the leaves of the new tree. Go back to Step 3.

Fig. 6.1 The complete
solution tree for selecting 3
features out of 6 by the
branch-and-bound algorithm.
The solution subset is found
by partially traversing the tree
from *top* to *bottom* while
maximizing the number of
correspondences

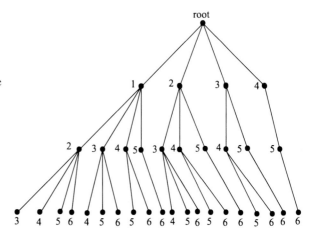

In Step 2, instead of creating D nodes only $D - d + 1$ nodes are created. Because d features are required, the distance of a node at level 1 to a leaf of the tree should be d to produce d features. After using d features, there will be $D - d$ features remaining, each creating a new branch in the tree and each branch defining the solution subset. This results in $D - d + 1$ nodes at level 1. At each level in the tree, the leftmost node has $D - d + 1$ branches, but the branch to the right of it at the same level has one fewer branches. This is because the order of features in a set is not important. For example, once set $\{x_1, x_2\}$ is tested, there is no need to test $\{x_2, x_1\}$.

Step 3 returns an optimal subset containing d features, because if a path exists that can produce a higher number of correspondences, it is already found. We know this because the path with the highest number of correspondences is always on top of list L, and we know that our matching algorithm produces more correspondences with feature subset $(Y \cup \{x_l\})$ than with feature subset Y, where x_l is any feature that is not already in Y. The tree structure when X contains 6 features and Y is required to contain 3 features is shown in Fig. 6.1. Note that use of list L makes it possible to find the solution set without exploring the entire tree.

The above algorithm shows steps of a forward algorithm as the number of features is gradually increased until the desired number of features is obtained. A similar algorithm can be designed to eliminate features one at a time while minimizing the number of incorrect correspondences until the required number of features is obtained. It has been shown that the branch and bound algorithm works quite well even when the feature selection criterion is not monotonic [13].

A study carried out by Kittler [20] in a two-class problem with 20 features finds that the optimal branch-and-bound algorithm has the highest discriminatory power, closely followed by the GSFS and GSBS algorithms, and the discriminatory power of the two get closer as the number of features added to or removed from the subset increases in each iteration. The Max-Min algorithm is found to be the fastest but the least accurate when compared to the branch-and-bound and the GSFS and GSBS algorithms.

Although the ultimate goal of a feature selector is to take the fewest features to achieve a required recognition rate, a property of a feature selector that is important is its stability [17, 23, 24, 36]. If features are extracted of the same phenomenon under slightly different conditions, will the feature selector under consideration select the same features? The stability can be measured using the Hamming distance between selected features in two tests. Stability shows robustness and ensures similar results under small perturbations in data.

6.2   Selecting the Best Features for Image Matching

Tables 4.1 and 4.2 in Chap. 4 identify the most invariant and repeatable features. If the features are to be selected individually, the tables are useful. However, if a combination of d features is to be selected for image matching, we do not know which d features to choose.

A set of features performing well on a class of images may perform poorly on another class of images. To determine optimal features in image matching, a training step is required that finds the optimal features for a class of images. Given two representative images and a number of corresponding windows in the images, we would like to find the set of d features that can find most corresponding windows in the images?

We start with the features suggested in Tables 4.1 and 4.2. That is, we assume the features available to us are $X = \{x_1:$ mean intensity (L_2), $x_2:$ second-order moment 1 (L_{23}), $x_3:$ second-order moment 2 (L_{24}), $x_4:$ third-order moment 2 (L_{26}), $x_5:$ normalized complex moment invariant of order $(1, 1)$ (L_{50c}), $x_6:$ Beaudet's cornerness measure (L_{64}), $x_7:$ local frequency domain entropy (L_{75}), $x_8:$ steerable filter response (L_{78}), $x_9:$ correlation response to Laws mask B_{11} (L_{86a}), $x_{10}:$ correlation response to Laws mask B_{22} (L_{86b}), $x_{11}:$ smoothed intensity with a Gaussian of standard deviation 2 pixels (L_{88}), $x_{12}:$ Laplacian after smoothing with a Gaussian of standard deviation 2 pixels (L_{90}), $x_{13}:$ center contrast (L_{96}), and $x_{14}:$ fractal dimension $(L_{111})\}$.

If different windows in the same image contain the same pattern, we will distinguish them from each other by using two features that provide external information about the windows. As external information, we will use $x_{15}:$ MST degree and $x_{16}:$ triangulation degree. The degree of a control point is considered the number of edges connected to the control point in the MST or in the triangulation of the control points. Local features are measured within circular windows of radius r pixels centered at the points. In the following experiments, r is taken to be 8 pixels.

Given a set of corresponding control points in two images, we take a circular window of radius $r = 8$ pixels centered at each control point and determine the above-mentioned 16 features using intensities in the window. As control points, we choose local extrema of the response of the Laplacian of Gaussian (LoG) of standard deviation 2 pixels in an image. Then we calculate the 16 features for windows centered at each control point. In the following, we will then determine the smallest subset $d < 16$ features that can determine the most correspondences. Sequential

(a)   (b)   (c)

(d)   (e)   (f)

Fig. 6.2 (**a**) Image of a coin, used as the reference image. The reference image after (**b**) blurring, (**c**) addition of noise, (**d**) histogram equalization, (**e**) rotation, and (**f**) scaling

forward selection (SFS) algorithm will be used to search for the best suboptimal features.

To demonstrate the search process, the simple coin image shown in Fig. 6.2a is used as the reference image. The image is then blurred with a Gaussian of standard deviation 1.5 pixels to obtain the image shown in Fig. 6.2b. Next, Gaussian noise of standard deviation 20 is added to the reference image to obtain the noisy image shown in Fig. 6.2c. Values higher than 255 are set to 255 and values below 0 are set to 0. The reference image after histogram equalization is shown in Fig. 6.2d. This can be considered a nonlinear but monotone intensity transformation of the reference image. Finally, we rotate the reference image by 30° clockwise to obtain the image in Fig. 6.2e, and scale the reference image by a factor of 1.5 to obtain the image in Fig. 6.2f.

The 100 strongest and well dispersed points determined in these images by the LoG detector are shown in Fig. 6.3. Details about point detection are provided in Chap. 3. The problem to be solved is to locate the points of the reference image in images (b)–(f) using the 16 or fewer features calculated within circular windows of radius 8 pixels centered at the points.

Knowing the geometric relations between image (a) and images (b)–(f) in Fig. 6.2, the coordinates of corresponding points in the images will be known. Therefore, given 100 points in each image, we know which point in image (a) corresponds to which point in any of the other images. Mapping the points in image (a) to the space of images (b)–(f), we obtain images (b)–(f) shown in Fig. 6.4. The points in image (a) are shown in red, while those in images (b)–(f) in Fig. 6.3 are shown in green. points that are perfectly aligned in these images appear in yellow.

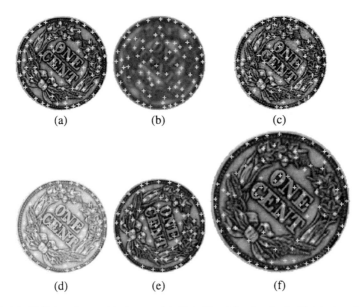

(a)   (b)   (c)

(d)   (e)   (f)

Fig. 6.3 (a)–(f) Points detected in images (a)–(f) in Fig. 6.2 using the LoG detector of standard deviation 2 pixels. Only the 100 strongest and well dispersed points are used in the experiments

(a)   (b)   (c)

(d)   (e)   (f)

Fig. 6.4 (a) Same as image (a) in Fig. 6.3. (b)–(f) Points in image (a) when overlaid with images (b)–(f) in Fig. 6.3. In these images, points of image (a) are shown in *red*, while points in images (b)–(f) in Fig. 6.3 are shown in *green*. Perfectly aligned points appear as *yellow*

Fig. 6.5 Performances of various image features in image matching under various image changes. The numbers along a plot indicate the order in which the particular features are selected as the number of features is increased

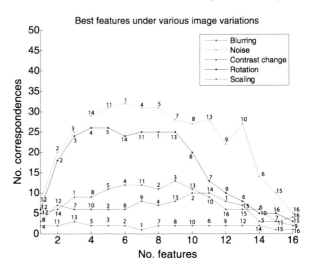

Out of 100 points in these images, 66, 60, 68, 48, and 28 of the points in blurred image (b), noisy image (c), contrast enhanced image (d), rotated image (e), and scaled image (f) in Fig. 6.3 are the same as those in the image (a). We consider points that are within distance $\sqrt{2}$ of each other as corresponding points to compensate for the digital errors caused by image rotation and scaling.

Knowing the true correspondence between points in these images, we will take circular windows of radius 8 pixels centered at each point, calculate the 16 features listed above from each window, and through feature selection determine the best feature subsets that can find the most correspondences between image (a) and images (b)–(f) in Fig. 6.2.

The matching results are summarized in Fig. 6.5. The graph shows the number of correspondences obtained for a particular set of features obtained by the SFS algorithm. As the number of features increases, the number of correspondences initially increases up to a point, but then it decreases as more features are added. The features selected early appear to contain the right information for a particular image variation and improve matching result. However, features selected later in the process contain misleading information and instead of improving the matching, worsen the process, increasing the number of mismatches.

Under blurring, the best features are (1) x_{12}: Laplacian of Gaussian intensity, (2) x_{14}: fractal dimension, (3) x_1: mean intensity, (4) x_8: steerable filter response, (5) x_5: normalized complex moment 2, (6) x_4: third-order moment 2, (7) x_{11}: smoothed Gaussian intensity, (8) x_2: second order moment 1, and (9) x_3: second-order moment 2. These features not only remain relatively unchanged under image blurring or change in resolution, they contain sufficient discriminatory power to recognize various patterns.

The worst features under image blurring are x_9: correlation response to Laws mask B_{11} and x_7: local frequency domain entropy. These features appear to be very sensitive to image blurring and should be avoided when matching images obtained at different resolutions. 66 of the 100 landmarks detected in the coin image and its

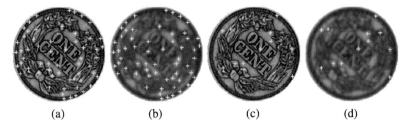

Fig. 6.6 (**a**), (**b**) 66 true corresponding points existing between the coin image and its blurred version. (**c**), (**d**) 13 of the correspondences are found when using the first 9 features as selected by the SFS algorithm

Fig. 6.7 (**a**), (**b**) 60 true corresponding points exist in the coin image and its noisy version. (**c**), (**d**) 32 of the 60 correspondences are found using the first 6 features as selected by the SFS algorithm

blurred version truly correspond to each other. This is depicted in Fig. 6.6a and b. Two points are considered corresponding points if they appear at the same pixel location or at adjacent pixel locations. 13 of the 66 correspondences are found when using the above 9 features as depicted in (c) and (d) in Fig. 6.6. Use of more features actually reduces the number of correspondences as can be observed in the graph in Fig. 6.5.

Under noise, the most effective feature are: (1) x_{12}: Laplacian of Gaussian intensity, (2) x_2: second-order moment 1, (3) x_3: second-order moment 2, (4) x_{14}: fractal dimension, (5) x_{11}: Gaussian smoothed intensity, and (6) x_1: mean intensity. These feature remain relatively unchanged under noise. They also carry the most information when matching the noisy images used in this experiment. The worst features under noise are x_{16}: triangulation degree and x_{15}: MST degree. Since noise can change the number of points and their locations, the triangulation and the MST of the points will differ, making these features unsuitable for matching noisy images. 60 out of the 100 points in the coin image an in its noisy version, as shown in the images in Figs. 6.7a, b are the same. Using the first 6 features as selected by the SFS algorithm, 32 of the correspondences are found as shown in Figs. 6.7c, d. Use of more features reduces the number of correspondences.

Under monotone intensity transformation, the most effective features for image matching are found to be: (1) x_8: steerable filter response, (2) x_{12}: Laplacian of Gaussian intensity, (3) x_7: local frequency domain entropy, (4) x_{10}: correlation re-

(a)   (b)   (c)   (d)

Fig. 6.8 (**a**), (**b**) 68 corresponding landmarks are detected in the coin image and its contrast enhanced version. (**c**), (**d**) 10 of the correspondences are identified using the first 10 features as selected by the SFS algorithm

sponse to Laws mask B_{22}, (5) x_3: second order moment 2, (6) x_6: Beaudet's cornerness measure, (7) x_9: correlation response to Laws B_{11} mask, (8) x_4: third-order moment 2, (9) x_{13}: center contrast, and (10) x_2: second-order moment 1. Observing the graph in Fig. 6.5, we see that the number of correspondences rises to 7 and then falls to 6 and again rises to 10. This behavior is a side effect of the suboptimal feature selection algorithm of SFS.

The worst features under monotone change in image contrast are x_{16}: triangulation degree, x_{11}: Gaussian smoothed intensity, and x_5: normalized complex moment. 68 features out of the 100 points in the coin image and its contrast enhanced version truly correspond to each other as shown in Figs. 6.8a, b. Using the first 10 features as selected by the SFS algorithm the process finds 10 of the correspondences as shown in Figs. 6.8c, d.

Images that have rotational differences are best matched using features (1) x_{12}: Laplacian of Gaussian intensity, (2) x_2: second-order moment 1, (3) x_3: second-order moment 2, and (4) x_4: third-order moment 2. These features are known to be rotation invariant. Among all rotationally invariant features, these features capture sufficient non-overlapping information to enable effective recognition/matching of local neighborhoods. The worst features to be used in matching of images with rotational differences are x_{15}: MST degree and x_{16}: triangulation degree.

It is interesting to note that the MST and triangulation degrees are not very reliable under image rotation. Although MST and triangulation of a set of points are invariant to rotation of the points, the point detector that has been used has found only 48 corresponding points out of 100 in the coin image and its rotated version as shown in Figs. 6.9a, b. As a result, the MST and the triangulation of control points in the images look very different from each other, producing very little useful information for matching. The process has been able to find 26 of the correspondences using the first 4 features as detected by the SFS algorithm.

Finally, examining the matching result of images with scaling differences, we find that the best features are: (1) x_4: third-order moment 2, (2) x_{11}: Gaussian smoothed intensity, and (3) x_{13}: center contrast. The worst features are: x_{16}: triangulation degree, x_{15}: MST degree, and x_1: mean intensity. It is interesting to see that under change in scale, mean intensity is not a reliable feature for use in image matching. Not knowing the scale difference between two images, averaging a fixed

Fig. 6.9 (**a**), (**b**) 48 true corresponding landmarks exist between the coin image and its rotated version. (**c**), (**d**) 26 of the correspondences are found when using the first 4 features as selected by the SFS algorithm

Fig. 6.10 (**a**), (**b**) 28 true corresponding points are present in the coin image and its scaled version. (**c**), (**d**) 3 of the correspondences are identified when using the first 3 features as selected by the SFS algorithm

neighborhood of 3×3 pixels centered at a point results in considerably different intensities that are not reliable in image matching.

The point detector has been able to find only 28 common points out of 100 in both images. Using the first 3 features as detected by the SFS algorithm, 3 of the correspondences are identified (Fig. 6.10). Using more features actually reduces the number of correspondences as the remaining features do not contain useful information when the images to be matched have unknown scaling differences.

Overall, worst matching results are obtained when the images have unknown scaling differences. A very small number of correspondences are obtained when considering all combinations of features. This can be attributed to (1) sensitivity of the features to change in scale, and (2) sensitivity of the point detector to change in scale. If a sufficiently large number of the same points is not detected in the images, the matching process cannot find a large number of correspondences.

Examining all these results, we see that various moments perform the best, and if the images do not have scaling difference, Laplacian of Gaussian intensity is also a very effective feature in image matching. It should be mentioned that the results obtained by the simple experiments above cannot be used to make a general conclusion about the power of the features. The performance of a feature can vary from image to image and it depends on the size of the window used in the calculations.

If the type of images to be registered is known, a number of the images may be used to identify those features that most effectively find the same points in the images and find correspondence between the points using the features of windows centered at the points. Once the best features are identified, they can be used in a custom system that can effectively register images in that class.

An important conclusion that can be reached from the above experiments is that use of more features does not necessarily mean a more accurate matching. Some features vary under certain image changes and do not contain useful information to help matching, and if used, they may confuse the matching process and reduce match rating.

When it comes to finding correspondence between windows in two images, in addition to the features of the windows, relations between the windows can be used as constraints to reject the false correspondences. Use of constraints in matching is discussed in detail in the next chapter.

References

1. Aha, D.W., Bankert, R.L.: A comparative evaluation of sequential feature selection algorithms. In: Proc. 5th Int'l Workshop Artificial Intelligence and Statistics, pp. 1–7 (1995)
2. Backer, E., Schipper, J.A.D.: On the max-min approach for feature ordering and selection. In: Seminar Series on Pattern Recognition, Liège University, Sart-Tilman, Belgium, pp. 2.4.1–2.4.7 (1977)
3. Beale, E.M.L., Kendall, M.G., Mann, D.W.: The discarding of variables in multivariate analysis. Biometrika 53(3/4), 357–366 (1967)
4. Bell, D.A., Wang, H.: A formalism for relevance and its application in feature subset selection. Mach. Learn. 41, 175–195 (2000)
5. Bonnlander, B.V., Weigend, A.S.: Selecting input variables using mutual information and nonparametric density estimation. In: Proc. International Symposium on Artificial Neural Networks (ISANN), pp. 42–50 (1996)
6. Cover, T.M.: The best two independent measurements are not the two best. IEEE Trans. Syst. Man Cybern. 4(1), 116–117 (1974)
7. Das, S.K.: Feature selection with a linear dependence measure. IEEE Trans. Comput. 20(9), 1106–1109 (1971)
8. Das, S.: Filters, wrappers and a boosting-based hybrid for feature selection. In: Proc. 18th Int'l Conf. Machine Learning, pp. 74–81 (2001)
9. Dash, M., Liu, H.: Feature selection for classification. Inell. Data Anal. 1, 131–156 (1997)
10. Ding, C., Peng, H.C.: Minimum redundancy feature selection from microarray gene expression data. In: Proc. 2nd IEEE Conf. Computational Systems Bioinformatics, pp. 523–528 (2003)
11. Duncan, T.E.: On the calculation of mutual information. SIAM J. Appl. Math. 19(1), 215–220 (1970)
12. Elashoff, J.D., Elashoff, R.M., Goldman, G.E.: On the choice of variables in classification problems with Dichotomous variables. Biometrika 54, 668–670 (1967)
13. Hamamoto, Y., Uchimura, S., Matsunra, Y., Kanaoka, T., Tomita, S.: Evaluation of the branch and bound algorithm for feature selection. Pattern Recognit. Lett. 11, 453–456 (1990)
14. Heydorn, R.P.: Redundancy in feature extraction. IEEE Trans. Comput. 20(9), 1051–1054 (1971)
15. John, G.H., Kohavi, R., Pfleger, K.: Irrelevant features and the subset selection problem. In: Proc. 11th Int'l Conf. Machine Learning, pp. 121–129 (1994)

16. Jolliffe, I.T.: Discarding variables in a principal component analysis. I: Artificial data. J. R. Stat. Soc., Ser. C, Appl. Stat. **21**(2), 160–173 (1972)

17. Kalousis, A., Prados, J., Hilario, M.: Stability of feature selection algorithms. In: Proc. 5th IEEE Int'l Conf. Data Mining, pp. 218–225 (2005)

18. Ke, C.-H., Yang, C.-H., Chuang, L.-Y., Yang, C.-S.: A hybrid filter/wrapper approach of feature selection for gene expression data. In: IEEE Int'l Conf. Systems, Man and Cybernetics, pp. 2664–2670 (2008)

19. King, B.: Step-wise clustering procedures. J. Am. Stat. Assoc. **62**(317), 86–101 (1967)

20. Kittler, J.: Feature set search algorithms. In: Chen, C.H. (ed.) Pattern Recognition and Signal Processing, pp. 41–60 (1978)

21. Kohavi, R., John, G.H.: Wrappers for feature subset selection. Artif. Intell. **97**, 273–324 (1997)

22. Koller, D., Sahami, M.: Toward optimal feature selection. In: Proc. 13th Int'l Conf. Machine Learning, pp. 284–292 (1996)

23. Křížek, P., Kittler, J., Hlaváč, V.: Improving stability of feature selection methods. In: Proc. 12th Int'l Conf. Computer Analysis of Images and Patterns, pp. 929–936 (2007)

24. Kuncheva, L.I.: A stability index for feature selection. In: Proc. 25th IASTED Int'l Multi-Conf. Artificial Intelligence and Applications, pp. 421–427 (2007)

25. Lawler, E.L., Wood, D.E.: Branch-and-bound methods: A survey. Oper. Res. **14**(4), 699–719 (1966)

26. Lewis, P.M. II: Characteristic selection problem in recognition systems. IRE Trans. Inf. Theory **8**(2), 171–178 (1962)

27. Liu, H., Yu, L.: Toward integrating feature selection algorithms for classification and clustering. IEEE Trans. Knowl. Data Eng. **17**(4), 491–502 (2005)

28. Marill, T., Green, D.M.: On the effectiveness of receptors in recognition systems. IEEE Trans. Inf. Theory **9**(1), 11–17 (1963)

29. Michael, M., Lin, W.-C.: Experimental study of information measure and inter-intra class distance ratios on feature selection and ordering. IEEE Trans. Syst. Man Cybern. **3**(2), 172–181 (1973)

30. Mitra, P., Murthy, C.A., Pal, S.K.: Unsupervised feature selection using feature similarity. IEEE Trans. Pattern Anal. Mach. Intell. **24**(3), 301–312 (2002)

31. Narendra, P.M., Fukunaga, K.: A branch and bound algorithm for feature subset selection. IEEE Trans. Comput. **26**(9), 917–922 (1977)

32. Ng, A.Y.: On feature selection: Learning with exponentially many irrelevant features as training examples. In: Proc. 15th Int'l Conf. Machine Learning, pp. 404–412 (1998)

33. Peng, H., Ding, C., Long, F.: Minimum redundancy maximum relevance feature selection. In: IEEE Intelligent Systems, Nov./Dec., pp. 70–71 (2005)

34. Peng, H., Long, F., Ding, C.: Feature selection based on mutual information: Criteria of max-dependency, max-relevance, and min-redundancy. IEEE Trans. Pattern Anal. Mach. Intell. **27**(8), 1226–1238 (2005)

35. Pudil, P., Novovičová, J., Kittler, J.: Floating search methods in feature selection. Pattern Recognit. Lett. **15**(11), 1119–1125 (1994)

36. Somol, P., Novovičová, J.: Evaluation stability and comparing output of feature selectors that optimize feature subset cardinality. IEEE Trans. Pattern Anal. Mach. Intell. **32**(11), 1921–1939 (2010)

37. Somol, P., Pudil, P., Novovičová, J., Paclík, P.: Adaptive floating search methods in feature selection. Pattern Recognit. Lett. **20**, 1157–1163 (1999)

38. Stearns, S.D.: On selecting features for pattern classifiers. In: 3rd Int'l Conf. Pattern Recognition, pp. 71–75 (1976)

39. Talavera, L.: Feature selection as a preprocessing step for hierarchical clustering. In: Proc. 16th Int'l Conf. Machine Learning, pp. 389–397 (1999)

40. Theodoridis, S., Koutroumbas, K.: Pattern Recognition, 4th edn. Academic Press, San Diego (2009), pp. 602, 605, 606

41. Toussaint, G.T.: Note on the optimal selection of independent binary features for pattern recognition. IEEE Trans. Inf. Theory **17**(5), 618 (1971)

42. Toussaint, G.T., Vilmansen, T.R.: Comments on feature selection with a linear dependence measure. IEEE Trans. Comput. **21**(4), 408 (1972)
43. Vidal-Naquet, M., Ullman, S.: Object recognition with informative features and linear classification. In: Proc. Int'l Conf. Computer Vision, pp. 281–288 (2003)
44. Wang, H., Bell, D., Murtagh, F.: Axiomatic approach to feature subset selection based on relevance. IEEE Trans. Pattern Anal. Mach. Intell. **21**(3), 271–277 (1999)
45. Wei, H.-L., Billings, S.A.: Feature subset selection and ranking for data dimensionality reduction. IEEE Trans. Pattern Anal. Mach. Intell. **29**(1), 162–166 (2007)
46. Whitney, A.: A direct method for nonparametric measurement selection. IEEE Trans. Comput. **20**, 1100–1103 (1971)
47. Xing, E., Jordan, M., Karp, R.: Feature selection for high-dimensional genomic microarray data. In: Proc. 15th Int'l Conf. Machine Learning, pp. 601–608 (2001)
48. Yu, L., Liu, H.: Efficiently handling feature redundancy in high-dimensional data. In: Proc. ACM SIGKDD Int'l Conf. Knowledge Discovery and Data Mining (KDD), pp. 685–690 (2003)
49. Yu, L., Liu, H.: Feature selection for high-dimensional data: A fast correlation-based filter solution. In: Proc. 20th Int'l Conf. Machine Learning, pp. 856–863 (2003)
50. Yu, L., Liu, H.: Efficient feature selection via analysis of relevance and redundancy. J. Mach. Learn. Res. **5**, 1205–1224 (2004)
51. Yu, B., Yuan, B.: A more efficient branch and bound algorithm for feature selection. Pattern Recognit. **26**(6), 883–889 (1993)
52. Zhu, Z., Ong, Y.-S., Dash, M.: Wrapper-filter feature selection algorithm using a memetic framework. IEEE Trans. Syst. Man Cybern., Part B, Cybern. **37**(1), 70–76 (2007)

Chapter 7
Point Pattern Matching

In previous chapters, methods for determining control points in images and methods for finding features of the control points were discussed. Some control points, known as outliers, appear in only one of the images, and some control points are slightly displaced from their true positions due to noise or other factors. Methods that establish correspondence between such control points in two images of a scene are discussed in this chapter.

The control points in an image may have associating features but due to intensity and geometric differences between the images and the presence of noise, the features may be inaccurate. We will use features at the control points and/or the geometric constraint that holds between corresponding points in two images of a scene to determine the correspondence between the points.

More specifically, the problem to be solved is as follows: Given points $\{\mathbf{p}_i = (x_i, y_i) : i = 1, \ldots, m\}$ in the reference image and points $\{\mathbf{P}_i = (X_i, Y_i) : i = 1, \ldots, n\}$ in the sensed image, we would like to determine the correspondence between the points. Each point may have an associating descriptor or feature vector. We will denote the descriptor or feature vector associated with point $\mathbf{p}_i$ by $\mathbf{f}_i = \{f_{ij} : j = 1, \ldots, n_f\}$ and the descriptor or feature vector associated with $\mathbf{P}_i$ by $\mathbf{F}_i = \{F_{ij} : j = 1, \ldots, n_f\}$. n_f is the number of features in each descriptor or feature vector. It is also assumed that the descriptor or feature vector associated with each point is normalized to have magnitude 1. Methods for finding homogeneous and heterogeneous descriptors at the control points were discussed in Chaps. 5 and 6.

Point pattern matching algorithms typically use the geometric constraint that holds between corresponding points in the images to distinguish correct correspondences from incorrect ones. The geometric constraint depends on the imaging geometry and the geometry of the scene. It may be known that the images represent different views of a flat scene. Since images of a flat scene are related by a projective transformation, projective constraint is used to find the correspondences. If the images represent distant views of a flat scene, instead of projective constraint, affine constraint may be used to find the correspondences.

A.A. Goshtasby, *Image Registration*,
Advances in Computer Vision and Pattern Recognition,
DOI 10.1007/978-1-4471-2458-0_7, © Springer-Verlag London Limited 2012

7.1 Random Sample and Consensus (RANSAC)

Suppose two images are related by a transformation with p parameters. For instance, if the images are known to have translational, rotational, and scaling differences, a similarity transformation with 4 parameters can spatially align the images. Since each point in a 2-D image has two coordinates, from the coordinates of 2 corresponding points a system of 4 equations can be produced and solved to determine the transformation parameters. Knowing the transformation that relates the geometries of two point sets, the geometry of one point set can be transformed to that of the other, aligning the point sets. Points falling within a distance tolerance of each other after this alignment are considered corresponding points.

When the type of transformation that relates the geometry of one point set to that of another point set is known, RANSAC can estimate the parameters of the transformation and use the transformation to establish correspondence between the remaining points in the two sets [18]. If the transformation has p parameters, a minimum of $q = \lceil p/2 \rceil$ non-colinear points are needed to determine the parameters. If p is an odd number, $(p + 1)/2$ points are selected from each point set but only the x- or the y-coordinate of the last point is used to produce p equations.

If a subset of q points is selected from each point set randomly, then when the two subsets contain corresponding points, the transformation obtained from them will align many other points in the two sets. If $\mathbf{f}$ is the function that transforms the geometry of the sensed set to that of the reference set, then $\mathbf{f}$ has two components (f_x, f_y), relating coordinates of points in the sensed set to coordinates of points in the reference set as follows:

$$x = f_x(X, Y), \tag{7.1}$$

$$y = f_y(X, Y). \tag{7.2}$$

Given sensed point $\mathbf{P}_i = (X_i, Y_i)$, the above transformation estimates the location of the corresponding point $\mathbf{f}(\mathbf{P}_i)$ in the reference space. If $\mathbf{f}(\mathbf{P}_i)$ is within distance ε of a reference point $\mathbf{p}_l$, that is, if $\|\mathbf{p}_l - \mathbf{f}(\mathbf{P}_i)\| \leq \varepsilon$, then $\mathbf{p}_l$ and $\mathbf{P}_i$ are considered corresponding points.

If the transformation function obtained from two point subsets finds t correspondences from among n points in the sensed set, the subsets are considered to contain corresponding points if $r = t/n$ is sufficiently high. If noise is present and r is set too high, the process may miss detecting the correct correspondences since the parameters estimated from noisy points may not be accurate enough to map the sensed points sufficiently close to the corresponding reference points. To avoid failure, if after N iterations corresponding point subsets are not found, from among the N cases the subsets producing the most correspondences are chosen as the subsets containing corresponding points. Then the transformation function mapping the sensed points to the reference points is determined by the least-squares (Chap. 8) using the available correspondences. The obtained transformation is then used to find the remaining correspondences between the point sets.

The performance of RANSAC is affected by three parameters: ε, r, and N. Parameter ε depends on the accuracy of point locations. If the points are accurately located, this parameter should be small, such as 1 pixel. However, if point coordinates are not accurately determined due to noise or other factors, this parameter should be set proportionately higher. However, it should not be set higher than half the distance between closest points in the reference set; otherwise, incorrect correspondences could be counted as correct ones.

Parameter r depends on the number of inliers. If there are i inliers among m points in the reference set and n points in the sensed set, there will be $m - i$ outliers in the reference set and $n - i$ outliers in the sensed set, and $r \leq i/n$. If there are as many outliers as inliers, $r \leq 0.5$. If no outliers are present so that all points in the sensed set appear in the reference set, then $r \leq 1$.

If r is selected too high and points are noisy, the process may miss identifying point subsets that truly correspond to each other when all N iterations are exhausted. This is because the iterations may not produce a sufficiently high number of correspondences from the obtained transformations. If r is set too low and there is a large number of outliers, since it is possible to obtain accidental correspondences from the outliers, the process may prematurely halt, reporting correspondences that are incorrect.

When the maximum number of iterations is reached, the iteration producing the highest number of correspondences is revisited and the correspondences are used to determine the transformation parameters. The smaller the N, the greater the likelihood that the process stops prematurely, resulting in an incorrect transformation. The larger the N, the more time consuming the process will be, but the higher the likelihood that the obtained transformation will be correct. Parameters ε, r, and N are estimated through a training process using a number of representative data sets where the true correspondence between the points is known.

Algorithm F1 (Point pattern matching by RANSAC) Given (1) a reference point set containing m points and a sensed point set containing n points, (2) knowing that coordinates of points in the sensed set are related to coordinates of points in the reference set by a transformation function with p parameters, (3) knowing the distance tolerance ε to consider two points as corresponding points after the sensed point set is transformed to align the reference point set, (4) knowing the minimum ratio r of number of correspondences found and the number of points in the sensed set to consider the correspondences correct, and (5) knowing the maximum number of iterations N that can be afforded to hypothesize and test various transformation functions, one of which can find correspondence between the point sets, we want to find the transformation that establishes the most correspondence between the point sets.

In the following, n_i denotes the iteration number, n_c is the largest number of correspondences obtained up to iteration n_i, and $\mathbf{f}$ denotes the transformation function with p parameters that will align points in the two sets.

1. Let $n_i = 0$ and $n_c = 0$.
2. Take a random subset containing $q = \lceil p/2 \rceil$ points from each point set.
3. Hypothesize a correspondence between points in the two subsets. There are $q!$ such cases. For each case:

   (a) From the q corresponding points, set up a system of p linear equations
      by substituting the coordinates of corresponding points into the x- and y-
      components of the transformation function ((7.1) and (7.2)). If p is an odd
      number, use the x- or the y-component of the last point in each subset.
   (b) Solve the system of p equations to determine the p parameters of transfor-
      mation $\mathbf{f}$.
   (c) For each point $\mathbf{P}_i$ in the sensed set, determine the corresponding point $\mathbf{f}(\mathbf{P}_i)$
      in the reference set with the obtained transformation. If $\|\mathbf{p}_l - \mathbf{f}(\mathbf{P}_i)\| \le \varepsilon$ for
      some l, then consider point $\mathbf{p}_l$ in the reference set corresponding to point
      $\mathbf{P}_i$ in the sensed set. Suppose t correspondences are obtained in this manner
      while changing $i = 1, \ldots, n$.
   (d) If $t > n_c$, let $n_c = t$ and save the obtained transformation $\mathbf{f}$. If $n_c/n \ge r$, go
      to Step 5.
4. Increment n_i by 1. If $n_i \le N$ go to Step 2.
5. Find points in the sensed set that fall within distance ε of points in the reference
   set after transformation with $\mathbf{f}$. There should be n_c correspondences. Use the
   coordinates of corresponding points to calculate a new transformation, $\mathbf{f}_n$, by the
   least-squares method.
6. Determine the correspondences obtained from $\mathbf{f}_n$ and return transformation $\mathbf{f}_n$
   and the obtained correspondences.

In Step 3, when q points are selected from each set, points in the reference subset
are kept fixed and points in the sensed subset are permuted and each case is considered to correspond to points in the reference subset. For instance, if the point sets
are related by an affine transformation with 6 unknown parameters, point subsets
containing 3 points are selected from each set. Suppose points in the reference subset are ABC and points in the sensed subset are DEF. Then point sequence ABC
is matched to point subsets {DEF, DFE, EDF, EFD, FDE, FED}, one at a time. In
each case, Steps 3a–d are performed until a point sequence from the sensed subset is
found that matches the point sequence from the reference subset. By matching the
reference point sequence and a sensed point sequence the transformation relating
the point subsets is determined. If the same transformation can relate a sufficiently
large number of other points in the two sets, a jump is made to Step 5 to find all
correspondences and return them. If a sufficient number of correspondences is not
found after N iterations, the process is stopped and the transformation producing
the most correspondences and with the obtained correspondences are returned.

When the point sets are very large, it may require a large number of iterations
before randomly selected point subsets correspond. For example, if the point sets
have only translational differences, a pair of corresponding points can determine
the translational difference between the point sets. Even in the absence of outliers,
given a point in the reference set, there is a need to take an average of $n/2$ points
in the sensed set until a correspondence to a selected reference point is found. In
the presence of outliers, this number increases. Since points are randomly selected,
the same non-matching point can be selected over and over while the sensed point
corresponding to the reference point may be missed even after a very large number
of iterations.

When the point sets are related by a similarity transformation, two points randomly selected from each set are needed to find the transformation parameters. The number of average iterations required for two points selected from the sensed set to correspond to two points selected in the reference set is on the order of n^2. The number of average iterations required to successfully find the parameters of an affine transformation using 3 points from each set is on the order of n^3, and the number of iterations required to find the parameters of a projective transformation is on the order of n^4. When n is small, such as 10, computations by RANSAC can be afforded; however, when n is on the order of hundreds or thousands, determination of point correspondence by RANSAC becomes impractical.

Approaches to speed up RANSAC have been proposed. In an algorithm known as *randomized* RANSAC or R-RANSAC, Matas and Chum [31] suggested first verifying the correctness of a hypothesized transformation using a small number of points d, and if the d points are found to satisfy the transformation, then the correctness of the transformation is verified using the remaining points. They derived d based on prior knowledge of the fraction of outliers. Later they showed how to estimate this fraction online [12]. d is typically a small number such as 1, 2, or 3.

To implement R-RANSAC, a step is inserted between Steps 3b and 3c in Algorithm F1 to first test the transformation for d randomly selected points, and if the test succeeds, then a further test is performed in Step 3c. Otherwise, a jump is made to Step 4 to increment the iteration number and repeat the process until a sufficiently large number of correspondences is obtained.

A speed-up method proposed by Van Wamelen et al. [51] initially finds the k-nearest points of each point in the two sets. Then for each point pair $\mathbf{p}_i$ and $\mathbf{q}_j$ in the two sets, the k-nearest points of $\mathbf{p}_i$ and $\mathbf{q}_j$ are matched, and if the neighborhoods are found to correspond, the obtained local transformation is tested globally to determine the number of points in the two sets that match with the provided distance tolerance ε. This can be considered a hierarchical search where the first search for the transformation is performed locally using small point subsets and when one is found the transformation is verified globally using all points. Optimal k depends on m, n, and ε [51] and is typically a small number such as 10. A similar approach is proposed by Denton and Beveridge [15] by clustering the point and matching points within clusters.

An *early bail-out* test proposed by Capel [5] abandons testing of all points against a hypothesized transformation if after testing a sufficient number of points the percentage of inliers obtained is much smaller than the best percentage of inliers obtained thus far. For instance, if the test is performed on n_1 randomly selected points and the largest number of points satisfying the transformation thus far is n_2, and if a new transformation is tested against n_1 points and $n_3 < \alpha n_2$ correspondences are obtained, further testing against the transformation is abandoned. α and n_1 depend on the parameters of RANSAC. α is a number such as 0.5 and n_1 is a number such as 100 or $n/100$, whichever is smaller. n is the number of points in the sensed set. This early bail-out test can also be added to the above RANSAC algorithm right before Step 3c. Therefore, after it is determined that the hypothesized transformation can match d points, the hypothesis is verified using n_1 points. If the number of points passing the test $n_3 < \alpha n_2$, a jump is made to Step 4. Otherwise, testing is continued by going to Step 3c.

In an algorithm known as *preemptive* RANSAC, Nistér [33] proposed generating a predetermined number of transformations. This can be achieved either using random subsets from the two sets or knowing the possible transformations between the two sets. A counter is associated with each transformation and initialized to 0. A point from each set is tested against all transformations, and the counter for the transformation that matches the points is incremented by 1. If a randomly selected point pair truly corresponds, they satisfy the correct transformation. If they do not correspond, they will not satisfy any of the transformations; however, they may accidentally satisfy and contribute to an incorrect transformation. The incorrect correspondences either randomly satisfy a transformation or they do not satisfy any of the transformations. Correct correspondences, however, contribute to the same transformation. After testing a sufficiently large number of randomly selected point pairs from the two sets, the transformation receiving the highest score is considered the correct transformation and is used to determine the correspondence between points in the two sets. The main difficulty in this approach is to come up with the smallest number of transformations that contain the correct transformation.

In the *maximum likelihood estimation sample consensus* (MLESAC) proposed by Torr and Zisserman [49], correspondence is established between point sets by maximizing the likelihood of finding the solution rather than maximizing the number of inliers. In a *guided-sampling* approach proposed by Tordoff and Murray [48], a feature matching quality is added to MLESAC to assist in the search for the maximum likelihood solution. Guided sampling enables selecting subsets that are more likely to find the solution. Subset selection or hypothesis generation in guided sampling relies on additional information about the points. The information can be in the form of features, such as the number of points with a fixed radius of a point, the degree of a point in the minimum spanning tree of the points, the intensity of a point, etc. By choosing point subsets that have similar features, point subsets are selected that are more likely to produce the correct transformation.

An extension to guided sampling proposed by Chum and Matas is known as *progressive sample consensus* (PROSAC) [11]. The idea is to create a small subset of points from each set based on the similarity of features/descriptors associated with the points. Initially, small subsets from each set are selected from points with the most similar features/descriptors. The size of the subset is progressively increased to generate hypotheses until the solution transformation is found.

In a RANSAC algorithm developed by Serradell et al. [42], initial correspondence is established between points in two images using their intensity features. Since lack of uniqueness among intensity features could result in some incorrect correspondences, to remove the incorrect correspondences, geometric information (constraint) holding between the images is used. In particular, homography is used as the geometric constraint between points in the images to remove the incorrect and ambiguous correspondences and arrive at unique ones.

In the generalized RANSAC framework developed by Zhang and Košecká [57], initially multiple correspondences of sensed points are considered for each reference point using the similarity between the features of the points [37]. Then, unique correspondences are determined between the reference and sensed points using additional information in the images. Hsiao et al. [24] have shown that keeping ambiguities among the correspondences and removing them later during hypothesis testing using global information in addition to the local information provided by the features of the points improves match rating among the points. Use of image features to find the putative correspondences before finding the final correspondences has been found to speed up RANSAC by two orders of magnitude. Use of image features to aid determination of correspondence between point sets is further discussed in Sect. 7.4.

A variant of RANSAC, known as *geometric hashing*, uses a table look-up to simultaneously compare one sensed point set to many reference point sets. For each reference set a point pair, called a *basis pair*, is selected and mapped to $(0, 0)$ and $(1, 0)$. The transformation obtained as a result is used to transform the remaining points in the reference set. Each transformed point is then mapped to an entry in a 2-D array called the *hash table*. The identity of the reference set and the basis point pair are then added to that entry. The process is repeated for other point pairs. After processing all point pairs, entries in the hash table will contain the name of the reference set. The same is repeated for other reference sets. Note that the process may save the identities of many reference sets in the same table entry.

To determine the reference point set best matching a sensed point set, point pairs are selected from the sensed set and mapped to $(0, 0)$ and $(1, 0)$. The transformation is then used to map the remaining points in the sensed set to the table. The model name most frequently encountered in the hash table during this mapping identifies the reference point matching the sensed point set. The basis point pairs in the reference and sensed point sets are used to determine the correspondence between remaining points by the similarity transformation [26, 54]. Note that this limits usage of the hash table to point sets that are related by only similarity transformation.

The performance of geometric hashing degrades quickly with noise [22, 27]. Also, since each reference point pair should be used to prepare the hash table, the point sets cannot be very large. Otherwise, preparation of the hash table from many point sets becomes impractical. Geometric hashing is suitable when each point set contains a small number of points, there is a small number of point sets, and the reference point sets are known ahead of time so that a hash table can be prepared from them off-line.

7.2 Graph-Based Point Pattern Matching

A graph representation of a set of points in the plane is independent of the position and orientation of the points within the plane. Examples are the complete graph, triangulation, minimum-spanning tree (MST), and the convex-hull of the points (Fig. 7.1). One of the earliest point correspondence algorithms determined the maximal *cliques* (connected subgraphs) in two point sets that satisfied the same geometric relation [2, 4]. Although matching in this manner is efficient for small point sets, due to its backtracking nature, its computational complexity increases

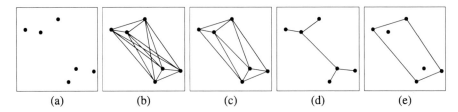

Fig. 7.1 (**a**) A set of points in the plane. (**b**) Complete graph, (**c**) triangulation, (**d**) MST, and (**e**) convex-hull of the points

exponentially with the number of points. To increase speed, Lavine et al. [28] correlated sorted edge lengths of subgraphs and Ahuja [1] correlated sorted areas of connected Voronoi polygons to establish correspondence between subgraphs.

To establish correspondence between two point sets, Zhan [56] matched an edge in the MST of one point set to an edge in the MST of another point set to determine the translational, rotational, and scaling differences between the point sets. The obtained transformation was then used to determine the correspondence between remaining points in the two sets.

The complete graph of a set of n points contains $n(n - 1)/2$ edges. Therefore, if two point sets that contain m and n points are related by the similarity transformation, the exhaustive search using the complete graph of the point sets requires hypothesizing and testing $n(n - 1)m(m - 1)/2$ or on the order of $n^2 m^2$ different transformations. Note that each edge in the reference graph should be matched against a sensed edge twice by reordering the edge endpoints in the sensed set. If instead of the complete graph edges the MST edges are used, because a point set with n points has an MST with $n - 1$ edges, the exhaustive search involves hypothesizing and testing $2(n - 1)(m - 1)$ or on the order of nm transformations. Use of MST edges, therefore, considerably reduces search time for the correspondences when compared to the complete graph edges. Since each hypothesis requires mapping n points in the sensed set to points in the reference, and finding which of the m points in the reference is closest to each of the mapped points from the sensed set, on the order of mn distance computations is needed. This makes the computational complexity of the graph-based algorithm using MST edges on the order of $m^2 n^2$.

Further speed-up can be achieved by matching an edge in the reference set to a small number of edges that have about the same length or length ratio in the sensed set rather than to all edges. It is not likely that the longest edge in one MST will produce correct correspondences when matched against the smallest edge in the other MST. Therefore, edges in the sensed set are ordered according to their lengths, and for each edge in the reference set, matching is performed between that edge and $k \ll m - 1$ edges in the sensed set that have the closest edge ratio. Edge ratio is considered to be the length of an edge divided by the average length of edges in an MST. Matching in this manner reduces the number of hypothesized and tested transformations from $2(n - 1)(m - 1)$ to $2(m - 1)k$ but with overhead of $(n - 1)\log_2(n - 1)$, the time needed to order the $(n - 1)$ edges of the MST in the sensed set. Considering each hypothesized transformation requires on the order of mn distance calculations to verify its correctness, the overall computational complexity of the process in this case will be $O(m^2nk)$.

Instead of MST edges, convex-hull edges can be used to match the points [21]. The maximum number of convex-hull edges of a set of n points is n and the minimum number is 3. Therefore, in general, there are fewer edges in the convex-hull than in the MST of a set of points. Edges in the convex-hull of a set of points are generally longer than MST edges (Fig. 7.1e). Therefore, matching of convex-hull edges generally results in more accurate transformation parameters than matching of MST edges.

When the point sets contain considerable outliers and noise, the likelihood that a tested edge pair finds the correct correspondences is low. The fewer the number of outliers and noisy points, the higher will be the likelihood that a tested edge pair finds the correct correspondences. Therefore, one may start by matching the convex-hull edges, and if that does not find a sufficient number of correspondences, then the MST edges are matched. If that also does not succeed, then the triangulation edges are matched, and if that also fails, an exhaustive search is performed using the complete-graph edges. In rare cases where the same convex hull, MST, or triangulation edges are not found in the two point sets due to a large number of outliers, the exhaustive search should be able to find the correspondences. Exhaustive search should be used as the last resort though, as it is very time consuming.

Similar to RANSAC, graph-based matching can have parameters ε, r, and N. r shows the ratio of the number of inliers and the number of points in the sensed set under a hypothesized transformation. For instance, if a transformation finds correspondence for 1/4th of the points in the sensed set, one may stop the process. In the event that r is not selected properly, the process may not stop even though the correct transformation is found. In that case, when the process stops after N iterations, the transformation producing the most correspondences is taken as the correct transformation and the correspondences obtained from it are returned.

If the point sets are related by an affine transformation, three corresponding points are needed to determine the transformation parameters. In such a situation, each point set is triangulated [16] and vertices of triangle pairs are used to determine the transformation parameters. If a point set contains n points, k of which fall on the convex-hull of the points, there will be $T = 2n - 2 - k$ triangles. Therefore, if there are T_1 triangles in the reference set and T_2 triangles in the sensed set, there will be T_1T_2 triangle pairs that can be tested. Note that each reference triangle should be matched with the sensed triangle 6 times by reordering the vertices of the sensed triangle.

To limit the search space when using triangulated points, the sensed triangles can be ordered according to their area sizes, largest angles, or ratio of largest and smallest sides. Then, given a reference triangle, a small number of sensed triangles most similar to it can be identified in the ordered list and used in matching. This will reduce the number of hypothesized transformations from T_1T_2 to kT_1, where $k \ll T_2$.

If the point sets are related by the projective transformation, four points are required from each set to determine the transformation parameters. If a point set is triangulated, except for the convex-hull edges, each interior edge is shared by two triangles that form a quadrilateral. If a point set contains n points, k of which fall on the convex-hull of the points, there will be $E = 3n - 3 - k$ edges in the triangulation. Since k edges fall on the convex-hull of the points, there will be $Q = 3n - 3 - 2k$ interior edges, so there will be Q quadrilaterals. Consequently, if there are Q_1 quadrilaterals in the reference set and Q_2 quadrilaterals in the sensed set, there will $Q_1 Q_2$ quadrilateral pairs that can be used to hypothesize and test the projective transformation relating the point sets.

Some quadrilateral pairs are unlikely to produce correspondences. Therefore, if the sensed quadrilaterals are ordered according to a predefined property, then quadrilaterals of similar property from the two sets can be matched. For example, a simple convex-concave categorization of the quadrilaterals can reduce the number of matches by a factor of 4. Other invariant properties of quadrilaterals under homography can be used to order the quadrilaterals and reduce computation time. Selecting similar quadrilaterals in reference and sensed sets increases the likelihood that the matched quadrilateral vertices find the correspondences, and that reduces the number of hypothesized transformations from $Q_1 Q_2$ to $k Q_1$, where $k \ll Q_2$. To avoid verification of a hypothesized transformation using all points, an early bail-out step like that used in RANSAC can be used here also to avoid further testing of a transformation function that is not likely to produce a solution.

In graph-based approaches, the local information provided by an edge, a triangle, or a quadrilateral is used to estimate a local transformation that is hypothesized to be the global transformation and verified using all points in the two sets. For the process to work, a locally estimated transformation should be the same or very close to the global transformation. This requires that points in the two sets be related to each other by a globally rigid, linear, or projective transformation. Moreover, noise among point coordinates should be smaller than half distances between closest points in the reference set. Otherwise, the local transformation determined from local MST edges, triangles, or quadrilaterals may not be able to correctly count corresponding points in the two sets during hypothesis and testing.

The correspondences reported by a graph-based method can be used to determine refined transformation parameters by the least-squares method. Least-squares will use more global information and produce a more accurate estimation of the transformation parameters than the parameters estimated using local point coordinates. The obtained global transformation can then be used to determine more correspondences in the two sets.

Outliers produce matches that can mislead the process if there are a sufficiently large number of them. Presence of too many outliers may produce completely different convex-hulls, MSTs, triangles, and quadrilaterals, causing the process that uses them to fail. Therefore, it is critical to include, as a last resort, an exhaustive search that uses the complete graph edges of the points to find the correspondences.

Graph-based approaches are similar to RANSAC in the way the transformation parameters are determined from point subsets. The two are different in the way the point subsets are selected. In graph-based approaches, point subsets are chosen in a structured manner. Since the number of such cases is much smaller than the number of random cases that produce subsets containing corresponding points, there rarely is a need to stop the process after N iterations. However, if N is available, it can be used in graph-based matching also.

The speed-up techniques discussed in RANSAC can be applied to graph-based matching also. For instance, the randomized, preemptive, and early bail-out schemes used in RANSAC can be used to speed up graph-based matching algorithms in the same manner.

7.3 Performance Measures in Point Pattern Matching

To characterize a matching algorithm and to evaluate its performance, a number of point sets with known correspondences is required. To demonstrate the evaluation process, the point sets obtained in the coin images in Fig. 6.2 will be used. Since the geometric relations between images (b)–(f) and image (a) are known, given a point in image (a), we will know its correspondence in images (b)–(f). 100 points detected in each image are used in the experiments. Due to the geometric and intensity differences between image (a) and images (b)–(f), some points detected in (a) do not appear in (b)–(f). Due to noise and other factors, some points detected in (a) are slightly displaced in (b)–(f). Assuming the geometric relation between image (a) and image (x) is $\mathbf{f}$, where (x) is one of (b)–(f), point $\mathbf{p}$ in (a) is considered corresponding to point $\mathbf{P}$ in (x) if $\|\mathbf{p} - \mathbf{f}(\mathbf{P})\| \leq \varepsilon$. We let $\varepsilon = 1.5$ pixels.

The 100 strongest points that are also the most widely spread over images (a)–(f) in Fig. 6.2 are detected and points in (b)–(f) falling within $\varepsilon = 1.5$ pixels of points in (a) after a transformation are considered to be corresponding points. If point $\mathbf{P}$ in (b)–(f) falls horizontally, vertically, or diagonally adjacent to or at point $\mathbf{p}$ in (a) after transformation, it is considered corresponding to point $\mathbf{p}$.

Since these images are related by the similarity transformation, two corresponding control points in the images are sufficient to align the images and find the correspondence between the points in the images. After determining the MST edges of points in each set, the MST edges are ordered from the longest to the shortest. Then, for the ith reference MST edge, a search is made among the sensed MST edges from $i - \delta n + 1$ to $i + \delta n + 1$ edges, where δn represents the difference between the number of points in the two sets. That is, $\delta n = |m - n|$. If no successful match is found, each reference MST edge is then matched with all sensed MST edges, and if that fails, each reference MST edge is matched with all triangulation edges of sensed points. If that also fails, each reference MST edge is matched against all edges in the complete graph of points in the sensed set.

The matching results obtained by edge matching are depicted in Fig. 7.2. Yellow lines connect the true correspondences found by the algorithm, red lines connect the correspondences found that are false, and green lines connect the true correspondences missed by the algorithm.

Matching the MST edges of points in the coin image and points in its blurred version (Fig. 7.2a) 67 correspondences are obtained, of which 66 are correct and 1 is incorrect. The algorithm finds 61 correspondences between points in the coin

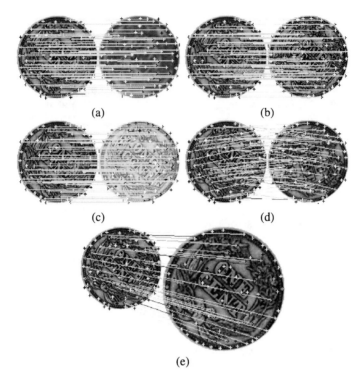

(a)   (b)

(c)   (d)

(e)

Fig. 7.2 (**a**)–(**e**) Correspondences obtained between points in the original coin image and points in its (**a**) blurred, (**b**) noisy, (**c**) contrast-enhanced, (**d**) rotated, and (**e**) scaled versions by MST edge matching. *Yellow lines* connect the true correspondences obtained by the algorithm, *red lines* connect correspondences found by the algorithm that are false, and *green lines* connect the true correspondences missed by the algorithm

image and its noisy version (Fig. 7.2b), of which 60 are correct and 1 is incorrect. The algorithm finds 68 correspondences between points in the coin image and its contrast-enhanced version (Fig. 7.2c), all of which are correct. The algorithm finds 48 correspondences between points in the coin image and its rotated version (Fig. 7.2d), of which 47 are correct and 1 is incorrect.

MST edges failed to match points in the coin image and its scaled version due to the absence of common edges in the MSTs of the points while satisfying $\varepsilon = 1.5$ pixels and $r = 0.25$. The process failed to find the correspondences by matching edges in the triangulation of the points also because of the same reason; however, it was able to find the correspondence between the point sets when matching the complete graph edges of the points. It found 28 correspondences between points in the coin image and its scaled version (Fig. 7.2e), of which 23 are correct and 5 are incorrect. It also misses 5 of the true correspondences.

To measure the performance of the graph-based matching algorithm on the coin images, true positive (*TP*): number of correspondences found that are correct; true negative (*TN*): correctly not selecting correspondences that do not exist; false positive (*FP*): number of correspondences found that are incorrect; false negative (*FN*):

number of correspondences missed. $P' = TP + FP$ is the *number of detected correspondences*, $N' = FN + TN$ is the *number of predicted non-correspondences*, $P = TP + FN$ is the *number of true correspondences* or *inliers*, $N = FP + TN$ is the *number of true non-correspondences* or *outliers*.

The example in Fig. 7.2a shows matching of points in the original coin image and in its blurred version. In this example, $TP = 66$, $FP = 1$, $TN = 33$, and $FN = 0$. Therefore, the number of predicted correspondences $P' = 67$ and the number of predicted non-correspondences $N' = 33$. The number of true correspondences $P = 66$ and the number of true non-correspondences $N = 34$. Note that $P' + N' = P + N = 100$.

Other measures used to characterize the performance of a correspondence algorithm are:

$$\text{true positive rate:} \quad TPR = \frac{TP}{P}, \tag{7.3}$$

$$\text{false positive rate:} \quad FPR = \frac{FP}{N}, \tag{7.4}$$

$$\text{accuracy:} \quad ACC = \frac{TP + TN}{P + N}. \tag{7.5}$$

Therefore, in the above example we find $TPR = 66/66 = 1.0$, $FPR = 1/33 = 0.03$, and $ACC = (66 + 33)/(66 + 34) = 0.99$.

As the error tolerance ε is increased, the number of missed correspondences (FN) decreases but the number of false correspondences (FP) increases. As ε is decreased, the number of false correspondences decrease but the number of missed correspondences increases. For image registration purposes, having fewer false correspondences is preferred over having fewer missed correspondences because missed correspondences can be recovered once the transformation to align the point sets is estimated from the correspondences. Presence of false correspondences degrades the estimated transformation, missing the correct correspondences.

Although accuracy is the most important performance measure in a correspondence algorithm, speed is also very important. Some applications demand high speed and speed becomes a critical factor. The speed of a matching algorithm depends on the average number of hypothesized transformations tested before finding a correct one. The computation times required to find the correspondence between points in the coin image and its blurred, noisy, contrast-enhanced, rotated, and scaled versions are 0.52, 0.51, 0.48, 0.40, and 30.22 seconds, respectively, on a Windows PC with a 2.2 GHz processor.

The excessive time needed to find the correspondence between points in the coin image and points in its scaled version is due to the fact that the MST and the triangulation edges in the sensed image could not find sufficient correspondences with the imposed $\varepsilon = 1.5$ pixels and $r = 0.25$, requiring matching of MST edges in the reference image to complete-graph edges in the sensed image to find the correspondences.

7.4 Feature-Based Matching

If a descriptor is associated with each control point, we can determine the sensed descriptor that is the most similar (or the least dissimilar) to each reference descriptor. Knowing that features within a descriptor can be inaccurate, the correspondences obtained from the descriptors of the points can contain correct and incorrect correspondences. The important point to note is that if among the obtained correspondences some are correct, those correspondences can be used to determine the remaining correspondences using the geometric constraint holding between the point sets. For example, if the point sets are known to be related by a similarity transformation, two correct correspondences are sufficient to determine the parameters of the transformation. The obtained transformation can then be used to find the remaining correspondences. If the point sets are related by an affine transformation, three corresponding points are sufficient to find the remaining correspondences, and if the point sets are related by a projective transformation (homography), four corresponding points are sufficient to find the remaining correspondences.

As the geometric relation between the point sets becomes more complex, a larger number of correspondences is needed to determine the parameters of the transformation. We will deal with this problem later in this chapter by developing a correspondence algorithm that gradually adapts to the local geometric difference between the point sets. In this section, we will consider cases where a similarity, an affine, or a projective transformation can align inliers in two point sets.

Let $\mathbf{A}$ be a proximity matrix with m rows and n columns with A_{ij} showing the dissimilarity (such as, Euclidean distance) between the descriptors of points $\mathbf{p}_i$ and $\mathbf{P}_j$. Suppose $\mathbf{b}$ is an array of length m with $b_i = j$ if the descriptor of $\mathbf{p}_i$ is closest to the descriptor of $\mathbf{P}_j$ among all sensed descriptors. Also suppose $\mathbf{e}$ is an array of length m of distances with $e_i = d_{ij} = \min_l(d_{il})$. d_{ij} is the distance between descriptors of $\mathbf{p}_i$ and $\mathbf{P}_j$, where $\mathbf{P}_j$ is the point in the sensed set with a descriptor that is closest to the descriptor of $\mathbf{p}_i$ when considering the descriptors of all points in the sensed set.

Algorithm F2 (Feature-based point pattern matching) It is assumed that the point sets are related by a similarity transformation and L denotes a sorted list of point pairs obtained from the correspondence array $\mathbf{b}$. The point pairs are used to estimate the parameters of the similarity transformation. If $\mathbf{b}$ has m entries, L will have $m(m-1)$ entries, showing all permutations of point pairs that can possibly find the correspondence between the point sets. n_m denotes the maximum number of correspondences found so far. Therefore, initially $n_m = 0$. h denotes the index of list L, thus it varies between 1 and $m(m-1)$ and is initially set to 0. r denotes the ratio of the number of correspondences found in an iteration and the number of points in the sensed set (m), r_m denotes the largest r found so far and so is initially set to 0, and r_t is a threshold ratio showing the smallest r to consider a hypothesized transformation correct and is provided by the user.

1. Normalize the features of the descriptors so they all vary between 0 and 1.

2. Compute proximity matrix $\mathbf{A}$:

$$A_{ij} = \left\{ \sum_{k=1}^{n_f} (f_{ik} - F_{jk})^2 \right\}^{\frac{1}{2}}, \quad i = 1, \ldots, m, \; j = 1, \ldots, n, \qquad (7.6)$$

where n_f is the number of features in a descriptor.

3. Compute the correspondence array $\mathbf{b}$ from the proximity matrix $\mathbf{A}$ by letting $b_i = j$, for $i = 1, \ldots, m$, with j being the smallest element in row i. That is, j is found such that

$$A_{ij} = \min_{l=1}^{n} (A_{il}). \qquad (7.7)$$

4. Compute distance array $\mathbf{e}$ of length m with entry e_i showing the Euclidean distance between descriptors of $\mathbf{p}_i$ and $\mathbf{P}_{b_i}$.
5. Compute entries of list L. This involves: (a) finding the MST of points in the reference set, (b) for each MST edge $\mathbf{p}_i \mathbf{p}_j$, hypothesizing sensed corresponding points $\mathbf{P}_k \mathbf{P}_l$ by letting $k = b_i$ and $l = b_j$, (c) finding the sum of Euclidean distances between descriptors of $\mathbf{p}_i$ and $\mathbf{P}_k$ and between descriptors of $\mathbf{p}_j$ and $\mathbf{P}_l$ for each such point pair in the list, and (d) ordering the point pairs according to the sum of their Euclidean distances from the smallest to the largest in the list.
6. Take the point pair from entry h in list L and denote the points by ($\mathbf{p}_i$, $\mathbf{P}_k$; $\mathbf{p}_j$, $\mathbf{P}_l$).
7. Determine the similarity transformation parameters by letting $\mathbf{p}_i$ correspond to $\mathbf{P}_k$ and $\mathbf{p}_j$ correspond to $\mathbf{P}_l$.
8. Using the obtained transformation, transform the sensed points and find the number of the transformed points that fall within distance tolerance ε of reference points, n_p.
9. If $n_p/m \geq r_t$, go to Step 11. Otherwise, if $n_p/m > r_m$, let $r_m = n_p/m$ and save the obtained correspondences.
10. If L is not empty, increment h by 1 and go to Step 6.
11. From the obtained correspondences, recalculate the transformation parameters, this time by a robust estimator (Chap. 8).
12. From the obtained transformation, find the correspondences and return the transformation and the correspondences.

In Step 1, each feature is normalized to vary between 0 and 1. This normalization is essential when descriptors containing heterogeneous features are used, because it prevents a feature with a larger range from influencing the matching outcome more than a feature with a smaller range.

The reason for using point pairs representing MST edges in Step 5 rather than all combinations of point pairs is to reduce the length of list L while ensuring all reference points participate in the matching process. When $m \leq 100$, instead of MST edges, all point pairs may be used to search for the correspondences. For a very large m, in the interest of time, point pairs representing the MST edges should be used to find the correspondences.

The point sets used in Algorithm F2 should be related by a similarity transformation. If the point sets are related by an affine transformation, three corresponding points are needed to find the transformation parameters. In that case, Step 5 of the algorithm should be changed to triangulate the points, insert vertices of triangles into list L, and find the affine transformation parameters by using corresponding point triples.

If the point sets are related by homography, points in the reference set should be triangulated, interior edges should be identified, and vertices of triangles sharing each edge should be used along with the initial correspondences saved in **b** to determine the projective transformation parameters. The transformation that finds the most correspondences with distance tolerance ε is then chosen as the transformation to find correspondence between the remaining points in the two sets.

In Step 8, instead of adding 1 to the count when a transformed sensed point falls within the distance threshold of ε of a reference point, a weight between 0 and 1 can be added to the count. For instance, if the distance between reference point $\mathbf{p}_i$ and the transformed sensed point $\mathbf{P}_j$ closest to it is r_{ij}, the weight can be considered $\exp(-r_{ij}^2/\varepsilon^2)$. When two transformations produce the same number of correspondences, use of continuous weights makes it possible to select the transformation that more closely aligns corresponding points.

Step 9 stops the iterations if a sufficiently high proportion of the points in the two sets are found to correspond to each other. Threshold value r_t, which determines this proportionality is provided by the user. r_t and ε can be determined through a training process using a number of representative data sets with known correspondences. The algorithm is set up in such a way that if r_t is too high, it will exhaustively search list L for the best answer. If r_t is too low, it may stop the search prematurely with an incorrect answer.

Parameter ε depends on noise and geometric difference between the images. If it is set too low, it may miss finding the correspondences. If it is set too high, it may find some incorrect correspondences. The robust estimator in Step 11 is used to determine the transformation parameters at the presence of some incorrect correspondences.

Since in the feature-based algorithm a graph is formed from points in the reference set only and the graph in the sensed set is obtained from the correspondences estimated by the features saved in **b**, far fewer transformations are hypothesized by the feature-based algorithm than by the graph-based algorithm.

To evaluate the performance of the feature-based matching algorithm, the point sets obtained from the coin images in Fig. 6.2 are used. Point correspondences obtained by Algorithm F2 are shown in Fig. 7.3. As features, L_{23}, L_{24}, L_{26}, L_{50c}, L_{90}, and L_{96} (see Chap. 4) calculated at each point within a circular window of radius 8 pixels were used. The correspondences found by the algorithm are connected by red lines while the true correspondences are drawn with green lines. Yellow lines, which are obtained when red and green lines coincide, show the correspondences found by the algorithm that are correct.

Algorithm F2 finds 68 correspondences between the original coin image and its blurred version, of which 66 are correct and 2 are incorrect. It finds 62 correspondences between the coin image and its noisy version, of which 60 are correct and 2

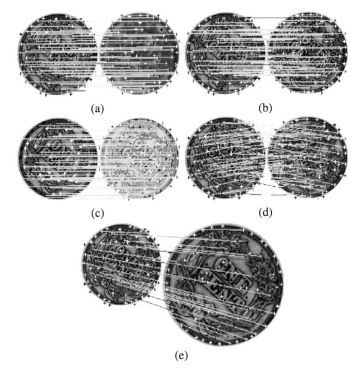

Fig. 7.3 Correspondences obtained between points in the original coin image and points in its (**a**) blurred, (**b**) noisy, (**c**) contrast-enhanced, (**d**) rotated, and (**e**) scaled versions when matching the MST edges using the descriptors of the points

are incorrect. It finds 69 correspondences between points in the coin image and its contrast-enhanced version, of which 68 are correct and 1 is incorrect. The algorithm finds 51 correspondences between points in the coin image and its rotated version, of which 48 are correct and 3 are incorrect. Finally, the algorithm finds 30 correspondences between points in the coin image and its scaled version, of which 26 are correct and 4 are incorrect. It also misses 2 correct correspondences.

If the reference set contains m points, the MST of the points will contain $(m-1)$ edges. This will produce $(m-1)$ different hypothesized transformations that need to be tested for correctness. Each transformation requires mapping points in the sensed set to the space of the reference set and finding the reference point set closest to each mapped point. This requires mn distance calculations for each hypothesized transformation. If the reference MST has $(m-1)$ edges, there will be $O(m^2n)$ distance calculation to find correspondence between points in the two sets. The actual computational time of Algorithm F2 depends on parameter r_t. The smaller it is, the faster the algorithm will find an answer and halt. However, it should be noted that if r_t is too small, it may stop the process prematurely, producing incorrect correspondences. An exhaustive search by Algorithm F2 ($r_t = 1$) when using all MST edges in the reference set has computational complexity $O(m^2n)$. This shows that we should let the smaller set represent the reference set to achieve a higher speed in finding the correspondences.

An early bailout approach like that used in RANSAC can be used here also to speed up the computations. Instead of testing a hypothesized transformation using all sensed points, the transformation can be first tested on a small fraction of the sensed points, and if the transformation finds correspondence for a large proportion of the points, then the transformation can be tested on all sensed points. If $k \ll n$, then this will reduce computational complexity of the feature-based algorithm to $O(mkn)$.

The results produced in Fig. 7.3 were obtained with $r_t = 0.25$. The time required to produce the correspondences depicted in (a)–(e) are 0.18, 0.21, 0.45, 0.18, and 0.16 seconds, respectively. These times include computation of the descriptors at the points. We see that computation times for the feature-based matching and graph-based matching are close for cases (a)–(d); however, due to excessive outliers, if the MSTs of two point sets do not contain matching edges, graph-based matching fails. In feature-based matching, since the MST in one of the point sets is used and the corresponding MST is obtained through correspondences guessed through feature matching, the likelihood that all point pairs representing the MST edges in the reference set incorrectly predict their correspondences is very low; therefore, the process has a very high likelihood of finding the correct correspondences.

In situations where MST edges in feature-based matching do not produce a solution, similar to graph-based matching, triangulation edges can be used, and if that fails, an exhaustive search using all complete graph edges can be used to find the correspondences. Note that when complete graph edges are used in feature-based matching, the exhaustive search by feature-based matching takes on the order of $m^3 n$ distance calculations. In feature-based matching, once an edge is selected in the complete graph of reference points, the corresponding edge in the sensed set is provided by the contents of array **b**, requiring only mn additional distance calculations to verify the correspondences.

7.5 Clustering-Based Matching

In RANSAC, graph-based, and feature-based matching, transformation parameters that relate the geometries of point sets are determined in such a way as to maximize the number of correspondences. Considering the fact that all point subsets that truly correspond to each other produce the same or very close transformation parameters and other point subsets produce parameters that randomly fill the parameter space, the parameters representing the strongest cluster center in the parameter space match the most points in the two sets.

If the point sets are related by a similarity transformation, a 4-D parameter space is required to find the parameters of the transformation that matches most points in the two sets. If the largest cluster formed in the 4-D space can be approximated by a 4-D Gaussian, since a 4-D Gaussian can be decomposed into 4 1-D Gaussians, the location of the 4-D Gaussian can be determined by locating 4 Gaussians in the 4 1-D spaces.

Consider selecting 2 points from each set and determining the scale ratio s of the line segments connecting the points in the two sets and the rotational difference θ between the line segments. Suppose 2 1-D accumulator arrays to record various values for s and θ are created and their entries are initialized to 0. Then, for each point pair from each set, parameters (s, θ) are estimated and corresponding entries of the accumulator arrays are incremented by 1. If there aren't too many outliers in the point sets, the most dominant peak within each array will identify the parameter that produces the most correspondences. After finding s and θ, parameters t_x and t_y are determined in the same manner.

Presence of zero-mean noise among point positions will produce a wider cluster but will not change the location of the peak and, therefore, the process performs well under zero-mean noise. As the number of outliers increases, a larger number of point subsets is needed to form a well-defined peak within each accumulator array.

Algorithm F3 (Point pattern matching by clustering) Given (1) reference point set $\{\mathbf{p}_i = (x_i, y_i) : i = 1, \ldots, m\}$ and sensed point set $\{\mathbf{P}_j = (X_j, Y_j) : j = 1, \ldots, n\}$, (2) knowing that the transformation mapping the sensed point set to the reference point set is a similarity transformation, and (3) knowing that a sensed point is considered to correspond to a reference point if it falls within distance ε of the reference point after being transformed with the obtained transformation, the following algorithm determines the correspondence between points in the two sets by clustering.

1. Create accumulator arrays $\{\mathbf{A}_k : k = 1, \ldots, 4\}$ of sufficient size and initialize the entries of the arrays to 0.
2. Select 2 points from the reference set and 2 points from the sensed set. Keep the order of the points in the reference subset fixed but permute the order of points in the sensed subset and for each permutation determine the rotation and scale parameters of the transformation using the point subsets. Then, map the obtained parameters to the corresponding array entries and increment the entries by 1.
3. Repeat Step 2 a sufficient number of times until a clear peak emerges in each array.
4. Detect the location of the cluster peak in the rotation and scale accumulator arrays. Knowing rotation and scale parameters, repeat Steps 2–4 in the same manner to find the translation parameters.
5. Use parameters corresponding to the peak entries in the accumulator arrays to define the transformation that maps the sensed points to the reference points.
6. Using the obtained transformation, find points in the sensed set that fall within distance tolerance ε of points in the reference set after the transformation and return the obtained correspondences.

The length of the accumulator arrays determines the accuracy of the estimated parameters. If arrays with 100 entries are selected, the range of value of a parameter is mapped to 0–99. Therefore, if parameter a varies between a_{min} and a_{max}, a particular value of a is mapped to entry $\lfloor 99(a - a_{min})/(a_{max} - a_{min}) \rfloor$.

The number of iterations required for Step 2 to form a clear cluster in an accumulator array depends on factors such as noise, ratio of outliers and inliers, and the complexity of the transformation function. A measure that determines the quality of a peak is kurtosis (4.9). The larger the kurtosis, the more clearly defined the obtained Gaussian will be.

To form peaks in the accumulator arrays faster, the points should be selected in a structured manner rather than randomly. Moreover, distances between points should be used to filter out cases that are not likely to produce correct parameters. For instance, if the images are related by the similarity transformation and the MST edges are used to determine the transformation parameters, the MST edges should be ordered from the largest to the smallest in both sets. Then, when an edge is selected from the reference list, it should be matched to a small number of edges that have about the same length in the sensed list. This will increase the likelihood that the matched edges produce correct parameters and contribute to the peaks in the accumulator arrays.

Note that the location of a peak within an accumulator array can be determined with floating point accuracy by fitting a Gaussian to a small number of entries surrounding the peak. If the peak location of accumulator $\mathbf{A}_k$ is a, the parameter corresponding to the peak entry in the array will be $a(a_{max} - a_{min})/99 + a_{min}$.

Wang and Chen [52] and Chang et al. [8] used 2-D accumulator arrays to determine the parameters of a similarity transformation to align the point sets by clustering. By selecting two points from each point set, the ratio of distances between the points in the two sets and the angle between lines connecting the points were determined and indexed into a 2-D accumulator array. With each point pair, an entry of the accumulator array is incremented by 1. After trying a large number of point pairs, a cluster forms at the parameters representing the scale ratio and the rotational difference between the point sets. Using the scale ratio and rotational difference parameters at the cluster center, the scale and orientation of one point set is corrected with respect to the other. The translational difference between the point sets is determined again by clustering using a 2-D accumulator array.

The parameters determined by clustering are less influenced by noise than parameters estimated by least-squares, especially when noise is not zero-mean. Parameters estimated by clustering are also less influenced by outliers than by RANSAC, graph-based, and feature-based approaches, because the transformation parameters are obtained from a small set of points that correspond to each other accurately rather than a large number of points, some of which only approximately correspond.

Point pattern matching by clustering is generally slower than RANSAC, graph-based, and feature-based methods. This is because a single correct match between point subsets finds the transformation parameters by RANSAC, graph-based, and feature-based methods, while a large number of correct subset matches are needed by clustering to form a well-defined cluster from which the parameters of the transformation are estimated. Presence of too many outliers hides peaks in the accumulators, making it difficult or impossible to find the transformation parameters.

The idea of clustering in parameter estimation was introduced by Stockman et al. [47]. The clustering approach to point pattern matching has been extended to localization and recognition of predefined objects in an image [17, 45, 46].

7.6 Geometric Invariance-Based Matching

Some properties of a point set are invariant under certain geometric transformations. Invariance under affine transformation and projective transformation are well-known. Geometric invariance can be used as a means to verify the correctness of correspondences between two point sets.

When two point sets are related by an affine transformation, given three non-colinear points $\mathbf{p}_1$, $\mathbf{p}_2$, and $\mathbf{p}_3$ in the reference set, any other point $\mathbf{p}$ in the reference set can be defined in terms of the three points by [19]:

$$\mathbf{p} = \mathbf{p}_1 + \alpha_1(\mathbf{p}_2 - \mathbf{p}_1) + \alpha_2(\mathbf{p}_3 - \mathbf{p}_1). \tag{7.8}$$

If $\mathbf{A}$ is the affine transformation that maps the sensed point set to the reference point set, we have

$$\mathbf{p} = \mathbf{A}\mathbf{P}, \tag{7.9}$$

where $\mathbf{p}$ and $\mathbf{P}$ are corresponding points in the reference and sensed sets. Substituting (7.9) into (7.8), we obtain

$$\mathbf{AP} = \left[\mathbf{AP}_1 + \alpha_1(\mathbf{AP}_2 - \mathbf{AP}_1) + \alpha_2(\mathbf{AP}_3 - \mathbf{AP}_1)\right] \tag{7.10}$$

$$= \mathbf{A}\left[\mathbf{P}_1 + \alpha_1(\mathbf{P}_2 - \mathbf{P}_1) + \alpha_2(\mathbf{P}_3 - \mathbf{P}_1)\right]. \tag{7.11}$$

Multiply both sides by $\mathbf{A}^{-1}$, we obtain

$$\mathbf{P} = \mathbf{P}_1 + \alpha_1(\mathbf{P}_2 - \mathbf{P}_1) + \alpha_2(\mathbf{P}_3 - \mathbf{P}_1). \tag{7.12}$$

This implies that the same relation holds between corresponding points in the sensed set. Therefore, if a subset containing 3 points are selected from each set and the points truly correspond to each other, for each point $\mathbf{p}$ in the reference set the correspondence to it $\mathbf{P}$ can be found in the sensed set. The same parameters α_1 and α_2 are obtained by substituting the coordinates of $\mathbf{p}$ into (7.8) and the coordinates of point $\mathbf{P}$ into (7.12) and solving the obtained equations. Note that each point in the reference or sensed set has two coordinates, producing two equations when substituted into (7.8) or (7.12).

Taking advantage of this property, a 2-D accumulator array is created for each point set, one dimension showing α_1 and the second dimension showing α_2. The array entries are initially set to 0. Then, a subset containing 3 points is selected from the reference set and for each additional point in that set α_1 and α_2 are determined and the corresponding entry in the accumulator array is incremented by 1. The same is repeated for a combination of 3 points in the sensed set, creating a second accumulator array. The accumulator arrays appear like images where intensities show the counts. The similarity/dissimilarity between the images (accumulator arrays) determine whether the point triples selected from the two sets truly correspond to each other or not. The process is repeated until the obtained accumulator arrays become sufficiently similar.

Algorithm F4 (Point pattern matching using affine invariance) Given (1) reference point set $\{\mathbf{p}_i = (x_i, y_i) : i = 1, \ldots, m\}$ and sensed point set $\{\mathbf{P}_j = (X_j, Y_j) : j = 1, \ldots, n\}$, (2) knowing the distance tolerance ε to consider two points corresponding, and (3) knowing that the two point sets are related by an affine transformation, the following steps outline the affine-invariance-based point pattern matching algorithm.

1. Create two 2-D accumulator arrays $\mathbf{H}_1$ and $\mathbf{H}_2$ and let S_m denote the maximum similarity achieved thus far between $\mathbf{H}_1$ and $\mathbf{H}_2$. Initially, let $S_m = -1$.
2. Triangulate the points in each set.
3. Take a reference triangle and perform the following:
   (a) Initialize all entries of $\mathbf{H}_1$ to 0. Then, for each point in the reference set that is not a vertex of the reference triangle, calculate α_1 and α_2, map the obtained values to the indices of $\mathbf{H}_1$, and increment the obtained entry by 1.
   (b) Take a sensed triangle and initialize all entries of $\mathbf{H}_2$ to 0. Then, for each point in the sensed set that is not a vertex of the sensed triangle, calculate α_1 and α_2, map the obtained values to the indices of $\mathbf{H}_2$, and increment the obtained entry by 1.
   (c) Determine the similarity S between $\mathbf{H}_1$ and $\mathbf{H}_2$ using normalized cross-correlation. If $S > S_m$, let $S_m = S$ and save the corresponding triangle vertices.
   (d) Permute the vertices of the sensed triangle (there are 6 such cases), and for each case repeat Steps 3b and 3c.
4. If $S_m > S_t$, go to Step 5. Otherwise, if unprocessed sensed triangles are available, go to Step 3b. If all sensed triangles are tested but untested reference triangles remain, go to Step 3a.
5. Use the coordinates of saved corresponding triangle vertices to determine the parameters of the affine transformation.
6. Using the obtained affine transformation, for each point $\mathbf{P}_i$ in the sensed set, determine point $\mathbf{p}$ in the reference set. If the point in the reference set closest to $\mathbf{p}$ is $\mathbf{p}_l$ and $\|\mathbf{p} - \mathbf{p}_l\| < \varepsilon$, consider points $\mathbf{P}_i$ and $\mathbf{p}_l$ as corresponding points. Repeat this step for $i = 1, \ldots, n$ to determine all corresponding points in the two sets. Suppose n_p corresponding points are obtained.
7. Use the coordinates of the n_p correspondences to calculate a new transformation by the least-squares method.
8. Determine the correspondences with the new transformation and return the transformation and the correspondences.

The size of the accumulator arrays should be chosen taking into consideration the cardinalities of the point sets. If $M = \min(m, n)$, dimensions of $\mathbf{H}_1$ and $\mathbf{H}_2$ should be $N \times N$, where $N = \sqrt{M}$. If much larger arrays are used, patterns formed in the arrays will be sparse, making correlation of the arrays inaccurate. If much smaller arrays are chosen, the estimated affine parameters may not be sufficiently accurate.

Mapping of particular values of α_1 and α_2 into the array indices can be achieved by finding the acceptable ranges of values for each parameter by testing a number of representative point sets. Once the maximum and minimum values for each parameter are determined, newly observed α_1 and α_2 can be mapped to $[0, N-1]$ using

$$(\alpha_1 - \alpha_{min_1}) \frac{N-1}{\alpha_{max_1} - \alpha_{min_1}}, \tag{7.13}$$

$$(\alpha_2 - \alpha_{min_2}) \frac{N-1}{\alpha_{max_2} - \alpha_{min_2}}, \tag{7.14}$$

where α_{max_1} and α_{min_1} are maximum and minimum values of α_1 and α_{max_2} and α_{min_2} are maximum and minimum values of α_2.

After finding corresponding points, instead of returning them they are used in Step 7 to find the transformation parameters more accurately by least-squares. The newly obtained transformation is then used to determine the final set of correspondences in Step 8.

The computational complexity of invariance-based point pattern matching is similar to that of graph-based matching in the sense that 3 or 4 point subsets from each set produce the hypothesized transformations. But unlike graph-based matching, points in each set are used independently to produce arrays $\mathbf{H}_1$ and $\mathbf{H}_2$ that are then correlated. Therefore, invariance-based matching is faster than graph-based matching using affine and projective transformation by a factor of $mn/(m+n)$.

If two point sets are related by the projective transformation, we have

$$X = \frac{ax + by + c}{gx + hy + 1}, \tag{7.15}$$

$$Y = \frac{dx + ey + f}{gx + hy + 1}. \tag{7.16}$$

Under the projective transformation, the following two properties remain invariant between five non-colinear points in the plane [14]:

$$I_1 = \frac{\det[\mathbf{m}_{431}] \det[\mathbf{m}_{521}]}{\det[\mathbf{m}_{421}] \det[\mathbf{m}_{531}]}, \tag{7.17}$$

$$I_2 = \frac{\det[\mathbf{m}_{421}] \det[\mathbf{m}_{532}]}{\det[\mathbf{m}_{432}] \det[\mathbf{m}_{521}]}. \tag{7.18}$$

For the sensed set, $\det[\mathbf{m}_{ijk}]$ is defined by

$$\det[\mathbf{m}_{ijk}] = \begin{vmatrix} X_i & X_j & X_k \\ Y_i & Y_j & Y_k \\ 1 & 1 & 1 \end{vmatrix}. \tag{7.19}$$

Substituting the X's and Y's calculated from (7.15) and (7.16) into (7.17) and (7.18) and simplifying the relations, we obtain

$$I_1 = \frac{\det[\mathbf{n}_{431}] \det[\mathbf{n}_{521}]}{\det[\mathbf{n}_{421}] \det[\mathbf{n}_{531}]},$$

$$(7.20)$$

$$I_2 = \frac{\det[\mathbf{n}_{421}] \det[\mathbf{n}_{532}]}{\det[\mathbf{n}_{432}] \det[\mathbf{n}_{521}]}$$

$$(7.21)$$

where

$$\det[\mathbf{n}_{ijk}] = \begin{vmatrix} x_i & x_j & x_k \\ y_i & y_j & y_k \\ 1 & 1 & 1 \end{vmatrix}.$$

$$(7.22)$$

If the point subsets truly correspond to each other, I_1 and I_2 determined by the two subsets will be the same or very close. Letting ΔI_1 represent the absolute difference between I_1 determined by the two subsets and letting ΔI_2 represent the absolute difference between I_2 obtained from the two subsets, then $\Delta I = \sqrt{\Delta I_1^2 + \Delta I_2^2}$ can be used as a distance measure to determine the degree of dissimilarity between the two point subsets. The point subsets producing the smallest distance are used to determine the projective transformation parameters.

To increase the likelihood that a selected subset of 4 points from the two sets correspond to each other, rather than taking the points randomly, they should be selected in a prespecified manner. For example, each point set can be triangulated, interior edges can be identified, and triangle vertices sharing interior edges in the two sets can be used in matching. Therefore, if triangulation of reference and sensed sets produce m_e and n_e interior edges, there will be $m_e n_e$ such matches. To further reduce the number of irrelevant matches, the interior edges in both sets are ordered and for each reference edge, only sensed edges that have similar properties are matched. Examples of these properties are convexity/concavity of the quadrilateral obtained with the edge, the ratio of areas of triangles sharing the edge, etc.

In addition to the five-point projective invariance discussed above, a number of other invariance properties have been found between point sets from images of flat scenes. For further information about geometric invariance, the reader is referred to the collection of papers edited by Mundy and Zisserman [32].

Under projective invariance, interior triangle edges are identified and vertices of triangles sharing each interior edge are used to hypothesize a projective transformation. Since the number of interior edges of a triangulation is a linear function of the number of points in a set, the computational complexity of projective matching is on the order of $mn(m+n)$. To reduce the computational complexity of projective matching, rather than using all interior edges of a triangulation, only those falling on the MST of the points may be used. The computational complexity of the process will still be on the order of $mn(m+n)$ but with a smaller coefficient.

Note that as the search space is reduced, the likelihood of missing the correct solution increases. The matching process can start by matching quadrilaterals obtained from MST edges in each set, and if that did not produce a solution, then all interior edges in the triangulation of the point sets can be tried. If that also failed, quadrilaterals with diagonals representing complete graph edges of the points in each set should be used to find the correspondences. If quadrilaterals obtained from the complete graph edges are used in the search, the computational complexity of the algorithm will increase to $m^2n^2(m+n)$.

7.7 Axis of Minimum Inertia-Based Matching

The axis of minimum inertia of a set of points is a line that (1) passes through the centroid (center of gravity) of the points and (2) the sum of squared distances of the points to it is minimum. A line passing through the centroid of the points and normal to the axis of minimum inertia is the axis of maximum inertia. Denoting the sum of squared distances of the given points to its axis of minimum inertia by M_{min} and the sum of squared distances of points to the axis of maximum inertia by M_{max}, by (1) stretching the coordinate space along the axis of maximum inertia or shrinking the coordinate space along the axis of minimum inertia in such a way that $M_{min} = M_{max}$, and (2) isotropically scaling the point coordinates with respect to the centroid in such a way that distance of the farthest point to the centroid is 1, a canonical representation for the points will be obtained.

Hong and Tan [23] showed that if the axis of minimum inertia makes angle ϕ with the x-axis, the relation between M, the sum of squared distances of points to the x-axis, and angle ϕ can be written as

$$M = a + b\cos(\phi). \tag{7.23}$$

Note that when $\phi = 0$, $M = a + b$ and the x-axis aligns with the axis of minimum inertia, and when $\phi = \pi/2$, $M = a - b$ and the x-axis aligns with axis of maximum inertia. The three unknowns a, b, and ϕ can be determined by rotating the coordinate system with respect to the centroid of the points three times and each time determining M. For example, when rotating the coordinate system by 0, $2\pi/3$, and $4\pi/3$, we obtain

$$M_1 = a + b\cos(\phi), \tag{7.24}$$
$$M_2 = a + b\cos(\phi + 2\pi/3), \tag{7.25}$$
$$M_3 = a + b\cos(\phi + 4\pi/3), \tag{7.26}$$

from which we find

$$a = (M_1 + M_2 + M_3)/3, \tag{7.27}$$
$$b = \sqrt{2\big[(M_1 - a)^2 + (M_2 - a)^2 + (M_3 - a)^2\big]/3}, \tag{7.28}$$
$$\phi = \arccos(M_1 - a)/b. \tag{7.29}$$

By scaling the coordinate space of the point set in direction ϕ by $\sqrt{(a-b)/(a+b)}$ and scaling the points with respect to their centroid so that the farthest point is of distance 1 to the centroid, the canonical form of the points will be obtained.

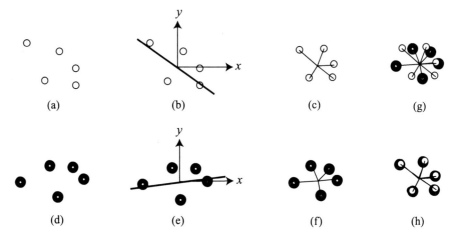

Fig. 7.4 (**a**), (**d**) Two point sets. (**b**), (**e**) The axis of minimum inertia and the coordinate axes centered at the centroid of each point set. (**c**), (**f**) Canonical transformation of the point sets. (**g**) Aligning the canonical point sets at their centroids. (**h**) Rotating one canonical set with respect to the other about their coinciding centroids so that points in the two sets farthest from the centroid align

If the given point sets do not contain outliers and points in the two sets are related by the affine transformation, then by converting each point set into canonical form, aligning the canonical forms at their centroids (Fig. 7.4), rotating one point set with respect to the other about the centroid such that the point farthest from the centroid in each set aligns, the remaining points in the two sets will align also.

When each point set contains n points, the computational complexity of this method is on order of n^2, making this method the fastest thus far. However, this method has many limitations. First, although it remains stable under zero-mean noise, it is very sensitive to outliers, especially when an outlier happens to be the point farthest from the centroid. Also, the method cannot align symmetric or nearly symmetric point sets that have undefined or non-unique axis of minimum inertia.

7.8 Relaxation-Based Matching

Relaxation labeling is an iterative approach that starts with an initial correspondence using features of the points. Then, the geometric constraint holding between the point sets is used to reduce ambiguity among the correspondences and arrive at a unique correspondence. A relaxation labeling approach to point pattern matching treats the matching problem as a consistent labeling problem where points in one set are considered objects and points in the second set are considered labels. Unique labeling of the objects is achieved iteratively by finding labels that are consistent with some world knowledge. The geometric relation between points in the reference set is considered world knowledge.

In a probabilistic relaxation labeling process developed by Goshtasby and Page [20], reference points $\{\mathbf{p}_i : i = 1, \ldots, m\}$ are considered objects and sensed points $\{\mathbf{q}_i : i = 1, \ldots, n\}$ are considered labels. An additional label $\mathbf{q}_0$ is considered a non-existent-object label. Since it is possible that some points in the reference set do not appear in the sensed set, the label for such points is considered $\mathbf{q}_0$.

It is assumed that each point has an associating feature vector. Suppose the similarity measure between the feature vector of point $\mathbf{p}_i$ in the reference set and the feature vector of point $\mathbf{q}_j$ in the sensed set is s_{ij}. Let's also suppose the similarity measures obtained for each point $\mathbf{p}_i$ in the reference set are normalized to have a sum of 1. That is

$$P_i^{(0)}(j) = \frac{s_{ij}}{\sum_{j=1}^{m} s_{ij}}. \tag{7.30}$$

$P_i^{(0)}(j)$ is considered the initial probability that object $\mathbf{p}_i$ will have label $\mathbf{q}_j$, implying that point $\mathbf{p}_i$ in the reference set corresponds to point $\mathbf{q}_j$ in the sensed set. Note that this will initially set $P_i^{(0)}(0) = 0$. That is, each point in the reference set corresponds to some point in the sensed set, although there may be more than one point in the reference set that corresponds to a point in the sensed set. The label probabilities are gradually revised until a consistent labeling is reached.

The probability that object $\mathbf{p}_i$ has label $\mathbf{q}_j$ at the $(k+1)$st iteration is defined by

$$P_i^{(k+1)}(j) = \frac{P_i^{(k)}(j)[1 + Q_i^{(k)}(j)]}{\sum_j P_i^{(k)}(j)[1 + Q_i^{(k)}(j)]}, \tag{7.31}$$

where $Q_i^{(k)}(j)$ is the support for object $\mathbf{p}_i$ having label $\mathbf{q}_j$ at the kth iteration and is in the range $[-1, 1]$. It is the compatibility of point $\mathbf{p}_i$ in the reference set corresponding to point $\mathbf{q}_j$ in the sensed set considering the correspondences of other points in the sets. If the vector of distances $\mathbf{D}_i = \{d_{ii'} : i' = 1, \ldots, m\}$ shows distances of point $\mathbf{p}_i$ to each point in the reference set. Suppose the label with the highest probability at point i' is j'. This will identify for each point in the reference set a point in the sensed set. Then, create a second distance vector showing distances of points in the sensed set to point $\mathbf{q}_j$. That is, $\mathbf{D}_j = \{d_{jj'} : j' = 1, \ldots, m\}$, where j' is the label with the highest probability at point i' in the reference set. Then, $Q_i^{(k)}(j)$ can be considered the normalized correlation between $\mathbf{D}_i$ and $\mathbf{D}_j$.

Since $Q_i^{(k)}(0)$ cannot be calculated in this manner because distances of points to a point that does not exist cannot be calculated. If reference point $\mathbf{p}_i$ does not truly exist in the sensed set, then by assigning label $\mathbf{q}_0$ to $\mathbf{p}_i$, the label probabilities of points with labels other than $\mathbf{q}_0$ should increase, otherwise, the probabilities should decrease. If m' objects out of m whose highest probability labels are not $\mathbf{q}_0$, and if by assigning label $\mathbf{q}_0$ to $\mathbf{p}_i$ the probabilities of m_1 of the labels increase and the probabilities of m_2 of the labels decrease, $Q_i^{(k)}(0) = (m_1 - m_2)/m'$. Note that $m_1 + m_2 = m'$ and when $m_2 = 0$, $Q_i^{(k)}(0) = 1$ and when $m_1 = 0$, $Q_i^{(k)}(0) = -1$.

Starting from the initial label probabilities $P_i^{(0)}(j)$, the label probabilities are iteratively revised according to (7.31) until label probabilities converge to either 0

Fig. 7.5 (a) The reference and (b) sensed point sets used in the relaxation labeling point pattern matching example. These points represent the centers of regions in two segmented images of a scene

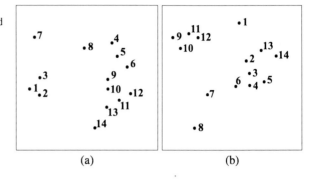

(a)   (b)

or 1. For each object, there will be one label with probability 1 and all remaining label probabilities 0. The above relaxation labeling algorithm relies on distances between points rather than their coordinates to find the correspondence between them. By correlating the distances, the process can find correspondence between point sets that have translational, rotational, and scaling differences.

Point pattern matching by relaxation labeling is generally slower than the methods described above. When very large point sets are given and the ratio of outliers and inliers is high, the process may take a long time to converge. The success of the method is very much dependent on the initial probabilities. For relatively small point sets (a dozen or so) where most of the highest initial label probabilities correctly identify the correspondences, the process could find the correspondences relatively quickly. However, the process can take a very long time to converge if the initial probabilities of many points obtained from inaccurate features incorrectly identify the correspondences. Therefore, this method is suitable for small point sets with accurate features.

An example of this method on a small set of points is given below. Consider the 14 points given in the reference and sensed sets in Fig. 7.5. The correct correspondences are $(1, 9)$, $(2, 10)$, $(3, 11)$, $(5, 13)$, $(6, 14)$, $(8, 1)$, $(9, 2)$, $(10, 3)$, $(11, 4)$, $(12, 5)$, and $(13, 6)$. Other points represent outliers. Using features at the points, the initial label probabilities shown in Table 7.1 were obtained. Label probabilities after 10 and 100 iterations are shown in Tables 7.2 and 7.3, respectively. By taking the label with the highest probability at each reference point as the corresponding sensed point, we see that the process finds all corresponding points correctly. In addition, it correctly identifies point 7 in the reference set as an outlier.

Relaxation labeling was introduced to computer vision by Rosenfeld and colleagues [39]. Ranade and Rosenfeld [38] described a relaxation labeling process that pairs points in the two sets and finds the number of other points that also match as the support. The process can handle only translational difference between point sets, although it has been shown to withstand a small amount of rotational difference between the points also.

In a relaxation labeling algorithm developed by Cheng [9], at each iteration the highest probability label of each object is used to guess a correspondence. From three of the correspondences, an affine transformation is determined and for each

Table 7.1 Initial probabilities of each point in the reference set having labels of each of the points in the sensed set depicted in Fig. 7.5

	0	1	2	3	4	5	6	7	8	9	10	11	12	13	14
1	0.00	0.07	0.08	0.08	0.05	0.06	0.08	0.08	0.08	0.09	0.05	0.06	0.07	0.06	0.07
2	0.00	0.07	0.06	0.07	0.09	0.07	0.06	0.06	0.07	0.07	0.10	0.07	0.06	0.07	0.08
3	0.00	0.06	0.08	0.08	0.04	0.07	0.08	0.09	0.08	0.05	0.05	0.10	0.07	0.08	0.07
4	0.00	0.05	0.08	0.07	0.05	0.07	0.08	0.08	0.10	0.06	0.05	0.07	0.07	0.07	0.06
5	0.00	0.07	0.08	0.08	0.06	0.07	0.06	0.08	0.06	0.07	0.05	0.07	0.06	0.10	0.08
6	0.00	0.09	0.07	0.07	0.06	0.07	0.07	0.07	0.08	0.06	0.07	0.06	0.06	0.07	0.09
7	0.00	0.06	0.08	0.07	0.06	0.07	0.08	0.08	0.09	0.06	0.06	0.06	0.07	0.08	0.08
8	0.00	0.10	0.07	0.08	0.06	0.07	0.07	0.08	0.08	0.05	0.06	0.06	0.06	0.07	0.08
9	0.00	0.08	0.09	0.07	0.06	0.07	0.08	0.08	0.08	0.05	0.06	0.05	0.06	0.07	0.08
10	0.00	0.08	0.07	0.10	0.06	0.07	0.07	0.08	0.08	0.05	0.06	0.06	0.06	0.06	0.09
11	0.00	0.07	0.06	0.07	0.09	0.06	0.05	0.07	0.07	0.07	0.08	0.07	0.05	0.08	0.08
12	0.00	0.06	0.06	0.05	0.09	0.10	0.06	0.06	0.08	0.08	0.09	0.05	0.07	0.07	0.07
13	0.00	0.07	0.07	0.06	0.06	0.08	0.10	0.07	0.10	0.05	0.07	0.05	0.07	0.07	0.08
14	0.00	0.08	0.08	0.08	0.05	0.06	0.07	0.10	0.08	0.05	0.05	0.07	0.06	0.07	0.09

Table 7.2 Label probabilities after 10 iterations

	0	1	2	3	4	5	6	7	8	9	10	11	12	13	14
1	0.00	0.00	0.00	0.00	0.00	0.00	0.00	0.00	0.00	0.35	0.20	0.24	0.21	0.00	0.00
2	0.00	0.00	0.00	0.00	0.00	0.00	0.00	0.00	0.00	0.26	0.37	0.22	0.15	0.00	0.00
3	0.00	0.00	0.00	0.00	0.00	0.00	0.00	0.00	0.00	0.19	0.16	0.39	0.27	0.00	0.00
4	0.29	0.08	0.11	0.03	0.01	0.02	0.00	0.00	0.00	0.00	0.00	0.00	0.00	0.31	0.16
5	0.00	0.06	0.16	0.07	0.02	0.04	0.00	0.00	0.00	0.00	0.00	0.00	0.00	0.39	0.26
6	0.00	0.01	0.16	0.12	0.05	0.12	0.01	0.00	0.00	0.00	0.00	0.00	0.00	0.18	0.34
7	0.42	0.01	0.00	0.00	0.00	0.00	0.00	0.00	0.00	0.12	0.09	0.18	0.19	0.00	0.00
8	0.09	0.70	0.02	0.00	0.00	0.00	0.00	0.00	0.00	0.00	0.00	0.00	0.00	0.14	0.04
9	0.00	0.01	0.28	0.19	0.09	0.14	0.05	0.00	0.00	0.00	0.00	0.00	0.00	0.09	0.16
10	0.00	0.00	0.12	0.29	0.16	0.19	0.12	0.00	0.00	0.00	0.00	0.00	0.00	0.02	0.09
11	0.00	0.00	0.06	0.02	0.32	0.18	0.17	0.01	0.01	0.00	0.00	0.00	0.00	0.01	0.04
12	0.00	0.00	0.08	0.14	0.27	0.29	0.11	0.00	0.00	0.00	0.00	0.00	0.00	0.02	0.07
13	0.02	0.00	0.03	0.10	0.16	0.13	0.44	0.07	0.04	0.00	0.00	0.00	0.00	0.00	0.01
14	0.07	0.00	0.00	0.02	0.03	0.02	0.19	0.49	0.18	0.00	0.00	0.00	0.00	0.00	0.00

reference point the location of the sensed point is estimated and distance of the estimated sensed point to the sensed point represented by the object label is calculated. If the average of the distances falls below a prespecified error tolerance, the process is stopped and the obtained correspondences are reported. Otherwise, the relaxation

Table 7.3 Label probabilities after 100 iterations

	0	1	2	3	4	5	6	7	8	9	10	11	12	13	14
1	0.00	0.00	0.00	0.00	0.00	0.00	0.00	0.00	0.00	0.69	0.17	0.11	0.03	0.00	0.00
2	0.00	0.00	0.00	0.00	0.00	0.00	0.00	0.00	0.00	0.23	0.69	0.02	0.00	0.00	0.00
3	0.00	0.00	0.00	0.00	0.00	0.00	0.00	0.00	0.00	0.06	0.03	0.62	0.29	0.00	0.00
4	0.69	0.00	0.00	0.00	0.00	0.00	0.00	0.00	0.00	0.00	0.00	0.00	0.00	0.31	0.00
5	0.00	0.00	0.00	0.00	0.00	0.00	0.00	0.00	0.00	0.00	0.00	0.00	0.00	0.97	0.03
6	0.00	0.00	0.01	0.00	0.00	0.00	0.00	0.00	0.00	0.00	0.00	0.00	0.00	0.02	0.97
7	0.98	0.00	0.00	0.00	0.00	0.00	0.00	0.00	0.00	0.00	0.00	0.00	0.02	0.00	0.00
8	0.12	0.88	0.00	0.00	0.00	0.00	0.00	0.00	0.00	0.00	0.00	0.00	0.00	0.00	0.00
9	0.00	0.00	0.95	0.04	0.00	0.00	0.00	0.00	0.00	0.00	0.00	0.00	0.00	0.00	0.00
10	0.00	0.00	0.01	0.77	0.11	0.12	0.00	0.00	0.00	0.00	0.00	0.00	0.00	0.00	0.00
11	0.00	0.00	0.00	0.04	0.84	0.07	0.05	0.00	0.00	0.00	0.00	0.00	0.00	0.00	0.00
12	0.00	0.00	0.00	0.06	0.24	0.70	0.00	0.00	0.00	0.00	0.00	0.00	0.00	0.00	0.00
13	0.06	0.00	0.00	0.00	0.00	0.00	0.93	0.00	0.00	0.00	0.00	0.00	0.00	0.00	0.00
14	0.29	0.00	0.00	0.00	0.00	0.00	0.00	0.57	0.14	0.00	0.00	0.00	0.00	0.00	0.00

is continued and the label probabilities are revised using the inter-point distances until object labels change enough so the largest probability label of each reference point uniquely identifies a sensed point.

Ogawa [34], using distances between point pairs in each set as the information source, developed a relaxation labeling process that can find correspondence between point sets with translational, rotational, and scaling differences. By using rotation and scale invariant descriptor at the points, Zhao et al. [59] revised the relaxation-based correspondence algorithm of Ranade and Rosenfeld [38] to find the correspondence between point sets with translational, rotational, and scaling differences.

Relaxation labeling was used by Lee and Won [29] to determine the correspondence between point sets with nonlinear geometric differences. Correlation of logarithm distances and polar angles formed by connecting a point to a number of points nearest to it in each point set were used to define the support or compatibility coefficients. Logarithmic distances de-emphasize differences between distances of corresponding point pairs in images and correlation of polar angles measured at corresponding points in images de-emphasizes spacing difference between corresponding points in images caused by local stretching or shrinking of one image with respect to the other. Choi and Kweon [10] required that not only the relaxation labeling process maximize an objective function but also to satisfy the required geometric constraint between images. Using some knowledge about the correspondences in the form of constraints a process was set up to find correspondence between point sets with nonlinear geometric differences.

7.9 Spectral Graph Theory-Based Matching

A number of correspondence algorithms analyze the singular values of inter-image proximity matrix or eigenvalues of the intra-image proximity matrices to find the correspondence between the points. These algorithms are known as spectral graph theory algorithms. An excellent overview of concepts relating to spectral graph theory is provided by Chung [13]. These algorithms take advantage of the following properties of eigen/singular values and eigenvectors of proximity matrices to find the correspondences: (1) A small perturbation in the positions of points in one set results in small changes in the created proximity matrix, which translates to small changes in the obtained eigen/singular values. More importantly, the changes appear in the trailing eigen/singular values [44]. Therefore, the process captures the global similarity between the point sets and makes it possible to establish correspondence between many of the points. (2) The orthogonal property of the decomposition ensures that the obtained correspondences are unique.

7.9.1 Matching Using Inter-image Proximity Matrix

A correspondence algorithm developed by Scott and Longuet-Higgins [41] relies on the principles of proximity and exclusion. These are the principles the human visual system is believed to use to establish correspondence between points in consecutive video frames. To implement the proximity principle, a correspondence that results in the least motion of a point from one frame to the next is given a higher preference than correspondences that result in larger motions. To implement the exclusion principle, the correspondences are ensured to be unique.

Given m points in the reference set and $n \geq m$ points in the sensed set, an $m \times n$ proximity matrix $\mathbf{G}$ is created with entry ij containing a value inversely proportional to the distance of point i in the reference set to point j in the sensed set when considering the same coordinate system for both point sets. A proximity matrix determined in this manner assigns a higher value to closer points. Note that if $m > n$, the point sets should be switched so that reference set has fewer points than the sensed set. The inverse proportionality function is taken to be a Gaussian:

$$G_{ij} = \exp\{-r_{ij}^2/2\sigma^2\}, \tag{7.32}$$

where r_{ij} is the distance between point i in the reference set and point j in the sensed set. σ is a scale factor and represents the average distance between corresponding points in the two sets and has to be provided by the user based on a-priori knowledge about the motion of points in the sensed set with respect to motion of points in the reference set.

Next, the obtained proximity matrix is subjected to singular value decomposition:

$$\mathbf{G} = \mathbf{TDU}, \tag{7.33}$$

where $\mathbf{T}$ and $\mathbf{U}$ are orthogonal matrices and $\mathbf{D}$ is a diagonal matrix with dimensions similar to those of $\mathbf{G}$ and diagonal entries equal to the singular values of $\mathbf{G}$.

The exclusion constraint is implemented by replacing matrix $\mathbf{D}$ with matrix $\mathbf{E}$ of the same size but with all diagonal elements equal to 1 and other entries equal to 0. Then the assignment matrix is computed from [41]:

$$\mathbf{P} = \mathbf{TEU}. \tag{7.34}$$

The rows of $\mathbf{P}$, like rows of $\mathbf{G}$, identify points in the reference set and the columns of $\mathbf{P}$ identify points in the sensed set. Note that because of the way $\mathbf{E}$ is set up, P_{ij} will show the correlation between row i of $\mathbf{T}$ and column j of $\mathbf{U}$. Therefore, P_{ij} shows the confidence that point i in the reference set would correspond to point j in the sensed set. Consequently, if P_{ij} is the largest element in row i and the largest element in column j, then point i in the reference set will most likely correspond to point j than to other points in the sensed set.

Scott and Longuet-Higgins [41] show that the correspondences obtained in this manner maximize the inner-product between $\mathbf{P}$ and $\mathbf{G}$,

$$\mathbf{P} : \mathbf{G} = \sum_{i} \sum_{j} P_{ij} G_{ij}. \tag{7.35}$$

By maximizing the inner product of proximity and exclusion matrices, the obtained correspondences will maximize the correlation between the proximity and exclusion measures. It has been shown that if the point sets are related by an affine transformation that involves only very small rotational and scaling differences, this method can effectively determine the correspondence between the point sets.

Pilu [36] augmented the proximity measure G_{ij} proposed by Scott and Longuet-Higgins with correlation coefficient C_{ij} of windows centered at points i and j in the reference and sensed images to produce a correlation-weighted proximity measure,

$$g_{ij} = \frac{C_{ij} + 1}{2} G_{ij}. \tag{7.36}$$

g_{ij} still varies between 0 and 1 as C_{ij} varies between -1 and 1. It is shown that in stereo images with very little to no rotational differences, proximity measure g_{ij} produces a higher correspondence rate than G_{ij}.

Parameter σ should be set equal to the average distance between corresponding points in the two sets. σ shows the radius of interaction between points in the two sets and may be taken larger than the average distance between corresponding points, but not smaller. If the average distance between corresponding points is not known, σ may be taken large enough to capture sufficient local information about geometries of the point patterns. A very small σ will use information in the immediate neighborhood of a point when finding the correspondences, which may not be sufficient to arrive at unique correspondences. At the other extreme, a very large σ can dull the process and also result in incorrect correspondences.

A number of correspondence examples using the singular values of inter-image proximity matrix are given in Fig. 7.6. As data, the coin images depicted in Fig. 6.2 are used. Image (a) in Fig. 6.2 is used as the reference and images (b)–(f) in the same figure are used as the sensed, one at a time. The correspondences obtained by the method of Scott and Longuet-Higgins [41] are depicted in Fig. 7.6. One-hundred

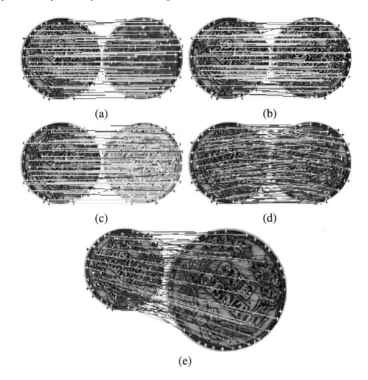

(a)   (b)

(c)   (d)

(e)

Fig. 7.6 Correspondences obtained between points in the coin image and points in its (**a**) smoothed, (**b**) noisy, (**c**) contrast-enhanced, (**d**) rotated, and (**e**) scaled versions. *Red lines* connect correspondences obtained by the method of Scott and Longuet-Higgins [41], *green lines* connect points that truly correspond to each other, and complete *yellow lines*, which are obtained when *red* and *green lines* coincide, identify those correspondences found by the program that are correct

landmarks obtained in these images as depicted in Fig. 6.3 are used. The correspondences found by the program are connected by red lines, while the true correspondences are connected by green lines. Yellow lines connect correspondences found by the program that are correct. The absence of green lines in an image is indication that all correct correspondences are found. Presence of red is indication that some additional correspondences are obtained that are incorrect. Yellow line segments in these figures are obtained when red and green lines cross each other. Complete yellow lines show correspondences found by the program that are correct.

In the examples in Figs. 7.6a–c, σ was 2 pixels, since we know correct correspondences cannot fall farther than 2 pixels from each other. When matching points in the original coin image and points in its smoothed version, the program finds 94 correspondences (the red + yellow lines). We know that only 66 true correspondences exist among the points in these images. The process has been able to find all correct correspondences; however, it has picked 28 incorrect correspondences (false positive). The process has been able to successfully reject 6 correspondences that do not exist (true negative).

When matching points from the original coin image and points from its noisy version (Fig. 7.6b), again 94 correspondences are found, among which 60 are correct (true positive) and 34 are incorrect (false positive). Matching of the coin image and its contrast-enhance version (Fig. 7.6c) resulted in 93 correspondences, among which 68 are correct and 25 are incorrect. These experiments show that when the true correspondences have the same or close coordinates, the process is able to find them; however, when outliers are present the process assigns some incorrect correspondences.

It is interesting to note that most of the incorrect correspondences (the red lines) have the same general direction as the correct correspondences (yellow lines). This can be the main source of confusion when trying to distinguish correct from incorrect correspondences. If additional information, such as features at the points, is available, correlation of features at the points can be used to detect some of the incorrect correspondences and remove them. This, however, will be at the cost of removing some correct correspondences also. For instance, in the example in Fig. 7.6c, if we calculate and use features L_{23}, L_{24}, L_{26}, L_{50c}, L_{90}, and L_{96} (see Chap. 4) at each point with a circular window of radius 8 pixels, and if we discard correspondences that produce a correlation coefficient smaller than 0.8, we detect 72 correspondences, among which 58 are correct and 14 are incorrect. Using correlation of features at the points, the process has been able to detect and remove 11 of the incorrect correspondences, but this has been at the cost of removing 10 correct correspondences.

When matching the coin image with its 30° rotated version (Fig. 7.6d), the program finds 90 correspondences, none of which are correct. There are 48 true correspondences among the points in these images. One reason for this failure is that among the 100 points in each image, there are 52 outliers. The second reason is the fact that the performance of this correspondence algorithm quickly declines as the rotational difference between the images increases. Changing the value of σ from 1 to 100 pixels reduces the number of correspondences found, but it does not change the number of true correspondences found. Similar results are obtained when matching images with scaling differences, as depicted in Fig. 7.6e. Sixty-six correspondences are obtained, among which none are correct. This correspondence algorithm, therefore, should be avoided when the point sets have rotational and/or scaling differences.

Note that r_{ij} does not have to show the Euclidean distance between points i and j, and it can show a measure of dissimilarity between the points. For example, if each point comes with a feature vector, the distance between the feature vectors associated with points $\mathbf{p}_i$ and $\mathbf{P}_j$ can be taken as r_{ij}. If the points come with feature vectors, instead of using the distance between point coordinates, the distance between feature vectors of the points can be used as r_{ij} to compute the proximity matrix.

Using features L_{23}, L_{24}, L_{26}, L_{50c}, L_{90}, and L_{96} at each point, and using the Euclidean distance between the six features at the points, we obtain the correspondences depicted in Figs. 7.7a and 7.7b for the case of images with rotational and scaling differences, respectively. Eighty-two correspondences are found in Fig. 7.7a,

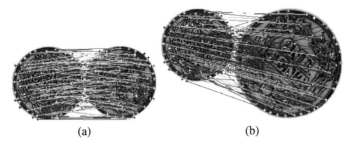

| (a) | (b) |

Fig. 7.7 (**a**), (**b**) Same as (**d**) and (**e**) in Fig. 7.6 but using the distance between feature vectors at the points rather than the distance between coordinates of points

among which 17 are correct and 65 are incorrect. In Fig. 7.7b, 71 correspondences are found, among which 2 are correct. The reason for this is two-fold. First, only 28 points among 100 in each image are present in both images, and second, the six features measured in images with scaling differences are not accurate enough to uniquely identify the correspondences.

A correspondence method developed by Leordeanu and Hebert [30] uses the similarity between descriptors of the points to create the proximity matrix. The proximity matrix is augmented with the geometric constraint that holds between point pairs in the images to arrive at consistent correspondences. If there are m points in the reference set and n points in sensed set, initially a proximity matrix $\mathbf{M}$ of dimension $mn \times mn$ is created.

Letting $a = (i, i')$ denote assignment of reference point $\mathbf{p}_i$ to sensed point $\mathbf{P}_{i'}$, entry (a, a) in the proximity matrix is set to the similarity between descriptors associated with points $\mathbf{p}_i$ and $\mathbf{P}_{i'}$. If $M(a, a)$ is not sufficiently high, row and column a of the matrix are eliminated, reducing the size of M by 1 row and 1 column. The actual size of M at the end, therefore, can be much smaller than $nm \times nm$. Smaller entries (a, a) in the matrix can be removed until a proximity matrix of a desired size is obtained. Entry (a, b) in the matrix is set to the degree of compatibility of pairwise geometric relations from assignments a and b. That is, if $b = (j, j')$, entry (a, b) is set to the similarity of geometric relation between points $\mathbf{P}_{i'}$ and $\mathbf{P}_{j'}$ in the sensed set and geometric relation between points $\mathbf{p}_i$ and $\mathbf{p}_j$ in the reference set. If a and b are both correct assignments, $M(a, b)$ will be high; otherwise, it will be low. $M(a, b)$ can simply be the product or the smaller of the similarity measures for assignments a and b.

The correspondence problem is treated as one of finding a set of assignments C that maximizes the matching score

$$S = \sum_{a,b \in C} M(a, b). \tag{7.37}$$

The problem is solved by considering an indicator vector $\mathbf{x}$ with the number of entries equal to the number of assignments in $\mathbf{M}$ and letting entry a in $\mathbf{x}$ be 1 if a is in C and 0 otherwise. Then,

$$S = \mathbf{x}^t \mathbf{M} \mathbf{x} \tag{7.38}$$

is calculated and according to Raleigh's ratio theorem [30], the maximum matching score is obtained when $\mathbf{x}$ is the principle eigenvector of $\mathbf{M}$. To summarize, the steps of this correspondence algorithm are [30]:

1. Given two point sets with associating descriptors, create proximity matrix $\mathbf{M}$ as outlined above.
2. Compute the principal eigenvector of $\mathbf{M}$, denote it by $\mathbf{x}^*$, and initialize the solution vector $\mathbf{x}$ to $\mathbf{0}$. Also, let L represent the set of assignments in $\mathbf{M}$.
3. Let a^* be that assignment in L that has the highest value in $\mathbf{x}^*$. If the highest value is 0, return the assignments saved in $\mathbf{x}$. Otherwise, set entry a of $\mathbf{x}$ to 1 and remove a^* from L.
4. Remove from L all assignments that are in conflict with assignment a^*. If L becomes empty as a result, return $\mathbf{x}$. Otherwise, go to Step 3.

The computational complexity of the spectral point pattern matching algorithm of Scott and Longuet-Higgins [41] is on the order of m^3 or n^3, whichever is higher. That is the time required to compute the singular values of the proximity matrix obtained from m or n points. The computational complexity of the algorithm of Leordeanu and Hebert [30] is even higher because it starts with a much larger proximity matrix. These algorithms are suitable when the given point sets are relatively small and the ratio of outliers and inliers is very small.

7.9.2 Matching Using Intra-image Proximity Matrices

Shapiro and Brady [43] used the structural information present in the proximity matrices of point sets to establish correspondence between the sets. Denoting the Euclidean distance between points $\mathbf{p}_i$ and $\mathbf{p}_j$ in the reference set by $r_{ij,1}$, a proximity matrix can be defined for the reference set with entry ij representing

$$H_{ij,1} = \exp\{-r_{ij,1}^2 / 2\sigma_1^2\}. \tag{7.39}$$

σ_1 controls the amount of local/global information used in matching. Denoting the kth eigenvalue of $\mathbf{H}_1$ by $\lambda_{k,1}$, the kth eigenvector of $\mathbf{H}_1$ by $\mathbf{v}_{k,1}$, and creating matrix $\mathbf{V}_1$ with its kth column representing $\mathbf{v}_{k,1}$, we obtain

$$\mathbf{H}_1 = \mathbf{V}_1 \mathbf{D}_1 \mathbf{V}_1^t, \tag{7.40}$$

where t denotes matrix transpose. If we create $\mathbf{V}_2$ in the same manner but discard the eigenvectors corresponding to the smallest $n - m$ eigenvalues of $\mathbf{H}_2$, we obtain

$$\mathbf{H}_2 \approx \mathbf{V}_2 \mathbf{D}_2 \mathbf{V}_2^t. \tag{7.41}$$

The ith row of $\mathbf{V}_1$ represents feature vector $\mathbf{f}_{i,1}$ and the jth row of $\mathbf{V}_2$ represents feature vector $\mathbf{f}_{j,2}$. The ijth entry of an assignment matrix $\mathbf{Z}$ is then computed from:

$$Z_{ij} = \|\mathbf{f}_{i,1} - \mathbf{f}_{j,2}\|^2 \tag{7.42}$$

$$= (\mathbf{f}_{i,1} - \mathbf{f}_{j,2})^t (\mathbf{f}_{i,1} - \mathbf{f}_{j,2}) \tag{7.43}$$

$$= 2[1 - (\mathbf{f}_{i,1})^t \mathbf{f}_{j,2}]. \tag{7.44}$$

Point $\mathbf{p}_i$ in the reference set is considered to correspond to point $\mathbf{P}_j$ in the sensed set if Z_{ij} is the smallest entry in row i and column j in $\mathbf{Z}$. Z_{ij} will have values between 0 and 2, with 0 showing the highest confidence level and 2 showing the lowest confidence level in matching.

Note that the signs of the eigenvectors of a proximity matrix are not unique, but when calculating the distance between two feature vectors in (7.44), signs play a critical role and there is a need to change the signs of the feature vector components in the sensed set so that they match those of the feature vectors in the reference set. Given feature vector $\mathbf{f}_{i,1}$, the feature vector $\mathbf{f}_{j,2}$ best matching it is considered to be the one minimizing $\|\mathbf{f}_{i,1} - \mathbf{f}_{j,2}\|$ when the signs of components of $\mathbf{f}_{j,2}$ are set to match the signs of components of $\mathbf{f}_{i,1}$.

If $\mathbf{H}_1$ represents the proximity matrix of a set of points and $\mathbf{H}_2$ represents the proximity matrix of the same set of points after reordering the labels of the points, the two proximity matrices will contain the same measures but at different entries. Consequently, the eigenvalues obtained from the two matrices will be the same except that they will be in different order. When $m \neq n$, the eigenvalues obtained from $\mathbf{H}_1$ and $\mathbf{H}_2$ are both ordered from the largest to the smallest. Similarly, the eigenvectors obtained from $\mathbf{H}_1$ and $\mathbf{H}_2$ are reordered so their orders match those of their eigenvalues. Then, m or fewer eigenvectors from $\mathbf{H}_1$ and $\mathbf{H}_2$ are used to create the feature vectors, from which the assignment matrix $\mathbf{Z}$ is calculated.

Parameters σ_1 and σ_2 should be proportional to the spacing between points in set 1 and set 2. If they are taken too small, the information used to match the points can be easily influenced by noise. If they are taken too large, the process may not capture sufficient local structural information among the points to correctly establish correspondence between them. σ_1 and σ_2 should make it possible to capture local structural information within each point set.

Since density and organization of points can vary across an image, instead of taking a fixed standard deviation, it is better to use a standard deviation at a point that reflects the density of points locally. For instance, the standard deviation at a point can be set equal to its distance to the kth point closest to it. Parameter k, if not given, can be set to $\sqrt{m}$ where m is the cardinality of the point set. The process will produce a small standard deviation where the density of points is high and a large standard deviation where the density of points is low. Adaption of σ to the local organization of the points can be implemented by replacing (7.39) with

$$H_{ij,1} = \frac{\exp\{-r_{ij,1}^2/2\sigma_{i,1}^2\}}{\sum_k \exp\{-r_{ik,1}^2/2\sigma_{i,1}^2\}}. \tag{7.45}$$

The denominator is a normalization factor that sets the sum of influences of the k closest points to a particular point to 1. Similarly entries of the proximity matrix for the sensed set can be adapted to the local density and organization of the points.

To determine the performance of the eigen-decomposition algorithm of Shapiro and Brady [43] in determining correspondence between points in real images, the images depicted in Fig. 6.2 were used. Points in image (a) were used as the reference set and points in images (b)–(f) were used as the sensed set, one set at a time. The correspondences obtained in these images by the method of Shapiro and Brady are

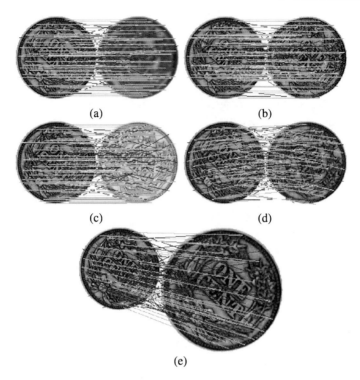

(a)   (b)

(c)   (d)

(e)

Fig. 7.8 The number of correspondences obtained by the method of Shapiro and Brady [43] using the coin image and its (**a**) smoothed, (**b**) noisy, (**c**) contrast-enhanced, (**d**) rotated, and (**e**) scaled versions are 1, 2, 0, 0, and 0, respectively

depicted in Fig. 7.8. Due to the large number of outliers, the number of correspondences obtained is too few to be useful. True correspondences are linked with green lines and the correspondences obtained by this method are shown in red. When full red and green lines fall on top of each other, they produce yellow lines, showing correspondences obtained by the program that are correct. Note that when red and green lines cross each other yellow segments are obtained, which do not correspond to correct correspondences.

Experiments on the method of Shapiro and Brady [43] show that the method is very sensitive to outliers; therefore the process quickly deteriorates as the difference between m and n increases. When $m \approx n$ and the point sets are related by a rigid transformation, the process finds the correspondences in one shot. This is in contrast to RANSAC and other methods that require a large number of iterations before finding the correspondences. The only drawback of the eigen-decomposition is that its computational complexity is already a cubic function of the number of points. Therefore, considering the fact that it requires $m \approx n$ and it can handle only a very small number of outliers, the method has very limited uses.

Carcassoni and Hancock [6, 7] suggested a number of refinements to the method of Shapiro and Brady to make it robust under noise and outliers. First, the correspondence problem is formulated as an expectation maximization (EM) problem. This enables the identification and removal of outliers by properly selecting the weights in the expectation step. Second, new proximity measures are introduced that are more robust under noise and outliers than the Gaussian-weighted proximity measures used by Shapiro and Brady. The new proximity measures reduce influence of a single measurement on the correspondence outcome, lowering the influence of an outlier on the final correspondence result.

If two point sets contain m points each and denoting the proximity matrices computed from the point sets by $\mathbf{H}_1$ and $\mathbf{H}_2$, Umeyama [50] proposed finding the correspondence between the point sets by first transforming the proximity matrices to complex Hermitian matrices

$$\mathbf{H}_1^h = \frac{\mathbf{H}_1 + \mathbf{H}_1^t}{2} + \sqrt{-1}\frac{\mathbf{H}_1 - \mathbf{H}_1^t}{2}, \tag{7.46}$$

$$\mathbf{H}_2^h = \frac{\mathbf{H}_2 + \mathbf{H}_2^t}{2} + \sqrt{-1}\frac{\mathbf{H}_2 - \mathbf{H}_2^t}{2}, \tag{7.47}$$

and then subjecting the Hermitian matrices to eigen-decomposition to obtain

$$\mathbf{H}_1^h = \mathbf{W}_1\mathbf{D}_1\mathbf{W}_1^*, \tag{7.48}$$

$$\mathbf{H}_2^h = \mathbf{W}_2\mathbf{D}_2\mathbf{W}_2^*, \tag{7.49}$$

where $*$ implies complex conjugate, and $\mathbf{D}_1$ and $\mathbf{D}_2$ are diagonal matrices of the eigenvalues of $\mathbf{H}_1^h$ and $\mathbf{H}_2^h$. Finally, computing a permutation matrix from

$$\mathbf{R} = Hungarian\left(|\mathbf{W}_2||\mathbf{W}_1|^t\right), \tag{7.50}$$

where $|\mathbf{W}_1|$ and $|\mathbf{W}_2|$ denote matrices whose entries are absolute values of entries of $\mathbf{W}_1$ and $\mathbf{W}_2$, respectively, and $Hungarian(\cdot)$ denotes the Hungarian algorithm [25], which is a combinatorial optimization algorithm that determines permutation matrix $\mathbf{R}$ from matrices $|\mathbf{W}_1|$ and $|\mathbf{W}_2|$ in $O(n^3)$ time [35]. Entries of the permutation matrix take values 0 and 1. When a 1 appears at entry ij in $\mathbf{R}$, it indicates that point $\mathbf{p}_i$ in the reference set corresponds to point $\mathbf{P}_j$ in the target set.

Through experimentation Zhao et al. [58] found that the method of Umeyama [50] works well when (1) noise is sufficiently low, (2) the eigenvalues of the proximity matrix for each point set are not very close to each other, and (3) any two rows of matrices $|\mathbf{W}_1|$ and $|\mathbf{W}_2|$ are sufficiently different from each other. If these conditions are not met, the process may incorrectly assign some of the correspondences.

Sclaroff and Pentland [40] made the method of Shapiro and Brady more robust under noise and local deformations by making the following modifications: (1) Correspondences with high confidence are used to determine the global transformation between the images. The global transformation is then used to find the remaining correspondences. (2) The eigenvectors corresponding to the lowest 75% of eigenvalues that are sensitive to noise are truncated, using only the top 25% low-order eigenvalues to the correspondences. (3) A correspondence is considered correct if obtained in both directions; that is, the match between reference point $\mathbf{p}_i$ and sensed point $\mathbf{P}_j$ is considered correct if Z_{ij} assumes the minimum value at its ith row and

jth column, and when the point sets are switched and the calculations are repeated, Z_{ji} will assume the minimum value at row j and column i.

If two point sets have translational and rotational differences, their proximity matrices will be the same. If the point sets have translational, rotational, and scaling differences, corresponding entries in the proximity matrices of the point sets will have scaling differences, which will only affect the eigenvalues and not the eigenvectors of the proximity matrices. Wang and Hancock [53] determine the correspondence to point $\mathbf{p}_i$ in the reference set by finding the feature vector $\mathbf{f}_{j,2}$ in the sensed set that is closest to feature vector $\mathbf{f}_{i,1}$ in the reference set. Note that point $\mathbf{p}_i$ in the reference set is associated with the ith row (feature vector) of $\mathbf{V}_1$ in (7.40). Similarly, point $\mathbf{P}_j$ in the sensed set is associated with the jth row (feature vector) of $\mathbf{V}_2$.

7.10 Coarse-to-Fine Matching

The common characteristic of the above matching algorithms is that they use all points in matching. Although graph-based and feature-based algorithms reduce the search space by avoiding matching of point subsets that are not likely to produce a solution, verification is done using all points. When the point sets are small, containing up to 100 points, these algorithms are practical; however, when point sets are large, containing thousands of points, the matching speed of the algorithms may not be high enough to be useful in some applications.

Even when the speed restriction is lifted, these algorithms are limited to point sets that are related by rigid, similarity, affine, and projective transformations. For point sets that are related by more complex transformation functions, a matching algorithm is required that can adapt to the local geometric difference between the images. Large images representing different views of a scene have local geometric differences. Consequently, points extracted from such images cannot be related by a single rigid, similarity, affine, or projective transformation. As a result, the above algorithms cannot find the correspondence between point sets with local geometric differences even without outliers and noise.

To determine the correspondence between large point sets with local geometric differences, a coarse-to-fine approach is needed. Initially, the images are reduced in scale sufficiently to produce a few dozen points in each image. It is assumed that at such a low resolution, corresponding points in the images when aligned by an affine transformation will fall within a distance tolerance ε of each other. When $4K \times 4K$ images of a natural scene are reduced to 32×32 images, this is not an unreasonable assumption when $\varepsilon = 1$ or 2 pixels. Correspondence will be established between points in the lowest resolution images by any one of the above methods. By tessellating the points in the reference image into triangular or Voronoi regions, and by knowing the corresponding points in the sensed image, corresponding triangular or Voronoi regions will be obtained in the sensed image.

As the resolution of the images is increased, more points will be obtained. By knowing the correspondence between triangular or Voronoi regions in the images at one level, we can determine the correspondence between points in corresponding regions at one level higher resolution, again, by using one of the preceding algorithms. The process can be repeated in this manner until correspondence is established between points in the images at the highest resolution. The process at each resolution requires determining correspondence between a small number of points that fall within small corresponding regions.

Let's denote the reference and sensed images at the highest resolution by A^0 and B^0, respectively. Suppose after reducing the scale of the images by a factor of 2^k, we obtain images A^k and B^k. The resolution of the images is reduced with steps of 2 in scale to produce two image pyramids. Then, points are detected in images at each resolution. To produce the image pyramid, the scale of the images is reduced until the number of points detected in each image will be a few dozen. Suppose images on top of the two pyramids represent reduction in scale of images A^0 and B^0 by 2^N. Also, suppose points in images A^k and B^k are denoted by $\mathbf{p}^k$ and $\mathbf{P}^k$, respectively. Moreover, let's suppose by tessellating $\mathbf{p}^k$ into triangular or Voronoi regions we obtain regions $\mathbf{t}^k$ and by tessellating $\mathbf{P}^k$ we obtain regions $\mathbf{T}^k$. Then, the following steps outline the coarse-to-fine matching algorithm.

Algorithm F5 (Coarse-to-fine point pattern matching) Given two image pyramids along with points in the images at each resolution, this algorithm finds the correspondence between the points in the images at the highest resolution. L_p denotes a list containing corresponding points in the images at a particular resolution, and L_t denotes a list containing corresponding regions in the images at the same resolution. Initially, both lists are empty.

1. Find correspondence between point sets $\mathbf{p}^N$ and $\mathbf{P}^N$ using a feature-based matching, graph-based matching, or a RANSAC algorithm under affine transformation and enter the obtained correspondences into list L_p. Also, let $k = N$.
2. If $k = 0$, return the list of corresponding points. Otherwise, tessellate the inliers in $\mathbf{p}^k$ and through correspondence between inliers in $\mathbf{p}^k$ and $\mathbf{P}^k$ find the corresponding regions in $\mathbf{P}^k$. Enter corresponding points into L_p and corresponding regions into list L_t (Fig. 7.9a).
3. Decrement k by 1.
4. Scale up coordinates of vertices of regions in L_t by a factor of 2 to obtain approximating region vertices in images at new resolution k.
5. Assign points in the images at resolution k to the regions in list L_t. This will assign to each point the label of the region the point belongs to (Fig. 7.9b).
6. Clear list L_p and find the correspondence between points in corresponding regions and enter the obtained correspondences into L_p. Repeat this step for all corresponding regions and then go to Step 2.

In Step 1, if points have associating features, a feature-based matching algorithm is used to find the correspondences. In the absence of features, a graph-based matching or RANSAC algorithm is used to find the correspondences.

In Step 6, list L_p is cleared and replaced with new point correspondences obtained for images at the kth level in the pyramid.

Fig. 7.9 (**a**) Determination
of correspondence between
inliers and tessellation of
inliers in the reference image.
Tessellation of inliers in the
sensed image is obtained
using correspondence
between the inliers in the
images. Points shown in
smaller size are the outliers.
(**b**) The same regions when
drawn in images at one-level
higher resolution.
Corresponding regions in the
images are given the same
label and correspondence is
established between points in
corresponding regions

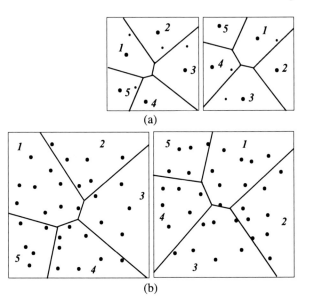

Since the regions obtained at resolution $k + 1$ approximately locate the regions
at resolution k, due to the local geometric difference between images, points near
region edges on one side of a region edge in the reference image may belong to
the region from the other side in the sensed image. Since points only within corresponding regions are subjected to matching, some points near region boundaries
may be grouped to different regions. Consequently, such points may be incorrectly
classified into outliers, contributing to false negatives. To reduce the number of false
negatives, points within a pixel or two of a region edge obtained at the highest resolution ($k = 0$) are considered fuzzy points and included in both regions that share
an edge. After matching, if a fuzzy point is found to satisfy the transformations for
both regions, it is assigned to the region with the transformation best satisfying the
point.

An example of point patter matching by the coarse-to-fine matching of Algorithm
F5 is given in Fig. 7.10. The original images are given in Figs. 7.10a and 7.10b. The
correspondences obtained at the lowest resolution are shown in yellow and green
in Figs. 7.10c and d. The points shown in yellow in the images define the affine
transformation used to obtained the remaining correspondences shown in green.
The points shown in red do not have correspondences and are considered outliers.

Using the correspondences obtained at the lowest resolution, the images at
one level higher resolution are subdivided into Voronoi regions [3] as shown in
Figs. 7.10e and f. Then correspondence is established between points within corresponding regions. The subdivision and correspondence processes are repeated in
sequence until correspondence is established between points in corresponding regions at the highest resolution. The coarse-to-fine subdivision result when using
image pyramids, each with 5 levels, is depicted in Figs. 7.10g and h. Resolution
increases from blue to green to red, and finally to black. As the resolution increases,

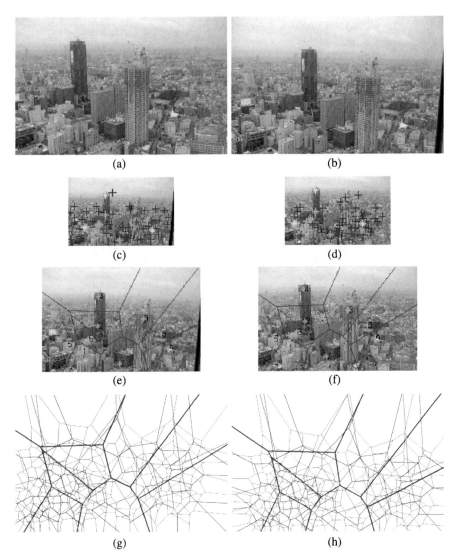

Fig. 7.10 (**a**), (**b**) Typical images considered for registration by the coarse-to-fine matching algorithm. These images are of size 2016×1280 pixels. (**c**), (**d**) The control points detected at the top level in the images. The correspondences are shown in *yellow* and *green* and the outliers are shown in *red*. (**e**), (**f**) Subdivision of the images at one level higher resolution using the correspondences obtained a the top level. (**g**), (**h**) Progressive subdivision of images (**a**) and (**b**), respectively, into finer regions while going from low to high resolution

more points and regions are produced, keeping the number of points within each region small and manageable.

Registration of the images in Figs. 7.10a and b using the correspondences obtained by Algorithm F5 within the convex hull of the control points in the overlap

Fig. 7.11 Registration of the images in Figs. 7.10a and b when using the point correspondences obtained by Algorithm F5 and using a piecewise-linear transformation function (Chap. 9)

area between the images is shown in Fig. 7.11. The reference image is shown in the green band and the resampled sensed image is shown in the red and blue bands of a color image. Therefore, when the images register perfectly, all three color bands at a pixel will have the same or similar values, producing gray scale. In areas where the images do not register well, the pixels will appear green or purple. Occluded pixels also appear in green or purple. These images provide visual or qualitative evaluation of registration results. Quantitative results as well as further information about this coarse-to-fine matching method have been reported elsewhere [55].

References

1. Ahuja, N.: Dot pattern processing using Voronoi neighborhoods. IEEE Trans. Pattern Anal. Mach. Intell. **4**(3), 336–343 (1982)
2. Bolles, R.C.: Robust feature matching through maximal cliques. In: SPIE Conf. Imaging Applications for Automated Industrial Inspection and Assembly, vol. 182, pp. 140–149 (1979)
3. Bowyer, A.: Computing Dirichlet tessellations. Comput. J. **24**(2), 162–166 (1981)
4. Bron, C., Kerbosch, J.: Algorithm 547: Finding all cliques of an undirected graph. Commun. ACM **16**(9), 575–577 (1973)
5. Capel, D.: An effective bail-out test for RANSAC consensus scoring. In: Proc. British Machine Vision Conf., pp. 629–638 (2005)
6. Carcassoni, M., Hancock, E.R.: Point pattern matching with robust spectral correspondence. In: IEEE Conf. Computer Vision and Pattern Recognition, vol. 1, pp. 649–655 (2000)
7. Carcassoni, M., Hancock, E.R.: Spectral correspondence for point pattern matching. Pattern Recognit. **36**, 193–204 (2003)
8. Chang, S.-H., Cheng, F.-H., Hsu, W.-H., Wu, G.-Z.: Fast algorithm for point pattern matching: Invariant to translations, rotations, and scale changes. Pattern Recognit. **30**(2), 311–320 (1997)

9. Cheng, F.-H.: Point pattern matching algorithm invariant to geometrical transformation and distortion. Pattern Recognit. Lett. **17**, 1429–1435 (1996)
10. Choi, O., Kweon, I.S.: Robust feature point matching by preserving local geometric consistency. Comput. Vis. Image Underst. **113**, 726–742 (2009)
11. Chum, O., Matas, J.: Matching with PROSAC–progressive sample consensus. In: Proc. Computer Vision and Pattern Recognition, vol. 1, pp. 220–226 (2005)
12. Chum, O., Matas, J.: Optimal randomized RANSAC. IEEE Trans. Pattern Anal. Mach. Intell. **30**(8), 1472–1482 (2008)
13. Chung, F.R.K.: Spectral Graph Theory, 2nd edn., pp. 1–22. Am. Math. Soc., Providence (1997)
14. Coelho, C., Heller, A., Mundy, J.L., Forsyth, D.A., Zisserman, A.: An experimental evaluation of projective invariants. In: Mundy, J.L., Zisserman, A. (eds.) Geometric Invariance in Computer Vision, pp. 87–104. The MIT Press, Cambridge (1992)
15. Denton, J.A., Beveridge, J.R.: An algorithm for projective point matching in the presence of spurious points. Pattern Recognit. **40**, 586–595 (2007)
16. Dwyer, R.A.: A faster divide-and-conquer algorithm for constructing Delaunay triangulations. Algorithmica **2**, 137–151 (1987)
17. Fang, T.J., Huang, Z.H., Kanal, L.N., Lavine, B.D., Stockman, G., Xiong, F.L.: Three-dimensional object recognition using a transform clustering technique. In: Proc. 6th Int'l Conf. Pattern Recognition, pp. 678–681 (1982)
18. Fischler, M.A., Bolles, R.C.: Random sample consensus: A paradigm for model fitting with applications to image analysis and automated cartography. Commun. ACM **24**(6), 381–395 (1981)
19. Forsyth, D., Ponce, J.: Computer Vision: A Modern Approach. Prentice Hall, New York (2002)
20. Goshtasby, A., Page, C.V.: Image matching by a probabilistic relaxation labeling process. In: Proc. 7th Int'l Conf. Pattern Recognition, vol. 1, pp. 307–309 (1984)
21. Goshtasby, A., Stockman, G.C.: Point pattern matching using convex hull edges. IEEE Trans. Syst. Man Cybern. **15**(5), 631–637 (1985)
22. Grimson, W.E.L., Huttenlocher, D.P.: On the sensitivity of geometric hashing. In: Proc. 3rd Int'l Conf. Computer Vision, pp. 334–338 (1990)
23. Hong, J., Tan, X.: A new approach to point pattern matching. In: Proc. 9th Int'l Conf. Pattern Recognition, vol. 1, pp. 82–84 (1988)
24. Hsiao, E., Collet, A., Hebert, M.: Making specific features less discriminative to improve point-based 3D object recognition. In: Int'l Conf. Computer Vision and Pattern Recognition, pp. 2653–2660 (2010)
25. Kuhn, H.W.: The Hungarian method for the assignment problem. Nav. Res. Logist. Q. **2**, 83–97 (1955)
26. Lamdan, Y., Wolfson, H.J.: Geometric hashing: A general and efficient model-based recognition scheme. In: Proc. 2nd Int'l Conf. Computer Vision, pp. 238–249 (1988)
27. Lamdan, Y., Wolfson, H.J.: On the error analysis of geometric hashing. In: Proc. IEEE Conf. Computer Vision and Pattern Recognition, pp. 22–27 (1991)
28. Lavine, D., Lambird, B.A., Kanal, L.N.: Recognition of spatial point patterns. Pattern Recognit. **16**(3), 289–295 (1983)
29. Lee, J.-H., Won, C.-H.: Topology preserving relaxation labeling for nonrigid point matching. IEEE Trans. Pattern Anal. Mach. Intell. **33**(2), 427–432 (2011)
30. Leordeanu, M., Hebert, M.: A spectral technique for correspondence problems using pairwise constraints. In: Proc. Int'l Conf. Computer Vision, vol. 2, pp. 1482–1489 (2005)
31. Matas, J., Chum, O.: Randomized RANSAC with Td:d test. Image Vis. Comput. **22**(10), 837–842 (2004)
32. Mundy, J.L., Zisserman, A.: Geometric Invariance in Computer Vision. The MIT Press, Cambridge (1992)
33. Nister, D.: Preemptive RANSAC for live structure and motion estimation. In: Proc. Int'l Conf. Computer Vision, Oct., vol. 1, pp. 199–206 (2003)

34. Ogawa, H.: Labeled point pattern matching by fuzzy relaxation. Pattern Recognit. **17**(5), 569–573 (1984)
35. Papadimitriou, C.H., Steiglitz, K.: Combinatorial Optimization: Algorithms and Complexity. Prentice-Hall, Englewood Cliffs (1982)
36. Pilu, M.: A direct method for stereo correspondence based on singular value decomposition. In: IEEE Conf. Computer Vision and Pattern Recognition, pp. 261–266 (1997)
37. Rabin, J., Delon, J., Gousseau, Y.: A statistical approach to the matching of local features. SIAM J. Imaging Sci. **2**(3), 931–958 (2008)
38. Ranade, S., Rosenfeld, A.: Point pattern matching by relaxation. Pattern Recognit. **12**(4), 269–275 (1980)
39. Rosenfeld, A., Hummel, R.A., Zucker, S.W.: Scene labeling by relaxation operations. IEEE Trans. Syst. Man Cybern. **6**(6), 420–433 (1976)
40. Sclaroff, S., Pentland, A.P.: Model matching for correspondence and recognition. IEEE Trans. Pattern Anal. Mach. Intell. **17**(6), 545–561 (1995)
41. Scott, G.L., Longuet-Higgins, H.C.: An algorithm for associating the features of two images. Proc. R. Soc. Lond. B **244**, 21–26 (1991)
42. Serradell, E., Özuysal, M., Lepetit, V., Fua, P., Moreno-Noguer, F.: Combining geometric and appearance priors for robust homography estimation. In: Proc. European Conf. Computer Vision (2010)
43. Shapiro, L.S., Brady, J.M.: Feature-based correspondence: An eigenvector approach. Image Vis. Comput. **10**(5), 283–288 (1992)
44. Stewart, G.W.: On the early history of the singular value decomposition. SIAM Rev. **35**(4), 551–566 (1993)
45. Stockman, G.: Object recognition and localization via pose clustering. Comput. Vis. Graph. Image Process. **40**, 361–387 (1987)
46. Stockman, G., Esteva, J.C.: Use of geometrical constraints and clustering to determine 3-D object pose. In: Proc. 7th Int'l Conf. Pattern Recognition, vol. 2, pp. 742–744 (1984)
47. Stockman, G., Kopstein, S., Benett, S.: Matching images to models for registration and object detection via clustering. IEEE Trans. Pattern Anal. Mach. Intell. **4**(3), 229–241 (1982)
48. Tordoff, B., Murray, D.W.: Guided sampling and consensus for motion estimation. In: Proc. European Conf. Computer Vision, pp. 82–98 (2002)
49. Torr, P., Zisserman, A.: MLESAC: A new robust estimator with application to estimating image geometry. In: Computer Vision and Image Understanding, pp. 138–156 (2000)
50. Umeyama, S.: An eigendecomposition approach to weighted graph matching problems. IEEE Trans. Pattern Anal. Mach. Intell. **10**(5), 695–703 (1988)
51. van Wamelen, P.B., Li, Z., Iyengar, S.S.: A fast expected time algorithm for the 2-D point pattern matching problem. Pattern Recognit. **37**, 1699–1711 (2004)
52. Wang, W.-H., Chen, Y.-C.: Point pattern matching by line segments and labels. Electron. Lett. **33**(6), 478–479 (1997)
53. Wang, H., Hancock, E.R.: A kernel view of spectral point pattern matching. In: Proc. IAPR Int'l Workshop Structural, Syntactic, and Statistical Pattern Recognition, pp. 361–369 (2004)
54. Wolfson, H.J., Rigoutsos, I.: Geometric hashing: An overview. In: IEEE Computational Science & Engineering, Oct.–Dec., pp. 10–21 (1997)
55. Wu, Z., Goshtasby, A.: A subdivision approach to image registration. Technical Report, Intelligent Systems Laboratory, Department of Computer Science and Engineering, Wright State University, January 2011
56. Zhan, C.T. Jr.: An algorithm for noisy template matching. In: Information Processing 74, pp. 698–701. North-Holland, Amsterdam (1974)
57. Zhang, W., Košecká, J.: Generalized RANSAC framework for relaxed correspondence problems. In: Proc. Int'l Sym. 3D Data Processing, Visualization, and Transmission (2006)
58. Zhao, Z., Liu, H.: Searching for interacting features. In: Proc. Int'l J. Conf. Artificial Intelligence (IJCAI), January (2007)
59. Zhao, J., Zhou, S., Sun, J., Li, Z.: Point pattern matching using relative shape context and relaxation labeling. In: Proc. 2nd Int'l Conf. Advanced Computer Control (ICACC), vol. 5, pp. 516–520 (2010)

Chapter 8
Robust Parameter Estimation

In the previous chapters, methods for detecting control points in two images of a scene and methods for determining the correspondence between the control points were discussed. In this chapter, robust methods that use the control-point correspondences to determine the parameters of a transformation function to register the images are discussed. Transformation functions for image registration will be discussed in the following chapter.

Although inaccuracies in the coordinates of corresponding points can be managed if the inaccuracies have a normal distribution with a mean of zero, but presence of even one incorrect correspondence can break down the parameter estimation process. When using image features/descriptors to find the correspondence between control points in two images, presence of noise, repeated patterns, and geometric and intensity differences between the images can result in some incorrect correspondences. Not knowing which correspondences are correct and which ones are not, the job of a robust estimator is to identify some or all of the correct correspondences and use their coordinates to determine the transformation parameters.

In the previous chapter, RANSAC, a robust estimator widely used in the computer vision community was reviewed. In this chapter, mathematically well-known robust estimators that are not widely used in computer vision and image analysis applications are reviewed. As we will see, these estimators can often replace RANSAC and sometimes outperform it.

The general problem to be addressed in this chapter is as follows. Given n corresponding points in two images of a scene:

$$\big\{(x_i, y_i), (X_i, Y_i) : i = 1, \ldots, n\big\}, \tag{8.1}$$

we would like to find the parameters of a transformation function with two components f_x and f_y that satisfy

$$\begin{aligned} X_i &\approx f_x(x_i, y_i), \\ Y_i &\approx f_y(x_i, y_i), \end{aligned} \qquad i = 1, \ldots, n. \tag{8.2}$$

A.A. Goshtasby, *Image Registration*,
Advances in Computer Vision and Pattern Recognition,
DOI 10.1007/978-1-4471-2458-0_8, © Springer-Verlag London Limited 2012

If the components of the transformation are independent of each other, their parameters can be determined separately. In such a situation, it is assumed that

$$\{(x_i, y_i, F_i) : i = 1, \ldots, n\} \tag{8.3}$$

is given and it is required to find the parameters of function f to satisfy

$$F_i \approx f(x_i, y_i), \quad i = 1, \ldots, n. \tag{8.4}$$

By letting $F_i = X_i$, the estimated function will represent f_x and by letting $F_i = Y_i$, the estimated function will represent f_y. If the two components of a transformation are dependent, such as the component of a projective transformation, both components of the transformation are estimated simultaneously.

f can be considered a single-valued surface that approximates the 3-D points given by (8.3). If the points are on or near the model to be estimated, f will approximate the model closely. However, if some points are away from the model to be estimated, f may be quite different from the model. The role of a robust estimator is to find the model parameters accurately even in the presence of distant points (outliers).

We assume each component of the transformation to be determined can be represented by a linear function of its parameters. That is

$$f = \mathbf{x}^t \mathbf{a}, \tag{8.5}$$

where $\mathbf{a} = \{a_1, \ldots, a_m\}$ are the m unknown parameters of the model and $\mathbf{x}$ is a vector with m components, each a function of x and y. For instance, when f represents a component of an affine transformation, we have

$$f = a_1 x + a_2 y + a_3, \tag{8.6}$$

and so $\mathbf{x}^t = [x \ y \ 1]$ and $\mathbf{a}^t = [a_1 \ a_2 \ a_3]$. When f represents a quadratic function, we have

$$f = a_1 x^2 + a_2 y^2 + a_3 xy + a_4 x + a_5 y + a_6, \tag{8.7}$$

and so $\mathbf{x}^t = [x^2 \ y^2 \ xy \ x \ y \ x \ 1]$ and $\mathbf{a}^t = [a_1 \ a_2 \ a_3 \ a_4 \ a_5 \ a_6]$.

When the observations given by (8.3) are contaminated, the estimated parameters will contain errors. Substituting (8.5) into (8.4) and rewriting it to include errors at the observations, we obtain

$$F_i = \mathbf{x}_i^t \mathbf{a} + e_i, \quad i = 1, \ldots, n, \tag{8.8}$$

where e_i is the vertical distance of F_i to the surface to be estimated at (x_i, y_i) as shown in Fig. 8.1. This is the estimated positional error in a component of the ith point in the sensed image. Not knowing which correspondences are correct and which ones are not, an estimator finds the model parameters in such a way as to minimize some measure of error between the given data and the estimated model.

In the remainder of this chapter, first the ordinary least squares (OLS) estimation is described. OLS performs well when the errors have a normal distribution. When errors have a long-tailed distribution, often caused by outliers, it performs poorly. Next, robust estimators that reduce or eliminate the influence of outliers on estimated parameters are discussed.

Fig. 8.1 Linear parameter estimation using contaminated data

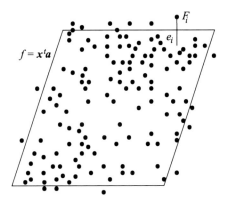

To evaluate and compare the performances of various estimators, 100 control points detected in each of the coin images in Fig. 6.2 will be used. The coordinates of the points are shown in Table 8.1. The points in the original coin image (Fig. 6.2a) are used as the reference points and denoted by (x, y). The control points detected in the blurred, noisy, contrast-enhanced, rotated, and scaled versions of the coin image are considered sensed points and are denoted by (X, Y).

Correspondence was established between the reference point set and each of the sensed point sets by a graph-based matching algorithm with a rather large distance tolerance ($\varepsilon = 10$ pixels) to allow inaccurate and incorrect correspondences enter the process. The correspondences established between each sensed point set and the reference point set are marked with a '+' or a '−' in Table 8.1. A '+' indicates a correspondence that is correct, while a '−' indicates a correspondence that is incorrect.

The algorithm found 95, 98, 98, 96, and 78 correspondences between the coin image and its blurred, noisy, contrast-enhanced, rotated, and scaled versions, respectively. Among the obtained correspondences, only 66, 60, 68, 48, and 28 are correct. Due to the large distance tolerance used in matching, the process has picked all of the correct correspondences (true positives). However, due to the large distance tolerance, it has also picked a large number of incorrect correspondences (false positives).

Establishing correspondence between points by the closest-point criterion resulted in some reference points being assigned to two or more sensed points. Although multiple assignments are easy to detect and remove, by removing such assignments, we run the risk of eliminating some correct correspondences, something that we want to avoid. Therefore, we keep the contaminated correspondences found by our matching algorithm and use them to determine the parameters of the transformation between each sensed image and the reference image by various estimators. After finding the transformation parameters by a robust estimator, we will then separate the correct correspondences from the incorrect ones.

The parameters of the affine transformations truly relating the blurred, noisy, contrast-enhanced, rotated, and scaled images to the original image are listed in Table 8.2. Knowing the true transformation parameters between each sensed image

Table 8.1 The point sets used to evaluate the performances of various estimators. (x, y) denote the column and row numbers of control points in the reference image, and (X, Y) denote the column and row numbers of control points in a sensed image. A sensed point that is found to correctly corresponds to a reference point is marked with a '+'. The remaining points represent outliers. A sensed point marked with a '−' is a point that is incorrectly assigned to a reference point by the matching algorithm

Point #	Original x	y	Blurred X	Y	Noisy X	Y	Enhanced X	Y	Rotated X	Y	Scaled X	Y
1	5	77	5+	76+	5+	77+	5+	76+	13−	105−	5	94
2	7	84	8+	85+	7+	84+	7+	84+	25+	109+	11+	126+
3	8	41	4−	36−	9−	39−	6−	47−	5−	77−	11−	63−
4	9	61	15−	64−	12−	55−	9+	61+	15+	88+	20−	87−
5	9	100	13−	105−	15−	99−	9+	99+	34+	121+	17	139
6	12	33	12+	34+	9−	39−	12+	34+	4+	62+	18+	50+
7	12	94	13+	95+	15−	99−	12+	93+	34+	115+	17−	139−
8	13	105	13+	105+	13+	105+	9−	99−	34−	121−	28−	155−
9	16	47	4	65	16+	47+	16+	47+	15	88	24+	72+
10	18	77	6	48	14−	74−	18+	77+	34−	95−	28+	155+
11	20	23	21+	22+	21+	22+	14−	21−	6−	46−	35−	29−
12	20	87	5	93	15−	85−	20+	87+	20	14	34	161
13	21	105	21−	105−	22+	106+	21+	105+	47+	120+	28−	155−
14	24	115	28−	111−	29−	112−	28−	111−	56−	122−	36	116
15	26	67	26+	67+	26+	67+	26+	67+	32+	85+	39+	102+
16	28	16	28+	16+	27+	17+	33−	20−	9+	39+	40	72
17	28	55	25−	58−	28+	55+	28+	55+	28+	73+	40−	72−
18	28	73	26−	67−	26−	67−	26−	67−	43−	86−	39−	102−
19	29	46	33−	41−	29+	46+	29+	47+	25+	65+	40−	72−
20	30	32	30+	31+	35−	33−	36−	33−	23−	51−	47+	48+
21	32	6	33	121	32+	6+	32+	7+	9−	26−	45−	12−
22	32	21	31+	22+	33+	21+	33+	20+	15+	41+	57−	35−
23	32	114	28−	111−	29−	112−	34−	115−	56−	122−	51−	174−
24	33	121	33+	121+	33+	121+	34+	121+	72−	122−	51−	174−
25	34	101	35+	101+	34+	101+	34+	101+	56+	110+	51+	152+
26	35	85	36+	84+	35+	86+	31−	80−	49+	96+	52−	128−
27	39	16	39+	16+	33−	21−	33−	20−	18+	34+	59+	24+
28	40	49	46−	52−	40+	48+	40+	48+	35+	62+	63−	69−
29	41	62	36−	60−	41+	62+	41−	70−	47−	73−	60−	95−
30	42	105	42+	105+	41+	105+	42+	105+	69−	106−	63	69
31	42	119	42+	119+	45−	120−	41+	119+	72+	122+	62−	179−
32	43	29	42+	30+	43+	29+	43+	29+	28+	43+	67−	43−
33	44	99	44−	105−	41−	105−	42−	105−	69−	106−	69−	148−
34	46	13	47−	7−	47	72	28	111	20−	22−	71−	10−

Table 8.1 (Continued)

Point #	Original		Blurred		Noisy		Enhanced		Rotated		Scaled	
	x	y	X	Y	X	Y	X	Y	X	Y	X	Y
35	46	52	46+	52+	46+	52+	40−	48−	42+	61+	71+	10+
36	46	86	46+	85+	46+	86+	46−	86−	59+	91+	75	183
37	47	7	47+	7+	45−	1−	46−	1−	20+	22+	71−	10−
38	52	35	53+	34+	53+	34+	53+	35+	40−	50−	79−	59−
39	53	122	52+	121+	54+	122+	53−	122−	90−	121−	75−	183−
40	54	96	54+	97+	54+	96+	45	125	71+	96+	82+	144+
41	56	21	55+	21+	56+	21+	56+	21+	36−	25−	86+	33+
42	56	72	56+	72+	56+	72+	54−	68−	61+	74+	87−	107−
43	56	114	57+	114+	56+	114+	57+	115+	81−	105−	79−	172−
44	58	12	58+	12+	58+	12+	58+	12+	36−	25−	84−	24−
45	59	52	59+	52+	56−	54−	59+	52+	59−	52−	90−	70−
46	60	5	60+	5+	59+	5+	58−	12−	31+	14+	91+	7+
47	63	78	56−	72−	65−	87−	64+	78+	61−	74−	99−	122−
48	63	104	61	122	63	26	63+	104+	81−	105−	90	70
49	65	52	59−	52−	65+	52+	65+	52+	59+	52+	90	172
50	67	114	68+	114+	68+	113+	67+	114+	90−	115−	98−	178−
51	68	15	68−	15−	64−	11−	74−	12−	42+	19+	112−	18−
52	68	27	67−	21−	63−	26−	68+	27+	54−	27−	111−	42−
53	68	93	69+	93+	69+	93+	68+	93+	82+	86+	102−	148−
54	73	112	68−	114−	68−	113−	73+	113+	104−	105−	111−	169−
55	74	12	74+	12+	74+	12+	74+	12+	46−	7−	112+	18+
56	74	28	81−	22−	75−	21−	74+	28+	54+	27+	111+	42+
57	75	38	75+	38+	76+	38+	76+	38+	61+	35+	101	7
58	75	49	75+	49+	76+	49+	75−	49−	65+	44+	102	148
59	75	90	75+	90+	75+	90+	76−	89−	92−	81−	114−	131−
60	77	61	76+	61+	76+	61+	76+	61+	73+	54+	112−	92−
61	77	121	79−	120−	79−	120−	78+	121+	104+	105+	112	18
62	78	7	78+	7+	80−	7−	78−	1−	46−	7−	120−	10−
63	78	105	78+	105+	79+	106+	77−	101−	73	111	113−	155−
64	81	22	81+	22+	81+	22+	81+	22+	58−	12−	129−	34−
65	83	50	83+	50+	83+	50+	75−	49−	73+	41+	126+	75+
66	85	74	77−	73−	84+	75+	83−	81−	87+	61+	125−	114−
67	87	36	87−	36−	87+	36+	87+	36+	69+	27+	129−	54−
68	87	63	87−	62−	87+	63+	87+	63+	82+	50+	118	97
69	87	110	87+	110+	86+	111+	87+	111+	107+	92+	127	179
70	88	11	88−	11−	89+	12+	87+	11+	58+	5+	133−	15−
71	88	90	88+	90+	88+	90+	80−	94−	97+	73+	133+	134+
72	91	54	91+	53+	91+	53+	91+	53+	77−	36−	137+	81+

Table 8.1 (Continued)

Point #	Original		Blurred		Noisy		Enhanced		Rotated		Scaled	
	x	y	X	Y	X	Y	X	Y	X	Y	X	Y
73	91	121	91−	121−	91+	121+	91+	121+	114+	92+	138−	174−
74	92	6	92+	6+	92+	6+	92+	7+	58−	5−	135	72
75	92	115	93+	114+	91−	121−	92+	115+	114−	92−	138+	174+
76	93	40	88+	36+	94+	39+	93+	40+	77+	27+	146−	52−
77	94	14	98−	17−	89−	12−	94+	14+	58−	5−	130	25
78	95	84	94+	85+	95+	84+	96+	78+	106−	66−	143+	125+
79	96	65	87+	62+	99−	62−	87−	63−	93−	43−	146	52
80	96	78	96+	77+	96+	78+	96−	78−	98+	59+	146+	118+
81	97	93	97+	94+	97+	94+	97+	94+	107+	72+	147+	139+
82	101	115	105−	112−	105−	112−	105−	112−	122−	87−	152	76
83	104	14	104+	14+	104+	14+	103+	14+	78−	7−	155	30
84	104	106	103+	106+	105−	112−	105−	112−	117−	86−	157+	160+
85	106	50	106+	50+	101−	51−	106+	50+	88−	33−	152−	76−
86	106	88	106+	87+	106+	88+	106+	88+	106−	66−	158	88
87	108	70	108+	70+	108−	75−	108+	71+	105	31	157−	111−
88	109	28	111−	21−	114−	25−	111−	30−	84+	9+	163−	38−
89	111	106	111+	106+	108−	101−	105−	112−	125+	77+	171	69
90	112	96	112+	95+	112+	96+	112+	96+	121+	67+	169+	145+
91	115	37	113−	34−	121−	37−	121−	38−	95−	8−	174−	53−
92	115	68	115+	68+	115+	67+	115+	67+	116−	40−	173+	101+
93	116	57	106−	95−	121−	58−	115−	67−	105+	31+	175−	83−
94	117	86	117+	85+	116−	88−	117+	86+	120−	54−	177+	130+
95	118	44	117−	42−	121−	37−	118+	44+	100+	18+	178−	63−
96	119	79	119+	78+	123−	84−	119+	78+	120−	54−	181−	116−
97	121	37	121+	37+	121+	37+	121+	38+	95−	8−	178−	63−
98	121	70	121+	70+	121+	71+	121+	70+	116+	40+	183+	105+
99	123	84	117−	85−	123+	84+	123+	84+	120−	54−	177−	130−
100	124	45	120−	51−	121−	37−	124+	46+	100−	18−	182−	72−

and the reference image, we would like to see how accurately various estimators can find these parameters using the contaminated correspondences shown in Table 8.1

8.1 OLS Estimator

Letting x_{ij} represent the jth element of $\mathbf{x}$ when evaluated at the ith data point, relation (8.8) can be written as

Table 8.2 True linear transformation parameters between the blurred, noisy, contrast-enhanced, rotated, and scaled coin images and the original coin image

Data set	a	b	c	d	e	f
Blurred	1.000	0.000	0.000	0.000	1.000	0.000
Noisy	1.000	0.000	0.000	0.000	1.000	0.000
Enhanced	1.000	0.000	0.000	0.000	1.000	0.000
Rotated	0.866	−0.500	39.94	0.500	0.866	−23.06
Scaled	1.500	0.000	0.000	0.000	1.500	0.000

$$F_i = \sum_{j=1}^{m} x_{ij} a_j + e_i, \quad i = 1, \ldots, n. \tag{8.9}$$

e_i is positive when the given data point falls above the approximating surface, and e_i is negative when the point falls below the surface. Assuming the error at a data point is independent of errors at other data points and the errors have a Gaussian distribution, the ordinary least-squares (OLS) estimator finds the parameters of the model by minimizing the sum of squared vertical distance between the data and the estimated surface:

$$R = \sum_{i=1}^{n} r_i^2, \tag{8.10}$$

where

$$r_i = F_i - \sum_{j=1}^{m} x_{ij} a_j. \tag{8.11}$$

Vertical distance or residual r_i can be considered an estimate of the actual error e_i at the ith point. If the components of a transformation depend on each other, the squared residual at the ith point will be

$$r_i^2 = \left(X_i - \sum_{j=1}^{m_x} x_{ij} a_j \right)^2 + \left(Y_i - \sum_{j=1}^{m_y} x_{ij} b_j \right)^2, \tag{8.12}$$

where $\{a_j : j = 1, \ldots, m_x\}$ are the parameters describing the x-component of the transformation, and $\{b_j : j = 1, \ldots, m_y\}$ are the parameters describing the y-component of the transformation. When the two components of a transformation function are interdependent, some parameters appear in both components. For instance, in the case of the projective transformation, we have

$$X = \frac{a_1 x + a_2 y + a_3}{a_7 x + a_8 y + 1}, \tag{8.13}$$

$$Y = \frac{a_4 x + a_5 y + a_6}{a_7 x + a_8 y + 1}, \tag{8.14}$$

or

$$a_7 x X + a_8 y X + X = a_1 x + a_2 y + a_3, \tag{8.15}$$

$$a_7 x Y + a_8 y Y + Y = a_4 x + a_5 y + a_6, \tag{8.16}$$

so the squared distance between the ith point and the transformation function will be

$$r_i^2 = (a_7 x_i X_i + a_8 y_i X_i + X_i - a_1 x_i - a_2 y_i - a_3)^2$$
$$+ (a_7 x_i Y_i + a_8 y_i Y_i + Y_i - a_4 x_i - a_5 y_i - a_6)^2. \qquad (8.17)$$

The linear parameters $a_1, \ldots, a_8$ are estimated by minimizing the sum of such squared distances or residuals.

To find the parameters that minimize the sum of squared residuals R, the gradient of R is set to 0 and the obtained system of linear equations is solved. For example, a component of an affine transformation ($m = 3$) is determined by solving

$$\frac{\partial R}{\partial a_1} = -2 \sum_{i=1}^{n} x_i (F_i - a_1 x_i - a_2 y_i - a_3) = 0,$$

$$\frac{\partial R}{\partial a_2} = -2 \sum_{i=1}^{n} y_i (F_i - a_1 x_i - a_2 y_i - a_3) = 0,$$

$$\frac{\partial R}{\partial a_3} = -2 \sum_{i=1}^{n} (F_i - a_1 x_i - a_2 y_i - a_3) = 0, \qquad (8.18)$$

which can be written as

$$\begin{pmatrix} \sum_{i=1}^{n} x_i^2 & \sum_{i=1}^{n} x_i y_i & \sum_{i=1}^{n} x_i \\ \sum_{i=1}^{n} x_i y_i & \sum_{i=1}^{n} y_i^2 & \sum_{i=1}^{n} y_i \\ \sum_{i=1}^{n} x_i & \sum_{i=1}^{n} y_i & n \end{pmatrix} \begin{pmatrix} a_1 \\ a_2 \\ a_3 \end{pmatrix} = \begin{pmatrix} \sum_{i=1}^{n} x_i F_i \\ \sum_{i=1}^{n} y_i F_i \\ \sum_{i=1}^{n} F_i \end{pmatrix}. \qquad (8.19)$$

In matrix form, this can be written as

$$\mathbf{A}^t \mathbf{A} \mathbf{X} = \mathbf{A}^t \mathbf{b}, \qquad (8.20)$$

where $\mathbf{A}$ is an $n \times 3$ matrix with $A_{i1} = x_i$, $A_{i2} = y_i$, and $A_{i3} = 1$; $\mathbf{b}$ is an $n \times 1$ array with $b_i = F_i$; and $\mathbf{X}$ is a 3×1 array of unknowns. Generally, when f is a function of m variables, A_{ij} represents the partial derivative of f with respect to the jth parameter when evaluated at the ith point.

We see that (8.20) is the same as left multiplying both sides of equation

$$\mathbf{A} \mathbf{X} = \mathbf{b} \qquad (8.21)$$

by $\mathbf{A}^t$, and (8.21) is an overdetermined system of equations for which there isn't an exact solution. Therefore, OLS finds the solution to this overdetermined system of linear equations in such a way that the sum of squared residuals obtained at the data points becomes minimum.

If (8.20) has full rank m, its solution will be

$$\hat{\mathbf{X}} = (\mathbf{A}^t \mathbf{A})^{-1} \mathbf{A}^t \mathbf{b}. \qquad (8.22)$$

Matrix $\mathbf{A}^\dagger = (\mathbf{A}^t \mathbf{A})^{-1} \mathbf{A}^t$ is known as the pseudo-inverse of $\mathbf{A}$ [4, 22]. Therefore,

$$\hat{\mathbf{X}} = \mathbf{A}^\dagger \mathbf{b}. \qquad (8.23)$$

Table 8.3 Estimated parameters by OLS for the five data sets in Table 8.1. $RMSE_a$ indicates RMSE when using all correspondences (marked with a '+' or a '−') and $RMSE_c$ indicates RMSE when using only the correct correspondences (marked with a '+'). The last column shows computation time in seconds when using all correspondences on a Windows PC with a 2.2 MHz processor

Data set	a	b	c	d	e	f	$RMSE_a$	$RMSE_c$	Time
Blurred	1.007	−0.004	0.676	−0.002	0.989	0.665	3.46	1.03	0.0001
Noisy	1.012	0.000	0.899	0.007	1.004	−0.652	3.56	0.88	0.0001
Enhanced	0.998	0.110	−0.353	−0.001	1.000	−0.274	3.70	0.84	0.0001
Rotated	0.872	−0.489	38.35	0.505	0.850	−22.78	4.31	0.83	0.0001
Scaled	1.501	0.017	−1.454	−0.021	1.485	2.899	5.01	1.75	0.0001

The OLS estimator was developed independently by Gauss and Legendre. Although Legendre published the idea in 1805 and Gauss published it in 1809, records show that Gauss has been using the method since 1795 [31]. It has been shown that if (1) data represent random observations from a model with linear parameters, (2) errors at the points have a normal distribution with a mean of zero, and (3) the variables are independent, then the parameters determined by OLS represent the best linear unbiased estimation (BLUE) of the model parameters [1]. Linear independence requires that the components of $\mathbf{x}$ be independent of each other. An example of dependence is x^2 and xy. This implies that when least squares is used to find parameters of functions like (8.7) with $\mathbf{x}$ containing interdependent components, the obtained parameters may not be BLUE.

Comparing the linear model with m parameters estimated by OLS with the first m principal components about the sample mean (Sect. 8.11), we see that OLS finds the model parameters by minimizing the sum of squared distances of the points to the surface vertically, while the parameters predicted by the first m principal components of the same data minimizes the sum of squared distances measured between the points and the surface in the direction normal to the surface. Although the two use the same error measure, OLS treats one dimension of the observations preferentially, while principal component analysis (PCA) treats all dimensions of observations similarly.

In addition to treating one dimension of data preferentially, OLS lacks robustness. A single outlier can drastically change the estimated parameters. The notion of *breakdown point* ε^*, introduced by Hampel [5], is the smallest fraction of outliers that can change the estimated parameters drastically. In the case of OLS, $\varepsilon^* = 1/n$.

Using the 95 points marked with '+' and '−' in Table 8.1 for the blurred image and the corresponding points in the original image, OLS estimated the six linear parameters shown in Table 8.3. The root-mean-squared error (RMSE) obtained at all correspondences and the RMSE obtained at the 66 correct correspondences are also shown. The estimated model parameters and RMSE measures between the noisy, contrast-enhanced, rotated, and scaled images and the original image are also shown in Table 8.3.

Due to the fact that the outliers are not farther than 10 pixels from the surface to be estimated, their adverse effect on the estimated parameters is limited. Since in image registration the user can control this distance tolerance, outliers that are very far from the surface model to be estimated can be excluded from the point correspondences. Therefore, although the correspondences represent contaminated data, the maximum error an incorrect correspondence can introduce to the estimation process can be controlled. Decreasing the distance tolerance too much, however, may eliminate some of the correct correspondences, something that we want to avoid. Therefore, we would like to have the distance tolerance large enough to detect all the correct correspondences but not so large as to introduce false correspondences that can irreparably damage the estimation process.

Having contaminated data of the kind shown in Table 8.1, we would like to identify estimators that can accurately estimate the parameters of an affine transformation model and produce as small an RMSE measure as possible.

Since points with smaller residuals are more likely to represent correct correspondences than points with larger residuals, one way to reduce the estimation error is to give lower weights to points that are farther from the estimated surface. This is discussed next.

8.2 WLS Estimator

The weighted least-squares (WLS) estimator gives lower weights to points with higher square residuals. The weights are intended to reduce the influence of outliers that are far from the estimated model surface. It has been shown that OLS produces the best linear unbiased estimation of the model parameters if all residuals have the same variance [20]. It has also been shown that when the observations contain different uncertainties or variances, least-squares error is reached when the square residuals are normalized by the reciprocals of the residual variances [2]. If σ_i^2 is the variance of the ith observation, by letting $w_i = 1/\sigma_i$, we can normalize the residuals by replacing $\mathbf{x}_i$ with $w_i \mathbf{x}_i$ and f_i with $w_i f_i$. Therefore, letting $A'_{ij} = A_{ij} w_i$ and $b'_i = b_i w_i$, (8.20) converts to

$$\mathbf{A}'^t \mathbf{A}' \mathbf{X} = \mathbf{A}'^t \mathbf{b}', \tag{8.24}$$

producing the least squares solution

$$\mathbf{X} = \left(\mathbf{A}'^t \mathbf{A}' \right)^{-1} \mathbf{A}'^t \mathbf{b}'. \tag{8.25}$$

If variances at the sample points are not known, w_i is set inversely proportional to the magnitude of residual at the ith observation. That is, if

$$r_i = F_i - \mathbf{x}_i \hat{\mathbf{a}}, \quad i = 1, \ldots, n, \tag{8.26}$$

then

$$w_i = \frac{1}{|r_i| + \varepsilon}, \quad i = 1, \ldots, n. \tag{8.27}$$

ε is a small number, such as 0.01, to avoid division by zero.

Table 8.4 Estimated parameters by WLS for the five data sets in Table 8.1 and the RMSE measures

Data set	a	b	c	d	e	f	$RMSE_a$	$RMSE_c$	Time
Blurred	1.001	−0.003	−0.108	0.001	0.998	0.063	3.52	0.79	0.001
Noisy	1.000	0.000	−0.038	0.000	1.000	0.089	3.59	0.75	0.001
Enhanced	0.997	0.005	−0.132	0.000	1.000	−0.043	3.73	0.69	0.001
Rotated	0.872	−0.489	38.36	0.505	0.850	−22.79	4.33	0.83	0.001
Scaled	1.501	−0.001	−0.082	−0.001	1.507	0.134	5.15	1.06	0.001

Since the weights depend on estimated errors at the points, better weights can be obtained by improving the estimated parameters. If (8.26) represents residuals calculated using the model surface obtained by OLS and denoting the initial model by $f_0(\mathbf{x})$, the residuals at the $(k+1)$st iteration can be estimated from the model obtained at the kth iteration:

$$r_i^{(k+1)} = F_i - f_k(\mathbf{x}_i), \quad i = 1, \ldots, n. \tag{8.28}$$

The process of improving the weights and the process of improving the model parameters are interconnected. From the residuals, weights at the points are calculated, and using the weights, the model parameters are estimated. The residuals are recalculated using the refined model and the process is repeated until the sum of square weighted residuals does not decrease noticeably from one iteration to the next.

Using the data in Table 8.1 and letting $\varepsilon = 0.01$, WLS finds the model parameters shown in Table 8.4 between the blurred, noisy, contrast-enhanced, rotated, and scaled images and the original image. Only a few to several iterations were needed to obtain these parameters. The estimation errors obtained by WLS using the correct correspondences are lower than those obtained by OLS. Interestingly, the parameters and the errors obtained by OLS and WLS on the rotated data set are almost the same. Results obtained on contaminated data by WLS are not any better than those obtained by OLS.

If some information about the uncertainties of the point correspondences is available, the initial weights can be calculated using that information. This enables estimating the initial model parameters by WLS rather than by OLS and achieving a more accurate initial model. For instance, if a point in each image has an associating feature vector, the distance between the feature vectors of the ith corresponding points can be used as $|r_i|$ in (8.27). The smaller the distance between the feature vectors of corresponding points, the more likely it will be that the correspondence is correct and, thus, the smaller the correspondence uncertainty will be.

The main objective in WLS estimation is to provide a means to reduce the influence of outliers on the estimation process. Although weighted mean can reduce the influence of distant outliers on estimated parameters, it does not diminish their influence. To completely remove the influence of distant outliers on estimated parameters, rather than using the weight function of (8.27), a weight function that cuts

Table 8.5 Estimated parameters by the weighted least squares with cut-off threshold $r_0 = 2$ pixels

Data set	a	b	c	d	e	f	RMSE$_a$	RMSE$_c$	Time
Blurred	1.001	−0.005	0.026	0.001	0.996	0.295	3.52	0.78	0.001
Noisy	1.000	0.000	0.030	0.000	0.999	0.202	3.60	0.75	0.001
Enhanced	0.998	0.006	−0.276	−0.001	0.999	0.180	3.74	0.69	0.001
Rotated	0.872	−0.489	38.36	0.505	0.850	−22.79	4.33	0.83	0.001
Scaled	1.502	−0.001	−0.067	−0.002	1.507	0.357	5.15	1.03	0.001

off observations farther away than a certain distance to the estimated surface can be used. An example of a weight function with this characteristic is

$$
w_i = \begin{cases} \frac{1}{|r_i|+\varepsilon} & |r_i| \leq r_0, \\ 0 & |r_i| > r_0, \end{cases} \tag{8.29}
$$

where r_0 is the required distance threshold to identify and remove the distant outliers.

The WLS estimator with a cut-off of $r_0 = 2$ pixels and $\varepsilon = 0.01$ produced the model parameters shown in Table 8.5. The errors when using the correct correspondences are either the same or only slightly lower than those found by the WLS estimator without a cut-off threshold. Removing points with larger residuals does not seem to change the results significantly when using the contaminated data. If the residuals obtained with and without the cut-off threshold both have the same distribution, the same results will be produced by OLS. Because the residuals initially estimated by OLS contain errors, by removing points with high residuals or weighting them lower, the distribution of the residuals does not seem to change, resulting in the same parameters by OLS and by WLS with and without a cut-off threshold distance in this example.

8.3 M Estimator

An M estimator, like the OLS estimator, is a maximum likelihood estimator [12], but instead of minimizing the sum of squared residuals, it minimizes the sum of functions of the residuals that increases less rapidly with increasing residuals when compared with squared residuals. Consider the objective function:

$$
\sum_{i=1}^{n} \rho(r_i), \tag{8.30}
$$

where $\rho(r_i)$ is a function of r_i that increases less rapidly with r_i when compared with the square of r_i. To minimize this objective function, its partial derivatives with respect to the model parameters are set to 0 and the obtained system of equations is solved. Therefore,

$$
\sum_{i=1}^{n} \frac{\partial \rho(r_i)}{\partial r_i} \frac{\partial r_i}{\partial a_k} = 0, \quad k = 1, \ldots, m. \tag{8.31}
$$

Since $\partial r_i/\partial a_k = x_{ik}$, and denoting $\partial \rho(r_i)/\partial r_i$ by $\psi(r_i)$, we obtain

$$\sum_{i=1}^{n} \psi(r_i)x_{ik} = 0, \quad k = 1, \ldots, m. \tag{8.32}$$

The residual at the ith observation, $r_i = F_i - \sum_{j=1}^{m} x_{ij}a_j$, depends on the measurement scale, another unknown parameter. Therefore, rather than solving (8.32), we solve

$$\sum_{i=1}^{n} \psi_k\left(\frac{r_i}{\sigma}\right)x_{ik} = 0, \quad k = 1, \ldots, m, \tag{8.33}$$

for the model parameters as well as for the scale parameter σ.

The process of determining the scale parameter and the parameters of the model involves first estimating the initial model parameters by OLS and from the residuals estimating the initial scale. A robust method to estimate scale from the residuals is the *median absolute deviation* [6, 12]:

$$b \, med_i\{|r_i - M_n|\}, \tag{8.34}$$

where $M_n = med_i\{r_i\}$ for $i = 1, \ldots, n$. To make the estimated scale comparable to the spread σ of a Gaussian distribution representing the residuals, it is required that we let $b = 1.483$.

Knowing the initial scale, the model parameters are estimated from (8.33) by letting $r_i = F_i - \sum_{j=1}^{m} x_{ij}a_j$. The process of scale and parameter estimation is repeated until the objective function defined by (8.30) reaches its minimum value.

A piecewise continuous ρ that behaves like a quadratic up to a point, beyond which it behaves linearly, is [11, 12]:

$$\rho(r) = \begin{cases} r^2/2 & \text{if } |r| < c, \\ c|r| - \frac{1}{2}c^2 & \text{if } |r| \geq c. \end{cases} \tag{8.35}$$

The gradient of this function is also piecewise continuous:

$$\psi(r) = \begin{cases} r & \text{if } |r| < c, \\ c \, sgn(r) & \text{if } |r| \geq c. \end{cases} \tag{8.36}$$

$\rho(r)$ and $\psi(r)$ curves, depicted in Fig. 8.2, reduce the effect of distant outliers by switching from quadratic to linear at the threshold distance c. To achieve an asymptotic efficiency of 95%, it is required that we set $c = 1.345\sigma$ when residuals have a normal distribution with spread σ.

The gradient of the objective function, known as the *influence function*, is a linear function of the residuals or a constant in this example. Therefore, the parameters of the model can be estimated by solving a system of linear equations. Although this M estimator reduces the influence of distant outliers and produces more robust parameters than those obtained by OLS, the breakdown point of this estimator is also $\varepsilon^* = 1/n$. This is because the objective function still monotonically increases with increasing residuals and a single distant outlier can arbitrarily change the estimated parameters.

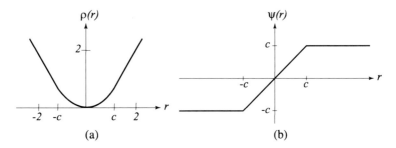

Fig. 8.2 (**a**) The plot of $\rho(r)$ curve of (8.35). (**b**) The plot of $\psi(r)$ curve of (8.36)

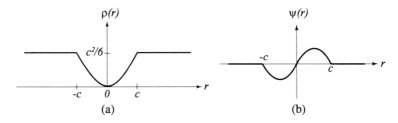

Fig. 8.3 (**a**) The plot of $\rho(r)$ of (8.37). (**b**) The plot of $\psi(r)$ of (8.38)

To further reduce the influence of outliers, consider [28]:

$$\rho(r) = \begin{cases} \frac{r^2}{2} - \frac{r^4}{2c^2} + \frac{r^6}{6c^4} & \text{if } |r| \le c, \\ \frac{c^2}{6} & \text{if } |r| > c. \end{cases} \tag{8.37}$$

This $\rho(r)$ is also a piecewise function. It is a function of degree six in r up to distance c, beyond which it changes to a constant, treating all residuals with magnitudes larger than c similarly. This estimator will, in effect, avoid distant outliers to arbitrarily change the estimated parameters. The gradient of $\rho(r)$ is:

$$\psi(r) = \begin{cases} r[1 - (\frac{r}{c})^2]^2 & \text{if } |r| \le c, \\ 0 & \text{if } |r| > c. \end{cases} \tag{8.38}$$

$\rho(r)$ and $\psi(r)$ curves are plotted in Fig. 8.3. Setting parameter $c = 4.685\sigma$, 95% asymptotic efficiency is reached when residuals have a normal distribution with spread of σ.

Note that the influence function in this example is a nonlinear function of the residuals, requiring the solution of a nonlinear system of equations to estimate the model parameters, which can be very time consuming. The objective function, by assuming a fixed value for residuals larger than a given magnitude, keeps the maximum influence an outlier can have on the estimated parameters under control. In this M estimator, a distant outlier can also adversely affect the estimated parameters, although the effect is not as damaging as the M estimator with the objective and influence curves defined by (8.35) and (8.36).

8.4 S Estimator

The scale (S) estimator makes estimation of the scale parameter σ in an M estimator the central problem [28]. An S estimator has the following properties:

1. The ρ curve in the objective function is continuously differentiable and symmetric, and it evaluates to 0 at 0 (i.e., $\rho(0) = 0$).
2. There exists an interval $[0, c]$ $(c > 0)$, where ρ is monotonically increasing, and an interval (c, ∞), where ρ is a constant.

3.
$$\frac{E(\rho)}{\rho(c)} = 0.5, \tag{8.39}$$

where $E(\rho)$ is the expected value of ρ.

An example of such an estimator is [28]:

$$\rho(r) = \begin{cases} \frac{r^2}{2} - \frac{r^4}{2c^2} + \frac{r^6}{6c^4} & \text{if } |r| \le c, \\ \frac{c^2}{6} & \text{if } |r| > c, \end{cases} \tag{8.40}$$

with influence curve

$$\psi(r) = \begin{cases} r[1 - (\frac{r}{c})^2]^2 & \text{if } |r| \le c, \\ 0 & \text{if } |r| > c. \end{cases} \tag{8.41}$$

The third property is achieved in this example by letting $c = 1.547$ [28].

Given residuals $\{r_i : i = 1, \ldots, n\}$ and letting $\hat{\mathbf{a}}$ be the model parameters estimated by OLS, the scale parameter σ is estimated by solving

$$\frac{1}{n} \sum_{i=1}^{n} \rho(r_i(\hat{\mathbf{a}})/\hat{\sigma}) = K, \tag{8.42}$$

where K is the expected value of ρ. If there is more than one solution, the largest scale is taken as the solution, and if there is no solution, the scale is set to 0 [28]. Knowing scale, $\mathbf{a}$ is estimated, and the process of estimating σ and $\mathbf{a}$ is repeated until dispersion among the residuals reaches a minimum.

A robust method for estimating the initial scale is the *median absolute deviation* described by (8.34) [6, 12]. An alternative robust estimation of the scale parameter is [25]:

$$1.193 \, med_i \{ med_j \{ |r_i - r_j| \} \}. \tag{8.43}$$

For each r_i, the median of $\{ |r_i - r_j| : j = 1, \ldots, n \}$ is determined. By varying $i = 1, \ldots, n$, n numbers are obtained, the median of which will be the estimated scale. The number 1.193 is to make the estimated scale consistent with the scale σ of the Gaussian approximating the distribution of the residuals.

If ρ possesses the three properties mentioned above, the breakdown point of the S estimator will be [28]:

$$\varepsilon^* = \frac{1}{n} \left(\left\lfloor \frac{n}{2} \right\rfloor - m + 2 \right). \tag{8.44}$$

As n approaches ∞, the breakdown point of the S estimator approaches 0.5. This high breakdown point of the S estimator is due to the second property of the ρ curve that is required to have a constant value beyond a certain point. This will stop a single outlier from influencing the outcome arbitrarily. Note that although an outlier in the S estimator is not as damaging as it can be, an outlier still adversely affects the estimated parameters and as the number of outliers increases, the estimations worsen up to the breakdown point, beyond which there will be a drastic change in the estimated parameters.

To summarize, an S estimator first determines the residuals using OLS or a more robust estimator. Then the scale parameter is estimated using the residuals. Knowing an estimation $\hat{\sigma}$ to the scale parameter, r_i is replaced with $r_i/\hat{\sigma}$ and the influence function is solved for the parameters of the model. Note that this requires the solution of a system of nonlinear equations. Having the estimated model parameters $\hat{\mathbf{a}}$, the process of finding the residuals, estimating the scale, and estimating the model parameters is repeated until a minimum is reached in the estimated scale, showing minimum dispersion of the obtained residuals.

8.5 RM Estimator

The repeated median (RM) estimator works with the median of the parameters estimated by different combinations of m points out of n [32]. If there are n points and m model parameters, there will be overall $n!/[m!(n-m)!]$ or $O(n^m)$ combinations of points that can be used to estimate the model parameters.

Now consider the following median operator:

$$M\{\tilde{\mathbf{a}}(i_1,\ldots,i_m)\} = med_{i_m}\{\tilde{\mathbf{a}}(i_1,\ldots,i_{m-1},i_m)\}, \tag{8.45}$$

where the right-hand side is the median of parameters $\tilde{\mathbf{a}}(i_1,\ldots,i_{m-1},i_m)$ as point i_m is replaced with all points not already among the m points. Every time the operator is called, it replaces one of its m points with all points not already in use. By calling the operator m times, each time replacing one of its points, the median parameters for all combinations of m points out of n will be obtained. The obtained median parameters are taken as the parameters of the model.

$$\hat{\mathbf{a}} = M^m\{\tilde{\mathbf{a}}(i_1,\ldots,i_m)\}, \tag{8.46}$$

$$= med_{i_1}\left(\cdots\left(med_{i_{m-1}}\left(med_{i_m}\tilde{\mathbf{a}}(i_1,\ldots,i_m)\right)\right)\cdots\right). \tag{8.47}$$

The process of estimating the model parameters can be considered m nested loops, where each loop goes through the n points except for the ones already in use by the outer loops and determines the parameters of the model for each combination of m points. The median of each parameter is used as the best estimate of that parameter.

When n is very large, an exhaustive search for the optimal parameters will become prohibitively time consuming, especially when m is also large. To reduce computation time without significantly affecting the outcome, only point combinations that are sufficiently far from each other in the (x, y) domain is used. Points distant

Table 8.6 The parameters estimated by the RM estimator along with RMSE measures and computation time for the five data sets in Table 8.1

Data set	a	b	c	d	e	f	$RMSE_a$	$RMSE_c$	Time
Blurred	1.000	0.000	0.000	0.000	1.000	0.000	3.57	0.79	133
Noisy	1.000	0.000	0.000	0.000	1.000	0.000	3.50	0.75	162
Enhanced	1.000	0.000	0.000	0.000	1.000	0.000	3.75	0.69	164
Rotated	0.871	−0.485	38.68	0.501	0.853	−22.70	4.32	0.79	144
Scaled	1.504	0.008	−0.049	−0.014	1.496	1.964	5.13	1.30	41

Table 8.7 Results obtained by the fast version of the RM estimator using only the convex-hull points in parameter estimation

Data set	a	b	c	d	e	f	$RMSE_a$	$RMSE_c$	Time
Blurred	0.999	0.000	0.000	0.000	1.000	0.000	3.38	0.83	0.035
Noisy	1.000	0.000	0.000	0.009	1.000	0.000	3.63	0.84	0.021
Enhanced	0.972	0.005	1.558	0.008	1.000	−0.497	3.65	1.10	0.009
Rotated	0.809	−0.485	41.64	0.507	0.845	−22.71	5.27	2.17	0.028
Scaled	1.458	0.034	1.712	0.003	1.474	0.039	4.91	2.90	0.011

from each other result in more accurate parameters as they are less influenced by small positional errors. For instance, points describing the convex hull of the points can be used. By discarding points inside the convex hull of the points, considerable savings can be achieved.

To evaluate the performance of the RM estimator on the data sets in Table 8.1 when using the full combination of 3 correspondences out of the marked correspondences in the table, the parameters listed in Table 8.6 are obtained. The RMSE measures and computation time required to find the parameters for each set are also shown.

The results obtained by the fast version of the RM estimator, which uses only the convex hull points in the reference image and the corresponding points are shown in Table 8.7. The fast RM estimator achieves a speed up factor of more than 1000 by introducing only small errors into the estimated parameters. The difference between the two is expected to reduce further with increasing n.

Although the RM estimator has a theoretical breakdown point of 0.5, we see that in the scaled data set there are only 28 true correspondences from among the 78 marked correspondences in Table 8.1, showing that more than half of the correspondences are incorrect. However, since all residuals are within 10 pixels, the RM estimator has been able to estimate the parameters of the model.

Table 8.8 The parameters estimated by the LMS estimator using the data sets in Table 8.1

Data set	a	b	c	d	e	f	RMSE$_a$	RMSE$_c$	Time
Blurred	1.000	−0.003	−0.097	−0.001	0.996	0.319	3.52	0.79	0.004
Noisy	1.012	0.000	−0.889	0.007	1.004	−0.562	3.56	0.88	0.003
Enhanced	0.997	0.11	−0.353	−0.001	1.001	−0.274	3.71	0.84	0.001
Rotated	0.869	−0.499	39.32	0.502	0.860	−23.54	4.37	0.58	0.001
Scaled	1.507	−0.007	−0.015	−0.005	1.509	0.612	5.18	1.02	0.001

8.6 LMS Estimator

The least median of squares (LMS) estimator finds the model parameters by minimizing the median of squared residuals [24]:

$$\min_{\hat{a}}\{med_i\left(r_i^2\right)\}. \tag{8.48}$$

When the residuals have a normal distribution with a mean of zero and when two
or more parameters are to be estimated ($m \geq 2$), the breakdown point of the LMS
estimator is [24]:

$$\varepsilon^* = \frac{1}{n}\left(\left\lfloor\frac{n}{2}\right\rfloor - m + 2\right). \tag{8.49}$$

As n approaches ∞, the breakdown point of the estimator approaches 0.5.

By minimizing the median of squares, the process, in effect, minimizes the sum
of squares of the smallest $\lfloor n/2 \rfloor$ absolute residuals. Therefore, first, the parameters
of the model are estimated by OLS or a more robust estimator. Then, points that
produce the $\lfloor n/2 \rfloor$ smallest magnitude residuals are identified and used in OLS to
estimate the parameters of the model. The process is repeated until the median of
squared residuals reaches a minimum.

Using the data sets shown in Table 8.1, the results in Table 8.8 are obtained. The
process in each case takes from a few to several iterations to find the parameters. The
LMS estimator has been able to find parameters between the transformed images
and the original image that are as close to the ideal parameters as the parameters
estimated by any of the estimators discussed so far.

8.7 LTS Estimator

The least trimmed squares (LTS) estimator [26] is similar to the LMS estimator
except that it uses fewer than half of the smallest squared residuals to estimate the
parameters. LTS estimates the parameters by minimizing

$$\sum_{i=1}^{h}\left(r^2\right)_{i:n}, \tag{8.50}$$

Table 8.9 Parameters estimated by the LTS estimator with $h = n/4$ using the data sets in Table 8.1

Data set	a	b	c	d	e	f	RMSE$_a$	RMSE$_c$	Time
Blurred	1.000	0.000	0.000	0.000	1.000	0.000	3.57	0.79	0.002
Noisy	1.000	0.000	0.000	0.000	1.000	0.000	3.60	0.75	0.001
Enhanced	1.000	0.000	0.000	0.000	1.000	0.000	3.75	0.69	0.002
Rotated	0.873	−0.496	38.90	0.503	0.857	−23.18	4.35	0.65	0.001
Scaled	1.510	−0.002	−0.579	−0.009	1.505	0.932	5.12	1.08	0.002

where $m \le h \le n/2 + 1$ and $(r^2)_{i:n} \le (r^2)_{j:n}$, when $i < j$. The process initially estimates the parameters of the model by OLS or a more robust estimator. It then orders the residuals and identifies points that produce the h smallest residuals. Those points are then used to estimate the parameters of the model. The squared residuals are recalculated using all points and ordered. The process of selecting points and calculating and ordering the residuals is repeated. The parameters obtained from the points producing the h smallest residuals are taken as estimates to the model parameters in each iteration. The process is stopped when the hth smallest squared residual reaches a minimum.

The breakdown point of the LTS estimator is [26]:

$$\varepsilon^* = \begin{cases} (h - m + 1)/n & \text{if } m \le h < \lfloor \frac{n+m+1}{2} \rfloor, \\ (n - h + 1)/n & \text{if } \lfloor \frac{n+m+1}{2} \rfloor \le h \le n. \end{cases} \qquad (8.51)$$

When n is not very large and if the number of parameters m is small, by letting $h = n/2 + 1$ we see that the breakdown point of this estimator is close to 0.5. When n is very large, by letting $h = n/2$, we see that irrespective of m a breakdown point close to 0.5 is achieved. Note that due to the ordering need in the objective function, each iteration of the algorithm requires $O(n \log_2 n)$ comparisons.

By letting $h = n/4$ and using the data in Table 8.1, we obtain the results shown in Table 8.9. Obtained results are similar to those obtained by the LMS estimator when using all the correspondences. When using only the correct correspondences, results obtained by the LTS estimator are slightly better than those obtained by the LMS estimator.

When the ratio of correct correspondences over all correspondences falls below 0.5, the parameters initially estimated by OLS may not be accurate enough to produce squared residuals that when ordered will place correct correspondences before the incorrect ones. Therefore, the obtained ordered list may contain a mixture of correct and incorrect correspondences from the very start. When the majority of correspondences is correct and there are no distant outliers, the residuals are ordered such that more correct correspondences appear at and near the beginning of the list. This enables points with smaller squared residuals to be selected, allowing more correct correspondences to participate in the estimation process, ultimately producing more accurate results.

8.8 R Estimator

A rank (R) estimator ranks the residuals and uses the ranks to estimate the model parameters [13]. By using the ranks of the residuals rather than their actual values, the influence of very distant outliers is reduced. By assigning weights to the residuals through a scoring function, the breakdown point of the estimator can be increased up to 0.5. Using a fraction α of the residuals in estimating the parameters of the model, Hossjer [9] reduced the influence of the $1 - \alpha$ largest magnitude residuals in parameter estimation. It is shown that a breakdown point of 0.5 can be achieved by letting $\alpha = 0.5$.

If R_i is the rank of the ith largest magnitude residual $|r_i|$ from among n residuals and if $b_n(R_i)$ is the score assigned to the ith largest magnitude residual from a score generating function, then the objective function to minimize is

$$\frac{1}{n}\sum_{i=1}^{n} b_n(R_i)r_i^2, \tag{8.52}$$

which can be achieved by setting its gradient to zero and solving the obtained system of linear equations. Therefore,

$$\sum_{i=1}^{n} b_n(R_i)r_i x_{ik} = 0, \quad k = 1, \ldots, m. \tag{8.53}$$

This is, in effect, a WLS estimator where the weight of the residual at the i point is $b_n(R_i)$.

Given ranks $\{R_i : i = 1, \ldots, n\}$, an example of a score generating function is

$$b_n(R_i) = h\big(R_i/(n+1)\big), \tag{8.54}$$

which maps the ranks to $(0, 1)$ in such a way that

$$\sup\{u; h(u) > \alpha\} = \alpha, \quad 0 < \alpha \le 1. \tag{8.55}$$

For example, if $\alpha = 0.25$ and letting $u = R_i/(n+1)$, then when $R_i/(n+1) \le \alpha$ the score is u, and when $R_i/(n+1) > \alpha$ the score is 0.25. This scoring function, in effect, assigns a fixed weight to a certain percentage of highest magnitude residuals. Therefore, when $\alpha = 0.25$, the highest 75% residuals are given a fixed weight that is lower than what they would otherwise receive. The scoring function can be designed to assign decreasing scores to increasing residuals from a point and to assign a score

Fig. 8.4 Plot of the scoring function of (8.56)

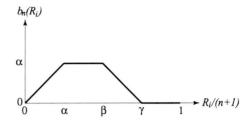

of 0 to a percentage of the largest magnitude residuals. For example, consider the scoring function depicted in Fig. 8.4 with $0 < \alpha \leq \beta \leq \gamma \leq 1$,

$$
b_n(R_i) = \begin{cases}
R_i/(n+1), & \text{if } R_i/(n+1) \leq \alpha, \\
\alpha, & \text{if } \alpha < R_i/(n+1) \leq \beta, \\
\alpha[\gamma - R_i/(n+1)]/(\gamma - \beta), & \text{if } \beta < R_i/(n+1) \geq \gamma, \\
0, & \text{if } R_i/(n+1) > \gamma.
\end{cases}
\tag{8.56}
$$

This scoring function discards the 100γ percentage of the points that produce the largest magnitude residuals. By discarding such points, the process removes the outliers. Hössjer [9] has shown that if the scoring function is nondecreasing, the process has a single global minimum. However, if the scoring function decreases in an interval, there may be more than one minima, and if the initial parameters estimated by OLS are not near the final parameters, the R estimator may converge to a local minimum rather than the global one.

To summarize, estimation by an R estimator involves the following steps:

1. Design a scoring function.
2. Estimate the model parameters by OLS or a more robust estimator and calculate the residuals.
3. Let initial weights at all points be $1/n$.
4. Rank the points according to the magnitude of the weighted residuals.
5. Find the score at each point using the scoring function, and let the score represent the weight at the point.
6. Find the model parameters by the WLS estimator.
7. Estimate the new residuals at the points. If a minimum is reached in the sum of weighted square residuals, stop. Otherwise, go to Step 4.

Using the nondecreasing scoring function in (8.54), the results shown in Table 8.10 are obtained for the data sets in Table 8.1. Using the scoring function (8.56) with $\alpha = 0.5$, $\beta = 0.75$, and $\gamma = 1.0$, the results shown in Table 8.11 are obtained for the same data sets.

Similar results are obtained by the two scoring functions. Comparing these results with those obtained by previous estimators, we see that the results by the R estimator are not as good as those obtained by some of the other estimators when using the data sets in Table 8.1. By using the ranks of the residuals rather than their magnitudes, the process reduces the influence of distant outliers. The process, however, may assign large ranks to very small residuals in cases where a great portion of

Table 8.10 Parameter estimation by the R estimator when using the scoring function of (8.54) with $\alpha = 0.5$ and the data sets in Table 8.1

Data set	a	b	c	d	e	f	$RMSE_a$	$RMSE_c$	Time
Blurred	1.000	0.002	−0.256	−0.006	1.000	0.036	3.55	0.95	0.001
Noisy	1.010	−0.004	−0.120	0.005	0.992	−0.044	3.61	0.92	0.001
Enhanced	0.996	0.003	0.038	−0.002	0.994	0.057	3.74	0.91	0.001
Rotated	0.872	−0.489	38.36	0.505	0.850	−22.79	4.33	0.83	0.001
Scaled	1.497	0.002	−0.249	−0.013	1.5001	0.604	5.13	1.59	0.001

Table 8.11 Parameter estimation by the R estimator when using the scoring function of (8.56) with $\alpha = 0.5$, $\beta = 0.75$, and $\gamma = 1.0$ and the data sets in Table 8.1

Data set	a	b	c	d	e	f	$RMSE_a$	$RMSE_c$	Time
Blurred	0.996	0.007	−0.220	−0.003	0.995	0.055	3.58	1.01	0.001
Noisy	1.009	−0.007	−0.053	0.003	0.994	−0.033	3.60	0.89	0.001
Enhanced	0.987	0.008	0.143	0.000	0.999	−0.070	3.75	0.90	0.001
Rotated	0.872	−0.489	38.36	0.505	0.850	−22.79	4.33	0.83	0.001
Scaled	1.484	0.012	−0.109	−0.007	1.500	0.438	5.13	1.67	0.001

the residuals are very small. This, in effect, degrades the estimation accuracy. Therefore, in the absence of distant outliers, as is the case for the data sets in Table 8.1, the R estimator does not produce results as accurate as those obtained by LMS and LTS estimators.

8.9 Effect of Distant Outliers on Estimation

If a correspondence algorithm does not have the ability to distinguish inaccurate correspondences from incorrect ones, some incorrect correspondences (outliers) may take part in estimation of the model parameters. In such a situation, the results produced by different estimators will be different from the results presented so far. To get an idea of the kind of results one may get from the various estimators in the presence of distant outliers, the following experiment is carried out.

The 28 correct corresponding points in the original and scaled images marked with '+' in Table 8.1 are taken. These correspondences are connected with yellow lines in Fig. 8.5a. In this correspondence set, points in the original set are kept fixed and points in the scaled set are switched one at a time until the breakdown point for each estimator is reached. To ensure that the outliers are far from the estimating model, the farthest points in the scaled set are switched. The correct correspondences, along with the outliers tested in this experiment, are shown in Figs. 8.5b–i. Red lines connect the incorrect correspondences and yellow lines connect the correct correspondences. Using point correspondences connected with yellow and red

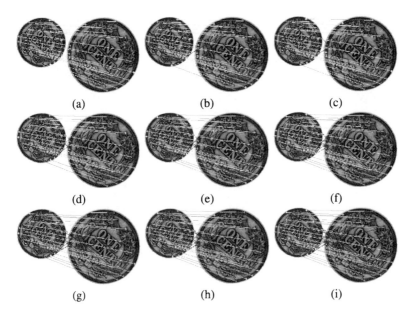

Fig. 8.5 (**a**) 28 corresponding points in the coin image and its scaled version. (**b**)–(**i**) Introduction of 1, 2, 4, 6, 8, 9, 10, and 14 outliers into the correspondence set of (**a**). *Red lines* are the outliers (false positives) and *green lines* are the missed correspondences (false negatives). The *yellow lines* are the correct correspondences (true positives). The *points* connected with the *yellow* and *red lines* are used as corresponding points in the experiments

lines, the results shown in Table 8.12 are obtained by the various estimators. The green lines indicate the correct correspondences that are not used in the estimation process.

From the results in Table 8.12, we can conclude the following:

1. For the data set in Fig. 8.5a where no outliers are present and data are simply corrupted with random noise, OLS performs as good as any other estimator by finding the maximum likelihood estimation of the parameters.
2. Because OLS can break down with a single distant outlier, the estimators that depend on OLS to find the initial residuals or initial parameters can also break down with a single distant outlier. WLS and R-1 estimators have exhibited this characteristic when using the data sets containing one or more outliers.
3. To improve the accuracy of the estimators, a means to either eliminate some of the distant outliers, as done by R-2, or to estimate the initial model parameters more robustly is required.
4. When using the data sets in Fig. 8.5, the clear winner is the R-2 estimator, which uses the scoring function in (8.56). By effectively removing some of the outliers, ordering the rest, and using points with low squared residuals, this estimator has been able to find correct model parameters from data containing up to 50% of distant outliers (Fig. 8.5i). LTS with $h = n/4$ and LMS have also been able to perform well under distant outliers.

Table 8.12 Breakdown points for various estimators in the presence of distant outliers. Table entries show RMSE at the correct correspondences. The point at which a sharp increase in RMSE is observed while gradually increasing the number of outliers is the breakdown point. WLS-1 and WLS-2 imply WLS estimation without and with a cut-off threshold of 2 pixels, RM-1 and RM-2 imply the regular and the fast RM estimators, and R-1 and R-2 imply the R estimator with the non-decreasing scoring function of (8.54) with $\alpha = 0.5$ and the decreasing scoring function of (8.56) with $\alpha = 0.25$, $\beta = 0.5$, and $\gamma = 0.75$, respectively. The numbers in the top row show the number of distant outliers used in a set of 28 corresponding points

Estimator	0	1	2	4	6	8	9	10	14
OLS	0.97	11.14	20.31	33.01	42.53	48.04	50.73	50.86	51.75
WLS-1	0.97	11.14	20.31	33.01	42.53	48.04	50.73	50.86	106.2
WLS-2	0.97	11.14	20.31	33.01	42.53	48.04	50.73	50.86	51.75
RM-1	0.98	1.01	1.06	1.19	5.88	67.07	47.46	47.63	58.30
RM-2	1.15	0.56	1.06	44.04	44.04	59.51	54.74	50.06	45.27
LMS	1.01	1.10	1.20	1.09	1.18	1.05	50.89	50.86	59.16
LTS	1.01	1.36	1.39	1.28	1.17	1.20	1.14	55.65	51.75
R-1	1.02	15.95	22.58	42.98	53.26	52.06	70.52	67.40	84.85
R-2	1.01	1.04	1.07	1.25	1.10	1.10	1.07	1.11	1.21

8.10 Additional Observations

For the data sets in Table 8.1, all tested estimators were able to find the parameters of the affine transformation to register the images with acceptable accuracies. These data sets do not contain distant outliers and errors at the points have distributions that are close to normal with a mean of 0. Among the estimators tested, RM, LMS, and LTS estimators produce the highest accuracies. Considering the high computational requirement of RM estimator, LMS and LTS stand out among the others in overall speed and accuracy in estimating model parameters when using the data sets of the kind shown in Table 8.1.

For the data sets of the kind depicted in Fig. 8.5, where distant outliers are present, results in Table 8.12 show that R estimator with the scoring function given in (8.56) is the most robust among the estimators tested, followed by LTS and LMS estimators. The OLS and WLS estimators are not to be used when the provided data contains distant outliers.

Although some estimators performed better than others on the limited tests performed in this chapter, it should be mentioned that one may be able to find a data set where any of the estimators can perform better than many of the other estimators. When data sets represent coordinates of corresponding points obtained by a point pattern matching algorithm, it is anticipated that the R-2 estimator will perform better than others when distant outliers are present, and LTS and LMS estimators will perform better than other estimators when the correspondences do not contain distant outliers.

When the ratio of outliers and inliers is small and the outliers are distant from the model, methods to remove the outliers have been developed. Hodge and Austin [8]

provided a survey of such methods. Outlier detection, however, without information about the underlying model is not always possible especially when the number of outliers is nearly the same as the number of inliers, or when outliers are not very far from the model to be estimated. Robust estimators coupled with the geometric constraint that hold between images of a scene can determine model parameters in the presence of a large number of outliers and without use of outlier detection methods.

The list of estimators discussed in this chapter is by no means exhaustive. For a more complete list of estimators, the reader is referred to excellent monographs by Andrews et al. [3], Huber [12], Hampel et al. [7], Rousseeuw and Leroy [27], and Wilcox [36].

8.11 Principal Component Analysis (PCA)

Suppose feature vector $\mathbf{x} = \{x_0, x_1, \ldots, x_{N-1}\}$ represents an observation from a phenomenon and there are m such observations: $\{\mathbf{x}^i : i = 0, \ldots, m - 1\}$. We would like to determine an $N \times N$ matrix $\mathbf{A}$ that can transform $\mathbf{x}$ to a new feature vector $\mathbf{y} = \mathbf{A}^t \mathbf{x}$ that has a small number of high-valued components. Such a transformation makes it possible to reduce the dimensionality of $\mathbf{x}$ while maintaining its overall variation.

Assuming each feature is normalized to have mean of 0 and a fixed scale, such as 1, then the expected value of $\mathbf{y}\mathbf{y}^t$ can be computed from

$$
\begin{aligned}
E(\mathbf{y}\mathbf{y}^t) &= E(\mathbf{A}^t \mathbf{x}\mathbf{x}^t \mathbf{A}) \\
&= \mathbf{A}^t E(\mathbf{x}\mathbf{x}^t) \mathbf{A} \\
&= \mathbf{A}^t \Sigma_x \mathbf{A}
\end{aligned}
\tag{8.57}
$$

where

$$
\Sigma_x =
\begin{bmatrix}
E(x_0 x_0) & E(x_0 x_1) & \cdots & E(x_0 x_{N-1}) \\
E(x_1 x_0) & E(x_1 x_1) & \cdots & E(x_1 x_{N-1}) \\
\cdot & & \cdots & \cdot \\
E(x_{N-1} x_0) & E(x_{N-1} x_1) & \cdots & E(N-1 x_{N-1})
\end{bmatrix}
\tag{8.58}
$$

is the covariance matrix with its ijth entry computed from

$$
E(x_i x_j) = \frac{1}{m} \sum_{k=0}^{m-1} (x_i^k x_j^k).
\tag{8.59}
$$

By letting the eigenvectors of Σ_x represent the columns of $\mathbf{A}$, $\mathbf{A}^t \Sigma_x \mathbf{A}$ will become a diagonal matrix with diagonal entries showing the eigenvalues of Σ_x.

Suppose the eigenvalues of Σ_x are ordered so that $\lambda_i \geq \lambda_{i+1}$ for $0 \leq i < N - 1$ and eigenvectors corresponding to the eigenvalues are $\mathbf{v}_0, \mathbf{v}_1, \ldots, \mathbf{v}_{N-1}$, we can then write

$$
y_i = \mathbf{v}_i^t \mathbf{x}, \quad i = 0, \ldots, N - 1.
\tag{8.60}
$$

If transformed features are known, the original features can be computed from

$$\mathbf{x} = \sum_{i=0}^{N-1} y_i \mathbf{v}_i.$$ (8.61)

An approximation to $\mathbf{x}$ using eigenvectors of Σ_x corresponding to its n largest eigenvalues is obtained from

$$\hat{\mathbf{x}} = \sum_{i=0}^{n-1} y_i \mathbf{v}_i.$$ (8.62)

Squared error in this approximation will be [23, 34]

$$E\left(\|\mathbf{x} - \hat{\mathbf{x}}\|^2\right) = \sum_{i=n}^{N-1} \mathbf{v}_i^t \lambda_i \mathbf{v}_i$$

$$= \sum_{i=n}^{N-1} \lambda_i$$ (8.63)

for using $y_0, y_1, \ldots, y_{n-1}$ instead of $x_0, x_1, \ldots, x_{N-1}$.

Since the eigenvalues depend on the scale of features, the ratio measure [23]

$$r_n = \sum_{i=n}^{N-1} \lambda_i \bigg/ \sum_{i=0}^{N-1} \lambda_i$$ (8.64)

may be used as a scale-independent error measure to select the number of principal components needed to achieve a required squared error tolerance in approximation.

To summarize, following are the steps to reduce the dimensionality of feature vector $\mathbf{x}$ from N to $n < N$ using a training data set containing m observations:

1. Estimate Σ_x from the m observations.
2. Find eigenvalues and eigenvectors of Σ_x. Order the eigenvalues from the largest to the smallest: $\lambda_0 \geq \lambda_1 \geq \cdots \geq \lambda_{N-1}$. Note that eigenvalue λ_i has an associating eigenvector, $\mathbf{v}_i$.
3. Find the largest n such that $\sum_{i=n}^{N-1} \lambda_i < \varepsilon$, where ε is the required squared error tolerance.
4. Given a newly observed feature vector $\mathbf{x}$, project $\mathbf{x}$ to the n-dimensions defined by the eigenvectors corresponding to the n largest eigenvalues of Σ_x. That is compute $y_i = \mathbf{v}_i^t \mathbf{x}$ for $i = 0, \ldots, n-1$. $\mathbf{y}$ represents a point in $n < N$ dimensions, thereby, reducing the dimensionality of $\mathbf{x}$ while ensuring the squared approximation error stays below the required tolerance.

PCA was first used by Pearson [21] to find the best-fit line or plane to high dimensional points. The best-fit line or plane was found to show the direction of most uncorrelated variation. Therefore, PCA transforms correlated values into uncorrelated values, called principal components. The components represent the direction of most uncorrelated variation, the direction of second most uncorrelated variation, and so on.

PCA is also called Karhunen–Loève (K–L) transform and Hotelling transform. Given a feature vector containing N features, in an attempt to create $n < N$ new features that carry about the same variance from the linear combinations of the features, Hotelling [10] (also see [16, 17]) found the linear coefficients relating the original features to new ones in such a way that the first new feature had the largest variance. Then, the second feature was created in such a way that it was uncorrelated with the first and had as large a variance as possible. He continued the process until n new features were created. The coefficients of the linear functions defining a new feature in terms of the original features transform the original features to the new ones.

Rao [23] provided various insights into the uses and extensions of PCA. Watanabe [35] showed that dimensionality reduction by PCA minimizes average classification error when taking only a finite number of coefficients in a series expansion of a feature vector in terms of orthogonal basis vectors. He also showed that PCA minimizes the entropy of average square coefficients of the principal components. These two characteristics make PCA a very efficient tool for data reduction. The dimensionality reduction power of PCA using artificial and real data has been demonstrated by Kittler and Young [18]. For a thorough treatment of PCA and its various applications, see the excellent monograph by Jolliffe [16].

Since PCA calculates a new feature using all original features, it still requires high-dimensional data collection. It would be desirable to reduce the number of original features while preserving sufficient variance in collected features without changing the number of principal components. Jolliffe [14, 15] suggested discarding features that contributed greatly to the last few principal components, or selecting features that contributed greatly to the first few principal components. Therefore, if

$$\mathbf{y} = \mathbf{A}^t \mathbf{x}, \tag{8.65}$$

or

$$y_i = \sum_{j=0}^{N-1} A_{ji} x_j, \quad i = 0, \ldots, N - 1, \tag{8.66}$$

where A_{ji} denotes the entry at column i and row j in matrix $\mathbf{A}$, then magnitude of A_{ji} determines the contribution of x_j to y_i.

Since this method finds ineffective features in the original set by focusing on the principal components one at a time, the influence of an original feature on a number of principal components is not taken into consideration. Mao [19] suggested finding the contribution of an original feature on all selected principal components. The significance of an original feature on the selected n principal components is determined by calculating the squared error in (8.63) once using all features and another time using all features except the feature under consideration. The feature producing the least increase in error is then removed from the original set and the process is repeated until the squared error among the remaining features reaches a desired tolerance.

Since each transformed feature in PCA is a linear combination of the original features, the process detects only linear dependency between features. If dependency between features is nonlinear, nonlinear approaches [29, 30, 33] should be used to reduce the number of features.

References

1. Abdi, H.: Least squares. In: Lewis-Beck, M., Bryman, A., Futing, T. (eds.) The Sage Encyclopedia of Social Sciences Research Methods, Thousand Oaks, CA, pp. 1–4 (2003)
2. Aitken, A.C.: On least squares and linear combinations of observations. Proc. R. Soc. Edinb. **55**, 42–48 (1935)
3. Andrews, D.F., Bickel, P.J., Hampel, F.R., Huber, P.J., Rogers, W.H., Tukey, J.W.: Robust Estimates of Location: Survey and Advances. Princeton University Press, Princeton (1972)
4. Golub, G., Kahan, W.: Calculating the singular values and pseudo-inverse of a matrix. J. SIAM Numer. Anal., Ser. B **2**(2), 205–224 (1965)
5. Hampel, F.R.: A general qualitative definition of robustness. Ann. Math. Stat. **42**(6), 1887–1896 (1971)
6. Hampel, F.R.: The influence curve and its role in robust estimation. J. Am. Stat. Assoc. **69**(346), 383–393 (1974)
7. Hampel, F.R., Ronchetti, E.M., Rousseeuw, P.J., Stahel, W.A.: Robust Statistics: The Approach Based on Influence Functions. Wiley, New York (1986)
8. Hodges, V.J., Austin, J.: A survey of outlier detection methodologies. Artif. Intell. Rev. **22**, 85–126 (2004)
9. Hossjer, P.: Rank-based estimates in the linear model with high breakdown point. J. Am. Stat. Assoc. **89**(425), 149–158 (1994)
10. Hotelling, H.: Analysis of a complex of statistical variables into principal components. J. Educ. Psychol. **24**, 417–441 (1933), also see pp. 498–520
11. Huber, P.J.: Robust regression: Asymptotics, conjectures and Monte Carlo. Ann. Stat. **1**(5), 799–821 (1973)
12. Huber, P.J.: Robust Statistics. Wiley, New York (1981)
13. Jaeckel, L.A.: Regression coefficients by minimizing the dispersion of the residuals. Ann. Math. Stat. **43**(5), 1449–1458 (1972)
14. Jolliffe, I.T.: Discarding variables in a principal component analysis. I: Artificial data. J. R. Stat. Soc., Ser. C, Appl. Stat. **21**(2), 160–173 (1972)
15. Jolliffe, I.T.: Discarding variables in a principal component analysis. II: Real data. J. R. Stat. Soc., Ser. C, Appl. Stat. **22**(1), 21–31 (1973)
16. Jolliffee, I.T.: Principal Component Analysis. Springer, New York (2002)
17. Kendall, M.G.: A Course in Multivariate Analysis, 4th Impression. Hafner, New York (1968)
18. Kittler, J., Young, P.C.: A new approach to feature selection based on the Karhunen–Loève expansion. Pattern Recognit. **5**, 335–352 (1973)
19. Mao, K.Z.: Identifying critical variables of principal components for unsupervised feature selection. IEEE Trans. Syst. Man Cybern., Part B, Cybern. **35**(2), 334–339 (2005)
20. McElroy, F.W.: A necessary and sufficient condition that ordinary least-squares estimators be best linear unbiased. J. Am. Stat. Assoc. **62**(320), 1302–1304 (1967)
21. Pearson, K.: On lines and planes of closest fit to systems of points in space. Philos. Mag. **2**(6), 559–572 (1901)
22. Penrose, R.: A generalized inverse for matrices. Math. Proc. Camb. Philos. Soc. **51**(3), 406–413 (1955)
23. Rao, C.R.: The use of interpretation of principal component analysis in applied research. Indian J. Stat., Ser. A **26**(4), 329–358 (1964)
24. Rousseeuw, P.J.: Least median of squares regression. J. Am. Stat. Assoc. **79**(388), 871–880 (1984)
25. Rousseeuw, P.J., Croux, C.: Alternatives to the median absolute deviation. J. Am. Stat. Assoc. **88**(424), 1273–1283 (1993)
26. Rousseeuw, P.J., Hubert, M.: Recent developments in PROGRESS. In: Lecture Notes on L_1-Statistical Procedures and Related Topics, vol. 31, pp. 201–214 (1997)
27. Rousseeuw, P.J., Leroy, A.M.: Robust Regression and Outlier Detection. Wiley, New York (1987)

28. Rousseeuw, P., Yohai, V.: Robust regression by means of S-estimators. In: Franke, J., Hördle, W., Martin, R.D. (eds.) Robust and Nonlinear Time Series Analysis. Lecture Notes in Statistics, vol. 26, pp. 256–274. Springer, New York (1984)

29. Roweis, S.T., Saul, L.K.: Nonlinear dimensionality reduction by locally linear embedding. Science **290**, 2323–2326 (2000)

30. Scholkopf, B., Smola, A., Muller, K.-R.: Nonlinear component analysis as a kernel eigenvalue problem. Neural Comput. **10**, 1299–1319 (1998)

31. Seal, H.L.: Studies in the history of probability and statistics XV: The historical development of the Gauss linear model. Biometrika **54**(1–2), 1–24 (1967)

32. Siegel, A.F.: Robust regression using repeated medians. Biometrika **69**(1), 242–244 (1982)

33. Tenenbaum, J.B., de Silva, V., Langford, J.C.: A global geometric framework for nonlinear dimensionality reduction. Science **290**, 2319–2323 (2000)

34. Theodoridis, S., Koutroumbas, K.: Pattern Recognition, 4th edn. Academic Press, San Diego (2009), pp. 602, 605, 606

35. Watanabe, S.: Karhunen–Loève expansion and factor analysis theoretical remarks and applications. In: Trans. Prague Conf. Information Theory, Statistical Decision Functions, Random Processes, pp. 9–26 (1965)

36. Wilcox, R.R.: Introduction to Robust Estimation and Hypothesis Testing. Academic Press, San Diego (1997)

Chapter 9
Transformation Functions

A transformation function uses the coordinates of corresponding control points in two images to estimate the geometric relation between the images, which is then used to transform the geometry of one image to that of the other to spatially aligned the images. Spatial alignment of images makes it possible to determine correspondence between points in overlapping areas in the images. This correspondence is needed in various image analysis applications, such as stereo depth perception, change detection, and information fusion.

Given the coordinates of n corresponding points in two images:

$$\{(x_i, y_i), (X_i, Y_i) : i = 1, \ldots, n\}, \tag{9.1}$$

we would like to find a transformation function with components f_x and f_y that satisfies

$$\begin{aligned} X_i &\approx f_x(x_i, y_i), \\ Y_i &\approx f_y(x_i, y_i), \end{aligned} \qquad i = 1, \ldots, n. \tag{9.2}$$

f_x is a single-valued function that approximates 3-D points

$$\{(x_i, y_i, X_i) : i = 1, \ldots, n\}, \tag{9.3}$$

and f_y is another single-valued function that approximates 3-D points

$$\{(x_i, y_i, Y_i) : i = 1, \ldots, n\}. \tag{9.4}$$

Each component of a transformation function is, therefore, a single-valued surface fitting to a set of 3-D points, representing the coordinates of control points in the reference image and the X- or the Y-component of corresponding control points in the sensed image. Many surface-fitting methods exist in the literature that can be chosen for this purpose. In this chapter, functions most suitable for the registration of images with local geometric differences will be examined.

If the type of transformation function relating the geometries of two images is known, the parameters of the transformation can be determined from the coordinates of corresponding points in the images by a robust estimator (Chap. 8). For example, if the images to be registered represent consecutive frames in an aerial

A.A. Goshtasby, *Image Registration*,
Advances in Computer Vision and Pattern Recognition,
DOI 10.1007/978-1-4471-2458-0_9, © Springer-Verlag London Limited 2012

video captured by a platform at a high altitude, the images will have translational and small rotational differences. The transformation function to register such images has only a few parameters, and knowing a number of corresponding points in the images, the parameters of the transformation can be determined. If the geometric relation between the images is not known, a transformation function is required that uses information present among the correspondences to adapt to the local geometric differences between the images.

In the following sections, first transformation functions that have a fixed number of parameters are discussed. These are *well-known transformation functions* that describe the global geometric relations between two images. Next, *adaptive transformations* that adapt to local geometric differences between images are discussed. The number of parameters in a component of an adaptive transformation varies with the severity of the geometric difference between two images and can be as high as the number of corresponding points. At the end of this chapter, the properties of various transformation functions will be reviewed, and their performances in registration of images with varying degrees of geometric differences will be measured and compared.

9.1 Well-Known Transformation Functions

9.1.1 Translation

If the sensed image is only translated with respect to the reference image, corresponding points in the images will be related by

$$X = x + h, \tag{9.5}$$

$$Y = y + k. \tag{9.6}$$

In matrix form, this can be written as

$$\begin{bmatrix} X \\ Y \\ 1 \end{bmatrix} = \begin{bmatrix} 1 & 0 & h \\ 0 & 1 & k \\ 0 & 0 & 1 \end{bmatrix} \begin{bmatrix} x \\ y \\ 1 \end{bmatrix}, \tag{9.7}$$

or simply by

$$\mathbf{P} = \mathbf{T}\mathbf{p}. \tag{9.8}$$

$\mathbf{P}$ and $\mathbf{p}$ are homogeneous coordinates of corresponding points in the sensed and reference images, respectively, and $\mathbf{T}$ is the transformation matrix showing that the sensed image is translated with respect to the reference image by (h, k).

By knowing one pair of corresponding points in the images, parameters h and k can be determined by substituting the coordinates of the points into (9.5) and (9.6) and solving the obtained system of equations for h and k. If two or more corresponding points are available, h and k are determined by one of the robust estimators discussed in the previous chapter. A robust estimator can determine the parameters of the transformation if some of the correspondences are incorrect. If the correspondences are known to be correct, the parameters can also be determined by the ordinary least-squares method [84].

9.1.2 Rigid

When the sensed image is translated and rotated with respect to the reference image, the distance between points and the angle between lines remain unchanged from one image to another. Such a transformation is known as *rigid* or *Euclidean* transformation and can be written as

$$X = x \cos\theta - y \sin\theta + h, \tag{9.9}$$

$$Y = x \sin\theta + y \cos\theta + k. \tag{9.10}$$

In matrix form, this will be

$$\begin{bmatrix} X \\ Y \\ 1 \end{bmatrix} = \begin{bmatrix} 1 & 0 & h \\ 0 & 1 & k \\ 0 & 0 & 1 \end{bmatrix} \begin{bmatrix} \cos\theta & -\sin\theta & 0 \\ \sin\theta & \cos\theta & 0 \\ 0 & 0 & 1 \end{bmatrix} \begin{bmatrix} x \\ y \\ 1 \end{bmatrix}, \tag{9.11}$$

or simply

$$\mathbf{P} = \mathbf{TRp}. \tag{9.12}$$

θ shows the difference in orientation of the sensed image with respect to the reference image when measured in the counter-clockwise direction. The coordinates of a minimum of two corresponding points in the images are required to determine parameters $\theta, h,$ and k. From a pair of points in each image, a line is obtained. The angle between the lines in the images determines θ. Knowing θ, by substituting the coordinates of the midpoints of the lines into (9.9) and (9.10) parameters h and k are determined.

If more than two corresponding points are available, parameters $\theta, h,$ and k are determined by one of the robust methods discussed in the previous chapter. For instance, if the RM estimator is used, parameter θ is calculated for various corresponding lines and the median angle is taken as the estimated angle. Knowing θ, parameters h and k are estimated by substituting corresponding points into (9.9) and (9.10), solving the obtained equations, and taking the median of h values and the median of k values as estimations to h and k.

9.1.3 Similarity

When the sensed image is translated, rotated, and scaled with respect to the reference image, coordinates of corresponding points in the images will be related by the *similarity transformation*, also known as the *transformation of the Cartesian coordinate system*, defined by

$$X = xs\cos\theta - ys\sin\theta + h, \tag{9.13}$$

$$Y = xs\sin\theta + ys\cos\theta + k, \tag{9.14}$$

where s shows scale, θ shows orientation, and (h, k) shows location of the coordinate system origin of the sensed image with respect to that of the reference image.

In matrix form, this can be written as

$$\begin{bmatrix} X \\ Y \\ 1 \end{bmatrix} = \begin{bmatrix} 1 & 0 & h \\ 0 & 1 & k \\ 0 & 0 & 1 \end{bmatrix} \begin{bmatrix} \cos\theta & -\sin\theta & 0 \\ \sin\theta & \cos\theta & 0 \\ 0 & 0 & 1 \end{bmatrix} \begin{bmatrix} s & 0 & 0 \\ 0 & s & 0 \\ 0 & 0 & 1 \end{bmatrix} \begin{bmatrix} x \\ y \\ 1 \end{bmatrix} \tag{9.15}$$

or simply by

$$\mathbf{P} = \mathbf{TRS}\mathbf{p}. \tag{9.16}$$

Under the similarity transformation, the angle between corresponding lines in the images remains unchanged. Parameters s, θ, h, and k are determined by knowing a minimum of two corresponding points in the images. The scale of the sensed image with respect to the reference image is determined using the ratio of the length of the line segment obtained from the two points in the sensed image over the length of the same line segment obtained in the reference image. Knowing s, parameters θ, h, and k are determined in the same way these parameters were determined under the rigid transformation.

If more than two corresponding points in the images are available, parameters s, θ, h, and k are determined by one of the robust methods discussed in the preceding chapter. For example, if the RM estimator is used, an estimation to parameter s is made by determining s for all combinations of two corresponding points in the images, ordering the obtained s values, and taking the mid value. Knowing s, parameters θ, h, and k are determined in the same way these parameters were determined under the rigid transformation.

9.1.4 Affine

Images that have translational, rotational, scaling, and shearing differences preserve parallelism. Such a transformation is defined by

$$\begin{bmatrix} X \\ Y \\ 1 \end{bmatrix} = \begin{bmatrix} 1 & 0 & h \\ 0 & 1 & k \\ 0 & 0 & 1 \end{bmatrix} \begin{bmatrix} \cos\theta & -\sin\theta & 0 \\ \sin\theta & \cos\theta & 0 \\ 0 & 0 & 1 \end{bmatrix} \begin{bmatrix} s & 0 & 0 \\ 0 & s & 0 \\ 0 & 0 & 1 \end{bmatrix} \begin{bmatrix} 1 & \alpha & 0 \\ \beta & 1 & 0 \\ 0 & 0 & 1 \end{bmatrix} \begin{bmatrix} x \\ y \\ 1 \end{bmatrix} \tag{9.17}$$

or by

$$\mathbf{P} = \mathbf{TRSE}\mathbf{p}. \tag{9.18}$$

An affine transformation has six parameters and can be written as a combination of a linear transformation and a translation. That is,

$$X = a_1 x + a_2 y + a_3, \qquad (9.19)$$

$$Y = a_4 x + a_5 y + a_6. \qquad (9.20)$$

In matrix form, this can be written as

$$\begin{bmatrix} X \\ Y \\ 1 \end{bmatrix} = \begin{bmatrix} a_1 & a_2 & a_3 \\ a_4 & a_5 & a_6 \\ 0 & 0 & 1 \end{bmatrix} \begin{bmatrix} x \\ y \\ 1 \end{bmatrix}, \qquad (9.21)$$

or

$$\mathbf{P} = \mathbf{L}\mathbf{p}. \qquad (9.22)$$

The two components of the transformation defined by (9.17) depend on each other while the two components of the transformation defined by (9.21) are independent of each other. Since transformation (9.17) is constrained by $\sin^2 \theta + \cos^2 \theta = 1$, it cannot represent all the transformations (9.21) can define. Therefore, the affine transformation allows more differences between two images than translation, rotation, scaling, and shearing. Use of affine transformation in image registration in 2-D and higher dimensions has been studied by Nejhum et al. [70].

To find the best affine transformation when $n > 3$ correspondences are available, a robust estimator should be used. For instance, if the RM estimator is available, from various combinations of 3 correspondences, the parameters of the transformation are determined. Then the median value obtained for each parameter is taken as a robust estimation to that parameter.

9.1.5 Projective

Projective transformation, also known as *homography*, describes the true imaging geometry. Corresponding points in a flat scene and its image, or corresponding points in two images of a flat scene, are related by a projective transformation. Under the projective transformation, straight lines remain straight. A projective transformation is defined by

$$X = \frac{a_1 x + a_2 y + a_3}{a_7 x + a_8 y + 1}, \qquad (9.23)$$

$$Y = \frac{a_4 x + a_5 y + a_6}{a_7 x + a_8 y + 1}. \qquad (9.24)$$

In matrix form, this can be written as

$$\begin{bmatrix} X \\ Y \\ 1 \end{bmatrix} = \begin{bmatrix} a_1 & a_2 & a_3 \\ a_4 & a_5 & a_6 \\ a_7 & a_8 & 1 \end{bmatrix} \begin{bmatrix} x \\ y \\ 1 \end{bmatrix}, \qquad (9.25)$$

or simply by

$$\mathbf{P} = \mathbf{H}\mathbf{p}. \qquad (9.26)$$

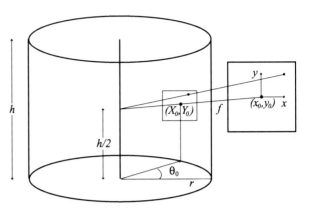

Fig. 9.1 The relation between cylindrical and planar image coordinates. h is the height and r is the radius of the cylindrical image. f is the focal length of the regular camera capturing the planar image, and (x_0, x_0) and (X_0, Y_0) are the intersections of the optical axis of the regular camera with the planar and cylindrical images, respectively

Images of a flat scene, or images of a 3-D scene taken from a distance where the heights of objects in the scene are negligible when compared with the distances of the cameras to the scene, are related by the projective transformation. A projective transformation has 8 parameters, requiring a minimum of 4 corresponding points in the images to determine them. The components of a projective transformation are interdependent due to the common denominator in (9.23) and (9.24). By substituting each corresponding point pair from the images into (9.23) and (9.24), two linear equations in terms of the unknown parameters are obtained. Having 4 corresponding points in the image, a system of 8 linear equations are obtained, from which the 8 parameters of the transformation can be determined.

Since the components of a projective transformation are interdependent, if more than 4 corresponding points are available, the residuals calculated by a robust estimator should include errors from both components as described by (8.17) in the preceding chapter.

9.1.6 Cylindrical

Suppose a cylindrical image of an environment is taken by a virtual camera with its center located in the middle of the axis of the cylinder. Also, suppose the camera has infinite optical axes that fall in a plane passing through the center of the camera and normal to the axis of the cylinder. A cylindrical image obtained in this manner can be saved as a rectangular image XY by letting $X = r\theta$ represent the image columns and $Y = i$ represent the image rows (Fig. 9.1). r is the radius of the cylinder and i varies between 0 and $h - 1$ in the discrete domain. Although such a camera does not exist in real life, images can be created that appear as if obtained by such a camera. To create a cylindrical image, images taken by a regular camera with its center fixed at the center of the cylinder and rotating about the axis of the cylinder are needed.

Suppose an image taken by a regular camera from view angle θ_0, as shown in Fig. 9.1, is available. If the optical axis of the regular camera is normal to the axis of the cylinder, the planar image will be parallel to the axis of the cylinder. The

Fig. 9.2 (a) A planar image of dimensions 256×256 and its corresponding cylindrical images (b) when $\theta_0 = 0$ and (c) when $\theta_0 = \pi/2$ in clockwise direction (or $-\pi/2$ in counter-clockwise direction). In these examples, $r = 128$, $h = 256$, and $f = 128$, all in pixels

coordinates of the center of the planar image (x_0, y_0) define the point where the optical axis of the regular camera intersects the planar image. Suppose this point maps to the cylindrical image at (X_0, Y_0). Then (X_0, Y_0) can be defined in terms of the radius of the cylinder r, the viewing angle θ_0, and the height of the cylinder h:

$$X_0 = r\theta_0, \tag{9.27}$$

$$Y_0 = h/2. \tag{9.28}$$

If the focal length of the regular camera is f, from the geometry in Fig. 9.1, we can write the following relations between the coordinates of a point (x, y) in the planar image and the coordinates of the corresponding point (X, Y) in the cylindrical image:

$$\frac{x - x_0}{f} = \tan\left(\frac{X}{r} - \theta_0\right), \tag{9.29}$$

$$\frac{Y - Y_0}{r} = \frac{y - y_0}{\sqrt{f^2 + (x - x_0)^2}}, \tag{9.30}$$

or

$$X = r\left\{\theta_0 + \tan^{-1}\left(\frac{x - x_0}{f}\right)\right\}, \tag{9.31}$$

$$Y = \frac{h}{2} + \frac{r(y - y_0)}{\sqrt{f^2 + (x - x_0)^2}}. \tag{9.32}$$

Therefore, given the coordinates of a point (x, y) in the planar image, we can find the coordinates of the corresponding point (X, Y) in the cylindrical image. Inversely, given the coordinates of a point (X, Y) in the cylindrical images, we can find the coordinates of the corresponding point (x, y) in the planar image from

$$x = x_0 + f \tan\left(\frac{X}{r} - \theta_0\right), \tag{9.33}$$

$$y = y_0 + \frac{Y - h/2}{r}\sqrt{f^2 + (x - x_0)^2}. \tag{9.34}$$

Using the planar image of dimensions 256×256 in Fig. 9.2a, the corresponding cylindrical image shown in Fig. 9.2b is obtained when letting $\theta_0 = 0$, $h = 256$, $r = 128$, and $f = 128$, all in pixel units. Changing the view angle to $\theta_0 = \pi/2$, the image shown in Fig. 9.2c is obtained. Note that in the above formulas, angle

θ increases in the clockwise direction. If θ is increased in the counter-clockwise direction, the cylindrical image will be vertically flipped with respect to the planar image.

If n planar images are taken with view angles $\theta_1, \ldots, \theta_n$, the images can be mapped to the cylindrical image and combined using formulas (9.33) and (9.34). For each regular image, mapping involves scanning the cylindrical image and for each pixel (X, Y) determining the corresponding pixel (x, y) in the planar image, reading the intensity there, and saving it at (X, Y). Since each planar image may cover only a small portion of the cylindrical image, rather than scanning the entire cylindrical image for each planar image, the midpoints of the four sides of the regular image are found in the cylindrical image using (9.31) and (9.32). Then the smallest bounding rectangle with horizontal and vertical sides is determined. This bounding rectangle will contain the entire image; therefore, the cylindrical image is scanned only within the bounding rectangle to find pixels in the planar image to map to the cylindrical image.

These formulas can be used to combine images captured from a fixed viewpoint and at different view angles to a cylindrical image. If gaps appear within the cylindrical image, and if the X-coordinate of the center of the gap is X_0, from (9.27), the view angle $\theta_0 = X_0/r$ can be determined and an image with that view angle obtained and mapped to the cylindrical image to fill the gap. The process can be repeated in this manner until all gaps are filled.

Formulas (9.31) and (9.32) can be used to map the cylindrical image to a planar image from any view angle θ_0. When planar images obtained in this manner are projected to planar screens of height h and at distance r to a viewer of height $h/2$ standing at the middle of the cylinder, the viewer will see a surround view of the environment without any geometric distortion. The cylindrical image can, therefore, be used as a means to visualize a distortion-free surround image of an environment through planar imaging and planar projection.

Note that this visualization does not require that the number of planar images captured and the number of planar projections used in viewing be the same. Therefore, if a number of video cameras are hinged together in such a way that they share the same center and their optical axes lie in the same plane, video frames of a dynamic scene simultaneously captured by the cameras can be combined into a cylindrical video and mapped to a desired number of planar images and projected to planar screens surrounding a viewer. The viewer will then see the dynamic scene from all directions.

9.1.7 Spherical

Consider a spherical image obtained by a virtual camera where the image center coincides with the camera center. Suppose the camera has infinite optical axes, each axis connecting the camera center to a point on the sphere. Points on the spherical image as well as directions of the optical axes can be represented by the angular

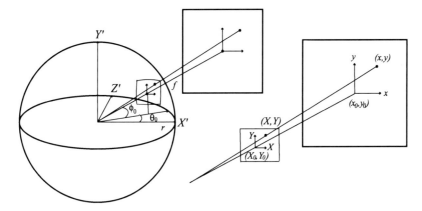

Fig. 9.3 The relation between the spherical image coordinates (X, Y) and the planar image coordinates (x, y). (x_0, y_0) is the center of the planar image and (X_0, Y_0) is the corresponding point in the spherical image. The ray connecting (x_0, y_0) to (X_0, Y_0) passes through the center of the spherical image and is normal to the planar image. θ_0 shows the angle the projection of this ray to the $X'Z'$-plane makes with the X'-axis, and ϕ_0 is the angle this ray makes with the $X'Z'$-plane. $X'Y'Z'$ is the coordinate system of the sphere

coordinates (θ, ϕ). If an image is obtained by a regular camera with an optical axis in direction $(0, 0)$, the relation between this planar image and the spherical image (Fig. 9.3) will be:

$$\theta = \tan^{-1}\left(\frac{x - x_0}{f}\right), \tag{9.35}$$

$$\phi = \tan^{-1}\left(\frac{y - y_0}{f}\right). \tag{9.36}$$

Values at (θ, ϕ) can be saved in an XY array for storage purposes, where

$$X = r\theta = r\tan^{-1}\left(\frac{x - x_0}{f}\right), \tag{9.37}$$

$$Y = r(\phi + \pi/2) = r\left[\tan^{-1}\left(\frac{y - y_0}{f}\right) + \frac{\pi}{2}\right]. \tag{9.38}$$

By varying θ from 0 to 2π and ϕ from $-\pi/2$ to $\pi/2$, and letting r represent the radius of the spherical image in pixel units, the obtained rectangular image (X, Y) will show the spherical image in its entirety.

If the planar image is obtained when the regular camera optical axis was in direction (θ_0, ϕ_0), as shown in Fig. 9.3, we first assume the image is obtained at direction $(0, 0)$, project it to the spherical image, and then shift the spherical image in such a way that its center moves to (θ_0, ϕ_0). This simply implies replacing θ in (9.37) with $\theta + \theta_0$ and ϕ in (9.38) with $\phi + \phi_0$. Therefore,

$$X = r\left[\theta_0 + \tan^{-1}\left(\frac{x_0 - x}{f}\right)\right], \tag{9.39}$$

$$Y = r\left[\phi_0 + \frac{\pi}{2} + \tan^{-1}\left(\frac{y - y_0}{f}\right)\right]. \tag{9.40}$$

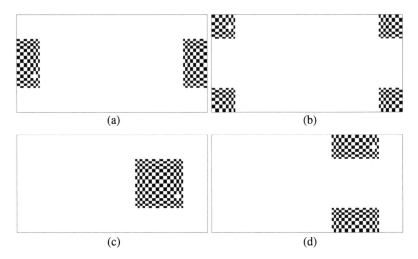

Fig. 9.4 (a)–(d) Spherical images corresponding to the planar image in Fig. 9.2a when viewing the planar image from directions $(\theta_0, \phi_0) = (0, 0)$, $(0, \pi/2)$, $(\pi/2, 0)$, and $(\pi/2, \pi/2)$, respectively

Conversely, knowing the coordinates (X, Y) of a point in the spherical image, the coordinates of the corresponding point in the planar image when viewed in direction (θ_0, ϕ_0) will be

$$x = x_0 + f \tan\left(\frac{X}{r} - \theta_0\right), \tag{9.41}$$

$$y = y_0 + f \tan\left(\frac{Y}{r} - \phi_0 - \frac{\pi}{2}\right). \tag{9.42}$$

The planar image of Fig. 9.2a when mapped to a spherical image of radius $r = 128$ pixels according to (9.41) and (9.42) with various values of (θ_0, ϕ_0) are shown in Fig. 9.4. Parameter f is set equal to r in these examples.

A rectangular image with XY coordinates and dimensions $2\pi r \times \pi r$ can be created by combining planar images taken at different orientations (θ_0, ϕ_0) of an environment. Having a spherical image created with coordinates (θ, ϕ), or equivalently (X, Y), we can project the spherical image to any plane and create a planar image. Such images, when projected to planes surrounding a viewer, will enable the viewer to see the environment from all directions.

Given a planar image that represents a particular view of a scene, its mapping to the spherical image is obtained by scanning the XY image and for each pixel (X, Y), locating the corresponding pixel (x, y) in the planar image from (9.41) and (9.42). If (x, y) falls inside the planar image, its intensity is read and saved at (X, Y). To avoid scanning XY areas where the planar image is not likely to produce a result, first, a bounding rectangle is found in the XY image where the planar image is mapped. This involves substituting the coordinates of the four corners of the image into (9.39) and (9.40) as (x, y) and finding the corresponding coordinates (X, Y) in the spherical image. This will create a rectangle inside which the planar image will be mapped. Then the bounding rectangle is scanned to determine the corresponding pixels in the planar image and mapped to the spherical image.

To find the projection of the spherical image to a planar image of a particular size and direction (θ_0, ϕ_0), the planar image is scanned and for each pixel (x, y) the corresponding pixel in the spherical image is located using (9.39) and (9.40). Then intensity at (X, Y) is read and saved at (x, y). Note that when $X > 2\pi r$, because $\theta \pm 2\pi = \theta$, we should let $X = X - 2\pi r$, and when $X < 0$, we should let $X = X + 2\pi r$. Similarly, we should let $\phi = -\pi - \phi$ when $\phi < -\pi/2$, $\phi = \pi - \phi$ when $\phi > \pi/2$, $Y = -Y$ when $Y < 0$, and $Y = 2Y - \pi r$ when $Y > \pi r$.

9.2 Adaptive Transformation Functions

9.2.1 Explicit

An explicit transformation function of variables x and y is defined by

$$F = f(x, y). \tag{9.43}$$

An explicit function produces a single value for each point in the xy domain. An explicit function of variables x and y can be considered a single-valued surface that spans over the xy domain. Therefore, given a set of 3-D points

$$\{(x_i, y_i, F_i) : i = 1, \ldots, n\}, \tag{9.44}$$

an explicit function interpolates the points by satisfying

$$F_i = f(x_i, y_i), \quad i = 1, \ldots, n, \tag{9.45}$$

and approximates the points by satisfying

$$F_i \approx f(x_i, y_i), \quad i = 1, \ldots, n. \tag{9.46}$$

If (x_i, y_i) are the coordinates of the ith control point in the reference image and F_i is the X or the Y coordinate of the corresponding control point in the sensed image, the surface interpolating/approximating points (9.44) will represent the X- or the Y-component of the transformation.

If corresponding points in the images are accurately located, an interpolating function should be used to ensure that the obtained transformation function maps corresponding points to each other. However, if the coordinates of corresponding points contain inaccuracies, approximating functions should be used to smooth the inaccuracies.

A chronological review of approximation and interpolation methods is provided by Meijering [68] and comparison of various approximation and interpolation methods is provided by Franke [25] and Renka and Brown [82]. Bibliography and categorization of explicit approximation and interpolation methods are provided by Franke and Schumaker [28, 93] and Grosse [40].

In the remainder of this chapter, transformation functions that are widely used or could potentially be used to register images with local geometric differences are reviewed.

9.2.1.1 Multiquadrics

Interpolation by radial basis functions is in general defined by

$$f(x, y) = \sum_{i=1}^{n} A_i R_i(x, y). \tag{9.47}$$

Parameters $\{A_i : i = 1, \ldots, n\}$ are determined by letting $f(x_i, y_i) = F_i$ for $i = 1, \ldots, n$ and solving the obtained system of linear equations. $R_i(x, y)$ is a radial function whose value is proportional to the distance between (x, y) and (x_i, y_i). A surface point is obtained from a weighted sum of these radial functions. Powell [75] has provided an excellent review of radial basis functions.

When

$$R_i(x, y) = \left[(x - x_i)^2 + (y - y_i)^2 + d^2 \right]^{\frac{1}{2}}, \tag{9.48}$$

$f(x, y)$ represents a multiquadric interpolation [42, 43]. As d^2 is increased, a smoother surface is obtained. In a comparative study carried out by Franke [25], multiquadrics were found to produce the best accuracy in the interpolation of randomly spaced data in the plane when compared with many other interpolation methods.

Multiquadric interpolation depends on parameter d^2. This parameter works like a stiffness parameter and as it is increased, a smoother surface is obtained. The best stiffness parameter for a data set depends on the spacing and organization of the data as well as on the data gradient. Carlson and Foley [10], Kansa and Carlson [47], and Franke and Nielson [29] have studied the role parameter d^2 plays on multiquadric interpolation accuracy.

An example of the use of multiquadric interpolation in image registration is given in Fig. 9.5. Images (a) and (b) represent multiview images of a partially snow covered rocky mountain. 165 corresponding points are identified in the images using the coarse-to-fine matching Algorithm F5 in Sect. 7.10. Corresponding points in corresponding regions that fall within 1.5 pixels of each other after transformation of a sensed region to align with its corresponding reference region by an affine transformation are chosen and used in the following experiments. About half (83 correspondences) are used to determine the transformation parameters and the remaining half (82 correspondences) are used to evaluate the registration accuracy. Images (a) and (b) will be referred to as the *Mountain image set*.

Resampling image (b) to align with image (a) by multiquadrics using the 83 correspondences (shown in red) produced the image shown in (c) when letting $d = 12$ pixels. Assigning values larger or smaller than 12 to d increases root-mean-squared error (RMSE) at the 82 remaining correspondences. Overlaying of images (a) and (c) is shown in (d). The reference image is shown in the red and blue bands and the resampled sensed image is shown in the green band of a color image. Pixels in the overlaid image where the images register well appear gray, while pixels in the overlaid image where the images are locally shifted with respect to each other appear purple or green. Although registration within the convex hull of the control points may be acceptable, registration outside the convex hull of the control points contain large errors and is not acceptable.

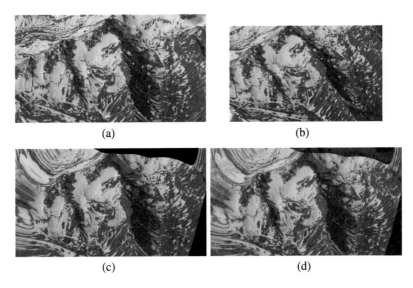

(a) (b)

(c) (d)

Fig. 9.5 (**a**) Reference and (**b**) sensed images used in image registration. The control points marked in *red* '+' are used to determine the registration parameters. The control points marked in *light blue* '+' are used to determine the registration accuracy. (**c**) Resampling of image (**b**) to align with image (**a**) using multiquadrics with $d = 12$ pixels. (**d**) Overlaying of the reference image (*purple*) and the resampled sensed image (*green*). Areas that are correctly registered appear in *gray*, while misregistered areas appear in *purple* or *green*. The reference image areas where there is no correspondence in the sensed image also appear in *purple* (the color of the reference image)

Multiquadrics use monotonically increasing basis functions. This implies that farther control points affect registration of a local neighborhood more than control points closer to the neighborhood. This is not a desirable property in image registration because we do not want a local error affect registration of distant points and would like to keep the influence of a control point local to its neighborhood. To obtain a locally sensitive transformation function, monotonically decreasing radial basis functions are needed.

If a transformation function is defined by monotonically decreasing radial basis functions, the farther a control point is from a neighborhood, the smaller will be its influence on that neighborhood. Radial basis functions that are monotonically decreasing are, therefore, more suitable for registration of images with local geometric differences. Moreover, monotonically decreasing basis functions keep the inaccuracy in a correspondence to a small neighborhood of the inaccuracy and will not spread the inaccuracy over the entire image domain.

Examples of radial basis functions with monotonically decreasing basis functions are Gaussians [37, 87],

$$R_i(x, y) = \exp\left\{-\frac{(x - x_i)^2 + (y - y_i)^2}{2\sigma_i^2}\right\} \tag{9.49}$$

and inverse multiquadrics [25, 43],

$$R_i(x, y) = \left[(x - x_i)^2 + (y - y_i)^2 + d^2\right]^{-\frac{1}{2}}. \tag{9.50}$$

Franke [25] has found through extensive experimentation that monotonically decreasing radial basis functions do not perform as well as monotonically increasing radial basis functions when data are accurate and are randomly spaced. Therefore, if the coordinates of corresponding points in the images are known to be accurate, multiquadric is preferred over inverse multiquadric in image registration. However, if some point coordinates are not accurate or the local geometric difference between some areas in the images is sharp, monotonically decreasing radial functions are preferred over monotonically increasing radial functions in image registration.

9.2.1.2 Surface Spline

Surface spline, also known as *thin-plate spline* (TPS), is perhaps the most widely used transformation function in nonrigid image registration. Harder and Desmarais [41] introduced it as an engineering mathematical tool and Duchon [20] and Meinguet [69] investigated its properties. It was used as a transformation function in the registration of remote sensing images by Goshtasby [33] and in the registration of medical images by Bookstein [6].

Given a set of points in the plane with associating values as described by (9.44), the surface spline interpolating the points is defined by

$$f(x, y) = A_1 + A_2 x + A_3 y + \sum_{i=1}^{n} B_i r_i^2 \ln r_i^2, \tag{9.51}$$

where $r_i^2 = (x - x_i)^2 + (y - y_i)^2 + d^2$. Surface spline is formulated in terms of an affine transformation and a weighted sum of radially symmetric (logarithmic) basis functions. In some literature, basis functions of form $r_i^2 \log r_i$ are used. Since $r_i^2 \log r_i^2 = 2r_i^2 \log r_i$, by renaming $2B_i$ by B_i we obtain the same equation. $r_i^2 \log r_i^2$ is preferred over $r_i^2 \log r_i$ as it avoids calculation of the square root of r_i^2.

Surface spline represents the equation of a plate of infinite extent deforming under point loads at $\{(x_i, y_i) : i = 1, \ldots, n\}$. The plate deflects under the imposition of the loads to take values $\{F_i : i = 1, \ldots, n\}$. Parameter d^2 acts like a stiffness parameter. As d^2 is increased, a smoother surface is obtained. When spacing between the points varies greatly in the image domain, a stiffer surface increases fluctuations in the interpolating surface. Franke [26] used a tension parameter as a means to keep fluctuations in interpolation under control.

Equation (9.51) contains $n + 3$ parameters. By substituting the coordinates of n points as described by (9.44) into (9.51), n equations are obtained. Three more

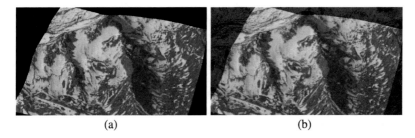

(a)   (b)

Fig. 9.6 Registration of the Mountain image set using surface spline as the transformation function. (**a**) Resampled sensed image. (**b**) Overlaying of the reference and resampled sensed images

equations are obtained from the following constraints:

$$\sum_{i=1}^{n} B_i = 0, \tag{9.52}$$

$$\sum_{i=1}^{n} x_i B_i = 0, \tag{9.53}$$

$$\sum_{i=1}^{n} y_i B_i = 0. \tag{9.54}$$

Constraint (9.52) ensures that the sum of the loads applied to the plate is 0 so that the plate will not move up or down. Constraints (9.53) and (9.54) ensure that moments with respect to the x- and y-axes are zero, so the surface will not rotate under the imposition of the loads.

Using surface spline transformation to register the Mountain image set in Fig. 9.5, the results shown in Fig. 9.6 are obtained when letting the stiffness parameter $d = 0$. Comparing these results with those obtained by multiquadric interpolation, we see that while within the convex hull of the control points similar results are obtained, outside the convex of the control points surface spline produces significantly better results than multiquadric. By increasing the stiffness parameter d^2, registration error increases.

When the control point correspondences contain errors and the density of control points in the reference image is not uniform, improved registration accuracy can be achieved by allowing each component of the transformation to approximate rather than interpolate the points. Rohr et al. [85] added a smoothing term to the interpolating spline while letting $d^2 = 0$ to obtain a surface that contained smaller fluctuations. As the smoothness term is increased, the obtained surface becomes smoother and fluctuations become smaller, but the surface moves away from some of the control points. The process, therefore, requires interaction by the user to specify a smoothness parameter that is large enough to reduce noise among control-point correspondences but not so smooth as to increase distances between the surface and the points it is approximating.

Monotonically increasing radial basis functions such as multiquadrics and surface splines that interpolate points produce a smooth mapping from one image to another. If the correspondences are accurate, surfaces representing the components of the transformation represent smoothly varying geometric differences between the images. However, when a function is defined in terms of monotonically increasing basis functions, a positional error in a pair of corresponding points in the images will influence the registration accuracy everywhere in the image domain.

Since radial basis functions are symmetric, when spacing between the control points varies greatly across the image domain, the transformation may produce large errors away from the control points. To increase registration accuracy, the density of the control points may be increased, but that will not only slow down the process, it will make the process unstable as it will require the solution of large systems of equations to find the parameters of the transformation.

Compactly supported radial basis functions, examined next, use local basis functions to keep errors and deformations local.

9.2.1.3 Compactly Supported Radial Basis Functions

Monotonically decreasing radial basis functions can be defined with local support in such a way that the data value at (x, y) is determined from data at a small number of points near (x, y). Interpolation by compactly supported radial basis functions is defined by

$$f(x, y) = \sum_{i=1}^{n} A_i R_i(x, y) = \sum_{i=1}^{n} A_i W(r_i),\tag{9.55}$$

where $r_i = \sqrt{(x - x_i)^2 + (y - y_i)^2}$. By replacing r_i with $\sqrt{(x - x_i)^2 + (y - y_i)^2}$, a function in (x, y) is obtained, which has been denoted by $R_i(x, y)$ in the above formula. $W(r_i)$ can take different forms. Wendland [102] defined it by

$$W(r_i) = \begin{cases} (a - r_i)^2, & 0 \le r_i \le a, \\ 0, & r_i > a, \end{cases}\tag{9.56}$$

while Buhmann [9] defined it by

$$W(r_i) = \begin{cases} \frac{112}{45}(a - r_i)^{\frac{9}{2}} + \frac{16}{3}(a - r_i)^{\frac{7}{2}} - 7(a - r_i)^4 - \frac{14}{15}(a - r_i)^2 + \frac{1}{9}, \\ \qquad 0 \le r_i \le a, \\ 0, \quad r_i > a. \end{cases}\tag{9.57}$$

In both cases, $W(r_i)$ not only vanishes at distance a from (x_i, y_i), but its gradient vanishes also. Therefore, the basis functions smoothly vanish at distance a from their centers and a weighted sum of them will create a surface that will be smooth everywhere in the image domain.

Parameter a should be large enough so that within each region of radius a, at least a few control points appear in the reference image. The unknown parameters $\{A_i : i = 1, \ldots, n\}$ are determined by solving the following system of linear equations:

$$F_j = \sum_{i=1}^{n} A_i R_i(x_j, y_j), \quad j = 1, \ldots, n.\tag{9.58}$$

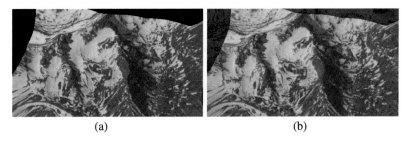

(a)	(b)

Fig. 9.7 Registration of the Mountain image set using Wendland's compactly supported radial basis functions with parameter $a = 5000$ pixels. (**a**) Resampled sensed image. (**b**) Overlaying of the reference and resampled sensed images

Note that although the basis functions have local support, a global system of equations has to be solved to find parameters $\{A_i : i = 1, \ldots, n\}$.

Using Wendland's compactly supported radial functions as the transformation to register the Mountain image set in Fig. 9.5, acceptable results are not obtained when a is small enough to consider the transformation local. As parameter a is increased, registration accuracy improves. Registration of the images when $a = 5000$ pixels is shown in Fig. 9.7. Results are acceptable within the convex hull of the control points, but they are inferior to those obtained by surface spline.

To overcome some of the weaknesses of compactly supported radial basis functions of a fixed support radius a, use of a hierarchy of compactly supported radial basis functions of varying support radii has been proposed [72]. Starting from basis functions of a large radius, basis functions of smaller radii are added to the approximation until residual errors in approximation fall within a desired range. A method proposed by Floater and Iske [23] uses a hierarchy of basis functions. The radii of basis functions at different levels are estimated by successive triangulation of the points and determination of the triangle sizes at each hierarchy. Wider basis functions are used to capture global structure in data while narrower basis functions are used to capture local details in data.

To avoid solving a system of equations, Maude [66] used weight functions with local support to formulate an approximation method to irregularly spaced data. Maude's weight functions are defined by:

$$W_i(x, y) = W(R_i) = \begin{cases} 1 - 3R_i^2 + 2R_i^3, & 0 \le R_i \le 1, \\ 0, & R_i > 1, \end{cases} \tag{9.59}$$

where $R_i = \sqrt{(x - x_i)^2 + (y - y_i)^2}/R_k$ and R_k is the distance of (x, y) to the kth point closest to it. Note that not only $W(R_i)$ vanishes at distance R_k to point (x, y), its first derivative vanishes there also. Then

$$f(x, y) = \frac{\sum_{i=1}^{k} F_i W_i(x, y)}{\sum_{i=1}^{k} W_i(x, y)} \tag{9.60}$$

is used as the approximating functional value at (x, y).

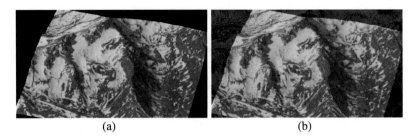

(a)   (b)

Fig. 9.8 Registration results using Maude's local interpolation formula with neighborhood size $k = 10$ points. (**a**) Resampling of sensed image to overlay the reference image. (**b**) Overlaying of the reference and resampled sensed images

Therefore, to estimate functional value at (x, y), the k points closest to (x, y) are identified. Let's suppose data values at the points are: $\{F_i : i = 1, \ldots, k\}$. Then a weighted sum of the values is calculated and used as the value at (x, y). The weights vanish at the kth point and the sum of the weights everywhere in a region of radius R_k centered at (x, y) is 1.

Note that the neighborhood size automatically adjusts to the local density of points. In areas where a high density of points is available, parameter R_k will be small, while in sparse areas, R_k will be large. The method does not require the solution of a system of equations, but it does require determination of the k control points that are closest to pixel (x, y) in the reference image.

Maude's weighted mean approximation uses rational weights, which is known to produce flat spots in the obtained surface at the control points. We will see later in this chapter how such errors can be reduced through parametric reformulation of the problem. Another way to remedy the flat-spot effect is to use data values as well as data gradients at the points. This can be achieved by replacing F_i in (9.60) with a linear function that evaluates to F_i at (x_i, y_i) and fits the k points closest to (x, y) by the least-squares method. Denoting such a linear function by $L_i(x, y)$, (9.60) becomes

$$f(x, y) = \frac{\sum_{i=1}^{k} L_i(x, y) W_i(x, y)}{\sum_{i=1}^{k} W_i(x, y)}. \tag{9.61}$$

This represents a local weighted linear approximation. Registering the mountain images using (9.61) as the components of the transformation with $k = 10$, the result shown in Fig. 9.8 is obtained. Except for areas with sharp geometric differences, the images are registered relatively well.

A local weighted mean method that interpolates irregularly spaced data is described by McLain [67]. In this method, first, the given points are triangulated. Then, the patch over each triangle is computed from the weighted sum of data at the vertices of the triangle. If data at the three vertices of a triangle are F_1, F_2, and F_3, the functional value at (x, y) inside the triangle is obtained from

$$f(x, y) = W_1(x, y) F_1 + W_2(x, y) F_2 + W_3(x, y) F_3, \tag{9.62}$$

Fig. 9.9 McLain [67]
interpolation over a triangle

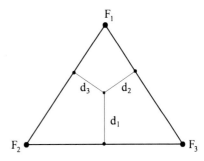

where W_1, W_2, and W_3 are weights associated with data at the vertices of the triangle
and are determined by first calculating the distance of point (x, y) to the three sides
of the triangle (Fig. 9.9):

$$d_i(x, y) = l_i x + m_i y + n_i, \quad \text{for } i = 1, 2, 3. \tag{9.63}$$

Coefficients l_i, m_i, and n_i are determined only once for each triangle side and are
normalized so that $d_i = 1$ when $(x, y) = (x_i, y_i)$. Then the weight associated with
a vertex is set proportional to the distance of (x, y) to the triangle side opposing it.
That is

$$W_i(x, y) = \frac{d_i^2}{d_1(x, y)^2 + d_2(x, y)^2 + d_3(x, y)^2}, \quad \text{for } i = 1, 2, 3. \tag{9.64}$$

Square weights are used to ensure continuous and smooth transition from one triangle to the next. If second derivative continuity is required across triangle edges, the
cubic power of distances is needed to define the weights [67].

Radial basis functions with local support are preferred over radial basis functions with global support when registering images with local geometric differences.
Remote sensing images of a 3-D scene captured from different views or serial images of a patient captured by a medical scanner have local geometric differences.
Compactly supported radial basis functions, by modeling the geometric difference
between corresponding local neighborhoods in images, use a small number of points
within corresponding areas to transform the geometry of the sensed image locally to
resemble that of the reference image. In this manner, global registration is achieved
via local registration.

A comparison between globally defined radial basis functions and compactly
supported radial basis functions in medical image registration has been provided by
Fornefett et al. [24]. Improved registration accuracy has been reported with compactly supported radial basis functions over globally defined radial basis functions
in the registration of serial brain images.

Although not a radial function, tensor-product functions that have local support,
such as B-splines, can be used in approximation/interpolation also. Lee et al. [57]
used multi-level B-splines with varying local support to interpolate data in the plane.
The control points of a B-spline surface are determined by the least-squares method
in such a way that the surface would interpolate given points. By using B-spline basis functions with different support levels, different levels of detail are reproduced in

the surface. By adding together B-spline basis functions at different support levels, a multi-level B-spline interpolation to scattered data is obtained.

For very large and irregularly spaced data, Bozzini et al. [7] laid a regular grid over the approximation domain and estimated the data at each grid point from the noisy and irregularly spaced data around it. Then, a B-spline surface was fitted to data at the regular grid. To produce B-splines that interpolate scattered data, Greiner et al. [39] first found parameter coordinates at the points to guarantee existence of an interpolating B-spline. Then, the control vertices of the interpolating B-spline surface were determined by an optimization process formulated in terms of surface fairness.

B-splines are a family of grid functions that are defined over regular grids of nodes (parameter coordinates). The process of generating grid functions that approximate scattered data is known as *gridding*. In spite of their limitations, in certain engineering applications, grid functions are preferred over other functions because of their ability to easily modify and visualize an approximation. Arge et al. [3] developed a three-step process for approximating scattered data by grid functions. The steps are: (1) Regularization: Identifying a subset of grid nodes in regions where density of data is high. (2) Approximation: Finding values at the grid nodes using approximation to nearby data. (3) Extrapolation: Extending the data values defined on the grid subset to the entire grid.

9.2.1.4 Moving Least-Squares

Suppose data points $\{\mathbf{p}_i = (x_i, y_i) : i = 1, \ldots, n\}$ with associating data values $\{F_i : i = 1, \ldots, n\}$ are given. A moving least-squares approximation is a function $f(\mathbf{p})$ that minimizes [52]:

$$\sum_{i=1}^{n} [f(\mathbf{p}_i) - F_i]^2 W_i(\mathbf{p}) \tag{9.65}$$

at each $\mathbf{p} = (x, y)$. $W_i(\mathbf{p})$ is a non-negative monotonically decreasing radial function centered at $\mathbf{p}_i$. This weight function ensures that a data point closer to $\mathbf{p}$ will influence the estimated value more than a data point that is farther away. If function f is a polynomial in x and y, the best polynomial for point (x, y) is determined by the weighted least squares in such a way as to minimize (9.65).

Note that relation (9.65) is specific to point $\mathbf{p}$. Therefore, function f determined according to (9.65) will be specific to point $\mathbf{p}$ and vary from point to point. Since the parameters of a new function have to be determined for each point in the approximation domain, f cannot be a very complex function. Typically, it is a polynomial of degree 1 or 2.

For interpolating moving least squares, it is required that the weight functions assume value ∞ at $\mathbf{p} = \mathbf{p}_i$. Some of the suggested weight functions are [53]:

$$W_i(\mathbf{p}) = \frac{1}{\|\mathbf{p} - \mathbf{p}_i\|^2}, \tag{9.66}$$

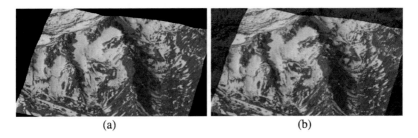

(a)   (b)

Fig. 9.10 Registration with moving least-squares using linear polynomials and weight functions of (9.66). (**a**) Resampling of the sensed image to overlay the reference image. (**b**) Overlaying of the reference and the resampled sensed images

$$W_i(\mathbf{p}) = \frac{1}{\|\mathbf{p} - \mathbf{p}_i\|^4}, \tag{9.67}$$

$$W_i(\mathbf{p}) = \frac{\alpha \exp(-\beta \|\mathbf{p} - \mathbf{p}_i\|^2)}{\|\mathbf{p} - \mathbf{p}_i\|^k}, \quad \alpha, \beta, k > 0. \tag{9.68}$$

To make the computations local, compactly supported weight functions are used. Examples are [53]:

$$W_i(\mathbf{p}) = \begin{cases} a\|\mathbf{p} - \mathbf{p}_i\|^{-k}(1 - \|\mathbf{p} - \mathbf{p}_i\|/d)^2, & \text{for } \|\mathbf{p} - \mathbf{p}_i\| \le d, \\ 0, & \text{for } \|\mathbf{p} - \mathbf{p}_i\| > d, \end{cases} \tag{9.69}$$

$$W_i(\mathbf{p}) = \begin{cases} a\|\mathbf{p} - \mathbf{p}_i\|^{-k}\cos(\pi\|\mathbf{p} - \mathbf{p}_i\|/2d), & \text{for } \|\mathbf{p} - \mathbf{p}_i\| \le d, \\ 0 & \text{for } \|\mathbf{p} - \mathbf{p}_i\| > d. \end{cases} \tag{9.70}$$

When f represents a polynomial of degree 1, the surface obtained by moving least-squares will be continuous and smooth everywhere in the approximation domain [51]. Levin [58] has found that moving least-squares are not only suitable for interpolation but are also useful in smoothing and derivatives estimation. For further insights into moving least-squares and its variations, see the excellent review by Belytschko et al. [4].

An example of image registration by moving least squares using the Mountain image set, linear polynomials, and weight functions of (9.66) is given in Fig. 9.10. The transformation is well-behaved outside the convex hull of the control points, and registration is acceptable at and near the control points; however, registration error is relatively large away from the control points.

9.2.1.5 Piecewise Polynomials

If control points in the reference image are triangulated [56, 91], by knowing the correspondence between the control points in the sensed and reference images, corresponding triangles will be known in the sensed image. This makes it possible to determine a transformation function for corresponding triangles and map triangles in the sensed image one by one to the corresponding triangles in the reference image.

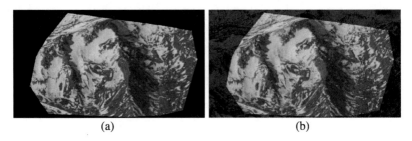

(a) (b)

Fig. 9.11 Registration of the Mountain image set using the piecewise linear transformation. (a) Resampling of the sensed image to the space of the reference image. (b) Overlaying of the reference and the resampled sensed images

If a linear function is used to do the mapping, the transformation becomes piecewise linear.

If coordinates of the vertices of the ith triangle in the reference image are (x_{i1}, y_{i1}), (x_{i2}, y_{i2}), and (x_{i3}, y_{i3}) and coordinates of the corresponding vertices in the sensed image are (X_{i1}, Y_{i1}), (X_{i2}, Y_{i2}), and (X_{i3}, Y_{i3}), the ith triangular regions in the images can be related by an affine transformation as described by (9.19) and (9.20). The six parameters of the transformation, $a-f$, can be determined by substituting the coordinates of three corresponding triangle vertices into (9.19) and (9.20) and solving the obtained system of linear equations.

Finding an affine transformation for each corresponding triangle produces a composite of local affine transformations or an overall piecewise linear transformation. An example of image registration by piecewise linear interpolation is depicted in Fig. 9.11. Registration is shown within the convex hull of the control points in the reference image. Although affine transformations corresponding to the boundary triangles can be extended to cover image regions outside the convex hull of the control points, registration errors outside the convex hull of the points could be large and so is not recommended. Piecewise linear transformation has been used in image registration before [31]. The method was later extended to piecewise cubic [32] to provide a smooth as well as continuous mapping within the convex hull of the control points.

Within the convex hull of the control points, registration by piecewise linear is comparable to surface spline or moving least-squares. Although piecewise linear transformation is continuous within the convex hull of the points, it is not smooth across the triangle edges. The affine transformations obtained over triangles sharing an edge may have different gradients, producing an overall transformation that is continuous but not smooth.

To ensure that a transformation is smooth as well as continuous across a triangle edge, a polynomial of degree two or higher is required to represent the component of a transformation over each triangle. The parameters of the polynomial are determined in such a way that adjacent triangular patches join smoothly and produce the same gradient at the two sides of an edge, and all patches sharing a vertex produce the same gradient at the vertex. Various triangular patches that provide this property have been proposed [2, 12, 14–17, 48, 50, 54, 63, 73, 76, 89, 97].

A factor that affects the registration accuracy is the choice of triangulation. As a general rule, elongated triangles should be avoided. Algorithms that maximize the minimum angle in triangles is know as Delaunay triangulation [38, 54]. A better approximation accuracy is achieved if triangulation is obtained in 3-D using the data values as well as the data points. Various data-dependent triangulation algorithms have been proposed [5, 8, 21, 22, 83, 92].

If the points are triangulated in 3-D, a subdivision method may be used to create a smooth approximation or interpolation to the triangle mesh. A subdivision method typically subdivides each triangle into four smaller triangles with a limiting smooth surface that approximates or interpolates the mesh vertices [64, 65, 74, 88, 98].

Loop [60] proposed a recursive subdivision algorithm that approximates a smooth surface to a triangle mesh, while Dyn et al. [22] proposed a recursive algorithm that generates a smooth surface interpolating the vertices of a triangle mesh. Doo [18] and Doo and Sabin [19] described a subdivision scheme that can approximate a mesh with triangular, quadrilateral, and, in general, n-sided faces. Subdivision surfaces contain B-spline, Bézier, and non-uniform B-spline (NURBS) as special cases [90]. Therefore, transformation functions can be created with each component representing a piecewise surface composed of B-spline, Bézier, or NURBS patches.

In the following, two of the popular subdivision algorithms that work with triangle meshes are described. The subdivision scheme developed by Loop [44, 60] generates an approximating surface, while the subdivision scheme developed by Dyn et al. [22] creates an interpolating surface. The Loop subdivision scheme is depicted in Fig. 9.12. Given a triangle mesh, at each iteration of the algorithm a triangle is replaced with four smaller triangles by (1) inserting a new vertex near the midpoint of each edge, (2) refining the old vertex positions, and (3) replacing each old triangle with four new triangles obtained by connecting the new and refined triangle vertices.

Assuming triangle vertices at iteration r surrounding vertex $\mathbf{v}^r$ are $\mathbf{v}_1^r, \mathbf{v}_2^r, \ldots, \mathbf{v}_k^r$ (Fig. 9.12d), new vertex $\mathbf{v}_i^{r+1}$ is inserted midway between $\mathbf{v}^r$ and $\mathbf{v}_i^r$ for $i = 1, \ldots, k$. The location of a newly inserted vertex is computed from

$$\mathbf{v}_i^{r+1} = \frac{3\mathbf{v}^r + 3\mathbf{v}_i^r + \mathbf{v}_{i-1}^r + \mathbf{v}_{i+1}^r}{8}, \quad i = 1, \ldots, k. \tag{9.71}$$

Then, vertex $\mathbf{v}^r$ is replaced with

$$\mathbf{v}^{r+1} = (1 - k\beta)\mathbf{v}^r + \beta\left(\mathbf{v}_1^2 + \cdots + \mathbf{v}_k^r\right), \tag{9.72}$$

where according to Loop [60]

$$\beta = \frac{1}{k}\left(\frac{5}{8} - \left(\frac{3}{8} + \frac{1}{4}\cos(2\pi/k)\right)^2\right). \tag{9.73}$$

A different set of subdivision rules are used along the boundary of the mesh to prevent the approximating open surface from shrinking towards its center after a number of iterations. Only points along the boundary are used in the rules as de-

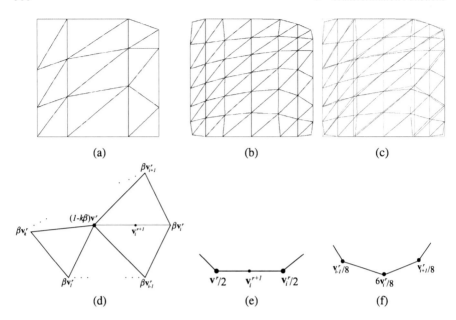

Fig. 9.12 (**a**) A triangle mesh. (**b**) The mesh after one iteration of Loop subdivision. (**c**) Overlaying of (**a**) and (**b**). (**d**) Loop vertex insertion and refinement rules for interior edges and vertices. (**e**) Loop vertex insertion for boundary edges and (**f**) vertex refinement for boundary vertices

picted in Figs. 9.12e, f. The vertex inserted between $\mathbf{v}^r$ and $\mathbf{v}_i^r$ along the boundary is computed from

$$\mathbf{v}_i^{r+1} = \frac{\mathbf{v}^r + \mathbf{v}_i^r}{2} \tag{9.74}$$

and vertex $\mathbf{v}_i^r$, which is between $\mathbf{v}_{i-1}^r$ and $\mathbf{v}_{i+1}^r$ along the boundary, is replaced with

$$\mathbf{v}_i^{r+1} = \frac{\mathbf{v}_{i-1}^r + 6\mathbf{v}_i^r + \mathbf{v}_{i+1}^r}{8}. \tag{9.75}$$

At the limit, the surface generated by Loop subdivision is C^1 continuous everywhere [95, 103]. That is, not only is the created surface continuous over the approximation domain, its first derivative is also continuous everywhere. For image registration purposes, the insertion and refinement steps should be repeated until the surface at iteration $r + 1$ is sufficiently close to that obtained at iteration r. Sufficiently close is when the maximum refinement among all vertices in an iteration is less than half a pixel and all newly inserted vertices are less than half a pixel away from their edge midpoints. This ensures that subdivision surfaces at two consecutive iterations produce the same resampled image when using the nearest-neighbor resampling rule.

Registration of the Mountain data set using the Loop subdivision surface is shown in Fig. 9.13. Although Loop subdivision surface produces a smoother resampled image due to gradient continuity of the transformation function within the

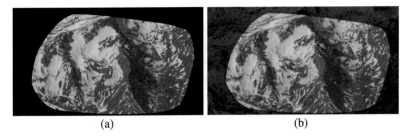

Fig. 9.13 Registration of the Mountain image set using Loop subdivision surfaces as the components of the transformation. (**a**) Resampling of the sensed image to the space of the reference image. (**b**) Overlaying of the reference and the resampled sensed images

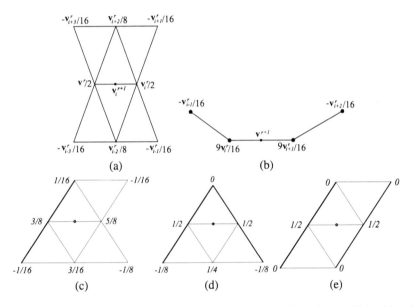

Fig. 9.14 Butterfly subdivision rules for (**a**) interior edges, (**b**) boundary edges, and (**c**)–(**e**) interior edges that touch the boundary or a crease

convex hull of the control points when compared with piecewise linear, there isn't a significant difference between the registration accuracy of the two methods.

The interpolative subdivision surface described by Dyn et al. [22] uses a neighborhood that has the shape of a butterfly as shown in Fig. 9.14a. Subdivision requires vertex insertion only. Existing vertices are not repositioned after each iteration because the original and newly inserted vertices are on the limiting surface. Vertex $\mathbf{v}_i^{r+1}$, which is newly inserted between vertices $\mathbf{v}^r$ and $\mathbf{v}_i^r$ when surrounded by the vertices shown in Fig. 9.14a, is computed from

$$\mathbf{v}_i^{r+1} = \frac{\mathbf{v}^r + \mathbf{v}_i^r}{2} + \frac{\mathbf{v}_{i-2}^r + \mathbf{v}_{i+2}^r}{8} - \frac{\mathbf{v}_{i-3}^r + \mathbf{v}_{i-1}^r + \mathbf{v}_{i+1}^r + \mathbf{v}_{i+3}^r}{16}. \tag{9.76}$$

Subdivision rules along the boundary are slightly different. Vertex $\mathbf{v}^{r+1}$, which is inserted between vertices $\mathbf{v}_i^r$ and $\mathbf{v}_{i+1}^r$ along the boundary, is computed from

$$\mathbf{v}^{r+1} = \frac{-\mathbf{v}_{i-1}^r + 9\mathbf{v}_i^r + 9\mathbf{v}_{i+1}^r - \mathbf{v}_{i+2}^r}{16}. \tag{9.77}$$

Vertex insertion at interior edges that touch the boundary or a crease is obtained using the rules shown in Figs. 9.14c–e.

The limiting surface produced by the butterfly subdivision scheme of Dyn et al. [22] is C^1-continuous everywhere when a regular mesh is provided. The surface, however, is not smooth at mesh vertices of valance $k = 3$ or $k > 7$ when an irregular mesh is given [103]. Zorin [103, 104] proposed a modified butterfly subdivision scheme that at the limit interpolates a smooth surface to any triangle mesh. Qu and Agarwal [77] described a 10-point interpolatory subdivision scheme over an arbitrary triangle mesh that has a limiting surface that is smooth everywhere, including at the mesh vertices.

9.2.2 Parametric

Parametric functions are of form

$$\mathbf{P}(u, v) = \mathbf{f}(u, v). \tag{9.78}$$

$\mathbf{P}(u, v)$ is the surface point at (u, v), defined as a function of parameters u and v. $\mathbf{f}(u, v)$ is a function with three independent components, each a function of (u, v); therefore,

$$x(u, v) = f_x(u, v), \tag{9.79}$$

$$y(u, v) = f_y(u, v), \tag{9.80}$$

$$F(u, v) = f_F(u, v). \tag{9.81}$$

Since the three components of a parametric surface are independent of each other, each can be determined separately.

Given $\{(x_i, y_i, F_i) : i = 1, \ldots, n\}$, to determine the surface value at (x, y), first, the corresponding (u, v) coordinates are determined from (9.79) and (9.80). Knowing (u, v), surface value F is then calculated. The nonlinear nature of the equations makes determination of exact surface values very time consuming. For image registration purposes, however, we will see that approximations to the surface values can be determined efficiently with sufficient accuracy.

Parametric surfaces used in geometric modeling require a regular grid of control points. The control points available in image registration are, however, irregularly spaced. Below, parametric surfaces suitable for interpolation/approximation to scattered data are explored.

Table 9.1 Coordinates of 9 uniformly spaced points in the xy domain with associating data values

i	1	2	3	4	5	6	7	8	9
x_i	0	1	2	0	1	2	0	1	2
y_i	0	0	0	1	1	1	2	2	2
F_i	0	1	2	0	1	2	0	1	2

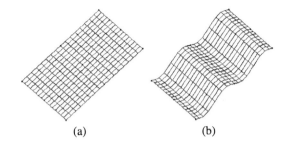

Fig. 9.15 Interpolation of the data in Table 9.1 by Shepard's method. (**a**) The ideal surface and (**b**) the surface obtained by Shepard's method

(a)   (b)

9.2.2.1 Parametric Shepard Interpolation

One of the earliest methods for the interpolation of scattered data is proposed by Shepard [96]. This is a weighted mean method with rational weights. Given data sites $\{(x_i, y_i) : i = 1, \ldots, n\}$ with associating data values $\{F_i : i = 1, \ldots, n\}$, Shepard's interpolation is defined by

$$f(x, y) = \sum_{i=1}^{n} W_i(x, y) F_i, \qquad (9.82)$$

where

$$W_i(x, y) = \frac{R_i(x, y)}{\sum_{j=1}^{n} R_j(x, y)}, \qquad (9.83)$$

and

$$R_i(x, y) = \left\{ (x - x_i)^2 + (y - y_i)^2 \right\}^{-\frac{1}{2}}. \qquad (9.84)$$

The surface interpolates the points, yet it does not require the solution of a system of equations. The interpolating surface is obtained immediately by substituting the coordinates of the data sites and the data values into (9.82).

Shepard's method is known to produce flat spots in the surface at and near the data sites. Consider the data in Table 9.1, showing coordinates of 3-D points in a plane as depicted in Fig. 9.15a. Shepard's method, however, produces the surface depicted in Fig. 9.15b.

The reason for the flat spots is the nonlinear relation between xy and f. The flat spots show increased surface point density near the data sites. This weakness can be overcome by subjecting x and y to the same nonlinear transformation that f is subjected to. By letting $(u_i, v_i) \propto (x_i, y_i)$ and defining the components of the parametric Shepard similarly by formula (9.82), we obtain

$$x(u, v) = \sum_{i=1}^{n} W_i(u, v) x_i, \tag{9.85}$$

$$y(u, v) = \sum_{i=1}^{n} W_i(u, v) y_i, \tag{9.86}$$

$$f(u, v) = \sum_{i=1}^{n} W_i(u, v) F_i, \tag{9.87}$$

where

$$W_i(u, v) = \frac{R_i(u, v)}{\sum_{j=1}^{n} R_j(u, v)}, \tag{9.88}$$

$$R_i(u, v) = \left\{ (u - u_i)^2 + (v - v_i)^2 \right\}^{-\frac{1}{2}}, \tag{9.89}$$

$u_i = x_i/(n_c - 1)$, and $v_i = y_i/(n_r - 1)$. n_c and n_r are, respectively, the number of columns and number of rows in the reference image. As x varies between 0 and $n_c - 1$, u will vary between 0 and 1, and as y varies between 0 and $n_r - 1$, v will vary between 0 and 1.

Parametric Shepard, however, requires the solution of two nonlinear equations to find (u, v) for a given (x, y). Then, it uses the obtained (u, v) to find the surface value F. For image registration purposes though, this is not necessary since exact surface coordinates are not required. Surface coordinates that are within half a pixel of the actual coordinates are sufficient to resample the sensed image to align with the reference image when using nearest neighbor resampling.

The following algorithm determines a component of a transformation function by the parametric Shepard method.

Algorithm PSI (Parametric Shepard Interpolation) Given points $\{(x_i, y_i, F_i) : i = 1, \ldots, n\}$, calculate image $F[x, y]$, showing the surface interpolating the points when quantized at discrete pixel coordinates in the reference image.

1. Let $u_i = x_i/(n_c - 1)$ and $v_i = y_i/(n_r - 1)$. This will ensure parameters in the image domain vary between 0 and 1.
2. Initially, let increments in u and v be $\Delta u = 0.5$ and $\Delta v = 0.5$.
3. For $u = 0$ to 1 with increment Δu and for $v = 0$ to 1 with increment Δv, repeat the following.

   - If $[x(u, v) + x(u + \Delta u, v)]/2! \in [x(u + \Delta u/2, v) \pm 0.5]$ or $[y(u, v) + y(u + \Delta u, v)]/2! \in [y(u + \Delta u/2, v) \pm 0.5]$ or $[F(u, v) + F(u + \Delta u, v)]/2! \in [F(u + \Delta u/2, v) \pm 0.5]$ or
     $[x(u, v) + x(u, v + \Delta v)]/2! \in [x(u, v + \Delta v/2) \pm 0.5]$ or $[y(u, v) + y(u, v + \Delta v)]/2! \in [y(u, v + \Delta v/2) \pm 0.5]$ or $[F(u, v) + F(u, v + \Delta v)] \neq [F(u, v + \Delta v/2) \pm 0.5]$ or
     $[x(u, v) + x(u + \Delta u, v) + x(u, v + \Delta v) + x(u + \Delta u, v + \Delta v)]/4! \in [x(u + \Delta u/2, v + \Delta v/2) \pm 0.5]$ or $[y(u, v) + y(u + \delta u, v) + y(u, v + \Delta v) + y(u + \Delta u, v + \Delta v)]/4! \in [y(u + \Delta u/2, v + \Delta v/2) \pm 0.5]$ or

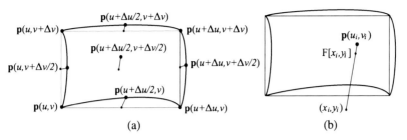

Fig. 9.16 (a) The subdivision scheme at Step 3. (b) Ensuring the approximating surface passes within half a pixel of the given points in Step 5

$[F(u, v) + F(u + \delta u, v) + x(u, v + \Delta v) + F(u + \Delta u, v + \Delta v)]/4! \in [F(u + \Delta u/2, v + \Delta v/2) \pm 0.5]$, then reduce Δu and Δv by a factor of 2 and go to Step 3.

4. If $F_i! \in [F[x_i, y_i] \pm 0.5]$ for any $i = 1, \ldots, n$, reduce Δu and Δv by a factor of 2 and repeat this step.
5. For $u = 0$ to 1 with increment Δu and for $v = 0$ to 1 with increment Δv, repeat the following.

   • Calculate $[x(u, v), y(u, v), F(u, v)], [x(u + \Delta u, v), y(u + \Delta u, v), F(u + \Delta u, v)], [x(u + \Delta u, v + \Delta v), y(u + \Delta u, v + \Delta v), F(u + \Delta u, v + \Delta v)], [x(u, v + \Delta v), y(u, v + \Delta v), F(u, v + \Delta v)]$. This defines a local patch. Estimate values within the patch using bilinear interpolation of values at its four corners.

By notation "$a! \in [b \pm 0.5]$," it is implied "if $a < b - 0.5$ or $a > b + 0.5$." In Step 3, for each patch defined within parameters (u, v) to $(u + \Delta u, v + \Delta v)$, the distances of the midpoints of the four sides and at the center of the patch to its bilinear approximation (Fig. 9.16a) are determined. Subdivision is continued until all distances become smaller than half a pixel.

Step 4 ensures that the obtained approximation is within half a pixel of the points it is supposed to interpolate. If it is not, subdivision is continued until the approximating surface falls within half a pixel of the given points. Note that in Step 3 the patches are not generated. Values at only edge midpoints and patch centers are calculated. In most situations, this finds the required increment in u and v that will obtain the required surface. In some rare cases, the process may not produce a surface sufficiently close to the given points. In such cases, Step 4 ensures that the obtained surface does, in fact, pass within half a pixel of the points it is supposed to interpolate (Fig. 9.16b).

The interpolating parametric Shepard defined in this manner may produce sharp edges and corners at the interpolating points. This problem can be alleviated by replacing the radial function defined in (9.89) by

$$R_i(u, v) = \left\{(u - u_i)^2 + (v - v_i)^2 + d^2\right\}^{-\frac{1}{2}}. \tag{9.90}$$

d^2 is a small positive number. The larger its value, the smoother the obtained surface will be, but also the farther the surface will fall from some of the points. Note that this is an inverse multiquadric weight. Therefore, Shepard weights can be considered rational inverse multiquadric weights. When $d^2 = 0$, the surface will interpolate the points and when $d^2 > 0$, the surface will approximate the points. W_i is a rational function in u and v when parametric Shepard is used with $u_i = x_i/(n_c - 1)$ and $v_i = y_i/(n_r - 1)$ for $i = 1, \ldots, n$.

Letting

$$R_i(u, v) = \exp\left\{ -\frac{(u - u_i)^2 + (v - v_i)^2}{2(s\sigma_i)^2} \right\}, \tag{9.91}$$

the obtained surface will be a rational Gaussian (RaG) surface [37] that approximates the points. The standard deviation of the Gaussian at the ith point, σ_i, shows spacing between the points surrounding it. It can be taken equal to the distance of that point to the kth point closest to it. The smoothness parameter s is a global parameter that will increase or decrease the standard deviations of all Gaussians simultaneously. The larger is the value for s, the smoother will be the obtained surface. The smaller is the s, the more closely the approximation will follow local data. Since the influence of a Gaussian vanishes exponentially, for small standard deviations and considering the digital nature of images, the weight functions, in effect, have only local support.

By setting the standard deviations of Gaussians proportional to the spacing between the points, the surface is made to automatically adapt to the spacing between the points. In areas where density of points is high, narrow Gaussians are used to keep the effect of the points local. In areas where the points are sparse, wide Gaussians are used to cover large gaps between the points.

As the standard deviations of Gaussians are increased, the surface gets smoother and moves away from some of the points. To ensure that a surface interpolates the points, new data values $\{A_i : i = 1, \ldots, n\}$ at $\{(u_i, v_i) : i = 1, \ldots, n\}$ are determined such that the surface obtained from the new data values will evaluate to the old data values at the parameter coordinates corresponding to the data sites. That is, the surface is obtained by solving

$$x_j = \sum_{i=1}^{n} A_i W_i(u_j, v_j), \tag{9.92}$$

$$y_j = \sum_{i=1}^{n} B_i W_i(u_j, v_j), \tag{9.93}$$

$$F_j = \sum_{i=1}^{n} C_i W_i(u_j, v_j), \tag{9.94}$$

for $\{A_i, B_i, C_i : i = 1, \ldots, n\}$, where $j = 1, \ldots, n$, and

$$W_i(u_j, v_j) = \frac{G_i(u_j, v_j)}{\sum_{k=1}^{n} G_k(u_j, v_j)} \tag{9.95}$$

is the ith basis function of the RaG surface evaluated at (u_j, v_j), and $G_i(u_j, v_j)$ is a 2-D Gaussian of standard deviation $s\sigma_i$ centered at (u_i, v_i) when evaluated at (u_j, v_j).

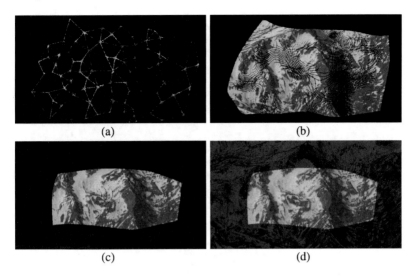

Fig. 9.17 (**a**)–(**c**) Resampling of the sensed image to the space of the reference image as the smoothness parameters is increased. Density of surface points is high at and near the control points as well as along edges connecting the points when smoothness parameter s is very small. Missing surface values are estimated by bilinear interpolation as outlined in Algorithm PSA. (**d**) Registration with parametric Shepard approximation when $s = 2.5$

It is important to note that due to the nonlinear relation between (x, y) and (u, v), by varying u and v from 0 to 1, x may not vary between 0 and $n_c - 1$ and y may not vary between 0 and $n_r - 1$. Consequently, it may be necessary to start u and v slightly below 0 and continue slightly past 1. If u and v are varied between 0 and 1, the sensed image may leave some gaps near the borders of the reference image.

Examples of parametric Shepard approximation using RaG weights are given in Fig. 9.17. The standard deviation of a Gaussian at a control point is set proportional to the distance of that control point to the control point closest to it in the reference image. Therefore, $k = 1$. Figure 9.17a shows resampling of the sensed image when $s = 0.25$. That is, the standard deviation at a control point is set to 0.25 times the distance of that control point to the control point closest to it. At such low standard deviations, the approximation is close to piecewise linear, and for uniformly spaced u and v, surface points primarily concentrate along edges and at vertices of the triangle mesh obtained from the points.

By increasing the smoothness parameter to 1, a smoother surface is obtained and for uniformly spaced u and v, points on the surface become more uniformly spaced as shown in (b). Increasing the smoothness parameter to 2.5 will further increase the smoothness of the surface, but it will shrink the surface at the same time when varying u and v from 0 to 1, as depicted in (c). It also moves the surface farther from some of the points, increasing approximation error. The registration result when $s = 2.5$ is depicted in (d).

In order to create a smooth surface that interpolates the points, we will find new coordinates $\{(A_i, B_i, C_i) : i = 1, \ldots, n\}$ such that the obtained surface would inter-

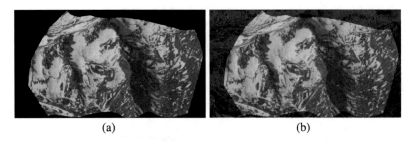

(a)   (b)

Fig. 9.18 Registration of the Mountain image set using parametric Shepard interpolation as the components of the transformation. (**a**) Resampling of the sensed image to the space of the reference image. (**b**) Overlaying of the reference and the resampled sensed images

polate 3-D points $\{(x_i, y_i, F_i) : i = 1, \ldots, n\}$. Doing so, we obtain the resampled image shown in Fig. 9.18a and the registration result shown in Fig. 9.18b. Ignoring its rough boundary, the quality of registration obtained by interpolative parametric Shepard is as good as any of the methods discussed so far.

Examining Shepard's interpolation as described by (9.82), we see that the surface that interpolates a set of points is obtained by a weighted sum of horizontal planes passing through the points. The plane passing through point (x_i, y_i, F_i) is $F(x, y) = F_i$. The reason for obtaining a high density of points near (x_i, y_i) is that many points near (x_i, y_i) produce values close to F_i. This formulation ignores the surface gradient at (x_i, y_i) and always uses horizontal plane $F(x, y) = F_i$ at (x_i, y_i). One remedy to this problem is to use a plane with a gradient equal to that estimated at (x_i, y_i) rather than using gradient 0 at every point.

Gradient vectors at the data points, if not given, can be estimated directly from the data. Typically, a surface is fitted to the points and the gradient vectors of the surface at the points are determined. Stead [99] found that gradient vectors produced by multiquadric surface fitting is superior to those estimated by other methods when using randomly spaced points. Goodman et al. [30] triangulated the points with their associating data values in 3-D and used a convex combination of gradient vectors of the triangle planes sharing a point as the gradient vector at the point.

To find the gradient vector at a point, we fit a plane to the that point and $k > 2$ other points nearest to it by the least-squares method. The gradients of the plane are then taken as estimates to the gradients of the surface at the point. Assuming the plane fitting to point (x_i, y_i, F_i) and a small number of points around it by the least-squares method is

$$F(x, y) = a_i x + b_i y + c_i, \tag{9.96}$$

we recalculate c_i in such a way that $F(x_i, y_i) = F_i$. Doing so, we find $c_i = F_i - a_i x_i - b_i y_i$. Therefore, the equation of the plane passing through the ith point will be

$$L_i(x, y) = a_i(x - x_i) + b_i(y - y_i) + F_i. \tag{9.97}$$

In the Shepard interpolation of (9.82), we replace F_i, which is a horizontal plane passing through point (x_i, y_i, F_i), with $L_i(x, y)$, which is a plane of a desired gra-

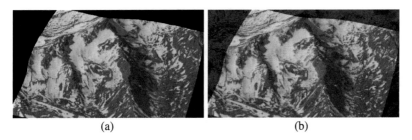

(a)   (b)

Fig. 9.19 Registration of the Mountain image set using weighted linear approximation as the components of the transformation. (**a**) Resampling of the sensed image to the space of the reference image. (**b**) Overlaying of the reference and the resampled sensed images. The smoothness parameter $s = 1$ in this example

dient passing through the same point. The weighted sum of such planes produces a weighted linear interpolation to the points:

$$f(x, y) = \frac{\sum_{i=1}^{n} R_i(x, y) L_i(x, y)}{\sum_{i=1}^{n} R_i(x, y)}. \tag{9.98}$$

This weighted linear function [34, 36] interpolates the points and provides desired gradients at the points. To make the surface approximate the points, instead of (9.89) we let the radial functions be (9.91) but define it in the xy space. If necessary, this surface can be made to interpolate the points by finding new data values at the points in such a way that the obtained surface would evaluate to the old data values at the control points by solving a system of equations similar to (9.94) but as a function of (x, y) rather than (u, v). Note that this new formulation is in explicit form; therefore, revising Shepard's method to use gradients at the points will make it possible to avoid formation of horizontal flat spots in the created surface without parametrizing it.

An example of the use of weighted linear approximation as the components of the transformation function in image registration is given in Fig. 9.19. RaG weights are used with the standard deviation of Gaussian at a point proportional to the distance of that point to the point closest to it. The smoothness parameter s is set to 1 in Fig. 9.19. Since this is an approximating surface, increasing s will create a smoother surface that gets farther from some of the given points. As s is decreased, the surface will more resemble a piecewise linear interpolation. Being an approximation method, weighted linear is particularly suitable in image registration when a large number of point correspondences is given. Registration results are better than those obtained by multiquadric and surface spline and are comparable to those obtained by parametric Shepard interpolation.

A number of modifications to the Shepard interpolation have been proposed. These modifications replace a data point with a function. Franke and Nielson [27] fitted a quadratic function, Renka and Brown [80] fitted a cubic function, Lazzaro and Montefusco [55] fitted a radial function, and Renka and Brown [81] fitted a 10-parameter cosine series to a small number of points in the neighborhood of a point as the nodal function at the point. The weighted sum of the functions were then used

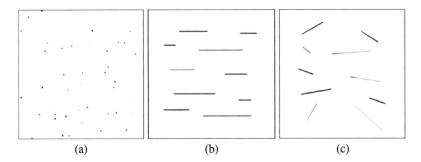

Fig. 9.20 (**a**) Scattered data points in the plane, showing 3-D points. (**b**) Scattered horizontal data lines, showing 3-D lines parallel to the x-axis. (**c**) Scattered data lines of arbitrary orientation with values along a line varying linearly. These represent scattered 3-D lines. Higher values are shown brighter in these images

to obtain the interpolation. Rational weights with local support are used, vanishing at a fixed distance of the data sites. Renka [78] further allowed the width of each weight function to vary with the density of local data and vanish at a distance equal to the distance of a data site to the kth data site closest to it.

Weights with local support are attractive because they are computationally efficient and do not allow a local deformation or inaccuracy to spread over the entire approximation domain. Weights with local support, however, may produce a surface with holes if spacing between the points varies greatly across the image domain.

9.2.2.2 Surface Approximation to Scattered Lines

Image registration methods rely on the coordinates of corresponding points in images to find the transformation function. Transformation functions defined in terms of points, however, cannot represent sharp geometric differences along edges, as found in images of man-made scenes taken from different views.

Line segments are abundant in images of indoor and outdoor scenes and methods to find correspondence between them have been developed [13, 46, 101]. Therefore, rather than defining a transformation function in terms of corresponding points, we would like to formulate the transformation function in terms of corresponding lines in images.

Suppose n corresponding line segments are obtained in two images. Let's denote the coordinates of the end points of the ith line segment by $(x_{i_1}, y_{i_1}, F_{i_1})$ and $(x_{i_2}, y_{i_2}, F_{i_2})$. We want to find a function $F = f(x, y)$ that approximates the lines.

The surface approximating a set of scattered lines is obtained by extending the equation of a surface that approximates a set of points [35]. Consider fitting a single-valued surface to data at scattered points in the plane $\{(x_i, y_i, F_i) : i = 1, \dots, n\}$. An example of scattered data in the plane is given in Fig. 9.20a. Intensities of the points represent the data values at the points. A weighted mean approximation to the data will be

$$f(x, y) = \sum_{i=1}^{n} F_i g_i(x, y).$$
(9.99)

$g_i(x, y)$ can be considered a rational basis function centered at (x_i, y_i) defined in such a way that the sum of n basis functions everywhere in the approximation domain is 1. One such example is rational Gaussian (RaG) basis functions [37]:

$$g_i(x, y) = \frac{w_i G_i(x, y)}{\sum_{j=1}^{n} w_j G_j(x, y)},$$
(9.100)

where $G_i(x, y)$ is a 2-D Gaussian centered at (x_i, y_i) and w_i is the weight associated with the ith data point. For point data, we let $w_i = 1$ for $i = 1, \ldots, n$. For a line, we let a weight be proportional to the length of the line it represents. The standard deviations of the Gaussians can be varied to generate surfaces at different levels of detail.

Now, consider using a data line in place of a data point. For the sake of simplicity, let's first assume that data along a line does not vary and all lines are parallel to the x-axis. An example of such data lines is given in Fig. 9.20b. Therefore, instead of point (x_i, y_i), we will have a line with end points (x_{i_1}, y_{i_1}) and (x_{i_2}, y_{i_2}) and the same data value F_i everywhere along the line. To fit a surface to these lines, we will horizontally stretch the Gaussian associated with a line proportional to its length.

If the coordinates of the midpoint of the ith line are (x_i, y_i), since a 2-D Gaussian can be decomposed into two 1-D Gaussians, we have

$$G_i(x, y) = \exp\left\{-\frac{(x - x_i)^2 + (y - y_i)^2}{2\sigma^2}\right\},$$
(9.101)

$$= \exp\left\{-\frac{(x - x_i)^2}{2\sigma^2}\right\} \exp\left\{-\frac{(y - y_i)^2}{2\sigma^2}\right\},$$
(9.102)

$$= G_i(x) G_i(y).$$
(9.103)

To stretch $G_i(x, y)$ along the x-axis, we scale σ by a factor proportional to the length of the line. Let's denote this scaling by $m_i > 1$. Then, we replace $G_i(x)$ with

$$H_i(x) = \exp\left\{-\frac{(x - x_i)^2}{2(m_i \sigma)^2}\right\},$$
(9.104)

where $m_i = (1 + \varepsilon_i)$ and ε_i is proportional to the length of the ith line. After this stretching, relation (9.99) becomes

$$f(x, y) = \frac{\sum_{i=1}^{n} w_i F_i H_i(x) G_i(y)}{\sum_{i=1}^{n} w_i H_i(x) G_i(y)}.$$
(9.105)

Now suppose data values along a line vary linearly, but the projections of the lines to the xy plane are still parallel to the x-axis. To fit a surface to such lines, instead of using a Gaussian of a fixed height F_i, we let the height of a Gaussian vary with data along the line. Assuming data at the endpoints of the ith line are F_{i_1} and F_{i_2} and the data value at the line midpoint is F_i, in (9.105) we will replace F_i with

$$F_i(x) = F_i + \frac{(x - x_i)}{(x_{i_2} - x_i)}(F_{i_2} - F_i). \tag{9.106}$$

This formula changes the height of the Gaussian along a line proportional to the data values on the line. The new approximation formula, therefore, becomes

$$f(x, y) = \frac{\sum_{i=1}^{n} w_i F_i(x) H_i(x) G_i(y)}{\sum_{i=1}^{n} w_i H_i(x) G_i(y)}. \tag{9.107}$$

To adapt the surface to data lines with arbitrary orientations, such as those shown in Fig. 9.20c, we rotate each data line about its center so that it becomes parallel to the x-axis. Then, we use the above formula to find its contribution to the surface. Finally, we rotate the values back. Doing this for each line and adding contributions from the lines, we obtain the approximating surface. If the projection of the ith line to the xy-plane makes angle θ_i with the x-axis, when rotating the coordinate system clockwise about the line's midpoint by θ_i so that it becomes parallel to the x-axis, denoting the coordinates of points on the line before and after this rotation by (X, Y) and (x, y), we have

$$x = (X - X_i)\cos\theta_i - (Y - Y_i)\sin\theta_i + x_i, \tag{9.108}$$

$$y = (X - X_i)\sin\theta_i + (Y - Y_i)\cos\theta_i + y_i. \tag{9.109}$$

Substituting relations (9.108) and (9.109) into the right side of (9.107), we obtain a relation in (X, Y). This relation finds the surface value at (X, Y) in the approximation domain. Renaming the approximating function by $F(X, Y)$, we will have

$$F(X, Y) = \frac{\sum_{i=1}^{n} w_i F_i(X, Y) H_i(X, Y) G_i(X, Y)}{\sum_{i=1}^{n} w_i H_i(X, Y) G_i(X, Y)}, \tag{9.110}$$

where

$$F_i(X, Y) = F_i + \frac{(X - X_i)\cos\theta_i - (Y - Y_i)\sin\theta_i}{D_i}(F_{i_2} - F_i), \tag{9.111}$$

$$H_i(X, Y) = \exp\left\{-\frac{[(X - X_i)\cos\theta_i - (Y - Y_i)\sin\theta_i]^2}{2(m_i\sigma)^2}\right\}, \tag{9.112}$$

$$G_i(X, Y) = \exp\left\{-\frac{[(X - X_i)\sin\theta_i + (Y - Y_i)\cos\theta_i]^2}{2\sigma^2}\right\}, \tag{9.113}$$

and

$$D_i = \sqrt{(x_{i_2} - x_i)^2 + (y_{i_2} - y_i)^2} = \sqrt{(X_{i_2} - X_i)^2 + (Y_{i_2} - Y_i)^2} \tag{9.114}$$

is half the length of the ith line segment in the xy or XY domain. Weight w_i of line L_i is set equal to $1 + 2D_i$. The 1 in the formula ensures that if points are used in addition to lines, the obtained surface will approximate the points as well as the lines. As the length of a line increases, the volume under the stretched Gaussian

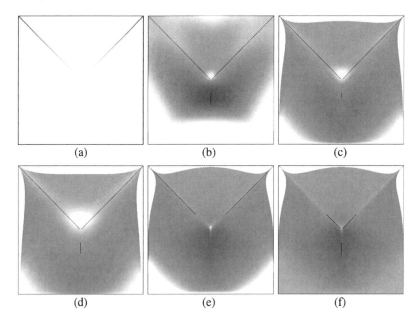

Fig. 9.21 (**a**) Data lines of Table 9.2. Higher values are shown brighter. (**b**) The single-valued surface of (9.110) approximating the data lines. (**c**) The parametric surface of (9.116)–(9.118) approximating the same data lines. (**d**) Same as (**c**) but using a larger σ. (**e**) Same as (**c**) but using a smaller σ. (**f**) Same as (**e**) but viewing from the opposite side. The lines and the approximating surface are overlaid for qualitative evaluation of the approximation

increases. To make the weight function dependent on the length of the line as well as on the data values along the line, we let

$$w_i = 1 + 2D_i = 1 + 2\sqrt{(X_{i_2} - X_i)^2 + (Y_{i_2} - X_i)^2 + (F_{i_2} - F_i)^2}. \qquad (9.115)$$

Substituting (9.111)–(9.113) into (9.110), a single-valued surface is obtained that approximates scattered line data in the plane.

An example of the kind of surfaces obtained by this method is shown in Fig. 9.21. Figure (a) shows seven data lines in the xy-plane. Intensities of points along a line show the data values. The coordinates of the line endpoints and the associating data values are shown in Table 9.2. Figure 9.21b shows the surface approximating the lines according to formula (9.110). Although the surface approximates the lines, flat spots are obtained along the lines. This is a known property of the weighted-mean method.

Since the sum of the weights is required to be 1 everywhere in the approximation domain, when the weight functions are rather narrow, flat spots are obtained at and near the data lines. To prevent such flat spots from appearing in the approximating surface, instead of a single-valued surface, as explained in the preceding section, a parametric surface should be used. Therefore, instead of the single-valued surface

Table 9.2 The coordinates of the endpoints of the lines in Fig. 9.21a and the associating data values

i	1	2	3	4	5	6	7
X_{i_1}	-50	50	50	-50	1	-1	0
Y_{i_1}	-50	-50	50	50	1	1	-10
F_{i_1}	0	0	0	0	50	50	40
X_{i_2}	50	50	-50	-50	50	-50	0
Y_{i_2}	-50	50	50	-50	50	50	-20
F_{i_2}	0	0	0	0	0	0	20

given by (9.110), we use the parametric surface defined by

$$F_x(u, v) = \frac{\sum_{i=1}^{n} w_i X_i(u, v) H_i(u, v) G_i(u, v)}{\sum_{i=1}^{n} w_i H_i(u, v) G_i(u, v)}, \tag{9.116}$$

$$F_y(u, v) = \frac{\sum_{i=1}^{n} w_i Y_i(u, v) H_i(u, v) G_i(u, v)}{\sum_{i=1}^{n} w_i H_i(u, v) G_i(u, v)}, \tag{9.117}$$

$$F_F(u, v) = \frac{\sum_{i=1}^{n} w_i F_i(u, v) H_i(u, v) G_i(u, v)}{\sum_{i=1}^{n} w_i H_i(u, v) G_i(u, v)}. \tag{9.118}$$

Doing so, we obtain the surface shown in Fig. 9.21c. F_x, F_y, and F_F are the x, y, and F components of the surface, each obtained by varying u and v from 0 to 1. Due to the nonlinear relation between (u, v) and (x, y), when varying u and v from 0 to 1, the obtained surface leaves gaps near the image borders. To recover surface values at and near the image borders, u and v need to be varied from values slightly below 0 to values slightly above 1.

In this example, parameter coordinates at the line midpoints and line end points were set proportional to the XY coordinates of the line midpoints and end points, respectively. That is,

$$u_i = (X_i - X_{\min})/(X_{\max} - X_{\min}), \tag{9.119}$$

$$u_{i_1} = (X_{i_1} - X_{\min})/(X_{\max} - X_{\min}), \tag{9.120}$$

$$u_{i_2} = (X_{i_2} - X_{\min})/(X_{\max} - X_{\min}), \tag{9.121}$$

$$v_i = (Y_i - Y_{\min})/(Y_{\max} - Y_{\min}), \tag{9.122}$$

$$v_{i_1} = (Y_{i_1} - Y_{\min})/(Y_{\max} - Y_{\min}), \tag{9.123}$$

$$v_{i_2} = (Y_{i_2} - Y_{\min})/(Y_{\max} - Y_{\min}), \tag{9.124}$$

where $X_{\min}$, $X_{\max}$, $Y_{\min}$, and $Y_{\max}$ define the range of coordinates in the approximation domain. In image registration, $X_{\min} = Y_{\min} = 0$, $X_{\max} = n_c - 1$, $Y_{\max} = n_r - 1$, and n_c and n_r are the image dimensions (i.e., number of columns and number of rows in the reference image).

The transformation with components described by (9.116)–(9.118) maps the sensed image to the reference image in such a way that corresponding lines in the images align. The transformation most naturally registers images containing sharp edges, such as close-range imagery of buildings and man-made structures. The accuracy of the method depends on the accuracy with which the endpoints of the lines are determined.

9.2.3 Implicit

Implicit functions are generally of the form

$$f(\mathbf{p}) = c. \tag{9.125}$$

Given point $\mathbf{p} = (x, y, F)$, the value at the point is $f(\mathbf{p})$. If this value happens to be c, the point will be on the surface. The process of determining an implicit surface involves producing a volumetric image and thresholding it at c. When $c = 0$, the obtained surface is called the *zero* surface or the *zero-crossing* surface.

Implicit surfaces are easy to generate, but if the function is not formulated carefully, multiple surface points can be obtained for the same (x, y), making resampling ambiguous. Implicit functions suitable for image registration are described next.

9.2.3.1 Interpolating Implicit Surfaces

If $\phi(\mathbf{p})$ is a radial function, a function of form

$$f(\mathbf{p}) = \sum_{i=1}^{n} A_i \phi(\|\mathbf{p} - \mathbf{p}_i\|) + L(\mathbf{p}) \tag{9.126}$$

will interpolate points $\{\mathbf{p}_i = (x_i, y_i, F_i) : i = 1, \ldots, n\}$ if it satisfies $f(\mathbf{p}_i) = h_i$ for $i = 1, \ldots, n$ [86, 100]. Since h_i can take any value, we will let it to be 0 for $i = 1, \ldots, n$. This will make the surface of interest be the zero surface of $f(\mathbf{p})$. $L(\mathbf{p})$ is an optional degree one polynomial in x, y, and F, with its coefficients determined in such a way that the surface would satisfy prespecified conditions. Carr et al. [11] used radial functions of form $\|\mathbf{p} - \mathbf{p}_i\|$, while Turk and O'Brien [100] used radial functions of form $\|\mathbf{p} - \mathbf{p}_i\|^3$. If logarithmic basis functions are used, $\phi(\|\mathbf{p} - \mathbf{p}_i\|) = \|\mathbf{p} - \mathbf{p}_i\|^2 \log(\|\mathbf{p} - \mathbf{p}_i\|^2)$.

Parameters $\{A_i : i = 1, \ldots, n\}$ are determined by letting $f(\mathbf{p}_i) = 0$ in (9.126) for $i = 1, \ldots, n$ and solving the obtained system of n linear equations. Note that the obtained system of equations will have a trivial solution $A_i = 0$ for $i = 1, \ldots, n$ when term $L(\mathbf{p})$ is not present. To avoid the trivial solution, additional constraints need to be provided. Since the surface traces the zeros of $f(\mathbf{p})$, one side of the surface will be positive, while the opposite side will be negative. To impose this constraint on the obtained surface, 2 virtual points $\mathbf{p}_{n+1}$ and $\mathbf{p}_{n+2}$ are added to the set of given points. $\mathbf{p}_{n+1}$ is considered a point below the surface and $\mathbf{p}_{n+2}$ is considered a point above the surface. Then, $f(\mathbf{p}_{n+1})$ is set to an appropriately large negative value and $f(\mathbf{p}_{n+2})$ is set to an appropriately large positive value.

Once the coefficients of the implicit surface are determined, the function is quantized within a volume where its xy domain covers the reference image and its F domain covers the columns (when $F = X$) or rows (when $F = Y$) of the sensed image. Then, the zero surface within the volume is obtained by thresholding the volume at 0 and tracing the zero values [61, 71].

An alternative approach to tracing the zero surface without creating an actual volume is to first find a point on the surface by scanning along F axis with discrete

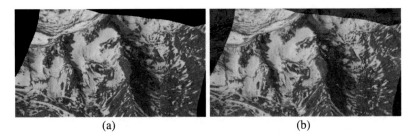

(a)   (b)

Fig. 9.22 Registration of the Mountain image set using interpolative implicit surfaces as the components of the transformation. (**a**) Resampling of the sensed image to align with the reference image. (**b**) Overlaying of the reference and resampled sensed images

steps within its possible range at an arbitrary point (x, y) in the image domain. Once the surface value F at (x, y) is determined, the surface value at a pixel adjacent to (x, y) is determined by using F as the start value and incrementing or decrementing it until a zero-crossing is detected. The process is propagated from one pixel to the next until surface points for all pixels in the reference image are determined.

An example of image registration using the interpolative implicit surface with $\phi(\|\mathbf{p} - \mathbf{p}_i\|) = \|\mathbf{p} - \mathbf{p}_i\|$ is given in Fig. 9.22. The two virtual points are assumed to be $(n_c/2, n_r/2, -n)$ and $(n_c/2, n_r/2, n)$, where n_r and n_c are the number of rows and columns, respectively, in the reference image and n is set to the number of columns of the sensed image when calculating the x-component and it is set to the number of rows of the sensed image when calculating the y-component of the transformation. A much larger n will require a longer time to calculate the surface points and a much smaller n will result in inaccurate surface values when incrementing and decrementing F by 1 to locate the zero-crossing at a particular (x, y). These virtual points are located in the middle of the image domain, one below and one above the surface. The registration result is shown in Fig. 9.22. Although the results may be acceptable within the convex hull of the control points, errors are rather large outside the convex hull of the points.

9.2.3.2 Approximating Implicit Surfaces

We are after an implicit function of form $f(x, y, F) = 0$ that can approximate points $\{\mathbf{p}_i = (x_i, y_i, F_i) : i = 1, \dots, n\}$. If a 3-D monotonically decreasing radial function, such as a Gaussian, is centered at each point, then by adding the functions we obtain

$$f_1(x, y, F) = \sum_{i=1}^{N} g_i(\sigma, x, y, F), \qquad (9.127)$$

where $g_i(\sigma, x, y, F)$ is a 3-D Gaussian of standard deviation σ centered at (x_i, y_i, F_i). f_1 in (9.127) generally increases towards the points and decreases away from the points. Therefore, by tracing locally maximum values of f_1, we can obtain a surface that passes near the points. When the points are uniformly spaced and the standard deviations are all equal to the spacing between the points, the process will work well, but when the points are irregularly spaced, the process will produce a fragmented surface.

Usually, control points in an image are not uniformly spaced. To find a surface that approximates a set of irregularly spaced points, we center a 3-D Gaussian at each point with its standard deviation proportional to the distance of that point to the kth point closest to it. Adding such Gaussians, we obtain

$$f_2(x, y, F) = \sum_{i=1}^{n} g_i(\sigma_i, x, y, F), \tag{9.128}$$

where $g_i(\sigma_i, x, y, F)$ is a 3-D Gaussian of magnitude 1 and standard deviation σ_i centered at point (x_i, y_i, F_i). By tracing the local maxima of f_2 in the direction of maximum gradient, a surface that approximates the points will be obtained.

When isotropic Gaussians are centered at the points and the points are irregularly spaced, local maxima of f_2 in the gradient direction will again produce a fragmented surface. We have to stretch the Gaussians toward the gaps in order to avoid fragmentation. This is achieved by replacing a 3-D isotropic Gaussian with a 3-D anisotropic Gaussian oriented in such a way that it stretches toward the gaps.

Letting XYZ represent the local coordinate system of a point, with the Z-axis pointing in the direction of surface normal and XY defining the tangent plane at the point, the relation between the global coordinate system xyF of the surface and the local coordinate system XYZ of a point will be a rigid transformation. The 3-D anisotropic Gaussian centered at $\mathbf{p}_i$ in the local coordinate system of the point can be defined by

$$G_i(\sigma_X, X)G_i(\sigma_Y, Y)G_i(\sigma_Z, Z), \tag{9.129}$$

where $G_i(\sigma_X, X)$, $G_i(\sigma_Y, Y)$, and $G_i(\sigma_Z, Z)$ are 1-D Gaussians centered at the origin and laid along X-, Y-, and Z-axes, respectively.

To determine the coordinate axes at point $\mathbf{p}_i$, first, the surface normal at the point is determined by identifying the k closest points of $\mathbf{p}_i$ and calculating from them the covariance matrix [1]:

$$\mathbf{M}_i = \frac{1}{k} \sum_{j=1}^{k} (\mathbf{p}_i^j - \mathbf{p}_i)(\mathbf{p}_i^j - \mathbf{p}_i)^t, \tag{9.130}$$

where $\mathbf{p}_i^j$ denotes the jth point closest to $\mathbf{p}_i$ and t denotes matrix transpose operation. The eigenvectors of the 3×3 matrix $\mathbf{M}_i$ define three orthogonal axes, which are taken as the local coordinate axes at $\mathbf{p}_i$. The eigenvector associated with the smallest eigenvalue is taken as the surface normal at $\mathbf{p}_i$. All normals are made to point upward. The surface normal is taken as the Z-axis and the eigenvector associated with the largest eigenvalue is taken as the Y-axis of the local coordinate system. The X-axis is taken normal to both Y and Z.

Letting the eigenvalues of $\mathbf{M}_i$ from the largest to the smallest be λ_1, λ_2, and λ_3, we define

$$\sigma_X^2 = a\lambda_2, \tag{9.131}$$

$$\sigma_Y^2 = a\lambda_1, \tag{9.132}$$

$$\sigma_Z^2 = b\lambda_3. \tag{9.133}$$

This will ensure that the 3-D Gaussian is stretched toward the gaps where the density of points is low. The process will automatically adapts local averaging to the local density and organization of points. Parameters a and b are global parameters that can be varied to produce surfaces at different levels of detail. Parameters a and b smooth the surface in the tangent and normal directions. A larger a will stretch a Gaussian at a data point in the tangent direction of the approximating surface, filling large gaps between points and avoiding the creation of holes. A larger b smoothes the surface more in the normal direction, reducing noise among the correspondences and also smoothing surface details.

A local coordinate system is considered at point $\mathbf{p}_i$ with coordinate axes representing the eigenvectors of the covariance matrix $\mathbf{M}_i$. The sum of the Gaussians at point (x, y, F) in the approximation can be computed from:

$$f_3(x, y, F) = \sum_{i=1}^{n} g_i(\sigma_X, x) g_i(\sigma_Y, y) g_i(\sigma_Z, F), \tag{9.134}$$

where $g_i(\sigma_X, x)$, $g_i(\sigma_Y, y)$, and $g_i(\sigma_Z, F)$, correspondingly, represent 1-D Gaussians $G_i(\sigma_X, X)$, $G_i(\sigma_Y, Y)$, and $G_i(\sigma_Z, Z)$ after coordinate transformation from XYZ to xyF. Note that parameters σ_X, σ_Y, and σ_Z are local to point $\mathbf{p}_i$ and, thus, vary from point to point.

The surface to be recovered is composed of points where function $f_3(x, y, F)$ becomes locally maximum in the direction of surface normal. To simplify the surface detection process, rather than finding local maxima of $f_3(x, y, F)$ in the direction of surface normal, we determine the zero-crossings of the first derivative of $f_3(x, y, F)$ in the direction of surface normal. To achieve this, we orient the first-derivative of Gaussian in the direction of surface normal at each point in such a way that its positive side always points upward. Then, zero-crossings of the sum of the first-derivative Gaussians are determined and used as the approximating surface. More specifically, we use the zeros of

$$f(x, y, F) = \sum_{i=1}^{n} g_i(\sigma_X, x) g_i(\sigma_Y, y) g_i'(\sigma_Z, F) \tag{9.135}$$

as the approximating surface, where $g_i'(\sigma_Z, F)$ is the coordinate transformation of $G_i'(\sigma_Z, Z)$ from XYZ to xyF, and $G_i'(\sigma_Z, Z)$ is the first derivative of 1-D Gaussian $G_i(\sigma_Z, Z)$ centered at the origin and along the Z-axis.

Note that a zero-point of function $f(x, y, F)$ can be a locally maximum or a locally minimum point of $f_3(x, y, F)$ in the normal direction. However, only locally maximum points of function $f_3(x, y, F)$ correspond to the true surface points, and locally minimum points of $f_3(x, y, F)$ represent false surface points that have to be discarded.

Zero surface points that correspond to local minima of $f_3(x, y, F)$ in the normal direction can be easily identified by examining the sign of the second derivative of $f_3(x, y, F)$ calculated in the direction of surface normal. At the point where $f_3(x, y, F)$ is maximum in the normal direction, the second derivative of $f_3(x, y, F)$ in the normal direction will be negative, and at the point where $f_3(x, y, F)$ is minimum in the normal direction, the second derivative of $f_3(x, y, F)$ in the normal direction will be positive. Therefore, at each zero-crossing of $f(x, y, F)$, we find the sign of the second derivative of $f_3(x, y, F)$ calculated in the normal direction. If the sign is negative, the zero-crossing is retained, otherwise it is discarded.

Note that the second derivative of $f_3(x, y, F)$ in the normal direction is obtained by replacing $g_i'(\sigma_Z, F)$ in (9.135) with $g_i''(\sigma_Z, F)$, the second derivative of $g_i(\sigma_Z, F)$ in the normal direction, which is the second derivative of $G_i(\sigma_Z, Z)$ after the coordinate transformation from XYZ to xyz.

To summarize, steps in the implicit surface detection algorithm are:

1. For each point $\mathbf{p}_i$, $i = 1, \ldots, n$, repeat (a)–(c) below.
   a. Find the k closest points of $\mathbf{p}_i$.
   b. Using the points determine the eigenvalues ($\lambda_1 > \lambda_2 > \lambda_3$) and the corresponding eigenvectors ($\mathbf{v}_1, \mathbf{v}_2, \mathbf{v}_3$) of the covariance matrix $\mathbf{M}_i$ defined by (9.130) and use the eigenvectors to define a local coordinate system XYZ at $\mathbf{p}_i$.
   c. Let $\sigma_X^2 = a\lambda_2$, $\sigma_Y^2 = a\lambda_1$, and $\sigma_Z^2 = b\lambda_3$. a and b are globally controlled smoothness parameters.
2. Create an xyF volume of sufficient size and initialize the entries to 0.
3. For each point $\mathbf{p}_i$, $i = 1, \ldots, n$, add the volume representing $g_i(\sigma_X, x)g_i(\sigma_Y, y) \times g_i'(\sigma_Z, F)$ to the xyF volume.
4. Find the zero-crossings of the obtained volume.
5. Discard zero-crossings where the second derivative of $f_3(x, y, F)$ is positive, as they represent false surface points. The remaining zero-crossings define the desired surface.

The computation of the second derivative of $f_3(x, y, F)$ can be avoided by simply checking the magnitude of $f_3(x, y, F)$. If at a zero-crossing of the first derivative of $f(x, y, F)$, the magnitude of $f_3(x, y, F)$ is sufficiently large (say $> \varepsilon$) the zero-crossing is considered authentic. Otherwise, it is considered false and discarded. ε is usually a very small number, determined experimentally.

The process of centering the first-derivative of a 3-D anisotropic Gaussian at point $\mathbf{p}_i$ and adding the Gaussians to volume xyF is achieved by resampling the first-derivative of a 3-D isotropic Gaussian centered at the origin by a similarity transformation. The first-derivative (with respect to Z) of an isotropic Gaussian of standard deviation σ and magnitude 1 centered at the origin is:

$$G(\sigma, X, Y, Z) = G(\sigma, X)G(\sigma, Y)G'(\sigma, Z), \tag{9.136}$$

where

$$G(\sigma, X) = \exp\left\{-\frac{X^2}{2\sigma^2}\right\}, \qquad G(\sigma, Y) = \exp\left\{-\frac{Y^2}{2\sigma^2}\right\}, \tag{9.137}$$

and

$$G'(\sigma, Z) = -\frac{Z}{\sigma^2} \exp\left\{-\frac{Z^2}{2\sigma^2}\right\}. \tag{9.138}$$

The first-derivative isotropic Gaussian centered at the origin in the XYZ coordinate system is then transformed to the first-derivative anisotropic Gaussian at (x, y, F). This involves (1) scaling the isotropic Gaussian of standard deviation σ along X, Y, and Z by σ_X/σ, σ_Y/σ, and σ_Z/σ, respectively, (2) rotating it about X-, Y-, and Z-axes in such a way that the X-, Y-, and Z-axes align with the eigenvectors $\mathbf{v}_2, \mathbf{v}_1$, and $\mathbf{v}_3$ of covariance matrix $\mathbf{M}_i$, and (3) translating the scaled and rotated Gaussian to (x_i, y_i, F_i). Let's denote this similarity transformation by $\mathbf{A}_i$. Then, for each point $\mathbf{P} = (X, Y, Z)$ in the local coordinate system of point $\mathbf{p}_i$, the coordinates of the same point $\mathbf{p} = (x, y, F)$ in the xyF coordinate system will be $\mathbf{p} = \mathbf{A}_i\mathbf{P}$. Conversely, given point $\mathbf{p}$ in the xyF coordinate system, the same point in the local coordinate system of point $\mathbf{p}_i$ will be

$$\mathbf{P} = \mathbf{A}_i^{-1}\mathbf{p}. \tag{9.139}$$

Therefore, if the given points are in xyF space, create the first-derivative (with respect to Z) of an isotropic 3-D Gaussian centered at the origin in a sufficiently large 3-D array XYZ with the origin at the center of the array. Then, resample array XYZ and add to array xyF by the similarity transformation given in (9.139). This involves scanning the xyF volume within a small neighborhood of $\mathbf{p}_i$ and for each entry (x, y, F), determining the corresponding entry (X, Y, Z) in isotropic volume XYZ using (9.139), reading the value in the isotropic volume, and adding it to the value at entry (x, y, F) in the xyF volume.

Since a Gaussian approaches 0 exponentially, it is sufficient to scan the xyF space within a sphere of radius r_i centered at $\mathbf{p}_i$ to find its effect. r_i is determined to satisfy

$$\exp\left\{-\frac{r_i^2}{2\sigma_i^2}\right\} < \varepsilon \tag{9.140}$$

where σ_i is the largest of σ_X, σ_Y, and σ_Z calculated at $\mathbf{p}_i$, ε is the required error tolerance, which should be smaller than half the voxel size in the xyF volume to meet digital accuracy.

For a given a and b, the subvolume centered at each point (x_i, y_i, F_i) is determined. The isotropic first-derivative Gaussian is mapped to the subvolume with transformation $\mathbf{A}_i$, the sum of the anisotropic first-derivative Gaussians is determined, and its zero-surface is calculated by thresholding the volume at 0. The obtained zero surface will approximate points $\{(x_i, y_i, F_i) : i = 1, \ldots, n\}$.

9.3 Properties of Transformation Functions

Transformation functions carry information about scene geometry as well as the relation of cameras with respect to each other and with respect to the scene. Camera geometry is global, while scene geometry is local. We would like to see if we can use information in a transformation function to estimate camera relations as well as scene geometry.

Because scene geometry is local in nature, it is reflected in the gradient of a transformation function. Camera geometry is either fixed across an image or it varies gradually; therefore, it has very little influence on the gradient of a transformation function.

If the components of a transformation function are

$$X = f_x(x, y), \tag{9.141}$$

$$Y = f_y(x, y), \tag{9.142}$$

the gradients of f_x with respect to x and y are

$$\frac{\partial X}{\partial x} = \frac{\partial f_x(x, y)}{\partial x}, \tag{9.143}$$

$$\frac{\partial X}{\partial y} = \frac{\partial f_x(x, y)}{\partial y}. \tag{9.144}$$

Therefore, the gradient magnitude of X at (x, y) can be computed from

$$\left| X'(x, y) \right| = \left\{ \left(\frac{\partial X}{\partial x} \right)^2 + \left(\frac{\partial X}{\partial y} \right)^2 \right\}^{\frac{1}{2}}. \tag{9.145}$$

Similarly, the gradient magnitude of the Y-component of the transformation is

$$\left| Y'(x, y) \right| = \left\{ \left(\frac{\partial Y}{\partial x} \right)^2 + \left(\frac{\partial Y}{\partial y} \right)^2 \right\}^{\frac{1}{2}}. \tag{9.146}$$

When the images are translated with respect to each other in a neighborhood, the components of the transformation that register the images in that neighborhood are defined by (9.5) and (9.6), from which we find $|X'(x, y)| = 1$ and $|Y'(x, y)| = 1$. Therefore, the gradient magnitude of each component of the transformation in the neighborhood under consideration is equal to 1 independent of (x, y).

When the images in a neighborhood have translational and rotational differences (rigid transformation) as defined by (9.9) and (9.10), the gradient magnitude for each component of the transformation in that neighborhood will be $\sqrt{\sin^2 \theta + \cos^2 \theta} = 1$. Therefore, the gradient magnitude of each component of the transformation in the neighborhood under consideration is also equal to 1 independent of (x, y).

When two images in a neighborhood are related by an affine transformation as defined by (9.19) and (9.20), the gradient magnitude of each component of the transformation in that neighborhood will be

$$\left| X'(x, y) \right| = \sqrt{a_1^2 + a_2^2}, \tag{9.147}$$

$$\left| Y'(x, y) \right| = \sqrt{a_3^2 + a_4^2}. \tag{9.148}$$

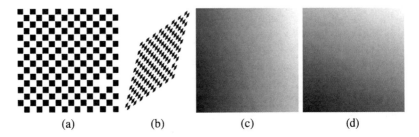

(a)   (b)   (c)   (d)

Fig. 9.23 (**a**), (**b**) An image and its transformation by an affine transformation. (**c**), (**d**) The X-component and the Y-component of the transformation, respectively. Values in the components of the transformation are appropriately scaled for viewing purposes

This shows that the X-component and the Y-component of an affine transformation have different gradient magnitudes unless $\sqrt{a_1^2 + a_2^2} = \sqrt{a_3^2 + a_4^2}$, implying the images are related by the similarity transformation. Therefore, gradient magnitudes of the two components of the similarity transformation are also the same. However, the gradient magnitude may be smaller than or larger than 1. The gradient magnitude, in fact, is equal to the $\sqrt{2}$ of the scale of the sensed image with respect to that of the reference image.

When two images are locally related by an affine transformation, gradient magnitudes $\sqrt{a_1^2 + a_2^2}$ and $\sqrt{a_3^2 + a_4^2}$, in addition to containing scale information, contain information about shearing of the sensed image with respect to the reference image. A larger shearing is obtained when the scene makes a larger angle with the direction of view. Therefore, the gradient of an affine transformation can be used to guess the orientation of the planar scene with respect to the view direction. The gradients of the X-component and the Y-component contain information about foreshortening of the scene horizontally and vertically with respect to the view.

Transforming the image in Fig. 9.23a by an affine transformation with $a_1 = 1.5$, $a_2 = 0.5, a_3 = 0, a_4 = 1, a_5 = 2$, and $a_6 = 0$, we obtain the image shown in Fig. 9.23b. The X-component and the Y-component of this transformation are shown in Figs. 9.23c and 9.23d, respectively. The gradient magnitude for the X-component transformation computed digitally is 1.581, which is the same as its theoretical value $\sqrt{a_1^2 + a_2^2} = \sqrt{2.5}$. The gradient magnitude of the Y-component transformation determined digitally is 2.236, which is the same as its theoretical value $\sqrt{a_3^2 + a_4^2} = \sqrt{5}$.

When two images are locally related by the projective transformation as defined by (9.23) and (9.24), the gradients of the two components become

$$\frac{\partial X}{\partial x} = \frac{a_1(a_7 x + a_8 y + 1) - a_7(a_1 x + a_2 y + a_3)}{(a_7 x + a_8 y + 1)^2}, \tag{9.149}$$

$$\frac{\partial X}{\partial y} = \frac{a_2(a_7 x + a_8 y + 1) - a_8(a_1 x + a_2 y + a_3)}{(a_7 x + a_8 y + 1)^2}, \tag{9.150}$$

$$\frac{\partial Y}{\partial x} = \frac{a_4(a_7x + a_8y + 1) - a_7(a_4x + a_5y + a_3)}{(a_7x + a_8y + 1)^2}, \qquad (9.151)$$

$$\frac{\partial Y}{\partial y} = \frac{a_5(a_7x + a_8y + 1) - a_8(a_4x + a_5y + a_3)}{(a_7x + a_8y + 1)^2}, \qquad (9.152)$$

or

$$\frac{\partial X}{\partial x} = \frac{a_1 - a_7X}{a_7x + a_8y + 1}, \qquad (9.153)$$

$$\frac{\partial X}{\partial y} = \frac{a_2 - a_8X}{a_7x + a_8y + 1}, \qquad (9.154)$$

$$\frac{\partial Y}{\partial x} = \frac{a_4 - a_7Y}{a_7x + a_8y + 1}, \qquad (9.155)$$

$$\frac{\partial Y}{\partial y} = \frac{a_5 - a_8Y}{a_7x + a_8y + 1}, \qquad (9.156)$$

or

$$\frac{\partial X}{\partial x} = A_1 + A_2X, \qquad (9.157)$$

$$\frac{\partial X}{\partial y} = A_3 + A_4X, \qquad (9.158)$$

$$\frac{\partial Y}{\partial x} = A_5 + A_2Y, \qquad (9.159)$$

$$\frac{\partial Y}{\partial y} = A_6 + A_4Y, \qquad (9.160)$$

therefore,

$$\left|X'(x, y)\right| = \sqrt{(A_1 + A_2X)^2 + (A_3 + A_4X)^2}, \qquad (9.161)$$

$$\left|Y'(x, y)\right| = \sqrt{(A_5 + A_2Y)^2 + (A_6 + A_4Y)^2}. \qquad (9.162)$$

The gradient magnitude for the X-component of the projective transformation is not only dependent on (x, y), it depends on X. Similarly, the gradient magnitude of the Y-component of the transformation is a function of Y as well as (x, y). Also, the gradient magnitudes of the two components of the projective transformation depend on each other. The gradient magnitudes become independent of (x, y) when $a_7 = a_8 = 0$, and that happens when the projective transformation becomes an affine transformation.

Since $\partial X/\partial x$ and $\partial X/\partial y$ are linear functions of X, their derivatives with respect to X will be constants. Denoting $\partial X/\partial x$ by X_x and denoting $\partial X/\partial y$ by X_y, we find $dX_x/dX = A_2$ and $dX_y/dX = A_4$. Let's define

$$\left|(dX)'\right| \equiv \sqrt{(dX_x/dX)^2 + (dX_y/dX)^2} = \sqrt{A_2^2 + A_4^2}. \qquad (9.163)$$

Similarly, denoting $\partial Y/\partial x$ by Y_x and denoting $\partial Y/\partial y$ by Y_y, we find

$$\left|(dY)'\right| \equiv \sqrt{(dY_x/dY)^2 + (dY_y/dY)^2} = \sqrt{A_2^2 + A_4^2}, \qquad (9.164)$$

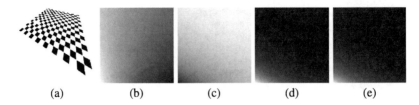

Fig. 9.24 (**a**) A projective transformation of the image in Fig. 9.23a. (**b**), (**c**) The X-component and the Y-component of the transformation. (**d**), (**e**) Images representing $|(dX)'|$ and $|(dY)'|$. In (**b**)–(**e**) the values are appropriately scaled to range $[0, 255]$ for enhanced viewing

we find that $|(dX)'| = |(dY)'|$. This implies that the gradient of the X-component of a projective transformation calculated in the xy domain has a gradient magnitude with respect to X that is the same as the gradient of the Y-component of the transformation calculated in the xy domain when its gradient magnitude is calculated with respect to Y. However, this amount varies from pixel to pixel as A_2 and A_4 both depend on (x, y).

An example showing this property is given in Fig. 9.24. Using the image in Fig. 9.23a and letting the parameters of the projective transformation be $a_1 = 1.5$, $a_2 = -0.5, a_3 = 0, a_4 = 1, a_5 = 2, a_6 = 0, a_7 = 0.005$, and $a_8 = 0.01$, we obtain the transformed image shown in Fig. 9.24a. The X- and Y-components of this transformation are shown in 9.24b and 9.24c. The gradient magnitude of the gradient of the two components of the transformation, $|(dX)'|$ and $|(dY)'|$, as shown in 9.24d and 9.24e, are exactly the same. This property can be used to determine whether a transformation in a neighborhood is projective or not.

When the geometric difference between two images varies locally, the above mentioned properties hold within corresponding local neighborhoods in the images. At each (x, y), $|X'|$ and $|Y'|$ can be determined and based on their values, the geometric difference between the images at and in the neighborhood of (x, y) can be guessed. The parameters of the transformation mapping images in the neighborhood of (x, y) can be estimated using the X and the Y values at (x, y) and at pixels around it. Knowing the X- and the Y-components of a transformation, algorithms can be developed to examine $X, Y, |X'|$, and $|Y'|$ at each pixel and derive information about the geometry of the scene.

Consider the example in Fig. 9.25. Images (a) and (b) show the X-component and the Y-component of the transformation obtained by the weighted-linear (WLIN) method to register the Mountain image set. Images (c) and (d) represent $|X'|$ and $|Y'|$. We see a larger variation in gradient magnitudes of the X-component transformation than the Y-component transformation. This is typical of stereo images, showing a larger change in foreshortening horizontally than vertically. Variation in local geometry of the sensed image with respect to the reference image is reflected in the components of the transformation. Images $|X'|$ and $|Y'|$ not only contain information about the geometry of the scene, they contain information about the relation of the cameras with respect to each other and with respect to the scene.

Darker areas in $|X'|$ and $|Y'|$ are indicative of areas that are going out of view horizontally and vertically from the sensed image to the reference image. Brighter

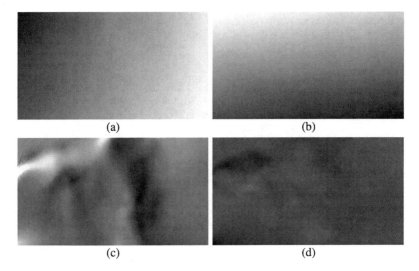

(a)   (b)

(c)   (d)

Fig. 9.25 (**a**), (**b**) The X-component and the Y-component of the transformation obtained by the weighted-linear (WLIN) method to register the Mountain images. (**c**), (**d**) Plots of $|X'|$ and $|Y'|$. Intensities in the images have been appropriately scaled for better viewing

areas show regions that are coming into view and expanding in size in the sensed image when compared to the reference image. Such regions point towards the view while darker regions point away from the view. The sensed image, therefore, has been obtained to the left of the reference image. Using the transformation function obtained for the registration of two images, some characteristics of the scene as well as the relation between the cameras and the scene can be determined.

9.4 Evaluation

Various interpolating/approximating functions suitable for representing the components of a transformation function in image registration were discussed. Each transformation has its strengths and weaknesses. It is hard to find a single transformation function that performs the best on all types of images; however, there are transformation functions that perform better than others on many image types. The desired properties of a transformation function for image registration are:

1. *Monotonicity, convexity, and nonnegativity preserving*: These properties ensure that the function is well behaved and it does not produce high fluctuations and overshoots away from the control points. The properties can be obtained by formulating the surface in terms of not only the data values but also the data gradients at the points. The properties are easier to achieve when a function is formulated in such a way that its variations can be more easily controlled. Lu and Schumaker [62] and Li [59] derived monotonicity-preserving conditions, Renka [79] and Lai [49] derived convexity-preserving conditions, and Schumaker and

Speleers [94] and Hussain and Hussain [45] derived nonnegativity preserving conditions for piecewise smooth surface interpolation to scattered data. These methods typically constrain gradient vectors at the points to ensure a desired property in the created surface.

2. *Linearity preserving*: If data values in the image domain vary linearly, the function interpolating/approximating the data should also vary linearly. This property ensures that a transformation function would not introduce nonlinearity into the resampling process when corresponding reference and sensed areas are related linearly.

3. *Adaptive to the density and organization of points*: Since control points in an image are rarely uniformly spaced, a transformation function should have the ability to adapt to the local density and organization of the points. Density of points across the image domain can vary greatly and so can the spacing between the points. If the transformation function is defined by radial basis functions, the widths of the functions should adapt to the local density of points and the shape of the basis functions should adapt to the irregular spacing of the points. Generally, monotonically decreasing rational basis functions adapt well to the organization of points. Rational basis functions, however, should be used in parametric form. If used in explicit form, flat spots appear in the components of the transformation, producing large errors in registration.

To determine the strengths and weaknesses of the transformation functions described in this chapter and to determine their performances in image registration, experiments were carried out using the images depicted in Fig. 9.26. Corresponding points in the images are also shown. The images have various degrees of geometric differences.

Images (a) and (b) are captured from different views and different distances of an art piece. They are of dimensions 520×614 and 505×549, respectively. The geometric difference between the images varies from point to point. We will refer to these images as *Face* images. The images contain 80 corresponding points. Images (c) and (d) show aerial images, again, taken from different views and different distances to the scene. They are of dimensions 412×244 and 469×274, respectively. The images contain small local and global geometric differences. We will refer to them as *Aerial* images. There are 31 corresponding points in these images.

Images (e) and (f) show two views of a terrain. These images are of dimensions 655×438 and 677×400, respectively. There is depth discontinuity near the center of the images at about 120 degrees. There are 46 corresponding points in the images. We will call these *Terrain* images. Images (g) and (h) show a close up of a small area in the terrain. The images are of dimensions 409×531 and 402×542, respectively. There are 58 corresponding points in these images. These images will be referred to as the *Rock* images. The geometric difference between these images vary across the image domain.

Images (i) and (j) show two views of a partially snow-covered, rocky mountain. These images are of dimensions 719×396 and 565×347, respectively. There are 165 corresponding points in theses images. This is called the *Mountain* data set. The geometric difference between these images varies considerably across the image

Fig. 9.26 (**a**), (**b**) Face, (**c**), (**d**) Aerial, (**e**), (**f**) Terrain, (**g**), (**h**) Rock, (**i**), (**j**) Mountain, and (**k**), (**l**) Parking images used to evaluate the performances of various transformation functions in image registration. The number of corresponding points in these image sets are 80, 31, 46, 58, 165, and 32. The control points are marked with '+' in the images. Points marked in *red* are used to determine the transformation parameters, and points marked in *light blue* are used to quantify registration accuracy

domain. Finally, (k) and (l) are images of a parking lot taken from the same viewpoint but with different view angles. These images are of dimensions 450×485 and 449×480, respectively. They contain only global geometric differences, defined by a projective transformation. Local geometric differences between the images are negligible. The images contain 32 corresponding points. We will refer to these images as the *Parking* images.

The control points in these images were determined using the Harris point detector and correspondence between the points were determined by the coarse-to-fine matching Algorithm F5 in Chap. 7 using error tolerance of 1.5 pixels.

We will compare the speeds and accuracies of various transformation functions in the registration of these images using the provided correspondences. For each transformation, the time to determine its parameters and the time to resample the sensed image to the geometry of the reference image are determined. Since the true transformation function between the images is not known, we will use half of the correspondences to determine the transformation and use the remaining half to measure the registration accuracy. Points marked in red in Fig. 9.26 are used to determine a transformation and points marked in light blue are used to determine the registration accuracy with the obtained transformation.

The transformation functions used in this evaluation are (1) multiquadric, (2) surface or thin-plate spline, (3) Wendland's compactly supported interpolation (9.55), (9.56), (4) Maude's local weighted linear (9.61), (5) moving least squares (9.65) using polynomials of degree 1 and inverse square distance weights (9.66), (6) piecewise-linear interpolation, (7) approximating subdivision surface of Loop, (8) parametric Shepard interpolation using rational Gaussian weights with smoothness parameter $s = 0.75$ (9.92)–(9.95), (9) weighted-linear approximation (9.98), and (10) interpolating implicit surface (9.126) with Euclidean ($\|\mathbf{p} - \mathbf{p}_i\|$) basis functions without a linear term.

Results are tabulated in Table 9.3. Examining the results, we see that surface or thin-plate spline (TPS) has the highest speed in spite of the fact that it solves a global system of equations to find each component of a transformation. A single method could not produce the best RMSE for all images and methods vary in accuracy depending on the organization of the points and the severity of the geometric difference between the images.

For images with small to moderate geometric differences, Maude's weighted linear approximation (MAUD) produced the best result, while for images with large local geometric differences, Loop subdivision method (LOOP) and implicit interpolation produced the smallest MAX errors. Weighted-linear (WLIN) and parametric Shepard (SHEP) also produce low MAX errors.

Considering both speed and accuracy, overall best results are obtained by moving least-squares (MLQ) followed by weighted-linear (WLIN) and parametric Shepard (SHEP). These methods are especially attractive because they have the ability to resample image regions outside the convex hull of the control points. Registration results for the six image sets in Fig. 9.26 by the moving least-square method are shown in Fig. 9.27 for qualitative evaluation. The reference image is shown in the red and blue bands and the sensed image is shown in the green band of a color image. At pixels where the images perfectly align gray values are obtained, and at pixels where the images do not align well green or purple are obtained. Scene areas visible in only one of the images also appear in green or purple.

9.5 Final Remarks

To register two images, not only is a set of corresponding points in the images required, a transformation function is required that can use information about the correspondences to find the geometric relations between the images. A transformation function makes it possible to spatially align the images and determine the correspondence between all points in the images. It also provides the means to infer the geometric characteristics of the underlying scene.

Table 9.3 Performance measures for various transformation functions used to register the images shown in Fig. 9.26. The transformation functions tested are: multiquadric (MQ), surface or thin-plate spline (TPS), Wendland's compactly supported radial basis functions (WEND), Maude's local weighted linear formula (MAUD), moving least squares (MLQ), piecewise linear (PWL), Loop subdivision surface (LOOP), parametric Shepard interpolation (SHEP), weighted linear approximation (WLIN), and interpolative implicit surface with Euclidean basis functions (IMPL). Performance measures are: computation time (TIME) in seconds, root-mean-squared error (RMSE) in pixels, and maximum (MAX) registration error, also in pixels. The transformation parameters are determined using half of the provided control-point correspondences and registration errors are determined using the remaining correspondences. Best results are shown in **bold**

Method	Measure	Face	Aerial	Terrain	Rock	Mountain	Parking
MQ	TIME	1.34	0.19	0.73	0.70	2.48	0.39
	RMSE	4.05	6.80	10.28	4.08	4.62	5.89
	MAX	9.00	13.89	26.38	9.10	30.62	14.33
TPS	TIME	**1.09**	**0.14**	**0.58**	**0.61**	**1.93**	**0.31**
	RMSE	3.85	1.34	2.16	1.51	4.47	0.98
	MAX	10.68	2.43	4.26	3.34	32.18	1.79
WEND	TIME	1.54	0.23	0.81	0.81	3.28	0.48
	RMSE	3.59	5.22	5.59	4.22	4.57	6.71
	MAX	7.26	10.01	12.57	12.16	30.05	12.88
MAUD	TIME	4.32	1.06	3.30	2.64	5.32	2.31
	RMSE	4.09	**1.07**	**1.38**	1.50	**4.40**	**0.93**
	MAX	9.34	**1.88**	3.12	3.35	27.55	1.69
MLQ	TIME	1.98	0.41	1.15	1.06	3.35	0.67
	RMSE	3.96	1.16	1.62	1.52	5.46	0.95
	MAX	9.32	2.13	3.40	3.69	33.17	**1.45**
PWL	TIME	2.20	0.30	1.26	1.16	4.71	0.61
	RMSE	4.08	1.28	1.70	1.48	4.55	0.94
	MAX	10.94	2.49	4.33	3.23	30.10	1.47
LOOP	TIME	6.86	7.16	8.5	6.68	4.52	8.13
	RMSE	4.13	1.24	**1.45**	1.59	4.46	0.95
	MAX	10.33	2.53	3.61	3.75	**25.49**	1.64
SHEP	TIME	1.93	0.27	1.05	1.05	2.98	0.69
	RMSE	4.32	1.38	1.79	1.59	4.91	1.13
	MAX	11.64	2.35	5.10	**3.04**	33.97	1.70
WLIN	TIME	1.95	0.27	1.01	1.03	3.06	0.69
	RMSE	4.25	1.28	1.58	1.51	4.47	0.96
	MAX	12.96	2.44	**3.01**	3.33	26.29	1.72
IMPL	TIME	6.80	0.91	3.74	3.50	12.22	2.01
	RMSE	**3.48**	5.58	8.55	3.93	4.43	6.14
	MAX	**6.96**	14.23	27.75	13.46	28.8	15.30

(a)   (b)   (c)

(d)   (e)   (f)

Fig. 9.27 (a)–(f) Registration of the Face, Aerial, Terrain, Rock, Mountain, and Parking images by the moving least-squares transformation function

If the geometry of a scene and the relations of the cameras to each other and to the scene are known, the type of transformation function most suitable to relate the geometries of the images can be selected. The parameters of the transformation can then be determined from the coordinates of corresponding points in the images. However, often information about the scene and the cameras is not available. In such a situation, the employed transformation function should be able to adapt to the local geometric differences between the images.

Comparing the performances of a number of adaptive transformation functions on various images with varying degrees of local and global geometric differences, we observe that although a single transformation does not exist that can outperform all other transformations, but some transformations clearly perform better than others. Among the tested transformation functions, weighted-linear, moving least-squares, and parametric Shepard methods generally perform better than other methods in both speed and accuracy.

The quality of a resampled image depends on the resampling method used. Image resampling is discussed in the next chapter. When registering two images, there is sometimes a need to combine the images into a larger image mosaic. To create a seamless mosaic, intensities in the overlap area in the images should be blended in such a way that intensities in the images smoothly merge. Image blending is also discussed in the next chapter.

References

1. Adamson, A., Alexa, M.: On normals and projection operators for surfaces defined by point sets. In: Eurographics Symposium on Point-based Graphics, pp. 149–155 (2004)

2. Akima, H.: A method of bivariate interpolation and smooth surface fitting for irregularly distributed data points. ACM Trans. Math. Softw. **4**, 148–159 (1978)

3. Arge, E., Dæhlen, M., Tveito, A.: Approximation of scattered data using smooth grid functions. J. Comput. Appl. Math. **59**, 191–205 (1995)

4. Belytschko, T., Krongauz, Y., Organ, D., Fleming, M., Krysl, P.: Meshless methods: An overview and recent developments. Comput. Methods Appl. Mech. Eng. **139**, 3–47 (1996)

5. Bertram, M., Barnes, J.C., Hamann, B., Joy, K.I., Pottmann, H., Wushour, D.: Piecewise optimal triangulation for the approximation of scattered data in the plane. Comput. Aided Geom. Des. **17**, 767–787 (2000)

6. Bookstein, F.L.: Principal warps: Thin-plate splines and the decomposition of deformations. IEEE Trans. Pattern Anal. Mach. Intell. **11**(6), 567–585 (1989)

7. Bozzini, M., Lenarduzzi, L., Rossini, M.: Polyharmonic splines: An approximation method for noisy scattered data of extra-large size. Appl. Math. Comput. **216**, 317–331 (2010)

8. Brown, J.L.: Vertex based data dependent triangulations. Comput. Aided Geom. Des. **8**, 239–251 (1991)

9. Buhmann, M.D.: A new class of radial basis functions with compact support. Math. Comput. **70**(233), 307–318 (2000)

10. Carlson, R.E., Foley, T.A.: The parameter R^2 in multiquadric interpolation. Comput. Math. Appl. **21**(9), 29–42 (1991)

11. Carr, J.C., Beatson, R.K., Cherrie, J.B., Mitchell, T.J., Fright, W.R., McCallum, B.C., Evans, T.R.: Reconstruction and representation of 3D objects with radial basis functions. In: Proc. SIGGRAPH '01 Conf., pp. 67–76 (2001)

12. Chang, L.H.T., Said, H.B.: A C^2 triangular patch for the interpolation of functional scattered data. Comput. Aided Des. **29**(6), 407–412 (1997)

13. Choi, Y.-L., Yoo, K.-W., Cho, N.-I., Lee, J.-H.: Line based image matching method. US Patent 9,884,079, Filed 20 Jun. 2001, Patented 29 Aug. 2002

14. Chui, C.K., Lai, M.-J.: Filling polygonal holes using C^1 cubic triangular spline patches. Comput. Aided Geom. Des. **17**, 297–307 (2000)

15. Constantini, P., Manni, C.: On a class of polynomial triangular macro-elements. Comput. Appl. Math. **73**, 45–64 (1996)

16. Dahmen, W., Meyling, R.H.J.G., Ursem, J.H.M.: Scattered data interpolation by bivariate C^1-piecewise quadratic functions. Approx. Theory Appl. **6**(3), 6–29 (1990)

17. Davydov, O., Schumaker, L.L.: Stable approximation and interpolation with C^1 quartic bivariate splines. SIAM J. Numer. Anal. **39**(5), 1732–1748 (2002)

18. Doo, D.W.H.: A subdivision algorithm for smoothing down irregular shaped polyhedrons. In: Proc. Interactive Techniques in Computer Aided Design, vol. 1, pp. 157–165 (1978)

19. Doo, D., Sabin, M.: Behavior of recursive division surfaces near extraordinary points. In: Computer Aided Design, pp. 356–360 (1978)

20. Duchon, J.: Splines minimizing rotation-invariant seminorms in Sobolov spaces. In: Constructive Theory of Functions of Several Variables. Lecture Notes in Math., vol. 571, pp. 85–100. Springer, Berlin (1977)

21. Dyn, N., Levin, D., Rippa, S.: Algorithms for the construction of data dependent triangulation. In: Mason, J.S., Cox, M.G. (eds.) Algorithms for Approximation II, pp. 185–192. Chapman and Hall, New York (1988)

22. Dyn, N., Levin, D., Gregory, J.A.: A butterfly subdivision scheme for surface interpolation with tension control. ACM Trans. Graph. **9**(2), 160–169 (1990)

23. Floater, M.S., Iske, A.: Multistep scattered data interpolation using compactly supported radial basis functions. J. Comput. Appl. Math. **73**, 65–78 (1996)

24. Fornefett, M., Rohr, K., Stiehl, H.S.: Radial basis functions with compact support for elastic registration of medical images. Image Vis. Comput. **19**, 87–96 (2001)

25. Franke, R.: Scattered data interpolation: Tests of some methods. Math. Comput. **38**(157), 181–200 (1982)

26. Franke, R.: Thin plate splines with tension. Comput. Aided Geom. Des. **2**, 87–95 (1985)

27. Franke, R., Nielson, G.: Smooth interpolation of large sets of scattered data. Int. J. Numer. Methods Eng. **15**, 1691–1704 (1980)

28. Franke, R., Schumaker, L.L.: A bibliography of multivariate approximation. In: Chui, C., Schumaker, L., Utrerus, F. (eds.) Topics in Multivariate Approximation, pp. 79–98. Academic Press, San Diego (1987)

29. Franke, R., Hagen, H., Nielson, G.M.: Least squares surface approximation to scattered data using multiquadric functions. Adv. Comput. Math. **2**, 81–99 (1994)

30. Goodman, T.N.T., Said, H.B., Chang, L.H.T.: Local derivative estimation for scattered data interpolation. Appl. Math. Comput. **68**, 41–50 (1995)

31. Goshtasby, A.: Piecewise linear mapping functions for image registration. Pattern Recognit. **19**(6), 459–466 (1986)

32. Goshtasby, A.: Piecewise cubic mapping functions for image registration. Pattern Recognit. **20**(5), 525–533 (1987)

33. Goshtasby, A.: Registration of image with geometric distortion. IEEE Trans. Geosci. Remote Sens. **26**(1), 60–64 (1988)

34. Goshtasby, A.: A weighted linear method for approximation of irregularly spaced data. In: Lucian, M.M., Neamtu, M. (eds.) Geometric Modeling and Computing, pp. 285–294. Nashboro Press, Brentwood (2004)

35. Goshtasby, A.: Surface approximation to scattered lines. Comput-Aided Des. Appl. **4**(1–4), 277–286 (2007)

36. Goshtasby, A.: Registration of multi-view images. In: LeMoigne, J., Netanyahoo, N.S., Eastman, R.D. (eds.) Image Registration for Remote Sensing, pp. 153–178. Cambridge University Press, Cambridge (2011)

37. Goshtasby, A.: Design and recovery of 2-D and 3-D shapes using rational Gaussian curves and surfaces. Int. J. Comput. Vis. **10**(3), 233–256 (1993)

38. Green, P.J., Sibson, R.: Computing Dirichlet tessellation in the plane. Comput. J. **21**, 168–173 (1978)

39. Greiner, G., Kolb, A., Riepl, A.: Scattered data interpolation using data dependent optimization techniques. Graph. Models **64**, 1–18 (2002)

40. Grosse, E.: A catalogue of algorithms for approximation. In: Mason, J., Cox, M. (eds.) Algorithms for Approximation II, pp. 479–514. Chapman and Hall, London (1990)

41. Harder, R.L., Desmarais, R.N.: Interpolation using surface splines. J. Aircr. **9**(2), 189–191 (1972)

42. Hardy, R.L.: Multiquadric equations of topography and other irregular surfaces. J. Geophys. Res. **76**(8), 1905–1915 (1971)

43. Hardy, R.L.: Theory and applications of the multiquadric-biharmonic method—20 years of discovery—1969–1988. Comput. Math. Appl. **19**(8/9), 163–208 (1990)

44. Hoppe, H., DeRose, T., Duchamp, T., Halstead, M., Jin, H., McDonald, J., Schweitzer, J., Stuetzle, W.: Piecewise smooth surface reconstruction. In: SIGGRAPH'94: Proc. 21st Annual Conference on Computer Graphics and Interactive Techniques, pp. 295–302 (1994)

45. Hussain, M.Z., Hussain, M.: C^1 positive scattered data interpolation. Comput. Math. Appl. **59**, 457–567 (2010)

46. Kamgar-Parsi, B., Kamgar-Parsi, B.: Algorithms for matching 3D line sets. IEEE Trans. Pattern Anal. Mach. Intell. **26**(5), 582–593 (2004)

47. Kansa, E.J., Carlson, R.E.: Improved accuracy of multiquadric interpolation using variable shape parameters. Comput. Math. Appl. **24**, 99–120 (1992)

48. Klucewicz, I.M.: A piecewise C^1 interpolant to arbitrarily spaced data. Comput. Graph. Image Process. **8**, 92–112 (1978)

49. Lai, M.-J.: Convex preserving scattered data interpolation using bivariate C^1 cubic spline. J. Comput. Appl. Math. **119**, 249–258 (2000)

50. Lai, M.-J., Wenston, P.: L_1 spline methods for scattered data interpolation and approximation. Adv. Comput. Math. **21**, 293–315 (2004)

51. Lancaster, P.: Moving weighted least-squares methods. In: Sahney, B.N. (ed.) Polynomial and Spline Approximation, pp. 103–120 (1979)

52. Lancaster, P., Šalkauskas, K.: Surfaces generated by moving least squares methods. Math. Comput. **37**(155), 141–158 (1981)

53. Lancaster, P., Šalkauskas, K.: Curve and Surface Fitting: An Introduction. Academic Press, San Diego (1986), pp. 55–62, 225–244
54. Lawson, C.L.: Software for C^1 surface interpolation. In: Rice, J.R. (ed.) Mathematical Software III, pp. 161–194. Academic Press, San Diego (1977)
55. Lazzaro, D., Montefusco, L.B.: Radial basis functions for the multivariate interpolation of large scattered data sets. J. Comput. Appl. Math. **140**, 521–536 (2002)
56. Lee, D.T., Schachter, B.J.: Two algorithms for constructing a Delaunay triangulation. Int. J. Comput. Inf. Sci. **9**, 219–242 (1980)
57. Lee, S., Wolberg, G., Shin, S.Y.: Scattered data interpolation with multilevel B-splines. IEEE Trans. Vis. Comput. Graph. **3**(3), 228–244 (1997)
58. Levin, D.: The approximation power of moving least-squares. Math. Comput. **67**(224), 1517–1531 (1998)
59. Li, A.: Convexity preserving interpolation. Comput. Aided Geom. Des. **16**, 127–147 (1999)
60. Loop, C.: Smooth subdivision surfaces based on triangles. Master's thesis, Department of Mathematics, University of Utah (1987)
61. Lorensen, W.E., Cline, H.E.: Marching cubes: A high resolution 3D surface construction algorithm. In: Proc. SIGGRAPH, pp. 71–78. ACM Press/ACM SIGGRAPH, New York (1992)
62. Lu, H., Schumaker, L.L.: Monotone surfaces to scattered data using C^1 piecewise cubics. SIAM J. Numer. Anal. **34**(2), 569–585 (1997)
63. Luo, Z., Peng, X.: A C^1-rational spline in range restricted interpolation of scattered data. J. Comput. Appl. Math. **194**, 255–266 (2006)
64. Maillot, J., Stam, J.: A unified subdivision scheme for polygonal modeling. In: Chalmers, A., Rhyne, T.-M. (eds.) EUROGRAPHICS, vol. 20(3) (2001)
65. Marinov, M., Kobbelt, L.: Optimization methods for scattered data approximation with subdivision surfaces. Graph. Models **67**, 452–473 (2005)
66. Maude, A.D.: Interpolation—mainly for graph plotters. Comput. J. **16**(1), 64–65 (1973)
67. McLain, D.H.: Two dimensional interpolation from random data. Comput. J. **19**(2), 178–181 (1976)
68. Meijering, E.: A chronology of interpolation: From ancient astronomy to modern signal and image processing. Proc. IEEE **90**(3), 319–342 (2002)
69. Meinguet, J.: An intrinsic approach to multivariate spline interpolation at arbitrary points. In: Sahney, B.N. (ed.) Polynomial and Spline Approximation, pp. 163–190. Reidel, Dordrecht (1979)
70. Nejhum, S.M.S., Chi, Y.-T., Yang, M.-H.: Higher-dimensional affine registration and vision applications. IEEE Trans. Pattern Anal. Mach. Intell. **33**(7), 1324–1338 (2011)
71. Nielson, G.M.: Dual marching cubes. In: Proc. IEEE Visualization, pp. 489–496 (2004)
72. Ohtake, Y., Belyaev, A., Seidel, H.-P.: 3D scattered data interpolation and approximation with multilevel compactly supported RBFs. Graph. Models **67**, 150–165 (2005)
73. Percell, P.: On cubic and quartic Clough-Tocher finite elements. SIAM J. Numer. Anal. **13**, 100–103 (1976)
74. Peters, J., Reif, U.: The simplest subdivision scheme for smoothing polyhedra. ACM Trans. Graph. **16**(4), 420–431 (1997)
75. Powell, M.J.D.: Radial basis functions for multivariate interpolation: A review. In: Mason, J.C., Cox, M.G. (eds.) Algorithms for Approximation, pp. 143–167. Clarendon Press, Oxford (1987)
76. Powell, M.J.D., Sabin, M.A.: Piecewise quadratic approximation on triangles. ACM Trans. Math. Softw. **3**, 316–325 (1977)
77. Qu, R., Agarwal, R.P.: Smooth surface interpolation to scattered data using interpolatory subdivision algorithms. Comput. Math. Appl. **32**(3), 93–110 (1996)
78. Renka, R.J.: Multivariate interpolation of large sets of scattered data. ACM Trans. Math. Softw. **14**(2), 139–148 (1988)
79. Renka, R.J.: Algorithm 833: CSRFPAXK—Interpolation of scattered data with a C^1 convexity-preserving surface. ACM Trans. Math. Softw. **30**(2), 200–211 (2004)
80. Renka, R.J., Brown, R.: Algorithm 790: CSHEP2D: Cubic Shepard method for bivariate interpolation of scattered data. ACM Trans. Math. Softw. **25**(1), 70–73 (1999)

81. Renka, R.J., Brown, R.: Algorithm 791: TSHEP2D: Cosine series Shepard method for bivariate interpolation of scattered data. ACM Trans. Math. Softw. **25**(1), 74–77 (1999)
82. Renka, R.J., Brown, R.: Algorithm 792: Accuracy tests of ACM algorithms for interpolation of scattered data in the plane. ACM Trans. Math. Softw. **25**(1), 78–94 (1999)
83. Rippa, S.: Scattered data interpolation using minimum energy Powell-Sabin elements and data dependent triangulations. Numer. Algorithms **5**, 577–587 (1993)
84. Rivlin, T.J.: Least-squares approximation. In: An Introduction to the Approximation of Functions, pp. 48–61. Dover, New York (1969)
85. Rohr, K., Stiehl, H.S., Sprengel, R., Buzug, T.M., Weese, J., Kuhn, M.H.: Landmark-based elastic registration using approximating thin-plate splines. IEEE Trans. Med. Imaging **20**(6), 526–534 (2001)
86. Savchenko, V.V., Pasko, A.A., Okunev, O.G., Kunii, T.L.: Function representation of solids reconstructed from scattered surface points and contours. Comput. Graph. Forum **14**(4), 181–188 (1995)
87. Schagen, I.P.: The use of stochastic processes in interpolation and approximation. Int. J. Comput. Math., Sect. B **8**, 63–76 (1980)
88. Scheib, V., Haber, J., Lin, M.C., Seidel, H.-P.: Efficient fitting and rendering of large scattered data sets using subdivision surfaces. Eurographics **21**(3), 353–362 (2002)
89. Schmidt, J.W.: Scattered data interpolation applying regional C^1 splines on refined triangulations. Math. Mech. **80**(1), 27–33 (2000)
90. Schröder, P., Zorin, D.: Subdivision for modeling and animation. SIGGRAPH Course No. 36 Notes (1998)
91. Schumaker, L.L.: Triangulation methods. In: Chui, C.K., Schumaker, L.L., Utreras, F. (eds.) Topics in Multivariate Approximation, pp. 219–232. Academic Press, San Diego (1987)
92. Schumaker, L.L.: Computing optimal triangulations using simulated annealing. Comput. Aided Geom. Des. **10**, 329–345 (1993)
93. Schumaker, L.L.: Multivariate spline bibliography. In: Chui, C., Neamtu, M., Schumaker, L.L. (eds.) Approximation Theory XI: Gatlinburg. Nashboro Press, Brentwood (2005)
94. Schumaker, L.L., Speleers, H.: Nonnegativity preserving macro-element interpolation of scattered data. Comput. Aided Geom. Des. **27**(3), 245–261 (2010)
95. Schweitzer, J.E.: Analysis and application of subdivision surfaces. Ph.D. Dissertation, University of Washington, Seattle (1996)
96. Shepard, D.: A two-dimensional interpolation function for irregularly spaced data. In: Proc. 23rd Nat'l Conf. ACM, pp. 517–524 (1968)
97. Shirman, L.A., Sequin, C.H.: Local surface interpolation with shape parameters between adjoining Gregory patches. Comput. Aided Geom. Des. **7**, 375–388 (1990)
98. Stam, J.: On subdivision schemes generalizing uniform B-spline surfaces of arbitrary degree. Comput. Aided Geom. Des. **18**, 383–396 (2001)
99. Stead, S.E.: Estimation of gradients from scattered data. Rocky Mt. J. Math. **14**, 265–279 (1984)
100. Turk, G., O'Brien, J.F.: Modeling with implicit surfaces that interpolate. ACM Trans. Graph. **21**(4), 855–873 (2002)
101. Wang, L., Neumann, U., You, S.: Image matching using line signature. US Patent 12,486,506, Filed 17 Jun. 2009, Patented 23 Dec. 2010
102. Wendland, H.: Piecewise polynomial, positive definite and compactly supported radial functions of minimal degree. Adv. Comput. Math. **4**, 389–396 (1995)
103. Zorin, D.: Subdivision and multiresolution surface representations. Ph.D. Dissertation, Caltech, Pasadena (1997)
104. Zorin, D., Schröder, P., Sweldens, W.: Interpolating subdivision for meshes with arbitrary topology. In: Computer Graphics Proceedings (SIGGRAPH 96), pp. 189–192 (1996)

Chapter 10
Image Resampling and Compositing

10.1 Image Resampling

The transformation

$$X = f(x, y), \tag{10.1}$$

$$Y = g(x, y) \tag{10.2}$$

relates the coordinates of points in the reference image to the coordinates of corresponding points in the sensed image. Given the (x, y) coordinates of a point in the reference image, relations (10.1) and (10.2) determine the (X, Y) coordinates of the same point in the sensed image. By reading the intensity at (X, Y) in the sensed image and saving at (x, y) in a new image, the sensed image is point-by-point resampled to the geometry of the reference image. Therefore, to resample the sensed image, the reference image is scanned and, for each pixel (x, y), the corresponding point (X, Y) is determined in the sensed image. Although coordinates (x, y) are integers, coordinates (X, Y) are floating-point numbers. Since intensities at only integer coordinates are available in the sensed image, the intensity at point (X, Y) has to be estimated from the intensities of a small number of pixels surrounding (X, Y).

If the sensed image were a continuous image, the intensity of any point (X, Y) in the image would be known. However, a sensed image $I(u, v)$ contains only uniformly spaced samples of a continuous image $C(X, Y)$. A resampling method has to estimate the intensity at (X, Y) from the intensities at discrete locations surrounding it. Figure 10.1 depicts the resampling process. Pixel a in the reference image maps to point A in the continuous sensed image. To estimate the intensity at A, intensities in a small neighborhood of A in the discrete sensed image are used. Different methods to achieve this estimation have been developed. In the following sections, nearest-neighbor, bilinear interpolation, cubic convolution, cubic spline interpolation, and radially symmetric resampling methods are discussed.

A.A. Goshtasby, *Image Registration*,
Advances in Computer Vision and Pattern Recognition,
DOI 10.1007/978-1-4471-2458-0_10, © Springer-Verlag London Limited 2012

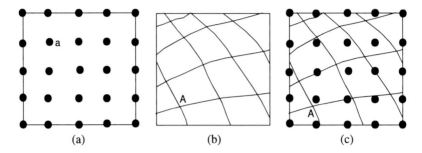

Fig. 10.1 The resampling process. (**a**) Pixels in the reference image. (**b**) A continuous sensed image. The *grid points* in this image correspond to the pixels in the reference image. (**c**) Overlaying of the continuous and discrete sensed images. The continuous sensed image is determined from intensities in the discrete sensed image. Resampling involves scanning the reference image and, for each pixel *a*, determining the intensity of the corresponding grid point *A* in the continuous sensed image. Intensity at *A* in the continuous image is estimated from the intensities of a small number of pixels surrounding *A* in the discrete sensed image

10.1.1 Nearest-Neighbor

Given the coordinates (X, Y) of a point, where X and Y are floating-point numbers, and assuming u is the integer part of X and v is the integer part of Y, the rectangular neighborhood defined by pixels (u, v), $(u, v + 1)$, $(u + 1, v)$, and $(u + 1, v + 1)$ contain point (X, Y). Among the four pixels, the one closest to (X, Y) is determined and its intensity is used as the intensity at (X, Y). There is actually no need to calculate the distances to achieve this. If $X - u < 0.5$, u is considered the X-coordinate of the pixel to be used, otherwise $u + 1$ is used. If $Y - v < 0.5$, the Y-coordinate of the pixel to be used is v, otherwise $v + 1$ is used. This is actually a rounding operation; therefore, the intensity at pixel $[round(X), round(Y)]$ is taken and considered the intensity at (X, Y).

Nearest neighbor resampling preserves the image intensities. Therefore, the histograms of an image before and after resampling will be very similar. If certain intensities do not exist in an image, they will not be present in the resampled image. The process does not blur an image, but it may produce aliasing effects. Horizontal and vertical edges in an image may appear jagged after rotation of the image by angles that are not a multiple of 90 degrees. Figure 10.2 shows a resampling example by the nearest-neighbor method. Figure 10.2a is an image of a penny and Fig. 10.2b is the penny after being rotated by 10 degrees counterclockwise about the image center and resampled by the nearest-neighbor method. The jagged appearance of the penny, especially along its boundary, is quite evident in the resampled image.

The computational complexity of nearest-neighbor resampling is on the order of n comparisons if reference image containing n pixels.

Fig. 10.2 (a) A penny and
(b) its rotation by 10 degrees
counterclockwise when using
nearest-neighbor resampling

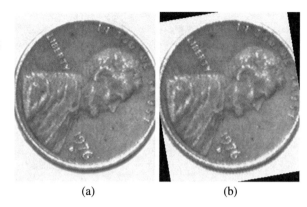

(a)   (b)

10.1.2 Bilinear Interpolation

In bilinear interpolation, the intensity at a point is determined from the weighted sum of intensities of the four pixels closest to it. Therefore, given location (X, Y) and assuming u is the integer part of X and v is the integer part of Y, the intensity at (X, Y) is estimated from the intensities at (u, v), $(u + 1, v)$, $(u, v + 1)$, and $(u + 1, v + 1)$. This resampling involves first finding the intensity at (X, v) from the linear interpolation of intensities at (u, v) and $(u + 1, v)$. Let this intensity be $I(X, v)$. Then, finding the intensity at $(X, v + 1)$ from the linear interpolation of intensities at $(u, v + 1)$ and $(u + 1, v + 1)$. Let this intensity be $I(X, v + 1)$. Finally, finding the intensity at (X, Y) from the linear interpolation of intensities at (X, v) and $(X, v + 1)$. This can be summarized as

$$I(X, Y) = W_{u,v}I(u, v) + W_{u+1,v}I(u + 1, v) + W_{u,v+1}I(u, v + 1)$$
$$+ W_{u+1,v+1}I(u + 1, v + 1), \tag{10.3}$$

where

$$W_{u,v} = (u + 1 - X)(v + 1 - Y), \tag{10.4}$$

$$W_{u+1,v} = (X - u)(v + 1 - Y), \tag{10.5}$$

$$W_{u,v+1} = (u + 1 - X)(Y - v), \tag{10.6}$$

$$W_{u+1,v+1} = (X - u)(Y - v), \tag{10.7}$$

and $I(u, v)$, $I(u + 1, v)$, $I(u, v + 1$, and $I(u + 1, v + 1)$ are intensities at (u, v), $(u + 1, v)$, $(u, v + 1)$, and $(u + 1, v + 1)$, respectively. Figure 10.3a depicts this estimation process. Figure 10.3b shows resampling of Fig. 10.2a after rotation counterclockwise by 10 degrees about the image center by bilinear interpolation. Compared to Fig. 10.2b, we see that the aliasing effect has mostly disappeared. One should also note that this anti-aliasing is at the cost of blurring the image. Therefore, if repeated resampling of an image is required, the process will gradually smooth image details. Bilinear interpolation changes image intensities, thereby changing the histogram of the image.

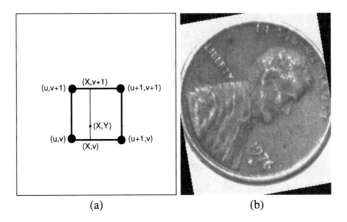

(a)   (b)

Fig. 10.3 (a) Estimating the intensity at (X, Y) from intensities at (u, v), $(u + 1, v)$, $(u, v + 1)$, and $(u + 1, v + 1)$ by bilinear interpolation. (b) The penny shown in Fig. 10.2a after rotation by 10 degrees counterclockwise about its center and resampling by bilinear interpolation

Computationally, resampling by bilinear interpolation requires on the order of n multiplications if the reference image contains n pixels. Therefore, nearest-neighbor and bilinear interpolation have the same computational complexity, although nearest-neighbor is several times faster than bilinear interpolation.

10.1.3 Cubic Convolution

In cubic convolution, the intensity at point (X, Y) is estimated from the intensities of a 4×4 grid of pixels closest to it as depicted in Fig. 10.4a. Just like a separable 2-D convolution that can be performed via 1-D convolutions row-by-row and then column-by-column, cubic convolution can be carried out in 1-D first along the rows and then along the columns [8]. Therefore, first, 1-D interpolation is carried out along the four image rows in the 4×4 neighborhood of (X, Y). This will determine values at $(X, v - 1)$, (X, v), $(X, v + 1)$, and $(X, v + 2)$. Then interpolation is carried out along column X to find the intensity at (X, Y). Figure 10.4a depicts this computation graphically.

If u denotes the integer part of X in a 1-D image, and assuming intensities at $u - 1, u, u + 1$, and $u + 2$ are $I(u - 1)$, $I(u)$, $I(u + 1)$, and $I(u + 2)$, respectively, a function $f(t)$ that interpolates the four intensities should satisfy $f(t_i) = I(t_i)$, where t_i is one of $u - 1, u, u + 1$, or $u + 2$. Function f is defined in terms of a weighted sum of four local functions, the weights representing the intensities at the pixels. That is,

$$f(X) = I(u - 1)f_{-1} + I(u)f_0 + I(u + 1)f_1 + I(u + 2)f_2, \qquad (10.8)$$

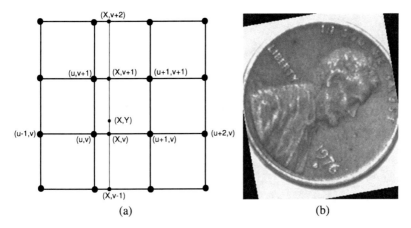

Fig. 10.4 (**a**) Cubic convolution uses intensities in a 4 × 4 neighborhood to estimate the intensity at a point. To determine the intensity at (X, Y), first 1-D interpolation is carried out along the 4 rows to determine intensities at X in each row. Then 1-D interpolation is carried out along column X to determine the intensity at (X, Y). (**b**) Resampling of Fig. 10.2a by cubic convolution

where

$$f_{-1} = -\frac{1}{2}t^3 + t^2 - \frac{1}{2}t, \tag{10.9}$$

$$f_0 = \frac{3}{2}t^3 - \frac{5}{2}t^2 + 1, \tag{10.10}$$

$$f_1 = -\frac{3}{2}t^3 + 2t^2 + \frac{1}{2}t, \tag{10.11}$$

$$f_2 = \frac{1}{2}t^3 - \frac{1}{2}t^2, \tag{10.12}$$

and $t = X - u$. Note that the sum of the local functions for any t in the range from 0 to 1 is 1. $f(X)$ evaluates to $I(u)$ when $X = u$ and it evaluates to $I(u + 1)$ when $X = u + 1$. In a 1-D image with n pixels, the pixel positions are $u = 0, 1, \ldots, n - 1$ with corresponding intensities $I(u)$. At the two image borders, it is assumed that $I(-1) = 3I(0) - 3I(1) + I(2)$ and $I(n) = 3I(n - 1) - 3I(n - 2) + I(n - 3)$. Resampling of the coin image of Fig. 10.2a after rotation counterclockwise by 10 degrees by cubic convolution is shown in Fig. 10.4b.

Although resampling by cubic convolution appears visually similar to that of bilinear interpolation, by a closer examination it becomes apparent that intensities estimated by the two methods are not the same. An example is given in Fig. 10.5. The image of Fig. 10.2a is rotated by 10 degrees 36 times. This is expected to produce the original image if no resampling errors existed. However, due to resampling errors, the obtained image is different from the original one. The absolute difference between the intensities of the obtained image and the intensities of the original image show the magnitude of resampling error.

Figures 10.5a–c show absolute errors when nearest-neighbor, bilinear interpolation, and cubic convolution, respectively, are used. Only errors within the circle

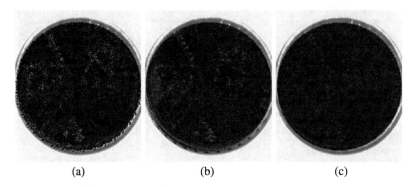

(a)   (b)   (c)

Fig. 10.5 (a)–(c) Resampling errors when rotating the image in Fig. 10.2a 36 times with 10-degree increments and computing the absolute difference between corresponding pixels in the original and resampled images using nearest-neighbor, bilinear interpolation, and cubic convolution, respectively. Higher intensities show larger errors

touching the image borders can be computed. As the image is rotated, areas near image corners move outside the image, causing them to be cut off. Consequently, after a 360-degree rotation, only pixels within the largest circle that can be contained in the image remain. Pixels outside this circle will all assume a value of zero. Therefore, when subtracting the resampled image from the original image, intensities of pixels outside this circle become equal to the intensities of the original image. This experiment reveals that among the three methods, cubic convolution is the most accurate method, while nearest-neighbor is the least accurate method.

Computational complexity of cubic convolution is $O(n)$ multiplications when reference image contains n pixels. Cubic convolution is several times slower than bilinear interpolation.

10.1.4 Cubic Spline

Given intensities $\{I_i : i = -1, 0, 1, 2\}$ of pixels at $\{u_i : i = -1, 0, 1, 2\}$ in a 1-D image, the intensity at point $0 \leq u < 1$ in the image can be estimated using a B-spline curve of order four (degree three) from:

$$f(u) = \sum_{i=-1}^{2} I_i b_i(u), \tag{10.13}$$

where

$$b_{-1}(u) = \left(-u^3 + 3u^2 - 3u + 1\right)/6, \tag{10.14}$$

$$b_0(u) = \left(3u^3 - 6u^2 + 4\right)/6, \tag{10.15}$$

$$b_1(u) = \left(-3u^3 + 3u^2 + 3u + 1\right)/6, \tag{10.16}$$

$$b_2(u) = u^3/6 \tag{10.17}$$

are the B-spline basis functions of order 4 and I_is are the control points of the curve. Note that the sum of the B-spline basis functions is 1 everywhere in the range $0 \le u \le 1$. The basis functions, when evaluated at a particular point u, show the contributions of the control points in the computation of the intensity at that point. The intensity at point u in a 1-D image is, therefore, a weighted sum of the intensities of the four pixels closest to it.

Formula (10.13) shows an approximation, thus $f(u)$ will only approximately evaluate to the intensities at the pixels. In order to interpolate the intensities, it is required to find new intensities such that, when they are used as the control points, the obtained B-spline curve will evaluate to the intensities at the pixels. That is $\{I'_j : j = -1, \ldots, 2\}$ should be determined such that

$$I_i = \sum_{j=-1}^{2} I'_j b_j(u_i), \quad i = -1, \ldots, 2. \tag{10.18}$$

Since two adjacent B-spline segments of order four share three control points (pixel intensities in our case), we cannot determine the control points of an interpolating B-spline by repeated use of formula (10.18). Instead, it is required to determine the entire set of control points collectively. This would require the solution of a system of n equations if a 1-D image with n pixels is given.

Estimation of the intensity at point (u, v) requires use of intensities of pixels at the 4×4 grid closest to the point. To make this estimation, first, new intensities should be determined so that when used as the control points in a bicubic B-spline surface, the obtained surface will interpolate the given intensities. Computation of the control points of a bicubic B-spline surface interpolating the intensities in an image with n pixels requires the solution of a system of n equations. This computation is on the order of n^2 multiplications. A parallel algorithm to calculate the control points of an interpolating B-spline surface with a smaller computational complexity is given by Cheng and Goshtasby [1].

Properties of B-splines as filters have been explored by Ferrari et al. [3]. Noticing that a B-spline curve acts like a digital filter when intensities of uniformly spaced pixels in a 1-D image are used as its control points; the control points of the B-spline curve interpolating the intensities can be obtained through an inverse filtering operation [6]. This involves finding the Fourier transform of the image and dividing it point-by-point by the Fourier transform of the B-spline filter. The inverse Fourier transform of the result will produce the control points of the interpolating B-spline. If FFT algorithm is used to compute the Fourier transform coefficients, it will take on the order of $n \log n$ multiplications to find the n control points of the interpolating B-spline. This is a reduction in computation time from $O(n^2)$ to $O(n \log n)$ multiplications.

The cubic spline method is computationally more expensive than cubic convolution; however, cubic spline has been found to produce more accurate results than cubic convolution [7].

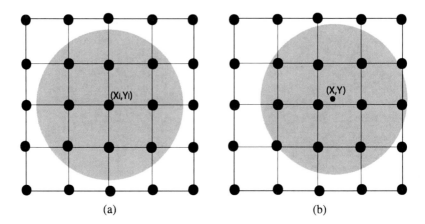

Fig. 10.6 (**a**) A radial function with local support of radius 1.8 pixels centered at pixel (X_i, Y_i). This function shows the influence of pixel (X_i, Y_i) on the interpolating function within the *shaded area*. (**b**) The intensity at (X, Y) is estimated from the intensities of pixels whose distances to (X, Y) are less than a. The pixels used in the calculation are those falling in the *shaded area* in this figure when $a = 1.8$ pixels

10.1.5 Compactly Supported Radial Functions

Cubic spline, cubic convolution, and bilinear interpolation are not radially symmetric functions. In general, locally defined separable functions are not radially symmetric because they approximate rectangular domains. The effect of such functions on an image depends on the orientation of the image. For a resampling operation to be rotationally invariant, the function used in resampling should be radially symmetric. Consider centering the compactly supported radial function,

$$f(r_i) = \begin{cases} 1 - 3r_i^2 + 2r_i^3, & 0 \le r_i \le 1, \\ 0, & r_i > 1, \end{cases} \tag{10.19}$$

at pixel (X_i, Y_i), where

$$r_i = \frac{\sqrt{(X - X_i)^2 + (Y - Y_i)^2}}{a} \tag{10.20}$$

and a is the radius of the domain where the function is nonzero (Fig. 10.6a). Function $f(r_i)$ will then show the influence of the intensity at (X_i, Y_i) on intensity at (X, Y). Note that since $df(r_i)/dr_i = 0$ at $r_i = 1$, not only does $f(r_i)$ vanish at $r_i = 1$, its derivative vanishes at $r_i = 1$. Therefore, if radial function f is centered at each pixel and a weighted sum of the functions is computed, the obtained surface will be smooth everywhere in the image domain.

Assuming intensity at (X_i, Y_i) in the sensed image is I_i, for the surface to interpolate the intensities in a circular neighborhood of radius a centered at point of

Table 10.1 Computational complexities of nearest-neighbor, bilinear interpolation, cubic convolution, cubic spline, and radial functions with local support in image resampling. It is assumed that the sensed image is resampled to a reference image of size n pixels

Type of resampling	Computational complexity
Nearest-neighbor	$O(n)$
Bilinear interpolation	$O(n)$
Cubic convolution	$O(n)$
Cubic spline, direct computation	$O(n^2)$
Cubic spline, using FFT	$O(n \log n)$
Compactly supported radial functions	$O(nm^2)$

interest (X, Y) (Fig. 10.6b), new intensities I_i' should be computed at the pixels within the neighborhood so that when

$$I(X, Y) = \sum_{r_i < a} I_i' f(r_i), \qquad (10.21)$$

is evaluated at the pixels within that neighborhood produce the original intensities, that is $I(X_i, Y_i) = I_i$ for all pixels (X_i, Y_i) within the circular neighborhood of radius a centered at (X, Y). Knowing I_i' at the pixels, the intensity at (X, Y) can then be determined from (10.21).

If there are m pixels within a circular neighborhood of radius a pixels, determination of new intensities at the pixels within the neighborhood requires on the order of m^2 multiplications. Since this should be repeated for each pixel, if reference image contains n pixels, resampling the sensed image to register with the reference image requires on the order of nm^2 multiplications.

10.1.6 Summary

Nearest-neighbor, bilinear interpolation, cubic convolution, cubic spline, and compactly supported radial functions in image resampling were discussed. The computational complexities of these resampling methods are summarized in Table 10.1. Nearest-neighbor is the fastest while compactly supported radial functions is the slowest.

Nearest-neighbor resampling does not change the image intensities; it preserves them. However, it can cause aliasing. Bilinear interpolation reduces the aliasing effect by slightly smoothing image intensities. Among all resampling methods, bilinear interpolation is perhaps the best compromise between speed and accuracy. Cubic convolution requires several times more time than bilinear interpolation, but it produces less aliasing. Cubic spline is considerably slower than cubic convolution, especially when the control points of the spline are determined by solving a system of equations. However, resampling accuracy of cubic spline is found to be better than that of cubic convolution [8].

Also discussed was use of radially symmetric kernels in image resampling. Considering the fact that the neighborhood size used in radial functions is adjustable,

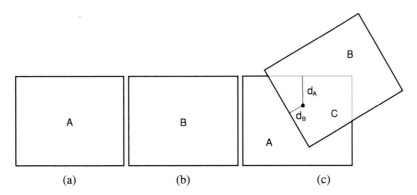

Fig. 10.7 (**a**), (**b**) Reference image A and sensed image B. (**c**) Registration and intensity blending of images A and B using inverse-distance weighting. C is the area of overlap between images A and B

this resampling method can be adapted to the level of details in an image. If cubic spline is used, since a fixed neighborhood size is used independent of the spatial frequency contents in an image, the matrix of coefficients may become singular for some images, making image resampling impossible. In resampling by compactly supported radial functions since the equations to be solved are for the determination of local intensities, the systems are relatively small and the likelihood of becoming singular reduces significantly. However, since a system of equations need be solved for resampling the intensity at each pixel, the process is the slowest among the resampling methods discussed.

10.2 Image Compositing and Mosaicking

After registering two images, there often is a need to combine the images into a larger image called a *composite* or a *mosaic*. Intensities at corresponding pixels in the overlap area of registered images may be different due to differences in environmental and sensor parameters during image acquisition. Different-view images of a scene record different intensities at the same scene point if the scene has specular characteristics. Change in scene brightness due to difference in time of day or weather conditions results in intensity differences between corresponding points in images.

The problem to be solved is as follows: Given reference image A and sensed image B, by registering B to A, we would like to create a mosaic that covers scene areas contained in both A and B as depicted in Fig. 10.7c. Denoting the area of overlap between the images by C, we would like to find intensities in C in such a way that they vary smoothly from region C to both regions A and B, creating a seamless mosaic.

10.2.1 *Intensity blending*

Intensities in region A in Fig. 10.7c are those of the reference image, intensities in region B are those of the sensed image, and intensities in region C are computed from a weighted sum of intensities of corresponding pixels in the reference and sensed images. To make sure that a seamless mosaic is obtained, the weights at a pixel in region C are set inversely proportional to the distances of that pixel to pixels closest to it in regions A and B. The closer the pixel in C is to region A, the higher the contribution of the pixel in the reference image will be to the computed intensity. If the distance of a pixel in region C to the pixel closest to it in region A is d_A and its distance to the pixel closest to it in region B is d_B, the intensity at the pixel in C is estimated from

$$I^C = \frac{I^A d_B^{-1} + I^B d_A^{-1}}{d_A^{-1} + d_B^{-1}}, \tag{10.22}$$

where I^A and I^B are intensities of corresponding pixels in the reference and sensed images in the overlap area, and I^C is the estimated intensity there. Distances d_A and d_B can be calculated ahead of time efficiently by finding the distance transform [2, 4, 9] of the mosaic image using the border pixels in each image as the object pixels and the remaining pixels as the background pixels.

Intensity blending by weighted averaging has been referred to as *feathering* [10]. Intensity blending in this manner can cause ghosting effects if images in the overlap area have differences due to occlusion or other factors. One way to reduce the ghosting effect is to use a higher power of distances. This will assign the intensities in most areas of C to either those of image A or image B, reducing the areas in C affected by ghosting. If too high a power is used, however, transition of intensities from one image to another becomes rather sharp and visible when the images have large intensity differences.

An alternative method for overcoming ghosting is to find a function that maps intensities of the sensed image to those of the reference image so that, rather than blending intensities of both images in the overlap area, intensities of only the reference image are used everywhere. The process assigns intensities of the reference image to region C, and since intensities in region A are already those of the reference image and intensities of region B are converted to those of the reference image, the composite image will have only intensities of the reference image. The process, in effect, by not blending intensities in region C, avoids the ghosting effect. This is explained in more detail next.

10.2.2 *Intensity Mapping*

Sometimes intensities in the images to be registered represent different scene properties, and averaging the properties is not meaningful. Consider the reference and sensed images shown in Figs. 10.8a and 10.8b. They represent aerial images of a city

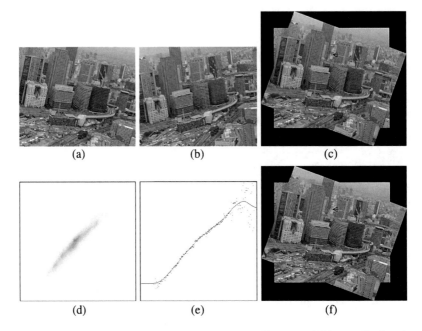

Fig. 10.8 (a), (b) Aerial images of a city downtown in different modalities. (c) Registration of the images and blending of image intensities by inverse-distance weighting. (d) Joint probability density (JPD) of intensities in sensed and reference images. (e) Intensity map of the sensed image with respect to the reference image. A *black dot* identifies the row with the highest value in each column of JPD. The curve shows approximation of the *black dots* by a rational Gaussian (RaG) curve. The curve maps intensities in the sensed to intensities in the reference images. (f) Compositing images (a) and (b) after registering them and mapping the intensities of the sensed image to those of the reference image (without intensity blending)

downtown in different modalities. While 10.8a is obtained by a sensor with spectral frequencies centered at red, the image in Fig. 10.8b is obtained by a sensor with frequencies centered at green. Registering the images and blending the intensities by the inverse-distance weighting method produces the composite image shown in Fig. 10.8c.

Although the images are seamlessly combined, the obtained intensities are no longer meaningful. We would like to map intensities of the sensed image to those of the reference image so that the combined image shows intensities of only the reference image. To achieve this, a mapping function that relates intensities of the sensed image to those of the reference images is required.

To find this mapping function, first, the joint probability density (JPD) of intensities in the images is calculated. A matrix is created with its entry (i, j) showing the number of pixels in the overlap area in the images where the intensity in the reference image is i and the intensity in the sensed image is j. Therefore, the columns in this matrix index to the intensities in the sensed image, while the rows index to the intensities in the reference image. The entries of the matrix are divided by the number of pixels in the overlap area to obtain probabilities.

The JPD of intensities in images in Figs. 10.8a and 10.8b is shown in Fig. 10.8d. Higher probabilities are shown darker in this image. This JPD shows that an intensity in the sensed image maps to a number of relatively close intensities in the reference image. This occurs due to noise and resampling side effects. When bilinear interpolation is used to resample the sensed image to register the reference image, most often intensities of four adjacent pixels in the sensed image are used to calculate the intensity of a pixel in the resampled image. Even when intensities in the sensed image uniquely map to intensities in the reference image, the resampling process destroys this uniqueness and makes the mapping ambiguous. Noise and other factors worsen the situation.

To obtain a unique mapping, at each column j in the JPD, the row i with the highest probability is identified. i will be the intensity in the reference image most frequently corresponding to intensity j in the sensed image. The JPD entries identified in this manner are shown by black dots in Fig. 10.8e. The black dots provide a unique mapping from intensities in the sensed image to those in the reference image, because each intensity j in the sensed image has a unique value i in the reference image. Such a mapping, however, is very noisy as can be observed in Fig. 10.8e. Adjacent intensities in the sensed image do not map to adjacent intensities in the reference image.

To reduce the effect of noise and map adjacent intensities in the sensed image to adjacent intensities in the reference image, a rational Gaussian (RaG) curve [5] is fitted to the points as shown in Fig. 10.8e. The curve provides a unique mapping from intensities in the sensed image to intensities in the reference image.

The image composite obtained after converting intensities of the sensed image to those of the reference image in this manner is shown in Fig. 10.8f. Intensities across the composite image measure the same scene properties. Although the images in Figs. 10.8c and 10.8f appear similar, looking more closely, we see that intensities in 10.8f follow the intensities in 10.8a, while those in 10.8c are a blending of the intensities in 10.8a and 10.8b. For instance, this difference is seen in Figs. 10.8c and 10.8f in the areas pointed to by the arrows.

References

1. Cheng, F., Goshtasby, A.: A parallel B-spline surface fitting algorithm. ACM Trans. Graph. **8**(1), 41–50 (1989)
2. Cuisenaire, O., Macq, B.: Fast Euclidean distance transformation by propagation using multiple neighborhoods. Comput. Vis. Image Underst. **76**(2), 163–172 (1999)
3. Ferrari, L.A., Sankar, P.V., Sklansky, J., Leeman, S.: Efficient two-dimensional filters using B-spline functions. Comput. Vis. Graph. Image Process. **35**, 152–169 (1986)
4. Goshtasby, A.: 2-D and 3-D Image Registration for Medical, Remote Sensing, and Industrial Applications. Wiley, New York (2005)
5. Goshtasby, A.: Design and recovery of 2-D and 3-D shapes using rational Gaussian curves and surfaces. Int. J. Comput. Vis. **10**(3), 233–256 (1993)
6. Goshtasby, A., Cheng, F., Barksy, B.A.: B-spline curves and surfaces viewed as digital filters. Comput. Vis. Graph. Image Process. **52**, 264–275 (1990)

7. Hou, H.S., Andrews, H.C.: Cubic splines for image interpolation and digital filtering. IEEE Trans. Acoust. Speech Signal Process. **26**(6), 508–517 (1978)

8. Keys, E.G.: Cubic convolution interpolation for digital image processing. IEEE Trans. Acoust. Speech Signal Process. **29**(6), 1153–1160 (1981)

9. Shih, F.Y., Wu, Y.-T.: Fast Euclidean distance transformation in two scans using a 3×3 neighborhood. Comput. Vis. Image Underst. **93**, 195–205 (2004)

10. Szeliski, R.: Computer Vision: Algorithms and Applications. Springer, London (2011)

Chapter 11
Image Registration Methods

In the preceding chapters, various tools for image registration were discussed. In this chapter, methods that use these tools to register various types of images are discussed. We start with methods that register images rigidly and continue to methods that register images nonrigidly. Also discussed in this chapter are multiresolution and adaptive registration methods as well as evaluation of the performance of a registration method.

11.1 Principal Axes Registration

If two images have translational and rotational differences, they can be registered by a rigid transformation. Suppose the images are segmented to contain the same scene parts, and coordinates of pixels belonging to the segmented regions in the reference image are:

$$\{\mathbf{p}_i = (x_i, y_i) : i = 1, \ldots, m\} \tag{11.1}$$

and coordinates of pixels belonging to the same regions in the sensed image are:

$$\{\mathbf{P}_j = (X_j, Y_j) : j = 1, \ldots, n\}. \tag{11.2}$$

Then the coordinates of the centroid of the reference image will be

$$\bar{x} = \frac{1}{m} \sum_{i=1}^{m} x_i,$$
$$\bar{y} = \frac{1}{m} \sum_{i=1}^{m} y_i, \tag{11.3}$$

A.A. Goshtasby, *Image Registration*,
Advances in Computer Vision and Pattern Recognition,
DOI 10.1007/978-1-4471-2458-0_11, © Springer-Verlag London Limited 2012

and the coordinates of the centroid of the sensed image will be

$$\bar{X} = \frac{1}{n} \sum_{j=1}^{n} X_j,$$
$$\bar{Y} = \frac{1}{n} \sum_{j=1}^{n} Y_j. \tag{11.4}$$

If the centroids of two images correspond to the same scene point, by moving the coordinate system origin in each image to its centroid, coordinates of points in both images will be measured with respect to the same coordinate system origin. This transformation requires replacing $\mathbf{p}_i$ with $\mathbf{T}_1 \mathbf{p}_i$ and replacing $\mathbf{P}_j$ with $\mathbf{T}_2 \mathbf{P}_j$, where

$$\mathbf{T}_1 = \begin{bmatrix} 1 & 0 & -\bar{x} \\ 0 & 1 & -\bar{y} \\ 0 & 0 & 1 \end{bmatrix}, \tag{11.5}$$

$$\mathbf{T}_2 = \begin{bmatrix} 1 & 0 & -\bar{X} \\ 0 & 1 & -\bar{Y} \\ 0 & 0 & 1 \end{bmatrix}, \tag{11.6}$$

$$\mathbf{p}_i = \begin{bmatrix} x_i \\ y_i \\ 1 \end{bmatrix}, \tag{11.7}$$

$$\mathbf{P}_j = \begin{bmatrix} X_j \\ Y_j \\ 1 \end{bmatrix} \tag{11.8}$$

in homogeneous coordinates.

Once the coordinate systems of the images are moved to their centroids, the rotational difference between them can be determined by finding the axis of minimum inertia [24, 38] of each image and calculating the angle between them. The axis of minimum inertia of a set of points, also known as the *major axis* of the points, is a line that passes through the centroid of the points, and the sum of squared distances of the points to that line is minimum. Using points in the reference image, the angle between the major axis of the points and the x-axis is [38]:

$$\alpha = 0.5 \tan^{-1} \left\{ \frac{2 \sum_{i=1}^{m} (x_i - \bar{x})(y_i - \bar{y})}{\sum_{i=1}^{m} (x_i - \bar{x})^2 - \sum_{i=1}^{m} (y_i - \bar{y})^2} \right\}. \tag{11.9}$$

Note that (11.9) is ambiguous and the sign of the term within the bracket can be obtained by two different sign combinations of the numerator and denominator. Since the same line will be obtained when rotating the points about the centroid by π, there is an ambiguity in determination of α. This ambiguity cannot be resolved unless some additional information about the points is provided. In the absence of such information, after finding α, $\pi + \alpha$ should also be considered a solution, and among the two the one producing a higher match rating between reference and sensed images should be chosen as the answer.

The angle between the major axis of points in the sensed image and the X-axis can be computed similarly from

$$\beta = 0.5 \tan^{-1} \left\{ \frac{2 \sum_{j=1}^{n} (X_j - \bar{X})(Y_j - \bar{Y})}{\sum_{j=1}^{n} (X_j - \bar{X})^2 - \sum_{j=1}^{n} (Y_j - \bar{Y})^2} \right\}. \tag{11.10}$$

Having selected α and β, the rotational difference between the images will be

$$\theta = \alpha - \beta. \tag{11.11}$$

Keeping α fixed, among the two choices of β the one that produces the lower registration error is chosen.

The problem of determining the major axis of a set of points can be solved from a different point of view. Consider finding the direction along which the largest spread among the points is observed in the image. The direction of maximum spread can be determined by finding the covariance matrix of the points and calculating the eigenvectors and eigenvalues of the matrix [2, 49]. Then, the eigenvector corresponding to the larger eigenvalue defines the major axis of the points. The other eigenvector, which is normal to the major axis is known as the *minor axis*. Major and minor axes of a set of points are known as the *principal axes* of the set of points.

The covariance matrix of the reference image is computed from

$$c = \frac{1}{m} \begin{bmatrix} \sum_{i=1}^{m} (x_i - \bar{x})^2 & \sum_{i=1}^{m} (x_i - \bar{x})(y_i - \bar{y}) \\ \sum_{i=1}^{m} (x_i - \bar{x})(y_i - \bar{y}) & \sum_{i=1}^{m} (y_i - \bar{y})^2 \end{bmatrix}, \tag{11.12}$$

while the covariance matrix for the sensed image is obtained from

$$C = \frac{1}{n} \begin{bmatrix} \sum_{j=1}^{n} (X_j - \bar{X})^2 & \sum_{j=1}^{n} (X_j - \bar{X})(Y_j - \bar{Y}) \\ \sum_{j=1}^{n} (X_j - \bar{X})(Y_j - \bar{Y}) & \sum_{j=1}^{n} (Y_j - \bar{Y})^2 \end{bmatrix}. \tag{11.13}$$

Denoting the eigenvector associated with the larger eigenvalue of c by $v = [v_1 \ v_2 \ v_3]^t$ and the eigenvector associated with the larger eigenvalue of C by $V = [V_1 \ V_2 \ V_3]^t$, the angle v makes with the x-axis can be computed from

$$\alpha = \tan^{-1} \left(\frac{v_2}{v_1} \right). \tag{11.14}$$

There is ambiguity in this α also, which can be resolved by taking into consideration the signs of v_1 and v_2 individually rather than collectively as discussed above. Similarly, the angle vector V makes with the X-axis can be computed from

$$\beta = \tan^{-1} \left(\frac{V_2}{V_1} \right). \tag{11.15}$$

Therefore, if the x-axis and X-axis have the same direction, then the sensed image will be rotated with respect to the reference image by

$$\theta = \beta - \alpha. \tag{11.16}$$

Letting

$$R = \begin{bmatrix} \cos\theta & -\sin\theta & 0 \\ \sin\theta & \cos\theta & 0 \\ 0 & 0 & 1 \end{bmatrix}, \tag{11.17}$$

if the reference and sensed images have only translational and rotational differences, the transformation that maps point $\mathbf{p}$ in the reference image to the corresponding point $\mathbf{P}$ in the sensed image will be

$$\mathbf{T}_2^{-1}\mathbf{RT}_1. \tag{11.18}$$

Therefore,

$$\mathbf{P} = \mathbf{T}_2^{-1}\mathbf{RT}_1\mathbf{p}. \tag{11.19}$$

This transformation involves translating each point $\mathbf{p}$ in the reference image by $\mathbf{T}_1$ so that the coordinate system origin of the reference image moves to its centroid and then rotating the coordinate system about the origin by θ. This is equivalent to rotating the coordinate system by $-\alpha$ so that the major axis of the image aligns horizontally, then rotating it by β so that the major axis of the reference image aligns with that of the sensed image, and then translating the point so that the centroid of the sensed image moves to its coordinate system origin. Denoting the obtained point by $\mathbf{P}$, finally, the intensity at $\mathbf{P}$ in the sensed image is read and saved at $\mathbf{p}$ in the resampled image. In this manner, by scanning the reference image, corresponding locations in the sensed image are found and the sensed image is resampled to align with the reference images. Note that in formulas (11.18) and (11.19)

$$\mathbf{T}_2^{-1} = \begin{bmatrix} 1 & 0 & \bar{X} \\ 0 & 1 & \bar{Y} \\ 0 & 0 & 1 \end{bmatrix}. \tag{11.20}$$

If the sensed image, in addition to being translated and rotated, it is also scaled with respect to the reference image by a factor of s, the larger eigenvalue of $\mathbf{C}$ will be scaled with respect to the larger eigenvalue of $\mathbf{c}$ by s^2. Therefore, if the larger eigenvalues of $\mathbf{c}$ and $\mathbf{C}$ are λ_1 and λ_2, respectively, the sensed image will be scaled with respect to the reference image by $s = \sqrt{\lambda_2/\lambda_1}$. Therefore, letting

$$\mathbf{S} = \begin{bmatrix} s & 0 & 1 \\ 0 & s & 1 \\ 0 & 0 & 1 \end{bmatrix}, \tag{11.21}$$

the transformation used to resample the sensed image to the geometry of the reference image will be

$$\mathbf{T}_2^{-1}\mathbf{SRT}_1. \tag{11.22}$$

Therefore,

$$\mathbf{P} = \mathbf{T}_2^{-1}\mathbf{SRT}_1\mathbf{p}. \tag{11.23}$$

An example of global registration using principal axes of segmented images is given in Fig. 11.1. Images (a) and (b) show the boundary contours of two gray-scale images with only translational and rotational differences. Registering (b) to (a) so that the centroids of the images coincide and their major axes align, the result shown in (c) is obtained.

If the images are not segmented but contain the same object or objects and the images are related by the rigid or similarity transformation, the parameters of the

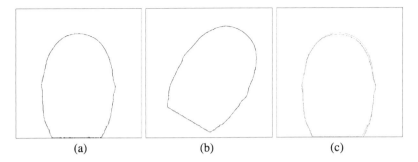

(a)   (b)   (c)

Fig. 11.1 (**a**), (**b**) Binary images that have only translational and rotational differences. (**c**) Registration of the images by the principal-axes method

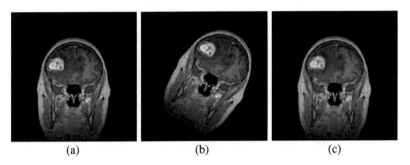

(a)   (b)   (c)

Fig. 11.2 Image (**b**) is translated and rotated with respect to image (**a**). Registration and overlaying of the images by the principal-axes method. The reference image is shown in *green* and the resampled sensed image is shown in *purple*. Pixels in images that perfectly align appear in *gray*. Otherwise, they appear *green* or *purple*

transformation can be determined using the intensities as the weights at the points. Therefore, if intensity at (x_i, y_i) in the reference image is f_i and the intensity at (X_j, Y_j) in the sensed image is F_j, all that needs to be done is to replace x_i, y_i with $x_i f_i$ and $y_i f_i$, and replace X_j and Y_j with $X_j F_j$ and $Y_j F_j$, respectively. It is also required to replace coefficient $1/m$ in (11.3) and (11.12) with $1/\sum_{i=1}^{m} f_i$. Similarly, it is required to replace coefficient $1/n$ in (11.4) and (11.13) with $1/\sum_{j=1}^{n} F_j$.

An example of gray-scale image registration by principal axes method is given in Fig. 11.2. The reference image is shown in green and the resampled sensed image is shown in purple in Fig. 11.2c. When the images perfectly align, a gray pixel is obtained. Otherwise, a purple or green pixel is obtained. Some green and purple colors can be observed in neighborhoods where intensity gradient is high. Some of this error is due to resampling error and the digital nature of images.

It is often the case that the given images do not cover exactly the same parts of a scene; therefore, registration by principal axes will not be accurate. In such a situation, the principal axes method is used to only approximately align the images. Approximate alignment of the images makes it possible to limit the computations to the area of overlap between the images and gradually improve registration accuracy.

Fig. 11.3 The
multiresolution image
registration paradigm. Levels
0, i, and n are shown. Level 0
is the bottom level and shows
images at the highest
resolution. Level n is the top
level and shows images at the
lowest resolution. Level i
represents any level
between 0 and n

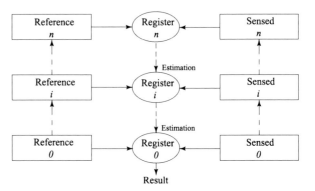

The process can be repeated until the overlap area between the images would not
change. This method is known as *iterative principal axes* registration [16].

Being a global registration method, the principal axes method can be used to
approximately align images that have nonlinear geometric differences [2]. Once the
images are approximately aligned, a nonrigid registration method can be used to
refine the registration so that the images will align locally as well as globally.

11.2 Multiresolution Registration

Multiresolution methods have also been called *coarse-to-fine*, *hierarchical*, and
pyramidal in the literature. Multiresolution methods create from each image two or
more images of increasingly smaller sizes. Smaller images reduce image geometric
differences and speed up the registration process.

The structure of a typical multiresolution image registration method is depicted
in Fig. 11.3. The original images at level 0 are decreased in size, typically by a factor
of 2, to obtain new images at level 1. The images at level 1 are reduced in size by the
same factor to obtain the images at level 2. The process is repeated until the desired
lowest-resolution images are obtained. The number of levels n is either provided
by the user or determined automatically by satisfying a prespecified condition. For
instance, it may be required to reduce the sizes of images until the number of control
points detected in each image falls below 30.

Registration is first achieved between images at the lowest resolution (level n).
By reducing the sizes of the images sufficiently, local geometric differences between
the images are reduced sufficiently to register the images by a global transformation
function. Smaller images simplify the correspondence process because of presence
of fewer control points in the images. The registration result at level n is then used
to estimate registration parameters at level $n - 1$.

Knowing that two images approximately register at a given resolution, it is possible to (1) subdivide the images at one level higher resolution into corresponding
subimages and (2) refine the registration parameters using information within corresponding subimages. Subdivision makes it possible to deal with smaller images and

have a more focused search. Knowledge about the approximate registration parameters makes it possible to find the ultimate registration parameters faster.

Information about the registration of images at level i is used to guide registration at level $i - 1$, and the process is repeated until registration at the highest resolution (level 0) is achieved. Multiresolution is the method of choice when registering images with local geometric differences. One of the earliest multiresolution methods to elastically register a CT brain image to a brain atlas was proposed by Bajcsy and Kovačič [2].

After registering images at the lowest resolution, Likar and Pernuš [29] subdivided the overlap area between the images into four subimages, and the subimages were registered again to improve registration within the quadrants. The process was repeated until subimages were small enough that the geometric difference between local image neighborhoods could be approximated by a rigid transformation. Centers of corresponding subimages at the bottom level were then used to determine an elastic transformation function (thin-plate spline) that could globally register the images. Buerger et al. [7] extended the method of Likar and Pernus to 3-D to register volumetric thoracic images.

In a multiresolution approach developed by Wu and Goshtasby [60], the images to be registered are subdivided into corresponding regions based on image content. In homogenous image areas where change in geometry is unlikely, an image is subdivided into large regions while in highly detailed areas where the images are likely to have local geometric differences, the images are subdivided into smaller regions. Subdivision is performed using Dirichlet tessellation [6], decomposing an image into corresponding Voronoi regions. Using the correspondences at one resolution, the images at one level higher resolution are subdivided into corresponding Voronoi regions. Then correspondence is established between control points within corresponding regions and the process is repeated until correspondence is established between points in images at the highest resolution.

An example of image registration by Dirichlet subdivision is given in Fig. 7.10. The images in Figs. 7.10a and 7.10b show different views of a city downtown. At the top level (level n), using a small number of corresponding points in the images, the images are subdivided into Voronoi regions (shown in blue in Fig. 7.10g, h). At the next higher resolution, correspondence is established between points within corresponding Voronoi regions and the correspondences are used to subdivide the images at the next higher resolution (shown in green). The subdivision process is repeated in this manner from low to high resolution, always keeping the sizes of corresponding regions small and manageable.

Corresponding Voronoi regions shown in blue, green, red, and black, respectively, show corresponding regions at levels 3, 2, 1, and 0 in the multiresolution method. At the top level (level 4), a small number of correspondences is obtained. The correspondences are then used to subdivide the images at level 3 into corresponding Voronoi regions. Level 0 is the bottom level, showing the subdivision of the original images into corresponding Voronoi regions. By focusing on small regions in images when finding point correspondences, not only is the likelihood of obtaining incorrect correspondences reduced, the search for the correspondences is made more efficient.

Registration of the images in Figs. 7.10a, b by this multiresolution method is shown in Fig. 7.11. Areas within the convex hull of corresponding control points in the images are registered. In Fig. 7.11, the reference image is treated as the green band and the resampled sensed image is treated as the red and blue bands of a color image. Therefore, areas in the images that register perfectly appear in gray, while in areas where there is misregistration, green or purple is obtained. Green or purple is also obtained around the boundaries of tall buildings due to occlusion.

For images that are not very large but have nonlinear geometric differences, multi-stage methods have been developed. In these methods, first the images are approximately registered by an affine transformation. Then registration accuracy is improved by subdividing the image into quadrants and registering each by an affine transformation [1]. The local affine transformations are then blended to create a global transformation and register the images nonrigidly. Martín et al. [35] achieved nonrigid registration in this manner by using local affine transformations to register individual bones in hand radiographs and then using a weighted sum of the affine transformations to register entire radiographs.

The multiresolution approach has also been used to register images with only global geometric differences. The aim in such cases has been to achieve a higher speed in registration. At a coarse resolution, the approximate translational [20, 47, 56] and rotational [21, 42] differences between the images are determined and the parameters are refined using information in higher resolution images.

11.3 Optimization-Based Registration

A registration may be considered optimal if it maximizes a measure of similarity or minimizes a measure of dissimilarity between the images. In an optimization-based registration, it is required to (1) define the similarity/dissimilarity measure, (2) find initial parameters that approximately register the images, and (3) develop an algorithm that takes the initial registration to the final one.

A proper measure of similarity/dissimilarity between two images can be chosen by knowing some properties of the images. For instance, if the images are in the same modality, cross-correlation coefficient may be used to measure the similarity between images and sum of squared intensity differences may be used to measure the dissimilarity between images. If the images are in different modalities, mutual information may be used as the similarity measure and joint entropy may be used as the dissimilarity measure to quantify the degree of match between two images.

The initial transformation parameters may be specified interactively or determined automatically. An interactive method allows the user to drag one image over the other and approximately align them. An automatic method will achieve the same without user interaction. For example, if the images are in the same modality, initial registration can be achieved by aligning the principal axes of the images as outlined in Sect. 11.1. If the images are in different modalities, the entire parameter space can be searched with relatively large steps to find the best approximate registration and use that as the initial registration.

The initial registration parameters are then refined iteratively until optimal registration is reached. The refinement step involves measuring the similarity/dissimilarity between registered images and revising the registration parameters in such a way that similarity is increased or dissimilarity is decreased at each iteration.

For instance, if the images to be registered are related by a rigid transformation, there are 3 parameters to be estimated: translation along the x-axis, translation along the y-axis, and rotation about the origin. The 3 registration parameters are used to create a 3-D digital space where the initial registration parameters represent a point in that space. Starting from the initial point, the similarity/dissimilarity between images when registered using the parameters at each of the 26 neighbors of the initial point is calculated and the parameters of the neighbor producing the highest similarity or lowest dissimilarity are chosen to represent the refined parameters. The refinement process is continued until no more refinement is possible.

Rather than examining all neighbors of a point in the parameter space to refine the registration parameters, a steepest gradient-descent method may be used to refine the parameters. A gradient-descent method relies on past search history to guess future registration parameters without examining all possible values. Maes et al. [31] and Zhu [62] used a gradient-based method [43] to find optimal parameters to register multimodality images. Maes et al. [32, 33] compared a number of gradient-based and non-gradient-based multiresolution methods, finding that the Levenberg-Marquardt [27, 34] algorithm performs the best when using mutual information as the similarity measure to register MR and CT brain images. A review of gradient-descent methods in image registration has been provided by Cole-Rode and Eastman [11].

The measure to be optimized depends on the similarity/dissimilarity used to determine the degree of match between the images. Maes et al. [31] used mutual information as the similarity measure, while Bajcsy and Kovačič [2] used cross-correlation coefficient as the similarity measure. If feature points are available in images, Hausdorff distance [48] between the points may be used as a measure of dissimilarity between images. Rather than optimizing the similarity between registered images, Chen et al. [8] optimized a measure of fusion between registered images through expectation maximization.

Jenkinson and Smith [25] found that local search for the optimal registration parameters in a multiresolution scheme may not find globally optimal parameters and suggested a two-step approach to the problem. In the first step, a fast local optimizer, such as Powell's optimizer [43], is used to find the initial registration parameters. In the second step, the transformation parameters are perturbed to escape a possible local minimum and reach the global optimum.

To achieve a globally optimal registration, simulated annealing [55] may be used. Simulated annealing perturbs the parameters in a stochastic manner to avoid converging to a local optimum. An evolutionary algorithm may be used to achieve the same. Winter et al. [58] developed an evolutionary registration algorithm that performed better than gradient-based optimization methods in both speed and precision when registering CT and ultrasound images of the spine.

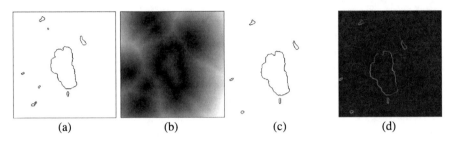

Fig. 11.4 (a) Region boundaries in the reference image. (b) Distance transform of (a). (c) Region boundaries in the sensed image. (d) Distance values in (b) coinciding with the boundary pixels in (c). As (c) is moved over (b), the distance values in (b) coinciding with the boundary pixels in (c) change

Of similar nature are genetic algorithms that search for the registration parameters globally. A genetic registration algorithm has been proposed by Staib and Lei [51] that first identifies promising areas of the search space very quickly. Then it searches for the globally optimal solution in finer steps. The rate of convergence of this algorithm near the solution is very slow though. Therefore, after finding the most promising regions of the parameter space, the search is switched to a gradient-based locally convergent method. By combining the global nature of the genetic algorithm and the high speed of the gradient-based search algorithm, Press et al. [43] developed a fast globally optimal registration method.

11.4 Boundary Registration

In the presence of outliers or a difference in the modality of images, it may not be possible to register the images using their intensities. If boundaries of the same objects can be determined in the images, the images can be registered using their boundaries. When the images have only translational and rotational differences, the principal axes of the boundaries can be used to register the images as outlined in Sect. 11.1. If the same boundaries are not detected in the images, the principal axes method will not be able to register the images.

When region boundaries in one image are a subset of region boundaries in another image, a more robust registration method is chamfer matching. Chamfer matching involves converting the boundary images into intensity images with the intensity at a pixel showing the distance of that pixel to the boundary pixel closest to it. The process is known as distance transform computation [12].

An example showing conversion of a boundary image to a distance image is given in Fig. 11.4. Image (b) shows the distance transform of boundary image (a). The value at a pixel in (b) is equal to the Euclidean distance of that pixel to the boundary pixel in (a) closest to it. Suppose image (c) shows region boundaries of another image of the same scene. Then, by translating and rotating image (c) over image (a), and determining the sum of the distances of points in (a) closest to points in (c), the degree of match between the two images can be measured.

This involves finding for each boundary pixel in (c) the boundary pixel in (a) closest to it and adding such distances over all boundary pixels in (c). If the distance transform of (a) is available, as shown in (b), this sum can be calculated very efficiently by simply adding the intensities in (b) that coincide with boundary pixels in (c). Therefore, as (c) is moved over (b), the sum of intensities coinciding with the boundary pixels in (c) is determined. The translation and rotation parameters that produce the smallest such sum determine the best rigid parameters registering the images.

Boundary registration was called chamfer matching by Barrow et al. [3]. Borgefors [4] provided an efficient means for calculating approximate Euclidean distances and extended it to 3-D for registration of volumetric images [5]. Levin et al. [28], Pelizzari et al. [39], and Van Herk and Kooy [54] used chamfer matching to register volumetric images using bounding surfaces of rigid bodies in images, and Kozinska et al. [26] used the Levenberg-Marquardt algorithm [34] to search for the optimal registration parameters more efficiently.

Davatzikos et al. [14, 15] used a length-preserving energy minimizing contour to delineate the outer cortical boundaries in two images. Correspondence was established between points in the boundary images by aligning the contours at a small number of points manually and letting the remaining points fall into correspondence using their distances to the selected points. The correspondences were then used to nonlinearly transform one image to align with the other.

If all boundaries are closed, rather than Euclidean distances, signed Euclidean distances may be used to reduce the number of local minima in the search domain and enable registration of more complex boundaries. Distance of a point inside a boundary to the boundary point closest to it is given a positive (negative) value, while distance of a point outside the boundary to the boundary point closest to it is given a negative (positive) value. This reduces inside/outside ambiguity and enables a quicker search for the registration parameters. When signed distances are used, rather than moving a boundary over a distance image, one signed distance image is moved over the other to locate the best-match position and find the registration parameters. Masuda [36] used signed distances to rigidly register range images in this manner.

Note that the edges in (c) should be a subset of the edges in (a). If the images contain many boundaries, one of the boundaries in one image may be chosen and searched for in another image. The obtained transformation can then be used to verify other boundaries in the images and ensure that the same transformation aligns other boundaries in the images.

11.5 Model-Based Registration

In certain applications, intensities in the images to be registered are so different that traditional similarity/dissimilarity measures cannot find an initial or approximate registration of the images. In such a situation, additional information about the images may be used to guide the registration.

One form of information is the model of the object or objects in the images. For instance, the shape of the human skull in a brain CT image, the shape of myocardial walls in a cardiac MR image, or the shape of ribs in a CT chest image is known. This shape information may be used to guide the registration and make sure that the shape of interest in the images align. A model-based method can use information about the shapes of objects in images to verify the correctness of a registration.

Constraints have been used to guide registration also. Giessen et al. [53] used the fixed distances between carpal bones that slide against each other as the constraint to achieve nonrigid registration of wrist joint images while preserving the rigidity of individual bones.

Symmetry can be used as a constraint to guide the registration also. The human body is symmetric for the most part. For example, when registering brain images, the registration parameters for the left and right sides of the brain should be similar. If similar parameters are not obtained, steps should be taken to guide the process to achieve a more symmetric result.

Certain images have strong orientational information. For instance, images of indoor and outdoor scenes often contain a large number of lines. Images of buildings contain lines that are either nearly parallel or nearly normal to each other. If histograms of gradient directions in such images are obtained, dominant peaks will be observed that enable estimation of initial registration parameters and facilitate a search for the optimal parameters.

11.6 Adaptive Registration

An adaptive registration method has access to a collection of tools and uses information about the geometric and intensity differences between the images to choose the right tools to register the images. Image information may be provided by the user or determined automatically. For instance, the user may let the system know that the images to be registered are of the same modality, they represent different views of a relatively flat scene, or they contain a large number of lines.

An adaptive registration method chooses a sequence of increasingly more powerful but less efficient tools. Initially, the fastest tools are tested, and if they fail, the next fastest tools are used and the process is continued until tools are chosen that successfully register the images. Such systems, by utilizing the outcomes of various tools, can learn the characteristics of the given images and finally choose the tools that can effectively register the images.

In a registration method proposed by Park et al. [37], the number of control points used to register two images is adapted to the geometric difference between the images. Initially, a small number of corresponding points is used to register the images with thin-plate spline [17, 23]. Then the quality of registration is evaluated using mutual information and additional control points are selected in areas where registration error exceeds a prespecified tolerance. The process is repeated until local registration error within the image domain falls below the required tolerance.

Fig. 11.5 Forward and
backward resampling to
calculate RMSE

If parts of two images are related rigidly while the other parts are related non-rigidly, the transformation function that is used to register the images should respond to different parts of the images differently. A transformation function defined by Little et al. [30] provides this functionality. It registers bones in the images rigidly while registering the soft tissues nonrigidly.

Rohr et al. [46] achieved simultaneous rigid and nonrigid registration by revising the formulation for thin-plate spline so it could assume desired gradients at the interpolating points. Gradients at the boundaries of rigid bodies were determined from the relation between corresponding rigid regions in the images. Then by requiring the nonrigid transformation to assume specified gradients at boundaries of rigid regions, rigid and nonrigid transformations are smoothly joined to register two images, part rigidly and part nonrigidly.

11.7 Evaluation of Registration Methods

Suppose the transformation function to register image S to image R is $\mathbf{f} = (f_x, f_y)$ (Fig. 11.5). f_x and f_y are the two components of transformation $\mathbf{f}$. Knowing $\mathbf{f}$, for any point $\mathbf{p} = (x, y)$ in image R, we can determine the corresponding point $\mathbf{P} = (X, Y)$ in image S from

$$\mathbf{P} = \mathbf{f}(\mathbf{p}). \tag{11.24}$$

Now, suppose the images are switched and transformation $\mathbf{g}$ that registers image R to image S is determined so that given any point in S we can estimate the location of the corresponding point in image R. Therefore, given point $\mathbf{P}$ in S we can find its correspondence in image R from

$$\mathbf{p}' = \mathbf{g}(\mathbf{P}). \tag{11.25}$$

Substituting $\mathbf{P}$ from (11.24) into (11.25), we obtain

$$\mathbf{p}' = \mathbf{g}(\mathbf{f}(\mathbf{p})). \tag{11.26}$$

If registration did not include any errors, points $\mathbf{p}$ and $\mathbf{p}'$ would coincide. At the presence of inaccuracies, points $\mathbf{p}$ and $\mathbf{p}'$ will be displaced with respect to each other, and the distance between them will measure registration error. The closer points $\mathbf{p}$ and $\mathbf{p}'$ are, the more accurate the registration will be. If N control points in image R after forward transformation by $\mathbf{f}$ fall inside image S and then after backward transformation with $\mathbf{g}$ fall inside image R, then

$$RMSE = \left\{ \frac{1}{N} \sum_{i=1}^{N} \left\| \mathbf{p}_i - \mathbf{g}(\mathbf{f}(\mathbf{p}_i)) \right\|^2 \right\}^{\frac{1}{2}} \tag{11.27}$$

Fig. 11.6 Forward and
backward transformation to
calculate *AAID*

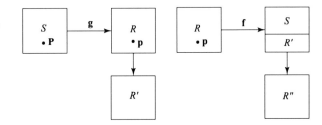

and

$$MAX = \max_{i=1}^{N} \left\| \mathbf{p}_i - \mathbf{g}\big(\mathbf{f}(\mathbf{p}_i)\big) \right\|, \tag{11.28}$$

respectively, quantify root-mean-squared error (RMSE) and maximum error (MAX) in registration.

If the images are in the same modality and corresponding points in the images have the same intensity, another measure that can be used to quantify registration error is the intensity difference between the reference image and its transformed version, first to register with the sensed image and then back to register with itself. Therefore, if the intensity at point $\mathbf{p}$ in the reference image is $R(\mathbf{p})$ and if point $\mathbf{p}$ in image R corresponds to point $\mathbf{P}$ in image S, then transforming image R to align with image S will create an image R' that has the geometry of image S but has the intensities of image R (Fig. 11.6).

Let's denote the intensity at $\mathbf{P}$ in this image by $R'(\mathbf{P})$. Now since transformation $\mathbf{f}$ registers image S to image R, and image R' has the same geometry as image S, we can use $\mathbf{f}$ to register image R' to image R. Suppose image R' after transformation to register with image R is denoted by R'' (Fig. 11.6). Then, if the registration is perfect, we obtain $R = R''$ in the overlap area between images R and S. If registration contains errors, the images will be locally shifted with respect to each other. The smaller the local shift between the images, the smaller the intensity difference between R and R'' is expected to be.

Therefore,

$$AAID = \frac{1}{N} \sum_{i=1}^{N} \left| R(\mathbf{p}_i) - R''(\mathbf{p}_i) \right| \tag{11.29}$$

can be used to represent the *average absolute intensity difference* between the reference image and its resampled version after a forward transformation followed by a backward transformation. Christensen et al. [10] have referred to this error measure as the *inverse consistency error*.

Note that *AAID* is meaningful only when the images are in the same modality. Otherwise, a smaller *AAID* may not necessarily imply a more accurate registration. When the images are in different modalities, the joint-probability density (JPD) of the images contain information about the quality of registration. If the registration is accurate, intensities of corresponding pixels in the images will form a JPD that contains a narrow band. However, if the registration is not accurate, the obtained JPD will contain a wider distribution. Measures that quantify the spread of a probability

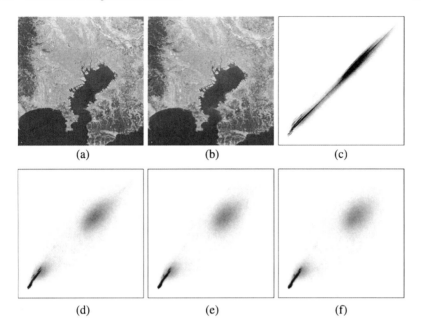

Fig. 11.7 (**a**), (**b**) Two bands of a Landsat image of the Tokyo Bay. (**c**) The JPD of the images. (**d**)–(**f**) JPDs of image (**b**) when shifted with respect to image (**a**) by $(1, 1)$, $(2, 2)$, and $(3, 3)$ pixels, respectively

distribution are joint entropy and joint energy. Denoting joint entropy by P and joint energy by E, we have

$$P = -\sum_{i=0}^{255}\sum_{j=0}^{255} p_{ij} \log_2 p_{ij}, \tag{11.30}$$

$$E = \sum_{i=0}^{255}\sum_{j=0}^{255} p_{ij}^2. \tag{11.31}$$

The smaller the P (the larger the E) is, the better the registration will be. These two measures can be used to quantify registration accuracy when the images are in the same modality or in different modalities. Both measures carry similar information. Therefore, if one is used, use of the other will be redundant.

An example demonstrating use of these measures in quantifying registration accuracy is given in Fig. 11.7. (a) and (b) show two bands of a Landsat image of the Tokyo Bay. These images are perfectly registered. The JPD of the images is shown in (c). Shifting image (b) with respect to image (a) by $(1, 1)$, $(2, 2)$, and $(3, 3)$ pixels changes the JPD to those shown in (d)–(f), respectively. The entropies of the JPDs in (c)–(f) are 8.1110, 9.2638, 9.4224, and 9.4887, while the energies of the same JPDs are 0.00149, 0.00101, 0.00083, and 0.00073, respectively. We see that as misregistration between the images increases, their joint entropy increases, while their joint energy decreases.

RMSE, *AAID*, *P*, and *E* are overall measures of registration accuracy/error. It is not clear which component of a registration method is causing most of the errors. To determine the weakest component, it is necessary to evaluate each component separately. The components represent the tools that build the method. They include a point detector, a point descriptor or feature extractor, a point matcher, and a transformation function. Evaluation of each tool was mentioned in the respective chapters. If an image registration method is found not to provide sufficient accuracy for a particular application, tools representing the weaker components may be replaced with stronger ones to achieve a higher registration accuracy.

In addition to accuracy, repeatability is an important performance measure. How stable is a method under noise? Can the same accuracy be achieved when the method is applied to different images of the same type? For instance, having developed a method for registering MR and PET brain images of the same patient, what is the mean and variance in registration error that can be expected when applying the method to a new set of images? Therefore, having designed a method, the variances of *RMSE, AAID* (if the images are in the same modality), and *P* and *E* (if the images are in different modalities) should be determined on a number of representative images. These variances characterize the repeatability of the method, which shows the degree of stability or reliability of the method.

Although the above measures were defined over the entire image domain, to obtain a more localized measure of error, the measures can be calculated within windows of interest in the image domain. For instance, the image domain may be subdivided into windows of size $d \times d$ pixels and the error measures can be calculated within those windows. This process will make it possible to determine variation in errors across the image domain. This variation can be used as a feedback to an adaptive registration method and improve registration accuracy in neighborhoods that have errors higher than a prespecified tolerance. Registration accuracy in a neighborhood can be improve by, for example, finding more control points in that neighborhood.

Measures *RMSE, AAID*, *P*, and *E* use the reference image as the gold standard. The reference image is first transformed to the geometry of the sensed image, then it is transformed back to itself. The process involves carrying out transformation twice. Therefore, the estimated registration error is normally higher than the actual error, which involves registration only in the forward direction.

Arguing that in an ideal registration forward and backward transformations are the inverse of each other, Christensen and Johnson [9] found the transformation function for the registration of two images in such a way that the forward transformation was the inverse of the backward transformation. This constraint, however, should be used with care, as error in one direction may force error in the opposite direction to satisfy the inverse constraint.

Attempts to create gold standards for the purpose of measuring registration accuracy have been made. Rohlfing et al. [45] and Strother et al. [52] used a stereotactic frame with fiducial markers that were visible in both images as the gold standard. Fitzpatrick and West et al. [18, 57] screwed fiducials to the skull of a patient and used the images of the fiducials as the gold standard, and Penney et al. [40] screwed fiducials to the femur and pelvis of a cadaver and used their images as the gold standard.

Attempts have also been made to find bounds on registration accuracy in well-defined situations. Robinson and Milanfar [44] determined the bounds on registration accuracy of gradient-based methods and suggested improvement in registration accuracy in multiresolution methods. Yetik and Nehorai [61] found bounds on the accuracy of point-based and intensity-based registration methods when the images were related by the affine transformation.

If fiducial markers are fixed to a rigid frame and the locations of corresponding fiducials in images have negligible positional errors, rigid registration error can be determined by (1) registering the images without the fiducials, (2) using the obtained transformation to map the fiducials in one image to the space of the other, (3) determining the distance between corresponding fiducials, and (4) using the mean and maximum of distances between corresponding fiducials to quantify registration accuracy. The fiducial markers take away user bias in measurement of registration accuracy.

The gold standard proposed by Schnabel et al. [50] is a finite-element-based system that learns the characteristics of the medium being imaged and evaluates the accuracy of a registration by taking the deformation obtained in the medium by registration and comparing it against the deformation predicted by the system. The discrepancy between the predicted and the estimated deformations is used as a metric to quantify registration accuracy. This gold standard has been found effective in validating registration of elastic breast images that lack clearly defined features.

A gold standard makes objective evaluation of a registration method possible as it takes user bias out of the registration process by providing the true locations of a set of corresponding points in the images. In certain applications, however, it is critical to include an expert in the process. Due to noise, outliers, and other image differences, quantifiable measures may not reliably determine registration accuracy and an expert observer, such as a radiologist, is required to judge the outcome of a registration and decide whether the registration is suitable for a diagnostic or treatment task. Fitzpatrick et al. [19] considered visual assessment when registration error was high. Pietrzyk et al. [41] studied inter-individual and intra-individual variability in visual registration assessment and concluded that influence of subjectivity in visual assessment is not significant.

Visual evaluation by an expert alone may be used to qualitatively measure registration accuracy. Although subjective in nature, this is the method of choice to accept or reject the result of an automatic registration method. Various visual aides to facilitate visual evaluation [22] or assist [13] the quantitative assessment of registration methods have been developed. Woods [59] has discussed the role of visual inspection in image registration and has reviewed the options and strategies that a user has to validate the accuracy of an image registration method.

Speed is another important performance measure. If sufficient accuracy can be achieved with different tools, the tools with the highest speed should be chosen to build the system. Computational complexity of the tools used in image registration were discussed in the respective chapters.

References

1. Ardizzone, E., Gambino, O., La Cascia, M., Lo Presti, L., Pirrone, R.: Multi-modal non-rigid registration of medical images based on mutual information maximization. In: 14th Int'l Conf. Image Analysis and Processing, pp. 743–750 (2007)
2. Bajcsy, R., Kovačič, S.: Multiresolution elastic matching. Comput. Vis. Graph. Image Process. **46**, 1–21 (1989)
3. Barrow, G., Tenenbaum, J.M., Bolles, R.C., Wolf, H.C.: Parametric correspondence and chamfer matching: Two new techniques for image matching. In: Proc. 5th Int'l J. Conf. Artificial Intelligence, pp. 659–663 (1977)
4. Borgefors, G.: An improved version of the chamfer matching algorithm. Int. J. Conf. Pattern Recognit. **2**, 1175–1177 (1986)
5. Borgefors, G.: On digital distance transforms in three dimensions. Comput. Vis. Image Underst. **64**(3), 368–376 (1996)
6. Bowyer, A.: Computing Dirichlet tessellations. Comput. J. **24**(2), 162–166 (1981)
7. Buerger, C., Schaeffer, T., King, A.P.: Hierarchical adaptive local affine registration for fast and robust respiratory motion estimation. Med. Image Anal. **15**, 551–564 (2011)
8. Chen, S., Guo, Q., Leung, H., Bossé, E.: A maximum likelihood approach to joint image registration and fusion. IEEE Trans. Image Process. **20**(5), 1365–1372 (2011)
9. Christensen, G.E., Johnson, H.J.: Consistent image registration. IEEE Trans. Med. Imaging **20**(7), 568–582 (2001)
10. Christensen, G.E., Geng, X., Kuhl, J.G., et al.: Introduction to the non-rigid image registration evaluation project. In: Pluim, J.P.W., Likar, B., Gerritsen, F.A. (eds.) Biomedical Image Registration. Lecture Notes in Computer Science, vol. 4057, pp. 128–135 (2006)
11. Cole-Rodes, A.A., Eastman, R.D.: Gradient descent approaches to image registration. In: Le Moigne, J., Netanyahu, N.S., Eastman, R.D. (eds.) Image Registration for Remote Sensing, pp. 265–275. Cambridge University Press, Cambridge (2011)
12. Cuisenaire, O., Macq, B.: Fast Euclidean distance transformation by propagation using multiple neighborhoods. Comput. Vis. Image Underst. **76**(2), 163–172 (1999)
13. Dann, R., Hoford, J., Kovacic, S., Reivich, M., Bajcsy, R.: Evaluation of elastic matching system for anatomic (CT, MR) and functional (PET) cerebral images. J. Comput. Assist. Tomogr. **13**(4), 603–611 (1989)
14. Davatzikos, C., Prince, J.L.: Brain image registration based on curve mapping. In: Proc. IEEE Workshop Biomedical Image Analysis, pp. 245–254 (1994)
15. Davatzikos, C.A., Prince, J.L., Bryan, R.N.: Image registration based on boundary mapping. IEEE Trans. Med. Imaging **15**(1), 112–115 (1996)
16. Dhawan, A.P., Levy, L.K.A.V., Mantil, J.: Iterative principal axes registration method for analysis of MR-PET brain images. IEEE Trans. Biomed. Eng. **42**(11), 1079–1087 (1995)
17. Dryden, I., Mardia, K.: Statistical Shape Analysis. Wiley, New York (1998)
18. Fitzpatrick, J.M., West, J.B.: The distribution of target registration error in rigid-body point-based registration. IEEE Trans. Med. Imaging **20**(9), 917–927 (2001)
19. Fitzpatrick, J.M., Hill, D.L.G., Shyr, Y., West, J., Studholme, C., Maurer, C.R. Jr.: Visual assessment of the accuracy of retrospective registration of MR and CT images of the brain. IEEE Trans. Med. Imaging **17**(4), 571–585 (1998)
20. Goshtasby, A., Gage, S., Bartholic, J.: A two-stage cross-correlation approach to template matching. IEEE Trans. Pattern Anal. Mach. Intell. **6**(3), 374–378 (1984)
21. Goshtasby, A.: Template matching in rotated images. IEEE Trans. Pattern Anal. Mach. Intell. **7**(3), 338–344 (1985)
22. Guéziec, A., Wu, K., Kalvin, A., Williamson, B., Kazandides, P., Van Vorhis, R.: Providing visual information to validate 2-D to 3-D registration. Med. Image Anal. **4**, 357–374 (2000)
23. Harder, R.L., Desmarais, R.N.: Interpolation using surface splines. J. Aircr. **9**(2), 189–191 (1972)
24. Horn, B.K.P.: Robot Vision, p. 432. The MIT Press, Cambridge (1986)

25. Jenkinson, M., Smith, S.: A global optimisation method for robust affine registration of brain images. Med. Image Anal. **5**, 143–156 (2001)
26. Kozinska, D., Tretiak, O.J., Nissanov, J., Ozturk, C.: Multidimensional alignment using the Euclidean distance transform. Graph. Models Image Process. **59**(6), 373–387 (1997)
27. Levenberg, K.: A method for the solution of certain non-linear problems in least squares. Q. Appl. Math. **2**, 164–168 (1944)
28. Levin, D.N., Pelizzari, C.A., Chen, G.T.Y., Chen, C.-T., Cooper, M.D.: Retrospective geometric correlation of MR, CT, and PET images. Radiology **169**(3), 817–823 (1988)
29. Likar, B., Pernuš, F.: A hierarchical approach to elastic registration based on mutual information. Image Vis. Comput. **19**, 33–44 (2001)
30. Little, A.A., Hill, D.L.G., Hawkes, D.J.: Deformations incorporating rigid structures. Comput. Vis. Image Underst. **66**(2), 223–232 (1997)
31. Maes, F., Collignon, A., Vandermeulen, D., Marchal, G., Suetens, P.: Multimodality image registration by maximization of mutual information. IEEE Trans. Med. Imaging **16**(2), 187–198 (1997)
32. Maes, F., Vandermeulen, D., Marchal, G., Suetens, P.: Fast multimodality image registration using multiresolution gradient-based maximization of mutual information. In: NASA Workshop on Image Registration, pp. 191–200 (1997)
33. Maes, F., Vandermeulen, D., Suetens, P.: Comparative evaluation of multiresolution optimization strategies for multimodality image registration by maximization of mutual information. Med. Image Anal. **3**(4), 373–386 (1999)
34. Marquardt, D.: An algorithm for least-squares estimation of nonlinear parameters. SIAM J. Appl. Math. **11**, 431–444 (1963)
35. Martín, M.A., Ćardenes, R., Muñoz-Moreno, E., de Luis-García, R., Martín-Fernández, M., Alberola-López, C.: Automatic articulated registration of hand radiographs. Image Vis. Comput. **27**, 1207–1222 (2009)
36. Masuda, T.: Registration and integration of multiple range images by matching signed distance fields for object shape modeling. Comput. Vis. Image Underst. **87**, 51–65 (2002)
37. Park, H., Bland, P.H., Brock, K.K., Meyer, C.R.: Adaptive registration using local information measures. Med. Image Anal. **8**, 465–473 (2004)
38. Parui, S.K., Majumder, D.D.: A new definition of shape similarity. Pattern Recognit. Lett. **1**(1), 37–42 (1982)
39. Pelizzari, C.A., Chen, G.T.Y., Spelbring, D.R., Weichselbaum, R.R., Chen, C.-T.: Accurate three-dimensional registration of CT, PET, and/or MR images of the Brain. J. Comput. Assist. Tomogr. **13**(1), 20–26 (1989)
40. Penney, G.P., Barratt, D.C., Chan, C.S.K., Slomczykowski, M., Carter, T.J., Edwards, P.J., Hawkes, D.J.: Cadaver validation of intensity-based ultrasound to CT registration. Med. Image Anal. **10**, 385–395 (2006)
41. Pietrzyk, U., Herholz, K., Fink, G., Jacobs, A., Mielke, R., Slansky, I., Wurker, M., Heiss, W.-D.: An interactive technique for three-dimensional image registration: Validation for PET, SPECT, MRI, and CT brain studies. J. Nucl. Med. **35**(12), 2011–2018 (1994)
42. Pluim, J.P.W., Maintz, J.B.A., Viergever, M.A.: Mutual information matching in multiresolution contexts. Image Vis. Comput. **19**, 45–52 (2001)
43. Press, W.H., Teukolsky, S.A., Vetterling, W.T., Flannery, B.P.: In: Numerical Recipes: The Art of Scientific Computing. Cambridge University Press, Cambridge (1999)
44. Robinson, D., Milanfar, P.: Fundamental performance limits in image registration. IEEE Trans. Image Process. **13**(9), 1185–1199 (2004)
45. Rohlfing, T., West, J.B., Beier, J., Liebig, T., Taschner, C.A., Thomale, U.-W.: Registration of functional and anatomical MRI: Accuracy assessment and application in navigated neurosurgery. Comput. Aided Surg. **5**, 414–425 (2000)
46. Rohr, K., Forenefett, M., Stiehl, H.S.: Spline-based elastic image registration: Integration of landmark errors and orientation attributes. Comput. Vis. Image Underst. **90**, 153–168 (2003)
47. Rosenfeld, A., Vanderburg, G.J.: Coarse-fine template matching. IEEE Trans. Syst. Man Cybern. **7**(2), 104–107 (1977)

48. Rucklidge, W.J.: Efficiently locating objects using the Hausdorff distance. Int. J. Comput. Vis.
     24(3), 251–270 (1997)
49. Sanchez-Marin, F.: Image registration of gray-scale images using the Hotelling transform. In:
     EC-VIP-MC 4th EURASIP Conf. Video/Image Processing and Multimedia Communications,
     Zagreb, Croatia, pp. 119–123 (2003)
50. Schnabel, J.A., Christine, T., Castellano-Smith, A.D., et al.: Validation of nonrigid image reg-
     istration using finite-element methods: Application to breast MR images. IEEE Trans. Med.
     Imaging **22**(2), 238–247 (2003)
51. Staib, L.H., Lei, X.: Intermodality 3D medical image registration with global search. In: Proc.
     IEEE Workshop Biomedical Image Analysis, pp. 225–234 (1994)
52. Strother, S.C., Anderson, J.R., Xu, X.-L., Liow, J.-S., Bonar, D.C., Rottenberg, D.A.: Quan-
     titative comparisons of image registration techniques based on high-resolution MRI of the
     brain. J. Comput. Assist. Tomogr. **18**(6), 954–962 (1994)
53. van de Giessen, M., Streekstra, G.J., Strackee, S.D., Maas, M., Grimbergen, K.A., van Vliet,
     L.J., Vos, F.M.: Constrained registration of the wrist joint. IEEE Trans. Med. Imaging **28**(12),
     1861–1869 (2009)
54. van Herk, M., Kooy, H.M.: Automatic three-dimensional correlation of CT-CT, CT-MRI, and
     CT-SPECT using chamfer matching. Med. Phys. **21**(7), 1163–1178 (1994)
55. van Laarhoven, P.J.M., Aarts, E.H.L.: Simulated Annealing: Theory and Applications. Kluwer
     Academic, Dordrecht (1989)
56. Vanderburg, G.J., Rosenfeld, A.: Two-stage template matching. IEEE Trans. Comput. **26**, 384–
     393 (1977)
57. West, J., Fitzpatrick, J.M., Wang, M.Y., et al.: Comparison and evaluation of retrospective
     intermodality brain image registration techniques. J. Comput. Assist. Tomogr. **21**(4), 554–568
     (1997)
58. Winter, S., Brendel, B., Pechlivanis, I., Schmieder, K., Igel, C.: Registration of CT and intra-
     operative 3D ultrasound images of the spine using evolutionary and gradient-based methods.
     IEEE Trans. Evol. Comput. **12**(3), 284–296 (2008)
59. Woods, R.: Validation of registration accuracy. In: Handbook of Medical Imaging: Processing
     and Analysis, pp. 491–497. Academic Press, San Diego (2000)
60. Wu, Z., Goshtasby, A.: A subdivision approach to image registration. Technical Report, Intel-
     ligent Systems Laboratory, Department of Computer Science and Engineering, Wright State
     University, January 2011
61. Yetik, I.S., Nehorai, A.: Performance bounds on image registration. IEEE Trans. Signal Pro-
     cess. **54**(5), 1737–1749 (2006)
62. Zhu, Y.-M.: Volume image registration by cross-entropy optimization. IEEE Trans. Med.
     Imaging **21**(2), 174–180 (2002)

Glossary

Affine transformation A transformation that is a combination of linear transformation and translation. Under the affine transformation, parallel lines remain parallel.

Control point A locally unique point in the reference or sensed image. A control point can be the point where two or more lines join, the centroid of a region or a blob, or a locally peak curvature point along a contour in an image. Control point is also referred to as *critical point, interest point, key point, extremal point, anchor point, landmark, tie point, corner, vertex,* and *junction* in the literature.

Geometric feature A feature that characterizes the geometric layout of intensities in an image or subimage.

Axis of minimum inertia Given a set of points, the axis of minimum inertia of the points is a line that (1) passes through the center of gravity of the points and (2) produces the smallest sum of squared distances of the points to it.

Dissimilarity measure Given two sequences of numbers, the dissimilarity measure between the sequences determines the independency between the sequences. The more independent the sequences the higher will be the dissimilarity measure. Dissimilarity measure is also referred to as *distance measure.*

Metric dissimilarity Given two sequences of numbers, the dissimilarity measure between the sequences becomes a metric if the dissimilarity measure between the sequences increases as the sequences become more independent.

Metric similarity Given two sequences of numbers, the similarity measure between the sequences becomes a metric if the similarity measure increases as the dependency between the sequences increases.

Reference image The first image in a set of two used in image registration. This is the image that is kept unchanged and used as the reference. The second image, known as the *sensed image*, is geometrically transformed and resampled to align with the reference image. Reference image is also known as source image.

Sensed image This is the second image in a set of two used in image registration. It is a newly sensed image that should be geometrically transformed to spatially align with the first image, known as the *reference image*. Sensed image is also known as *target image* and *test image.*

A.A. Goshtasby, *Image Registration,*
Advances in Computer Vision and Pattern Recognition,
DOI 10.1007/978-1-4471-2458-0, © Springer-Verlag London Limited 2012

Similarity measure Given two sequences of numbers, the similarity measure between the sequences determines the dependency between the sequences. The more dependent the sequences are the higher will be the similarity measure between them.

Statistical feature A feature that is computed from the first-order or second-order statistic of an image. A histogram represents a first-order statistic and a co-occurrence matrix represents a second-order statistic.

Index

A.A. Goshtasby, *Image Registration*,
Advances in Computer Vision and Pattern Recognition,
DOI 10.1007/978-1-4471-2458-0, © Springer-Verlag London Limited 2012